Course   BA 101
INTRODUCTION TO BUSINESS
CENTRAL OREGON COMMUNITY COLLEGE
Business Department

http://create.mcgraw-hill.com

ISBN-10: 1121754600   ISBN-13: 9781121754607

Contents

Credits

Taking Risks and Making Profits within the DYNAMIC BUSINESS Environment

LEARNING goals

After you have read and studied this chapter, you should be able to

1 Describe the relationship between profit and risk, and show how businesses and nonprofit organizations can raise the standard of living for all.

2 Compare and contrast being an entrepreneur and working for others.

3 Analyze the effects of the economic environment and taxes on businesses.

4 Describe the effects of technology on businesses.

5 Demonstrate how businesses can meet and beat competition.

6 Analyze the social changes affecting businesses.

7 Identify what businesses must do to meet global challenges, including war and terrorism.

8 Review how past trends are being repeated in the present and what those trends mean for tomorrow's college graduates.

profile

Getting to Know
X *Monif Clarke*
of Monifc.com

What do you do when you are a full-figured woman and want nice clothes to wear, especially a flattering bathing suit? Few designers offer fashionable clothing in larger sizes, making shopping for clothes very frustrating for plus-sized women. That was the issue facing Monif Clarke. She decided to fill the need for such clothes by designing her own line. Using a $30,000 loan from her father and help from her mother (her business partner), she started Monif C. Contemporary Plus Sizes.

As a plus-sized woman, Clarke understands the need for a new point of view in the plus-size market. "It took me many years to appreciate my curves and recognize them as a plus and NOT a minus . . . I was tired of buying the standard uniform that every woman has, I needed luxurious feminine clothes that make a statement . . . Who says plus size can't be sexy, luxurious, and feminine?" Clarke's designs are heavily inspired by her love of the Caribbean, the glamour of New York City nightlife, and European style. Recognizing the importance of versatility, she makes certain that the clothes work well for day and night . . . dressed up or down. Fabrics, trims, and treatments are carefully selected. The Monif C. collection is targeted to young, contemporary women. You can go to www.Monifc.com to see her collection for yourself.

Clarke earned her degree from Rutgers University where she majored in math and computer science. She signed up for classes at New York's Fashion Institute of Technology and started networking (meeting people) and attending trade shows. She met a manufacturer who she tried to convince to produce her collection, but her order was too small to be profitable for him. However, he was so impressed with Clarke's enthusiasm and persistence that he gave her the contact information of the manufacturer, fabric vendors, and trim vendors who she still works with today. All of her garments are made in New York's garment district. That makes sense for local, new designers because such factories will take lower minimum orders.

Clarke got a lot of good publicity when her outfits appeared on TLC's *What Not to Wear* television show, which featured her clothing as a good option for plus-sized women. Despite the good publicity, Monif C. had trouble getting merchandise into leading department stores since they were looking for more traditional designs (black or tan that try to conceal curves). Clarke turned to the Internet and developed an e-commerce site to distribute her creative collection. She also teamed up with other online retailers such as Overstock.com and Ideeli.com to carry her fashions. Some customers helped her spread the word by modeling her clothes on YouTube.

Monif C. now sells her clothing to retailers throughout the United States and around the world. Like all businesses, Monif C. was affected by the economic downturn, but Clarke was able to set prices and adapt products to meet the changing needs of the market. When her mother died, Clarke was forced to hire new people, and she became even more motivated to succeed. Monifc.com has been around since 2005, so it has proven successful. Be sure to check out the swimsuit models on her website. Swimsuits now make up over 40 percent of sales.

Businesses are constantly trying to adapt to the wants and needs of their customers and to the technologies that those customers are using. This chapter will introduce you to entrepreneurship in general and some of the many changes occurring in businesses today. As you learn more about businesses and nonprofit organizations, you will see that adapting to changing times is a constant necessity.

Sources: Tamara E. Holmes, "Plus-Sized Profits," *Black Enterprise*, April 2011, and www.Monifc.com, accessed April 2011.

NAME THAT company

This microlending organization provides small loans to entrepreneurs too poor to qualify for traditional loans. The person who started the organization has started 30 of what he calls social businesses that do not have profit as their goal. Name that organization and its founder. (Find the answers in the chapter.)

LEARNING goal 1

Describe the relationship between profit and risk, and show how businesses and nonprofit organizations can raise the standard of living for all.

business
Any activity that seeks to provide goods and services to others while operating at a profit.

goods
Tangible products such as computers, food, clothing, cars, and appliances.

services
Intangible products (i.e., products that can't be held in your hand) such as education, health care, insurance, recreation, and travel and tourism.

entrepreneur
A person who risks time and money to start and manage a business.

revenue
The total amount of money a business takes in during a given period by selling goods and services.

profit
The amount of money a business earns above and beyond what it spends for salaries and other expenses.

loss
When a business's expenses are more than its revenues.

ENTREPRENEURSHIP AND WEALTH BUILDING

One thing you can learn from the chapter-opening Profile is that success in business is based on constantly adapting to the market. A **business** is any activity that seeks to provide goods and services to others while operating at a profit. To earn that profit, you provide desired goods, jobs, and services to people in the area. **Goods** are *tangible* products such as computers, food, clothing, cars, and appliances. **Services** are *intangible* products (i.e., products that can't be held in your hand) such as education, health care, insurance, recreation, and travel and tourism. Once you have developed the right goods and services, based on consumer wants and needs, you need to reach those consumers using whatever media they prefer, including blogs, tweets, Facebook, TV advertising, and more.[1]

Although you don't need to have wealth as a primary goal, one result of successfully filling a market need is that you can make money for yourself, sometimes a great deal, by giving customers what they want. Sam Walton of Walmart began by opening one store in Arkansas and, over time, became one of the richest people in the United States.[2] There are over 11 million millionaires in the world.[3] Maybe you will be one of them some day if you start your own business. An **entrepreneur** is a person who risks time and money to start and manage a business.

Revenues, Profits, and Losses

Revenue is the total amount of money a business takes in during a given period by selling goods and services. **Profit** is the amount of money a business earns above and beyond what it spends for salaries and other expenses needed to run the operation. A **loss** occurs when a business's expenses are more than its revenues. If a business loses money over time, it will likely have to close, putting its employees out of work. About 80,000 businesses in the United States close each year; even more close during a slowdown like the United States experienced starting in 2008.[4]

As noted above, the business environment is constantly changing. What seems like a great opportunity one day—for example, online grocery shopping or SUVs—may become a huge failure when the economy changes. Starting a business may thus come with huge risks.[5] But huge risks often result in huge profits. We'll explore that concept next.

Matching Risk with Profit

Risk is the chance an entrepreneur takes of losing time and money on a business that may not prove profitable. Profit, remember, is the amount of money a business earns *above and beyond* what it pays out for salaries and other expenses. For example, if you were to start a business selling hot dogs from a cart in the summer, you would have to pay for the cart rental. You would also have to pay for the hot dogs and other materials and for someone to run the cart while you were away. After you paid your employee and yourself, paid for the food and materials you used, paid the rent on the cart, and paid your taxes, any money left over would be profit.

Keep in mind that profit is over and above the money you pay yourself in salary. You could use any profit to rent or buy a second cart and hire other employees. After a few summers, you might have a dozen carts employing dozens of workers.

Not all enterprises make the same amount of profit. Those that take the most risk may make the most profit. There is high risk, for example, in making a new kind of automobile.[6] It's also risky to open a business in an inner city, because insurance and rent are usually higher than in suburban areas, but reduced competition makes substantial profit possible. Irish entrepreneur Denis O'Brien, of Digicel, makes billions of dollars selling cell phones in the poorest, most violent countries in the world. Big risk, big profits.

Standard of Living and Quality of Life

Entrepreneurs such as Sam Walton (Walmart) and Bill Gates (Microsoft) not only became wealthy themselves; they also provided employment for many other people. Walmart is currently the nation's largest private employer.

Businesses and their employees pay taxes that the federal government and local communities use to build hospitals, schools, libraries, playgrounds, roads, and other public facilities. Taxes also help to keep the environment clean, support people in need, and provide police and fire protection. Thus, the wealth businesses generate and the taxes they pay help everyone in their communities. A nation's businesses are part of an economic system that contributes to the standard of living and quality of life for everyone in the country (and, potentially, the world). How has the recent economic slowdown affected the standard of living and quality of life in your part of the world?

The term **standard of living** refers to the amount of goods and services people can buy with the money they have. For example, the United States has one of the highest standards of living in the world, even though workers in some other countries, such as Germany and Japan, may on average make more money per hour. How can that be? Prices for goods and services in Germany and Japan are higher than in the United States, so a person in those countries can buy less than what a person in the United States can buy with the same amount of money. For example, a bottle of beer may cost $7 in Japan and $3 in the United States.

risk
The chance an entrepreneur takes of losing time and money on a business that may not prove profitable.

standard of living
The amount of goods and services people can buy with the money they have.

Mary Kate and Ashley Olsen are now the head designers of their company Dualstar which has three clothing lines ranging from the high-end to the more affordable. Today the business is worth over $1 billion. What risks and rewards did the twins face when they started their business?

Often, goods cost more in one country than another because of higher taxes and stricter government regulations. Finding the right level of taxes and regulation is important in making a country or city prosperous. We'll explore that issue more deeply in Chapter 2. At this point, it is enough to understand that the United States enjoys a high standard of living largely because of the wealth created by its businesses.

The term **quality of life** refers to the general well-being of a society in terms of its political freedom, natural environment, education, health care, safety, amount of leisure, and rewards that add to the satisfaction and joy that other goods and services provide. Maintaining a high quality of life requires the combined efforts of businesses, nonprofit organizations, and government agencies. The more money businesses create, the more is potentially available to improve the quality of life for everyone. It's important to be careful, however. Working to build a higher standard of living may lower the quality of life if it means less time with family or more stress.[7]

quality of life
The general well-being of a society in terms of its political freedom, natural environment, education, health care, safety, amount of leisure, and rewards that add to the satisfaction and joy that other goods and services provide.

Responding to the Various Business Stakeholders

Stakeholders are all the people who stand to gain or lose by the policies and activities of a business and whose concerns the business needs to address.[8] They include customers, employees, stockholders, suppliers, dealers (retailers), bankers, people in the surrounding community, the media, environmentalists, and elected government leaders (see Figure 1.1).

A primary challenge for organizations of the 21st century will be to recognize and respond to the needs of their stakeholders. For example, the need for the business to make profits may be balanced against the needs of employees to earn sufficient income or the need to protect the environment.[9] Ignore the media, and they might attack your business with articles that hurt sales. Oppose the local community, and it may stop you from expanding.

stakeholders
All the people who stand to gain or lose by the policies and activities of a business and whose concerns the business needs to address.

figure 1.1

A BUSINESS AND ITS STAKEHOLDERS
Often the needs of a firm's various stakehoders will conflict. For example, paying employees more may cut into stockholders' profits. Balancing such demands is a major role of business managers.

STAKEHOLDERS

Staying competitive may call for outsourcing. **Outsourcing** means contracting with other companies (often in other countries) to do some or all the functions of a firm, like its production or accounting tasks. Outsourcing has had serious consequences in some states where jobs have been lost to overseas competitors. We discuss outsourcing in more detail in Chapter 3.

The other side of the outsourcing coin is *insourcing*.[10] Many foreign companies are setting up design and production facilities here in the United States. For example, Korea-based Hyundai operates design and engineering headquarters in Detroit, Michigan, and produces cars in Montgomery, Alabama. Japanese automakers Honda and Toyota have been producing cars in the United States for years. Insourcing creates many new U.S. jobs and helps offset those being outsourced.[11]

It may be legal and profitable to outsource, but is it best for all the stakeholders? Business leaders must make outsourcing decisions based on all factors. Pleasing stakeholders is not easy and often calls for trade-offs.

Using Business Principles in Nonprofit Organizations

Despite their efforts to satisfy their stakeholders, businesses cannot do everything needed to make a community all it can be. Nonprofit organizations—such as public schools, civic associations, charities like United Way and Salvation Army, and groups devoted to social causes—also make a major contribution to the welfare of society. A **nonprofit organization** is an organization whose goals do not include making a personal profit for its owners or organizers. Nonprofit organizations often do strive for financial gains, but they use them to meet their social or educational goals rather than for personal profit.[12]

Social entrepreneurs are people who use business principles to start and manage not-for-profits and help address social issues. Muhammad Yunus won the Nobel Prize for starting the Grameen Bank, a microlending organization that provides small loans to entrepreneurs too poor to qualify for traditional loans. Yunus has started 30 of what he calls social businesses that do not have profit as their goal. One, for example, provides cataract operations for a fraction of the usual cost.[13]

outsourcing
Contracting with other companies (often in other countries) to do some or all of the functions of a firm, like its production or accounting tasks.

nonprofit organization
An organization whose goals do not include making a personal profit for its owners or organizers.

The goals of nonprofit organizations are social and educational, not profit-oriented. The Red Cross, for instance provides assistance to around 30 million people annually from refugees to victims of natural disasters. Why do good management principles apply equally to businesses and nonprofit organizations?

Your interests may lead you to work for a nonprofit organization such as those started by Yunus. That doesn't mean, however, that you shouldn't study business in college. You'll still need to learn business skills such as information management, leadership, marketing, and financial management. The knowledge and skills you acquire in this and other business courses are useful for careers in any organization, including nonprofits. We'll explore entrepreneurship in more detail right after the Progress Assessment.

progress assessment

- What is the difference between *revenue* and *profit?*
- What is the difference between *standard of living* and *quality of life?*
- What is risk, and how is it related to profit?
- What do the terms *stakeholders, outsourcing,* and *insourcing* mean?

> *To create wealth for its citizens, a country requires more than natural resources. It needs the efforts of entrepreneurs and the skill and knowledge to produce goods and services. How can government support entrepreneurship and the spread of knowledge?*

LEARNING goal 2

Compare and contrast being an entrepreneur and working for others.

ENTREPRENEURSHIP VERSUS WORKING FOR OTHERS

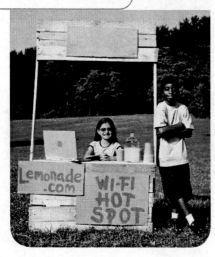

There are two ways to succeed in business. One is to rise through the ranks of large companies. The advantage of working for others is that somebody else assumes the company's entrepreneurial risk and provides you with benefits like paid vacation time and health insurance.[14] It's a good option, and many people choose it.

The other, riskier path is to become an entrepreneur. The national anthem, "The Star Spangled Banner," says that the United States is the "land of the free and the home of the brave." Part of being free is being able to own your own business and reap the profits from it. But freedom to succeed also means freedom to fail, and many small businesses fail each year. It takes a brave person to start one. As an entrepreneur, you don't receive any benefits such as paid vacation time, day care, a company car, or health insurance. You have to provide them for yourself! But what you gain—freedom to make your own decisions, opportunity, and possible wealth—is often worth the effort.

Before you take on the challenge, you should study successful entrepreneurs to learn the process. You can talk to them personally and read about them in Chapter 6, as well as in other books and magazines.

Opportunities for Entrepreneurs

Millions of people from all over the world have taken the entrepreneurial challenge and succeeded. For example, the number of Hispanic-owned businesses in the United States has grown dramatically (Hispanics are now the largest ethnic group in the United States). Both Hispanic men and women are doing

SPOTLIGHT ON SMALL
business

Networking of Minority Businesses

The Black Enterprise Entrepreneurs Conference attracts about 2,000 accomplished business owners each year. Earl Graves, the publisher of *Black Enterprise* magazine says, "We cannot build businesses of size, scale and significance in the global marketplace without aggressively and effectively building and leveraging our relationships with others." He goes on to say, "You need to establish mutually beneficial relationships within your industry, with customers, suppliers, other business owners, bankers, lawyers, financiers, and corporate managers to grow your business."

A good example of black entrepreneurs relying on others as vendors, customers, investors, and partners is the story of Carol's Daughter, the hair care and beauty products company founded as an online and mail-order business by Lisa Price. Price started out by experimenting with homemade fragrances and bath products in her Brooklyn kitchen. When she met music industry executive Steve Stoute, he grew so convinced of the potential of her business that he encouraged others like celebrities Will Smith and Shawn "Jay-Z" Carter to invest in her company. Carol's Daughter is now a nationally recognized brand with a store in Harlem and retail partnerships with Sephora, Macy's, and Home Shopping Network.

Sources: Earl G. Graves, "To Build Our Businesses, We Must Leverage Our Relationships," *Black Enterprise,* March 2011; and artgoodiesonline, accessed March 2011.

particularly well. Similar successes are true of businesses owned by Asians, Pacific Islanders, Native Americans, and Alaskan Natives.

Women now own over a third of all businesses. Names you may know include Oprah Winfrey, Donna Karan, and Lillian Vernon. Andrea Jung is the CEO of Avon Products. The world's most powerful women include Ho Ching, the chief executive of Temasek Holdings in Singapore; Indra Nooyi, chief executive of Pepsico, U.S.; and Cynthia Carroll, chief executive of Anglo American in the United Kingdom.

Businesses owned by minority women are growing faster than those owned by men or nonminority women. Women of color are establishing businesses at twice the rate of their male counterparts and more than four times that of nonminority entrepreneurs.[15] Read the nearby Spotlight on Small Business box to learn more about minority entrepreneurs.

The Importance of Entrepreneurs to the Creation of Wealth

Have you ever wondered why some countries are relatively wealthy and others poor? Economists have been studying the issue of wealth creation for many years. They began by identifying five **factors of production** that seemed to contribute to wealth (see Figure 1.2):

1. Land (or natural resources).
2. Labor (workers).

factors of production
The resources used to create wealth: land, labor, capital, entrepreneurship, and knowledge.

3. Capital. (This includes machines, tools, buildings, or whatever else is used in the production of goods. It may not include money; money is used to buy factors of production but is not always considered a factor by itself.)
4. Entrepreneurship.
5. Knowledge.

Traditionally, business and economics textbooks emphasized only four factors of production: land, labor, capital, and entrepreneurship. But the late management expert and business consultant Peter Drucker said the most important factor of production in our economy is and always will be *knowledge.*

What do we find when we compare the factors of production in rich and poor countries? Some poor countries have plenty of land and natural resources. Russia, for example, has vast areas of land with many resources such as timber and oil, but it is not considered a rich country (yet). Therefore, land isn't the critical element for wealth creation.

Most poor countries, such as Mexico, have many laborers, so it's not labor that's the primary source of wealth today. Laborers need to find work to make a contribution; that is, they need entrepreneurs to create jobs for them. Furthermore, capital—machinery and tools—is now fairly easy for firms to find in world markets, so capital isn't the missing ingredient either. Capital is not productive without entrepreneurs to put it to use.

What makes rich countries rich today is a combination of *entrepreneurship* and the effective use of *knowledge.* Entrepreneurs use what they've learned (knowledge) to grow their businesses and increase wealth. Economic and political freedom also matter.

The business environment either encourages or discourages entrepreneurship. That helps explain why some states and cities in the United States grow rich while others remain relatively poor. In the following section, we'll explore what makes up the business environment and how to build an environment that encourages growth and job creation.

figure 1.2

THE FIVE FACTORS OF PRODUCTION

Land

Land and other natural resources are used to make homes, cars, and other products.

Labor

People have always been an important resource in producing goods and services, but many people are now being replaced by technology.

Capital

Capital includes machines, tools, buildings, and other means of manufacturing.

Entrepreneurship

All the resources in the world have little value unless entrepreneurs are willing to take the risk of starting businesses to use those resources.

Knowledge

Information technology has revolutionized business, making it possible to quickly determine wants and needs and to respond with desired goods and services.

progress assessment

- What are some of the advantages of working for others?
- What benefits do you lose by being an entrepreneur, and what do you gain?
- What are the five factors of production? Which ones seem to be the most important for creating wealth?

THE BUSINESS ENVIRONMENT

The **business environment** consists of the surrounding factors that either help or hinder the development of businesses. Figure 1.3 shows the five elements in the business environment:

business environment
The surrounding factors that either help or hinder the development of businesses.

1. The economic and legal environment.
2. The technological environment.
3. The competitive environment.
4. The social environment.
5. The global business environment.

figure 1.3

TODAY'S DYNAMIC BUSINESS ENVIRONMENT

Businesses that create wealth and jobs grow and prosper in a healthy environment. Thus, creating the right business environment is the foundation for social benefits of all kinds, including good schools, clean air and water, good health care, and low rates of crime. Businesses normally can't control their environment, but they need to monitor it carefully and do what they can to adapt as it changes.

LEARNING goal 3

Analyze the effects of the economic environment and taxes on businesses.

The Economic and Legal Environment

People are willing to start new businesses if they believe the risk of losing their money isn't too great. The economic system and the way government works with or against businesses can have a strong impact on that level of risk. For example, a government can *minimize spending* and *keep taxes and regulations to a minimum,* policies that tend to favor business. Much of the debate in recent elections has focused on whether or not to raise taxes and how to lower government spending.[16] President Obama is increasing government spending with the idea of getting the economy moving faster. Some economists agree with such a stimulus, but some do not.[17] One way for government to actively promote entrepreneurship is to *allow private ownership of businesses.* In some countries, the government owns most businesses, and there's little incentive for people to work hard or create profit. Around the world today, however, some governments are selling those businesses to private individuals to create more wealth. One of the best things the governments of developing countries can do is to *minimize interference with the free exchange of goods and services.*

The government can further lessen the risks of entrepreneurship by *passing laws that enable businesspeople to write enforceable contracts.* In the United

Starting a business is much harder in some countries than in others. In India, for example, it requires a time-consuming and bureaucratic process to obtain government permission. Nonetheless, new businesses can become a major source of wealth and employment; this sari shop is one small example. What do you think would be the effect of a little more freedom to create business opportunities in this country of over a billion people?

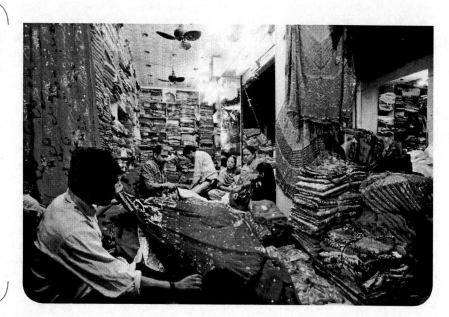

States, the Uniform Commercial Code, for example, regulates business agreements like contracts and warranties so that firms know they can rely on one another. In countries that don't yet have such laws, the risks of starting a business are that much greater. You can read more about business laws in Bonus Chapter A at the end of this book.

The government can also *establish a currency that's tradable in world markets.* That is, the currency lets you buy and sell goods and services anywhere in the world when it is easily exchanged for that of the other countries where you do business. If the Chinese did not want to trade their yuan for the U.S. dollar, for instance, it's hard to imagine how Coca-Cola or Disney would have been able to sell their products and services there.

Finally, the government can help *minimize corruption* in business and in its own ranks. Where governments are corrupt, it's difficult to build a factory or open a store without a government permit, which is obtained largely through bribery of public officials. Among businesses themselves, unscrupulous leaders can threaten their competitors and unlawfully minimize competition.

Many laws in the United States attempt to minimize corruption. Nonetheless, corrupt and illegal activities at some companies do negatively affect the business community and the economy as a whole.[18] The news media widely reports these scandals. Ethics is so important to the success of businesses and the economy as a whole that we feature stories about ethics in most chapters and devote Chapter 4 to the subject.

The capitalist system relies heavily on honesty, integrity, and high ethical standards. Failure of those fundamentals can weaken the whole system. The faltering economy that began in 2008 was due in large part to such failure. Some mortgage lenders, for instance, failed to do the research necessary to ensure their borrowers' creditworthiness. Many subprime borrowers (people with low credit ratings) forfeited their loans. The ripple effects of these unpaid debts not only cost many people their homes but also reduced the value of housing across the world and made it difficult even for business borrowers to get new loans. Part of the blame for this economic disaster can be placed on the borrowers who didn't tell the truth about their income or who otherwise deceived the lenders.

It is easy to see the damage caused by the poor moral and ethical behavior of some businesspeople.[19] What is not so obvious is the damage caused by the moral and ethical lapses of the everyday consumer—that is, you and me. The nearby Making Ethical Decisions box discusses that issue in more depth.

LEARNING goal 4

Describe the effects of technology on businesses.

The Technological Environment

Since prehistoric times, humans have felt the need to create tools that make work easier. Few technological changes have had a more comprehensive and lasting impact on businesses, however, than the emergence of information technology (IT): computers, networks, cell phones, and especially the Internet.

The iPod, iPhone, BlackBerry and other smartphones, as well as social media like MySpace, Facebook, and Twitter, have completely changed the way people communicate with one another. Advertisers and other businesspeople

MAKING ethical decisions

Ethics Begins with You

It is easy to criticize the ethics of people whose names appear in the headlines. It is more difficult to see the moral and ethical misbehavior of your own social group. Do you find some of the behaviors of your friends morally or ethically questionable?

A survey found that the number of employees calling in sick had reached a five-year high, and three-fifths were not sick at all. Other employees have been caught conducting personal business at work, such as doing their taxes. And others play video games on their work computers. We're sure you can add many more examples.

Many companies today are creating ethics codes to guide their employees' behavior. We believe the trend toward improving ethical behavior is so important that we've made it a major theme of this book. Throughout the text you'll see boxes like this one, called Making Ethical Decisions, that pose ethical dilemmas and ask what you would do to resolve them. The idea is for you to think about the moral and ethical dimensions of every decision you make.

Here is your first one: You have become addicted to your electronic gadgets. Some days at work you spend most of the time playing games, watching TV, texting, sending e-mails to friends, or reading a book or magazine on your devices. What is the problem in this situation? What are your alternatives? What are the consequences of each alternative? Which alternative will you choose? Is your choice ethical?

have created ways of using these tools to reach their suppliers and customers. Even politicians have harnessed the power of the Internet to advance their causes. See the nearby Social Media in Business box for an example of how a well-established company uses these tools to interact with customers.

IT is such a major force in business today that we discuss its impact on businesses throughout the entire text.

How Technology Benefits Workers and You One of the advantages of working for others is that the company often provides the tools and technology to make your job more productive. **Technology** means everything from phones and copiers to computers, medical imaging devices, personal digital assistants, and the

technology
Everything from phones and copiers to computers, medical imaging devices, personal digital assistants, and the various software programs that make business processes more effective, efficient, and productive.

Technology makes workers more productive. Instead of spending hours traveling to meet, for instance, this doctor is using teleconferencing to consult with a colleague about diagnosis and treatment options. Are some workers likely to be more comfortable with new technology than others?

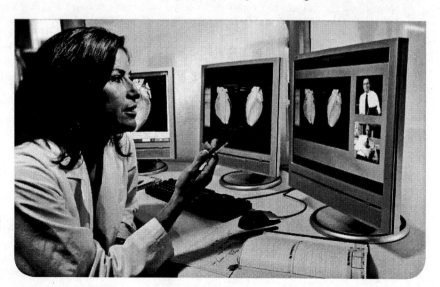

SOCIAL MEDIA IN
business

JCPenney Keeps in Touch

Nothing highlights the dynamic nature of business more than the number of new electronic devices people carry today, including iPads, iPhones, e-readers, and cell phones of all kinds. People seem to be constantly texting, tweeting, and talking to each other. You cannot help but notice them in restaurants, on buses, and even walking down the street. Hopefully, though, you don't see them doing it while they're driving.

In order to reach the coveted 18-to-35-year-olds, JCPenney ran local ads featuring fashion blogger Geri Hirsh. In the spots, Hirsh showcased the retailer's spring line as she was preparing for an Oscar party. JCPenney's social media team then posted clothing selected by Hirsh to the brand's Facebook page, which includes a shopping app.

During the Oscar broadcast, JCPenny incorporated Twitter and Facebook into the spring campaign using seven commercials. JCPenney was the only retail sponsor for the show and wanted to reach young women. During the show, the company posted mini-blogs with trivia questions about

fashion. The first person to send in a correct answer received a $20 gift card from the retailer. Before the show, the company also sent warm-up tweets with questions like, "Which film should win for Best Costume?"

The store also launched a "Shop Like a Celebrity" sweepstakes on Facebook. Winners received a free trip to New York complete with a two-night hotel stay, a $500 JCPenney gift card, and fashion advice from blogger Mia Morgan (The Fashion Alchemist). Other digital components of the campaign included a design contest on social shopping site Polyvore and an original video series on Olsenboye.com. JCPenney is a great example of how successful well-established businesses continue to adapt to the wants and needs of their customers and to the technology they use.

Sources: Christopher Heine, "JCPenney Hopes Twitter Contest Creates Oscar Buzz," *Department Store Retailing News* online, accessed March 3, 2011; and Marilyn Much, "The Changing Face (book) of Internet Commerce," *Investor's Business Daily,* February 2, 2011.

---

various software programs that make business processes more effective, efficient, and productive. *Effectiveness* means producing the desired result. *Efficiency* means producing goods and services using the least amount of resources.

Productivity is the amount of output you generate given the amount of input, such as the number of hours you work. The more you can produce in any given period, the more money you are worth to companies. The average worker in the United States contributes $63,885 to GDP, making U.S. workers some of the world's most productive employees. The problem with productivity today is that workers are so productive that fewer are needed, and that is contributing to the high unemployment rate we are now experiencing.[20]

Technology affects people in all industries. For example, Don Glenn, a farmer in Decatur, Alabama, uses his personal computer to compare data from the previous year's harvest with infrared satellite photos of his farm that show which crops are flourishing. He has a desktop terminal called a DTN that allows him to check the latest grain prices, and he uses AgTalk, a web-based bulletin board, to converse with other farmers from all over the world. He also bids for bulk fertilizer on XSAg.com, an online agricultural exchange. High-tech equipment tells Glenn how and where to spread fertilizer and seed, tracks yields yard by yard, and allows him to maintain high profit margins.

The Growth of E-Commerce **E-commerce** is the buying and selling of goods over the Internet. There are two major types of e-commerce transactions: business-to-consumer (B2C) and business-to-business (B2B). As important as the Internet has been to retailers like Amazon.com in the consumer market, it has become even more important in the B2B market, where businesses sell

productivity
The amount of output you generate given the amount of input (e.g., hours worked).

e-commerce
The buying and selling of goods over the Internet.

goods and services to one another, such as IBM selling consulting services to a local bank. Websites have become the new stores.[21]

Traditional businesses must deal with the competition from B2B and B2C firms, and vice versa. Many new parents would just as soon buy used items posted on Craigslist than shop in a baby-goods store. Starting a business on eBay has never been easier. More than 450 million Chinese citizens are using the Internet. This is about double the number of U.S. users.[22] And what did people do before they could google? E-commerce has become so important that we will discuss it throughout the text.

Using Technology to Be Responsive to Customers   A major theme of this text is that those businesses most responsive to customer wants and needs will succeed. That realization points to one way in which even traditional retailers can use Internet technology. For example, businesses use bar codes to identify products you buy and their size, quantity, and color. The scanner at the checkout counter identifies the price but can also put all your purchase information into a **database**, an electronic storage file for information.

database
An electronic storage file for information.

Databases enable stores to carry only the merchandise their local population wants. But because companies routinely trade database information, many retailers know what you buy and from whom you buy it. Thus they can send you catalogs and other direct mail advertising offering the kind of products you might want, as indicated by your past purchases. We discuss other ways businesses use technology to be responsive to consumers throughout the text.

identity theft
The obtaining of individuals' personal information, such as Social Security and credit card numbers, for illegal purposes.

Unfortunately, the legitimate collection of personal customer information also opens the door to identity theft. **Identity theft** is the obtaining of individuals' personal information, such as Social Security and credit card numbers, for illegal purposes. The Federal Trade Commission says millions of U.S. consumers are victims of identity theft each year. What you should learn from these examples is to limit those to whom you give personal information. You also need antivirus software on your computer as well as a firewall and antispyware software.[23] You may also want to monitor your credit report. It is important for you to understand identity theft, security, privacy, stability, and other important IT issues.

LEARNING goal 5

Demonstrate how businesses can meet and beat competition.

The Competitive Environment

Competition among businesses has never been greater. Some have found a competitive edge by focusing on quality. The goal for many companies is zero defects—no mistakes in making the product. However, even achieving a rate of zero defects isn't enough to stay competitive in world markets. Companies now have to offer both high-quality products and good value—that is, outstanding service at competitive prices.

Competing by Exceeding Customer Expectations   Today's customers want not only good quality at low prices but great service as well. Every manufacturing and service organization in the world should have a sign over its door telling its workers that the customer is king. Business is becoming customer-driven, not management-driven as often occurred in the past. Successful organizations must now listen more closely to customers to determine their wants and needs, and then adjust the firm's products, policies, and practices accordingly. We will explore these ideas in more depth in Chapter 13.

Competing by Restructuring and Empowerment   To meet the needs of customers, firms must give their frontline workers—for example, office clerks, front-desk people at hotels, and salespeople—the responsibility, authority, freedom, training, and equipment they need to respond quickly to customer requests. They also must allow workers to make other decisions essential to producing high-quality goods and services. The process is called **empowerment**, and we'll be talking about it throughout this book.

As many companies have discovered, it sometimes takes years to restructure an organization so that managers can and will give up some of their authority, and employees will assume more responsibility. We'll discuss such organizational changes in Chapter 8.

> **empowerment**
> Giving frontline workers the responsibility, authority, freedom, training, and equipment they need to respond quickly to customer requests.

LEARNING goal 6

Analyze the social changes affecting businesses.

> **demography**
> The statistical study of the human population with regard to its size, density, and other characteristics such as age, race, gender, and income.

The Social Environment

Demography is the statistical study of the human population with regard to its size, density, and other characteristics such as age, race, gender, and income. In this text, we're particularly interested in the demographic trends that most affect businesses and career choices. The U.S. population is going through major changes that are dramatically affecting how people live, where they live, what they buy, and how they spend their time. Furthermore, tremendous population shifts are leading to new opportunities for some firms and to declining opportunities for others. For example, there are many more retired workers than in the past, creating new markets for all kinds of goods and services.[24]

Managing Diversity   *Diversity* has come to mean much more than recruiting and keeping minority and female employees. Diversity efforts now include seniors, people with disabilities, homosexuals, atheists, extroverts, introverts, married people, singles, and the devout. It also means dealing sensitively with workers and cultures around the world.

Legal and illegal immigrants have had a dramatic effect on many cities. Schools and hospitals have been especially affected. Some local governments are making every effort to adapt, including changing signs, brochures, websites, and forms to include other languages. Has your city experienced such changes? What are some of the impacts you've noticed?

The Increase in the Number of Older Citizens
People ages 65 to 74 are currently the richest demographic group in the United States. They thus represent a lucrative market for companies involved with food service, transportation, entertainment, education, lodging, and so on. By 2020, the percentage of the population over 60 will be 22.8 percent (versus

The U.S. boasts enormous ethnic and racial diversity. Its workforce is also widely diverse in terms of age, which means managers must adopt to the generational demographics of the workplace. What are some challenges of working with someone much younger or much older than yourself?

More and more working families consist of single parents who must juggle the demands of a job and responsibilities of raising children. What can managers do to try to retain valued employees who face such challenges?

16 percent in 2000). What do these changes mean for you and for businesses in the future? Think of the products and services that middle-aged and elderly people will need—medicine, nursing homes, assisted-living facilities, adult day care, home health care, recreation, and the like—and you'll see opportunities for successful businesses of the 21st century. Don't rule out computer games and Internet services, even Wii. Businesses that cater to older consumers will have the opportunity for exceptional growth in the near future. The market is huge.[25]

On the other hand, retired people will be draining the economy of wealth. Social Security has become a major issue. The pay-as-you-go system (in which workers today pay the retirement benefits for today's retirees) operated just fine in 1940, when 42 workers supported each retiree; but by 1960, there were only 5 workers per retiree, and today, as the baby-boom generation (born between 1946 and 1964) begins to retire, that number is under 3 and dropping. In addition, the government has been spending the accumulated Social Security money instead of leaving it in a Social Security account.

Soon, less money will be coming into Social Security than will be going out. The government will have to do something to make up for the shortfall: raise taxes, reduce Social Security benefits (e.g., raise the retirement age at which people qualify for payments), reduce spending elsewhere (e.g., in other social programs like Medicare or Medicaid), or borrow on the world market.

In short, paying Social Security to senior citizens in the future will draw huge amounts of money from the working population. That is why there is so much discussion in the media today about what to do with Social Security.

The Increase in the Number of Single-Parent Families   It is a tremendous task to work full-time and raise a family. Thus, the rapid growth of single-parent households has also had a major effect on businesses. Single parents, including those forced by welfare rules to return to work after a certain benefit period, have encouraged businesses to implement programs such as family leave (giving workers time off to attend to a sick child or elder relative) and flextime (allowing workers to arrive or leave at selected times). You will read about such programs in more detail in Chapter 11.

LEARNING goal 7

Identify what businesses must do to meet global challenges, including war and terrorism.

The Global Environment

The global environment of business is so important that we show it as surrounding all other environmental influences (see again Figure 1.3). Two important changes here are the growth of global competition and the increase of free trade among nations.

World trade, or *globalization,* has grown thanks to the development of efficient distribution systems (we'll talk about these in Chapter 15) and communication advances such as the Internet. Globalization has greatly improved living standards around the world. China and India have become major U.S. competitors. Lenovo, a Chinese firm, bought IBM's PC unit. Shop at Walmart and most other U.S. retail stores, and you can't help but notice the number of "Made in China" stickers you see. Call for computer help, and you are as likely to be talking with someone in India as someone in the United States.

World trade has its benefits and costs. You'll read much more about its importance in Chapter 3 and in the Reaching Beyond Our Borders boxes throughout the text.

War and Terrorism   The wars in Iraq and Afghanistan have drawn billions of dollars from the U.S. economy. Some companies—like those that make bullets, tanks, and uniforms—have benefited greatly. Others, however, have lost workers to the armed forces, and still others (e.g., tourism) have grown more slowly as money has been diverted to the war effort. The threat of other wars and terrorism leads the government to spend even more money on the military. Such expenditures are subject to much debate, especially as the United States responds to an economic recession. Note the increased unrest in the world as people in other nations are demanding more freedom.

The threat of terrorism also adds greatly to organizational costs, including the cost of insurance. In fact, some firms are finding it difficult to get insurance against terrorist attacks. Security, too, is costly. Airlines, for example, have had to install stronger cockpit doors and add more passenger screening devices.

Like all citizens, businesspeople benefit from a peaceful and prosperous world. One way to lessen international tensions is to foster global economic growth among both profit-making and nonprofit organizations.

How Global Changes Affect You   As businesses expand to serve global markets, new jobs will be created in both manufacturing and service industries. Global trade also means global competition. The students who will prosper will be those prepared for the markets of tomorrow. Rapid changes create a need for continuous learning, so be prepared to continue your education throughout your career. You'll have every reason to be optimistic about job opportunities in the future if you prepare yourself well.

The Ecological Environment   Few issues have captured the attention of the international business community more than climate change. **Climate change** is the movement of the temperature of the planet up or down over time. The issue now is global warming, but the issue may become global cooling. Some of the world's largest firms—including General Electric, Coca-Cola, Shell, Nestlé, DuPont, Johnson & Johnson, British Airways, and Shanghai Electric— say the evidence for climate change is overwhelming. Saving energy and producing products that cause less harm to the environment is a trend called **greening**.[26] Greening has become such a pervasive issue that we devote boxes to that subject throughout the text. (See the nearby Thinking Green box for things you can do to contribute to the cause.)

climate change
The movement of the temperature of the planet up or down over time.

greening
The trend toward saving energy and producing products that cause less harm to the environment.

progress assessment

- What are four ways the government can foster entrepreneurship?
- What's the difference between effectiveness, efficiency, and productivity?
- What is *empowerment?*
- What are some of the major issues affecting the economy today?

THINKING green

Getting Involved Personally

There is little doubt humans can take action to protect the environment. What can we do now to start?

It's not necessary to change your lifestyle radically in order to make a difference. Simply heating or cooling your apartment or house more efficiently is a good start. Why not buy a reusable grocery bag? You can recycle paper and containers. You can walk or ride a bike instead of driving. You can reduce your use of electrical equipment and of water (pumping water takes a lot of electricity). Buy produce that is grown locally to save the energy used in shipping food from faraway places. If you're in the market for a car, you could "go green" by buying a hybrid or a small, fuel-efficient car.

The idea is to become more ecologically aware and join others throughout the world in using less energy and emitting less carbon into the atmosphere. Everyone benefits when the air is cleaner. That's part of what the green movement is all about.

LEARNING goal **8**

Review how past trends are being repeated in the present and what those trends mean for tomorrow's college graduates.

THE EVOLUTION OF U.S. BUSINESS

Businesses in the United States have become so productive that they need fewer workers than ever before to produce goods. If global competition and improved technology are putting skilled people out of work, should we be concerned about the prospect of high unemployment rates and low incomes? Where will the jobs be when you graduate? These important questions force us all to look briefly at the U.S. economy and its future.

Progress in the Agricultural and Manufacturing Industries

The United States has experienced strong economic development since the 1800s. The agricultural industry led the way, providing food for the United States and much of the world. Cyrus McCormick's invention of the harvester in 1834, other inventions such as Eli Whitney's cotton gin, and modern improvements on such equipment did much to make large-scale farming successful. Technology has made modern farming so efficient that the number of farmers has dropped from about 33 percent of the population to about 1 percent today. However, average farm size is now about 450 acres versus 160 acres in the past.

Agriculture is still a major industry in the United States. What has changed is that the millions of small farms that existed previously have been replaced by some huge farms, some merely large farms, and some small but highly specialized farms. The loss of farm workers over the past century is not a negative sign. It is instead an indication that U.S. agricultural workers are the most productive in the world.

Most farmers who lost their jobs during the 19th and 20th centuries went to work in factories springing up around the country. Manufacturers, like farms, began using technology like tools and machines to become more productive. Eventually the consequence in manufacturing, as in farming, was the elimination of many jobs.

Again, the loss to society is minimized if the wealth created by increased productivity and efficiency creates new jobs elsewhere—and that's exactly what has happened over the past 50 years. Many workers in the industrial sector found jobs in the growing service sector. Most of those who can't find work today are people who need retraining and education to become qualified for jobs that now exist or will exist in the near future, like building wind farms or making electric automobiles. We'll discuss the manufacturing sector and production in more detail in Chapter 9.

Agriculture is one of the largest and most important industries in the US. Technology has increased productivity and made farmers more efficient, allowing for larger farms. This trend has reduced the price of food for consumers, but has also reduced the number of small, family-run farms. Does the new technology also help smaller farms compete? How?

Progress in Service Industries

In the past, the fastest-growing industries in the United States produced goods like steel, automobiles, and machine tools. Today, the fastest-growing firms provide services in areas like law, health, telecommunications, entertainment, and finance.

Together, services make up about 70 percent of the value of the U.S. economy. Since the mid-1980s, the service industry has generated almost all the increases in employment. Although service-sector growth has slowed, it remains the largest area of growth. Chances are very high that you'll work in a service job at some point in your career. Figure 1.4 lists many service-sector jobs; look it over to see where the careers of the future are likely to be. Retailers like American Eagle are part of the service sector. Each new retail store can create managerial jobs for college graduates.

Another bit of good news is that there are *more* high-paying jobs in the service sector than in the goods-producing sector. High-paying service-sector jobs abound in health care, accounting, finance, entertainment, telecommunications, architecture, law, software engineering, and more. Projections are that some areas of the service sector will grow rapidly, while others may have much slower growth. The strategy for college graduates is to remain flexible, find out where jobs are being created, and move when appropriate.[27]

Your Future in Business

Despite the growth in the service sector we've described above, the service era now seems to be coming to a close as a new era is beginning. We're in the midst of an information-based global revolution that will alter all sectors of the economy: agricultural, industrial, and service. It's exciting to think about the role you'll play in that revolution. You may be a leader who will implement the changes and accept the challenges of world competition based on world quality standards. This book will introduce you to some of the concepts that make such leadership possible, not just in business but also in government agencies and nonprofit organizations. Business can't prosper in the future without the cooperation of government and social leaders throughout the world.

There's much talk about the service sector, but few discussions actually list what it includes. Here's a representative list of services as classified by the government:

Lodging Services

Hotels, rooming houses, and other lodging places
Sporting and recreation camps
Trailer parks and camp sites for transients

Personal Services

Laundries	Child care
Linen supply	Shoe repair
Diaper service	Funeral homes
Carpet cleaning	Tax preparation
Photographic studios	Beauty shops
Health clubs	

Business Services

Accounting	Exterminating
Ad agencies	Employment agencies
Collection agencies	Computer programming
Commercial photography	Research & development labs
Commercial art	Management services
Stenographic services	Public relations
Window cleaning	Detective agencies
Consulting	Interior design
Equipment rental	Web design
Tax preparation	Trash collection

Automotive Repair Services and Garages

Auto rental	Tire retreading
Truck rental	Exhaust system shops
Parking lots	Car washes
Paint shops	Transmission repair

Miscellaneous Repair Services

Radio and television	Welding
Watch	Sharpening
Reupholstery	Septic tank cleaning

Motion Picture Industry

Production	Theaters
Distribution	Drive-ins

Amusement and Recreation Services

Restaurants	Racetracks
Symphony orchestras	Golf courses
Pool halls	Amusement parks
Bowling alleys	Carnivals
Fairs	Ice skating rinks
Botanical gardens	Circuses
Video rentals	Infotainment

Health Services

Physicians	Nursery care
Dentists	Medical labs
Chiropractors	Dental labs

Legal Services

Educational Services

Libraries	Computer schools
Schools	Online schools

Social Services

Child care	Family services
Job training	Elder care

Noncommercial Museums, Art Galleries, and Botanical and Zoological Gardens

Selected Membership Organizations

Business associations	Civic associations

Financial Services

Banking	Real estate agencies
Insurance	Investment firms (brokers)

Miscellaneous Services

Architectural	Surveying
Engineering	Utilities
Telecommunications	Lawn care
Vending	Delivery

figure I.4

WHAT IS THE SERVICE SECTOR?

progress assessment

- What major factor caused people to move from farming to manufacturing and from manufacturing to the service sector?
- What does the future look like for tomorrow's college graduates?

summary

Learning Goal 1. Describe the relationship between profit and risk, and show how businesses and nonprofit organizations can raise the standard of living for all.

- **What is the relationship of businesses' profit to risk assumption?**

Profit is money a business earns above and beyond the money that it spends for salaries and other expenses. Businesspeople make profits by taking risks. *Risk* is the chance an entrepreneur takes of losing time and money on a business that may not prove profitable. A loss occurs when a business's costs and expenses are higher than its revenues.

- **Who are stakeholders, and which stakeholders are most important to a business?**

Stakeholders include customers, employees, stockholders, suppliers, dealers, bankers, the media, people in the local community, environmentalists, and elected government leaders. The goal of business leaders is to try to recognize and respond to the needs of these stakeholders and still make a profit.

Learning Goal 2. Compare and contrast being an entrepreneur and working for others.

- **What are the advantages and disadvantages of entrepreneurship?**

Working for others means getting benefits like paid vacations and health insurance. Entrepreneurs take more risks and lose those benefits. They gain the freedom to make their own decisions, more opportunity, and possible wealth.

- **What are the five factors of production?**

The five factors of production are land, labor, capital, entrepreneurship, and knowledge. Of these, the most important are entrepreneurship and knowledge. Entrepreneurs are people who risk time and money to start and manage a business. What makes rich countries rich today is a combination of *entrepreneurship* and the effective use of *knowledge*.

Learning Goal 3. Analyze the effects of the economic environment and taxes on businesses.

- **What can governments in developing countries do to reduce the risk of starting businesses and thus help entrepreneurs?**

The government may allow private ownership of businesses, pass laws that enable businesspeople to write contracts that are enforceable in court, establish a currency that's tradable in world markets, help to lessen corruption in business and government, and keep taxes and regulations to a minimum. From a business perspective, lower taxes mean lower risks, more growth, and thus more money for workers and the government.

Learning Goal 4. Describe the effects of technology on businesses.

- **How has technology benefited workers, businesses, and consumers?**

Technology enables workers to be more effective, efficient, and productive. *Effectiveness* means doing the right thing in the right way. *Efficiency* means producing items using the least amount of resources. *Productivity* is the amount of output you generate given the amount of input (e.g., hours worked).

Learning Goal 5. Demonstrate how businesses can meet and beat competition.
*   **What are some ways in which businesses meet and beat competition?**
Some companies have found a competitive edge by focusing on making high-quality products, all the way to zero defects. Companies also aim to exceed customer expectations. Often that means *empowering* frontline workers by giving them more training and more responsibility and authority.

Learning Goal 6. Analyze the social changes affecting businesses.
*   **How have social changes affected businesses?**
Diversity has come to mean much more than recruiting and keeping minority and female employees. Diversity efforts now include seniors, disabled people, homosexuals, atheists, extroverts, introverts, married people, singles, and the devout. It also means dealing sensitively with workers and cultures around the world. Providing Social Security benefits to senior citizens in the future will draw huge amounts of money from the working population. That is why there is so much discussion about Social Security in the media today.

Learning Goal 7. Identify what businesses must do to meet global challenges, including war and terrorism.
*   **Which countries are creating the greatest challenges?**
China and India are two major competitors.
*   **What will be the impacts of future wars and terrorism?**
Some businesses, such as those in the defense industry, may prosper. Others, such as tourism, may suffer. One way to minimize world tensions is to help less developed countries to become more prosperous.

Learning Goal 8. Review how past trends are being repeated in the present and what those trends mean for tomorrow's college graduates.
*   **What is the history of our economic development in the United States, and what does it tell us about the future?**
Agricultural workers displaced by improved farm technology went to work in factories. Improved manufacturing productivity and increased competition from foreign firms contributed to the development of a service economy in the United States. The service era is now giving way to an information-based global revolution that will affect all sectors of the economy. The secret to long-term success in such an economy is flexibility and continuing education to be prepared for the opportunities that are sure to arise.
*   **What job opportunities for college graduates exist in the service sector?**
Check over Figure 1.4, which outlines the service sector. That is where you are most likely to find the fast-growing firms of the future.

key terms

business 4	e-commerce 15	greening 19
business environment 11	empowerment 17	identity theft 16
climate change 19	entrepreneur 4	loss 4
database 16	factors of production 9	nonprofit organization 7
demography 17	goods 4	outsourcing 7

critical thinking

Imagine you are thinking of starting a restaurant in your community. Answer the following questions:

1. Who will be the various stakeholders of your business?

2. What are some of the things you can do to benefit your community other than providing jobs and tax revenue?

3. How will you establish good relationships with your suppliers? With your employees?

4. Do you see any conflict between your desire to be as profitable as possible and your desire to pay employees a living wage?

5. Which of the environmental factors outlined in this chapter might have the biggest impact on your business? How?

developing workplace skills

1. Poll the class and determine which students believe that climate change is primarily caused by humans and which believe that other factors, such as climate cycles or sun spots, are the primary cause. Discuss what students can do to minimize human effects on the environment regardless of the primary causes of climate change. Are there any negative consequences to trying to minimize humans' impact on the environment?

2. Imagine you are a local businessperson who has to deal with the issue of outsourcing. You want to begin with the facts. How many, if any, jobs have been lost to outsourcing in your area? Are there any foreign firms in your area that are creating jobs (insourcing)? You may want to use the Internet to find the data you need.

3. What indicates that you and other people in the United States have a high standard of living? What are some signs that maintaining such a high standard of living may have a negative impact on quality of life?

4. Look through your local phone book to find five businesses that provide services in your area. List those businesses and, for each, describe how social trends might affect them in both positive and negative ways. Be prepared to explain your descriptions.

5. Form into teams of four or five and discuss the technological and e-commerce revolutions. How many students now shop for goods and services online? What have been their experiences? What other high-tech equipment do they use (iPhones, iPads, laptops, etc.)?

taking it to the net

Purpose

To learn what changes are occurring in the business environment today and how those changes are affecting businesses.

Exercise

1. Go to the National Taxpayers Union website (www.ntu.org) "Who Pays Income Taxes? See Who Pays What." Study the tables showing what percent of taxes the various income groups pay. Do you think that business-people pay their fair share? What percent of taxes does the top 1 percent of earners pay? What about the top 5 percent? The lowest 50 percent? How do such tax rates affect incentives to become a successful entrepreneur?

2. Go to the Census Bureau's website (www.census.gov) and learn what the population of the United States is at this moment. While at the site, you may want to look up the population in your town or city. Explore what other data are available at this site. What trends seem most important to you and to businesspeople in general?

3. Do a Google search for "business blogs" and check out some of the available results. Go to one of the blogs that seems interesting to you and write a brief paragraph about it—including such things as who sponsors it, who contributes the posts, and what other features it has—and how it may help a student in an introductory business course.

casing the web

To access the case "Moving Up the Corporate Ladder," visit **www.mhhe.com/ubl0e**

video case

To access the video case featuring Redbox, visit **www.mhhe.com/ubl0e**

Understanding
ECONOMICS and How It
AFFECTS Business

LEARNING
goals

After you have read and studied this chapter, you should be able to

1 Explain basic economics.

2 Explain what capitalism is and how free markets work.

3 Compare socialism and communism.

4 Analyze the trend toward mixed economies.

5 Describe the economic system of the United States, including the significance of key economic indicators (especially GDP), productivity, and the business cycle.

6 Contrast fiscal policy and monetary policy, and explain how each affects the economy.

If you listened to much of the recent debates about the state of the nation's economy and what to do about it, you've probably heard people mention Keynes or Keynesian economics and wondered what they were talking about. John Maynard Keynes (pronounced *Canes*) was one of the economists who had a great influence on U.S. economic policy. It was Keynes who advocated stabilizing the economy by the use of fiscal policy (policy related to taxes and spending). He believed that if the economy was in a recession, the government should increase *spending* (e.g., on infrastructure—roads, bridges, schools, and utilities) and cut taxes in order to stimulate the economy. The goal of cutting taxes would be to increase consumer spending to revive businesses. Conversely, when the economy seems to be growing too fast and inflation results, Keynesian theory suggests cutting back on government spending and increasing taxes. Such government intervention is supposed to be a short-term solution to wide swings in the business cycle. Once the economy was stabilized, Keynes believed, free economic principles could be restored.

Keynes published his most famous book, *The General Theory of Employment, Interest and Money,* in 1936. Until that time U.S. economic thinking was dominated by Adam Smith's classic economics. Smith believed that the economy would automatically function at full employment if there was minimal government intervention. The depression of the 1930s changed that view, and Keynesian economics took over.

While Keynesian economics has been in and out of favor since the 1930s, it was Keynesian theory that Presidents Bush and Obama had in mind when they attempted to stimulate the economy by spending money. While there are signs that the economy is now on the road to recovery, the $787 billion stimulus package did not lead to the job growth expected, and unemployment stayed about 9 percent.

The economic environment is critical to the success of business. That is what this chapter is all about. You will learn to compare different economic systems to see the benefits and the drawbacks of each. You will learn how the free-market system of the United States works. And you will learn more about what makes some countries rich and other countries poor. By the end of the chapter, you should understand the direct effect economic systems have on the wealth and happiness of communities throughout the world.

profile

Getting to Know

X *John Maynard Keynes*

Economist

Sources: Paul Johnson, "There Is No Keynesian Miracle," *Forbes,* March 1, 2010; Daniel Fisher, "Keynes Who?" *Forbes,* August 9, 2010; Peter Coy, "The Keynes Solution," *Bloomberg Businessweek,* November 1–November 7, 2010; and Peter Coy, "Keynes vs. Alesina; Alesina Who?" *Bloomberg Businessweeek,* July 5–July 11, 2010.

NAME THAT
company

This organization lends small amounts of money to people in poor countries. For example, it loaned a woman in Uganda enough to buy a refrigerator. She was able to sell fresh food from the refrigerator and make enough money for her family to succeed. Name this organization. (The answer is in the chapter.)

LEARNING goal 1

Explain basic economics.

HOW ECONOMIC CONDITIONS AFFECT BUSINESSES

Compared to, say, Mexico, the United States is a relatively wealthy country. Why? Why is South Korea comparatively wealthy and North Korea suffering economically, with many of its people starving?[1] Such questions are part of the subject of economics. In this chapter, we explore the various economic systems of the world and how they either promote or hinder business growth, the creation of wealth, and a higher quality of life for all.

A major part of the United States' business success in the past was due to an economic and social climate that allowed most businesses to operate freely. People were free to start a business anywhere, and just as free to fail and start again. That freedom motivated people to try until they succeeded because the rewards were often so great.[2]

Any change in the U.S. economic or political system has a major influence on the success of the business system. For example, the recent increase in government involvement in business will have an economic effect.[3] What that effect will be in the long run, however, remains to be seen.

Global economics and global politics also have a major influence on businesses in the United States. Therefore, to understand business, you must also understand basic economics and politics.

What Is Economics?

Economics is the study of how society chooses to employ resources to produce goods and services and distribute them for consumption among various competing groups and individuals. There are two major branches of economics: **macroeconomics** looks at the operation of a nation's economy as a whole (the whole United States), and **microeconomics** looks at the behavior of people and organizations in markets for particular products or services. A question in macroeconomics might be: What should the United States do to lower its national debt?[4] Macroeconomic topics in this chapter include gross

economics
The study of how society chooses to employ resources to produce goods and services and distribute them for consumption among various competing groups and individuals.

microeconomics
The part of economics study that looks at the behavior of people and organizations in particular markets.

macroeconomics
The part of economics study that looks at the operation of a nation's economy as a whole.

domestic product (GDP), the unemployment rate, and price indexes. A question in microeconomics might be: Why do people buy smaller cars when gas prices go up?

Some economists define economics as the study of the allocation of *scarce* resources. They believe resources need to be carefully divided among people, usually by the government. However, there's no way to maintain peace and prosperity in the world by merely dividing the resources we have today among the existing nations. There aren't enough known resources to do that. **Resource development** is the study of how to increase resources (say, by getting oil from shale and tar sands) and create conditions that will make better use of them (like recycling and conservation).[5]

Businesses can contribute to an economic system by inventing products that greatly increase available resources. For example, they can discover new energy sources (hydrogen fuel for autos), new ways of growing food (hydroponics), and new ways of creating needed goods and services (nanotechnology). Mariculture, or raising fish in pens out in the ocean, could lead to more food for everyone and more employment. It is believed that the United States could monopolize the shrimp industry using aquaculture.[6] Now we import about a billion pounds of shrimp a year.[7] The nearby Thinking Green box explores some new ventures that have been created to help lessen climate change.

The Secret to Creating a Wealthy Economy

Imagine the world when kings and other rich landowners had most of the wealth, and the majority of the people were peasants. The peasants had many children, and it may have seemed a natural conclusion that if things went on as usual there would soon be too many people and not enough food and other

The economic contrast is remarkable. Business is booming in Seoul, South Korea (pictured on the left). But North Korea, a communist country, is not doing well, as the picture on the right of thousands of workers using old-fashioned tools in a work-for-food program shows. What do you think accounts for the dramatic differences in the economies of these two neighboring countries?

resource development
The study of how to increase resources and to create the conditions that will make better use of those resources.

THINKING green

Bringing in the Green with Green Products

Adjusting to climate changes creates as many opportunities as it does challenges. Companies that help lower carbon emissions can prosper as people become more concerned about climate change. Toyota has had success selling its hybrid Prius, and most automakers now offer similar hybrids, which get better mileage with less pollution than gas-only vehicles. Some all-electric cars are now available. And several firms are offering cars half the size of regular cars—to get better fuel economy.

Farmers are growing more corn and other crops for use as biofuels. That creates more demand for tractors and other farm equipment, and helps the economy grow. It also causes food prices to skyrocket. Given these outcomes, would you recommend an increase in the use of biofuels?

It's amazing what you find when you begin looking for greener businesses There are now "green" tennis shoes and "green" jeans. Have you ever seen hot-dog wrappers blowing around the ballpark? In the future, they'll be recycled. *Reduce. Reuse. Recycle.* These have become the tenets of a greener, more environmentally responsive lifestyle.

Sources: Christina Binkley, "How Green Is My Sneaker?" *The Wall Street Journal*, July 22, 2010; Jason B. White, "The Confusing Shades of Green Cars," *The Wall Street Journal*, October 13, 2010; and Paul H. Rubin, "Why Is the Gulf Cleanup So Slow?" *The Wall Street Journal*, July 2, 2010.

resources. Economist Thomas Malthus made this argument in the late 1700s and early 1800s, leading the writer Thomas Carlyle to call economics "the dismal science."

Followers of Malthus today (who are called neo-Malthusians) still believe there are too many people in the world and that the solution to poverty is radical birth control, including forced abortions and sterilization. The latest world statistics, however, show population growing more slowly than expected. In some industrial countries—like Japan, Germany, Italy, Russia, and the United States—population growth may be so slow that eventually there will be too many old people and too few young people to care for them.[8] In the developing world, on the other hand, population will climb relatively quickly and may lead to greater poverty and more unrest. Studies about the effects of population growth on the economy are part of macroeconomics.

Some macroeconomists believe that a large population, especially an educated one, can be a valuable resource. You've probably heard the saying "Give a man a fish and you feed him for a day, but teach a man to fish and you feed him for a lifetime." You can add to that: "Teach a person to start a fish farm, and he or she will be able to feed a village for a lifetime." *The secret to economic development is contained in this last statement.* Business owners provide jobs and economic growth for their employees and communities as well as for themselves.

The challenge for macroeconomists is to determine what makes some countries relatively wealthy and other countries relatively poor, and then to implement policies and programs that lead to increased prosperity for everyone in all countries. One way to begin understanding this challenge is to consider the theories of Adam Smith.

New ways of producing goods and services add resources to the economy and create more employment. Fish farms, for instance, create both food and jobs. Can you think of other innovations that can help increase economic development?

Adam Smith and the Creation of Wealth

Rather than believing fixed resources had to be divided among competing groups and individuals, Scottish economist Adam Smith envisioned creating more resources so that everyone could become wealthier. Smith's book *An Inquiry into the Nature and Causes of the Wealth of Nations* (often called simply *The Wealth of Nations*) was published in 1776.

Smith believed *freedom* was vital to the survival of any economy, especially the freedom to own land or property and to keep the profits from working the land or running a business.[9] He believed people will work long and hard if they have incentives for doing so—that is, if they know they'll be rewarded. As a result of those efforts, the economy will prosper, with plenty of food and all kinds of products available to everyone.[10] Smith's ideas were later challenged by Malthus and others who believed economic conditions would only get worse, but Smith, not Malthus, is considered the *father of modern economics*.

How Businesses Benefit the Community

In Adam Smith's view, businesspeople don't necessarily deliberately set out to help others. They work primarily for their own prosperity and growth. Yet as people try to improve their own situation in life, Smith said, their efforts serve as an "invisible hand" that helps the economy grow and prosper through the production of needed goods, services, and ideas. Thus, the phrase **invisible hand** is used to describe the process that turns self-directed gain into social and economic benefits for all.

How do people working in their own self-interest produce goods, services, and wealth for others? The only way farmers can become wealthy is to sell some of their crops to others. To become even wealthier, they have to hire workers to produce more food. So the farmers' self-centered efforts to become wealthy lead to jobs for some and food for almost all. Think about that process for a minute, because it is critical to understanding economic growth in the United States and other free countries. The same principles apply to everything from clothing to houses to iPads.

invisible hand
A phrase coined by Adam Smith to describe the process that turns self-directed gain into social and economic benefits for all.

According to Adam Smith's theory, business owners are motivated to work hard because they know they will earn, and keep, the rewards of their labor. When they prosper, as the owner of this store has, they are able to add employees and grow, indirectly helping the community and the larger economy grow in the process. What might motivate you to start your own business?

Corruption's Effect on the Economy

There are numerous forces in poor countries that hinder economic growth and development. One of those forces is corruption. In many countries, a businessperson must bribe government officials to get permission to own land, build on it, and conduct normal business operations.

The United States has seen much corruption among businesspeople, such as use of prostitutes, illegal drug use, alcohol addiction, and gambling. Imagine you need a permit to add liquor to your restaurant menu to increase your profit.

You have tried for years to get one, with no results. You have a friend in the government who offers to help you if you make a large contribution to his or her reelection campaign. Would you be tempted to make a campaign contribution? What are your alternatives? What are the consequences of each?

Sources: Alina Dizik, "Social Concerns Gain New Urgency," *The Wall Street Journal,* March 4, 2010; and Carol Loomis, "The $600 Billion Challenge," *Fortune,* July 5, 2010.

Smith assumed that as people became wealthier, they would naturally reach out to help the less fortunate in the community. That has not always happened. Today, however, many businesspeople are becoming more concerned about social issues and their obligation to return to society some of what they've earned.[11] As we mentioned in Chapter 1, it is important for businesses to be ethical as well as generous. Unethical practices undermine the whole economic system. The nearby Making Ethical Decisions box explores what universities are now doing about this.

progress assessment

- What is the difference between macroeconomics and microeconomics?
- What is better for an economy than teaching a man to fish?
- What does Adam Smith's term *invisible hand* mean? How does the invisible hand create wealth for a country?

LEARNING goal 2

Explain what capitalism is and how free markets work.

UNDERSTANDING FREE-MARKET CAPITALISM

Basing their ideas on free-market principles such as those of Adam Smith, businesspeople in the United States, Europe, Japan, Canada, and other countries began to create more wealth than ever before. They hired others to work on their farms and in their factories, and their nations began to prosper as a result. Businesspeople soon became the wealthiest people in society.

However, great disparities in wealth remained or even increased. Many businesspeople owned large homes and fancy carriages while most workers lived in humble surroundings. Nonetheless, there was always the promise of better times. One way to be really wealthy was to start a successful business of your own. Of course, it wasn't that easy—it never has been. Then and now, you have to accumulate some money to buy or start a business, and you have to work long hours to make it grow. But the opportunities are there.[12]

The economic system that has led to wealth creation in much of the world is known as capitalism.[13] Under **capitalism** all or most of the factors of production and distribution—such as land, factories, railroads, and stores—are owned by individuals. They are operated for profit, and businesspeople, not government officials, decide what to produce and how much, what to charge, and how much to pay workers. They also decide whether to produce goods in their own countries or have them made in other countries. No country is purely capitalist, however. Often the government gets involved in issues such as determining minimum wages, setting farm prices, and lending money to some failing businesses—as it does in the United States. But capitalism is the *foundation* of the U.S. economic system, and of the economies of England, Australia, Canada, and most other industrialized nations. There have been many suggestions as to how the United States could improve its capitalist system, especially given the recession that began on 2008.[14]

Some countries are practicing state capitalism. *State capitalism* is where the state runs some businesses instead of private owners. The most obvious example is China, but the same concepts are being used in Russia and some of the Arab nations of the Middle East.[15] These countries have experienced some success using capitalist principles, but the future is still uncertain.[16]

The root word of *capitalism* is "capital." The Spotlight on Small Business box on page 36 shows how a little capital can help small businesses grow in the poorest countries in the world.

> **capitalism**
> An economic system in which all or most of the factors of production and distribution are privately owned and operated for profit.

The Foundations of Capitalism

Under free-market capitalism people have four basic rights:

1. *The right to own private property.* This is the most fundamental of all rights under capitalism. Private ownership means that individuals can buy, sell, and use land, buildings, machinery, inventions, and other forms of property. They can also pass property on to their children. Would farmers work as hard if they didn't own the land and couldn't keep the profits from what they earned? More than 90 percent of Egyptians hold their property without legal title. This is one reason they can't build wealth and why they protested in the streets in 2011.[17]

2. *The right to own a business and keep all that business's profits.* Recall from Chapter 1 that profits equal revenues minus expenses (salaries, materials, taxes). Profits act as important incentives for business owners.

3. *The right to freedom of competition.* Within certain guidelines established by the government, individuals are free to compete with other individuals or businesses in selling and promoting goods and services.

4. *The right to freedom of choice.* People are free to choose where they want to work and what career they want to follow. Other choices people are free to make include where to live and what to buy or sell.

> *The right to own private property and the right to own a business and keep its profits are two of the fundamental rights that exist in the economic system called free-market capitalism. Would either of these rights be viable without the other?*

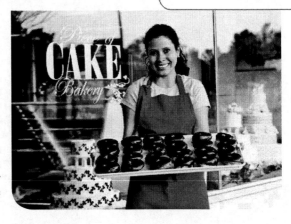

SPOTLIGHT ON SMALL business

www.villagebanking.org

A Small Loan Can Make a Big Difference

One way people in industrialized countries can help people in developing countries is to create a local "bank" that lends money to budding entrepreneurs so they can begin or expand their business. The entrepreneurs must pay the money back, with interest, and often must keep some money in the bank. Such banks don't necessarily have to be in a bank building. Village women often assume the role of banker and decide which women will get the loans. The "bankers" meet in a community building of some sort.

Such banks are sponsored by the Foundation for International Community Assistance (FINCA). In its 10-year history, FINCA has loaned more than $447 million to over 600,000 small-scale entrepreneurs in some of the world's poorest countries. Its borrowers have a 97.6 percent loan repayment rate.

The story of one small entrepreneur will help you understand the process. Pros Magaga lives in Kampala, Uganda. She had a tiny shop in town, but it carried very little inventory. She did not make enough to send her four children to school or to feed them more than once a day. FINCA lent her $50; she used it to buy a refrigerator, which allowed her to carry fresh foods and cold snacks. Later she added a freezer. Now her children are all in school, and the family enjoys two meals a day. Magaga has built a small home with two rooms and plans to add another room soon. She can borrow more money from FINCA because she has already paid back her $50 loan.

Sources: Ruth David, "In a Microfinance Boom, Echoes of Subprime," *Bloomberg Businessweek*, June 21–June 27, 2010; and Daniel Fisher, "Bullish on Harare," *Forbes*, November 22, 2010.

One benefit of the four basic rights of capitalism is that people are willing to take more risks than they might otherwise. President Franklin Roosevelt believed four additional freedoms were essential to economic success: freedom of speech and expression, freedom to worship in your own way, freedom from want, and freedom from fear. Do you see the benefits of these additional freedoms?

Now let's explore how the free market works. What role do consumers play in the process? How do businesses learn what consumers need and want? These questions and more are answered next.

How Free Markets Work

A free market is one in which decisions about what and how much to produce are made by the market—by buyers and sellers negotiating prices for goods and services. You and I and other consumers send signals to tell producers what to make, how many, in what color, and so on. We do that by choosing to buy (or not to buy) certain products and services.

For example, if all of us decided we wanted T-shirts supporting our favorite baseball team, the clothing industry would respond in certain ways. Manufacturers and retailers would increase the price of those T-shirts, because they know people are willing to pay more for the shirts they want. They would also realize they could make more money by making more of those T-shirts. Thus, they have an incentive to pay workers to start earlier and end later. Further, the number of companies making T-shirts would increase. How many T-shirts they make depends on how many we request or buy in the stores. Prices and quantities will continue to change as the number of T-shirts we buy changes.

The same process occurs with most other products. The *price* tells producers how much to produce. If something is wanted but isn't available, the price tends to go up until someone begins making more of that product, sells the ones already on hand, or makes a substitute. As a consequence, there's rarely a long-term shortage of goods in the United States.

How Prices Are Determined

In a free market, prices are not determined by sellers; they are determined by buyers and sellers negotiating in the marketplace. A seller may want to receive $50 for a T-shirt, but the quantity buyers demand at that high price may be quite low. If the seller lowers the price, the quantity demanded is likely to increase. How is a price determined that is acceptable to both buyers and sellers? The answer is found in the microeconomic concepts of supply and demand. We shall explore both next.

The Economic Concept of Supply

Supply refers to the quantities of products manufacturers or owners are willing to sell at different prices at a specific time. Generally speaking, the amount supplied will increase as the price increases, because sellers can make more money with a higher price.

    Economists show this relationship between quantity supplied and price on a graph. Figure 2.1 shows a simple supply curve for T-shirts. The price of the shirts in dollars is shown vertically on the left of the graph. The quantity of shirts sellers are willing to supply is shown horizontally at the bottom of the graph. The various points on the curve indicate how many T-shirts sellers would provide at different prices. For example, at a price of $5 a shirt, a T-shirt vendor would provide only 5 shirts, but at $50 a shirt the vendor would supply 50 shirts. The supply curve indicates the relationship between the price and the quantity supplied. All things being equal, the higher the price, the more the vendor will be willing to supply.

The Economic Concept of Demand

Demand refers to the quantity of products that people are willing to buy at different prices at a specific time. Generally speaking, the quantity demanded will increase as the price decreases. Again, we can show the relationship between price and quantity demanded in a graph. Figure 2.2 shows a simple demand curve for T-shirts. The various points on the graph indicate the quantity demanded at various prices. For example, at $45, buyers demand just 5 shirts, but at $5, the quantity demanded would increase to 35 shirts. All things being equal, the lower the price, the more buyers are willing to buy.

The Equilibrium Point, or Market Price

You might realize from Figures 2.1 and 2.2 that the key factor in determining the quantities supplied and demanded is *price*. If you were to lay the two graphs one on top of the other, the supply curve and the demand curve would cross where quantity demanded and quantity supplied are equal. Figure 2.3 illustrates that point. At a price of $15, the quantity of T-shirts demanded and the quantity supplied are equal (25 shirts). That crossing point is known as the *equilibrium point* or *equilibrium price*. In the long run, that price will become the market price. **Market price**, then, is determined by supply and demand. It is the price toward which the market will trend.

supply
The quantity of products that manufacturers or owners are willing to sell at different prices at a specific time.

demand
The quantity of products that people are willing to buy at different prices at a specific time.

market price
The price determined by supply and demand.

figure 2.1

THE SUPPLY CURVE AT VARIOUS PRICES
The supply curve rises from left to right. Think it through. The higher the price of T-shirts goes (the vertical axis), the more sellers will be willing to supply.

figure 2.2

THE DEMAND CURVE AT VARIOUS PRICES
This is a simple demand curve showing the quantity of T-shirts demanded at different prices. The demand curve falls from left to right. It is easy to understand why. The lower the price of T-shirts, the higher the quantity demanded.

figure 2.3

THE EQUILIBRIUM POINT
The place where quantity demanded and quantity supplied meet is called the equilibrium point. When we put both the supply and demand curves on the same graph, we find that they intersect at a price where the quantity supplied and the quantity demanded are equal. In the long run, the market price will tend toward the equilibrium point.

Proponents of a free market argue that, because supply and demand interactions determine prices, there is no need for the government to set prices. If quantity supplied exceeds quantity demanded, the resulting surplus signals sellers to lower the price. If shortages develop because the quantity supplied is less than quantity demanded, it signals sellers to increase the price. Eventually, supply will again equal demand if nothing interferes with market forces.

When supplies of oil were lower because of the Gulf oil spill, for instance, the price of gasoline went up. When supplies were again plentiful, the price of gas fell a little. The price of gas rose again when there was turmoil in the Middle East (e.g., Libya) and the supply of oil was suspect. Note, too, how many alternative fuel sources (wind, solar, tar sands shale gas, etc.) were tried when the price of gas approached $4 a gallon.[18]

In countries without a free market, there is no mechanism to reveal to businesses (via price) what to produce and in what amounts, so there are often shortages (not enough products) or surpluses (too many products). In such countries, the government decides what to produce and in what quantity, but without price signals it has no way of knowing what the proper quantities are. Furthermore, when the government interferes in otherwise free markets, such as when it subsidizes farm goods, surpluses and shortages may develop. Competition differs in free markets, too. We shall explore that concept next.

The economic concept of demand measures the quantities of goods and services that people are willing to buy. Judging from this photo of people waiting to buy the iPad on the first day it was available for sale, how would you describe the demand for this product? Did the introduction of the iPad 2 generate similar demand?

Competition within Free Markets

Economists generally agree there are four different degrees of competition: (1) perfect competition, (2) monopolistic competition, (3) oligopoly, and (4) monopoly.

Perfect competition exists when there are many sellers in a market and none is large enough to dictate the price of a product. Sellers' products appear to be identical, such as agricultural products like apples, corn, and potatoes. There are no true examples of perfect competition. Today, government price supports and drastic reductions in the number of farms make it hard to argue that even farming represents perfect competition.

Under **monopolistic competition** a large number of sellers produce very similar products that buyers nevertheless perceive as different, such as hot dogs, sodas, personal computers, and T-shirts. Product differentiation—the attempt to make buyers think similar products are different in some way—is a key to success. Think about what that means. Through advertising, branding, and packaging, sellers try to convince buyers that their products are different from competitors', though they may be very similar or even interchangeable. The fast-food industry, with its pricing battles among hamburger offerings and the like, offers a good example of monopolistic competition.[19]

An **oligopoly** is a degree of competition in which just a few sellers dominate a market, as we see in tobacco, gasoline, automobiles, aluminum, and aircraft. One reason some industries remain in the hands of a few sellers is that the initial investment required to enter the business often is tremendous. Think, for example, of how much it would cost to start a new airplane manufacturing facility.

In an oligopoly, products from different companies tend to be priced about the same. The reason is simple: Intense price competition would lower profits for everyone, since a price cut by one producer would most likely be matched by the others. As in monopolistic competition, product differentiation, rather than price, is usually the major factor in market success in an oligopoly. Note, for example, that most cereals are priced about the same, as are soft drinks.

perfect competition
The degree of competition in which there are many sellers in a market and none is large enough to dictate the price of a product.

monopolistic competition
The degree of competition in which a large number of sellers produce very similar products that buyers nevertheless perceive as different.

oligopoly
A degree of competition in which just a few sellers dominate the market.

Thus, advertising is a major factor determining which of the few available brands consumers buy, because often it is advertising that creates the perceived differences.[20]

monopoly
A degree of competition in which only one seller controls the total supply of a product or service, and sets the price.

A **monopoly** occurs when one seller controls the total supply of a product or service, and sets the price. In the United States, laws prohibit the creation of monopolies. Nonetheless, the U.S. legal system has permitted monopolies in the markets for public utilities that sell natural gas, water, and electric power. These companies' prices and profits are usually controlled by public service commissions to protect the interest of buyers. For example, the Florida Public Service Commission is the administering agency over the Florida Power and Light utility company. Legislation ended the monopoly status of utilities in some areas, letting consumers choose among providers. The intention of such *deregulation* is to increase competition among utility companies and, ultimately, lower prices for consumers.

Benefits and Limitations of Free Markets

One benefit of the free market is that it allows open competition among companies. Businesses must provide customers with high-quality products at fair prices with good service. If they don't, they lose customers to businesses that do. Do government services have the same incentives?

The free market—with its competition and incentives—was a major factor in creating the wealth that industrialized countries now enjoy. Some people even talk of the free market as an economic miracle. Free-market capitalism, more than any other economic system, provides opportunities for poor people to work their way out of poverty. Capitalism also encourages businesses to be more efficient so they can successfully compete on price and quality.

Yet, even as free-market capitalism has brought prosperity to the United States and to much of the rest of the world, it has brought inequality as well.[21] Business owners and managers usually make more money and have more wealth than lower-level workers. Yet people who are old, disabled, or sick may not be able to start and manage a business, and others may not have the talent or the drive. What should society do about such inequality? Not everyone in the United States is as generous as Bill Gates, founder of Microsoft, who with his wife has established the Bill and Melinda Gates Foundation to support world health and education.[22] In fact, the desire to create as much wealth as possible has led some businesspeople throughout history, and still today, to exploit such practices as slavery and child labor.

One of the dangers of free markets is that some people let greed dictate how they act. Criminal charges brought against some big businesses in banking, oil, accounting, telecommunications, insurance, and pharmaceuticals indicate the scope of the potential problem. Some businesspeople have deceived the public about their products; others have deceived stockholders about the value of their stock, all in order to increase executives' personal assets.[23]

Clearly, some government laws and regulations are necessary to protect businesses' stakeholders and make sure people who cannot work get the basic care they need.[24] To overcome some of capitalism's limitations, some countries have adopted an economic system called socialism. It, too, has its good and bad points. We explore these after you review the following Progress Assessment questions.

progress assessment

- What are the four basic rights that people have under free-market capitalism?
- How do businesspeople know what to produce and in what quantity?
- How are prices determined?
- What are the four degrees of competition, and what are some examples of each?

LEARNING goal **3**

Compare socialism and communism.

socialism
An economic system based on the premise that some, if not most, basic businesses should be owned by the government so that profits can be more evenly distributed among the people.

UNDERSTANDING SOCIALISM

Socialism is an economic system based on the premise that some, if not most, basic businesses (e.g., steel mills, coal mines, and utilities) should be owned by the government so that profits can be more evenly distributed among the people. Entrepreneurs often own and run smaller businesses, and individuals are often taxed relatively steeply to pay for social programs. The top federal personal income tax rate in the United States, for example, was 35 percent recently, but in some socialist countries the top rate can be as much as 60 percent. While U.S. shoppers pay sales taxes ranging from over 10 percent in Chicago to zero in Delaware, socialist countries charge a similar value-added tax of 15 to 20 percent or more. Socialists acknowledge the major benefit of capitalism—wealth creation—but believe that wealth should be more evenly distributed than occurs in free-market capitalism. They believe the government should carry out the distribution and be much more involved in protecting the environment and providing for the poor.

The Benefits of Socialism

The major benefit of socialism is supposed to be social equality.[25] Ideally it comes about because the government takes income from wealthier people, in the form of taxes, and redistributes it to poorer people through various government programs. Free education through college, free health care, and free child care are some of the benefits socialist governments, using the money from taxes, may provide to their people. Such education benefits helped Finland become the world leader in student achievement.[26] Workers in socialist countries usually get longer vacations, work fewer hours per week, and have more employee benefits (e.g., generous sick leave) than those in countries where free-market capitalism prevails.

Socialism has been more successful in some countries than in others. This photo shows Denmark's clean and modern public transportation system. In Greece, overspending caused a debt crisis that forced the government to impose austerity measures that many Greeks oppose. What other factors might lead to slower growth in socialist countries?

The Negative Consequences of Socialism

Socialism may create more equality than capitalism, but it takes away some of businesspeople's incentives. For example, tax rates in some socialist nations once reached 83 percent. Today, doctors, lawyers, business owners, and others who earn a lot of money pay very high tax rates. As a consequence, many of them leave socialist countries for capitalistic countries with lower taxes, such as the United States. This loss of the best and brightest people to other countries is called a **brain drain**.

Imagine an experiment in socialism in your own class. Imagine that after the first exam, those with grades of 90 and above have to give some of their points to those who make 70 and below so that everyone ends up with grades in the 80s. Would those who got 90s study as hard for the second exam? What about those who got 70s? Can you see why workers may not work as hard or as well if they all get the same benefits regardless of how hard they work?

Socialism also tends to result in fewer inventions and less innovation, because those who come up with new ideas usually don't receive as much reward as they would in a capitalist system. Communism may be considered a more intensive version of socialism. We shall explore that system next.

brain drain
The loss of the best and brightest people to other countries.

UNDERSTANDING COMMUNISM

Communism is an economic and political system in which the government makes almost all economic decisions and owns almost all the major factors of production. It intrudes further into the lives of people than socialism does. For example, some communist countries have not allowed their citizens to practice certain religions, change jobs, or move to the town of their choice.

One problem with communism is that the government has no way of knowing what to produce, because prices don't reflect supply and demand as they do in free markets. The government must guess what the people need. As a result, shortages of many items, including food and clothing, may develop. Another problem is that communism doesn't inspire businesspeople to work hard because the incentives are not there. Therefore, communism is slowly disappearing as an economic form.

Most communist countries today are suffering severe economic depression. In North Korea, many people are starving. In Cuba, people suffer a lack of goods and services readily available in most other countries, and some fear the government. Even so, there seems to be a movement toward communist principles in Venezuela, following the Cuban model.

While some parts of the former Soviet Union remain under communist ideals, Russia itself now has a flat tax of only 13 percent. Yet this low rate increased the government's tax revenues by nearly 30 percent, because more people were willing to pay. The trend toward free markets is growing in Vietnam and parts of China as well. The regions of China that are most free have prospered rapidly, while the rest of the country has grown relatively slowly. Remnants of China's communist system, such as political and religious oppression, still exist, however.

communism
An economic and political system in which the government makes almost all economic decisions and owns almost all the major factors of production.

LEARNING goal 4

Analyze the trend toward mixed economies.

THE TREND TOWARD MIXED ECONOMIES

The nations of the world have largely been divided between those that followed the concepts of capitalism and those that adopted the concepts of communism or socialism. We can now contrast the two major economic systems as follows:

1. **Free-market economies** exist when the market largely determines what goods and services get produced, who gets them, and how the economy grows. *Capitalism* is the popular term for this economic system.
2. **Command economies** exist when the government largely decides what goods and services will be produced, who gets them, and how the economy will grow. *Socialism* and *communism* are variations on this economic system.

Although all countries actually have some mix of the two systems, neither free-market nor command economies have resulted in optimal economic conditions. Free-market mechanisms don't seem to respond enough to the needs of the poor, the old, or the disabled. Some people also believe that businesses in free-market economies have not done enough to protect the environment. (We shall discuss that issue throughout the text.) Over time, voters in mostly free-market countries, such as the United States, have elected officials who have adopted many social and environmental programs such as Social Security, welfare, unemployment compensation, and various clean air and water acts. What new or enhanced social policies do you know of that are being considered today?

Socialism and communism haven't always created enough jobs or wealth to keep economies growing fast enough. Thus, communist governments are disappearing, and some socialist governments have been cutting back on social programs and lowering taxes on businesses and workers to generate more business growth and more revenue.[27] The Reaching Beyond Our Borders box discusses how the economy of China has been growing despite its communist base.

The trend, then, has been for mostly capitalist countries (like the United States) to move toward socialism (i.e. more government involvement in health care), and for mostly socialist countries, such as France and China, to move toward capitalism

free-market economies Economic systems in which the market largely determines what goods and services get produced, who gets them, and how the economy grows.

command economies Economic systems in which the government largely decides what goods and services will be produced, who will get them, and how the economy will grow.

Since the communist system in Russia has largely collapsed, the country has been moving toward a viable market economy. As poverty begins to decline, a middle class is emerging. More jobs are being created like the ones in this Hewlett-Packard manufacturing facility. Do you think the Russian economy will continue to grow?

REACHING BEYOND
our borders

China's Changing Economy

It is important, when studying economics, to look at countries throughout the world to see how they are doing economically. One country that has been in the news a lot lately is China. China's economy is growing two or three times faster than the United States. As a consequence of that rapid growth, China is worried about inflation and the possibility of a housing crash and market drop much like the one experienced recently in the U.S.

China is now the world's second largest economy, replacing Japan. China's GDP grew 10.3 percent in 2010, up from 9.2 percent in 2009. The rapid rise in the Chinese economy creates opportunities for companies that sell them goods and services, but the rapid growth in Chinese manufacturing also creates problems for countries trying to compete. There is much discussion in the United States about losing jobs to Chinese workers whose pay is much lower than in the United States.

Although it is known for its socialist and communist foundations, one reason China is growing so rapidly is because it has adopted capitalist principles. This is an interesting time

to watch world economies to see what kind of system proves to be the most beneficial to the most people.

Sources: Jason Dean and Aaron Back, "China Growth Shows Contrast with U.S.," *The Wall Street Journal,* January 21, 2011; and Kevin D. Williamson, "The Other National Debt," *National Review,* June 21, 2010.

(more private businesses, lower taxes). All countries have some mix of the two systems. Thus, the long-term global trend is toward a blend of capitalism and socialism. This trend likely will increase with the opening of global markets made easier by the Internet. The net effect is the emergence throughout the world of mixed economies.

mixed economies
Economic systems in which some allocation of resources is made by the market and some by the government.

Mixed economies exist where some allocation of resources is made by the market and some by the government. Most countries don't have a name for such a system. If free-market mechanisms allocate most resources, the leaders call their system capitalism. If the government allocates most resources, the leaders call it socialism. Figure 2.4 compares the various economic systems.

Like most other nations of the world, the United States has a mixed economy. The U.S. government has now become the largest employer in the country, which means there are more workers in the public sector (government) than in any of the major businesses in the United States. Do you see the government growing or declining in the coming years?

progress assessment

- What led to the emergence of socialism?
- What are the benefits and drawbacks of socialism?
- What countries still practice communism?
- What are the characteristics of a mixed economy?

	CAPITALISM* (United States)	SOCIALISM (Sweden)	COMMUNISM (North Korea)	MIXED ECONOMY (Germany)
Social and Economic Goals	Private ownership of land and business. Liberty and the pursuit of happiness. Free trade. Emphasis on freedom and the profit motive for economic growth.	Public ownership of major businesses. Some private ownership of smaller businesses and shops. Government control of education, health care, utilities, mining, transportation, and media. Very high taxation. Emphasis on equality.	Public ownership of all businesses. Government-run education and health care. Emphasis on equality. Many limitations on freedom, including freedom to own businesses and to assemble to protest government actions.	Private ownership of land and business with government regulation. Government control of some institutions (e.g., mail). High taxation for defense and the common welfare. Emphasis on a balance between freedom and equality.
Motivation of Workers	Much incentive to work efficiently and hard because profits are retained by owners. Workers are rewarded for high productivity.	Capitalist incentives exist in private businesses. Government control of wages in public institutions limits incentives.	Very little incentive to work hard or to produce quality goods or services.	Incentives are similar to capitalism except in government-owned enterprises, which may have fewer incentives.
Control over Markets	Complete freedom of trade within and among nations. Some government control of markets.	Some markets are controlled by the government and some are free. Trade restrictions among nations vary and include some free-trade agreements.	Total government control over markets except for illegal transactions.	Some government control of trade within and among nations (trade protectionism).
Choices in the Market	A wide variety of goods and services is available. Almost no scarcity or over-supply exists for long because supply and demand control the market.	Variety in the marketplace varies considerably from country to country. Choice is directly related to government involvement in markets.	Very little choice among competing goods.	Similar to capitalism, but scarcity and oversupply may be caused by government involvement in the market (e.g., subsidies for farms).
Social Freedoms	Freedom of speech, press, assembly, religion, job choice, movement, and elections.	Similar to mixed economy. Governments may restrict job choice, movement among countries, and who may attend upper-level schools (i.e., college).	Very limited freedom to protest the government, practice religion, or change houses or jobs.	Some restrictions on freedoms of assembly and speech. Separation of church and state may limit religious practices in schools.

*The United States is a mixed economy based on a foundation of capitalism.

figure 2.4

COMPARISONS OF KEY ECONOMIC SYSTEMS

gross domestic product (GDP)
The total value of final goods and services produced in a country in a given year.

LEARNING goal 5

Describe the economic system of the United States, including the significance of key economic indicators (especially GDP), productivity, and the business cycle.

UNDERSTANDING THE U.S. ECONOMIC SYSTEM

The following sections will introduce the terms and concepts that you, as an informed citizen, will need to understand in order to grasp the issues facing government and business leaders in the United States.

Key Economic Indicators

Three major indicators of economic conditions are (1) the gross domestic product (GDP), (2) the unemployment rate, and (3) price indexes. Another important statistic is the increase or decrease in productivity. When you read business literature, you'll see these terms used again and again. Let's explore what they mean.

The overall unemployment rate in the U.S. fluctuates. Over the last decade, it has been as low as less than 5 percent and as high as more than 10 percent. Unemployment insurance goes only so far to relieve the loss of income caused by losing your job. How high is the unemployment rate in your area today?

Gross Domestic Product   **Gross domestic product (GDP)**, which we mentioned briefly in Chapter 1, is the total value of final goods and services produced in a country in a given year. Both domestic and foreign-owned companies can produce the goods and services included in GDP, as long as the companies are located within the country's boundaries. For example, production values from Japanese automaker Honda's factory in Ohio are included in U.S. GDP. Revenue generated by Ford's factory in Mexico is included in Mexico's GDP, even though Ford is a U.S. company.

Almost every discussion about a nation's economy is based on GDP. If growth in GDP slows or declines, businesses may feel many negative effects, such as the slowdown in retail sales experienced beginning in 2008. A major influence on the growth of GDP is the productivity of the workforce—that is, how much output workers create with a given amount of input. The total U.S. GDP is about $14 trillion. The level of U.S. economic activity is actually larger than the GDP figures show, because those figures don't take into account illicit activities such as sales of illegal drugs. The high GDP in the United States is what enables its citizens to enjoy a high standard of living.

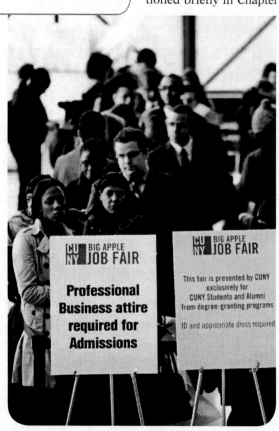

The Unemployment Rate   The **unemployment rate** refers to the percentage of civilians at least 16 years old who are unemployed *and tried to find a job within the prior four weeks*. In 2000, the U.S. unemployment rate reached its lowest point in over 30 years, falling as low as 3.9 percent, but by 2010

figure 2.5

U.S. UNEMPLOYMENT RATE 1989–2011

the rate had risen to over 9.5 percent (see Figure 2.5). The unemployment rate fell to below 9 percent in 2011, but many people had given up looking for jobs (people who are not actively looking for work are not included in the unemployment figures).

Figure 2.6 describes the four types of unemployment: frictional, structural, cyclical, and seasonal. The United States tries to protect those who are unemployed because of recessions (defined later in the chapter), industry shifts, and other cyclical factors. Nonetheless, the *underemployment* figure in 2010 was about 17 percent (this includes those who are working part time and want to work full time and those who stopped looking for work).[28]

If you worry about the U.S. unemployment rate, consider this: the unemployment rate in Zimbabwe is way over 80 percent, and the inflation rate is spectacular. You would enjoy cashing in your dollars in Zimbabwe; one dollar will get you billions of Zimbabwean dollars. Actually, the situation is getting much worse. Do you suppose Zimbabwe is a capitalist economy?

Inflation and Price Indexes   Price indexes help gauge the health of the economy by measuring the levels of inflation, disinflation, deflation, and stagflation. **Inflation** is a general rise in the prices of goods and services over time.

unemployment rate
The number of civilians at least 16 years old who are unemployed and tried to find a job within the prior four weeks.

inflation
A general rise in the prices of goods and services over time.

figure 2.6

FOUR TYPES OF UNEMPLOYMENT

- *Frictional unemployment* refers to those people who have quit work because they didn't like the job, the boss, or the working conditions and who haven't yet found a new job. It also refers to those people who are entering the labor force for the first time (e.g., new graduates) or are returning to the labor force after significant time away (e.g., parents who reared children). There will always be some frictional unemployment because it takes some time to find a first job or a new job.

- *Structural unemployment* refers to unemployment caused by the restructuring of firms or by a mismatch between the skills (or location) of job seekers and the requirements (or location) of available jobs (e.g., coal miners in an area where mines have been closed).

- *Cyclical unemployment* occurs because of a recession or a similar downturn in the business cycle (the ups and downs of business growth and decline over time). This type of unemployment is the most serious.

- *Seasonal unemployment* occurs where demand for labor varies over the year, as with the harvesting of crops.

figure 2.7

HOW THE CONSUMER PRICE INDEX IS PUT TOGETHER

1. 400 data collectors visit stores and gather 80,000 retail price quotes and 5,000 housing rent quotes, transmitting data daily to Washington.

2. 40 commodity analysts at the Bureau of Labor Statistics review about a quarter of this avalanche of price data.

3. About nine days before the release of the CPI, the office is locked down—with bright red RESTRICTED AREA signs posted on all the doors.

4. 90 people—a mix of commodity analysts and other economists who specialize in assembling the CPI—compute basic indexes for 211 item categories, which are divided into 38 index areas.

5. Final results are released at 8:30 a.m., Eastern time, about two weeks after the end of the month in question.

disinflation
A situation in which price increases are slowing (the inflation rate is declining).

deflation
A situation in which prices are declining.

stagflation
A situation when the economy is slowing but prices are going up anyhow.

consumer price index (CPI)
Monthly statistics that measure the pace of inflation or deflation.

producer price index (PPI)
An index that measures prices at the wholesale level.

The official definition is "a persistent increase in the level of consumer prices or a persistent decline in the purchasing power of money, caused by an increase in available currency and credit beyond the proportion of goods and services." Thus, it is also described as "too many dollars chasing too few goods." Go back and review the laws of supply and demand to see how that works. Rapid inflation is scary. If the prices of goods and services go up by just 7 percent a year, they will double in about 10 years. Think of how much fear was generated by the rapid increase in the price of gasoline in 2011.

Disinflation occurs when price increases are slowing (the inflation rate is declining). That was the situation in the United States throughout the 1990s. **Deflation** means that prices are declining.[29] It occurs when countries produce so many goods that people cannot afford to buy them all (too few dollars are chasing too many goods). Some experts believed that deflation could occur in 2011.[30] **Stagflation** occurs when the economy is slowing but prices are going up anyhow. Some economists fear the United States may face stagflation in the near future.

The **consumer price index (CPI)** consists of monthly statistics that measure the pace of inflation or deflation. The government computes costs of goods and services—including housing, food, apparel, and medical care—to see whether they are going up or down (see Figure 2.7). The CPI is an important figure because some wages and salaries, rents and leases, tax brackets, government benefits, and interest rates are based on it. You may see the term *core inflation*. That means the CPI minus food and energy costs. Since food and energy have been going up rapidly, the core inflation figure is actually much lower than the real CPI.

The **producer price index (PPI)** measures prices at the wholesale level. Other indicators of the economy's condition include housing starts, retail sales, and changes in personal income. You can learn more about such indicators by reading business periodicals, listening to business broadcasts on radio and television, and exploring business sites on the Internet.

Productivity in the United States

An increase in productivity means a worker can produce more goods and services than before in the same time period, usually thanks to machinery or other equipment. Productivity in the United States has risen because computers and other technology have made production faster and easier. The higher is productivity, the lower are the costs of producing goods and services, and the lower prices can be. Therefore, businesspeople are eager to increase productivity. Remember, however, that high productivity can lead to high unemployment.[31]

Certainly, that is what the United States in now experiencing.

Now that the U.S. economy is a service economy, productivity is an issue because service firms are so labor-intensive. Spurred by foreign competition, productivity in the manufacturing sector is rising rapidly. In the service sector, productivity is growing more slowly because service workers—like teachers, clerks, lawyers, and barbers—have fewer new technologies available than there are for factory workers.

Productivity in the Service Sector

One problem with the service industry is that an influx of machinery may add to the *quality* of the service provided but not to the *output per worker*. For example, you've probably noticed how many computers there are on college campuses. They add to the quality of education but don't necessarily boost professors' productivity. The same is true of some equipment in hospitals, such as CAT scanners, PET scanners, and MRI scanners. They improve patient care but don't necessarily increase the number of patients doctors can see. In other words, today's productivity measures in the service industry fail to capture the increase in quality caused by new technology.

Clearly, the United States and other countries need to develop new measures of productivity for the service economy that include quality as well as quantity of output. Despite productivity improvement, the economy is likely to go through a series of ups and downs, much as it has over the past few years. We'll explore that process next.

It can be difficult to measure productivity in the service sector. New technology can improve the quality of services without necessarily increasing the number of people served. A doctor can make more accurate diagnoses with scans, for instance, but still can only see so many patients in a day. How can productivity measures capture improvements in the quality of service?

The Business Cycle

Business cycles are the periodic rises and falls that occur in economies over time. Economists look at a number of business cycles, from seasonal cycles that occur within a year to cycles that occur every 48–60 years.

Economist Joseph Schumpeter identified the four phases of long-term business cycles as boom–recession–depression–recovery:

1. An *economic boom* is just what it sounds like—business is booming.
2. **Recession** is two or more consecutive quarters of decline in the GDP. In a recession prices fall, people purchase fewer products, and businesses fail. A recession brings high unemployment, increased business failures, and an overall drop in living standards. The recession that started in 2008 is an example.
3. A **depression** is a severe recession, usually accompanied by deflation. Business cycles rarely go through a depression phase. In fact, while there were many business cycles during the 20th century, there was only one severe depression (1930s). Nonetheless some economists are predicting a depression in the coming years.
4. A *recovery* occurs when the economy stabilizes and starts to grow. This eventually leads to an economic boom, starting the cycle all over again.

One goal of some economists is to predict such ups and downs. That is very difficult to do. Business cycles are identified according to facts, but we can explain those facts only by using theories. Therefore, we cannot predict

business cycles
The periodic rises and falls that occur in economies over time.

recession
Two or more consecutive quarters of decline in the GDP.

depression
A severe recession, usually accompanied by deflation.

with certainty. But one thing is certain: over time, the economy *will* rise and fall as it has done lately.

Since dramatic swings up and down in the economy cause all kinds of disruptions to businesses, the government tries to minimize such changes. It uses fiscal policy and monetary policy to try to keep the economy from slowing too much or growing too rapidly.

LEARNING goal 6

Contrast fiscal policy and monetary policy, and explain how each affects the economy.

Stabilizing the Economy through Fiscal Policy

fiscal policy
The federal government's efforts to keep the economy stable by increasing or decreasing taxes or government spending.

Fiscal policy refers to the federal government's efforts to keep the economy stable by increasing or decreasing taxes or government spending. The first fiscal policy tool is taxation. Theoretically, high tax rates tend to slow the economy because they draw money away from the private sector and put it into the government. High tax rates may discourage small-business ownership because they decrease the profits businesses can earn and make the effort less rewarding.[32] It follows, then, that low tax rates will theoretically give the economy a boost.

In the United States, the percentage of GDP the government takes through taxes at all levels (federal, state, and local) is about 28 percent. When you count all fees, sales taxes, and more, taxes on the highest-earning citizens could exceed 50 percent. Is that figure too high or not high enough in your opinion? Why?

The second fiscal policy tool is government spending on highways, social programs, education, infrastructure (e.g., roads and utilities), defense, and so on. The *national deficit* is the amount of money the federal government spends beyond what it gathers in taxes for a given fiscal year. The deficit is expected to be over $1 trillion for the next several years. Such deficits increase the national debt. The **national debt** is the sum of government deficits over time. Recently, the national debt was over $14 trillion (see Figure 2.8). That is a rather misleading number, however, since the unfunded obligation for Medicare alone is about $34 trillion. The unfunded debt to Social Security is on top of that. If the government takes in more revenue than it spends (i.e., tax revenues exceed expenditures), there is a *national surplus*. That is not likely to happen soon.

national debt
The sum of government deficits over time.

One way to lessen deficits is to cut government spending. Many presidents and those in Congress have promised to make the government "smaller," that is, to reduce government spending—but that doesn't happen very often. There seems to be a need for more social programs or more defense spending (such as for the wars in Iraq, Afghanistan, and Libya) each year, and thus the deficits continue and add to the national debt. Some people believe that government spending helps the economy grow. Others believe that the money the government spends comes out of the pockets of consumers and businesspeople, and thus slows growth. What do you think?

Keynesian economic theory
The theory that a government policy of increasing spending and cutting taxes could stimulate the economy in a recession.

Fiscal Policy in Action during the Economic Crisis that Began in 2008

monetary policy
The management of the money supply and interest rates by the Federal Reserve.

For most of his presidency, George W. Bush followed the basic economic principles of free markets. By the end of his term, however, the economy was facing a dire economic crisis and President Bush approved the spending of almost $1 trillion of government money in an effort to revive the failing economy (including helping out banks, the auto industry, and others). (A trillion dollars

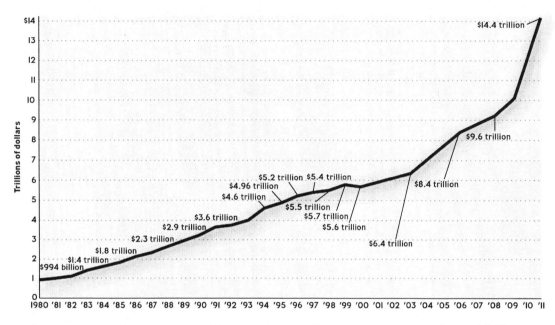

figure 2.8

THE NATIONAL DEBT

is about $3,272 per person in the United States.) President Barack Obama promised to spend additional funds. Both presidents were following the basic economic theory of Keynes discussed in the Profile.[33] As you recall, **Keynesian economic theory** is the theory that a government policy of increasing spending and cutting taxes could stimulate the economy in a recession.

Using Monetary Policy to Keep the Economy Growing

Have you ever wondered what organization adds money to or subtracts money from the economy? The answer is the Federal Reserve Bank (the Fed). The Fed is a semiprivate organization that is not under the direct control of the government but does have members appointed by the president. We will discuss the Fed in detail when we look at banking in Chapter 20. Now we simply introduce monetary policy and the role of the Fed in controlling the economy.

Monetary policy is the management of the money supply and interest rates by the Federal Reserve Bank. The Fed's most visible role is the raising and lowering of interest rates. When the economy is booming, the Fed tends to raise interest rates. This makes money more expensive to borrow. Businesses thus borrow less, and the economy slows as businesspeople spend less money on everything they need to grow, including labor and machinery. The opposite is true when the Fed lowers interest rates. Businesses tend to borrow more, and the economy is expected to grow. Raising and lowering interest rates should therefore help control the rapid ups and downs of the economy.[34] In 2010–2011, the Fed kept interest rates near zero,

The economic crisis beginning in 2008 caused much anguish among Wall Street workers and people in general. How effective was the government's response?

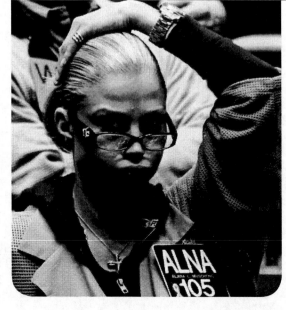

but the economy remained sluggish. You can imagine the pressure that put on the head of the Federal Reserve.[35]

The Fed also controls the money supply. A simple explanation of this function is that the more money the Fed makes available to businesspeople and others, the faster the economy is supposed to grow. To slow the economy (and prevent inflation), the Fed lowers the money supply. The Fed poured money into the economy in 2008–2011. What would you expect the result to be?

To sum up, there are two major tools for managing the economy of the United States: fiscal policy (government taxes and spending) and monetary policy (the Fed's control over interest rates and the money supply). The goal is to keep the economy growing so that more people can rise up the economic ladder and enjoy a higher standard of living and quality of life.

progress assessment

- Name the three economic indicators and describe how well the United States is doing based on each indicator.
- What's the difference between a recession and a depression?
- How does the government manage the economy using fiscal policy?
- What does the term *monetary policy* mean? What organization is responsible for monetary policy?

summary

Learning Goal 1. Explain basic economics.

- **What is economics?**

Economics is the study of how society chooses to employ resources to produce goods and services and distribute them for consumption among various competing groups and individuals.

- **What are the two branches of economics?**

There are two major branches of economics: macroeconomics studies the operation of a nation's economy as a whole, and microeconomics studies the behavior of people and organizations in particular markets (e.g., why people buy smaller cars when gas prices go up).

- **How can we be assured of having enough resources?**

Resource development is the study of how to increase resources and create the conditions that will make better use of them.

- **How does capitalism create a climate for economic growth?**

Under capitalism, businesspeople don't often deliberately set out to help others; they work mostly for their own prosperity and growth. Yet people's efforts to improve their own situation in life act like an *invisible hand* to help the economy grow and prosper through the production of needed goods, services, and ideas.

Learning Goal 2. Explain what capitalism is and how free markets work.

- **What is capitalism?**

Capitalism is an economic system in which all or most of the means of production and distribution are privately owned and operated for profit.

- **Who decides what to produce under capitalism?**

In capitalist countries, businesspeople decide what to produce, how much to pay workers, and how much to charge for goods and services. They also decide whether to produce certain goods in their own countries, import those goods, or have them made in other countries.

- **What are the basic rights people have under capitalism?**

The four basic rights under capitalism are (1) the right to private property, (2) the right to own a business and to keep all of that business's profits after taxes, (3) the right to freedom of competition, and (4) the right to freedom of choice. President Franklin D. Roosevelt felt that other economic freedoms were also important: the right to freedom of speech and expression, the right to worship in your own way, and freedom from want and fear.

- **How does the free market work?**

The free market is one in which buyers and sellers negotiating prices for goods and services influence the decisions about what gets produced and in what quantities. Buyers' decisions in the marketplace tell sellers what to produce and in what quantity. When buyers demand more goods, the price goes up, signaling suppliers to produce more. The higher the price, the more goods and services suppliers are willing to produce. Price is the mechanism that allows free markets to work.

Learning Goal 3. Compare socialism and communism.

- **What is socialism?**

Socialism is an economic system based on the premise that some businesses should be owned by the government.

- **What are the advantages and disadvantages of socialism?**

Socialism intends to create more social equity. Workers in socialist countries usually receive more education, health care, and other benefits and also work fewer hours, with longer vacations. The major disadvantage of socialism is that it lowers the incentive to start a business or to work hard. Socialist economies tend to have a higher unemployment rate and a slower growth rate than capitalist economies.

- **How does socialism differ from communism?**

Under communism, the government owns almost all major production facilities and dictates what gets produced and by whom. Communism is also more restrictive when it comes to personal freedoms, such as religious freedom.

Learning Goal 4. Analyze the trend toward mixed economies.

- **What is a mixed economy?**

A mixed economy is part capitalist and part socialist. Some businesses are privately owned, but taxes tend to be high to distribute income more evenly among the population.

- **What countries have mixed economies?**

The United States has a mixed economy, as do most other industrialized countries.

- **What are the benefits of mixed economies?**

A mixed economy has most of the benefits of wealth creation that free markets bring plus the benefits of greater social equality and concern for the environment that socialism promises.

Learning Goal 5. Describe the economic system of the United States, including the significance of key economic indicators (especially GDP), productivity, and the business cycle.

• **What are the key economic indicators in the United States?**

Gross domestic product (GDP) is the total value of final goods and services produced in a country in a given year. The *unemployment rate* refers to the percentage of civilians at least 16 years old who are unemployed and tried to find a job within the most recent four weeks. The *consumer price index (CPI)* measures changes in the prices of about 400 goods and services that consumers buy.

• **What are the four phases of business cycles?**

In an *economic boom*, businesses do well. A *recession* occurs when two or more quarters show declines in the GDP, prices fall, people purchase fewer products, and businesses fail. A *depression* is a severe recession. *Recovery* occurs when the economy stabilizes and starts to grow.

Learning Goal 6. Contrast fiscal policy and monetary policy, and explain how each affects the economy.

• **What is fiscal policy?**

Fiscal policy consists of government efforts to keep the economy stable by increasing or decreasing taxes or government spending.

• **What is the importance of monetary policy to the economy?**

Monetary policy is the management of the money supply and interest rates. When unemployment gets too high, the Federal Reserve Bank (the Fed) may put more money into the economy and lower interest rates. That is supposed to provide a boost to the economy as businesses borrow and spend more money and hire more people.

key terms

critical thinking

U.S. Supreme Court ruled that cities could have school voucher programs that give money directly to parents, who could then choose between competing schools, public or private. The idea was to create competition among schools. Like businesses, schools were expected to improve their services (how effectively they teach) to win students from competitors. The result would be improvement in all schools, private and public, to benefit many students.

1. Do you believe economic principles like competition apply in both private and public organizations? Be prepared to defend your answer.

2. Are there other public functions that might benefit from more competition, including competition from private firms?

3. Many people say that businesspeople do not do enough for society. Some students choose to go into the public sector instead of business because they want to help others. However, businesspeople say that they do more to help others than nonprofit groups do because they provide jobs for people rather than giving them charity. Furthermore, they believe businesses create all the wealth that nonprofit groups distribute.

   a. How can you find some middle ground in this debate to show that both businesspeople and those who work for nonprofit organizations contribute to society and need to work together more closely to help people?

   b. How could you use the concepts of Adam Smith to help illustrate your position?

developing workplace skills

1. In teams, develop a list of the advantages of living in a capitalist society. Then develop lists headed "What are the disadvantages?" and "How could such disadvantages be minimized?" Describe why a poor person in a socialist country might reject capitalism and prefer a socialist state.

2. Show your understanding of the principles of supply and demand by looking at the oil market today. Why does the price of gas fluctuate so greatly? What will happen as more and more people in China and India decide to buy automobiles? What would happen if most U.S. consumers decided to drive electric cars?

3. This exercise will help you understand socialism from different perspectives. Form three groups. Each group should adopt a different role in a socialist economy: one group will be the business owners, another group will be workers, and another will be government leaders. Within your group discuss and list the advantages and disadvantages to you of lowering taxes on businesses. Then have each group choose a representative to go to the front of the class and debate the tax issue with the representatives from the other groups.

4. Draw a line and mark one end "Free-Market Capitalism" and the other end "Central Planning." Mark where on the line the United States is now.

Explain why you marked the spot you chose. Students from other countries may want to do this exercise for their own countries and explain the differences to the class.

5. Break into small groups. In your group discuss how the following changes have affected people's purchasing behavior and attitudes toward the United States and its economy: the wars in Iraq and Afghanistan, the increased amount spent on homeland security, the government involvement in banking and other industries, and the growth of the Internet. Have a group member prepare a short summary for the class.

taking it to the net

Purpose

To familiarize you with the sources of economic information that are important to business decision makers.

Exercise

Imagine that your boss asked you to help her to prepare the company's sales forecast for the coming two years. In the past, she felt that such trends in the nation's GDP, U.S. manufacturing, and manufacturing in Illinois were especially helpful in forecasting sales. She would like you to do the following:

1. Go to the Bureau of Economic Analysis's website (www.bea.gov) and locate the gross domestic product data. Compare the annual figure for the last four years. What do the figures indicate for the next couple of years?

2. At the Bureau of Labor Statistics' website (www.bls.gov) under Industries, click on Industries at a Glance to find the information about the manufacturing industry. What is the employment trend in manufacturing over the last four years (percentage change from preceding period)?

3. Return to the Bureau of Labor Statistics' home page and use the Search feature to find trends in employment for the state of Illinois. Look around the website to see what other information is available. Plot the trend in manufacturing employment in Illinois over the last four years. On your own, discuss what economic changes may have influenced that trend.

4. Based on the information you have gathered, write a brief summary of what may happen to company sales over the next couple of years.

casing the web

To access the case "The Rule of 72," visit **www.mhhe.com/ub10e**

video case

To access the video case featuring Oppurtunity International, visit **www.mhhe.com/ubl0e**

HOW to Form a Business

After you have read and studied this chapter, you should be able to

1 Compare the advantages and disadvantages of sole proprietorships.

2 Describe the differences between general and limited partners, and compare the advantages and disadvantages of partnerships.

3 Compare the advantages and disadvantages of corporations, and summarize the differences between C corporations, S corporations, and limited liability companies.

4 Define and give examples of three types of corporate mergers, and explain the role of leveraged buyouts and taking a firm private.

5 Outline the advantages and disadvantages of franchises, and discuss the opportunities for diversity in franchising and the challenges of global franchising.

6 Explain the role of cooperatives.

profile

Getting to Know

X *Mary Ellen Sheets*

Founder of Two Men and a Truck

Regardless of background or experience, every successful entrepreneur shares at least one thing in common: they each identified a need and filled it. For Mary Ellen Sheets, all she wanted when she started her business was for her sons Brig and Jon Sorber to get out of the house and earn some money during their summer vacation. Sheets gave the boys an old pickup truck and soon they had an ad in the paper that read, "Two men and a truck." The simple slogan eventually became the name of the moving business Sheets' sons ran throughout their high school years.

Once Brig and Jon went off to college, Sheets continued to receive phone calls from customers asking for her sons' services. Recognizing the demand, Sheets purchased a used moving van for $350 and hired two employees to do the lifting. Her minimal initial investment turned out to be the only money Sheets ever had to take out of her own pocket for the business. As Two Men and a Truck steadily grew, Sheets took a big risk and quit her job in state government (forgoing her retirement) to work on the business full time. The gamble paid off within a year when Sheets granted the first Two Men and a Truck franchise to her daughter Melanie in Atlanta, GA.

Since then Sheets and her family have expanded their brand to more than 215 locations across the country, earning $193.3 million annually. The key to the company's success is its simplicity. The name says it all, as does the straightforward stick-figure logo drawn by Sheets when the business was still her sons' summer jobs. The brand is so effective that the company is now expanding overseas with franchises in the United Kingdom.

Besides its financial success, Two Men and a Truck also remains committed to giving back to each community it serves. Every truck in its system sports the slogan, "The Movers Who Care." Two Men and a Truck's record of service goes back to the company's beginnings. After generating a $1,000 profit in its first year, Sheets was so pleased that she gave away the money to 10 different charities, giving each $100. Two Men and a Truck continues to donate generously to those original organizations. The company also contributes a portion of every move completed to the American Cancer Society. With 317,841 moves completed in 2010 alone, that's certainly no small donation. Nevertheless, Sheets and her family see charity and service as integral parts of their business plan. The corporate office even grants a Humanitarian Award each year to the franchisee that performs the most community service. The Omaha, NE, franchise took home the prize in 2010 after donating more than 2,000 hours of service.

Sheets herself is no stranger to accolades. In 2004 she became the first woman to win the International Franchise Association's Entrepreneur of the Year award. She was honored with a number of other recognitions over the years, including a Blue Chip Award and the Michigan Entrepreneur of the Year Award. With her kids in charge of most of the corporate leadership these days, Sheets operates the company's flagship location in Lansing, MI. She now manages 53 employees and completed more than 4,200 moves in 2010. Not bad for a $350 investment.

Just like Sheets, all business owners must decide for themselves which form of business is best for them. Whether you dream of starting a business for yourself, going into business with a partner, forming a corporation, or someday being a leading franchisor, it's important to know that each form of ownership has its advantages and disadvantages. You will learn about them all in this chapter.

Sources: Randy J. Stine, "A Long History of Giving," *The Greater Lansing Business Monthly*, April 2011; "Recent Interview with Mary Ellen Sheets," *Franchise Gator*, accessed April 2011; "Two Men and a Truck Leads the Way as It Arrives in the UK," *The Franchise Magazine*, accessed April 2011; and www.TwoMenAndATruck.com/mary-ellen-sheets, accessed April 2011.

NAME THAT company

Around April 15th every year, we are a very sought out company. With thousands of locations in the United States we make tax filing much easier. Most people are unaware that we are actually a Canadian franchise even though we have our headquarters in the United States. Who are we? (Find the answer in the chapter.)

BASIC FORMS OF BUSINESS OWNERSHIP

Like Mary Ellen Sheets, hundreds of thousands of people have started new businesses in the United States. In fact, more than 600,000 are started each year.[1] Chances are, you've thought of owning your own business or know someone who has.

How you form your business can make a tremendous difference in your long-term success. The three major forms of business ownership are (1) sole proprietorships, (2) partnerships, and (3) corporations. Each has advantages and disadvantages that we'll discuss.

It can be easy to get started in your own business. You can begin a lawn mowing service, develop a website, or go about meeting other wants and needs of your community. A business owned, and usually managed, by one person is called a **sole proprietorship**. That is the most common form of business ownership.

Many people do not have the money, time, or desire to run a business on their own. When two or more people legally agree to become co-owners of a business, the organization is called a **partnership**.

Sole proprietorships and partnerships are relatively easy to form, but there are advantages to creating a business that is separate and distinct from the owners. This is a **corporation**, a legal entity with authority to act and have liability apart from its owners. The almost 5 million corporations in the United

sole proprietorship
A business that is owned, and usually managed, by one person.

partnership
A legal form of business with two or more owners.

corporation
A legal entity with authority to act and have liability apart from its owners.

figure 5.1

FORMS OF BUSINESS OWNERSHIP
Although corporations make up only 20 percent of the total number of businesses, they make 81 percent of the total receipts. Sole proprietorships are the most common form (72 percent), but they earn only 6 percent of the receipts.
Source: U.S. Internal Revenue Service.

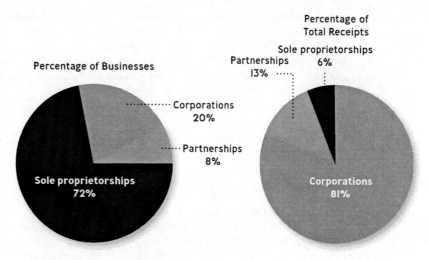

Percentage of Businesses

Corporations 20%

Partnerships 8%

Sole proprietorships 72%

Percentage of Total Receipts

Sole proprietorships 6%

Partnerships 13%

Corporations 81%

States make up only 20 percent of all businesses, but they earn 81 percent of total U.S. business receipts (see Figure 5.1).

Keep in mind that just because a business starts in one form of ownership, it doesn't have to stay in that form.[2] Many companies start out in one form, then add (or drop) a partner or two, and eventually become corporations, limited liability companies, or franchisors.[3] Let's begin our discussion by looking at the most basic form of ownership—the sole proprietorship.

LEARNING goal 1

Compare the advantages and disadvantages of sole proprietorships.

SOLE PROPRIETORSHIPS

Advantages of Sole Proprietorships

Sole proprietorships are the easiest kind of businesses to explore in your quest for an interesting career. Every town has sole proprietors you can visit and talk with about the joys and frustrations of being in business on their own.[4] Most will mention the benefits of being their own boss and setting their own hours. Other advantages include:

1. *Ease of starting and ending the business.* All you have to do to start a sole proprietorship is buy or lease the needed equipment (a saw, a laptop, a tractor, a lawn mower) and put up some announcements saying you are in business. You may have to get a permit or license from the local government, but often that is no problem. It is just as easy to get out of business; you simply stop. There is no one to consult or disagree with about such decisions.

2. *Being your own boss.* Working for others simply does not have the same excitement as working for yourself—at least, that's the way sole proprietors feel. You may make mistakes, but they are your mistakes—and so are the many small victories each day.

3. *Pride of ownership.* People who own and manage their own businesses are rightfully proud of their work. They deserve all the credit for taking the risks and providing needed goods or services.

4. *Leaving a legacy.* Owners can leave an ongoing business for future generations.

5. *Retention of company profits.* Owners not only keep the profits earned but also benefit from the increasing value as the business grows.

6. *No special taxes.* All the profits of a sole proprietorship are taxed as the personal income of the owner, and the owner pays the normal income tax on that money.[5] However, owners do have to pay the self-employment tax (for Social Security and Medicare). They also have to estimate their taxes and make quarterly payments to the government or suffer penalties for nonpayment.

Warren Brown's career is finally "rising." Brown left a promising law career to create Cakelove, a bustling bakery that specializes in making pastries from scratch using natural ingredients. Brown regularly appears on the Food Network. Do you have a passion you would like to pursue as a business?

Disadvantages of Sole Proprietorships

Not everyone is equipped to own and manage a business. Often it is difficult to save enough money to start a business and keep it going. The costs of inventory, supplies, insurance, advertising, rent, computers, utilities, and so on may be too much to cover alone. There are other disadvantages:

Being the sole proprietor of a company, like a dog-walking service, means making a major time commitment to run the business, including constantly seeking out new customers and looking for reliable employees when the time comes to grow. If you were a sole proprietor, what would you need to do if you wanted to take a week's vacation?

1. *Unlimited liability—the risk of personal losses.* When you work for others, it is their problem if the business is not profitable. When you own your own business, you and the business are considered one. You have **unlimited liability;** that is, any debts or damages incurred by the business are your debts and you must pay them, even if it means selling your home, your car, or whatever else you own. This is a serious risk, and undertaking it requires not only thought but also discussion with a lawyer, an insurance agent, an accountant, and others.

2. *Limited financial resources.* Funds available to the business are limited to what the one owner can gather. Since there are serious limits to how much money one person can raise, partnerships and corporations have a greater probability of obtaining the financial backing needed to start and equip a business and keep it going.

3. *Management difficulties.* All businesses need management; someone must keep inventory, accounting, and tax records. Many people skilled at selling things or providing a service are not so skilled at keeping records. Sole proprietors often find it difficult to attract qualified employees to help run the business because often they cannot compete with the salary and benefits offered by larger companies.

unlimited liability
The responsibility of business owners for all of the debts of the business.

4. *Overwhelming time commitment.* Though sole proprietors say they set their own hours, it's hard to own a business, manage it, train people, and have time for anything else in life when there is no one with whom to share the burden. The owner of a store, for example, may put in 12 hours a day at least six days a week—almost twice the hours worked by a nonsupervisory employee in a large company. Imagine how this time commitment affects the sole proprietor's family life. Many sole proprietors will tell you, "It's not a job, it's not a career, it's a way of life."

5. *Few fringe benefits.* If you are your own boss, you lose the fringe benefits that often come with working for others. You have no paid health insurance, no paid disability insurance, no pension plan, no sick leave, and no vacation pay. These and other benefits may add up to 30 percent or more of a worker's compensation.

6. *Limited growth.* Expansion is often slow since a sole proprietorship relies on its owner for most of its creativity, business know-how, and funding.

7. *Limited life span.* If the sole proprietor dies, is incapacitated, or retires, the business no longer exists (unless it is sold or taken over by the sole proprietor's heirs).

Talk with a few local sole proprietors about the problems they've faced in being on their own. They are likely to have many interesting stories about problems getting loans from the bank, problems with theft, and problems simply keeping up with the business. These are reasons why many sole proprietors choose to find partners to share the load.

progress assessment

- Most people who start businesses in the United States are sole proprietors. What are the advantages and disadvantages of sole proprietorships?
- Why would unlimited liability be considered a major drawback to sole proprietorships?

LEARNING goal 2

Describe the differences between general and limited partners, and compare the advantages and disadvantages of partnerships.

PARTNERSHIPS

A partnership is a legal form of business with two or more owners. There are several types: (1) general partnerships, (2) limited partnerships, and (3) master limited partnerships. In a **general partnership** all owners share in operating the business and in assuming liability for the business's debts. A **limited partnership** has one or more general partners and one or more limited partners. A **general partner** is an owner (partner) who has unlimited liability and is active in managing the firm. Every partnership must have at least one general partner. A **limited partner** is an owner who invests money in the business but does not have any management responsibility or liability for losses beyond his or her investment. **Limited liability** means that the limited partners' liability for the debts of the business is *limited* to the amount they put into the company; their personal assets are not at risk.

One form of partnership, the **master limited partnership (MLP)**, looks much like a corporation (which we discuss next) in that it acts like a corporation and is traded on the stock exchanges like a corporation, but is taxed like a partnership and thus avoids the corporate income tax.[6] Master Limited Partnerships are normally found in the oil and gas industry. For example, Sunoco Inc. formed the MLP Sunoco Logistics Partners (SXL) to acquire, own, and operate a group of crude oil and refined-product pipelines and storage facilities. Income received by SXL is not taxed before it is passed on to investors as dividends as it would be if SXL were a corporation.[7]

Another type of partnership was created to limit the disadvantage of unlimited liability. A **limited liability partnership (LLP)** limits partners' risk of losing their personal assets to the outcomes of only their own acts and omissions and those of people under their supervision. If you are a limited partner in an LLP, you can operate without the fear that one of your partners might commit an act of malpractice resulting in a judgment that takes away your house, car, retirement plan, even your collection of vintage Star Wars action figures, as would be the case in a general partnership. However, in many states this personal protection does not extend to contract liabilities such as bank loans, leases, and business debt the partnership takes on; loss of personal assets is still a risk if these are not paid. In states without additional contract liability protections for LLPs, the LLP is in many ways similar to an LLC (discussed later in the chapter).

All states except Louisiana have adopted the Uniform Partnership Act (UPA) to replace earlier laws governing partnerships. The UPA defines the

general partnership
A partnership in which all owners share in operating the business and in assuming liability for the business's debts.

limited partnership
A partnership with one or more general partners and one or more limited partners.

general partner
An owner (partner) who has unlimited liability and is active in managing the firm.

limited partner
An owner who invests money in the business but does not have any management responsibility or liability for losses beyond the investment.

limited liability
The responsibility of a business's owners for losses only up to the amount they invest; limited partners and shareholders (stockholders) have limited liability.

master limited partnership (MLP)
A partnership that looks much like a corporation (in that it acts like a corporation and is traded on a stock exchange) but is taxed like a partnership and thus avoids the corporate income tax.

limited liability partnership (LLP)
A partnership that limits partners' risk of losing their personal assets to only their own acts and omissions and to the acts and omissions of people under their supervision.

three key elements of any general partnership as (1) common ownership, (2) shared profits and losses, and (3) the right to participate in managing the operations of the business.

Advantages of Partnerships

Often, it is much easier to own and manage a business with one or more partners. Your partner may be skilled at inventory control and accounting, while you do the selling or servicing. A partner can also provide additional money, support, and expertise as well as cover for you when you are sick or on vacation. The Spotlight on Small Business box offers a few tips about choosing a partner.

Partnerships usually have the following advantages:

1. *More financial resources.* When two or more people pool their money and credit, it is easier to pay the rent, utilities, and other bills incurred by a business. A limited partnership is specially designed to help raise money. As mentioned earlier, a limited partner invests money in the business but cannot legally have management responsibility and has limited liability.

2. *Shared management and pooled/complementary skills and knowledge.* It is simply much easier to manage the day-to-day activities of a business with carefully chosen partners. Partners give each other free time from the business and provide different skills and perspectives..Some people find that the best partner is a spouse. Many husband-and-wife teams manage restaurants, service shops, and other businesses.[8]

3. *Longer survival.* One study that examined 2,000 businesses started since 1960 found that partnerships were four times more likely to succeed than sole proprietorships. Being watched by a partner can help a businessperson become more disciplined.

4. *No special taxes.* As with sole proprietorships, all profits of partnerships are taxed as the personal income of the owners, who pay the normal income tax on that money. Similarly, partners must estimate their taxes and make quarterly payments or suffer penalties for nonpayment.

Kate and Andy Spade started a business selling a $155 black nylon handbag in 1993. Their business has grown into a global brand. What makes the pair of Spades such great business partners? It's their differences: Kate is the creative soul who designs the products and Andy is the risk taker who shapes the brand. What problems might partners who share both business and home encounter that other partners might not?

The Ties That Bind

Before plunging into a partnership, ask yourself these questions regarding your potential partner: Do you share the same goals? Do you share the same vision for the company's future? What skills does the person have? Are those skills the same as yours, or do they complement your skills? What contacts, resources, or special attributes will the person bring to the business? What type of decision maker is the person? Is this someone with whom you could happily share authority for all major business decisions? Do you trust each other? How does the person respond to adversity? Does he or she try to solve the problem or try to defend his or her ego? Can the person accept constructive criticism without getting defensive? To what extent can you build fun and excitement into the partnership?

If the answers to many of these questions are negative, this person is not the partner for you. But remember, there's no such thing as a perfect partner, so allow for some imperfection (after all, you aren't going to be the perfect partner either). As in a good marriage, the best way to avoid major conflicts in a business partnership is to begin with an honest discussion of what each partner expects to give to and get from the endeavor.

Disadvantages of Partnerships

Anytime two people must agree, conflict and tension are possible. Partnerships have caused splits between relatives, friends, and spouses. Let's explore the disadvantages of partnerships:

1. *Unlimited liability.* Each *general* partner is liable for the debts of the firm, no matter who was responsible for causing them. You are liable for your partners' mistakes as well as your own. Like sole proprietors, general partners can lose their homes, cars, and everything else they own if the business loses a lawsuit or goes bankrupt.

2. *Division of profits.* Sharing risk means sharing profits, and that can cause conflicts. There is no set system for dividing profits in a partnership, and they are not always divided evenly. For example, if one partner puts in more money and the other puts in more hours, each may feel justified in asking for a bigger share of the profits.

3. *Disagreements among partners.* Disagreements over money are just one example of potential conflict in a partnership. Who has final authority over employees? Who hires and fires employees? Who works what hours? What if one partner wants to buy expensive equipment for the firm and the other partner disagrees? All terms of the partnership should be spelled out in writing to protect all parties and minimize misunderstandings.

4. *Difficulty of termination.* Once you have committed yourself to a partnership, it is not easy to get out of it. Sure, you can just quit. However, questions about who gets what and what happens next are often difficult to resolve when the partnership ends. Surprisingly, law firms often have faulty partnership agreements and find that breaking up is hard to do. How do you get rid of a partner you don't like? It is best to decide such questions up front in the partnership agreement. Figure 5.2 gives you ideas about what to include in partnership agreements.

figure 5.2

HOW TO FORM A PARTNERSHIP

It's not hard to form a partnership, but it's wise for each prospective partner to get the counsel of a lawyer experienced with such agreements. Lawyers' services are usually expensive, so would-be partners should read all about partnerships and reach some basic agreements before calling a lawyer.

For your protection, be sure to put your partnership agreement in writing. The Model Business Corporation Act recommends including the following in a written partnership agreement:

1. The name of the business. Many states require the firm's name to be registered with state and/or county officials if the firm's name is different from the name of any of the partners.

2. The names and addresses of all partners.

3. The purpose and nature of the business, the location of the principal offices, and any other locations where business will be conducted.

4. The date the partnership will start and how long it will last. Will it exist for a specific length of time, or will it stop when one of the partners dies or when the partners agree to discontinue?

5. The contributions made by each partner. Will some partners contribute money, while others provide real estate, personal property, expertise, or labor? When are the contributions due?

6. The management responsibilities. Will all partners have equal voices in management, or will there be senior and junior partners?

7. The duties of each partner.

8. The salaries and drawing accounts of each partner.

9. Provision for sharing of profits or losses.

10. Provision for accounting procedures. Who'll keep the accounts? What bookkeeping and accounting methods will be used? Where will the books be kept?

11. The requirements for taking in new partners.

12. Any special restrictions, rights, or duties of any partner.

13. Provision for a retiring partner.

14. Provision for the purchase of a deceased or retiring partner's share of the business.

15. Provision for how grievances will be handled.

16. Provision for how to dissolve the partnership and distribute the assets to the partners.

The best way to learn about the advantages and disadvantages of partnerships is to interview several people who have experience with them. They will give you insights and hints on how to avoid problems.

One fear of owning your own business or having a partner is the fear of losing everything you own if someone sues the business or it loses a lot of money. Many businesspeople try to avoid this and the other disadvantages of sole proprietorships and partnerships by forming corporations. We discuss this basic form of business ownership in the following section.

progress assessment

- What is the difference between a limited partner and a general partner?
- What are some of the advantages and disadvantages of partnerships?

LEARNING goal 3

Compare the advantages and disadvantages of corporations, and summarize the differences between C corporations, S corporations, and limited liability companies.

> **conventional (C) corporation**
> A state-chartered legal entity with authority to act and have liability separate from its owners.

CORPORATIONS

Many corporations—like General Electric, Microsoft, and Walmart—are big and contribute substantially to the U.S. economy. However, it's not necessary to be big to incorporate. Incorporating may be beneficial for small businesses as well.

A **conventional (C) corporation** is a state-chartered legal entity with authority to act and have liability separate from its owners—its *stockholders*. Stockholders are not liable for the debts or other problems of the corporation beyond the money they invest in it by buying ownership shares, or stock, in the company. They don't have to worry about losing their house, car, or other property because of some business problem—a significant benefit. A corporation not only limits the liability of owners but often enables many people to share in the ownership (and profits) of a business without working there or having other commitments to it.[9] Corporations may choose whether to offer ownership to outside investors or remain privately held. (We discuss stock ownership in Chapter 19.) Figure 5.3 on p. 124 describes various types of corporations.

Advantages of Corporations

Most people are not willing to risk everything to go into business. Yet for a business to grow, prosper, and create economic opportunity, many people have to be willing to invest money in it. One way to solve this problem is to create an artificial being, an entity that exists only in the eyes of the law—a corporation. Let's explore some of the advantages of corporations:

1. *Limited liability*. A major advantage of corporations is the limited liability of their owners. Remember, limited liability means that the owners of a business are responsible for its losses only up to the amount they invest in it.

2. *Ability to raise more money for investment*. To raise money, a corporation can sell shares of its stock to anyone who is interested. This means that millions of people can own part of major companies like IBM, Apple, and Coca-Cola, and smaller corporations as well. If a company sells 10 million shares of stock for $50 a share, it will have $500 million available to build plants, buy materials, hire people, manufacture products, and so on. Such a large amount of money would be difficult to raise any other way.

   Corporations can also borrow money by obtaining loans from financial institutions like banks. They can also borrow from individual investors by issuing bonds, which involve paying investor's interest until the bonds are repaid sometime in the future.[10] You can read about how corporations raise funds through the sale of stocks and bonds in Chapter 19.

Burton Baskin and Irvine Robbins ran their ice cream businesses separately for two years. Once they had succeeded apart, Baskin and Robbins became partners and were able to avoid many of the pitfalls of starting a new business from scratch. They flipped a coin to see whose name would come first. What factors besides the partners' individual success do you think contributed to their long-lasting partnership?

figure 5.3

CORPORATE TYPES

Corporations can fit in more than one category.

You may find some confusing types of corporations when reading about them. Here are a few of the more widely used terms:

An *alien corporation* does business in the United States but is chartered (incorporated) in another country.

A *domestic corporation* does business in the state in which it's chartered (incorporated).

A *foreign corporation* does business In one state but is chartered in another. About one-third of all corporations are chartered in Delaware because of its relatively attractive rules for incorporation. A foreign corporation must register in states where it operates.

A *closed (private) corporation* is one whose stock is held by a few people and isn't available to the general public.

An *open (public) corporation* sells stock to the general public. General Motors and ExxonMobil are examples of public corporations.

A *quasi-public corporation* is a corporation chartered by the government as an approved monopoly to perform services to the general public. Public utilities are examples of quasi-public corporations.

A *professional corporation* is one whose owners offer professional services (doctors, lawyers, etc.). Shares in professional corporations aren't publicly traded.

A *nonprofit (or not-for-profit) corporation* is one that doesn't seek personal profit for Its owners.

A *multinational corporation* is a firm that operates in several countries.

3. *Size.* "Size" summarizes many of the advantages of some corporations. Because they can raise large amounts of money to work with, big corporations can build modern factories or software development facilities with the latest equipment. They can hire experts or specialists in all areas of operation. They can buy other corporations in different fields to diversify their business risks. In short, a large corporation with numerous resources can take advantage of opportunities anywhere in the world.

   But corporations do not have to be large to enjoy the benefits of incorporating. Many doctors, lawyers, and individuals, as well as partners in a variety of businesses, have incorporated. The vast majority of corporations in the United States are small businesses.

4. *Perpetual life.* Because corporations are separate from those who own them, the death of one or more owners does not terminate the corporation.

5. *Ease of ownership change.* It is easy to change the owners of a corporation. All that is necessary is to sell the stock to someone else.

6. *Ease of attracting talented employees.* Corporations can attract skilled employees by offering such benefits as stock options (the right to purchase shares of the corporation for a fixed price).

7. *Separation of ownership from management.* Corporations are able to raise money from many different owners/stockholders without getting them involved in management. The corporate hierarchy in Figure 5.4 shows how the owners/stockholders are separate from the managers and employees. The owners/stockholders elect a board of directors, who hire the officers of the corporation and oversee major policy issues. The owners/stockholders thus have some say in who runs the corporation but have no real control over the daily operations.[11]

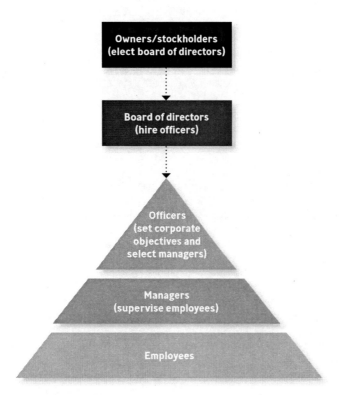

figure 5.4

HOW OWNERS AFFECT MANAGEMENT
Owners have an influence on how a business is managed by electing a board of directors. The board hires the top officers (and fires them if necessary). It also sets the pay for those officers. The officers then select managers and employees with the help of the human resources department.

Disadvantages of Corporations

There are so many sole proprietorships and partnerships in the United States that there must be some disadvantages to incorporating. Otherwise, everyone would do it. The following are a few of the disadvantages:

1. *Initial cost.* Incorporation may cost thousands of dollars and require expensive lawyers and accountants. There are less expensive ways of incorporating in certain states (see the following subsection), but many people do not have the time or confidence to go through this procedure without the help of a potentially expensive lawyer.

2. *Extensive paperwork.* The paperwork needed to start a corporation is just the beginning. A sole proprietor or partnership may keep rather broad accounting records. A corporation, in contrast, must keep detailed financial records, the minutes of meetings, and more. As noted in Figure 5.3, many firms incorporate in Delaware or Nevada because these state's business-oriented laws make the process easier than it is in other states.

3. *Double taxation.* Corporate income is taxed twice. First the corporation pays tax on its income before it can distribute any, as *dividends,* to stockholders. Then the stockholders pay income tax on the dividends they receive.[12] States often tax corporations more heavily than other enterprises, and some special taxes apply only to corporations.

4. *Two tax returns.* An individual who incorporates must file both a corporate tax return and an individual tax return. Depending on the size of the corporation, a corporate return can be quite complex and require the assistance of a certified public accountant (CPA).

You can be part owner of a corporation by buying shares of the company's stock on exchanges like the NASDAQ. What are the advantages and disadvantages of corporations?

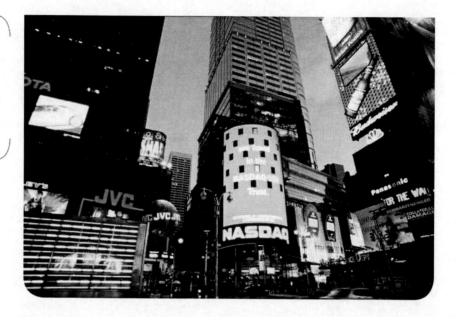

5. *Size.* Size may be one advantage of corporations, but it can be a disadvantage as well. Large corporations sometimes become too inflexible and tied down in red tape to respond quickly to market changes, and their profitability can suffer.

6. *Difficulty of termination.* Once a corporation has started, it's relatively hard to end.

7. *Possible conflict with stockholders and board of directors.* Conflict may brew if the stockholders elect a board of directors who disagree with management. Since the board of directors chooses the company's officers, entrepreneurs serving as managers can find themselves forced out of the very company they founded. This happened to Tom Freston, one of the founders of MTV, and Steve Jobs, a founder of Apple Computer (Jobs of course returned to the company later).

Many businesspeople are discouraged by the costs, paperwork, and special taxes corporations must pay. However, many others believe the advantages of incorporation outweigh the hassles.

Individuals Can Incorporate

Not all corporations are large organizations with hundreds of employees and thousands of stockholders. Truckers, doctors, lawyers, plumbers, athletes, and small-business owners of all kinds can also incorporate. Normally, individuals who incorporate do not issue stock to outsiders; therefore, they do not share all the advantages and disadvantages of large corporations (such as size and more money for investment). Their major advantages are limited liability and possible tax benefits. Although you are not required to file for incorporation through a lawyer, it is usually wise to consult one. In addition to lawyers' fees, the secretary of state's office charges a fee for incorporating a business, varying by state from a low of $50 (in Colorado, Iowa, Kentucky, Mississippi, and Oklahoma) to a high of $300 (in Texas).[13] Like the fee, the length of time it will take to actually have your business incorporated will vary by state. The average

figure 5.5

HOW TO INCORPORATE

The process of forming a corporation varies somewhat from state to state. The articles of incorporation are usually filed with the secretary of state's office in the state in which the company incorporates. The articles contain:

- The corporation's name.
- The names of the people who incorporated it.
- Its purposes.
- Its duration (usually perpetual).
- The number of shares that can be issued, their voting rights, and any other rights the shareholders have.
- The corporation's minimum capital.
- The address of the corporation's office.
- The name and address of the person responsible for the corporation's legal service.
- The names and addresses of the first directors.
- Any other public information the incorporators wish to include.

Before a business can so much as open a bank account or hire employees, it needs a federal tax identification number. To apply for one, get an SS-4 form from the IRS.

In addition to the articles of incorporation listed, a corporation has bylaws. These describe how the firm is to be operated from both legal and managerial points of view. The bylaws include:

- How, when, and where shareholders' and directors' meetings are held, and how long directors are to serve.
- Directors' authority.
- Duties and responsibilities of officers, and the length of their service.
- How stock is Issued.
- Other matters, including employment contracts.

time is approximately 30 days from the date of application. Figure 5.5 outlines how to incorporate.

S Corporations

An **S corporation** is a unique government creation that looks like a corporation but is taxed like sole proprietorships and partnerships. (The name comes from the fact that the rules governing them are in Subchapter S of Chapter 1 of the Internal Revenue Code.) The paperwork and details of S corporations are similar to those of conventional (C) corporations. S corporations have shareholders, directors, and employees, and the benefit of limited liability, but their profits are taxed only as the personal income of the shareholders—thus avoiding the double taxation of C corporations.

Avoiding double taxation is reason enough for approximately 3 million U.S. companies to operate as S corporations. Yet not all businesses can become S corporations. In order to qualify, a company must:

1. Have no more than 100 shareholders. (All members of a family count as one shareholder.)
2. Have shareholders that are individuals or estates, and who (as individuals) are citizens or permanent residents of the United States.
3. Have only one class of stock. (You can read more about the various classes of stock in Chapter 19.)
4. Derive no more than 25 percent of income from passive sources (rents, royalties, interest).

S corporation
A unique government creation that looks like a corporation but is taxed like sole proprietorships and partnerships.

An S corporation that loses its S status may not operate under it again for at least five years. The tax structure of S corporations isn't attractive to all businesses. For one thing, the benefits change every time the tax rules change. The best way to learn all the benefits or shortcomings for a specific business is to go over the tax advantages and liability differences with a lawyer, an accountant, or both.

Limited Liability Companies

limited liability company (LLC)
A company similar to an S corporation but without the special eligibility requirements.

A **limited liability company (LLC)** is similar to an S corporation, but without the special eligibility requirements. LLCs were introduced in Wyoming in 1977 and were recognized by the Internal Revenue Service as a partnership for federal income tax purposes in 1988. By 1996, all 50 states and the District of Columbia recognized LLCs.

The number of LLCs has risen dramatically since 1988, when there were fewer than 100 filings to operate them. Today more than half of new business registrations in some states are LLCs. The nearby Legal Briefcase box features a new type of LLC, a virtual company.

Why the drive toward forming LLCs? Advantages include:

1. *Limited liability.* Personal assets are protected. Limited liability was previously available only to limited partners and shareholders of C corporations.

2. *Choice of taxation.* LLCs can choose to be taxed as partnerships or as corporations. Partnership-level taxation was previously a benefit normally reserved for partners or S corporation owners.

3. *Flexible ownership rules.* LLCs do not have to comply with ownership restrictions as S corporations do. Owners can be a person, partnership, or corporation.

4. *Flexible distribution of profits and losses.* Profits and losses don't have to be distributed in proportion to the money each person invests, as in corporations. LLC members agree on the percentage to be distributed to each member.

5. *Operating flexibility.* LLCs do have to submit articles of organization, which are similar to articles of incorporation, but they are not required to keep minutes, file written resolutions, or hold annual meetings. An LLC also submits a written operating agreement, similar to a partnership agreement, describing how the company is to be operated.

Of course, LLCs have their disadvantages as well. These include:

PetZen Products LLC offers doggie treadmills to help the nation's overweight pets get back their puppy figures. What are the advantages and disadvantages of LLCs?

1. *No stock.* LLC ownership is nontransferable. LLC members need the approval of the other members in order to sell their interests in the company. In contrast, regular and S corporation stockholders can sell their shares as they wish.

2. *Limited life span.* LLCs are required to identify dissolution dates in the articles of organization (no more than 30 years in some states). The death of a member can cause LLCs to dissolve automatically. Members may choose to reconstitute the LLC after it dissolves.

3. *Fewer incentives.* Unlike corporations, LLCs can't deduct the cost of fringe benefits for

LEGAL briefcase

www.vermontvirtual.org

Virtual Companies

One of the benefits of cloud computing, social media, and the Internet in general is that businesses and their employees no longer have to come together in a physical place in order to work together. Most companies are still required by law to have a physical office and a management team, and to keep a physical paper trail of all transactions. However a recent Vermont law created a new form of LLC called a virtual company, that is, a company that can exist only online. Any documents required to register a company can be filed electronically, company meetings can be held using any type of online communication, and relationships among company members can be established electronically. They can make decisions together using voting structures managed by social networking software.

Traditional companies spend large amounts of money recruiting, hiring, and training employees to serve in various roles. In contrast, virtual companies can allow online contributors with different skills, availability, and interests to identify themselves and contribute as they choose. Members of the virtual company decide the value of each member's contribution and the percentage of the LLC's profits that should be passed to each.

Supporters of the Vermont law believe it will make the state so attractive for LLCs that it will become the "Delaware of the Net." (Delaware collects around $700 million a year in incorporation taxes and fees because of its attractive rules of incorporation.) It will be interesting to see whether Vermont does indeed become the Delaware of the Net.

Sources: Stanley P. Jaskiewicz, "Is a 'Virtual Company' Worth the Effort?" *Law Technology News,* April 16, 2010; and Christopher Steiner, "Five Ways to Build a Virtual Company," *Forbes,* September 21, 2010.

members owning 2 percent or more of the company. And since there's no stock, they can't use stock options as incentives to employees.

4. *Taxes.* LLC members must pay self-employment taxes—the Medicare/Social Security taxes paid by sole proprietors and partnerships—on their profits. In contrast, S corporations pay self-employment tax on owners' salaries but not on the entire profits.

5. *Paperwork.* While the paperwork required of LLCs is not as great as that required of corporations, it is more than required of sole proprietors.

The start-up cost for an LLC varies. Online legal services such as Legal Zoom (www.legalzoom.com) can file the necessary paperwork for as little as $150. Figure 5.6 on p. 130 summarizes the advantages and disadvantages of the major forms of business ownership.

progress assessment

- What are the major advantages and disadvantages of incorporating a business?
- What is the role of owners (stockholders) in the corporate hierarchy?
- If you buy stock in a corporation and someone gets injured by one of the corporation's products, can you be sued? Why or why not?
- Why are so many new businesses choosing a limited liability company (LLC) form of ownership?

	SOLE PROPRIETORSHIP	Partnerships		Corporations		
		GENERAL PARTNERSHIP	LIMITED PARTNERSHIP	CONVENTIONAL CORPORATION	S CORPORATION	LIMITED LIABILITY COMPANY
Documents Needed to Start Business	None; may need permit or license	Partnership agreement (oral or written)	Written agreement; must file certificate of limited partnership	Articles of incorporation, bylaws	Articles of incorporation, bylaws, must meet criteria	Articles of organization and operating agreement; no eligibility require-ments
Ease of Termination	Easy to terminate: just pay debts and quit	May be hard to terminate, depending on the partnership agreement	Same as general partnership	Hard and expensive to terminate	Same as conventional corporation	May be difficult, depending upon operating agreement
Length of Life	Terminates on the death of owner	Terminates on the death or withdrawal of partner	Same as general partnership	Perpetual life	Same as conventional corporation	Varies according to dissolution dates in articles of organization
Transfer of Ownership	Business can be sold to qualified buyer	Must have other partner(s)' agreement	Same as general partnership	Easy to change owners; just sell stock	Can sell stock, but with restrictions	Can't sell stock
Financial Resources	Limited to owner's capital and loans	Limited to partners' capital and loans	Same as general partnership	More money to start and operate; may sell stocks and bonds	Same as conventional corporation	Same as partnership
Risk of Losses	Unlimited liability	Unlimited liability	Limited liability	Limited liability	Limited liability	Limited liability
Taxes	Taxed as personal income	Taxed as per-sonal income	Same as general partnership	Corporate, double taxation	Taxed as personal income	Varies
Management Responsibilities	Owner manages *all* areas of the business	Partners share management	Can't participate in management	Separate management from ownership	Same as conventional corporation	Varies
Employee Benefits	Usually fewer benefits and lower wages	Often fewer benefits and lower wages; promising employee could become a partner	Same as general partnership	Usually better benefits and wages, advancement opportunities	Same as conventional corporation	Varies, but are not tax deductible

figure 5.6

**COMPARISON OF FORMS OF
BUSINESS OWNERSHIP**

LEARNING goal 4

Define and give examples of three types of corporate mergers, and explain the role of leveraged buyouts and taking a firm private.

CORPORATE EXPANSION: MERGERS AND ACQUISITIONS

The merger mania of the late 1990s reached its peak in 2000, when the total spent on mergers and acquisitions hit a stunning $3.4 trillion and a new deal was being struck every 17 minutes. It seemed as though each deal made was intended to top the one before. Most of the new deals involved companies trying to expand within their own fields to save costs, enter new markets, position for global competition, or adapt to changing technologies or regulations. Those proved to be unattainable goals for many of the merged giants; two-thirds of mergers of the late 1990s failed to meet their goals. By 2009, the bleak U.S. economy caused the volume of mergers and acquisitions to plummet 86 percent. 2010 offered some renewed optimism as mergers increased 14 percent.[14]

What's the difference between mergers and acquisitions? A **merger** is the result of two firms joining to form one company. It is similar to a marriage, joining two individuals as one family. An **acquisition** is one company's purchase of the property and obligations of another company. It is more like buying a house than entering a marriage.

There are three major types of corporate mergers: vertical, horizontal, and conglomerate. A **vertical merger** joins two firms operating in different stages of related businesses. A merger between a soft drink company and an artificial sweetener maker would ensure the merged firm a constant supply of an ingredient the soft drink manufacturer needs. It could also help ensure quality control of the soft drink company's products.

A **horizontal merger** joins two firms in the same industry and allows them to diversify or expand their products. A soft drink company and a mineral water company that merge can now supply a variety of drinking products.

A **conglomerate merger** unites firms in completely unrelated industries in order to diversify business operations and investments. A soft drink company and a snack food company would form a conglomerate merger. Figure 5.7 on p. 132 illustrates the differences among the three types of mergers.

Rather than merge or sell to another company, some corporations decide to maintain, or in some cases regain, control of a firm internally. By *taking a firm private*, management or a group of stockholders obtain all the firm's stock for themselves by buying it back from the other stockholders.[15] Burger King and Gymboree are firms that have been taken private. Suppose employees believe they may lose their jobs, or managers believe they could improve corporate performance if they owned the company. Does either group have an opportunity of taking ownership of the company? Yes—they might attempt a leveraged buyout.

A **leveraged buyout (LBO)** is an attempt by employees, management, or a group of private investors to buy out the stockholders in a company, primarily by borrowing the necessary funds. The

merger
The result of two firms forming one company.

acquisition
One company's purchase of the property and obligations of another company.

vertical merger
The joining of two companies involved in different stages of related businesses.

horizontal merger
The joining of two firms in the same industry.

conglomerate merger
The joining of firms in completely unrelated industries.

leveraged buyout (LBO)
An attempt by employees, management, or a group of investors to purchase an organization primarily through borrowing.

Mars, the maker of M&M's, acquired the Wm. Wrigley Jr. Company for $23 billion. What type of merger is this (vertical, horizontal, or conglomerate)?

figure 5.7

TYPES OF MERGERS

employees, managers, or investors now become the owners of the firm. LBOs have ranged in size from $50 million to $31 billion and have involved everything from small family businesses to giant corporations like Hertz Corporation, Toys "R" Us, Chrysler and the former RJR Nabisco.[16]

Today, business acquisitions are not limited to U.S. buyers. Foreign companies have found the fastest way to grow is often to buy an established operation that can enhance their technology or expand the number of brands they offer. Swiss drug maker Roche paid $43 billion to take control of biotechnology giant Genentech. Belgium's InBev purchased the largest U.S. brewer, Anheuser-Busch and its Budweiser and Bud Light brands, for $52 billion. Number two brewer Miller Brewing Company was acquired by London-based SAB.[17] In 2010, foreign investors poured over $300 billion into U.S. companies.

However, such deals are not always welcomed. In 2005, U.S. lawmakers feared the proposed purchase of U.S. oil company Unocal by a Chinese oil company might threaten American economic and national security interests. CNOOC, the Chinese company, eventually withdrew its bid.

LEARNING goal 5

Outline the advantages and disadvantages of franchises, and discuss the opportunities for diversity in franchising and the challenges of global franchising.

Play Ball but Play Green

Many people think the only type of franchises you can buy is restaurants. Franchising, however, goes beyond a local Subway or KFC. Hotels, schools, even teams in The National Football League and Major League Baseball, are franchises. While these sports franchises compete for fans, one area where both the NFL and MLB have reached common agreement is going green.

Washington, DC decided that the new home for the Nationals baseball team would be the first sports stadium to earn a Leadership in Energy and Environmental Design (LEED) rating from the U.S. Green Building Council. When the Nationals took the field on opening day in 2008, fans may not have noticed that 95 percent of the stadium's steel was recycled or that the low-flow toilets saved millions of gallons of water each season. They also may not have known that the wastewater system screens out organic debris such as peanut shells and hot-dog bits, or that the park's recycling center is large enough to handle glass, metal, and plastic recyclables amassed during a three-game home stand. This was just the beginning.

When the New York Mets finalized a deal for the team's new home they reached an agreement with the U.S. Environmental Protection Agency (EPA) to build their new ballpark using the latest green technologies and practices. The Regional

EPA Administrator boasted that the Mets deserved an environmental MVP award for their effort to reduce the carbon footprint and for the waste system at Citi Field. Not to be outdone, the New York Giants and the New York Jets joined with the EPA to make the New Meadowlands Stadium one of the nation's greenest sport's venues. Let's play ball! But let's play green!

Sources: www.epa.gov, accessed April 2011; www.mlb.com, accessed April 2011; and www.nfl.com, accessed April 2011.

FRANCHISES

In addition to the three basic forms of business ownership, there are two special forms: franchises and cooperatives. Let's look at franchises first. A **franchise agreement** is an arrangement whereby someone with a good idea for a business (the **franchisor**) sells the rights to use the business name and sell a product or service (the **franchise**) to others (the **franchisees**) in a given territory.

Some people, uncomfortable with the idea of starting their own business from scratch, would rather join a business with a proven track record through a franchise agreement. A franchise can be formed as a sole proprietorship, a partnership, or a corporation. The U.S. Census Bureau estimates that one out of every ten businesses in the United States is a franchise.[18] Some of the best-known franchises are McDonald's, Jiffy Lube, 7-Eleven, Weight Watchers, and Holiday Inn.

According to the International Franchising Association, the more than 825,000 franchised businesses operating in the United States create approximately 17.5 million jobs that produce a direct and indirect economic impact of $2.1 trillion in the U.S. economy.[19] The most popular businesses for franchising are restaurants (fast food and full service) and gas stations with convenience stores.[20] McDonald's, the largest restaurant chain in the United States in terms of sales, is often considered the gold standard of franchising.[21] Retail

franchise agreement
An arrangement whereby someone with a good idea for a business sells the rights to use the business name and sell a product or service to others in a given territory.

franchisor
A company that develops a product concept and sells others the rights to make and sell the products.

franchise
The right to use a specific business's name and sell its products or services in a given territory.

franchisee
A person who buys a franchise.

Merry Maids is the largest home cleaning franchise in the U.S. It cleans over 300,000 houses, apartments, and condos a month. The franchise fee includes a comprehensive eight-day training program followed by in-depth interaction with the franchise development team and assistance from an established franchise owner. The training helps new franchisees learn how to select, train, develop and compensate employees. What type of franchise might appeal to you as a business owner?

stores, financial services, health clubs, hotels and motels, and automotive parts and service centers are also popular franchised businesses. Today a fast-growing franchise sector is senior care. In fact, *Entrepreneur Magazine*'s 2011 list of 100 fastest-growing franchises included eight senior care concepts.[22] With roughly 40 million seniors in the United States today and projections the number will double in the next 20 years, it's a market that is not going to disappear.

The nearby Thinking Green box discusses a business that many people don't realize is a franchise system.

Advantages of Franchises

Franchising has penetrated every aspect of U.S. and global business life by offering products and services that are reliable, convenient, and competitively priced. Franchising clearly has some advantages:

1. *Management and marketing assistance.* Compared with someone who starts a business from scratch, a franchisee usually has a much greater chance of succeeding because he or she has an established product to sell, help choosing a location, and assistance in all phases of promotion and operation. It's like having your own store but with full-time consultants when you need them. Franchisors usually provide intensive training. For example, McDonald's sends all new franchisees and managers to Hamburger University in Oak Brook, Illinois.[23]

   Some franchisors help their franchisees with local marketing efforts rather than having them depend solely on national advertising. Franchisees also have a network of fellow franchisees facing similar problems who can share their experiences. The UPS Store provides its more than 4,500 franchisees with a software program that helps them build customer databases along with quick and personal one-on-one phone and e-mail support.

2. *Personal ownership.* A franchise operation is still your business, and you enjoy as much of the incentives and profit as any sole proprietor would. You are still your own boss, although you must follow more rules, regulations, and procedures than with your own privately owned business.

3. *Nationally recognized name.* It is one thing to open a gift shop or an ice cream store. It is quite another to open a new Hallmark store or a Baskin-Robbins. With an established franchise, you get instant recognition and support from a product group with established customers around the world.

4. *Financial advice and assistance.* Two major problems for small-business owners are arranging financing and learning to keep good records. Franchisees often get valuable assistance and periodic advice from people with expertise in these areas. In fact, some franchisors provide financing to potential franchisees they feel will be valuable parts of the franchise system. For example, Merry Maids, a leader in

the maid service business, offers up to 80 percent financial assistance with their franchise fee to promising franchisees.

5. *Lower failure rate.* Historically, the failure rate for franchises has been lower than that of other business ventures. However, franchising has grown so rapidly that many weak franchises have entered the field, so you need to be careful and invest wisely.

Disadvantages of Franchises

There are, however, some potential pitfalls to franchising. Check out any franchise arrangement with present franchisees and discuss the idea with an attorney and an accountant. Disadvantages of franchises include the following:

1. *Large start-up costs.* Most franchises demand a fee for the rights to the franchise. Start-up costs for a Jazzercise franchise range from $3,000, but if it's Dunkin Donuts you're after, you'd better have a lot more dough—approximately $2 million.[24]

2. *Shared profit.* The franchisor often demands either a large share of the profits in addition to the start-up fees or a percentage commission based on sales, not profit. This share is called a *royalty.* For example, if a franchisor demands a 10 percent royalty on a franchise's net sales, 10 cents of every dollar the franchisee collects (before taxes and other expenses) must be paid to the franchisor.

3. *Management regulation.* Management "assistance" has a way of becoming managerial orders, directives, and limitations. Franchisees feeling burdened by the company's rules and regulations may lose the drive to run their own business. Often franchisees will band together to resolve their grievances with franchisors rather than fighting their battles alone. For example, in 2010 the KFC National Council & Advertising Cooperative, which represents all U.S. franchisees, sued KFC to gain control of advertising strategies. The franchisees were angry over Yum Brands (owners of KFC) decision to implement an ad strategy that emphasized a shift to grilled chicken rather than fried chicken. The campaign centered around the slogan "Unthink KFC" which was exactly what customers did. Sales plummeted 7 percent that quarter and franchisees had to throw away up to 50 percent of their grilled chicken supplies.[25] In another case, Burger King franchisees filed suit over whether the franchisor could impose $1 pricing on them for double cheeseburgers they claim lost them money.[26]

4. *Coattail effects.* What happens to your franchise if fellow franchisees fail? The actions of other franchises have an impact on your future growth and profitability. Due to this *coattail effect,* you could be forced out of business even if your particular franchise has been profitable. For example, the customer passion for high-flying franchisor Krispy Kreme in the early 2000s sank as the market became flooded with new stores and the availability of the product at retail locations caused overexposure. McDonald's and Subway franchisees complain that due to the company's relentless growth, some new stores have taken business away from existing locations, squeezing franchisees' profits per outlet.

5. *Restrictions on selling.* Unlike owners of private businesses, who can sell their companies to whomever they choose on their own terms,

Since buying a franchise is a major investment, be sure to check out a company's financial strength before you get involved. Watch out for scams too. Scams called *bust-outs* usually involve people coming to town, renting nice offices, taking out ads, and persuading people to invest. Then they disappear with the investors' money. For example, in San Francisco a company called T.B.S. Inc. sold distributorships for in-home AIDS tests. It promised an enormous market and potential profits of $3,000 for an investment of less than $200. The "test" turned out to be nothing more than a mail-order questionnaire about lifestyle.

A good source of information about evaluating a franchise deal is the handbook *Investigate before Investing,* available from International Franchise Association Publications.

Checklist for Evaluating a Franchise

The Franchise

Did your lawyer approve the franchise contract you're considering after he or she studied it paragraph by paragraph?

Does the franchise give you an exclusive territory for the length of the franchise?

Under what circumstances can you terminate the franchise contract and at what cost to you?

If you sell your franchise, will you be compensated for your goodwill (the value of your business's reputation and other intangibles)?

If the franchisor sells the company, will your investment be protected?

The Franchisor

How many years has the firm offering you a franchise been in operation?

Does it have a reputation for honesty and fair dealing among the local firms holding its franchise?

Has the franchisor shown you any certified figures indicating exact net profits of one or more going firms that you personally checked yourself with the franchisee? Ask for the company's disclosure statement.

Will the firm assist you with
  A management training program?
  An employee training program?
  A public relations program?
  Capital?
  Credit?
  Merchandising ideas?

Will the firm help you find a good location for your new business?

Has the franchisor investigated you carefully enough to assure itself that you can successfully operate one of its franchises at a profit both to itself and to you?

You, the Franchisee

How much equity capital will you need to purchase the franchise and operate it until your income equals your expenses?

Does the franchisor offer financing for a portion of the franchising fees? On what terms?

Are you prepared to give up some independence of action to secure the advantages offered by the franchise? Do you have your family's support?

Does the industry appeal to you? Are you ready to spend much or all of the remainder of your business life with this franchisor, offering its product or service to the public?

Your Market

Have you made any study to determine whether the product or service that you propose to sell under the franchise has a market in your territory at the prices you'll have to charge?

Will the population in the territory given to you increase, remain static, or decrease over the next five years?

Will demand for the product or service you're considering be greater, about the same, or less five years from now than it is today?

What competition already exists in your territory for the product or service you contemplate selling?

Sources: U.S. Department of Commerce, *Franchise Opportunities Handbook;* and Steve Adams, "Buying a Brand," *Patriot Ledger* (Quincy, MA), March 1, 2008.

figure 5.8

BUYING A FRANCHISE

many franchisees face restrictions on the resale of their franchises. To control quality, franchisors often insist on approving the new owner, who must meet their standards.

6. *Fraudulent franchisors.* Most franchisors are not large systems like McDonald's and Subway. Many are small, rather obscure companies that prospective franchisees may know little about. Most are honest, but complaints to the Federal Trade Commission have increased about franchisors that delivered little or nothing of what they promised. Before you buy a franchise, make certain you check out the facts fully and remember the old adage "You get what you pay for." See Figure 5.8 for some tips on evaluating a franchisee.

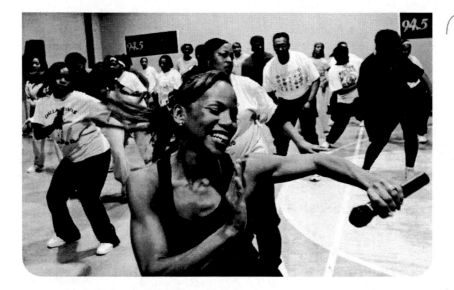

Judi Sheppard Missett started a dance-fitness program called Jazzercise in 1969. The worldwide franchise company now takes fitness-minded adults and kids in 32 countries through weekly classes blending jazz dance, resistance training, Pilates, yoga and kickboxing moves choreographed to the latest popular music. Jazzercise is consistently listed among Entrepreneur magazine's top 20 franchises. What accounts for its appeal?

Diversity in Franchising

A lingering issue in franchising is the number of women who own franchises. While women own about half of all U.S. companies and are opening businesses at double the rate of men, their ownership of franchises is about 25 percent.[27] Some think there is not so much a glass ceiling for women as a green ceiling—lack of money. Many experts believe more needs to be done to attract educated women business owners about the opportunities and forms of financing available for franchise growth. The International Franchise Association has increased its efforts to attract more women into franchising.[28]

Women are getting the message. In fact, women aren't just franchisees anymore; they're becoming franchisors as well. Think back to the opening Profile of Mary Ellen Sheets of Two Men and a Truck. Women are finding if they face difficulty getting financing for growing their business, turning to franchisees to help carry expansion costs can help. For example, top-rated franchise companies Auntie Anne's, Decorating Den, and Jazzercise are owned by women.

Minority-owned businesses are growing at more than six times the national rate. Franchisors are becoming more focused on recruiting minority franchisees. MinorityFran is an initiative by the International Franchise Association to build awareness of franchising opportunities within minority communities. The U.S. Commerce Department's Federal Minority Business Development Agency provides aspiring minority business owners with training in how to run franchises. Domino's Pizza launched a minority franchisee recruitment program called Delivering the Dream. The company provides financial support and a financing partner to help budding franchisees "realize their dream."

Today over 20 percent of franchises are owned by African Americans, Latinos, Asians, and Native Americans. Franchising opportunities seem perfectly attuned to the needs of aspiring minority businesspeople. For example, Junior Bridgeman was a basketball star in college and enjoyed a stellar career with the Milwaukee Bucks and Los Angeles Clippers in the NBA. He transferred his dedication on the court to dedication to building Bridgeman Foods. His company now owns several Wendy's franchises and runs 162 other Wendy's restaurants.[29]

Home-Based Franchises

Home-based businesses offer many obvious advantages, including relief from the stress of commuting, extra time for family activities, and low overhead expenses. One disadvantage is the feeling of isolation. Compared to home-based entrepreneurs, home-based franchisees feel less isolated. Experienced franchisors often share their knowledge of building a profitable enterprise with other franchisees.

Home-based franchises can be started for as little as $5,000. Today you can be a franchisee in areas ranging from cleaning services to tax preparation, child care, pet care, or direct mail services. But don't get the idea working at home is easy. Home-based franchisee Ralph Santisteban was excited by the challenge when he bought his CruiseOne franchise. What he didn't expect was the 12 to 14 hours per day he put in to get the business going.[30] Before investing in a home-based franchise it is helpful to ask yourself the following questions: Are you willing to put in long hours? Can you work in a solitary environment? Are you motivated and well organized? Does your home have the space you need for the business? Can your home also be the place you work? It's also important to check out the franchisor carefully.

E-Commerce in Franchising

Holiday Inn's InterContinental Amstel hotel in Amsterdam has been celebrated as the Netherlands' most beautiful and luxurious hotel. Holiday Inn franchises try to complement the environment of the area they serve. This hotel is on the crossroads of Amsterdam's financial and exclusive shopping districts. What do you think would have been the reaction if Holiday Inn had built the typical U.S-style Holiday Inn in this area?

The Internet has changed franchising in many ways. Most brick-and-mortar franchises have expanded their businesses online and created virtual storefronts to deliver increased value to customers. Franchisees like Carole Shutts, a Rocky Mountain Chocolate Factory franchisee in Galena, Illinois, increased her sales by setting up her own website. Many franchisors, however, prohibit franchisee-sponsored websites because conflicts can erupt if the franchisor creates its own website. Sometimes franchisors send "reverse royalties" to franchisees who believe their sales were hurt by the franchisor's Internet sales, but that doesn't always bring about peace. Before buying a franchise, read the small print regarding online sales.

Today potential franchisees can make a choice between starting an online business or a business requiring an office or storefront outside of the home.[31] Quite often the decision comes down to financing. Traditional brick-and-mortar franchises require finding real estate and often require a high franchise fee. Online franchises like Printinginabox.com charge no upfront franchise fee and require little training to start a business. Franchisees pay only a set monthly fee. Online franchises also do not set exclusive territories limiting where the franchisee can compete. An online franchisee can literally compete against the world.[32]

Using Technology in Franchising

Franchisors often use technology, including social media, to extend their brands, to meet the needs of both their customers and their franchisees, and even to expand their businesses.[33] For example, Candy Bouquet International, Inc., of Little Rock, Arkansas, offers franchises that sell candies in flowerlike arrangements. Franchisees have brick-and-mortar locations to serve walk-in customers, but they also are provided leads from the company's main website. All franchisees are kept up-to-date daily on company news via e-mail, and they use a chat room to discuss issues and product ideas with each other. The

SOCIAL MEDIA IN
business

www.haagen-dazs.com

Franchise Expansion on Facebook

Although social media is still a relatively young medium, companies across the board are using it to reach customers. While many businesses are using social marketing to communicate with customers, some are using the technology to reach out to potential investors and franchisees as well.

The ice cream company Häagen-Dazs, for instance, launched a Facebook game called Ice Cream Boss in 2010. The program simulates the day-to-day operations of a Häagen-Dazs store. Additionally, each week the game challenges users to offer feedback on a new story or situation occurring at the virtual store. The company ultimately hopes that players who become engaged with the game will move on to become franchisees of a real Häagen-Dazs store. Though it's found no new investors from Ice Cream Boss as of this writing, only time will tell if the scheme is a success.

Sources: Jason Ankeny, "Social Climbers," *Entrepreneur*, January 2011; and Lucy Fisher, "Fool's Gold?" *Marketing Week*, April 4, 2011.

company has found the Internet a great way of disseminating information that is revolutionizing franchisor support and franchisee communications. Candy Bouquet plans international expansion in the near future.

Some franchisors use social media not only to reach customers and current franchisees, but also to recruit new franchisees. See the nearby Social Media in Business box for an example of a company using a Facebook game to attract potential franchisees.

Franchising in Global Markets

Franchising today is truly a global effort. U.S. franchisors are counting their profits in euros, yuan, pesos, won, krona, baht, yen, and many other currencies. McDonald's has more than 13,500 restaurants in 117 countries serving over 50 million customers each day.[34]

Because of its proximity and shared language, Canada is the most popular target for U.S.-based franchises. Franchisors are finding it surprisingly easier now to move into China, South Africa, the Philippines, and the Middle East. Plus it's not just the large franchises like Subway and Marriott Hotels making the move. Newer, smaller franchises are going global as well. Auntie Anne's sells hand-rolled pretzels in 22 different countries including Indonesia, Malaysia, the Philippines, Singapore, Venezuela, and Thailand. Build-A-Bear Workshops has 63 franchisees in 12 countries including South Africa and the United Arab Emirates.[35] In 2005, 29-year-old Matthew Corrin launched Freshii, a sandwich, salad, and soup restaurant with fresh affordable food in trendy locations. He already has 45 locations in four countries with a new store in India on the horizon.[36]

What makes franchising successful in global markets is what makes it successful in the United States: convenience and a predictable level of service and quality. Franchisors, though, must be careful and do their homework before entering into global franchise agreements. Three questions to ask before forming a global franchise are: Will your intellectual property be protected? Can you give proper support to global partners? Are you able to adapt to franchise regulations in other countries? If the answer is yes to all three questions, global franchising creates great opportunities. It's also important to remember that adapting products and brand names to different countries creates challenges. In France, people thought a furniture-stripping franchise called Dip 'N' Strip was a bar that featured strippers.

Just as McDonald's and Subway have exported golden arches and sub sandwiches worldwide, foreign franchises see the United States as a popular target. Japanese franchises like Kumon Learning Centers and Canadian franchises like tax preparer H&R Block are very active in the United States.[37] H&R Block even has its headquarters in Kansas City, Missouri. Other franchises are hoping to change our tastes here. Ly Qui Trung would like to see his Pho 24 Noodle Bars become a part of the American landscape and Canada's Yogen Fruz frozen yogurt wants us to eat healthier desserts.

LEARNING goal 6

Explain the role of cooperatives.

COOPERATIVES

cooperative
A business owned and controlled by the people who use it—producers, consumers, or workers with similar needs who pool their resources for mutual gain.

Some people dislike the notion of owners, managers, workers, and buyers being separate individuals with separate goals. So they have formed cooperatives, a different kind of organization to meet their needs for electricity, child care, housing, health care, food, and financial services. A **cooperative**, or co-op, is owned and controlled by the people who use it—producers, consumers, or workers with similar needs who pool their resources for mutual gain. In many rural parts of the country, for example, the government sells wholesale power to electric cooperatives at rates 40 to 50 percent below the rates nonfederal utilities charge. Electric cooperatives serve 42 million U.S. consumer-members in 47 states—or 12 percent of the population.

Worldwide, some 750,000 cooperatives serve 730 million members—120 million of them in the United States.[38] Members democratically control these businesses by electing a board of directors that hires professional management. Some co-ops ask members/customers to work for a number of hours a month as part of their membership duties. You may have one of the country's 4,000 food co-ops near you. If so, stop by and chat to learn more about this growing aspect of the U.S. economy. If you are interested in knowing more about cooperatives, contact the National Cooperative Business Association at 202-638-6222 or visit its website at www.ncba.coop.

Another kind of cooperative in the United States is formed to give members more economic power as a group than they have as individuals.[39] The best example is a farm cooperative. The goal at first was for farmers to join together to get better prices for their food products. Eventually the idea expanded, and farm cooperatives now buy and sell fertilizer, farm equipment, seed, and other products in a multibillion-dollar industry. Cooperatives have an advantage in the marketplace because they don't pay the same kind of taxes corporations pay.

Cooperatives are still a major force in agriculture and other industries today. Some top co-ops have familiar names such as Land O Lakes, Sunkist, Ocean Spray, Blue Diamond, Associated Press, Ace Hardware, True Value Hardware, Riceland Foods, and Welch's.

WHICH FORM OF OWNERSHIP IS FOR YOU?

You can build your own business in a variety of ways. You can start your own sole proprietorship, partnership, corporation, LLC, or cooperative—or you can buy a franchise and be part of a larger corporation. There are advantages and disadvantages to each. Before you decide which form is for you, evaluate all the alternatives carefully.

The miracle of free enterprise is that the freedom and incentives of capitalism make risks acceptable to many people who go on to create the great corporations of America. You know many of their names and companies: James Cash Penney (JCPenney), Steve Jobs (Apple Computer), Sam Walton (Walmart), Levi Strauss (Levi Strauss), Henry Ford (Ford Motor Company), Thomas Edison (General Electric), Bill Gates (Microsoft), and so on. They started small, accumulated capital, grew, and became industrial leaders. Could you do the same?

progress assessment

- What are some of the factors to consider before buying a franchise?
- What opportunities are available for starting a global franchise?
- What is a cooperative?

summary

Learning Goal 1. Compare the advantages and disadvantages of sole proprietorships.

- **What are the advantages and disadvantages of sole proprietorships?**

The advantages of sole proprietorships include ease of starting and ending, ability to be your own boss, pride of ownership, retention of profit, and no special taxes. The disadvantages include unlimited liability, limited financial resources, difficulty in management, overwhelming time commitment, few fringe benefits, limited growth, and limited life span.

Learning Goal 2. Describe the differences between general and limited partners, and compare the advantages and disadvantages of partnerships.

- **What are the three key elements of a general partnership?**

The three key elements of a general partnership are common ownership, shared profits and losses, and the right to participate in managing the operations of the business.

- **What are the main differences between general and limited partners?**

General partners are owners (partners) who have unlimited liability and are active in managing the company. Limited partners are owners (partners) who have limited liability and are not active in the company.

- **What does *unlimited liability* mean?**

Unlimited liability means that sole proprietors and general partners must pay all debts and damages caused by their business. They may have to sell their houses, cars, or other personal possessions to pay business debts.

- **What does *limited liability* mean?**

Limited liability means that corporate owners (stockholders) and limited partners are responsible for losses only up to the amount they invest. Their other personal property is not at risk.

- **What is a master limited partnership?**

A master limited partnership is a partnership that acts like a corporation but is taxed like a partnership.

- **What are the advantages and disadvantages of partnerships?**

The advantages include more financial resources, shared management and pooled knowledge, and longer survival. The disadvantages include unlimited liability, division of profits, disagreements among partners, and difficulty of termination.

Learning Goal 3. Compare the advantages and disadvantages of corporations, and summarize the differences between C corporations, S corporations, and limited liability companies.

- **What is the definition of a corporation?**

A corporation is a state-chartered legal entity with authority to act and have liability separate from its owners.

- **What are the advantages and disadvantages of corporations?**

The advantages include more money for investment, limited liability, size, perpetual life, ease of ownership change, ease of drawing talented employees, and separation of ownership from management. The disadvantages include initial cost, paperwork, size, difficulty in termination, double taxation, and possible conflict with a board of directors.

- **Why do people incorporate?**

Two important reasons for incorporating are special tax advantages and limited liability.

- **What are the advantages of S corporations?**

S corporations have the advantages of limited liability (like a corporation) and simpler taxes (like a partnership). To qualify for S corporation status, a company must have fewer than 100 stockholders (members of a family count as one shareholder), its stockholders must be individuals or estates and U.S. citizens or permanent residents, and the company cannot derive more than 25 percent of its income from passive sources.

- **What are the advantages of limited liability companies?**

Limited liability companies have the advantage of limited liability without the hassles of forming a corporation or the limitations imposed by S corporations. LLCs may choose whether to be taxed as partnerships or corporations.

Learning Goal 4. Define and give examples of three types of corporate mergers, and explain the role of leveraged buyouts and taking a firm private.

- **What is a merger?**

A merger is the result of two firms forming one company. The three major types are vertical mergers, horizontal mergers, and conglomerate mergers.

- **What are leveraged buyouts, and what does it mean to take a company private?**

Leveraged buyouts are attempts by managers and employees to borrow money and purchase the company. Individuals who, together or alone, buy all the stock for themselves are said to take the company private.

Learning Goal 5. Outline the advantages and disadvantages of franchises, and discuss the opportunities for diversity in franchising and the challenges of global franchising.

- **What is a franchise?**

An arrangement to buy the rights to use the business name and sell its products or services in a given territory is called a franchise.

- **What is a franchisee?**

A franchisee is a person who buys a franchise.

- **What are the benefits and drawbacks of being a franchisee?**

The benefits include getting a nationally recognized name and reputation, a proven management system, promotional assistance, and pride of ownership. Drawbacks include high franchise fees, managerial regulation, shared profits, and transfer of adverse effects if other franchisees fail.

- **What is the major challenge to global franchises?**

It is often difficult to transfer an idea or product that worked well in the United States to another culture. It is essential to adapt to the region.

Learning Goal 6. Explain the role of cooperatives.

- **What is the role of a cooperative?**

Cooperatives are organizations owned by members/customers. Some people form cooperatives to acquire more economic power than they would have as individuals. Small businesses often form cooperatives to gain more purchasing, marketing, or product development strength.

key terms

acquisition 131	**general partner** 119	**limited partnership** 119
conglomerate merger 131	**general partnership** 119	**master limited partnership (MLP)** 119
conventional (C) corporation 123	**horizontal merger** 131	**merger** 131
cooperative 140	**leveraged buyout (LBO)** 131	**partnership** 116
corporation 116	**limited liability** 119	**S corporation** 127
franchise 133	**limited liability company (LLC)** 128	**sole proprietorship** 116
franchise agreement 133	**limited liability partnership (LLP)** 119	**unlimited liability** 118
franchisee 133	**limited partner** 119	**vertical merger** 131
franchisor 133		

critical thinking

Imagine you are considering starting your own business.

1. What kinds of products or services will you offer?

2. What talents or skills do you need to run the business?

3. Do you have all the skills and resources to start the business, or will you need to find one or more partners? If so, what skills would your partners need to have?

4. What form of business ownership would you choose—sole proprietorship, partnership, C corporation, S corporation, or LLC? Why?

developing workplace skills

1. Research businesses in your area and identify sole proprietorships, partnerships, corporations, and franchises. Arrange interviews with managers using each form of ownership and get their impressions, hints, and warnings. (If you are able to work with a team of fellow students, divide the interviews among team members.) How much does it cost to start? How many hours do they work? What are the specific benefits? Share the results with your class.

2. Have you thought about starting your own business? What opportunities seem attractive? Think of a friend or friends whom you might want for a partner or partners in the business. List all the financial resources and personal skills you will need to launch the business. Then make separate lists of the personal skills and the financial resources that you and your friend(s) might bring to your new venture. How much capital and what personal skills will be needed beyond those you already have? Develop an action plan for needed capital.

3. Let's assume you want to open one of the following new businesses. What form of business ownership would you choose for each? Why?

    a. Video game rental store.

    b. Wedding planning service.

    c. Software development firm.

    d. Online bookstore.

4. Successful businesses continually change hands. Methods of change discussed in this chapter include mergers, acquisitions, taking a firm private, and using leveraged buyouts. Search for an article online that illustrates how one of these methods changed an organization. What led to the change? How did this change affect the company's stakeholders? What benefits did the change provide? What new challenges were created?

5. Find information online about a business cooperative (i.e. Welch's, Land O Lakes, Sunkist). Research how it was formed, who can belong to it, and how it operates.

taking it to the net

Purpose

To explore franchising opportunities and to evaluate the strengths and weaknesses of a selected franchise.

Exercise

Go to Franchise Expo (www.franchiseexpo.com).

1. Take the self-test to see if franchising is a good personal choice for you. Find the test by clicking on Resources, then on Introduction to Franchising. Then, under Franchising Basics, click on Franchising—An Interactive Self-Test.

2. Go back to the home page and use the search tool to find a franchise that has the potential of fulfilling your entrepreneurial dreams. Navigate to the profile of the franchise you selected. Explore the franchise's website if a link is available. Refer to the questions listed in Figure 5.8 in this chapter and assess the strengths and weaknesses of your selected franchise. (Hint: The website also contains tips for evaluating a franchise listing.)

3. Did your search give you enough information to answer most of the questions in Figure 5.8? If not, what other information do you need, and where can you obtain it?

casing the web

To access the case "Stopped Cold," visit **www.mhhe.com/ubl0e**

video case

To access the video case featuring PODS, visit **www.mhhe.com/ubl0e**

Entrepreneurship
and STARTING A
Small Business

LEARNING
goals

After you have read and studied this chapter, you should be able to

1 Explain why people take the risks of entrepreneurship; list the attributes of successful entrepreneurs; and describe entrepreneurial teams, intrapreneurs, and home- and web-based businesses.

2 Discuss the importance of small business to the American economy and summarize the major causes of small-business failure.

3 Summarize ways to learn about how small businesses operate.

4 Analyze what it takes to start and run a small business.

5 Outline the advantages and disadvantages small businesses have in entering global markets.

Shawn Carter, aka Jay-Z, should be no stranger to hip hop fans. The 10-time Grammy winning artist has sold more than 45 million albums worldwide. He's bested only by the Beatles in terms of No. 1 albums on the Billboard charts. Although Jay-Z still releases an album from time to time, today he's more concerned with his business ventures than with rap. For good reason, too: his businesses have earned him a net worth of $450 million.

But Jay-Z didn't turn from rapper to media mogul overnight. Many musicians attempt to translate their artistic success into a business empire only to fail from either a lack of knowledge or unwillingness to adapt to the system. Jay-Z, on the other hand, used his entrepreneurial cunning along with his complete control over the Jay-Z brand to become one of the world's richest musicians. In fact, in a few years Jay-Z's fortune may exceed $1 billion, making him one of the richest people in the world.

Part of the reason Jay-Z has been so successful is that he's been involved in the business side of music almost as long as he's been rapping. In 1996 no labels wanted to sign a 26-year-old low profile personality known mostly through New York's local hip hop scene. Out of necessity, he and two others founded Roc-A-Fella Records. The risk of starting his own business paid off big both for his career and his brand. Since he owned the company he rapped for, that made him more attractive to cost-cutting labels wanting to avoid traditional contracts. He eventually entered a joint venture with Def Jam Recordings and together the two companies made millions from albums like *Reasonable Doubt* and *The Blueprint*.

As his stardom rose, Jay-Z did endorsements like any other pop star would. But unlike his industry peers, Jay-Z carefully considered which products he promoted all while obtaining creative control over each ad. In a spot for HP computers, for instance, Jay-Z played the role of a professional commanding his empire in a sharp suit with his trusty computer. Each ad that played up his business side slowly wore down his Brooklyn bad boy image from his rap days and replaced it with that of a slick corporate player. By the time Jay-Z took up the

mantle of CEO at Def Jam, few questioned the abilities of this rapper to take over the reins of a major company.

Jay-Z's branding expertise has served him as well in his clothing line. In the late 1990s he noticed that sales of Iceberg apparel rose after he mentioned the company in his raps. Jay-Z once again took the entrepreneurial route and started his own clothing brand called Rocawear. The line took off and in 2006 Jay-Z sold it to a brand licensing company for $204 million. Jay-Z continues to own a stake in the Rocawear name.

Today Jay-Z's business holdings are almost too numerous to count. The international 40/40 nightclub chain, a partial ownership in the New Jersey Nets basketball team, and a footwear line with Reebok account for just a portion of his wide portfolio. His most ambitious entrepreneurial venture at the moment is his role as the CEO of Roc Nation, a joint project with concert giant Live Nation.

As a testament to his success as a businessman, Jay-Z has talked shop with global leaders such as Bill Gates, Warren Buffett and former President Bill Clinton. Although his popularity as a rapper helped launch his valuable brand, Jay-Z wouldn't be the success he is today without the entrepreneurial risks he took throughout his career. As you read about such risk-takers in this chapter, maybe you'll be inspired to become an entrepreneur yourself.

profile

Getting to Know
Jay-Z
Rapper and Founder of Roc Nation

X

Sources: Daniel Gross, "Jay-Z's $450 Million Business Empire," *Yahoo Finance: The Daily Ticker,* March 25, 2011; John Jurgensen, "The State of Jay-Z's Empire," *The Wall Street Journal,* October 29, 2010; Lisa Taddeo, "Jay-Z: It Takes a Harmless, Hand-Built Gangster to Run this Town," *Esquire,* February 2010.

NAME THAT company

When this company's founder had financial problems in the business's early days, he asked his suppliers to help him out. They did and they were well rewarded for their risk. Today these suppliers still service this mammoth company that has franchises all over the world. Name that company. (Find the answer in the chapter.)

THE AGE OF THE ENTREPRENEUR

Mark Pincus is the founder and CEO of Zynga, maker of popular Facebook games FarmVille and Mafia Wars. The company pocketed $835 million in 2010 and has more than 100 million users. Zynga is by far the most successful company built on the Facebook platform. Do you have any ideas for other businesses that might be successful on Facebook?

Today most young people know it's unlikely they will get a job in a large corporation and stay 30 years. For those who want more control over their destiny, working in or starting a small business makes sense. **Entrepreneurship** is accepting the risk of starting and running a business. Explore this chapter and think about the possibility of entrepreneurship in your future.

THE JOB-CREATING POWER OF ENTREPRENEURS IN THE UNITED STATES

Well before the recent economic turmoil, one of the major issues in the United States has been the need to create more jobs. With the current high unemployment rate, job creation is even more critical. You can begin to understand the job-creating power of entrepreneurs when you look at some of the great U.S. entrepreneurs from the past and the present. The history of the United States is the history of its entrepreneurs. Consider just a few of the many who have helped shape the U.S. economy:[1]

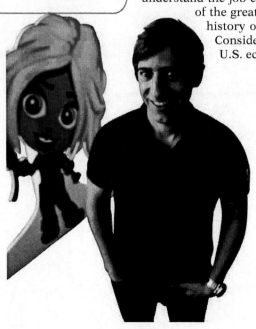

- DuPont, which manufactures thousands of products under such brand names as Teflon and Lycra, was started in 1802 by French immigrant Éleuthère Irénée du Pont de Nemours. Some 18 shareholders provided $36,000 in start-up money.

- Avon, the familiar beauty products retailer, started in 1886 with $500 David McConnell borrowed from a friend.

- George Eastman launched photographic giant Kodak in 1880 with a $3,000 investment.

- Procter & Gamble, now a multinational marketer of household products, was formed in 1837 by William Procter, James Gamble, and a total of $7,000 in capital.

- Ford Motor Company began with an investment of $28,000 by Henry Ford and 11 associates.

Success Knows No Age

Although fortunes are amassed over time, that doesn't mean they are exclusive to older people. Here are just a few examples of young entrepreneurs who found success in their college years:

Derek Johnson came up with the idea for his company, Tatango, during a lunch with a fellow undergrad. As the chair of communications for her sorority, his friend complained that even with Facebook and e-mail she couldn't get important announcements to her entire chapter quickly. Within months Johnson established a mass-texting business that generated more than $500,000 in sales in 2010.

Peter Findley stumbled into the business program of his college after trying a number of different majors. Inspired in an entrepreneurship class, Findley began writing the business plan for Giant Campus. The company organizes summer camps for middle- and high school age kids on college campuses where they learn new media skills like web design. Five years after his initial spark, Giant Campus grew to more than 70 colleges located across the world.

Sam Hogg opened his wallet one day after Christmas and stared at all the plastic gift cards he received. Troubled at the waste of plastic, Hogg was shocked when he learned that 75 million pounds of gift card plastic end up in landfills each year. In 2008 he started GiftZip.com, an electronic gift card aggregator site. With 275 retailers now onboard, use of the site has increased 2,100 percent since the company launched.

John Goscha lived in a dorm for student entrepreneurs in his freshman year at Babson College. He and his friends spent many nights in his room brainstorming on enormous sheets of paper spread across the wall. After a while Goscha wondered if it would be possible simply to write all their ideas directly on the wall. After years of development, he finally devised a paint that can turn any wall into a dry erase board. With help from his friends he launched IdeaPaint in 2002, and six years later the company won the Innovation Award at NeoCon, one of the design industry's largest showcases.

Sources: Joel Holland, "What's Your Problem?" *Entrepreneur,* May 2010; Jason Daley, "A Charter for New Courses," *Entrepreneur,* April 2010; Ivy Hughes, "Guilt Free Gifting," *Entrepreneur,* April 2010; Kasey Wehrum, "30 Under 30: IdeaPaint," *Inc.,* October 1, 2009.

- Amazon.com began with investments by founder Jeff Bezos's family and friends. Bezos's parents invested $300,000, a huge portion of their retirement account. Today they are billionaires.

These stories have much in common. One or a couple of entrepreneurs had a good idea, borrowed some money from friends and family, and started a business. That business now employs thousands of people and helps the country prosper.

The United States has plenty of entrepreneurial talent. Names such as Steve Jobs (Apple Computer), Mark Zuckerberg (Facebook), Michael Dell (Dell Inc.), Bill Gates (Microsoft), Howard Schultz (Starbucks), Jack Dorsey (Twitter), and Chad Hurley and Steve Chen (YouTube) have become as familiar as those of the great entrepreneurs of the past. The nearby Spotlight on Small Business box highlights several young entrepreneurs who started businesses while still in school.

entrepreneurship
Accepting the risk of starting and running a business.

LEARNING goal 1

> Explain why people take the risks of entrepreneurship; list the attributes of successful entrepreneurs; and describe entrepreneurial teams, intrapreneurs, and home- and web-based businesses.

WHY PEOPLE TAKE THE ENTREPRENEURIAL CHALLENGE

Taking the risks of starting a business can be scary and thrilling at the same time. One entrepreneur described it as almost like bungee jumping. You might be scared, but if you watch six other people do it and they survive, then you're more likely to do it yourself. Here are some reasons people are willing to take the entrepreneurial risk:

- *Opportunity.* The opportunity to share in the American dream is a tremendous lure. Many people, including those new to this country, may not have the skills for today's complex organizations, but they do have the initiative and drive to work the long hours demanded by entrepreneurship. The same is true of many corporate managers who leave corporate life (by choice or after downsizing) to run businesses of their own. Others, including an increasing number of women, minorities, older people, and people with disabilities, find that starting their own businesses offers them more opportunities than working for others.[2]

- *Profit.* Profit is another important reason to become an entrepreneur. Bill Gates, who cofounded Microsoft, is the richest man in the United States and one of the richest men in the world.[3]

- *Independence.* Many entrepreneurs simply do not enjoy working for someone else. Melissa Harvey, whose company Will n' Roses LLC produces all-natural nut and whole-grain Kizo bars, says one of the best things about being an entrepreneur is the freedom to pursue your passion: "It's about independence. You can take something that motivates you, that inspires you and act on it without roadblocks."[4]

- *Challenge.* Some people believe that entrepreneurs are excitement junkies who thrive on risk. Entrepreneurs take moderate, calculated risks; they don't just gamble. In general, though, entrepreneurs seek achievement more than power.[5]

What Does It Take to Be an Entrepreneur?

Would you succeed as an entrepreneur? You can learn about the managerial and leadership skills needed to run a firm. However, you may not have the personality to assume the risks, take the initiative, create the vision, and rally others to follow your lead. Such personality traits are harder to learn or acquire than academic skills are. A list of entrepreneurial attributes to look for in yourself includes:[6]

- *Self-directed.* You should be self-disciplined and thoroughly comfortable being your own boss. You alone will be responsible for your success or failure.

- *Self-nurturing.* You must believe in your idea even when no one else does, and be able to replenish your own enthusiasm. When Walt Disney suggested the possibility of a full-length animated feature film, *Snow White,* the industry laughed. His personal commitment and enthusiasm caused the Bank of America to back his venture. The rest is history.

- *Action-oriented.* Great business ideas are not enough. Most important is a burning desire to realize, actualize, and build your dream into reality.

- *Highly energetic.* It's your business, and you must be emotionally, mentally, and physically able to work long and hard. Employees have weekends and vacations; entrepreneurs often work seven days a week and don't take vacations for years. Working 18-hour days in your own business can be exhausting, but most entrepreneurs think it is better than working long hours for someone else.

- *Tolerant of uncertainty.* Successful entrepreneurs take only calculated risks (if they can help it). Still, they must be able to take *some* risks. Remember, entrepreneurship is not for the squeamish or those bent on security. You can't be afraid to fail. Many well-known entrepreneurs failed several times before achieving success. The late football coach Vince Lombardi summarized the entrepreneurial philosophy when he said, "We didn't lose any games this season, we just ran out of time twice." New entrepreneurs must be prepared to run out of time a few times before they succeed.

Turning Your Passions and Problems into Opportunities

As a young man in Queens, a borough of New York City, Russell Simmons channeled his passion for hip-hop culture into Def Jam Records. Today, his multimillion-dollar empire also includes Phat Farm clothing and Rush Management. Simmons used his time, money, and energy to turn his passion into a sustainable business.[7]

While many entrepreneurs' business ideas are inspired by their passions, many see business opportunities in their problems. For example, Anita Roddick started The Body Shop, which recycles its bottles and jars, because she hated paying for expensive packaging when she bought makeup.[8]

Most entrepreneurs don't get ideas for products and services from some flash of inspiration. The source of innovation is more like a *flashlight.* Imagine a search party walking in the dark, shining lights, looking around, asking questions, and looking some more. "That's how most creativity happens," says business author Dale Dauten. "Calling around, asking questions, saying 'What if?' till you get blisters on your tongue."

To look at problems and/or passions and see opportunities in them, ask yourself these questions: What do I want, but can never find? What product or service would improve my life? What really irritates me and what product or service would help?

Paula Deen had a dream that she could grow a business based on her passion for good country cooking. Her home-based catering business grew from a small family operation into multiple television shows, countless cookbooks, several restaurants, a bi-monthly magazine, and an ever-expanding product line. Do you have a passion that you could turn into a profitable business?

Keep in mind, however, that not all ideas are opportunities. If your idea doesn't meet anyone else's needs, the business won't succeed. You may have a business idea that is a good opportunity if:[9]

- It fills customers' needs.
- You have the skills and resources to start a business.
- You can sell the product or service at a price customers are willing and able to pay—and still make a profit.
- You can get your product or service to customers before your window of opportunity closes (before competitors with similar solutions beat you to the marketplace).
- You can keep the business going.

If you think you may have the entrepreneurial spirit in your blood, complete the Entrepreneurial Readiness Questionnaire on pages 153–154.

Entrepreneurial Teams

entrepreneurial team
A group of experienced people from different areas of business who join together to form a managerial team with the skills needed to develop, make, and market a new product.

An **entrepreneurial team** is a group of experienced people from different areas of business who join to form a managerial team with the skills to develop, make, and market a new product. A team may be better than an individual entrepreneur because team members can combine creative skills with production and marketing skills right from the start. Having a team also can ensure more cooperation and coordination later among functions in the business.

While Steve Jobs was the charismatic folk hero and visionary of Apple Computers, it was Steve Wozniak who invented the first personal computer model and Mike Markkula who offered business expertise and access to venture capital. The key to Apple's early success was that it was built around this "smart team" of entrepreneurs. The team wanted to combine the discipline of a big company with an environment in which people could feel they were participating in a successful venture. The trio of entrepreneurs recruited seasoned managers with similar desires. Everyone worked together to conceive, develop, and market products.[10]

Micropreneurs and Home-Based Businesses

micropreneurs
Entrepreneurs willing to accept the risk of starting and managing the type of business that remains small, lets them do the kind of work they want to do, and offers them a balanced lifestyle.

Not everyone who starts a business wants to grow a mammoth corporation. Some are interested in maintaining a balanced lifestyle while doing the kind of work they want to do. Such business owners are called **micropreneurs**. While other entrepreneurs are committed to the quest for growth, micropreneurs know they can be happy even if their companies never appear on a list of top-ranked businesses.

Many micropreneurs are home-based business owners. More than half of all small businesses are run from owners' homes.[11] Micropreneurs include consultants, video producers, architects, and bookkeepers. Many with professional skills such as graphic design, writing, and translating have found that one way of starting a freelance business is through websites such as Elance (www.elance.com) and oDesk (www.odesk.com) that link clients and freelancers. The sites post job openings and client feedback and serve as secure intermediaries for clients' payments.

ENTREPRENEUR READINESS QUESTIONNAIRE

Each of the following items describes something that you may or may not feel represents your personality or other characteristics about you. Read each item and then circle the response (1, 2, 3, 4, or 5) that most nearly reflects the extent to which you agree or disagree that the item seems to fit you.

Looking at My Overall Philosophy of Life and Typical Behavior, I Would Say That . . .	AGREE COMPLETELY (1)	MOSTLY AGREE (2)	PARTIALLY AGREE (3)	MOSTLY DISAGREE (4)	DISAGREE COMPLETELY (5)
1. I am generally optimistic.	1	2	3	4	5
2. I enjoy competing and doing things better than someone else.	1	2	3	4	5
3. When solving a problem, I try to arrive at the best solution first without worrying about other possibilities.	1	2	3	4	5
4. I enjoy associating with co-workers after working hours.	1	2	3	4	5
5. If betting on a horse race I would prefer to take a chance on a high-payoff "long shot."	1	2	3	4	5
6. I like setting my own goals and working hard to achieve them.	1	2	3	4	5
7. I am generally casual and easy-going with others.	1	2	3	4	5
8. I like to know what is going on and take action to find out.	1	2	3	4	5
9. I work best when someone else is guiding me along the way.	1	2	3	4	5
10. When I am right I can convince others.					
11. I find that other people frequently waste my valuable time.	1	2	3	4	5
12. I enjoy watching football, baseball, and similar sports events.	1	2	3	4	5
13. I tend to communicate about myself very openly with other people.	1	2	3	4	5
14. I don't mind following orders from superiors who have legitimate authority.	1	2	3	4	5
15. I enjoy planning things more than actually carrying out the plans.	1	2	3	4	5
16. I don't think it's much fun to bet on a "sure thing."	1	2	3	4	5
17. If faced with failure, I would shift quickly to something else rather than sticking to my guns.	1	2	3	4	5
18. Part of being successful in business is reserving adequate time for family.	1	2	3	4	5
19. Once I have earned something, I feel that keeping it secure is important.	1	2	3	4	5
20. Making a lot of money is largely a matter of getting the right breaks.	1	2	3	4	5
21. Problem solving is usually more effective when a number of alternatives are considered.	1	2	3	4	5
22. I enjoy impressing others with the things I can do.	1	2	3	4	5
23. I enjoy playing games like tennis and handball with someone who is slightly better than I am.	1	2	3	4	5
24. Sometimes moral ethics must be bent a little in business dealings.	1	2	3	4	5
25. I think that good friends would make the best subordinates in an organization.	1	2	3	4	5

(continued)

Scoring:

Give yourself one point for each 1 or 2 response you circled for questions 1, 2, 6, 8, 10, 11, 16, 17, 21, 22, 23.

Give yourself one point for each 4 or 5 response you circled for questions 3, 4, 5, 7, 9, 12, 13, 14, 15, 18, 19, 20, 24, 25.

Add your points and see how you rate in the following categories:

21–25   Your entrepreneurial potential looks great if you have a suitable opportunity to use it. What are you waiting for?

16–20   This is close to the high entrepreneurial range. You could be quite successful if your other talents and resources are right.

11–15   Your score is in the transitional range. With some serious work you can probably develop the outlook you need for running your own business.

6–10   Things look pretty doubtful for you as an entrepreneur. It would take considerable rearranging of your life philosophy and behavior to make it.

0–5   Let's face it. Entrepreneurship isn't really for you. Still, learning what it's all about won't hurt anything.

Source: Kenneth R. Van Voorhis, *Entrepreneurship and Small Business Management* (New York: Allyn & Bacon, 1980).

Micropreneur Jane Mason, of Virtuous Bread, teaches small bread-making classes in her home kitchen. She also created a network of "Bread Angels," people she taught to start their own home-based bread businesses. Her website contains a blog, a newsletter and recipes. Mason is more concerned with building positive relationships within communities than with building a huge baking company. Can you see why Mason is considered a micropreneur?

Many home-based businesses are owned by people combining career and family. Don't picture just moms with young children; nearly 60 percent are men. Here are more reasons for the growth of home-based businesses:[12]

- Computer technology has leveled the competitive playing field, allowing home-based businesses to look and act as big as their corporate competitors. Broadband Internet connections, smart phones such as the BlackBerry and the iPhone, and other technologies are so affordable that setting up a business takes a much smaller initial investment than it once did.

- Corporate downsizing has led many to venture out on their own. Meanwhile, the work of the downsized employees still needs to be done, and corporations are outsourcing much of it to smaller companies.

- Social attitudes have changed. Whereas home-based entrepreneurs used to be asked when they were going to get a "real" job, they are now likely to be asked for how-to-do-it advice.

- New tax laws have loosened restrictions on deducting expenses for home offices.

Working at home has its challenges, of course. Here are a few:[13]

- *Getting new customers.* Getting the word out can be difficult because you don't have a retail storefront.

- *Managing time.* You save time by not commuting, but it takes self-discipline to use that time wisely.

- *Keeping work and family tasks separate.* It's great to be able to throw a load of laundry in the washer in the middle of the workday if you need to, but you have to keep such distractions to a minimum. It also takes self-discipline to leave your work at the office if the office is at home.

- *Abiding by city ordinances.* Government ordinances restrict the types of businesses allowed in certain parts of the community and how much traffic a home-based business can attract to the neighborhood.

figure 6.1

POTENTIAL HOME-BASED BUSINESSES

Many businesses can be started at home. Listed below are I0 businesses that have low start-up costs, don't require an abundance of administrative tasks, and are in relatively high demand:

1. Cleaning service.
2. Gift-basket business.
3. Web merchant.
4. Mailing list service.
5. Microfarming (small plots of land for such high-value crops as mushrooms, edible flowers, or sprouts).
6. Tutoring.
7. Résumé service.
8. Web design.
9. Medical claims assistance.
10. Personal coaching.

Look for a business that meets these important criteria: (I) The job is something you truly enjoy doing; (2) you know enough to do the job well or you are willing to spend time learning it while you have another job; and (3) you can identify a market for your product or service.

- *Managing risk.* Home-based entrepreneurs should review their homeowner's insurance policy, since not all policies cover business-related claims. Some even void the coverage if there is a business in the home.

Home-based entrepreneurs should focus on finding opportunity instead of accepting security, getting results instead of following routines, earning a profit instead of earning a paycheck, trying new ideas instead of avoiding mistakes, and creating a long-term vision instead of seeking a short-term payoff. Figure 6.1 lists 10 ideas for potentially successful home-based businesses, and Figure 6.2 highlights clues for avoiding home-based business scams. You can find a wealth of online information about starting a home-based business at *Entrepreneur* magazine's website (www.entrepreneur.com).

figure 6.2

WATCH OUT FOR SCAMS

You've probably read many newspaper and magazine ads selling home-based businesses. You may have even received unsolicited e-mail messages touting the glory of particular work-at-home opportunities. Beware of work-at-home scams! Here are a few clues that tell you a home business opportunity is a scam:

1. The ad promises that you can earn hundreds or even thousands of dollars a week working at home.
2. No experience is needed.
3. You only need to work a few hours a week.
4. There are loads of CAPITAL LETTERS and exclamation points!!!!!
5. You need to call a 900 number for more information.
6. You're asked to send in some money to receive a list of home-based business opportunities.
7. You're pressured to make a decision NOW!!!!

Do your homework before investing in a business opportunity. Call and ask for references. Contact the Better Business Bureau (www.bbb.org), county and state departments of consumer affairs, and the state attorney general's office. Conduct an Internet search and ask people in forums or on social networking sites if they've dealt with the company. Visit Web sites such as Friends In Business (www.friendsinbusiness.com) to find advice on specific online scams. Most important, don't pay a great deal of money for a business opportunity until you've talked to an attorney.

Web-Based Businesses

Markus Frind operates his dating website, Plenty of Fish, out of his apartment. Apparently there really are plenty of fish since his site brings in $10 million a year.

affiliate marketing
An Internet-based marketing strategy in which a business rewards individuals or other businesses (affiliates) for each visitor or customer the affiliate sends to its website.

The Internet has sprouted a world of small web-based businesses selling everything from staplers to refrigerator magnets to wedding dresses. In 2010, online retail sales reached $172.9 billion, or approximately 7 percent of all retail sales. Online retail sales were up 11 percent in 2010, compared to just 2.5 percent for all retail sales. Forrester Research predicts that online retail sales will reach $250 billion by 2014.[14]

Web-based businesses have to offer more than the same merchandise customers can buy at stores—they must offer unique products or services. For example, Marc Resnik started his web-based distribution company after waking up one morning laughing about his business idea. Now ThrowThings.com makes money for him—he's shipped products to more than 44 countries. Although the company's offerings seem like a random collection of unrelated items, everything it sells can be thrown. You can buy promotional products in the "Throw Your Name Around!" section, ventriloquist dummies in the "Throw Your Voice!" section, and sporting equipment in the "Things to Throw!" section. Stranger products include fake vomit ("Throw Up!") and a $3.50 certificate that says you wasted your money ("Throw Your Money Away!"). Resnik doesn't sell very many of those certificates, but he does sell more dummies than anyone else in the United States. About two-thirds of the company's revenue comes from the promotional products section, which allows customers to add a logo to thousands of products. Why is Resnik's business so successful? As one frequent customer said, it's because of Resnik's exceptional service and quick turnaround time.[15]

One of the easiest ways to start a web-based business is through affiliate marketing. **Affiliate marketing** is an Internet-based marketing strategy in which a business rewards individuals or other businesses (affiliates) for each visitor or customer the affiliate sends to its website. For example, imagine you discovered a backpack online made of an extremely lightweight, amazingly strong fabric that holds everything you need for the day, is easy to carry, and looks great. You want to tell all your friends about it, so you register as an affiliate on the seller's website and download to your Facebook page a *widget*, a tiny application that links your page to the seller's site. Whenever anyone clicks on the widget (an image of the product) and buys a backpack, the seller pays you a commission.

If you can make a little money in commissions from sales of a single backpack, imagine setting up an online store with many products you love. Building such a store has become easier with the advent of social commerce services such as Lemonade Inc.'s Lemonade Stand (www.lemonade.com). Once partnered, an online retailer typically provides Lemonade Stand access to product information and images. Lemonade Stand then funnels that information through its website so that users can select which products they would like to appear in their widget product galleries on their websites, Facebook pages, or blogs. Widget users get commissions on sales generated through the widgets. Using social commerce services like Lemonade Stand saves users from the time-consuming task of registering as an affiliate with multiple sellers. Such services are allowing Internet users to become what amounts to peer-to-peer affiliates for e-retailers where the users can make money.

A web-based business isn't always a fast road to success.[16] It can sometimes be a shortcut to failure. Hundreds of high-flying dot-coms crashed after promising to revolutionize the way we shop. That's the bad news. The good news is that you can learn from someone else's failure and spare yourself some pain.

Entrepreneurship within Firms

Entrepreneurship in a large organization is often reflected in the efforts and achievements of **intrapreneurs,** creative people who work as entrepreneurs within corporations. The idea is to use a company's existing resources—human, financial, and physical—to launch new products and generate new profits.[17] At 3M, which produces a wide array of products from adhesives like Scotch tape to nonwoven materials for industrial use, managers are expected to devote 15 percent of their work time to thinking up new products or services.[18] You know those bright-colored Post-it Notes people use to write messages on just about everything? That product was developed by Art Fry, a 3M employee. He needed to mark the pages of his hymnal with something that wouldn't damage the book or fall out. He came up with the idea of the self-stick, repositionable paper slips. The labs at 3M produced a sample, but distributors were unimpressed and market surveys were inconclusive. Nonetheless, 3M kept sending samples to secretaries of top executives. Eventually, after a major sales and marketing program, the orders began pouring in, and Post-it Notes became a big winner. The company continues to update the product; making it from recycled paper is one of many innovations. Post-it Notes have gone international as well—the notepads sent to Japan are long and narrow to accommodate vertical writing. You can even use Post-it Notes electronically—the Post-it Software Notes program allows you to type messages onto brightly colored notes and store them on memo boards, embed them in documents, or send them through e-mail.

A classic intrapreneurial venture is Lockheed Martin Corporation's Skunkworks, a research and development center that turned out such monumental products as the United States' first fighter jet in 1943 and the Stealth fighter in 1991.[19]

Encouraging Entrepreneurship: What Government Can Do

Part of the Immigration Act passed by Congress in 1990 was intended to encourage more entrepreneurs to come to the United States. The act created a category of "investor visas" that allows 10,000 people to come to the United States each year if they invest $1 million in an enterprise that creates or preserves 10 jobs. Some people are promoting the idea of increasing the allowed number of such immigrants. They believe the more entrepreneurs that can be drawn to the United States, the more jobs will be created and the more the economy will grow.[20]

Another way to encourage entrepreneurship is **enterprise zones,** specific geographic areas to which governments attract private business investment by offering lower taxes and other government support. (These are also sometimes

intrapreneurs
Creative people who work as entrepreneurs within corporations.

When you come up with a winning idea, stick with it. That's certainly been the motto of 3M, the maker of Post-It Notes. The company encourages intrapreneurship among its employees by requiring them to devote at least 15 percent of their time to think about new products. How has this commitment to innovation paid off for 3M and its employees?

enterprise zones
Specific geographic areas to which governments try to attract private business investment by offering lower taxes and other government support.

Incubators, such as this one in Alabama, offer new businesses low-cost offices with basic business services such as accounting, legal advice, and secretarial help. Do you have such incubators in your area?

incubators
Centers that offer new businesses low-cost offices with basic business services.

called *empowerment zones* or *enterprise communities.*) The government could have a significant effect on entrepreneurship by offering tax breaks to businesses that make investments to create jobs.[21]

States are becoming stronger supporters of entrepreneurs and are creating programs that invest directly in new businesses. Often, state commerce departments serve as clearinghouses for such programs. States are also creating incubators and technology centers to reduce start-up capital needs. **Incubators** offer new businesses in the critical stage of early development low-cost offices with basic services such as accounting, legal advice, and secretarial help. According to a recent study conducted by the National Business Incubator Association (NBIA), 87 percent of incubator graduates remain in business.[22] To learn more about what incubators offer and to find links to incubators in your area, visit the NBIA's website (www.nbia.org).

There are a few states that offer assistance to qualified candidates under the Self-Employment Assistance (SEA) program. The program allows participants to collect unemployment checks while they build their businesses. Participants often get training and counseling as well. Unemployment checks may not seem like much, but many business owners say they are enough to help them launch their companies without depleting savings to pay for living expenses until their businesses are strong enough to support them. Rose Rios entered the New Jersey SEA program in 2007 when she was laid off from her job in market research. She collected benefits of about $450 while she started a medical communications and market research company. Since then she has brought in over $2.5 million in revenue and hired three full-time employees and several freelancers.[23]

The government can also join with private entities to promote entrepreneurship. For example, Startup America is a White House initiative to "celebrate, inspire, and accelerate high-growth entrepreneurship throughout the nation."[24] It is a public and private effort to bring together the country's most innovative entrepreneurs, corporations, universities, foundations, and other leaders, to work with federal agencies to increase the number and success of U.S. entrepreneurs. One of the core goals is to empower more Americans not just to get a job, but to create jobs. Learn more about the resources offered by Startup America at www.startupamericapartnership.org.[25]

progress assessment

- Why are people willing to take the risks of entrepreneurship?
- What are the advantages of entrepreneurial teams?
- How do micropreneurs differ from other entrepreneurs?
- What are some opportunities and risks of web-based businesses?

LEARNING goal 2

Discuss the importance of small business to the American economy and summarize the major causes of small-business failure.

GETTING STARTED IN SMALL BUSINESS

Let's suppose you have a great idea for a new business, you have the attributes of an entrepreneur, and you're ready to take the leap into business for yourself. How do you start? That's what the rest of this chapter is about.

It may be easier to identify with a small neighborhood business than with a giant global firm, yet the principles of management are similar for each. The management of charities, government agencies, churches, schools, and unions is much the same as the management of small and large businesses. So, as you learn about small-business management, you will take a giant step toward understanding management in general. All organizations demand capital, good ideas, planning, information management, budgets (and financial management in general), accounting, marketing, good employee relations, and good overall managerial know-how. We shall explore these areas as they relate to small businesses and then, later in the book, apply the concepts to large firms and even global organizations.

Small versus Big Business

The Small Business Administration (SBA) defines a **small business** as one that is independently owned and operated, is not dominant in its field of operation, and meets certain standards of size in terms of employees or annual receipts (such as under $2 million a year for service businesses). A small business is considered "small" only in relationship to other businesses in its industry. A wholesaler may sell up to $22 million and still be considered a small business by the SBA. In manufacturing, a plant can have 1,500 employees and still be considered small. Let's look at some interesting statistics about small businesses:[26]

> **small business**
> A business that is independently owned and operated, is not dominant in its field of operation, and meets certain standards of size (set by the Small Business Administration) in terms of employees or annual receipts.

- There are 27.8 million small businesses in the United States.
- Of all nonfarm businesses in the United States, almost 97 percent are considered small by SBA standards.
- Small businesses account for more than 50 percent of the gross domestic product (GDP).
- Nearly 600,000 tax-paying, employee-hiring businesses are started every year.
- Small businesses generate 60–80 percent of the new jobs each year.
- Small businesses employ about half of all private-sector employees.
- About 80 percent of U.S. workers find their first jobs in small businesses.

As you can see, small business is really a big part of the U.S. economy. How big? Let's find out.

Importance of Small Businesses

Since 60–80 percent of the nation's new jobs are in small businesses, there's a very good chance you'll either work in a small business someday or start one. In addition to providing employment opportunities, small firms believe they offer other advantages over larger companies—more personal customer service and the ability to respond quickly to opportunities.

Bigger is not always better. Picture a hole in the ground. If you fill it with boulders, there are many empty spaces between them. If you fill it with sand, there is no space between the grains. That's how it is in business. Big businesses don't serve all the needs of the market. There is plenty of room for small companies to make a profit filling those niches.

Small-Business Success and Failure

You can't be naïve about business practices, or you'll go broke. It's been reported that half of new businesses don't last five years.[27] Yet a study by economist Bruce Kirchhoff showed that the failure rate is only 18 percent over the first eight years. Kirchhoff contends that other reported failure rates are misinterpretations of Dun & Bradstreet statistics. When small-business owners closed down one business to start another, for instance, they were included in the "failure" category—even though they hadn't failed at all. Similarly, when a business changed its form of ownership or a sole proprietor retired, it was counted as a failure. The good news for entrepreneurs is that business failures are much lower than traditionally reported.[28]

Figure 6.3 lists reasons for small-business failures, among them managerial incompetence and inadequate financial planning. Keep in mind that when a business fails, it is important that the owners learn from their mistakes. Some entrepreneurs who have suffered flops are more realistic than novice entrepreneurs. Because of the lessons they've learned, they may be more successful in their future ventures.[29]

Choosing the right type of business is critical. Many businesses with low failure rates require advanced training to start—veterinary services, dental practices, medical practices,

Thirteen-year-old Madison Waldrop developed her own dress collection called Designs by Malyse, specializing in evening and bridal gowns. One of the young entrepreneur's bridal gowns was featured on the runway at the 2010 Bridal Fashion Week in New York City.

figure 6.3

CAUSES OF SMALL-BUSINESS FAILURE

The following are some of the causes of small-business failure:

- Plunging in without first testing the waters on a small scale.
- Underpricing or overpricing goods or services.
- Underestimating how much time it will take to build a market.
- Starting with too little capital.
- Starting with too much capital and being careless in its use.
- Going into business with little or no experience and without first learning something about the industry or market.
- Borrowing money without planning just how and when to pay it back.
- Attempting to do too much business with too little capital.

- Not allowing for setbacks and unexpected expenses.
- Buying too much on credit.
- Extending credit too freely.
- Expanding credit too rapidly.
- Failing to keep complete, accurate records, so that the owners drift into trouble without realizing it.
- Carrying habits of personal extravagance into the business.
- Not understanding business cycles.
- Forgetting about taxes, insurance, and other costs of doing business.
- Mistaking the freedom of being in business for oneself for the liberty to work or not, according to whim.

figure 6.4

**SITUATIONS FOR
SMALL-BUSINESS SUCCESS**

The following factors increase the chances of small-business success:

- The customer requires a lot of personal attention, as in a beauty parlor.

- The product is not easily made by mass-production techniques (e.g., custom-tailored clothes or custom auto-body work).

- Sales are not large enough to appeal to a large firm (e.g., a novelty shop).

- The neighborhood is not attractive because of crime or poverty. This provides a unique opportunity for small grocery stores and laundries.

- A large business sells a franchise operation to local buyers. (Don't forget franchising as an excellent way to enter the world of small business.)

- The owner pays attention to new competitors.

- The business is in a growth industry (e.g., computer services or web design).

and so on. While training and degrees may buy security, they do not tend to produce much growth—one dentist can fill only so many cavities. If you want to be both independent and rich, you need to go after growth. Often high-growth businesses, such as technology firms, are not easy to start and are even more difficult to keep going.

The easiest businesses to start have the least growth and greatest failure rate (like restaurants). The easiest to keep alive are difficult to get started (like manufacturing). And the ones that can make you rich are both hard to start and hard to keep going (like automobile assembly). See Figure 6.4 to get an idea of the business situations most likely to lead to success.

When you decide to start your own business, think carefully. You're unlikely to find everything you want—easy entry, security, and reward—in one business. Choose those characteristics that matter most to you; accept the absence of the others; plan, plan, plan; and then go for it!

LEARNING goal 3

Summarize ways to learn about how small businesses operate.

Jason White, owner of Crested Butte Angler, turned his love of fishing into a successful guide business. He learned to fish in the Ozarks of Missouri and Arkansas and now leads fishing excursions in Colorado, Mexico, and Thailand. What experiences do you have that would help you start and run a successful business?

LEARNING ABOUT SMALL-BUSINESS OPERATIONS

Hundreds of would-be entrepreneurs ask the same question: "How can I learn to run my own business?" Here are some hints.

Learn from Others

Investigate your local community college for classes on small business and entrepreneurship; there are thousands of such programs throughout the United States. Many bring together entrepreneurs from diverse backgrounds who form helpful support networks. Talk to others who have already

MAKING **ethical decisions**

Going Down with the Ship

Suppose you've worked for two years in a company and you see signs that it is beginning to falter. You and a co-worker have ideas about how to make a company like your boss's succeed. Rather than share your ideas with your boss, you and your friend are considering quitting your jobs and starting your own company together. Should you approach other co-workers about working for your new venture? Will you try to lure your old boss's customers to your own business? What are your alternatives? What are the consequences of each alternative? What's the most ethical choice?

done it. They'll tell you that location is critical and caution you not to be undercapitalized, that is, not to start without enough money. They'll warn you about the problems of finding and retaining good workers. And, most of all, they'll tell you to keep good records and hire a good accountant and lawyer before you start. Free advice like this is invaluable.

Get Some Experience

There is no better way to learn small-business management than by becoming an apprentice or working for a successful entrepreneur. Many small-business owners got the idea for their businesses from their prior jobs. The rule of thumb is: Have three years' experience in a comparable business first.[30]

Back in 1818, Cornelius Vanderbilt sold his own sailing vessels and went to work for a steamboat company so that he could learn the rules of the new game of steam. After learning what he needed to know, he quit, started his own steamship company, and became the first U.S. business owner to accumulate $100 million.

Running a small business part-time, during your off hours or on weekends, can bring the rewards of working for yourself while still enjoying a regular paycheck at another job. It may save you money too, because you're then less likely to make "rookie mistakes" when you start your own business. The Making Ethical Decisions box presents ethical questions about using the knowledge you've gained as an employee to start your own business.

Take Over a Successful Firm

Small-business owners work long hours and rarely take vacations. After many years, they may feel stuck and think they can't get out because they have too much time and effort invested. Thus millions of small-business owners are eager to get away, at least for a long vacation.

This is where you come in. Find a successful businessperson who owns a small business. Tell him or her you are eager to learn the business and would like to serve an apprenticeship, that is, a training period. Say that at the end of the training period (one year or so), you would like to help the owner or manager by becoming assistant manager. Thus you can free the owner to take off weekends and holidays and have a long vacation—a good deal for him or her. For another year or so, work very hard to learn all about the business—suppliers, inventory, bookkeeping, customers, promotion. At the end of two years, make this offer: The owner can retire or work only part-time, and you will take over management of the business. You can establish a profit-sharing plan with the owner plus pay yourself a salary. Be generous with yourself; you'll earn it if you manage the business. You can even ask for 40 percent or more of the profits.

The owner benefits by keeping ownership in the business and making 60 percent of what he or she earned before—without having to work. You benefit by making 40 percent of the profits of a successful firm. This is an excellent deal for an owner about to retire—he or she is able to keep the firm and a healthy profit flow. It is also a clever and successful way to share in the profits of a successful small business without making any personal monetary investment.

If profit sharing doesn't appeal to the owner, you may want to buy the business outright. How do you determine a fair price for a business? Value is based on (1) what the business owns, (2) what it earns, and (3) what makes it unique. Naturally, an accountant will need to help you determine the business's value.[31]

If you fail at your efforts to take over the business through either profit sharing or buying, you can quit and start your own business fully trained.

LEARNING goal 4

> Analyze what it takes to start and run a small business.

MANAGING A SMALL BUSINESS

According to the Small Business Administration, one of the major causes of small business failures is poor management. Keep in mind, though, that *poor management* covers a number of faults. It could mean poor planning, record keeping, inventory control, promotion, or employee relations. Most likely it includes poor capitalization. To help you succeed as a business owner, in the following sections we explore the functions of business in a small-business setting:

- Planning your business.
- Financing your business.
- Knowing your customers (marketing).
- Managing your employees (human resource development).
- Keeping records (accounting).

Although all the functions are important in both the start-up and management phases of the business, the first two—planning and financing—are the primary concerns when you start your business. The others are the heart of your operations once the business is under way.

Begin with Planning

Many people eager to start a small business come up with an idea and begin discussing it with professors, friends, and other businesspeople. At this stage the entrepreneur needs a business plan. A **business plan** is a detailed written statement that describes the nature of the business, the target market, the

business plan
A detailed written statement that describes the nature of the business, the target market, the advantages the business will have in relation to competition, and the resources and qualifications of the owner(s).

advantages the business will have over competition, and the resources and qualifications of the owner(s). A business plan forces potential small-business owners to be quite specific about the products or services they intend to offer. They must analyze the competition, calculate how much money they need to start, and cover other details of operation. A business plan is also mandatory for talking with bankers or other investors.

Lenders want to know everything about an aspiring business. First, pick a bank that serves businesses the size of yours. Have a good accountant prepare a complete set of financial statements and a personal balance sheet. Make an appointment before going to the bank and go to the bank with an accountant and all the necessary financial information. Demonstrate to the banker that you're a person of good character: civic minded and respected in business and community circles.[32] Finally, ask for *all* the money you need, be specific, and be prepared to personally guarantee the loan.

Writing a Business Plan

Modcloth co-founders Susan and Eric Koger started selling vintage clothes when they were in college. They entered a hastily written business plan in a school competition— and lost. While discouraging at first, the loss taught them that they needed to refocus and create a solid business plan if they were going to attract investors. Today their company has 100 full-time employees.

A good business plan takes a long time to write, but you've got only five minutes, in the *executive summary*, to convince readers not to throw it away. Since bankers receive many business plans every day, the summary has to catch their interest quickly. There's no such thing as a perfect business plan, but prospective entrepreneurs do think out the smallest details. An outline of a comprehensive business plan is shown on pages 165–166.

Many computer software programs can help you get organized. One highly rated business-plan program is Business Plan Pro by Palo Alto Software. To see samples of successful business plans for a variety of businesses go to www.bplans.com/sample_business_plans. You can also learn more about writing business plans on the Small Business Administration website at www.sba.gov/starting.

Getting the completed business plan into the right hands is almost as important as getting the right information into the plan. Finding funding requires research. Next we discuss sources of money available to new business ventures. All require a comprehensive business plan. The time and effort you invest before starting a business will pay off many times later. The big payoff is survival.

Getting Money to Fund a Small Business

An entrepreneur has several potential sources of capital: personal savings; relatives; former employers; banks; finance companies; venture capitalists; and government agencies such as the Small Business Administration (SBA), the Farmers Home Administration, the Economic Development Authority, and the Minority Business Development Agency. The most common source of funding after personal savings is friends and family.[33]

You may even want to consider borrowing from a potential supplier to your future business. Helping you get started may be in the supplier's interest if there is a chance you will be a big customer later. This is what Ray Kroc did in the early years of McDonald's. When Kroc didn't have the funds available to keep the company going, he asked his suppliers to help him with the necessary funds. These suppliers grew along with McDonalds. It's usually not a

OUTLINE OF A COMPREHENSIVE BUSINESS PLAN

A good business plan is between 25 and 50 pages long and takes at least six months to write.

Cover Letter

Only one thing is certain when you go hunting for money to start a business: You won't be the only hunter out there. You need to make potential funders want to read *your* business plan instead of the hundreds of others on their desks. Your cover letter should summarize the most attractive points of your project in as few words as possible. Be sure to address the letter to the potential investor by name. "To whom it may concern" or "Dear Sir" is not the best way to win an investor's support.

Section 1—Executive Summary

Begin with a two-page or three-page management summary of the proposed venture. Include a short description of the business, and discuss major goals and objectives.

Section 2—Company Background

Describe company operations to date (if any), potential legal considerations, and areas of risk and opportunity. Summarize the firm's financial condition, and include past and current balance sheets, income and cash flow statements, and other relevant financial records (you will read about these financial statements in Chapter 17). It is also wise to include a description of insurance coverage. Investors want to be assured that death or other mishaps do not pose major threats to the company.

Section 3—Management Team

Include an organization chart, job descriptions of listed positions, and detailed résumés of the current and proposed executives. A mediocre idea with a proven management team is funded more often than a great idea with an inexperienced team. Managers should have expertise in all disciplines necessary to start and run a business. If not, mention outside consultants who will serve in these roles and describe their qualifications.

Section 4—Financial Plan

Provide five-year projections for income, expenses, and funding sources. Don't assume the business will grow in a straight line. Adjust your planning to allow for funding at various stages of the company's growth. Explain the rationale and assumptions used to determine the estimates. Assumptions should be reasonable and based on industry/historical trends. Make sure all totals add up and are consistent throughout the plan. If necessary, hire a professional accountant or financial analyst to prepare these statements.

Stay clear of excessively ambitious sales projections; rather, offer best-case, expected, and worst-case scenarios. These not only reveal how sensitive the bottom line is to sales fluctuations but also serve as good management guides.

Section 5—Capital Required

Indicate the amount of capital needed to commence or continue operations, and describe how these funds are to be used. Make sure the totals are the same as the ones on the cash-flow statement. This area will receive a great deal of review from potential investors, so it must be clear and concise.

Section 6—Marketing Plan

Don't underestimate the competition. Review industry size, trends, and the target market segment. Sources like *American Demographics* magazine and the *Rand McNally Commercial Atlas and Marketing Guide* can help you put a plan together. Discuss strengths and weaknesses of the product or service. The most important things investors want to know are what makes the product more desirable than what's already available and whether the product can be patented. Compare pricing to the competition's. Forecast sales in dollars and units. Outline sales, advertising, promotion, and public relations programs. Make sure the costs agree with those projected in the financial statements.

Section 7—Location Analysis

In retailing and certain other industries, the location of the business is one of the most important factors. Provide a comprehensive demographic analysis of consumers in the area of the proposed business as well as a traffic-pattern analysis and vehicular and pedestrian counts.

(continued)

Section 8—Manufacturing Plan

Describe minimum plant size, machinery required, production capacity, inventory and inventory-control methods, quality control, plant personnel requirements, and so on. Estimates of product costs should be based on primary research.

Section 9—Appendix

Include all marketing research on the product or service (off-the-shelf reports, article reprints, etc.) and other information about the product concept or market size. Provide a bibliography of all the reference materials you consulted. This section should demonstrate that the proposed company won't be entering a declining industry or market segment.

If you would like to see sample business plans that successfully secured funding, go to Bplans.com (www.bplans .com). You can also learn more about writing business plans on the Small Business Administration website at www.sba.gov/starting.

Wouldn't it be great if money grew on trees? Unfortunately it doesn't, so prospective entrepreneurs must find other sources of capital such as personal savings, relatives, former employers, banks, finance companies, venture capitalists, and government agencies. What is the most common source of funding after personal savings?

good idea to ask such an investor for money at the outset. Begin by asking for advice; if the supplier likes your plan, he or she may be willing to help you with funding too.

The credit crunch spurred by the recent financial crisis made it necessary for small-business owners to do a little extra shopping to find a friendly lender. Many found that smaller community banks were more likely to grant loans than larger regional banks. Since small banks do business in a single town or cluster of towns, they know their customers better. They have more flexibility to make lending decisions based on everything they know about their customers, rather than on a more automated basis as larger banks must.[34]

Community development financial institutions (CDFIs) may be a source of funding for businesses in lower-income communities. Today CDFIs are playing a big role in the economic recovery. CDFIs were first formed in the early 1980s by socially motivated investors such as nuns investing their retirement funds. However, in 2009 more than $1 billion flowed into CDFIs from big investment companies and another $247 million from the government. CDFIs succeeded even after the credit bubble because they maintained the financial discipline other lenders lacked. They have the incentive to make sure their clients succeed because, if borrowers don't repay their loans, the CDFIs take the hit, not investors. Only 1 percent of their loans were not paid back in the last three decades. CDFIs don't just loan money. More importantly, they provide business counseling such as helping owners learn how to develop marketing strategies, manage inventory, and improve cash flow.[35]

Individual investors are also a frequent source of capital for most entrepreneurs. *Angel investors* are private individuals who invest their own money in potentially hot new companies before they go public.[36] A number of websites match people who want money with those willing to lend it; they include Prosper Marketplace, Zopa, Lending Club, Kiva, Virgin Money, CircleLending, and GlobeFunder. Other sites, such as GreenNote and People Capital, specialize in lending to students. This form of individual investing is called peer-to-peer (P2P) lending.[37] A creditworthy borrower often gets such money faster and easier than going to the bank. And the cost is often less than a bank

SOCIAL MEDIA IN
business

Social Lending

For aspiring entrepreneurs, having a good idea is only half the battle. The next hurdle is gathering enough capital to turn a business plan into reality. But bank loans are hard to come by these days. The failed speculation that spurred the financial crisis remains a vivid memory for many investors, making them reluctant to lend funds.

Although traditional avenues of investment may be closed to some, a number of new ventures online can help entrepreneurs acquire cash. Kickstarter.com, for instance, helps potential business owners, as well as musicians and artists, gather funds from a variety of backers. Instead of dealing in interest rates and equity, however, contributors pledge to give as little as $1 in exchange for free products or just a thank-you for helping make the project a reality. Although these may seem like small contributions, a little money from a lot of people can go a long way. Vidam Akimenko posted a $15,000 investment goal on Kickstarter in order to establish a Boston-area butcher shop specializing in meat from local farms. After donations from 201 different people, he surpassed his investment cap by $1,405 and soon opened Akimenko Meats.

For those investors wanting a larger return than a T-bone steak, peer-to-peer lending sites like Lending Club act as a sort of Facebook of money. But instead of collecting online friends, loan-seekers look for people who are willing to lend them money. Individuals set up a profile that outlines their credit history, how much cash they need, and what they intend to do with it. Administrators at Lending Club then assign an interest rate between 6.78 percent and 24.95 percent based on the criteria above. Many users, such as Karla Brazelton of Detroit, use the money to pay down debt. After facing rejection from banks across the board, Brazelton signed up to Lending Club in order to reduce her $7,000 credit card debt. After investment from a small collection of lenders, Brazelton eventually secured a 36-month personal loan at 7.74 percent interest. Not only does the loan help Brazelton, it also provides investors with a much higher rate of return on their money than any standard savings account could offer.

Sources: John Tozzi, "Eight Companies Kick-Started by Fans," *Bloomberg Businessweek*, June 28–July 4, 2010; and John Simons, "How to Get a Loan the Web 2.0 Way," *Black Enterprise*, December 1, 2010.

loan. The Social Media in Business box offers a number of examples of companies that started with P2P loans.

Venture capitalists may finance your project—for a price. Venture capitalists may ask for a hefty stake in your company (as much as 60 percent) in exchange for the cash to start your business. If the venture capitalist takes too large a stake, you could lose control of the business. Since the widespread failure of early web startups, venture capitalists have been willing to invest less and expect more return on their investment if the new company is sold.[38] Therefore, if you're a very small company, you don't have a very good chance of getting venture capital. You'd have a better chance finding an angel investor.

If your proposed venture does require millions of dollars to start, experts recommend that you talk with at least five investment firms and their clients in order to find the right venture capitalist. You may able to connect with potential investors through Angellist.com, a nonprofit service that helps entrepreneurs and venture capitalist get to know each other.[39] To learn more about how to find venture capitalists, visit the National Venture Capital Association's website (www.nvca.org).

venture capitalists
Individuals or companies that invest in new businesses in exchange for partial ownership of those businesses.

The Small Business Administration (SBA)

Small Business Administration (SBA)
A U.S. government agency that advises and assists small businesses by providing management training and financial advice and loans.

The **Small Business Administration (SBA)** is a U.S. government agency that advises and assists small businesses by providing management training and financial advice and loans (see Figure 6.5). The SBA started a microloan demonstration program in 1991. The program provides very small loans (up to $50,000) and technical assistance to small-business owners. It is administered through a nationwide network of nonprofit organizations chosen by the SBA. Rather than award loans based on collateral, credit history, or previous business success, the program judges worthiness on belief in the borrowers' integrity and the soundness of their business ideas.[40]

The SBA microloan program helps people like Ted Cooper, who owns Fresh Look Remodeling, a New York–based energy-audit business. Faced with laying off his six workers, Cooper searched for a loan to keep the business going. Before Cooper received a $10,000 SBA microloan, he applied to a few big banks, one of which asked for $15,000 worth of collateral. "If I had that, I wouldn't have needed to borrow it," Cooper said.[41]

Small Business Investment Company (SBIC) Program
A program through which private investment companies licensed by the Small Business Administration lend money to small businesses.

You may also want to consider requesting funds from the **Small Business Investment Company (SBIC) Program.** SBICs are private investment companies licensed by the SBA to lend money to small businesses. An SBIC must have a minimum of $5 million in capital and can borrow up to $2 from the SBA for each $1 of capital it has. It lends to or invests in small businesses that meet its criteria. Often SBICs are able to keep defaults to a minimum by identifying a business's trouble spots early, giving entrepreneurs advice, and in some cases rescheduling loan payments.[42]

Perhaps the best place for young entrepreneurs to start shopping for an SBA loan is a Small Business Development Center (SBDC). SBDCs are funded jointly by the federal government and individual states, and are usually associated with state and community colleges and universities. SBDCs can help you evaluate the feasibility of your idea, develop your business plan, and complete your funding application—all for no charge.

figure 6.5

TYPES OF SBA FINANCIAL ASSISTANCE

The SBA may provide the following types of financial assistance:

- *Guaranteed loans*—loans made by a financial institution that the government will repay if the borrower stops making payments. The maximum individual loan guarantee is capped at $5 million.

- *Microloans*—amounts ranging from $100 to $50,000 to people such as single mothers and public housing tenants.

- *Export Express*—loans made to small businesses wishing to export. The maximum guaranteed loan amount is $500,000.

- *Community Adjustment and Investment Program (CAIP)*—loans to businesses to create new, sustainable jobs or to preserve existing jobs in eligible communities that have lost jobs due to changing trade patterns with Mexico and Canada following the adoption of NAFTA.

- *Pollution control loans*—loans to eligible small businesses for the financing of the planning, design, or installation of a pollution control facility. This facility must prevent, reduce, abate, or control any form of pollution, including recycling.

- *504 certified development company (CDC) loans*—loans for purchasing major fixed assets, such as land and buildings for businesses in eligible communities, typically rural communities or urban areas needing revitalization. The program's goal is to expand business ownership by minorities, women, and veterans. The maximum guaranteed loan amount is $1.5 million.

The SBA reduced the size of its application from 150 pages to one page for loans under $50,000. In February 2011, the SBA introduced a new program called Community Advantage and Small Loan Advantage program, which is aimed at providing a simpler and easier way for lenders to make smaller loans to businesses in underserved areas. However, a month later the House Small Business Committee recommended the SBA budget be cut and that no money be used for the new program.[43] Confused? Since government regulations are constantly changing, you may want to go to the SBA's website (www.sba.gov) for the latest information about SBA programs and other business services.

Obtaining money from banks, venture capitalists, and government sources is very difficult for most small businesses. (You will learn more about financing in Chapter 18.) Those who do survive the planning and financing of their new ventures are eager to get their businesses up and running. Your success in running a business depends on many factors, especially knowing your customers, managing your employees, and keeping good records.

Knowing Your Customers

One of the most important elements of small-business success is knowing the **market**, which consists of consumers with unsatisfied wants and needs who have both resources and willingness to buy. Most of our students have the willingness to own a brand-new Maserati sports car. However, few have the resources necessary to satisfy this want. Would they be a good market for a luxury car dealer?

Once you have identified your market and its needs, you must set out to fill those needs. How? Offer top quality at a fair price with great service. Remember, it isn't enough to get customers—you have to *keep* them. As Victoria Jackson, founder of the $50 million company Victoria Jackson Cosmetics, says of the stars who push her products on television infomercials, "All the glamorous faces in the world wouldn't mean a thing if my customers weren't happy with the product and didn't come back for more." Everything must be geared to bring customers the satisfaction they deserve.

One of the greatest advantages small businesses have is the ability to know their customers better and adapt quickly to their ever-changing needs. You will gain more insights about markets in Chapters 13–16. Now let's consider effectively managing the employees who help you serve your market.

market
People with unsatisfied wants and needs who have both the resources and the willingness to buy.

Managing Employees

As a business grows, it becomes impossible for an entrepreneur to oversee every detail, even by putting in 60 hours per week. This means that hiring, training, and motivating employees are critical.

It is not easy to find good help when you offer less money, skimpier benefits, and less room for advancement than larger firms do. That's one reason employee relations is important for small-business management. Employees of small companies are often more satisfied with their jobs than are their counterparts in big business. Why? Quite often they find their jobs more challenging, their ideas more accepted, and their bosses more respectful.[44]

Often entrepreneurs are reluctant to recognize that to keep growing, they must delegate authority to others. Who should have this delegated authority, and how much?

This can be a particularly touchy issue in small businesses with long-term employees, and in family businesses. As you might expect, entrepreneurs who have built their companies from scratch often feel compelled to promote employees who have been with them from the start—even when they aren't qualified to serve as managers. Common sense tells you this could hurt the business. The idea that you must promote or can't fire people because "they're family" can also hinder growth. Entrepreneurs best serve themselves and the business if they gradually recruit and groom employees for management positions, enhancing trust and support between them. You'll learn more about managing employees in Chapters 7–12.

Keeping Records

Small-business owners often say the most important assistance they received in starting and managing their business was in accounting.[45] A businessperson who sets up an effective accounting system early will save much grief later. Computers simplify record keeping and enable a small-business owner to daily follow sales, expenses, and profits. An inexpensive computer system can also help owners with inventory control, customer records, and payroll.

Many business failures are caused by poor accounting practices that lead to costly mistakes. A good accountant can help you decide whether to buy or lease equipment and whether to own or rent a building. He or she may also help you with tax planning, financial forecasting, choosing sources of financing, and writing requests for funds.

Other small-business owners may tell you where to find an accountant experienced in small business. It pays to shop around for advice. You'll learn more about accounting in Chapter 17.

Not all small businesses stay small; some become business superstars. Take Mattel, for example. Mattel founders Ruth and Elliot Handler started their business in their garage—making picture frames. When they found that the dollhouse furniture they made with the wood scraps sold better than the frames, they changed their business. Today toys like Barbie helped Mattel grow into a $6.4 billion business.

Looking for Help

Small-business owners have learned, sometimes the hard way, that they need outside consulting advice early in the process. This is especially true of legal, tax, and accounting advice but also of marketing, finance, and other areas. Most small and medium-sized firms cannot afford to hire such experts as employees, so they must turn to outside assistance.

A necessary and invaluable aide is a competent, experienced lawyer who knows and understands small businesses. Lawyers can help with leases, contracts, partnership agreements, and protection against liabilities.[46] They don't have to be expensive. In fact, several prepaid legal plans offer services such as drafting legal documents for a low annual rate. Of course, you can find plenty of legal services online. The SBA offers plain-English guides and mini-tutorials that will help you gain a basic understanding of the laws that affect each phase of the life of a small business. FindForms.com offers a search tool that helps you find free legal forms from all over the web as well as advice, links, books, and more. Remember, "free" isn't a bargain if the information isn't correct, so check the sources carefully and double-check any legal actions with an attorney.

Make your marketing decisions long before you introduce a product or open a store. An inexpensive marketing research study may help you determine where to locate, whom to select as your target market, and what is an effective strategy for reaching it.

Small business owner Michelle Matta received several microloans from the SBA to start and expand her promotional products business. In addition to financing, what other forms of business assistance do entrepreneurs like Matta need?

Thus a marketing consultant with small-business experience can be of great help to you, especially one who has had experience with the Internet and social media.

Two other invaluable experts are a commercial loan officer and an insurance agent. The commercial loan officer can help you design an acceptable business plan and give you valuable financial advice as well as lend you money when you need it. An insurance agent will explain all the risks associated with a small business and how to cover them most efficiently with insurance and other means like safety devices and sprinkler systems.

An important source of information for small businesses is the **Service Corps of Retired Executives (SCORE)**. This SBA office has more than 10,500 volunteers from industry, trade associations, and education who counsel small businesses at no cost (except for expenses).[47] You can find a SCORE counselor by logging on to www.score.org. The SBA also offers a free, comprehensive online entrepreneurship course for aspiring entrepreneurs.

Often business professors from local colleges will advise small-business owners free or for a small fee. Some universities have clubs or programs that provide consulting services by master of business administration (MBA) candidates for a nominal fee. The University of Maryland and Virginia Tech have internship programs that pair MBA students with budding companies in local incubator programs. The incubator companies pay half the intern's salary, which is around $20 an hour.

It is also wise to seek the counsel of other small-business owners. The website YoungEntrepreneur.com offers experienced entrepreneurs and young start-ups an open forum to exchange advice and ideas. Visitors have access to articles on marketing, business planning, incorporation, and financial management.

Other sources of counsel include local chambers of commerce, the Better Business Bureau, national and local trade associations, the business reference section of your library, and many small-business-related sites on the Internet. Some can match your consulting needs with the proper consultant, like Company Expert (www.4consulting-services.com).

Service Corps of Retired Executives (SCORE)
An SBA office with volunteers from industry, trade associations, and education who counsel small businesses at no cost (except for expenses).

progress assessment

- A business plan is probably the most important document a small business owner will ever create. There are nine sections in the business plan outline on pages I65–I66. Can you describe at least five of those sections now?

LEARNING goal 5

Outline the advantages and disadvantages small businesses have in entering global markets.

GOING GLOBAL: SMALL-BUSINESS PROSPECTS

As we noted in Chapter 3, there are over 310 million people in the United States but more than 6.9 billion people in the world.[48] Obviously, the world market is a much larger, more lucrative market for small businesses than the United States alone. In spite of that potential, many small businesses still do not think globally. Only 1 percent of small businesses now export, but half are expected to engage in global trade by 2015. Small businesses are well on their way to meeting those expectations; small and medium-sized business accounted for 99 percent of the growth in exporting firms in recent years.[49]

Technological advances have helped increase small business exporting. PayPal makes it possible for small businesses to get paid automatically when they conduct global business online. The Internet also helps small businesses find customers without the expense of international travel. As people acquire more wealth, they often demand specialized products that are not mass-produced and are willing to pay more for niche goods that small businesses offer. Dave Hammond, inventor and founder of Wizard Vending, began to push his gumball machines into the global market via a website. In the site's first year, he sold machines in Austria, Belgium, and Germany. The nearby Reaching Beyond Our Borders box offers examples of entrepreneurs who are thriving in emerging markets.

Still, many small businesses have difficulty getting started in global business. Why are so many missing the boat to the huge global markets? Primarily, because the voyage includes a few major hurdles: (1) Financing is often difficult to find, (2) would-be exporters don't know how to get started and do not understand the cultural differences between markets, and (3) the bureaucratic paperwork can threaten to bury a small business.

Beside the fact that most of the world's market lies outside the United States, there are other good reasons for going global. Exporting can absorb excess inventory, soften downturns in the domestic market, and extend product lives. It can also spice up dull routines.

Small businesses have several advantages over large businesses in international trade:

- Overseas buyers often enjoy dealing with individuals rather than with large corporate bureaucracies.
- Small companies can usually begin shipping much faster.

REACHING BEYOND
our borders

Emerging Markets, Emerging Entrepreneurship

A good entrepreneur finds a need in the market and fills it with a new business. For emerging markets, entire industries and services are wide open for innovation. Given the technological advances of the past few decades, the amount of resources required to start a business venture in emerging markets is often lower now than in the past.

These factors are contributing to an entrepreneurial revolution in many developing nations. And the growth isn't just occurring in markets that economists have been watching for years like India and Brazil. In Lebanon's capital of Beirut, for instance, Christine Sfeir opened the country's first Dunkin' Donuts at age 22. More than 10 years later, Sfeir now owns 30 locations throughout Lebanon. Stories like Sfeir's are becoming more common as educated professionals hailing from the Middle East, Africa, and Southeast Asia return home with global experience and credentials. Many entrepreneurs in the developing world hold degrees and have worked at high-level companies like Toyota and Pepsi.

Opportunities for growth are so vast in emerging markets that entrepreneurs must often expand into different areas of business in order for their first venture to grow. When Aisha Natto wanted to expand her high-end eyewear chain in Saudi Arabia, the company first had to build a lens manufacturing plant just to keep up with demand. Not only did this help grow the business, it also provided Natto and her employees with knowledge about several fields of business. Such a wide range of expertise almost ensures that entrepreneurial expansion in the developing world should continue for years to come.

Sources: Anne S. Habiby and Deirdre M. Coyle, Jr., "The High-Intensity Entrepreneur," *Harvard Business Review,* September 2010; and Dayananda Yumlembam, "Foreigners Get Incubation Tips at EDI," *The Times of India,* April 4, 2011.

- Small companies can provide a wide variety of suppliers.
- Small companies can give customers personal service and undivided attention, because each overseas account is a major source of business to them.

A good place to start finding information about exporting is the Department of Commerce's Bureau of Industry and Security (www.bis.doc.gov). Other sources include the SBA's list of international business resources (www.sba.gov/hotlist/internat.html). The SBA's Export Express loan program provides export financing opportunities for small businesses. The program is designed to finance a variety of needs of small-business exporters, including participation in foreign trade shows, catalog translations for use in foreign markets, lines of credit for export purposes, and real estate and equipment for the production of goods or services to be exported.

progress assessment

- Why do many small businesses avoid doing business globally?
- What are some of the advantages small businesses have over large businesses in selling in global markets?

summary

Learning Goal 1. Explain why people take the risks of entrepreneurship; list the attributes of successful entrepreneurs; and describe entrepreneurial teams, intrapreneurs, and home- and web-based businesses.

- **What are a few of the reasons people start their own businesses?**

Reasons include profit, independence, opportunity, and challenge.

- **What are the attributes of successful entrepreneurs?**

Successful entrepreneurs are self-directed, self-nurturing, action-oriented, highly energetic, and tolerant of uncertainty.

- **What have modern entrepreneurs done to ensure longer terms of management?**

They have formed entrepreneurial teams with expertise in the many skills needed to start and manage a business.

- **What is a micropreneur?**

Micropreneurs are people willing to accept the risk of starting and managing the type of business that remains small, lets them do the kind of work they want to do, and offers them a balanced lifestyle.

- **What is intrapreneuring?**

Intrapreneuring is the establishment of entrepreneurial centers within a larger firm where people can innovate and develop new product ideas internally.

- **Why has there been such an increase in the number of home-based and web-based businesses in the last few years?**

The increase in power and decrease in price of computer technology have leveled the field and made it possible for small businesses to compete against larger companies—regardless of location.

Learning Goal 2. Discuss the importance of small business to the American economy and summarize the major causes of small business failure.

- **Why are small businesses important to the U.S. economy?**

Small business accounts for almost 50 percent of gross domestic product (GDP). Perhaps more important to tomorrow's graduates, 80 percent of U.S. workers' first jobs are in small businesses.

- **What does the *small* in small business mean?**

The Small Business Administration defines a small business as one that is independently owned and operated and not dominant in its field of operation, and that meets certain standards of size in terms of employees or sales (depending on the size of others in the industry).

- **Why do many small businesses fail?**

Many small businesses fail because of managerial incompetence and inadequate financial planning. See Figure 6.3 for a list of causes of small-business failure.

Learning Goal 3. Summarize ways to learn about how small businesses operate.

- **What hints would you give someone who wants to learn about starting a small business?**

First, learn from others. Take courses and talk with some small-business owners. Second, get some experience working for others. Third, take over a successful firm. Finally, study the latest in small-business management techniques, including the use of computers for functions like payroll, inventory control, and mailing lists.

Learning Goal 4. Analyze what it takes to start and run a small business.

- **What goes into a business plan?**

See the Business Plan on pages 165–166.

- **What sources of funds should someone wanting to start a new business consider investigating?**

A new entrepreneur has several potential sources of capital: personal savings, relatives, former employers, banks, finance companies, venture capital organizations, government agencies, and more.

- **What are some of the special problems that small-business owners have in dealing with employees?**

Small-business owners often have difficulty finding competent employees and grooming employees for management responsibilities.

- **Where can budding entrepreneurs find help in starting their businesses?**

Help can come from many sources: accountants, lawyers, marketing researchers, loan officers, insurance agents, the SBA, SBDCs, SBICs, and even college professors.

Learning Goal 5. Outline the advantages and disadvantages small businesses have in entering global markets.

- **What are some advantages small businesses have over large businesses in global markets?**

Foreign buyers enjoy dealing with individuals rather than large corporations because (1) small companies provide a wider variety of suppliers and can ship products more quickly and (2) small companies give more personal service.

- **Why don't more small businesses start trading globally?**

There are several reasons: (1) financing is often difficult to find, (2) many people don't know how to get started and do not understand the cultural differences in foreign markets, and (3) the bureaucratic red tape is often overwhelming.

key terms

affiliate marketing 156	intrapreneurs 157	Small Business Administration (SBA) 168
business plan 163	market 169	
enterprise zones 157	micropreneurs 152	
entrepreneurial team 152	Service Corps of Retired Executives (SCORE) 171	Small Business Investment Company (SBIC) Program 168
entrepreneurship 149	small business 159	venture capitalists 167
incubators 158		

critical thinking

1. Do you have the entrepreneurial spirit? What makes you think that?

2. Are there any similarities between the characteristics demanded of an entrepreneur and those of a professional athlete? Would an athlete be a good prospect for entrepreneurship? Why or why not? Could teamwork be important in an entrepreneurial effort? Why or why not?

3. Imagine yourself starting a small business. What kind of business would it be? How much competition is there? What could you do to make your business more attractive than those of competitors? Would you be willing to work 60 to 70 hours a week to make the business successful?

developing workplace skills

1. Find issues of *Entrepreneur, Black Enterprise,* and *Inc.* magazines in the library or on the Internet. Read about the entrepreneurs who are heading today's dynamic new businesses. Write a profile about one.

2. Select a small business that looks attractive as a career possibility for you. Talk to at least one person who manages such a business. Ask how he or she started it. Ask about financing; human resource management (hiring, firing, training, scheduling); accounting issues; and other managerial matters. Prepare a summary of your findings, including whether the person's job was rewarding, interesting, and challenging—and why or why not.

3. Contact the Small Business Administration by visiting a local office or the organization's website at www.sba.gov. Write a brief summary of the services the SBA offers.

4. Select a small business in your area or a surrounding area that has failed. List the factors you think led to its failure. Compile a list of actions the business owners might have taken to keep the company in business.

5. Choose a partner from among your classmates and put together a list of factors that might mean the difference between success and failure of a new company entering the business technology industry. Can small startups realistically hope to compete with companies such as Microsoft and Intel? Discuss the list and your conclusions in class.

taking it to the net

Purpose

To assess your potential to succeed as an entrepreneur and to evaluate a sample business plan.

Exercise

1. Go to www.bizmove.com/other/quiz.htm and take the interactive entrepreneurial quiz to find out whether you have the qualities to be a successful entrepreneur.

2. If you have entrepreneurial traits and decide you would like to start your own business, you'll need to develop a business plan. Go to www.bplans.com/sample_business_plans.cfm and click on Coffee Shops. Review the sample business plan for Internet Café. Although the plan may not follow the same format as the business plan outline on pages 165–166, does it contain all the necessary information listed in the outline? If not, what is missing?

casing the web

To access the case "BMOC; Starting a Small Business at School," visit **www.mhhe.com/ubl0e**

video case

To access the video case featuring Pillow Pets, visit **www.mhhe.com/ubl0e**

MANAGEMENT
and
Leadership

LEARNING goals

After you have read and studied this chapter, you should be able to

1 Describe the changes occurring today in the management function.

2 Describe the four functions of management.

3 Relate the planning process and decision making to the accomplishment of company goals.

4 Describe the organizing function of management.

5 Explain the differences between leaders and managers, and describe the various leadership styles.

6 Summarize the five steps of the control function of management.

John Mackey has become one of the more controversial and successful entrepreneurs and managers in America. After attending the University of Texas, Mackey went to work in a vegetarian co-op in Austin where he thought he could "meet some interesting women." Soon he became the co-op's food buyer and later went to work in a natural foods store.

Mackey and his girlfriend, Renee Lawson Hardy, borrowed $45,000 from friends and family and eventually opened their own store called SaferWay Natural Foods. (The name was a spoof of Safeway, which had several stores in Austin at the time.) Shortly after the store opened the couple was kicked out of their apartment for storing food there and they decided to move into the store. Since the building was zoned commercial, there was no shower so they bathed in the Hobart dishwasher that had an attached hose. (Nobody said entrepreneurship is easy!)

In 1980 SaferWay merged with a competitor and became Whole Foods Market. The first Whole Foods store opened with only 19 employees. There were less than a half dozen natural food stores in all of the United States at the time. Today Whole Foods Market is a world leader in natural and organic foods with over 300 stores in North America and the United Kingdom. Whole Foods Market is consistently listed as one of *Fortune* magazine's "100 Best Companies to Work For." Let's see why.

You would expect someone like Mackey to have a different view of management, and you would be right. At Whole Foods, titles don't count as much as the ability to get along with others and make decisions collectively. As a consequence, decisions may take longer to make, but implementation is faster. All the executives of the company make the same compensation. Mackey now shares

leadership of the company with Walter Robb as co-CEOs (Chief Executive Officers).

Mackey and his team say that their success is due largely to their focus on the company's mission: Whole Foods, Whole people, Whole planet. As you can see, one of the core values at Whole Foods is the happiness and excellence of its people. Whole Foods recruits the best people and empowers them to make their own decisions. They believe that their decentralized self-directed team culture creates a respectful workplace where people are treated fairly and are highly motivated to succeed. Mackey believes that business can be a "win-win" situation. For example, if Whole Foods hires good people and trains them well, then those people will treat customers well, and both will be happier as a result: win-win.

This chapter is all about leadership and management. You will learn that shared leadership is more widespread than you might have imagined. You will also learn about the functions of management and how management differs from leadership. All in all, you should get a better idea of what leaders and managers do and how they do it.

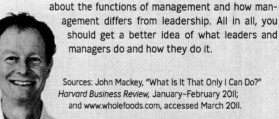

Getting to Know

X *John Mackey*

Founder of Whole Foods Market

Sources: John Mackey, "What Is It That Only I Can Do?" *Harvard Business Review*, January–February 2011; and www.wholefoods.com, accessed March 2011.

profile

Like many companies today, this company uses social media to communicate with customers. In one case, a customer complained on Twitter when the company sent a Blackberry to replace an iPhone that had failed. The company responded quickly with a replacement iPhone. The customer then tweeted about the company's great customer service. Name that company. (The answer is in the chapter.)

LEARNING goal **1**

Describe the changes occurring today in the management function.

MANAGERS' ROLES ARE EVOLVING

Managers, like John Mackey, must practice the art of getting things done through organizational resources, which include workers, financial resources, information, and equipment. At one time, managers were called "bosses" and their job consisted of telling people what to do, watching over them to be sure they did it, and reprimanding those who didn't. Many managers still behave that way. Perhaps you've witnessed such behavior; some coaches use this style.

Today, however, some managers tend to be more progressive. For example, they emphasize teams and team building; they create drop-in centers, team

Here a Best Buy manager rallies his employees just before opening the store's doors. Rather than telling employees exactly what to do, managers today tend to give their employees enough independence to make their own informed decisions about how best to please customers. How do you think most employees respond to this empowerment on the job?

spaces, and open work areas.[1] They may change the definition of *work* from a task you do for a specified period in a specific place to something you do anywhere, anytime. They tend to guide, train, support, motivate, and coach employees rather than tell them what to do.[2] Managers of high-tech firms, for instance, realize that many workers often know more about technology than they do.[3] Thus most modern managers emphasize teamwork and cooperation rather than discipline and order giving. They may also open their books to employees to share the company's financials.[4]

The years 2008–2011 were particularly hard on managers and workers. The financial crisis forced many leading firms—like Boeing, IBM, and Caterpillar— to fire managers and lower-level workers. PepsiCo's CEO Indra Nooyi won praise for rallying employees amid the gloom. But she too announced plans to cut some 3,000 employees. Furthermore, it became more difficult to get financing for new ventures or to modernize existing plants. Managers tended to be cautious in starting new ventures as they waited to see what the economy would do. That hesitancy contributed to the high unemployment the U.S. experienced in 2010–2011.[5]

The people entering management today are different from those who entered in the past.[6] Leaders of Fortune 100 companies tend to be younger, more of them are female, and fewer of them were educated at elite universities. Managers in the future are more likely to be working in teams and assuming completely new roles in the firm. For one thing, they'll be doing more expansion overseas. Further, they will be taking a leadership role in adapting to climate change. They will also be more concerned with recycling and other "green" issues.[7]

What these changes mean for you is that management will demand a new kind of person: a skilled communicator and team player as well as a planner, organizer, motivator, and leader. Future managers will need to be more globally prepared; that is, they need skills such as adaptability, foreign language skills, and ease in other cultures.[8] We'll address these trends in the next few chapters to help you decide whether management is the kind of career you would like.

Ursula Burns, for example, is the new CEO of Xerox. She is a mechanical engineer, and the first African-American woman to run a Fortune 500 company. She was outspoken and blunt in a culture that was probably overly genteel.[9] Burns was just one of the women who inspired an article called "The Year of the Business Woman" in *U.S. News and World Report*.[10] You will read more about Burns in the next chapter. In the following sections, we shall discuss management in general and the functions that Ursula Burns and other new managers are performing.

LEARNING goal **2**

Describe the four functions of management.

THE FOUR FUNCTIONS OF MANAGEMENT

The following definition of management provides the outline of this chapter: **Management** is the process used to accomplish organizational goals through planning, organizing, leading, and controlling people and other organizational resources (see Figure 7.1 on p. 182).

management
The process used to accomplish organizational goals through planning, organizing, leading, and controlling people and other organizational resources.

figure 7.1

WHAT MANAGERS DO
Some modern managers perform all of these tasks with the full cooperation and participation of workers. Empowering employees means allowing them to participate more fully in decision making.

Planning
- Setting organizational goals.
- Developing strategies to reach those goals.
- Determining resources needed.
- Setting precise standards.

Organizing
- Allocating resources, assigning tasks, and establishing procedures for accomplishing goals.
- Preparing a structure (organization chart) showing lines of authority and responsibility.
- Recruiting, selecting, training, and developing employees.
- Placing employees where they'll be most effective.

Leading
- Guiding and motivating employees to work effectively to accomplish organizational goals and objectives.
- Giving assignments.
- Explaining routines.
- Clarifying policies.
- Providing feedback on performance.

Controlling
- Measuring results against corporate objectives.
- Monitoring performance relative to standards.
- Rewarding outstanding performance.
- Taking corrective action when necessary.

planning
A management function that includes anticipating trends and determining the best strategies and tactics to achieve organizational goals and objectives.

organizing
A management function that includes designing the structure of the organization and creating conditions and systems in which everyone and everything work together to achieve the organization's goals and objectives.

Planning is what helps managers understand the environment in which their business must operate. When people's tastes and preferences for restaurant meals change, food services managers need to be ready to respond with menu alternatives. What changes have occurred in your own preferences?

Planning includes anticipating trends and determining the best strategies and tactics to achieve organizational goals and objectives. One of the major objectives of organizations is to please customers.[11] The trend today is to have *planning teams* to help monitor the environment, find business opportunities, and watch for challenges. *Planning* is a key management function because accomplishing the other functions depends heavily on having a good plan.

Organizing includes designing the structure of the organization and creating conditions and systems in which everyone and everything works together to achieve the organization's goals and objectives. Many of today's organizations are being designed around pleasing the customer at a profit. Thus they must remain flexible and adaptable, because when customer needs change, firms must change with them. Whole Foods Market, for example, is known for its high-quality, high-priced food items.[12] But it has introduced many lower-cost items to adjust to the financial losses of its customer base. General Motors lost much of its customer base to manufacturers of more fuel-efficient cars. It hopes to win back market share by offering hydrogen-powered or electric vehicles that cost less to run.[13] GM has had some success in doing that.

Leading means creating a vision for the organization and communicating, guiding, training, coaching, and motivating others to achieve goals and objectives in a timely manner. The trend is to empower employees, giving them as much freedom as possible to become self-directed and self-motivated. This function was once known as *directing*; that is, telling employees exactly what to do. In many smaller firms, that is still the manager's role. In most large firms, however, managers no longer tell people exactly what to do because knowledge workers and others often know how to do their jobs better than the manager does. Nonetheless, leadership is still necessary to keep employees focused on the right tasks at the right time.

Controlling establishes clear standards to determine whether an organization is progressing toward its goals and objectives, rewarding people for doing a good job, and taking corrective action if they are not. Basically, it means measuring whether what actually occurs meets the organization's goals.

Planning, organizing, leading, and controlling are the heart of management, so let's explore them in more detail. The process begins with planning; we'll look at that right after the Progress Assessment.

progress assessment

- What are some of the changes happening in management today?
- What's the definition of *management* used in this chapter?
- What are the four functions of management?

LEARNING goal 3

Relate the planning process and decision making to the accomplishment of company goals.

PLANNING AND DECISION MAKING

Planning, the first managerial function, is setting the organization's vision (including its mission statement), goals, and objectives. Executives find planning to be their most valuable tool. A **vision** is more than a goal; it's a broad explanation of why the organization exists and where it's trying to go. It gives the organization a sense of purpose and a set of values that unite workers in a common destiny. Managing an organization without first establishing a vision is like getting everyone in a rowboat excited about going somewhere, but not telling them exactly where. The boat will just keep changing directions rather than speeding toward an agreed-on goal.[14]

Top management usually sets the vision for the organization and then often works with others in the firm to establish a mission statement. A **mission statement** outlines the organization's fundamental purposes. It should address:

- The organization's self-concept.
- Its philosophy.
- Long-term survival needs.
- Customer needs.
- Social responsibility.
- Nature of the product or service.

The mission statement becomes the foundation for setting specific goals and objectives. **Goals** are the broad, long-term accomplishments an organization

leading
Creating a vision for the organization and guiding, training, coaching, and motivating others to work effectively to achieve the organization's goals and objectives.

controlling
A management function that involves establishing clear standards to determine whether or not an organization is progressing toward its goals and objectives, rewarding people for doing a good job, and taking corrective action if they are not.

vision
An encompassing explanation of why the organization exists and where it's trying to head.

mission statement
An outline of the fundamental purposes of an organization.

goals
The broad, long-term accomplishments an organization wishes to attain.

objectives
Specific, short-term statements detailing how to achieve the organization's goals.

wishes to attain. Because workers and management need to agree on them, setting goals is often a team process. **Objectives** are specific, short-term statements detailing *how to achieve* the organization's goals. One of your goals for reading this chapter, for example, may be to learn basic concepts of management. An objective you could use to achieve this goal is to answer the chapter's Progress Assessment questions.

Planning is a continuous process. A plan that worked yesterday may not be successful in today's market.[15] Most planning also follows a pattern. The procedure you'll follow in planning your life and career is basically the same as the one businesses use. It answers several fundamental questions:

1. *What is the situation now?* What are the success factors affecting the industry participants and how do we compare? What is the state of the economy and other environments?[16] What opportunities exist for meeting people's needs? What products and customers are most profitable? Who are our major competitors?[17] What threats are there to our business? These questions are part of **SWOT analysis,** which analyzes the organization's **s**trengths and **w**eaknesses, and the **o**pportunities and **t**hreats it faces, usually in that order. Opportunities and threats are often external to the firm and cannot always be anticipated.[18] See the Reaching Beyond Our Borders box for an example of how environmental threats affect businesses.

SWOT analysis
A planning tool used to analyze an organization's strengths, weaknesses, opportunities, and threats.

Weaknesses and strengths are more often internal and therefore more within reach of being measured and fixed. Figure 7.2 lists some of the general issues companies consider when conducting a SWOT analysis: What external success factors affect the industry? How does our firm measure up to other firms? What are our social objectives? What are our personal development objectives? What can we do to survive and prosper during a recession? For more on SWOT analysis, see the Taking It to the Net exercise at the end of this chapter.

2. *How can we get to our goal from here?* Answering this question is often the most important part of planning. It takes four forms: strategic, tactical, operational, and contingency (see Figure 7.3).

figure 7.2

SWOT MATRIX
This matrix identifies potential strengths, weaknesses, opportunities, and threats organizations may consider in a SWOT analysis.

Potential Internal STRENGTHS	Potential Internal WEAKNESSES
• Core competencies in key areas	• No clear strategic direction
• An acknowledged market leader	• Obsolete facilities
• Well-conceived functional area strategies	• Subpar profitability
• Proven management	• Lack of managerial depth and talent
• Cost advantages	• Weak market image
• Better advertising campaigns	• Too narrow a product line

Potential External OPPORTUNITIES	Potential External THREATS
• Ability to serve additional customer groups	• Entry of lower-cost foreign competitors
• Expand product lines	• Rising sales of substitute products
• Ability to transfer skills/technology to new products	• Slower market growth
• Falling trade barriers in attractive foreign markets	• Costly regulatory requirements
• Complacency among rival firms	• Vulnerability to recession and business cycles
• Ability to grow due to increases in market demand	• Changing buyer needs and tastes

REACHING BEYOND
our borders

The Japanese Crisis, Terrorism, and American Business

Few catastrophes can compare to the one that occurred in Japan in March 2011. A 9.0 magnitude earthquake followed by a tsunami completely devastated whole cities and ports. The looming failure of nuclear power plants only added to the devastation. Such disasters point out the need for contingency planning and for disaster planning. It will take a long time for Japanese companies to recover from the crisis. What about U.S. companies and other companies throughout the world that rely on Japan for parts and products?

Over 30 U.S. corporations (e.g., Rambus, Coach, Callaway, and Tiffany) get at least 15 percent of their sales from Japan. About 75 percent of Aflac's 2010 sales came from Japan. Texas Instruments had a silicon wafer plant in Japan that experienced substantial damage. Furthermore, the damage in Japan may disrupt the flow of auto and tech supplies from Japan to

U.S. and other foreign producers. Japanese companies supply 35 percent of Boeing's new 787 Dreamliner, for example.

The global supply chain not only is affected by natural disasters such as the one in Japan, but is constantly threatened by man-made and other disasters, such as the consequences of war and terrorism. You can see how strategic planning and contingency planning are critical to the long-term success of firms. That often means cooperating with companies across the globe and making plans for what to do when disasters happen.

Sources: Janet Napolitano, "How to Secure the Global Supply Chain," *The Wall Street Journal,* January 6, 2011; Thomas Black, "The Impact on American Companies," *Bloomberg Businessweek,* March 21–March 27, 2011; and Joseph Sternberg, "Now Comes the Global Revolution in Services," *The Wall Street Journal,* February 10, 2011.

Strategic planning is done by top management and determines the major goals of the organization and the policies, procedures, strategies, and resources it will need to achieve them. *Policies* are broad guidelines for action, and *strategies* determine the best way to use resources. At the strategic planning stage, top managers of the company decide which customers to serve, when to serve them, what products or services to sell, and the geographic areas in which to compete.[19] Take Taco Bell, for example. Recognizing the economic slump, the company introduced a "value menu" of items like cheese roll-ups and bean burritos with prices starting at 79 cents. It also went after the "fourth-meal" (late-night) crowd and introduced several low-calorie, low-fat Fresco items.

strategic planning
The process of determining the major goals of the organization and the policies and strategies for obtaining and using resources to achieve those goals.

FORMS OF PLANNING

figure 7.3

PLANNING FUNCTIONS
Very few firms bother to make contingency plans. If something changes the market, such companies may be slow to respond. Most organizations do strategic, tactical, and operational planning.

This strategy resulted in an 8 percent increase in sales. Blockbuster was not as successful in fighting off the introduction of new technology, making the company seemingly obsolete.[20]

In today's rapidly changing environment, strategic planning is becoming more difficult because changes are occurring so fast that plans—even those set for just months into the future—may soon be obsolete. Think of how the amusement park company Six Flags had to change its plans when gas went from a couple of dollars per gallon to over four dollars and then dropped back to the three-dollar range again. Think too of how Japanese companies had to respond to the earthquake and tsunami that created such devastation in a short period of time in 2011.[21]

Clearly, some companies are making shorter-term plans that allow for quick responses to customer needs and requests. The goal is to be flexible and responsive to the market.

Tactical planning is the process of developing detailed, short-term statements about what is to be done, who is to do it, and how. Managers or teams of managers at lower levels of the organization normally make tactical plans. Such plans can include setting annual budgets and deciding on other activities necessary to meet strategic objectives. If the strategic plan of a truck manufacturer, for example, is to sell more trucks in the South, the tactical plan might be to fund more research of southern truck drivers' wants and needs, and to plan advertising to reach them.

Operational planning is the process of setting work standards and schedules necessary to implement the company's tactical objectives. Whereas strategic planning looks at the organization as a whole, operational planning focuses on specific supervisors, department managers, and individual employees. The operational plan is the department manager's tool for daily and weekly operations. An operational plan may include, for example, the specific dates for certain truck parts to be completed and the quality specifications they must meet.

Contingency planning is the process of preparing alternative courses of action the firm can use if its primary plans don't work out. The economic and competitive environments change so rapidly that it's wise to have alternative

tactical planning
The process of developing detailed, short-term statements about what is to be done, who is to do it, and how it is to be done.

operational planning
The process of setting work standards and schedules necessary to implement the company's tactical objectives.

contingency planning
The process of preparing alternative courses of action that may be used if the primary plans don't achieve the organization's objectives.

Organizations of all kinds need contingency plans for unexpected events. Here Memphis firefighters help mock wounded during a drill preparing for a possible terrorist attack. What contingency plans are you aware of on your campus or at work?

plans of action ready in anticipation of such changes.[22] For example, if an organization doesn't meet its sales goals by a certain date, the contingency plan may call for more advertising or a cut in prices at that time. Crisis planning is a part of contingency planning that anticipates sudden changes in the environment. For example, many cities and businesses have developed plans to respond to terrorist attacks. You can imagine how important such plans would be to hospitals, airlines, the police, and public transportation authorities.

Instead of creating detailed strategic plans, the leaders of market-based companies (companies that respond quickly to changes in competition or to other environmental changes) often simply set direction. They want to stay flexible, listen to customers, and seize opportunities—expected or not. Think of how stores selling to teenagers must adapt to style changes.

The opportunities, however, must fit into the company's overall goals and objectives; if not, the company could lose its focus. Clearly, then, much of management and planning requires decision making.

Decision Making: Finding the Best Alternative

Planning and all the other management functions require decision making. **Decision making** is choosing among two or more alternatives, which sounds easier than it is. In fact, decision making is the heart of all the management functions.

The *rational decision-making model* is a series of steps managers often follow to make logical, intelligent, and well-founded decisions. Think of the steps as the seven Ds of decision making:

1. Define the situation.
2. Describe and collect needed information.
3. Develop alternatives.
4. Develop agreement among those involved.
5. Decide which alternative is best.
6. Do what is indicated (begin implementation).
7. Determine whether the decision was a good one, and follow up.

Managers don't always go through this seven-step process. Sometimes they have to make decisions *on the spot*—with little information available. They still must make good decisions in all such circumstances. **Problem solving** is less formal than decision making and usually calls for quicker action to resolve everyday issues. Both decision making and problem solving call for a lot of judgment.

Problem-solving teams are two or more workers assigned to solve a specific problem (e.g., Why aren't customers buying our service contracts?). Problem-solving techniques include **brainstorming**, that is, coming up with as many solutions as possible in a short period of time with no censoring of ideas. Another technique is called **PMI**, or listing all the **p**luses for a solution in one column, all the **m**inuses in another, and the **i**mplications in a third. The idea is to make sure the pluses exceed the minuses.

You can try using the PMI system on some of your personal decisions to get some practice. For example, should you stay home and study tonight? List all the pluses in one column: better grades, more self-esteem, more responsible behavior, and so on. In the other column, put the minuses: boredom, less fun, and so on. We hope the pluses outweigh the minuses most of the time and that you study often. But sometimes it's best to go out and have some fun, as long as doing so won't hurt your grades or job prospects.

decision making
Choosing among two or more alternatives.

problem solving
The process of solving the everyday problems that occur. Problem solving is less formal than decision making and usually calls for quicker action.

brainstorming
Coming up with as many solutions to a problem as possible in a short period of time with no censoring of ideas.

PMI
Listing all the Pluses for a solution in one column, all the Minuses in another, and the Implications in a third column.

progress assessment

- What's the difference between goals and objectives?
- What does a company analyze when it does a SWOT analysis?
- What are the differences between strategic, tactical, and operational planning?
- What are the seven Ds in decision making?

LEARNING goal **4**

Describe the organizing function of management.

organization chart
A visual device that shows relationships among people and divides the organization's work; it shows who reports to whom.

ORGANIZING: CREATING A UNIFIED SYSTEM

After managers have planned a course of action, they must organize the firm to accomplish their goals. That means allocating resources (such as funds for various departments), assigning tasks, and establishing procedures. An **organization chart** is a visual device that shows relationships among people and divides the organization's work; it shows who reports to whom (see Figure 7.4).[23]

top management
Highest level of management, consisting of the president and other key company executives who develop strategic plans.

Top management, the highest level, consists of the president and other key company executives who develop strategic plans. Job titles and abbreviations you're likely to see often are chief executive officer (CEO), chief operating officer (COO), chief financial officer (CFO), and chief information officer (CIO) or

figure 7.4

LEVELS OF MANAGEMENT
This figure shows the three levels of management. In many firms, there are several levels of middle management. Recently, however, firms have been eliminating middle-level managers because fewer are needed to oversee self-managed teams of employees.

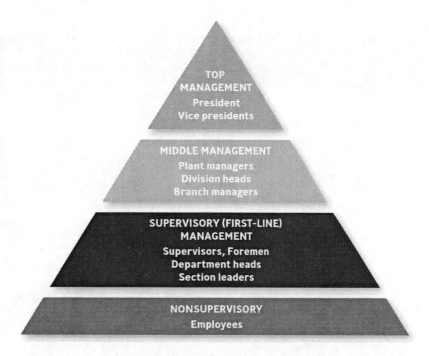

TOP MANAGEMENT
President
Vice presidents

MIDDLE MANAGEMENT
Plant managers
Division heads
Branch managers

SUPERVISORY (FIRST-LINE) MANAGEMENT
Supervisors, Foremen
Department heads
Section leaders

NONSUPERVISORY
Employees

in some companies chief knowledge officer (CKO). The CEO is often also the president of the firm and is responsible for all top-level decisions. The CEO and president are the same person in 65 percent of the S&P 500 companies, including big companies like United Parcel Service, John Deere, and General Electric.

CEOs are responsible for introducing change into an organization. The COO is responsible for putting those changes into effect. His or her tasks include structuring work, controlling operations, and rewarding people to ensure that everyone strives to carry out the leader's vision. Many companies today are eliminating the COO function as a cost-cutting measure and assigning that role to the CEO. Often, the CFO participates in the decision to cut the COO position. The CFO is responsible for obtaining funds, planning budgets, collecting funds, and so on. The CIO or CKO is responsible for getting the right information to other managers so they can make correct decisions. CIOs are more important than ever to the success of their companies given the crucial role that information technology has come to play in every aspect of business.[24]

Middle management includes general managers, division managers, and branch and plant managers (in colleges, deans and department heads) who are responsible for tactical planning and controlling. Many firms, as a result of the recession that began in 2008, have eliminated some middle managers through downsizing and have given their remaining managers more employees to supervise.[25] Nonetheless, middle managers are still considered very important to most firms.[26]

Supervisory management includes those directly responsible for supervising workers and evaluating their daily performance; they're often known as first-line managers (or supervisors) because they're the first level above workers. This is the first management position you are most likely to acquire after college.

Tasks and Skills at Different Levels of Management

Few people are trained to be good managers. Usually a person learns how to be a skilled accountant or sales representative or production-line worker, and then—because of her or his skill—is selected to be a manager. Such managers tend to become deeply involved in showing others how to do things, helping them, supervising them, and generally being active in the operating task.

The further up the managerial ladder a person moves, the less important his or her original job skills become. At the top of the ladder, the need is for people who are visionaries, planners, organizers, coordinators, communicators, morale builders, and motivators.[27] Figure 7.5 shows that a manager must have three categories of skills:

middle management
The level of management that includes general managers, division managers, and branch and plant managers who are responsible for tactical planning and controlling.

supervisory management
Managers who are directly responsible for supervising workers and evaluating their daily performance.

figure 7.5

SKILLS NEEDED AT VARIOUS LEVELS OF MANAGEMENT
All managers need human relations skills. At the top, managers need strong conceptual skills and rely less on technical skills. First-line managers need strong technical skills and rely less on conceptual skills. Middle managers need to have a balance between technical and conceptual skills.

technical skills
Skills that involve the ability to perform tasks in a specific discipline or department.

human relations skills
Skills that involve communication and motivation; they enable managers to work through and with people.

conceptual skills
Skills that involve the ability to picture the organization as a whole and the relationship among its various parts.

1. **Technical skills** are the ability to perform tasks in a specific discipline (such as selling a product or developing software) or department (such as marketing or information systems).
2. **Human relations skills** include communication and motivation; they enable managers to work through and with people. Skills associated with leadership—coaching, morale building, delegating, training and development, and supportiveness—are also human relations skills.
3. **Conceptual skills** let the manager picture the organization as a whole and see the relationships among its various parts. They are needed in planning, organizing, controlling, systems development, problem analysis, decision making, coordinating, and delegating.

Looking at Figure 7.5, you'll notice that first-line managers need to be skilled in all three areas. However, they spend most of their time on technical and human relations tasks, like assisting operating personnel and giving directions, and less time on conceptual tasks. Top managers, in contrast, need to use few technical skills. Instead, they spend almost all their time on human relations and conceptual tasks. A person who is competent at a low level of management may not be competent at higher levels, and vice versa. Different skills are needed at different levels.

Staffing: Getting and Keeping the Right People

staffing
A management function that includes hiring, motivating, and retaining the best people available to accomplish the company's objectives.

To get the right kind of people to staff an organization, the firm has to offer the right kind of incentives. For example, Google's gourmet chefs cook up free lunches, dinners, and snacks for employees. Would such an incentive appeal to you? How important to you is pay relative to other incentives?

Staffing is recruiting, hiring, motivating, and retaining the best people available to accomplish the company's objectives. Today, staffing is critical, especially in the Internet and high-tech areas. At most high-tech companies, like Google, Sony, and Microsoft, the primary capital equipment is brainpower. A firm with innovative and creative workers can go from start-up to major competitor in just a few years.[28]

Many people are not willing to work at companies unless they are treated well and get fair pay. They may leave to find a better balance between work and home. Staffing is becoming a greater part of each manager's assignment, and all managers need to cooperate with human resource management to win and keep good workers. Chapter 11 is devoted to human resource issues, including staffing.

LEARNING goal 5

Explain the differences between leaders and managers, and describe the various leadership styles.

LEADING: PROVIDING CONTINUOUS VISION AND VALUES

One person might be a good manager but not a good leader. Another might be a good leader without being a good manager. Managers strive to produce order and stability, whereas leaders embrace and manage change. Leadership is creating a

MAKING ethical decisions

To Share or Not to Share

First-line managers assist in the decisions made by their department heads. The department heads retain full responsibility for the decisions—if a plan succeeds, it's their success; if a plan fails, it's their failure. Now imagine this: As a first-line manager, you have new information that your department head hasn't seen yet. The findings in this report indicate that your manager's recent plans are sure to fail. If the plans do fail, the manager will probably be demoted and you're the most likely candidate to fill the vacancy. Will you give your department head the report? What is the ethical thing to do? What might be the consequences of your decision?

vision for others to follow, establishing corporate values and ethics, and transforming the way the organization does business in order to improve its effectiveness and efficiency.[29] Good leaders motivate workers and create the environment for them to motivate themselves. Management is carrying out the leader's vision.[30] Leaders must therefore:

- *Communicate a vision and rally others around that vision.* The leader should be openly sensitive to the concerns of followers, give them responsibility, and win their trust. A successful leader must influence the actions of others. Ellen Kullman took the reins at Dupont in the middle of a crisis. Nonetheless, she set the tone for growth and prosperity in the future.[31]

- *Establish corporate values.* These include concern for employees, for customers, for the environment, and for the quality of the company's products. When companies set their business goals, they're defining the company's values as well. The number one trait that others look for in a leader is honesty. The second requirement is that the leader be forward looking.

- *Promote corporate ethics.* Ethical behavior includes an unfailing demand for honesty and an insistence that everyone in the company gets treated fairly (see the Making Ethical Decisions box). That's why we stress ethical decision making throughout this text. Many businesspeople have made the news by giving away huge amounts to charity, thus setting a model of social concern for their employees and others.[32]

- *Embrace change.* A leader's most important job may be to transform the way the company does business so that it's more effective (does things better) and more efficient (uses fewer resources to accomplish the same objectives).[33]

- *Stress accountability and responsibility.* If there is anything we have learned from the failures of banking managers and other industry and government managers during the recession that began in 2008, it is that leaders need to be held accountable and need to

When Ellen Kullman took the reins at Dupont, the company was in crisis. Immediately Kullman oversaw two restructurings, dismissed thousands of employees, and asked the remaining employees to take a two- to three-week holiday without pay. Throughout it all Kullman never lost her ready sense of humor and set the tone for the company going forward.

transparency
The presentation of a company's facts and figures in a way that is clear and apparent to all stakeholders.

feel responsible for their actions. A key word that has emerged from the crisis is transparency. **Transparency** is the presentation of a company's facts and figures in a way that is clear and apparent to all stakeholders. Clearly it is time to make businessess and the government more transparent so that everyone is more aware of what is happening to the economy and to specific businesses and government agencies.[34]

All organizations need leaders, and all employees can help lead. You don't have to be a manager to perform a leadership function. That is, any employee can motivate others to work well, add to a company's ethical environment, and report ethical lapses when they occur. Some employees today are taking a leadership position through the use of social media. (You can read about them in the nearby Social Media in Business box.)

Leadership Styles

Nothing has challenged management researchers more than the search for the best leadership traits, behaviors, or styles. Thousands of studies have tried to identify characteristics that make leaders different from other people. Intuitively, you might conclude the same thing they did: leadership traits are hard to pin down. Some leaders are well groomed and tactful, while others are unkempt and abrasive—yet both may be just as effective.

Just as no one set of traits describes a leader, no one style of leadership works best in all situations. Even so, we can look at a few of the most commonly recognized leadership styles and see how they may be effective (see Figure 7.6):

autocratic leadership
Leadership style that involves making managerial decisions without consulting others.

figure 7.6

VARIOUS LEADERSHIP STYLES

Source: Reprinted by permission of the *Harvard Business Review.* An exhibit from "How to Choose a Leadership Pattern" by Robert Tannenbaum and Warren Schmidt (May/June 1973). Copyright © 1973 by the Harvard Business School Publishing Corporation. All rights reserved.

1. **Autocratic leadership** means making managerial decisions without consulting others. This style is effective in emergencies and when absolute followership is needed—for example, when fighting fires. Autocratic leadership is also effective sometimes with new, relatively unskilled workers who need clear direction and guidance. Coach Phil Jackson used an autocratic leadership style to take the Los Angeles Lakers to three consecutive National Basketball Association championships in his first three seasons. By following his leadership,

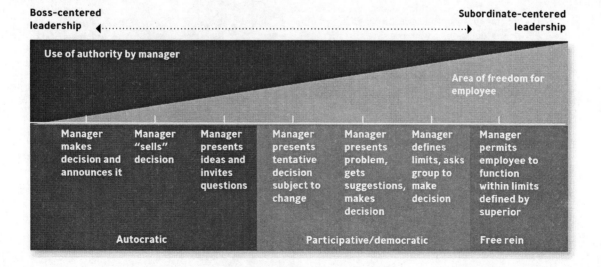

Boss-centered leadership ◄···► Subordinate-centered leadership

Use of authority by manager

Area of freedom for employee

| Manager makes decision and announces it | Manager "sells" decision | Manager presents ideas and invites questions | Manager presents tentative decision subject to change | Manager presents problem, gets suggestions, makes decision | Manager defines limits, asks group to make decision | Manager permits employee to function within limits defined by superior |

Autocratic   Participative/democratic   Free rein

SOCIAL MEDIA IN
business

Using Social Media to Build Customer Support

You probably know someone who has used social media to complain about products and services. One woman, for example, tweeted to complain about her Maytag washer. Another man expressed his irritation with an airline's baggage handling through a music video on YouTube that reached some 8 million viewers.

Of course, many companies use that same technology to proactively and reactively communicate with the public. Best Buy, for example, has 2,500 employees who can see consumer complaints and respond to them on Twitter. The system used at Best Buy is called Twelpforce. Here's an example of how it works. One person bought a cell phone and an insurance plan. When the iPhone stopped working, the customer was offered a BlackBerry as a loaner. The consumer was unhappy with that solution and began tweeting about his experience. A customer service rep from Best Buy quickly tweeted a reply and arranged to get a replacement iPhone to the customer. As a result, the customer got back on Twitter to talk about the good service at Best Buy. In another example, one person posted Best Buy's TV commercials on his blog before they were aired. After one customer complained about a commercial he saw on the blog, the spot was never aired.

Twitter, Facebook, blogs, YouTube, etc. have made it possible for companies to be proactive in reaching customers. Sadly, many companies with IT departments have been slow to implement such programs. As a result, there seem to be many more complaints on social media than positive support for companies. That is likely to change as more and more companies realize the importance and benefits of the two-way communication that is simplified by social media.

Sources: Josh Bernoff and Ted Schadler, "Empowered," *Harvard Business Review,* July–August 2010; and Sonya A. Donaldson, "Social Media: Things That Make You Go 'Oops?'" *Black Enterprise,* December 2010.

---

a group of highly skilled individuals became a winning team. How is the team doing now? What kind of leadership do you see being used most successfully in baseball, football, and other areas?

2. **Participative (democratic) leadership** involves managers and employees working together to make decisions. Research has found that employee participation in decisions may not always increase effectiveness, but it usually does increase job satisfaction.[35] Many large organizations like Google, Apple, IBM, Cisco, and AT&T, and most smaller firms have been highly successful using a democratic style of leadership that values traits such as flexibility, good listening skills, and empathy. Employees meet to discuss and resolve management issues by giving everyone some opportunity to contribute to decisions.

3. In **free-rein leadership** managers set objectives and employees are free to do whatever is appropriate

Mike Krzyewski, coach of Duke University's basketball team, has been successful as an autocratic leader. That makes sense, since you don't want basketball players deciding whether or not to play as a team. On the other hand, can you see why it is not so good to use autocratic leadership with a team of doctors?

participative (democratic) leadership Leadership style that consists of managers and employees working together to make decisions.

194 PART 3 ✳ Business Management: Empowering Employees to Satisfy Customers

free-rein leadership
Leadership style that involves managers setting objectives and employees being relatively free to do whatever it takes to accomplish those objectives.

enabling
Giving workers the education and tools they need to make decisions.

to accomplish those objectives. Free-rein leadership is often the most successful leadership style in certain organizations, such as those in which managers supervise doctors, professors, engineers, or other professionals. The traits managers need in such organizations include warmth, friendliness, and understanding. More and more firms are adopting this style of leadership with at least some of their employees.

Individual leaders rarely fit neatly into just one of these categories. We can think of leadership as a continuum along which employee participation varies, from purely boss-centered leadership to subordinate-centered leadership.

Which leadership style is best? Research tells us that it depends largely on what the goals and values of the firm are, who's being led, and in what situations.[36] A manager may be autocratic but friendly with a new trainee, democratic with an experienced employee, and free-rein with a trusted long-term supervisor.

There's no such thing as a leadership trait that is effective in all situations, or a leadership style that always works best. A successful leader in one organization may not be successful in another organization. For example, there was a question recently about whether or not Meg Whitman, eBay's former CEO, would make a good governor for California even though she oversaw eBay's growth from $4 million annual revenue and 30 employees to $8 billion and 15,000 employees in her ten-year tenure. In 2010, voters of California decided not to elect her.[37] A truly successful leader has the ability to adopt the leadership style most appropriate to the situation and the employees.

Fast-food restaurant employees often don't have the skill and experience to make empowerment work very well. Instead their managers generally have to supervise and direct them fairly closely. What do you think are some of the consequences for managers of not being able to empower their staff with decision-making authority?

Empowering Workers

Many leaders in the past gave explicit instructions to workers, telling them what to do to meet the goals and objectives of the organization. The term for this process is *directing*. In traditional organizations, directing includes giving assignments, explaining routines, clarifying policies, and providing feedback on performance. Many organizations still follow this model, especially fast-food restaurants and small retail establishments where the employees don't have the skill and experience needed to work on their own, at least at first.

Progressive leaders, such as those in some high-tech firms and Internet companies, empower employees to make decisions on their own. *Empowerment* means giving employees the authority to make a decision without consulting the manager and the responsibility to respond quickly to customer requests. Managers are often reluctant to give up their decision-making power and often resist empowerment. In firms that implement the concept, however, the manager's role is less that of a boss and director and more that of a coach, assistant, counselor, or team member.[38]

Enabling means giving workers the education and tools they need to make decisions. Clearly, it's the key to the success of empowerment. Without the right education, training, coaching, and tools, workers cannot assume the responsibilities and decision-making roles that make empowerment work.[39]

Managing Knowledge

"Knowledge is power." Empowering employees means giving them knowledge—that is, the information they need to do the best job they can. Finding the right information, keeping it in a readily accessible place, and making it known to everyone in the firm together constitute the tasks of **knowledge management.**

The first step to developing a knowledge management system is determining what knowledge is most important. Do you want to know more about your customers? Do you want to know more about competitors? What kind of information would make your company more effective or more efficient or more responsive to the marketplace? Once you've decided what you need to know, you set out to find answers to those questions.

Knowledge management tries to keep people from reinventing the wheel—that is, duplicating the work of gathering information—every time a decision must be made. A company really progresses when each person continually asks, "What do I still not know?" and "Whom should I be asking?" It's as important to know what's *not* working as it is to know what *is* working. Employees and managers now have texting, tweeting, and other means of keeping in touch with one another, with customers, and with other stakeholders. The key to success is learning how to process information effectively and turn it into knowledge that everyone can use to improve processes and procedures. The benefits are obvious.

knowledge management
Finding the right information, keeping the information in a readily accessible place, and making the information known to everyone in the firm.

LEARNING goal **6**

Summarize the five steps of the control function of management.

CONTROLLING: MAKING SURE IT WORKS

The control function measures performance relative to the planned objectives and standards, rewards people for work well done, and takes corrective action when necessary. Thus the control process (see Figure 7.7) provides the feedback that lets managers and workers adjust to deviations from plans and to changes in the environment that have affected performance.

figure 7.7

THE CONTROL PROCESS
The whole control process is based on clear standards. Without such standards, the other steps are difficult, if not impossible. With clear standards, performance measurement is relatively easy and the proper action can be taken.

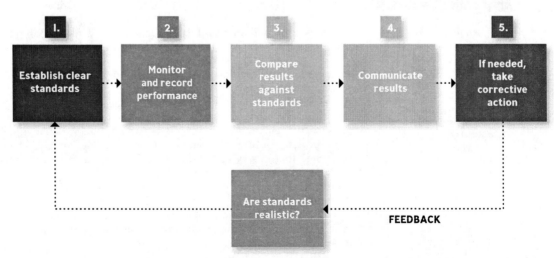

1. Establish clear standards
2. Monitor and record performance
3. Compare results against standards
4. Communicate results
5. If needed, take corrective action

Are standards realistic?

FEEDBACK

One way colleges and universities measure their performance is to track the number of students who complete their degrees or who graduate within a certain number of years. What are some of the factors that could affect the achievement of this performance standard, and how do college administrators take corrective action when necessary?

Controlling consists of five steps:

1. Establishing clear performance standards. This ties the planning function to the control function. Without clear standards, control is impossible.
2. Monitoring and recording actual performance or results.
3. Comparing results against plans and standards.
4. Communicating results and deviations to the appropriate employees.
5. Taking corrective action when needed and providing positive feedback for work well done.

For managers to measure results, the standards must be specific, attainable, and measurable. Setting such clear standards is part of the planning function. Vague goals and standards such as "better quality," "more efficiency," and "improved performance" aren't sufficient because they don't describe in enough detail what you're trying to achieve. For example, let's say you're a runner and you have made the following statement: "My goal is to improve my distance." When you started your improvement plan last year, you ran 2.0 miles a day; now you run 2.1 miles a day. Did you meet your goal? Well, you did increase your distance, but certainly not by very much.

A more appropriate statement would be "My goal is to increase my running distance from two miles a day to four miles a day by January 1." It's important to establish a time period for reaching goals. The following examples of goals and standards meet these criteria:

- Cutting the number of finished product rejects from 10 per 1,000 to 5 per 1,000 by March 31.
- Increasing the number of times managers praise employees from 3 per week to 12 per week by the end of the quarter.
- Increasing sales of product X from 10,000 per month to 12,000 per month by July.

One way to make control systems work is to establish clear procedures for monitoring performance. Accounting and finance are often the foundations for control systems because they provide the numbers management needs to evaluate progress.

A Key Criterion for Measurement: Customer Satisfaction

Traditional measures of success are usually financial; that is, they define success in terms of profits or return on investment. Certainly these measures are still important, but they're not the whole purpose of the firm. Other purposes may include pleasing employees, stakeholders, and customers—including both external and internal customers.

External customers include dealers, who buy products to sell to others, and ultimate customers (also known as end users) such as you and me, who buy products for their own personal use. **Internal customers** are individuals

external customers
Dealers, who buy products to sell to others, and ultimate customers (or end users), who buy products for their own personal use.

internal customers
Individuals and units within the firm that receive services from other individuals or units.

and units within the firm that receive services from other individuals or units. For example, the field salespeople are the internal customers of the marketing research people who prepare market reports for them.

One goal today is to go beyond simply satisfying customers to "delighting" them with unexpectedly good products and services. We'll discuss management in more detail in the next few chapters. Let's pause now, review, and do some exercises. Management is doing, not just reading.

progress assessment

- How does enabling help achieve empowerment?
- What are the five steps in the control process?
- What's the difference between internal and external customers?

summary

Learning Goal 1. Describe the changes occurring today in the management function.

- **What does management look like today?**

At one time, managers were called bosses, and their job consisted of telling people what to do, watching over them to be sure they did it, and reprimanding those who didn't. Many, if not most, managers still behave that way. Today, however, some managers tend to be more progressive. For example, they emphasize teams and team building; they create drop-in centers, team spaces, and open work areas. They tend to guide, train, support, motivate, and coach employees rather than tell them what to do.

- **What reasons can you give to account for changes in management?**

Leaders of Fortune 100 companies today tend to be younger, more of them are female, and fewer of them were educated at elite universities. They know that many of their employees know more about technology and other practices than they do. Therefore, they tend to put more emphasis on motivation, teamwork, and cooperation. Managers in the future are likely to be assuming completely new roles in the firm. For one thing, they will be taking a leadership role in adapting to climate change. Further, they'll be doing more expansion overseas.

Learning Goal 2. Describe the four functions of management.

- **What are the primary functions of management?**

The four primary functions are (1) planning, (2) organizing, (3) leading, and (4) controlling.

- **How do you define each of these functions?**

Planning includes anticipating trends and determining the best strategies and tactics to achieve organizational goals and objectives. Organizing includes designing the structure of the organization and creating conditions and systems in which everyone and everything works together to achieve the organization's goals and objectives. Leading means creating a vision for the organization, and communicating, guiding, training, coaching, and motivating others to achieve goals and objectives. Controlling means measuring whether what actually occurs meets the organization's goals.

Learning Goal 3. Relate the planning process and decision making to the accomplishment of company goals.

- **What's the difference between goals and objectives?**

Goals are broad, long-term achievements that organizations aim to accomplish, whereas objectives are specific, short-term plans made to help reach the goals.

- **What is a SWOT analysis?**

Managers look at the **S**trengths and **W**eaknesses of the firm and the **O**pportunities and **T**hreats facing it.

- **What are the four types of planning, and how are they related to the organization's goals and objectives?**

Strategic planning is broad, long-range planning that outlines the goals of the organization. *Tactical planning* is specific, short-term planning that lists organizational objectives. *Operational planning* is part of tactical planning and sets specific timetables and standards. *Contingency planning* is developing an alternative set of plans in case the first set doesn't work out.

- **What are the steps involved in decision making?**

The seven Ds of decision making are (1) define the situation; (2) describe and collect needed information; (3) develop alternatives; (4) develop agreement among those involved; (5) decide which alternative is best; (6) do what is indicated (begin implementation); and (7) determine whether the decision was a good one, and follow up.

Learning Goal 4. Describe the organizing function of management.

- **What is an organization chart?**

An organization chart is a visual device that shows relationships among people and divides the organization's work; it shows who is accountable for the completion of specific work and who reports to whom.

- **What are the three levels of management in the corporate hierarchy?**

The three levels of management are (1) top management (highest level consisting of the president and other key company executives who develop strategic plans); (2) middle management (general managers, division managers, and plant managers who are responsible for tactical planning and controlling); and (3) supervisory management (first-line managers/supervisors who evaluate workers' daily performance).

- **What skills do managers need?**

Managers must have three categories of skills: (1) technical skills (ability to perform specific tasks such as selling products or developing software), (2) human relations skills (ability to communicate and motivate), and (3) conceptual skills (ability to see organizations as a whole and how all the parts fit together).

- **Are these skills equally important at all management levels?**

Managers at different levels need different skills. Top managers rely heavily on human relations and conceptual skills and rarely use technical skills, while first-line supervisors need strong technical and human relations skills but use conceptual skills less often. Middle managers need to have a balance of all three skills (see Figure 7.5).

Learning Goal 5. Explain the differences between leaders and managers, and describe the various leadership styles.

- **What's the difference between a manager and a leader?**

A manager plans, organizes, and controls functions within an organization. A leader has vision and inspires others to grasp that vision, establishes corporate values, emphasizes corporate ethics, and doesn't fear change.

- **Describe the various leadership styles.**

Figure 7.6 shows a continuum of leadership styles ranging from boss-centered to subordinate-centered leadership.

- **Which leadership style is best?**

The most effective leadership style depends on the people being led and the situation. The challenge of the future will be to empower self-managed teams.

- **What does empowerment mean?**

Empowerment means giving employees the authority and responsibility to respond quickly to customer requests. Enabling is giving workers the education and tools they need to assume their new decision-making powers.

- **What is knowledge management?**

Knowledge management is finding the right information, keeping the information in a readily accessible place, and making the information known to everyone in the firm.

Learning Goal 6. Summarize the five steps of the control function of management.

- **What are the five steps of the control function?**

Controlling incorporates (1) setting clear standards, (2) monitoring and recording performance, (3) comparing performance with plans and standards, (4) communicating results and deviations to employees, and (5) providing positive feedback for a job well done and taking corrective action if necessary.

- **What qualities must standards possess to measure performance results?**

Standards must be specific, attainable, and measurable.

key terms

autocratic leadership 192

brainstorming 187

conceptual skills 190

contingency planning 186

controlling 183

decision making 187

enabling 194

external customers 196

free-rein leadership 194

goals 183

human relations skills 190

internal customers 196

knowledge management 195

leading 183

management 181

middle management 189

mission statement 183

objectives 184

operational planning 186

organization chart 188

organizing 182

participative (democratic) leadership 193

planning 182

PMI 187

problem solving 187

staffing 190

strategic planning 185

supervisory management 189

SWOT analysis 184

tactical planning 186

technical skills 190

top management 188

transparency 192

vision 183

critical thinking

Many students say they would like to be a manager someday. Here are some questions to get you started thinking like a manager:

1. Would you like to work for a large firm or a small business? Private or public? In an office or out in the field? Give your reasons for each answer.

2. What kind of leader would you be? Do you have evidence to show that?

3. Do you see any problems with a participative (democratic) leadership style? Can you see a manager getting frustrated when he or she can't control others?

4. Can someone who's trained to give orders (like a military sergeant) be retrained to be a participative leader? How? What problems may emerge?

developing workplace skills

1. Allocate time to do some career planning with a SWOT analysis of your present situation. Choose one career you are interested in and answer the following questions: What does the marketplace for your chosen career look like today? What skills do you have that will make you a winner in that type of career? What weaknesses might you target to correct? What are the threats to your career choice? What are the opportunities? Prepare a two-minute presentation to the class.

2. Bring several decks of cards to class and have the class break up into teams of four or so members. Each team should then elect a leader. Each leader should be assigned a leadership style and learn how to perform that style: autocratic, participative (democratic), or free rein. Have each team try to build a house of cards by stacking them on top of each other. The team with the tallest house wins. Each team member should report his or her experience under the selected style of leadership.

3. In class, discuss the advantages and disadvantages of becoming a manager. Does the size of the business make a difference? What are the advantages of a career in a profit-seeking business versus a career in a nonprofit organization?

4. Review Figure 7.6 and discuss managers you have known, worked for, or read about who have practiced each management style. Students from other countries may have interesting experiences to add. Which managerial style did you like best? Why? Which was or were most effective? Why?

5. Because of the illegal and unethical behavior of a few managers, managers in general are under suspicion for being greedy and dishonest. Discuss the fairness of such charges, and suggest what could be done to improve the opinion of managers among the students in your class.

taking it to the net

Purpose
To perform a simple SWOT analysis.

Exercise
Go to www.marketingteacher.com, locate the list of SWOT analyses, and click the link to go to the SWOT for Toys "R" Us.

1. What are Toys "R" Us's strengths, weaknesses, opportunities, and threats?

2. Analyze Toys "R" Us's weaknesses. How do you think the company's strengths might be used to overcome some of its weaknesses?

3. Analyze Toys "R" Us's opportunities and threats. What additional opportunities can you suggest? What additional threats can you identify?

casing the web

To access the case "Leading in a Leaderless Company," visit **www.mhhe.com/ubl0e**

video case

To access the video case featuring Zappos, visit **www.mhhe.com/ubl0e**

Structuring
Organizations
for Today's
Challenges

LEARNING
goals

After you have read and studied this chapter, you should be able to

1 Outline the basic principles of organization management.

2 Compare the organizational theories of Fayol and Weber.

3 Evaluate the choices managers make in structuring organizations.

4 Contrast the various organizational models.

5 Identify the benefits of interfirm cooperation and coordination.

6 Explain how organizational culture can help businesses adapt to change.

When Ursula Burns replaced Anne Mulcahy as CEO of Xerox in 2009, she had big shoes to fill. Mulcahy was one of the few women to run a top public company and the first woman to be chosen CEO of the Year by *Chief Executive* magazine. Mulcahy took Xerox back to the foundations of its corporate culture—innovation and customer care. "You need to change and adapt," she said.

Burns was certainly up to the task of taking the reins from Mulcahy and more. Recently *Forbes* magazine named Burns as the 14th most powerful woman in the world! She not only is the CEO at Xerox, but she's also on many boards, including the boards of American Express and MIT. President Obama named her to help lead the White House national program on STEM (science, technology, engineering and math), and V.P. Biden placed her on the Export Council in 2010. Burns is the only female African-American chief executive among the Fortune 500's top 150 companies.

Burns was born and raised in New York City. She earned her bachelor's degree from Polytechnic Institute of NYU and received her Master's degree from Columbia. She started with Xerox as a summer intern and joined the company a year later. From 1992 to 2000, she led several business teams including the office color and fax business and the office network printing business. She worked as an executive assistant for a while and eventually became president for global manufacturing in 1999. She worked closely with Mulcahy as

executive vice president until Mulcahy left in 2009.

When Burns took over as CEO, Xerox had to cut its employee ranks to 50,000. Around the same time, however, the company bought ACS, an IT services company with 80,000 employees. That acquisition took Xerox into a new services market and created a new challenge for Burns. Using ACS's base in IT and business process outsourcing, Xerox hopes to persuade its customers to give them a bigger slice of their document-related work.

This chapter is about changing and adapting organizations to today's markets, as Ursula Burns is doing at Xerox. Most managers never face challenges that big, but there are plenty of opportunities in every firm to use the principles of organizing to manage—and benefit from—change, especially today as firms adapt to the recent economic crisis.

profile

Getting to Know

X   *Ursula Burns*

CEO of Xerox

Sources: Diane Brady, "Hard Choices," *Bloomberg Businessweek,* April 26–May 2, 2010; Richard Waters, "Xerox Chief Sets Out the Big Picture," *Financial Times,* May 6, 2010; and Xerox Newsroom Bios, accessed online March 2011.

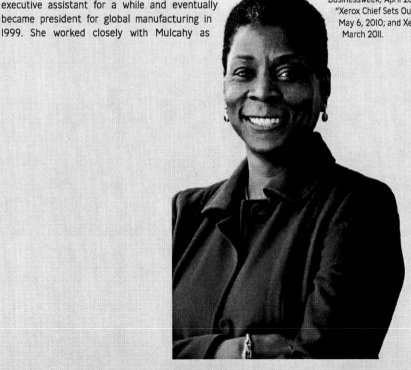

This sports equipment company studied the compact-disc industry and learned to use ultraviolet inks to print graphics on skis. It went to the cable television industry to learn how to braid layers of fiberglass and carbon, and adapted that knowledge to make its products. Name that company. (The answer can be found in this chapter.)

LEARNING goal 1

Outline the basic principles of organization management.

The principles of organization apply to businesses of all sizes. Structuring the business, making an appropriate division of labor using job specialization and departmentalization, establishing procedures, and assigning authority are tasks found in most firms. How do these principles operate at your current or most recent job?

EVERYONE'S REORGANIZING

You don't have to look far to find examples of companies reorganizing.[1] Xerox is just one of many—and sometimes the process is quite painful. A. G. Lafley, former CEO of legendary Procter & Gamble, transformed the company into one of the most innovative firms in the United States. Some entrepreneurial companies are organizing globally from the start and succeeding. Other organizations have been declining, including automobile makers, homebuilders, and banks. You have been hearing about such failures in the news. Clearly the challenge to reorganize is strong.

Few firms have established as strong an image in the United States as Starbucks, but even that company had to restructure to keep its customer base.[2] As the company expanded its menu to include more sandwiches, one of the unexpected results was a change in the smell of the stores (the odor of burning cheese was overwhelming the smell of coffee). The company restored the stores' aroma by cutting back on sandwiches for a while.[3] Many stores had to be closed and other stores were remodeled to recapture the feel of a Milan coffee bar. In the end, Starbucks regained its market image and is prospering again.[4]

You may be wondering what has happened to U.S. producers—so many seem to be failing. But adjusting to changing markets is a normal function in a capitalist economy. There will be big winners, like Google and Facebook, and big losers as well. The key to success is remaining flexible enough to adapt to the changing times.[5] Often that means going back to basic organizational principles and rebuilding the firm on a sound foundation. This chapter will discuss such basic principles.

MAKING **ethical decisions**

Safety versus Profit

Imagine you have begun a successful lawn-mowing service in your neighborhood. Other lawn-mowing services in the area seem to hire untrained workers, many from other countries. They pay only the minimum wage or slightly more. Most obviously, however, they often provide no safety equipment. Workers don't have ear protection against the loud mowers and blowers. Most don't wear goggles when operating the shredder. Very few wear masks when spraying potentially harmful fertilizers.

You are aware there are many hazards connected with yard work, but safety gear can be expensive and workers often prefer to work without it. You are interested in making as much money as possible, but you also are concerned about the safety and welfare of your workers. You know yard maintenance equipment creates noise pollution, but quiet equipment is expensive.

The corporate culture you create as you begin your service will last a long time. If you emphasize safety and environmental concern from the start, your workers will adopt your values. On the other hand, you can see the potential for making faster profits by ignoring safety rules and paying little attention to the environment as your competitors seem to do. What are the consequences?

Building an Organization from the Bottom Up

No matter the size of the business, the principles of organization are much the same. Let's say you and two friends plan to start a lawn-mowing business. One of the first steps is to organize your business. *Organizing,* or structuring, begins with determining what work needs to be done (mowing, edging, trimming) and then dividing up the tasks among the three of you; this is called a *division of labor.* One of you might have a special talent for trimming bushes, while another is better at mowing. The success of a firm often depends on management's ability to identify each worker's strengths and assign the right tasks to the right person. Many jobs can be done quickly and well when each person specializes. Dividing tasks into smaller jobs is called *job specialization.* For example, you might divide the mowing task into mowing, trimming, and raking.

If your business is successful, you'll probably hire more workers to help. You might organize them into teams or departments to do the various tasks. One team might mow while another uses blowers to clean up leaves and debris. If you're really successful over time, you might hire an accountant to keep records, various people to handle advertising, and a crew to maintain the equipment.

You can see how your business might evolve into a company with several departments: production (mowing and everything related to that), marketing, accounting, and maintenance. The process of setting up individual departments to do specialized tasks is called *departmentalization.* Finally, you'll assign authority and responsibility to people so that you can control the whole process. If something went wrong in the accounting department, for example, you would know who was responsible.

Structuring an organization, then, consists of devising a division of labor (sometimes resulting in specialization); setting up teams or departments to do specific tasks (like production and accounting); and assigning responsibility and authority to people. It also includes allocating resources (such as funds for various departments), assigning specific tasks, and establishing procedures for accomplishing the organizational objectives. From the start, you have to make ethical decisions about how you'll treat your workers and how you will benefit the community (see the nearby Making Ethical Decisions box).[6]

You may develop an *organization chart* that shows relationships among people: who is accountable for the completion of specific work, and who reports to whom. Finally, you'll monitor the environment to see what competitors are doing and what customers are demanding. Then you must adjust to the new realities. For example, a major lawn care company may begin promoting itself in your area. You might have to make some organizational changes to offer even better service at competitive prices. What would you do first if you began losing business to competitors?

LEARNING goal 2

Compare the organizational theories of Fayol and Weber.

THE CHANGING ORGANIZATION

Never before in the history of business has so much change been introduced so quickly—sometimes too quickly, as we saw with the earthquake and tsunami in Japan. Think of the effects these disasters have had on the nuclear power industry.[7] As we noted in earlier chapters, much change is due to the evolving business environment—more global competition, a declining economy, faster technological change, and pressure to preserve the natural environment.[8] Equally important to many businesses is the change in customer expectations. Consumers today expect high-quality products and fast, friendly service—at a reasonable cost.[9]

Managing change, then, has become a critical managerial function. That sometimes includes changing the whole organization structure. Such change may occur in nonprofit and government organizations as well as businesses.[10] Many organizations in the past were designed more to facilitate management than to please the customer. Companies designed many rules and regulations to give managers control over employees. As you'll learn later in this chapter, this reliance on rules is called *bureaucracy.* When Hurricane Katrina hit New Orleans in August 2005, the government seemed paralyzed and didn't respond quickly. The victims placed blame on federal, state, and local *bureaucracy.* Meanwhile, more flexible businesses in the area and in other states adjusted to the new conditions, reopened, and waited for the government to catch up. The local, state, and federal responses to the Gulf oil spill in 2010 were not much better. Yes, the government has to wrestle with bureaucracy as well as businesses.

To understand where we are in organization design, it helps to know where we've been. We'll look at that subject next.

The Development of Organization Design

Until the 20th century, most businesses were rather small, the processes for producing goods were relatively simple, and organizing workers was fairly easy. Organizing workers is still not too hard in most small firms, such as a lawn-mowing service or a small shop that produces custom-made boats. Not until the 1900s and the introduction of *mass production* (methods for efficiently producing large quantities of goods) did production processes and business organization become so complex. Usually, the bigger the plant, the more efficient production becomes.

Business growth led to **economies of scale**. This term refers to the fact that companies can reduce their production costs by purchasing raw

economies of scale
The situation in which companies can reduce their production costs if they can purchase raw materials in bulk; the average cost of goods goes down as production levels increase.

materials in bulk. The average cost of goods decreases as production levels rise. The cost of building a car, for example, declined sharply when automobile companies adopted mass production and GM, Ford, and others introduced their huge factories. Over time, such innovations became less meaningful as other companies copied the processes. You may have noticed the benefits of mass production in housing and computers.

During the era of mass production, organization theorists emerged. Two influential thinkers were Henri Fayol and Max Weber. Many of their principles are still being used in businesses throughout the world. Let's explore these principles.

Fayol's Principles of Organization   In France, economic theoretician Henri Fayol published his book *Administration industrielle et générale* in 1919. It was popularized in the United States in 1949 under the title *General and Industrial Management*. Fayol introduced such principles as the following:

- *Unity of command.* Each worker is to report to one, and only one, boss. The benefits of this principle are obvious. What happens if two different bosses give you two different assignments? Which one should you follow? To prevent such confusion, each person should report to only one manager. (Later we'll discuss an organizational plan that seems to violate this principle.)

- *Hierarchy of authority.* All workers should know to whom they report. Managers should have the right to give orders and expect others to follow. (As we discussed in Chapter 7, this concept has changed over time, and empowerment is often more important now.)

- *Division of labor.* Functions are to be divided into areas of specialization such as production, marketing, and finance. (This principle too is being modified, as you'll read later, and cross-functional teamwork is getting more emphasis.)

- *Subordination of individual interests to the general interest.* Workers are to think of themselves as a coordinated team. The goals of the team are more important than the goals of individual workers. (This concept is still very much in use.) Have you heard this concept being applied to football and basketball teams?

- *Authority.* Managers have the right to give orders and the power to enforce obedience. Authority and responsibility are related: whenever authority is exercised, responsibility arises. (This principle is also being modified as managers are beginning to empower employees.)

- *Degree of centralization.* The amount of decision-making power vested in top management should vary by circumstances. In a small organization, it's possible to centralize all decision-making power in the top manager. In a larger organization, however, some decision-making power, for both major and minor issues, should be delegated to lower-level managers and employees.

- *Clear communication channels.* All workers should be able to reach others in the firm quickly and easily.

- *Order.* Materials and people should be placed and maintained in the proper location.

- *Equity.* A manager should treat employees and peers with respect and justice. (That includes, of course, the treatment of women. Note, for

Henri Fayol introduced several management principles still followed today, including the idea that each worker should report to only one manager and that managers, in turn, should have the right to give orders for others to follow and the power to enforce them. Which of Fayol's principles have you observed?

example, the Walmart class-action lawsuit where women have claimed that the company did not treat them equally.)[11]

- *Esprit de corps.* A spirit of pride and loyalty should be created among people in the firm.

Management courses in colleges throughout the world taught Fayol's principles for years, and they became synonymous with the concept of management. Organizations were designed so that no person had more than one boss, lines of authority were clear, and everyone knew to whom to report. Naturally, these principles tended to be written down as rules, policies, and regulations as organizations grew larger.

That process of rule making has often led to rather rigid organizations that haven't always responded quickly to consumer requests. For example, in various cities, the Department of Motor Vehicles (DMV) and auto repair facilities have been slow to adapt to the needs of their customers. So where did the idea of *bureaucracy* come from? We talk about that next.

Max Weber and Organizational Theory   Max Weber's book *The Theory of Social and Economic Organizations,* like Fayol's, appeared in the United States in the late 1940s. Weber, a German sociologist and economist, promoted the pyramid-shaped organization structure that became popular in large firms. Weber put great trust in managers and felt the firm would do well if employees simply did what they were told. The less decision making they had to do, the better. Clearly, this is a reasonable way to operate if you're dealing with relatively uneducated and untrained workers. Such was generally the case at the time Weber was writing. Most employees today, however, have considerably more education and technical skills.

Weber's principles of organization resembled Fayol's. In addition, Weber emphasized:

- Job descriptions.
- Written rules, decision guidelines, and detailed records.
- Consistent procedures, regulations, and policies.
- Staffing and promotion based on qualifications.

Weber believed that large organizations demanded clearly established rules and guidelines to be followed precisely. In other words, he was in favor of *bureaucracy.* Although his principles made sense at the time, rules and procedures became so rigid in some companies that they grew counterproductive. Some organizations today still thrive on Weber's theories. United Parcel Service (UPS), for example, maintains strict written rules and decision guidelines. Those rules enable the firm to deliver packages quickly because employees don't have to pause to make decisions—procedures are clearly spelled out for them.

Some organizations that follow Weber's principles are less effective than UPS because they don't allow employees to respond quickly to new challenges. That has clearly been the case with disaster relief agencies in many areas. Later, we explore how to make organizations more responsive. First, let's look at some basic terms and concepts.

Turning Principles into Organization Design

Following theories like Fayol's and Weber's, managers in the latter 1900s began designing organizations so that managers could *control* workers. Many companies are still organized that way, with everything set up in a hierarchy. A **hierarchy** is a system in which

---

hierarchy
A system in which one person is at the top of the organization and there is a ranked or sequential ordering from the top down of managers who are responsible to that person.

Max Weber promoted an organizational structure composed of middle managers who implement the orders of top managers. He believed less-educated workers were best managed if managers or supervisors gave them strict rules and regulations to follow and monitored their performance. What industries or businesses today would benefit by using such controls?

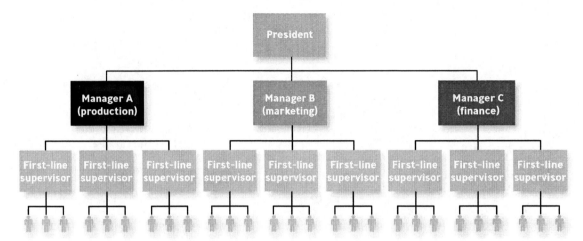

figure 8.1

TYPICAL ORGANIZATION CHART

This is a rather standard chart with managers for major functions and supervisors reporting to the managers. Each supervisor manages three employees.

one person is at the top of the organization and there is a ranked or sequential ordering from the top down of managers and others who are responsible to that person. Since one person can't keep track of thousands of workers, the top manager needs many lower-level managers to help. The **chain of command** is the line of authority that moves from the top of the hierarchy to the lowest level. Figure 8.1 shows a typical hierarchy.

Some organizations have a dozen or more layers of management between the chief executive officer (CEO) and the lowest-level employees. If employees want to introduce work changes, they ask a supervisor (the first level of management), who asks his or her manager, who asks a manager at the next level up, and so on. It can take weeks or months for a decision to be made and passed from manager to manager until it reaches employees.

Max Weber used the word *bureaucrat* to describe a middle manager whose function was to implement top management's orders. Thus, **bureaucracy** came to be the term for an organization with many layers of managers.

When employees in a bureaucracy of any size have to ask managers for permission to make a change, the process may take so long that customers become annoyed. Has this happened to you in a department store or other organization? Since customers want efficient service—and they want it *now*—slow service is simply not acceptable in today's competitive firms.[12]

Some companies are therefore reorganizing to let employees make decisions in order to please customers no matter what. Home Depot has adopted this approach to win more customers from competitors. Nordstrom employees can accept a return from a customer without managerial approval, even if the item was not originally sold at that store. As you read earlier in this book, giving employees such authority is called *empowerment*. Remember that empowerment works only when employees are given the proper training and resources to respond. Can you see how such training would help first responders in crisis conditions?

chain of command
The line of authority that moves from the top of a hierarchy to the lowest level.

bureaucracy
An organization with many layers of managers who set rules and regulations and oversee all decisions.

progress assessment

- What do the terms *division of labor* and *job specialization* mean?
- What are the principles of management outlined by Fayol?
- What did Weber add to the principles of Fayol?

LEARNING goal 3

Evaluate the choices managers make in structuring organizations.

centralized authority
An organization structure in which decision-making authority is maintained at the top level of management.

decentralized authority
An organization structure in which decision-making authority is delegated to lower-level managers more familiar with local conditions than headquarters management could be.

span of control
The optimal number of subordinates a manager supervises or should supervise.

A broad span of control allows one supervisor to be responsible for many workers whose work tasks are predictable and standardized. In addition to assembly lines, can you think of other management situations that might benefit from a broad span of control? What about in a service industry?

DECISIONS TO MAKE IN STRUCTURING ORGANIZATIONS

When designing responsive organizations, firms have to make decisions about several organizational issues: (1) centralization versus decentralization, (2) span of control, (3) tall versus flat organization structures, and (4) departmentalization.

Choosing Centralized or Decentralized Authority

Centralized authority occurs when decision making is concentrated at the top level of management. The retailing giant Target, for example, has a very centralized form of management. *Fortune* magazine commented that Target is so top-down that the CEO personally interviews candidates for the top 600 positions. That doesn't mean Target hasn't adapted to different circumstances, however, as you'll see later in this chapter.

McDonald's believes that purchasing, promotion, and other such decisions are best handled centrally. There's usually little need for each McDonald's restaurant in the United States to carry different food products. McDonald's thus leans toward centralized authority. However, today's rapidly changing markets, added to global differences in consumer tastes, tend to favor some decentralization and thus more delegation of authority, even at McDonald's.[13] Its restaurants in England offer tea, those in France offer a Croque McDo (a hot ham-and-cheese sandwich), those in Japan sell rice, and Chinese McDonald's offer taro and red bean desserts.

Decentralized authority occurs when decision making is delegated to lower-level managers and employees more familiar with local conditions than headquarters management could be. JCPenney customers in California, for example, demand clothing styles different from what customers in Minnesota or Maine like. It makes sense to delegate to store managers in various cities the authority to buy, price, and promote merchandise appropriate for each area. In response to the economic crisis that began in 2008, Macy's department store is also shifting to local tastes. The plan, called "My Macy's," proved successful in test markets. Both Home Depot and Lowe's also responded to the financial crisis with similar moves toward catering to local markets. Figure 8.2 lists some advantages and disadvantages of centralized and decentralized authority.

Choosing the Appropriate Span of Control

Span of control describes the optimal number of subordinates a manager supervises or should supervise. What is the "right" span of control? At

ADVANTAGES	DISADVANTAGES
Centralized	
• Greater top-management control	• Less responsiveness to customers
• More efficiency	• Less empowerment
• Simpler distribution system	• Interorganizational conflict
• Stronger brand/corporate image	• Lower morale away from headquarters
Decentralized	
• Better adaptation to customer wants	• Less efficiency
• More empowerment of workers	• Complex distribution system
• Faster decision making	• Less top-management control
• Higher morale	• Weakened corporate image

figure 8.2

ADVANTAGES AND DISADVANTAGES OF CENTRALIZED VERSUS DECENTRALIZED MANAGEMENT

lower levels, where work is standardized, it's possible to implement a broad span of control (15 to 40 workers). For example, one supervisor can be responsible for 20 or more workers assembling computers or cleaning movie theaters. The appropriate span gradually narrows at higher levels of the organization, because work becomes less standardized and managers need more face-to-face communication.

The trend today is to expand the span of control as organizations adopt empowerment, reduce the number of middle managers, and hire more talented and better educated lower-level employees. Information technology also allows managers to handle more information, so the span can be broader still.[14]

At Rowe Furniture in Salem, Virginia, the manufacturing chief dismantled the assembly line and empowered the people who had had limited functions—like sewing, gluing, and stapling—with the freedom to make sofas as they saw fit. Productivity and quality soared.

Choosing between Tall and Flat Organization Structures

In the early 20th century, organizations grew even bigger, adding layer after layer of management to create **tall organization structures**. Some had as many as 14 levels, and the span of control was small (few people reported to each manager).

Imagine how a message might be distorted as it moved up the organization and back down through managers, management assistants, secretaries, assistant secretaries, supervisors, trainers, and so on. The cost of all these managers and support people was high, the paperwork they generated was enormous, and the inefficiencies in communication and decision making were often intolerable.

More recently, organizations have adopted **flat organization structures** with fewer layers of management (see Figure 8.3) and a broad span of control

tall organization structure
An organizational structure in which the pyramidal organization chart would be quite tall because of the various levels of management.

flat organization structure
An organization structure that has few layers of management and a broad span of control.

figure 8.3

A FLAT ORGANIZATION STRUCTURE

figure 8.4

**ADVANTAGES AND
DISADVANTAGES OF A
NARROW VERSUS A BROAD
SPAN OF CONTROL**
The flatter the
organization, the broader
the span of control.

ADVANTAGES	DISADVANTAGES
Narrow	
• More control by top management	• Less empowerment
• More chances for advancement	• Higher costs
• Greater specialization	• Delayed decision making
• Closer supervision	• Less responsiveness to customers
Broad	
• Reduced costs	• Fewer chances for advancement
• More responsiveness to customers	• Overworked managers
• Faster decision making	• Loss of control
• More empowerment	• Less management expertise

(many people report to each manager).[15] Flat structures can respond readily to customer demands because lower-level employees have authority and responsibility for making decisions, and managers can be spared some day-to-day tasks. In a bookstore with a flat organization structure, employees may have authority to arrange shelves by category, process special orders for customers, and so on.

Large organizations use flat structures to try to match the friendliness of small firms, whose workers often know customers by name. The flatter organizations become, the broader their spans of control, which means some managers lose their jobs. Figure 8.4 lists advantages and disadvantages of narrow and broad spans of control.

Weighing the Advantages and Disadvantages of Departmentalization

departmentalization
The dividing of organizational functions into separate units.

Departmentalization divides organizations into separate units. The traditional way to departmentalize is by *function*—such as design, production, marketing, and accounting. Departmentalization groups workers according to their skills, expertise, or resource use so that they can specialize and work together more effectively. It may also save costs and thus improve efficiency. Other advantages include the following:

1. Employees can develop skills in depth and progress within a department as they master more skills.
2. The company can achieve economies of scale by centralizing all the resources it needs and locate various experts in that area.
3. Employees can coordinate work within the function, and top management can easily direct and control various departments' activities.

Disadvantages of departmentalization by function include the following:

1. Departments may not communicate well. For example, production may be so isolated from marketing that it does not get needed feedback from customers.
2. Employees may identify with their department's goals rather than the organization's. The purchasing department may find a good value somewhere and buy a huge volume of goods. That makes purchasing look good, but the high cost of storing the goods hurts overall profitability.

3. The company's response to external changes may be slow.

4. People may not be trained to take different managerial responsibilities; rather, they tend to become narrow specialists.

5. Department members may engage in groupthink (they think alike) and may need input from outside to become more creative.

Looking at Alternative Ways to Departmentalize   Functional separation isn't always the most responsive form of organization. So what are the alternatives? Figure 8.5 shows five ways a firm can departmentalize. One way is by product. A book publisher might have a trade book department (for books sold to the general public), a textbook department, and a technical book department, each with separate development and marketing processes. Such product-focused departmentalization usually results in good customer relations.

Some organizations departmentalize by customer group. A pharmaceutical company might have one department for the consumer market, another that calls on hospitals (the institutional market), and another that targets doctors. You can see how customer groups can benefit from having specialists satisfying their needs.

Some firms group their units by geographic location because customers vary so greatly by region. Japan, Europe, and South America may deserve separate departments, with obvious benefits.

The decision about how to departmentalize depends on the nature of the product and the customers. A few firms find that it's most efficient to separate activities by process. For example, a firm that makes leather coats may have one department cut the leather, another dye it, and a third sew the coat together. Such specialization enables employees to do a better job because they can focus on learning a few critical skills.

Some firms use a combination of departmentalization techniques to create *hybrid forms*. For example, a company could departmentalize by function, geographic location, *and* customer groups.

After the material for footballs has been cut and sewn in the Wilson Sporting Goods factory, it moves on to the lacing department where workers like this one open up the deflated balls and prepare them for lacing. What are the advantages and disadvantages of departmentalizing by process like this?

figure 8.5

WAYS TO DEPARTMENTALIZE
A computer company may want to departmentalize by geographic location (countries), a manufacturer by function, a pharmaceutical company by customer group, a leather manufacturer by process, and a publisher by product. In each case the structure must fit the firm's goals.

progress assessment

- Why are organizations becoming flatter?
- What are some reasons for having a narrow span of control in an organization?
- What are the advantages and disadvantages of departmentalization?
- What are the various ways a firm can departmentalize?

LEARNING goal 4

Contrast the various organizational models.

ORGANIZATIONAL MODELS

Now that we've explored the basic choices in organization design, let's look in depth at four ways to structure an organization: (1) line organizations, (2) line-and-staff organizations, (3) matrix-style organizations, and (4) cross-functional self-managed teams. You'll see that some of these models violate traditional management principles. The business community is in a period of transition, with some traditional organizational models giving way to new structures. Such transitions can be not only unsettling to employees and managers but also fraught with problems and errors.

Line Organizations

A **line organization** has direct two-way lines of responsibility, authority, and communication running from the top to the bottom of the organization, with everyone reporting to only one supervisor. Many small businesses are organized this way. For example, a locally owned pizza parlor might have a general manager and a shift manager. All the general employees report to the shift manager, and he or she reports to the general manager or owner.

A line organization does not have any specialists who provide managerial support. There is no legal department, accounting department, human resources department, or information technology (IT) department. Line organizations follow all of Fayol's traditional management rules. Line managers can issue orders, enforce discipline, and adjust the organization as conditions change.

In large businesses, a line organization may have the disadvantages of being too inflexible, of having few specialists or experts to advise people along the line, and of having lengthy lines of communication.[16] Thus they may be unable to handle complex decisions relating to thousands of products and tons of paperwork. Such organizations usually turn to a line-and-staff form of organization.

Line-and-Staff Organizations

To minimize the disadvantages of simple line organizations, many organizations today have both line and staff personnel. **Line personnel** are responsible for directly achieving organizational goals, and include production workers, distribution people, and marketing personnel. **Staff personnel** advise and assist line personnel in meeting their goals, and include those in marketing research, legal advising, information technology, and human resource management.

line organization
An organization that has direct two-way lines of responsibility, authority, and communication running from the top to the bottom of the organization, with all people reporting to only one supervisor.

line personnel
Employees who are part of the chain of command that is responsible for achieving organizational goals.

staff personnel
Employees who advise and assist line personnel in meeting their goals.

figure 8.6

A SAMPLE LINE-AND-STAFF
ORGANIZATION

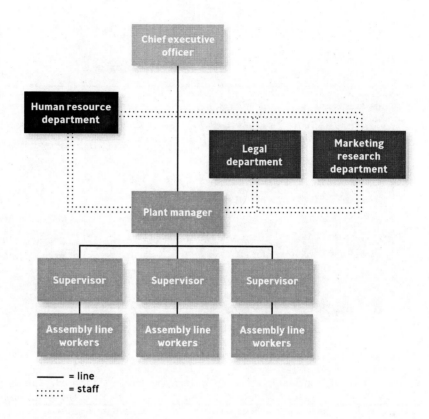

See Figure 8.6 for a diagram of a line-and-staff organization. One important difference between line and staff personnel is authority. Line personnel have formal authority to make policy decisions. Staff personnel have authority to advise line personnel and influence their decisions, but they can't make policy changes themselves. The line manager may seek or ignore the advice from staff personnel.

Many organizations benefit from expert staff advice on safety, legal issues, quality control, database management, motivation, and investing. Staff personnel strengthen the line positions and are like well-paid consultants on the organization's payroll.

Matrix-Style Organizations

Both line and line-and-staff organization structures may suffer from inflexibility. Both allow for established lines of authority and communication and work well in organizations with stable environments and slow product development (such as firms selling household appliances). In such firms, clear lines of authority and relatively fixed organization structures are assets that ensure efficient operations.

Today's economy, however, is dominated by high-growth industries like telecommunications, nanotechnology, robotics, biotechnology, and aerospace, where competition is stiff and the life cycle of new ideas is short.[17] Emphasis is on product development, creativity, special projects, rapid communication, and interdepartmental teamwork. From those changes grew the popularity of the **matrix organization**, in which specialists from different parts of the organization work together temporarily on specific projects, but still remain part of a line-and-staff structure (see Figure 8.7). In other words, a project manager

matrix organization
An organization in which specialists from different parts of the organization are brought together to work on specific projects but still remain part of a line-and-staff structure.

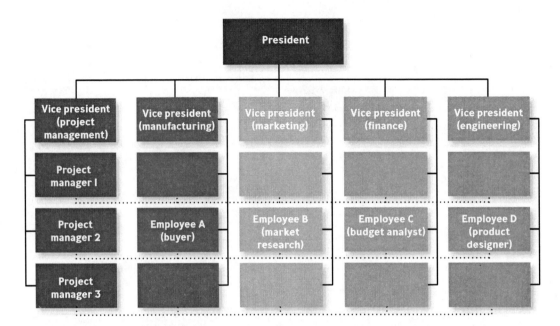

figure 8.7

can borrow people from different departments to help design and market new product ideas.

The matrix structure was developed in the aerospace industry and is now familiar in areas such as banking, management consulting firms, accounting firms, ad agencies, and school systems. Among its advantages:

- It gives managers flexibility in assigning people to projects.
- It encourages interorganizational cooperation and teamwork.
- It can produce creative solutions to product development problems.
- It makes efficient use of organizational resources.

As for disadvantages:

- It's costly and complex.
- It can confuse employees about where their loyalty belongs—with the project manager or with their functional unit.
- It requires good interpersonal skills as well as cooperative employees and managers to avoid communication problems.
- It may be only a temporary solution to a long-term problem.

If you're thinking that matrix organizations violate some traditional managerial principles, you're right. Normally a person can't work effectively for two bosses. Who has the real authority? Whose directive has first priority?

In reality, however, the system functions more effectively than you might imagine. To develop a new product, a project manager may be given temporary authority to "borrow" line personnel from production, marketing, and other line functions. The employees work together to complete the project and then return to their regular positions. Thus, no one actually reports to more than one manager at a time.

A potential real problem with matrix management, however, is that the project teams are not permanent. They form to solve a problem and then break

figure 8.7

A MATRIX ORGANIZATION
In a matrix organization, project managers are in charge of teams made up of members of several departments. In this case, project manager 2 supervises employees A, B, C, and D. These employees are accountable not only to project manager 2 but also to the head of their individual departments. For example, employee B, a market researcher, reports to project manager 2 *and* to the vice president of marketing.

In matrix organizations, specialists from different parts of the organization work together temporarily on specific projects. For example, a team developing a new product may have members from production, marketing, and finance who report to the team's project manager. When the project is over, the team members return to their regular positions.

up. There is little chance for cross-functional learning, because teams work together so briefly.

Decision making in the future will be distributed throughout the organization so that people can respond rapidly to change, says the *Harvard Business Review*. Global teams will collaborate on the Internet for a single project and then disband. Young people who play online games will feel quite comfortable working in such groups.

Cross-Functional Self-Managed Teams

One solution to the temporary nature of matrix teams is to establish long-lived teams and empower them to work closely with suppliers, customers, and others to quickly and efficiently bring out new, high-quality products while giving great service. *BusinessWeek* reports that some 82 percent of white-collar workers partner with co-workers. Over 80 percent say they prefer working in groups of three or more. Most work in groups to learn from others, but 30 percent use groups to accomplish a specific task.

cross-functional self-managed teams
Groups of employees from different departments who work together on a long-term basis.

Cross-functional self-managed teams are groups of employees from different departments who work together on a long-term basis (as opposed to the temporary teams established in matrix-style organizations). *Self-managed* means that they are empowered to make decisions without management approval. The barriers among design, engineering, marketing, distribution, and other functions fall when interdepartmental teams are created. Sometimes the teams are interfirm; that is, the members come from two or more companies.

Cross-functional teams work best when leadership is shared. An engineer may lead the design of a new product, but a marketing expert may take the leadership position once it's ready for distribution.

Going Beyond Organizational Boundaries

Cross-functional teams work best when the voice of the customer is brought in, especially in product development tasks. Suppliers and distributors should be on the team as well. A cross-functional team that includes customers, suppliers, and distributors goes beyond organizational boundaries. When suppliers and distributors are in other countries, cross-functional teams may share market information across national boundaries.[18] Government coordinators may assist such projects, letting cross-functional teams break the barriers between government and business.

Cross-functional teams are only one way businesses can interact with other companies. Next we look at others.

progress assessment

- What is the difference between line and staff personnel?
- What management principle does a matrix-style organization challenge?
- What is the main difference between a matrix-style organization's structure and the use of cross-functional teams?

LEARNING goal 5

Identify the benefits of interfirm cooperation and coordination.

MANAGING THE INTERACTIONS AMONG FIRMS

Whether it involves customers, suppliers, distributors, or the government, **networking** uses communications technology and other means to link organizations and allow them to work together on common objectives.[19] Let's explore this concept further.

networking
Using communications technology and other means to link organizations and allow them to work together on common objectives.

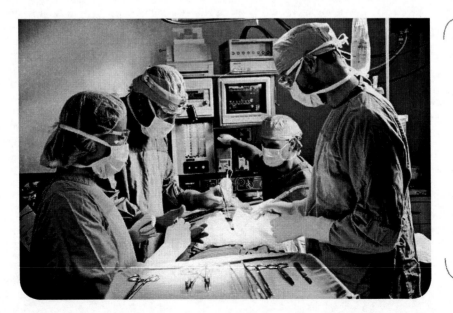

You can think of a team of medical specialists in an operating room as a cross-functional, self-managed team. Doctors, nurses, technicians, and anesthesiologists from different departments and areas in the hospital work together to complete successful operations. What kinds of tasks do cross-functional, self-managed teams complete in an office or retail environment?

220   PART 3   ✳   **Business Management: Empowering Employees to Satisfy Customers**

Transparency and Virtual Organizations

real time
The present moment or the actual time in which something takes place.

Networked organizations are so closely linked by the Internet that each can find out what the others are doing in real time. **Real time** simply means the present moment or the actual time in which an event takes place. The Internet has allowed companies to send real-time data to organizational partners as they are developed or collected. The result is transparency (see Chapter 7), which occurs when a company is so open to other companies that electronic information is shared as if the companies were one. With this integration, two companies can work as closely as two departments in traditional firms.

Can you see the implications for organizational design? Most organizations are no longer self-sufficient or self-contained. Rather, they are part of a vast network of global businesses that work closely together. An organization chart showing what people do within any one organization is simply not complete, because the organization is part of a much larger system of firms. A modern chart would show people in different organizations and indicate how they are networked. This is a relatively new concept, however, so few such charts are yet available. The nearby Spotlight on Small Business box offers an example of how a small business works with another company that performs production, fulfillment and shipping functions.

virtual corporation
A temporary networked organization made up of replaceable firms that join and leave as needed.

Networked organization structures tend to be flexible. A company may work with a design expert from another company in Italy for a year and then not need that person anymore. It may hire an expert from a company in another country for the next project. Such a temporary network, made of replaceable firms that join and leave as needed, is a **virtual corporation** (see Figure 8.8).[20] This is quite different from a traditional organization structure; in fact, traditional managers sometimes have trouble adapting to the speed of change and the impermanence of relationships in networking. We discuss adaptation to change below; first, we describe how organizations use benchmarking and outsourcing to manage their interactions with other firms.

figure 8.8

A VIRTUAL CORPORATION
A virtual corporation has no permanent ties to the firms that do its production, distribution, legal, and other work. Such firms are flexible enough to adapt to changes in the market quickly.

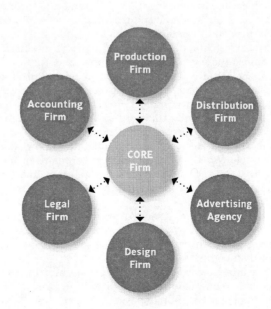

SPOTLIGHT ON SMALL business

When Your Workers Work for Someone Else

It was rather noisy where Douglas Pick lived near the University of Southern California. He found that earplugs were a great help. In fact, he decided that he could profit from making earplugs himself, so he launched DAP World from his apartment. After a few years, Pick found that he could not keep up with demand. His home-based office was simply not big enough to produce as many units as he needed.

Pick was hesitant to take on the overhead necessary to house and run his own manufacturing facility. About that time, however, he learned about an organization called New Horizons that assists and employs developmentally disabled adults. New Horizons not only could produce his earplugs, but could handle fulfillment and shipping as well. The organization was cost-competitive because the State of California and private contributions helped to subsidize the labor costs. Now Pick sells millions of pairs of earplugs to major outlets such as Walgreens and Rite Aid and supports some 200 workers. Can you see the benefit of being creative when planning, organizing, and structuring a business?

Source: Gwen Moran, "Sound Principles," *Entrepreneur*, April 2011; and www.dapworld.com, accessed April 2011.

Benchmarking and Core Competencies

Organizations historically tried to do all functions themselves. Each had its own department for accounting, finance, marketing, production, and so on. As we've noted, today's organizations look to other organizations for help in areas where they do not generate world-class quality.

Benchmarking compares an organization's practices, processes, and products against the world's best. As one example, K2 Skis is a company that makes skis, snowboards, in-line skates, and related products. It studied the compact-disc industry and learned to use ultraviolet inks to print graphics on skis. It went to the aerospace industry to get piezoelectric technology to reduce vibration in its snowboards (the aerospace industry uses the technology for wings on planes). It learned from the cable television industry how to braid layers of fiberglass and carbon, and adapted that knowledge to make skis. As another example, Wyeth, a pharmaceutical company, benchmarked the aerospace industry for project management, the shipping industry for standardization of processes, and computer makers to learn the most efficient way to make prescription drugs.

Benchmarking also has a more directly competitive purpose. In retailing, Target may compare itself to Walmart to see what, if anything, Walmart does better. Target will then try to improve its practices or processes to become even better than Walmart.

If an organization can't do as well as the best in, say, shipping, it will try to outsource the function to an organization like UPS or FedEx that specializes in shipping. Outsourcing, remember, means assigning one or more

benchmarking
Comparing an organization's practices, processes, and products against the world's best.

Nike's core competencies are designing and marketing athletic shoes. The company outsources other functions (i.e. manufacturing) to other companies that assemble shoes better and cheaper than Nike could do on its own. What are the advantages of focusing on the company's core competencies? What are the disadvantages?

functions—such as accounting, production, security, maintenance, and legal work—to outside organizations. Even small firms are getting involved in outsourcing. We've already discussed some problems with outsourcing, especially when companies outsource to other countries. Some functions, such as information management and marketing, may be too important to assign to outside firms. In that case, the organization should benchmark the best firms and restructure its departments to try to be equally good. It is important to remember that companies in other countries often outsource their functions to companies in the United States. We call that *insourcing* and it is the source of many jobs.[21]

When a firm has completed its outsourcing process, the remaining functions are its **core competencies**, those functions it can do as well as or better than any other organization in the world.[22] For example, Nike is great at designing and marketing athletic shoes. Those are its core competencies. It outsources manufacturing, however, to other companies that assemble shoes better and less expensively than Nike can. Similarly, Dell is best at marketing computers and outsources most other functions, including manufacturing and distribution.

After you have structured an organization, you must keep monitoring the environment (including customers) to learn what changes are needed. Dell, for example, recently reversed its practice of outsourcing customer support and now offers a premium service that allows U.S. customers to reach tech support in North America. The following section discusses organizational change in more detail.

core competencies
Those functions that the organization can do as well as or better than any other organization in the world.

ADAPTING TO CHANGE

Once you have formed an organization, you must be prepared to adapt the structure to changes in the market.[23] That's not always easy to do. Over time, an organization can get stuck in its ways. Employees have a tendency to say, "That's the way we've always done things. If it isn't broken, don't fix it." Managers also get complacent. They may say they have 20 years' experience when in fact they've had 1 year's experience 20 times. Do you think that slow adaptation to change was a factor in the decline of the manufacturing sector in the United States?

Introducing change is thus one of the hardest challenges facing any manager. Nonetheless, change is what's happening at General Motors (GM), Ford, Facebook, and other companies eager to become more competitive. If you have old facilities that are no longer efficient, you have to get rid of them. That's exactly what GM and other companies are doing. In fact, they have asked the government to lend them billions of dollars to help. You may have to cut your labor force to lower costs.

digital natives
Young people who have grown up using the Internet and social networking.

The Internet has created whole new opportunities, not only to sell to customers directly but also to ask them questions and provide them with any information they want. To win market share, companies must coordinate the efforts of their traditional departments and their Internet staff to create friendly, easy-to-manage interactions. Young people today are called **digital natives** because they grew up with the Internet. To reach them, companies are retraining older employees to be more tech-savvy. That means becoming

SOCIAL MEDIA IN
business

When Twitter and Facebook Are Old School

There was a day when many people were eager to hear about microchips and how they worked. Today, there aren't many people talking about microprocessors or other old high-tech innovations. Today, the focus is on Facebook, Twitter, cloud computing, and the like. People are still debating which eBook reader is the best. But soon people will become so accustomed to having these tools at their fingertips that they will no longer be newsworthy. Matt Ridley writes, "The very notion that we discussed the relative merits of text, email, social network messaging, and tweeting will seem quaint. In the future, my part of the cloud will get a message to a friend's part of the cloud by whichever method works best, and I will not even know which way it went."

There will be dozens of new high-tech gadgets to try. Many of them will be slight improvements on what is available today (just as the iPad 2 was a slight improvement on the original iPad), while others may be revolutionary. What is most relevant to this chapter is how social media will affect organizations in the future. There is likely to be an even greater increase in working from home. There will be closer and better relationships with customers and suppliers and dealers. All in all, social media will continue to have a major influence on how business gets done and where it gets done and who does it. The moral of the story for managers is: Keep up with the latest technology or be left behind.

Sources: Matt Ridley, "Microchips Are Old Hat, Can Tweets Be Far Behind?" *The Wall Street Journal,* March 5-6, 2011; and B. L. Ochman, " 3 Things You Need to Know about Social Media," www.mashable.com, accessed April 2011.

familiar with YouTube, Facebook, Wikis, Skype, Twitter, RSS, and more. The Social Media in Business box explores the future of such high-tech devices.

We've seen that Target is highly centralized. Nonetheless, the company reacts effectively to changes in consumer preferences throughout the country, in part by keeping in touch with an enormous web of people of all ages, interests, and nationalities—its "creative cabinet"—via the Internet. The members of the "cabinet," who never meet so they cannot influence each other, evaluate various new initiatives and recommend new programs to help Target figure out what belongs on store shelves.

Restructuring for Empowerment

To empower employees, firms often must reorganize dramatically to make frontline workers their most important people. **Restructuring** is redesigning an organization so it can more effectively and efficiently serve its customers.[24]

Until recently, department store clerks, bank tellers, and front-desk staff in hotels weren't considered key employees. Instead, managers were considered more important, and they were responsible for directing the work of the frontline people. The organization chart in a typical firm looked much like the pyramid in Figure 8.1.

A few service-oriented organizations have turned the traditional organization structure upside down. An **inverted organization** has contact people (like nurses) at the top and the chief executive officer at the bottom. Management layers are few, and the manager's job is to *assist and support* frontline people, not boss them around. Figure 8.9 illustrates the difference between an inverted and a traditional organizational structure.

restructuring
Redesigning an organization so that it can more effectively and efficiently serve its customers.

inverted organization
An organization that has contact people at the top and the chief executive officer at the bottom of the organization chart.

Traditional Organization   Inverted Organization

figure 8.9

COMPARISON OF AN INVERTED ORGANIZATIONAL STRUCTURE AND A TRADITIONAL ORGANIZATIONAL STRUCTURE

Companies based on this organization structure support frontline personnel with internal and external databases, advanced communication systems, and professional assistance. Naturally, this means frontline people have to be better educated, better trained, and better paid than in the past. It takes a lot of trust for top managers to implement such a system—but when they do, the payoff in customer satisfaction and profits is often well worth the effort.[25]

In the past, managers controlled information—and that gave them power. In more progressive organizations today, everyone shares information, often through an elaborate database system, and *among* firms as well as *within* them. No matter what organizational model you choose or how much you empower your employees, the secret to successful organization change is to focus on customers and give them what they want.

LEARNING goal 6

Explain how organizational culture can help businesses adapt to change.

Creating a Change-Oriented Organizational Culture

Any organizational change is bound to cause some stress and resistance among members. Firms adapt best when their culture is already change-oriented. **Organizational (or corporate) culture** is the widely shared values within an organization that foster unity and cooperation to achieve common goals. Usually the culture of an organization is reflected in its stories, traditions, and myths.

Each McDonald's restaurant has the same feel, look, and atmosphere; in short, each has a similar organizational culture. It's obvious from visiting almost any McDonald's that the culture emphasizes quality, service, cleanliness, and value.

An organizational culture can also be negative. Have you ever been in an organization where you feel no one cares about service or quality? The clerks may seem uniformly glum, indifferent, and testy. Their mood pervades the atmosphere, and patrons become unhappy or upset. It may be hard to believe

organizational (or corporate) culture
Widely shared values within an organization that provide unity and cooperation to achieve common goals.

an organization, especially a profit-making one, can be run so badly and still survive. Clearly then, when you search for a job, study the organizational culture to see whether you will thrive in it.

Some of the best organizations have cultures that emphasize service to others, especially customers. The atmosphere reflects friendly, caring people who enjoy working together to provide a good product at a reasonable price. Companies that have such cultures have less need for close supervision of employees. That usually means fewer policy manuals; organization charts; and formal rules, procedures, and controls. The key to a productive culture is mutual trust.[26] You get such trust by giving it. The very best companies stress high moral and ethical values such as honesty, reliability, fairness, environmental protection, and social involvement.

Empowering employees who deal directly with customers to solve problems without needing a manager's approval makes a higher level of customer service possible and helps employees grow as well. What kind of guest issues do you think a frontline hotel employee should be allowed to solve on his or her own?

We've been talking as if organizational matters were mostly controllable by management. In fact, the formal structure is just one element of the total organizational system, including its culture. The informal organization is of equal or even greater importance. Let's explore this notion next.

Managing the Informal Organization

All organizations have two organizational systems. The **formal organization** details lines of responsibility, authority, and position. It's the structure shown on organization charts. The other system is the **informal organization**, the system that develops spontaneously as employees meet and form cliques, relationships, and lines of authority outside the formal organization. It's the human side of the organization that doesn't show on any organization chart.

No organization can operate effectively without both types of organization. The formal system is often too slow and bureaucratic to let the organization adapt quickly, although it does provide helpful guides and lines of authority for routine situations.

The informal organization is often too unstructured and emotional to allow careful, reasoned decision making on critical matters. It's extremely effective, however, in generating creative solutions to short-term problems and creating camaraderie and teamwork among employees.[27]

In any organization, it's wise to learn quickly who is important in the informal organization. Following formal rules and procedures can take days. Who in the organization knows how to obtain supplies immediately without the normal procedures? Which administrative assistants should you see if you want your work given first priority? Answers to these questions help people work effectively in many organizations.

The informal organization's nerve center is the *grapevine*, the system through which unofficial information flows between and among managers and employees. Key people in the grapevine usually have considerable influence.

In the old "us-versus-them" system of organizations, where managers and employees were often at odds, the informal system hindered effective management. In more open organizations, managers and employees work together to set objectives and design procedures. The informal organization is an invaluable managerial asset that can promote harmony among workers and establish the corporate culture.

formal organization
The structure that details lines of responsibility, authority, and position; that is, the structure shown on organization charts.

informal organization
The system that develops spontaneously as employees meet and form cliques, relationships, and lines of authority outside the formal organization.

The informal organization is the system that develops as employees meet and form relationships. The grapevine, the unofficial flow of information among employees, is the nerve center of the informal organization. How does the informal organization affect the work environment?

As effective as the informal organization may be in creating group cooperation, it can still be equally powerful in resisting management directives. Employees may form unions, go on strike together, and generally disrupt operations. Learning to create the right corporate culture and work within the informal organization is thus a key to managerial success.[28]

progress assessment

- What is an inverted organization?
- Why do organizations outsource functions?
- What is organizational culture?

summary

Learning Goal 1. Outline the basic principles of organization management.
- **What is happening today to American businesses?**
They are adjusting to changing markets. That is a normal function in a capitalist economy. There will be big winners, like Google and Facebook, and big losers as well. The key to success is remaining flexible and adapting to the changing times.
- **What are the principles of organization management?**
Structuring an organization means devising a division of labor (sometimes resulting in specialization), setting up teams or departments, and assigning responsibility and authority. It includes allocating resources (such as funds), assigning specific tasks, and establishing procedures for accomplishing the organizational objectives. Managers also have to make ethical decisions about how to treat workers.

Learning Goal 2. Compare the organizational theories of Fayol and Weber.

- **What were Fayol's basic principles?**

Fayol introduced principles such as unity of command, hierarchy of authority, division of labor, subordination of individual interests to the general interest, authority, clear communication channels, order, and equity.

- **What principles did Weber add?**

Weber added principles of bureaucracy such as job descriptions, written rules and decision guidelines, consistent procedures, and staffing and promotions based on qualifications.

Learning Goal 3. Evaluate the choices managers make in structuring organizations.

- **What are the four major choices in structuring organizations?**

Choices to make in structuring and restructuring organizations cover (1) centralization versus decentralization, (2) breadth of span of control, (3) tall versus flat organization structures, and (4) type of departmentalization.

- **What are the latest trends in structuring?**

Departments are often replaced or supplemented by matrix organizations and cross-functional teams that decentralize authority. The span of control becomes larger as employees become self-directed. Another trend is to eliminate managers and flatten organizations.

Learning Goal 4. Contrast the various organizational models.

- **What are the two major organizational models?**

Two traditional forms of organization are (1) line organizations and (2) line-and-staff organizations. A line organization has clearly defined responsibility and authority, is easy to understand, and provides each worker with only one supervisor. The expert advice of staff assistants in a line-and-staff organization helps in areas such as safety, quality control, computer technology, human resource management, and investing.

- **What are the key alternatives to the major organizational models?**

Matrix organizations assign people to projects temporarily and encourage interorganizational cooperation and teamwork. Cross-functional self-managed teams have all the benefits of the matrix style and are long-term.

Learning Goal 5. Identify the benefits of interfirm cooperation and coordination.

- **What are the major concepts involved in interfirm communications?**

Networking uses communications technology and other means to link organizations and allow them to work together on common objectives. A virtual corporation is a networked organization of replaceable firms that join and leave as needed. Benchmarking tells firms how their performance measures up to that of their competitors in specific functions. The company may then *outsource* to companies that perform its weaker functions more effectively and efficiently. The functions that are left are the firm's *core competencies*.

- **What is an inverted organization?**

An inverted organization places employees at the top of the hierarchy; managers are at the bottom to train and assist employees.

Learning Goal 6. Explain how organizational culture can help businesses adapt to change.

- **What is organizational culture?**

Organizational (or corporate) culture consists of the widely shared values within an organization that foster unity and cooperation to achieve common goals.

- **What is the difference between the formal and informal organization of a firm?**

The formal organization details lines of responsibility, authority, and position. It's the structure shown on organization charts. The informal organization is the system that develops spontaneously as employees meet and form cliques, relationships, and lines of authority outside the formal organization. It's the human side of the organization. The informal organization is an invaluable managerial asset that often promotes harmony among workers and establishes the corporate culture. As effective as the informal organization may be in creating group cooperation, it can still be equally powerful in resisting management directives.

key terms

benchmarking 221	digital natives 222	matrix organization 216
bureaucracy 209	economies of scale 206	networking 219
centralized authority 210	flat organization structure 211	organizational (or corporate) culture 224
chain of command 209	formal organization 225	real time 220
core competencies 222	hierarchy 208	restructuring 223
cross-functional self-managed teams 218	informal organization 225	span of control 210
decentralized authority 210	inverted organization 223	staff personnel 215
departmentalization 212	line organization 215	tall organization structure 211
	line personnel 215	virtual corporation 220

critical thinking

Now that you have learned some of the basic principles of organization, pause and think about where you have already applied such concepts yourself or when you have been part of an organization that did.

1. Did you find a division of labor necessary and helpful?

2. Were you assigned specific tasks or left on your own to decide what to do?

3. Were promotions based strictly on qualifications, as Weber suggested? What other factors may have been considered?

4. What problems seem to emerge when an organization gets larger?

5. What organizational changes might you recommend to the auto companies? The airline industry?

developing workplace skills

1. There is no better way to understand the effects of having many layers of management on communication accuracy than the game of Message Relay. Choose seven or more members of the class and have them leave the classroom. Then choose one person to read the following paragraph and another student to listen. Call in one of the students from outside and have the "listener" tell him or her what information was in the paragraph. Then bring in another student and have the new listener repeat the information to him or her. Continue the process with all those who left the room. Do not allow anyone in the class to offer corrections as each listener becomes the storyteller in turn. In this way, all the students can hear how the facts become distorted over time. The distortions and mistakes are often quite humorous, but they are not so funny in organizations such as Ford, which once had 22 layers of management.

   Here's the paragraph:

   Dealers in the midwest region have received over 130 complaints about steering on the new Commander and Roadhandler models of our minivans. Apparently, the front suspension system is weak and the ball joints are wearing too fast. This causes slippage in the linkage and results in oversteering. Mr. Berenstein has been notified, but so far only 213 of 4,300 dealers have received repair kits.

2. Describe some informal groups within an organization with which you are familiar at school or work. What have you noticed about how those groups help or hinder progress in the organization?

3. Imagine you are working for Kitchen Magic, an appliance manufacturer that produces dishwashers. A competitor introduces a new dishwasher that uses sound waves not only to clean even the worst burned-on food but also to sterilize dishes and silverware. You need to develop a similar offering fast, or your company will lose market share. Write an e-mail to management outlining the problem and explaining your rationale for recommending use of a cross-functional team to respond quickly.

4. Divide the class into teams of five. Each team should imagine your firm, a producer of athletic shoes, has been asked to join a virtual network. How might you minimize the potential problems of joining? Begin by defining a virtual corporation and listing its advantages and disadvantages. Each team should report its solutions to the class.

5. Many work groups of the future, including management, will be cross-functional and self-managed. To practice working in such an organization, break into groups of five or so students, preferably with different backgrounds and interests. Each group must work together to prepare a report on the advantages and disadvantages of working in teams. Many of the problems and advantages of cross-functional, self-managed teams should emerge in your group as you try to complete this assignment. Each group should report to the class how it handled the problems and benefited from the advantages.

taking it to the net

Purpose

To learn more about the process of organizational change.

Exercise

Xerox is a very familiar corporate name in the United States. There was a time, however, when the company was faltering and needed to adapt to foreign competition. This exercise will help you see how complex such change can be.

1. Do an online search for Xerox Corporation.

2. Read through the history of the company and describe its current strengths, weaknesses, opportunities, and threats (a SWOT analysis; see Chapter 7).

3. Describe Xerox's reasons for success.

casing the web

To access the case "IBM Is Both an Outsourcer and a Major Outsource for Others," visit **www.mhhe.com/ubl0e**

video case

To access the video case featuring New Belgium Brewery, visit **www.mhhe.com/ubl0e**

Human Resource Management

FINDING AND KEEPING THE BEST EMPLOYEES

LEARNING
goals

After you have read and studied this chapter, you should be able to

1 Explain the importance of human resource management, and describe current issues in managing human resources.

2 Illustrate the effects of legislation on human resource management.

3 Summarize the five steps in human resource planning.

4 Describe methods that companies use to recruit new employees, and explain some of the issues that make recruitment challenging.

5 Outline the six steps in selecting employees.

6 Illustrate employee training and development methods.

7 Trace the six steps in appraising employee performance.

8 Summarize the objectives of employee compensation programs, and evaluate pay systems and fringe benefits.

9 Demonstrate how managers use scheduling plans to adapt to workers' needs.

10 Describe how employees can move through a company: promotion, reassignment, termination, and retirement.

profile

Getting to Know

X **Mark Parker**

CEO of Nike

Sometimes the relationship between managers and employees has an "us vs. them" quality. Wary staff may not respect superiors they view as out of touch with the day-to-day operations of the business. After all, many of today's upper managers did not work their way to the top of the companies they now lead. Moving from high-level positions at a number of different firms is common practice in some industries. Nevertheless, there are loyal veterans with decades of technical experience who run many of the world's most successful companies.

Such is the case for Nike's CEO Mark Parker. As a champion marathoner at Penn State, Parker often modified his running shoes to increase their performance. After graduating in 1977 he was hired by Nike's research and development department to turn his hobby into a career in footwear design. During his first years at the company, though, Nike R&D was little more than a shoe shop instead of a hotbed of innovation. By the mid-1980s the company's footwear division was in dire straits as Reebok's increasing market dominance caused Nike's net income to fall 75 percent.

In an effort to turn its fortunes around, the company turned to the R&D department for ideas. Parker and his design team worked feverishly on a project called Visible Air, a technology that placed a hole in the sole that showed Nike's unique cushioning at work. By 1986 the new line of Air shoes soon became a hit, not only with athletes but casual consumers too. Over the following decade Parker played an integral part in the development of other Nike footwear mainstays, such as the Air Jordan and Air Force One brands. Although admittedly remaining a designer at heart, he steadily ascended the corporate ladder until finally assuming the title of CEO in 2006. Parker's business goals for Nike are ambitious. By 2015 he hopes to increase revenues by more than 40 percent to $27 billion a year.

In order to hit his financial targets Parker knows he needs to keep the company's 33,000 employees motivated and thinking creatively. While he appreciates the respect the employees have for his own accomplishments at Nike, he wants to provide a work environment that helps employees flourish as well. Parker has certainly taken care of the latter for the 7,000 workers employed at Nike's world headquarters in Beaverton, Oregon. The sprawling 17-building campus is home to two employee gyms for the exercise-obsessed Nike staff. The Lance Armstrong gym alone is home to an Olympic-size pool as well as workout spaces for yoga, spinning classes and Pilates. Besides its ample exercise facilities, the headquarters also hosts five restaurants where employees can eat lunch and watch the big games of the day. Nike also offers free on-site childcare, paid leave and a 50 percent discount on its products to all employees. It's no wonder why Nike was named one of the 100 Best Places to Work by *Fortune* magazine in 2006, 2007, and 2008.

Still, it's impossible to talk about labor at Nike without recalling accusations of inhumane working conditions at the factories of the company's contractors overseas. Parker has taken active strides toward fixing the problem. Nike now employees more than 130 people to keep constant watch on the safety and energy impact of the 20 percent of its contractors who produce 80 percent of the company's goods. Parker and his team have made progress, although he admits that the process is a "never-ending challenge."

Really, though, the same thing could be said for almost every aspect of the manager–employee relationship. In this chapter, you'll learn how businesses that succeed like Nike recruit, manage, and make the most of their employees.

Sources: Ellen McGirt, "How Nike's CEO Shook Up the Shoe Industry," *Fast Company,* September 1, 2010; Jessica Flint, "Inside the Swoosh," *Bloomberg Businessweek,* November 29–December 5, 2010; and "Company Overview—Awards and Recognition," Nikebiz.com, accessed May 2011.

NAME THAT company

This company is one of the largest U.S. steel producers. It pays its teams bonuses that are calculated on quality—tons of steel that go out the door with no defects. There are no limits on bonuses a team can earn; they usually average around $20,000 per employee each year. Name that company. (Find the answer in the chapter.)

LEARNING goal 1

Explain the importance of human resource management, and describe current issues in managing human resources.

WORKING WITH PEOPLE IS JUST THE BEGINNING

Students often say they want to go into human resource management because they want to "work with people." Human resource managers do work with people, but they are also deeply involved in planning, record keeping, and other administrative duties. To begin a career in human resource management, you need a better reason than "I want to work with people." This chapter will tell you what else human resource management is all about.

Human resource management (HRM) is the process of determining human resource needs and then recruiting, selecting, developing, motivating, evaluating, compensating, and scheduling employees to achieve organizational goals (see Figure 11.1). For many years, human resource management was called "personnel" and involved clerical functions such as screening applications, keeping records, processing the payroll, and finding new employees when necessary. The roles and responsibilities of HRM have evolved primarily because of two key factors: (1) organizations' recognition of employees as their ultimate resource and (2) changes in the law that rewrote many traditional practices. Let's explore both.

human resource management (HRM)
The process of determining human resource needs and then recruiting, selecting, developing, motivating, evaluating, compensating, and scheduling employees to achieve organizational goals.

Developing the Ultimate Resource

One reason human resource management is receiving increased attention now is that the U.S. economy has experienced a major shift—from traditional manufacturing industries to service and high-tech manufacturing industries that require highly technical job skills. This shift means that many workers must be retrained for new, more challenging jobs. They truly are the ultimate resource. People develop the ideas that eventually become products to satisfy consumers' wants and needs. Take away their creative minds, and leading firms such as Disney, Apple, Procter & Gamble, Google, and General Electric would be nothing.

Legal Environment

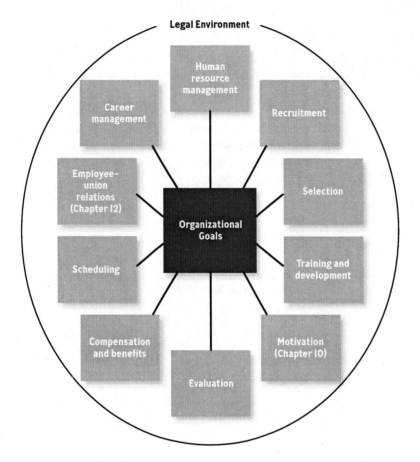

figure II.I

HUMAN RESOURCE MANAGEMENT
As this figure shows, human resource management is more than hiring and firing personnel. All activities are designed to achieve organizational goals within the laws that affect human resource management. (Note that human resource management includes motivation, as discussed in Chapter IO, and employee-union relations, as discussed in Chapter I2.)

In the past, human resources were plentiful, so there was little need to nurture and develop them. If you needed qualified people, you simply hired them. If they didn't work out, you fired them and found others. Most firms assigned the job of recruiting, selecting, training, evaluating, compensating, motivating, and, yes, firing people to the functional departments that employed them, like accounting, manufacturing, and marketing. Today the job of human resource management has taken on an increased role in the firm since *qualified* employees are much scarcer, which makes recruiting and retaining people more important and more difficult.[1]

In the future, human resource management may become the firm's most critical function, responsible for dealing with all aspects of a business's most critical resource—people. In fact, the human resource function has become so important that it's no longer the job of just one department; it's a responsibility of *all* managers. What are some human resource challenges all managers face? We'll outline a few next.

The Human Resource Challenge

Many of the changes that have had the most dramatic impact on U.S. business are those in the labor force. The ability to compete in global markets depends on new ideas, new products, and new levels of productivity—in other words, on people with good ideas. These are some of the challenges and opportunities in human resources:[2]

- Shortages of trained workers in growth areas, such as computer technology, biotechnology, robotics, green technology, and the sciences.
- An increasing number of skilled and unskilled workers from declining industries, such as steel and automobiles, who are unemployed or underemployed and need retraining. *Underemployed workers* are those who have more skills or knowledge than their current jobs require or those with part-time jobs who want to work full time.
- A growing percentage of new workers who are undereducated and unprepared for jobs in the contemporary business environment.
- A shortage of workers in skilled trades due to retirement of aging baby boomers.

U.S. firms face a shortage of workers skilled in areas like science, green technology, and the development of clean energy sources like this wind turbine. What other job markets do you think will grow as companies focus more on environmentally friendly policies? Which ones appeal to you?

- An increasing number of baby boomers who, due to the recession, delay retirement (preventing the promotion of younger workers) or move to lower-level jobs (increasing the supply of workers for such jobs).
- An increasing number of both single-parent and two-income families, resulting in a demand for job sharing, maternity leave, and special career advancement programs for women.
- A shift in employee attitudes toward work. Leisure time has become a much higher priority, as have flextime and a shorter workweek.
- A recession that took a toll on employee morale and increased the demand for temporary and part-time workers.
- A challenge from overseas labor pools whose members work for lower wages and are subject to fewer laws and regulations than U.S. workers. This results in many jobs being outsourced overseas.
- An increased demand for benefits tailored to the individual yet cost-effective to the company.
- Growing concerns over health care, elder care, child care, drug testing, workplace violence (all discussed in Chapter 12), and opportunities for people with disabilities.
- Changes in health care laws that have added a large number of new regulations that employers must read, interpret, implement, and track.
- A decreased sense of employee loyalty, which raises employee turnover and the cost of replacing lost workers.

Given these issues, you can see why human resource management has taken a central place in management thinking. However, significant changes in laws covering hiring, safety, unionization, equal pay, and affirmative action have also had a major influence. Let's look at their impact on human resource management.

LEARNING goal 2

Illustrate the effects of legislation on human resource management.

LAWS AFFECTING HUMAN RESOURCE MANAGEMENT

Until the 1930s, the U.S. government had little to do with human resource decisions. Since then, legislation and legal decisions have greatly affected all areas of human resource management, from hiring to training to monitoring working conditions (see Figure 11.2). These laws were passed because many businesses did not exercise fair labor practices voluntarily.

One of the more important pieces of social legislation passed by Congress was the Civil Rights Act of 1964. This act generated much debate and was amended 97 times before final passage. Title VII of that act brought the

National *Labor Relations Act of 1935.* Established collective bargaining in labor–management relations and limited management interference in the right of employees to have a collective bargaining agent.

Fair Labor Standards Act of 1938. Established a minimum wage and overtime pay for employees working more than 40 hours a week. Amendments expanded the classes of workers covered, raised the minimum wage, redefined regular-time work, raised overtime payments, and equalized pay scales for men and women.

Manpower Development and Training Act of 1962. Provided for the training and retraining of unemployed workers.

Equal Pay Act of 1963. Specified that men and women doing equal jobs must be paid the same wage.

Civil Rights Act of 1964. For firms with 15 or more employees, outlawed discrimination in employment based on sex, race, color, religion, or national origin.

Age Discrimination in Employment Act of 1967. Outlawed employment practices that discriminate against people 40 and older. An amendment outlaws requiring retirement by a specific age.

Occupational Safety and Health Act of 1970. Regulated the degree to which employees can be exposed to hazardous substances and specified the safety equipment the employer must provide.

Equal Employment Opportunity Act of 1972. Strengthened the Equal Employment Opportunity Commission (EEOC) and authorized the EEOC to set guidelines for human resource management.

Comprehensive Employment and Training Act of 1973 (CETA). Provided funds for training unemployed workers.

Employee Retirement Income Security Act of 1974 (ERISA). Regulated and insured company retirement plans.

Immigration Reform and Control Act of 1986. Required employers to verify employment eligibility of all new hires including U.S. citizens.

Supreme Court ruling against set-aside programs (affirmative action), 1989. Declared that setting aside 30 percent of contracting jobs for minority businesses was reverse discrimination and unconstitutional.

Older Workers Benefit Protection Act, 1990. Protects older people from signing away their rights to pensions and protection from illegal age discrimination.

Civil Rights Act of 1991. For firms with over 15 employees, extends the right to a jury trial and punitive damages to victims of intentional job discrimination.

Americans with Disabilities Act of 1990 (1992 implementation). Prohibits employers from discriminating against qualified individuals with disabilities in hiring, advancement, or compensation and requires them to adapt the workplace if necessary.

Family and Medical Leave Act of 1993. Businesses with 50 or more employees must provide up to 12 weeks of unpaid leave per year upon birth or adoption of an employee's child or upon serious illness of a parent, spouse, or child.

Americans with Disabilities Amendments Act of 2008 (ADA). Provides broader protection for disabled workers and reverses Supreme Court decisions deemed too restrictive. Adds disabilities such as epilepsy and cancer to ADA coverage.

figure II.2

GOVERNMENT LEGISLATION AFFECTING HUMAN RESOURCE MANAGEMENT

affirmative action
Employment activities designed to "right past wrongs" by increasing opportunities for minorities and women.

reverse discrimination
Discrimination against members of a dominant or majority group (e.g. whites or males) usually as a result of policies designed to correct previous discrimination against minority or disadvantaged groups.

The Americans with Disabilities Act guarantees that all U.S. workers have equal opportunity in employment. This legislation requires businesses to make "reasonable accommodations" on the job for people with disabilities. What required accommodations do you think would be reasonable?

government directly into the operations of human resource management. Title VII prohibits discrimination in hiring, firing, compensation, apprenticeships, training, terms, conditions, or privileges of employment based on race, religion, creed, sex, or national origin. Age was later added to the conditions of the act. The Civil Rights Act of 1964 was expected to stamp out discrimination in the workplace, but specific language in it made enforcement quite difficult. Congress took on the task of amending the law.

In 1972, the Equal Employment Opportunity Act (EEOA) was added as an amendment to Title VII. It strengthened the Equal Employment Opportunity Commission (EEOC), which was created by the Civil Rights Act, by giving it rather broad powers. For example, it permitted the EEOC to issue guidelines for acceptable employer conduct in administering equal employment opportunity. The EEOC also mandated specific record-keeping procedures, and Congress vested it with the power of enforcement to ensure these mandates were carried out. The EEOC became a formidable regulatory force in the administration of human resource management.

Perhaps the most controversial policy enforced by the EEOC was **affirmative action**, designed to "right past wrongs" by increasing opportunities for minorities and women. Interpretation of the affirmative action law led employers to actively recruit, and in some cases give preference to, women and minority group members. Questions persist about the legality of affirmative action and the effect it may have in creating a sort of reverse discrimination in the workplace. **Reverse discrimination** has been defined as discriminating against members of a dominant or majority group (e.g. whites or males) usually as a result of policies designed to correct previous discrimination against minority or disadvantaged groups. The issue has generated much heated debate as well as many lawsuits.[3]

The Civil Rights Act of 1991 expanded the remedies available to victims of discrimination by amending Title VII of the Civil Rights Act of 1964. Now victims of discrimination have the right to a jury trial and punitive damages. Human resource managers must follow court decisions closely to see how the law is enforced.[4] The Legal Briefcase box discusses a case that may change the way class action discrimination disputes are handled in the future.

The Office of Federal Contract Compliance Programs (OFCCP) ensures that employers comply with nondiscrimination and affirmative action laws and regulations when doing business with the federal government.

Laws Protecting Employees with Disabilities and Older Employees

As you read above, laws prohibit discrimination related to race, sex, or age in hiring, firing, and training. The Vocational Rehabilitation Act of 1973 extended protection to people with any physical or mental disability.

The Americans with Disabilities Act of 1990 (ADA) requires employers to give applicants with physical or mental disabilities the same consideration for employment as people without disabilities. It also requires making "reasonable accommodations" for employees with disabilities, such as modifying equipment or widening doorways. Accommodations are not always expensive; an inexpensive headset can allow someone with cerebral

LEGAL briefcase

The Million Woman Suit against Walmart

From the late 1990s until 2004, the retail giant Walmart relied on a "tap-on-the-shoulder" policy for management promotion. Rather than posting openings and accepting applications, it is charged that managers simply promoted their colleagues and friends from within. And since most of the company's upper staff consisted of men, the new crop of managers remained overwhelmingly male.

Such alleged unchecked gender dominance led to widespread bias, according to the plaintiffs of a class action discrimination suit filed by more than one million women. (Class-action lawsuits pool individual claims into a single case that creates the potential for a large judgment and increases the pressure on businesses to settle.) The case charges that not only did the company leapfrog over women for leadership roles, it engaged in pay inequality and harassment.

Walmart argued that with such a large field of plaintiffs it would be impossible for them to verify each individual claim. Those in the business community who supported Walmart agreed that a ruling in favor of the women would have led to

a flood of class-action lawsuits based on vague evidence. Supporters of the women, on the other hand, maintained that the huge number of litigants reflected the scope of Walmart's discriminatory policies.

On June 11, 2011, the U.S. Supreme Court (on a 5–4 vote) dismissed the enormous class-action suit that sought billions of dollars on behalf of the over one million women. The Court did not decide whether Walmart had, in fact, discriminated against the women, only that they could not proceed as a class. Walmart and business groups applauded the court's decision, while consumer groups strongly criticized it. Both sides agreed, however, that the decision was momentous.

Sources: Greg Stohr, "Wal-Mart Faces the Big Box of Bias Suits," *Bloomberg Businessweek,* March 24, 2011; James Oliphant and David G. Savage, "Supreme Court Appears Poised to Reject Class Action in Wal-Mart Sex-bias Case," *Los Angeles Times,* March 30, 2011; and Adam Liptak, "Justices Rule for Walmart in Class-Action Bias Case," *New York Times,* June 20, 2011.

palsy to talk on the phone.[5] The ADA also protects individuals with disabilities from discrimination in public accommodations, transportation, and telecommunications.[6]

Most companies have no trouble making structural changes to be accommodating. Some, however, find cultural changes difficult. Employers used to think that being fair meant treating everyone the same, but *accommodation* in fact means treating people *according to their specific needs.* That can include putting up barriers to isolate people readily distracted by noise, reassigning workers to new tasks, and making changes in supervisors' management styles.

In 2008, Congress passed the Americans with Disabilities Amendments Act, which overturned Supreme Court decisions that had reduced protections for certain people with disabilities such as diabetes, epilepsy, heart disease, autism, major depression, and cancer.[7] In 2011, the EEOC issued new regulations that widen the range of disabilities covered by the ADA and shifted the burden of proof of disability in labor disputes from employees to business owners.[8] Enforcement promises to be a continuing issue for human resource management. [9]

The Age Discrimination in Employment Act of 1967 (ADEA) protects individuals 40 or older from employment and workplace discrimination in hiring, firing, promotion, layoff, compensation, benefits, job assignments, and training. The ADEA is enforced by the EEOC, applies to employers with 20 or more employees, and protects both employees and job applicants. It also outlaws mandatory retirement in most organizations. It does, however, allow age restrictions for certain job categories such as airline pilot or bus driver if evidence shows that the ability to perform significantly diminishes with age or that age imposes a danger to society.

Effects of Legislation

Clearly, laws ranging from the Social Security Act of 1935 to the 2008 Americans with Disabilities Amendments Act require human resource managers to keep abreast of laws and court decisions to effectively perform their jobs. Choosing a career in human resource management offers a challenge to anyone willing to put forth the effort. Remember:

- Employers must know and act in accordance with the legal rights of their employees or risk costly court cases.
- Legislation affects all areas of human resource management, from hiring and training to compensation.
- Court cases demonstrate that it is sometimes legal to go beyond providing equal rights for minorities and women to provide special employment (affirmative action) and training to correct discrimination in the past.
- New court cases and legislation change human resource management almost daily; the only way to keep current is to read the business literature and stay familiar with emerging issues.

progress assessment

- What is human resource management?
- What did Title VII of the Civil Rights Act of 1964 achieve?
- What is the EEOC, and what was the intention of affirmative action?
- What does *accommodations* mean in the Americans with Disabilities Act of 1990?

LEARNING goal 3

Summarize the five steps in human resource planning.

DETERMINING A FIRM'S HUMAN RESOURCE NEEDS

All management, including human resource management, begins with planning. The five steps in the human resource planning process are:

1. *Preparing a human resource inventory of the organization's employees.* This inventory should include ages, names, education, capabilities, training, specialized skills, and other relevant information (such as languages spoken). It reveals whether the labor force is technically up-to-date and thoroughly trained.

2. *Preparing a job analysis.* A **job analysis** is a study of what employees do who hold various job titles. It's necessary in order to recruit and train employees with the necessary skills to do the job. The results of job analysis are two written statements: job descriptions and job specifications. A **job description** specifies the objectives of the job, the type of work, the responsibilities and duties, working conditions, and the job's relationship to other functions. **Job specifications** are a written summary of the minimal education and skills to do a particular job. In short, job descriptions are about the job, and job specifications are about the person who does the job. Visit the Occupational Information Network (O*NET) at www.onetcenter.org for detailed information about job analyses and job descriptions. See Figure 11.3 for a hypothetical job description and job specifications.

3. *Assessing future human resource demand.* Because technology changes rapidly, effective human resource managers are proactive; that is, they forecast the organization's requirements and train people ahead of time or ensure trained people are available when needed.

4. *Assessing future labor supply.* The labor force is constantly shifting: getting older, becoming more technically oriented, attracting more women. Some workers will be scarcer in the future, like computer and robotic repair workers, and others will be oversupplied, like assembly-line workers.

5. *Establishing a strategic plan.* The human resource strategic plan must address recruiting, selecting, training, developing, appraising, compensating, and scheduling the labor force. Because the first four steps lead up to this one, we'll focus on them in the rest of the chapter.

job analysis
A study of what employees do who hold various job titles.

job description
A summary of the objectives of a job, the type of work to be done, the responsibilities and duties, the working conditions, and the relationship of the job to other functions.

job specifications
A written summary of the minimum qualifications required of workers to do a particular job.

JOB ANALYSIS

Observe current sales representatives doing the job.

Discuss job with sales managers.

Have current sales reps keep a diary of their activities.

JOB DESCRIPTION	JOB SPECIFICATIONS
Primary objective is to sell company's products to stores in Territory Z. Duties include servicing accounts and maintaining positive relationships with clients. Responsibilities include: • Introducing the new products to store managers in the area. • Helping the store managers estimate the volume to order. • Negotiating prime shelf space. • Explaining sales promotion activities to store managers. • Stocking and maintaining shelves in stores that wish such service.	Characteristics of the person qualifying for this job include: • Two years' sales experience. • Positive attitude. • Well-groomed appearance. • Good communication skills. • High school diploma and two years of college credit.

figure II.3

JOB ANALYSIS
A job analysis yields two important statements: job descriptions and job specifications. Here you have a job description and job specifications for a sales representative.

Some companies use advanced technology to perform the human resource planning process more efficiently. IBM manages its global workforce of about 100,000 employees and 100,000 subcontractors with a database that matches employee skills, experiences, schedules, and references with jobs available. If a client in Quebec, Canada, has a month-long project requiring a consultant who speaks English and French, has an advanced degree in engineering, and is experienced with Linux programming, IBM's database can find the best-suited consultant available and put him or her in touch with the client.

LEARNING goal 4

Describe methods that companies use to recruit new employees, and explain some of the issues that make recruitment challenging.

RECRUITING EMPLOYEES FROM A DIVERSE POPULATION

recruitment
The set of activities used to obtain a sufficient number of the right employees at the right time.

Recruitment is the set of activities for obtaining the right number of qualified people at the right time. Its purpose is to select those who best meet the needs of the organization. You might think a continuous flow of new people into the workforce makes recruiting easy. On the contrary, it's become very challenging for several reasons:

- Some organizations have policies that demand promotions from within, operate under union regulations, or offer low wages, which makes recruiting and keeping employees difficult or subject to outside influence and restrictions.
- The emphasis on corporate culture, teamwork, and participative management makes it important to hire people who not only are skilled but also fit in with the culture and leadership style of the

Human resource managers today have the opportunity to recruit people from a wide range of cultural and ethnic backgrounds. What are some of the advantages of a diverse workforce?

External sources

- Private employment agencies
- Public employment agencies
- Personal applications
- Management consultants
- New graduates
- Former employees
- Part-time applicants
- Competing organizations
- Union organizations
- Advertisements
- Temporary help services
- Union halls
- Trade schools
- College placement offices
- Newspaper ads
- Trade associations
- Business associates
- College professors
- Internet
- Job fairs
- Cooperative education internships

Human Resource Department

Selection

Hiring

Orientation and training

Internal sources

- Transfers
- Promotions
- Employee recommendations
- Retrained employees
- Department reorganizations

organization.[10] Wegmans Food Markets (a perennial member of *Fortune* magazine's list of best companies to work for) encourages employees to do whatever they think is necessary to make a customer happy. For example, they don't have to ask a supervisor if they need to cook a Thanksgiving turkey at the store for a customer whose oven is too small or go to a customer's home to check a food order.

- Sometimes people with the necessary skills are not available; then workers must be hired and trained internally.

Human resource managers can turn to many sources for recruiting assistance (see Figure 11.4). *Internal sources* include current employees who can be transferred or promoted or who can recommend others to hire. Using internal sources is less expensive than recruiting from outside and helps maintain employee morale. However, it isn't always possible to find qualified workers within the company, so human resource managers also use *external sources* such as advertisements, public and private employment agencies, college placement bureaus, management consultants, Internet sites, professional organizations, referrals, and online and walk-in applications.

Recruiting qualified workers may be particularly difficult for small businesses with few staff members and less-than-competitive compensation to attract external sources. CareerBuilder.com and Monster.com have helped such firms. They attract more than 80 million visitors per month.[11] The Spotlight on Small Business box on p. 300 offers additional ways small businesses can recruit.

figure II.4

EMPLOYEE SOURCES

Internal sources are often given first consideration, so it's useful to get a recommendation from a current employee of the firm for which you want to work. College placement offices are also an important source. Be sure to learn about such facilities early so that you can plan a strategy throughout your college career.

It's Not Easy Being Small

To survive, it's critical for small businesses to recruit and retain qualified workers. However, competing for top talent is difficult when you can't afford corporate-level benefits or expensive recruiters to hunt down the best people. Despite these hurdles, small-business management consultants say there are many ways to lure desirable workers:

- *Transform ads into promotional tools.* Ecoprint, a small print shop in Maryland, touts the benefits of working for this collegial company in its regular advertisements.

- *Post job openings on the Internet.* Running an ad on an online service like CareerBuilder.com or Monster.com for 30 days costs about one-fourth the price of a comparable ad in the *New York Times* that runs for one week.

- *Let your staff help recruit and select hires.* The more staff is engaged in the search and interview process, the better chance to find recruits with the right personality and skills.

- *Create a dynamic workplace that attracts local, energetic applicants.* Sometimes word-of-mouth is the most effective recruiting tool.

- *Test-drive an employee.* Hiring contingent workers allows you to test candidates for a few months before deciding whether to make an offer of permanent employment.

- *Hire customers.* Loyal customers sometimes make the smartest employees. Build-A-Bear Workshop often hires customers who come into its stores and exhibit a real interest in the company and its products.

- *Check community groups and local government agencies.* Don't forget to check state-run employment agencies. Many nonprofit organizations serve immigrants new to a region or people in need of a job who become excellent candidates you can train.

- *Work hard for publicity in local media.* Publicity is more believable than advertising.

- *Lure candidates with a policy of promotions and raises.* Most employees want to know they can move up. Give employees an incentive for learning the business.

- *Outsource fringe benefit management to a professional employer organization (PEO).* It's tough to build a benefits program equivalent to those offered by large companies, but PEOs may offer lower insurance rates due to economies of scale. Face it, any way you can close the gap may help attract qualified workers.

Sources: "7 Tips for Motivating Employees," *Inc.*, April 20, 2010; Leigh Buchanan, "Opening the Books and Motivating the Workers," *Inc.*, June 8, 2010; and Lou DuBois, "How to Build a Corporate Culture of Trust," *Inc.*, August 2, 2010.

LEARNING goal 5

Outline the six steps in selecting employees.

SELECTING EMPLOYEES WHO WILL BE PRODUCTIVE

selection
The process of gathering information and deciding who should be hired, under legal guidelines, to serve the best interests of the individual and the organization.

Selection is the process of gathering information and deciding who should be hired, under legal guidelines, to serve the best interests of the individual and the organization. Selecting and training employees are extremely expensive processes in some firms. Just think what's involved: advertising or recruiting agency fees, interview time, medical exams, training costs, unproductive time spent learning the job, possible travel and moving expenses, and more. It can cost one and a half times the employee's annual salary to recruit, process, and train even an entry-level worker, and over six figures for a top manager. A typical selection process has six steps:

1. *Obtaining complete application forms.* Although equal employment laws limit the kinds of questions that can appear, applications help reveal the applicant's educational background, work experience, career objectives, and other qualifications directly related to the job.

    Large retail employers like Winn-Dixie and Finish Line make the application process more efficient by using an automated program called Workforce Acquisition. An applicant sits at a computer and answers questions about job experience, time available to work, and personality. The software e-mails a report to the hiring manager recommending whether to interview the applicant and, if so, suggesting questions to ask. Mike Marchetti, executive vice president of store operations for Finish Line, says his company processed 330,000 applications, eliminating 60,000 interview hours and reducing turnover 24 percent.[12]

2. *Conducting initial and follow-up interviews.* A staff member from the human resource department often screens applicants in a first interview. If the interviewer considers the applicant a potential hire, the manager who will supervise the new employee may interview the applicant as well. It's important that managers prepare adequately for the interview to avoid selection decisions they may regret.[13] No matter how innocent the intention, missteps such as asking about pregnancy or child care could later be evidence if the applicant files discrimination charges.

3. *Giving employment tests.* Organizations often use tests to measure basic competency in specific job skills like welding or firefighting, and to help evaluate applicants' personalities and interests. The tests should always be directly related to the job. Employment tests have been legally challenged as potential means of discrimination.[14] Many companies test potential employees in assessment centers where they perform actual job tasks. Such testing can make the selection process more efficient and will generally satisfy legal requirements.

4. *Conducting background investigations.* Most organizations now investigate a candidate's work record, school record, credit history, and references more carefully than in the past to help identify those most likely to succeed. It is simply too costly to hire, train, and motivate people only to lose them and have to start the process over. Services such as LexisNexis allow prospective employers not only to conduct speedy background checks of criminal records, driving records, and credit histories but also to verify work experience and professional and educational credentials.[15]

> *Choosing qualified employees is a challenge. Psychologist Turhan Canli believes he can tell what makes some people better suited to a job than others by using human physiology mechanisms. Canli uses brain scans to see how people react to certain word-image combinations and believes you can read personalities from them. What do you think are key criteria for evaluating job candidates?*

PART 4 ✳ **Management of Human Resources: Motivating Employees to Produce Quality Goods and Services**

5. *Obtaining results from physical exams.* There are obvious benefits to hiring physically and mentally healthy people. However, according to the Americans with Disabilities Act, medical tests cannot be given just to screen out individuals. In some states, physical exams can be given only after an offer of employment has been accepted. In states that allow pre-employment physical exams, they must be given to everyone applying for the same position. Pre-employment testing to detect drug or alcohol abuse has been controversial, as has screening to detect carriers of HIV, the virus that causes AIDS.

6. *Establishing trial (probationary) periods.* Often an organization will hire an employee conditionally to let the person prove his or her value on the job. After a specified probationary period (perhaps six months or a year), the firm can either permanently hire or discharge that employee on the basis of supervisors' evaluations. Although such systems make it easier to fire inefficient or problem employees, they do not eliminate the high cost of turnover.

contingent workers
Employees that include part-time workers, temporary workers, seasonal workers, independent contractors, interns, and co-op students.

The selection process is often long and difficult, but it is worth the effort to select new employees carefully because of the high cost of replacing them.[16] Care helps ensure that new employees meet all requirements, including communication skills, education, technical skills, experience, personality, and health.

Hiring Contingent Workers

A company with employment needs that vary—from hour to hour, day to day, week to week, or season to season—may find it cost-effective to hire contingent workers. **Contingent workers** include part-time workers (anyone who works 1 to 34 hours per week), temporary workers (workers paid by temporary employment agencies), seasonal workers, independent contractors, interns, and co-op students.

Companies may also hire contingent workers when full-timers are on some type of leave (such as maternity leave), when there is a peak demand for labor or products (like the holiday shopping season), or when quick service to customers is a priority. Companies also tend to hire more contingent workers in an uncertain economy, particularly when they are available and qualified, and when the jobs require minimal training.

Contingent workers receive few benefits; they are rarely offered health insurance, vacation time, or company pensions. They also tend to earn less than permanent workers do. On the positive side, many on temporary assignments are eventually offered full-time positions. Managers see using temporary workers as a way of weeding out poor workers and finding good hires. Although exact numbers are difficult to gather, the Bureau of Labor Statistics estimates there are approximately 5.7 million contingent workers in the United States, with the majority under age 25.[17] Experts say temps are filling openings in an increasingly broad range of jobs, from unskilled manufacturing and distribution positions to middle management. Increasing numbers of contingent workers are educated professionals such as accountants, attorneys, and engineers.

Seasonal businesses, such as Halloween stores and haunted houses, depend on hiring contingent (temporary) workers to help them through the limited times they are operational. What are the advantages and disadvantages of hiring contingent workers? What are the advantages and disadvantages of being a contingent worker?

Many companies include college students in their contingent workforce plan. Working with temporary staffing agencies, companies have easier access to workers who have already been screened. Of course, temp agencies benefit college students as well. Once the agencies have assessed the workers, their information is entered into their databases. Then when students are coming back in town for vacations or whatever, they can call the agency and ask them to put their names into the system for work assignments. No need to spend time searching for openings or running around town for interviews. Randstad USA, a global staffing services giant with over 350 branches in the United States, welcomes college students primarily because of their computer skills and familiarity with many of the popular software programs companies use.[18]

College interns can be considered temporary workers. However, when these internships are unpaid, ethical questions could arise (see the nearby Making Ethical Decisions box).

In an era of rapid change and economic uncertainty, some contingent workers have even found that temping can be more secure than full-time employment.

progress assessment

- What are the five steps in human resource planning?
- What factors make it difficult to recruit qualified employees?
- What are the six steps in the selection process?
- Who is considered a contingent worker, and why do companies hire such workers?

LEARNING goal 6

Illustrate employee training and development methods.

TRAINING AND DEVELOPING EMPLOYEES FOR OPTIMUM PERFORMANCE

As technology and other innovations change the workplace, companies must offer training programs that often are quite sophisticated. The term **training and development** includes all attempts to improve productivity by increasing an employee's ability to perform. A well-designed training program often leads to higher retention rates, increased productivity, and greater job satisfaction. Employers in the United States generally find that money for training is well spent. *Training* focuses on short-term skills, whereas *development* focuses on long-term abilities. Both include three steps: (1) assessing organization needs and employee skills to determine training needs; (2) designing training activities to meet identified needs; and (3) evaluating the training's effectiveness. Some common training and development activities are employee orientation, on-the-job training, apprenticeships, off-the-job training, vestibule training, job simulation, and management training.

- **Orientation** is the activity that initiates new employees into the organization; to fellow employees; to their immediate supervisors; and to the policies, practices, and objectives of the firm. Orientation programs

training and development
All attempts to improve productivity by increasing an employee's ability to perform. Training focuses on short-term skills, whereas development focuses on long-term abilities.

orientation
The activity that introduces new employees to the organization; to fellow employees; to their immediate supervisors; and to the policies, practices, and objectives of the firm.

MAKING ethical decisions

http://unpaidinternslawsuit.com

Are Unpaid Interns Too Interred?

Traditionally, unpaid internships have been a great way for young people to transition from college to the workforce. The sacrifice of financial benefits usually pays off in practical experience the interns otherwise would not get in a classroom. Businesses in turn risk nothing financially, but could end up benefiting in the long run if an intern eventually becomes a key paid employee. However, with entry-level positions scarce in today's job market, interns can end up in an unpaid position for as long as six months with no chance of advancement. At that point, interns may wonder if they are improving their chances for a rewarding career or simply performing free services for the company.

In order to distinguish a quality internship from a dead end, simply look at the tasks you're asked to do every day. If your central duties include keeping the coffee pot full or running errands, chances are that those jobs will not translate into valuable experience down the line. Interns should be taught about the day-to-day duties of a business, not how to be professional gofers. Management must also be sure to outline an intern's responsibilities explicitly and provide regular feedback. Even without a regular paycheck, internships can be beneficial as long as the person is compensated in experience.

Some businesses are quite willing to give interns plenty of professional responsibility. For example, one Toronto newspaper fired all of its paid staff writers and replaced them with unpaid interns.

Is it ethical for companies to use unpaid interns if they know they will not have any jobs to offer at the end of the internships or if the unpaid internships replace paid jobs? Why or why not?

Source: Knight Kiplinger, "Are Unpaid Interns Exploited by Employers?" *Kiplinger*, April 2011; Diane Brady, "Turmoil Strategies," *Bloomberg Businessweek*, February 10, 2009; and Bruce Weinstein, "Dos and Don'ts of Unpaid Internships," *Bloomberg Businessweek*, May 28, 2010.

---

range from informal talks to formal activities that last a day or more and often include scheduled visits to various departments and required reading of handbooks. For example, at Zappos every new employee in the online retailer's Henderson, Nevada, headquarters must spend two weeks answering customer calls, two weeks learning in a classroom, and a week shipping boxes in the company's Kentucky fulfillment center.[19]

on-the-job training
Training at the workplace that lets the employee learn by doing or by watching others for a while and then imitating them.

- **On-the-job training** lets the employee learn by doing, or by watching others for a while and then imitating them, right at the workplace. Salespeople, for example, are often trained by watching experienced salespeople perform (often called *shadowing*). Naturally, this can be either quite effective or disastrous, depending on the skills and habits of the person being observed. On-the-job training is the easiest kind of training to implement when the job is relatively simple (such as clerking in a store) or repetitive (such as collecting refuse, cleaning carpets, or mowing lawns). More demanding or intricate jobs require a more intense training effort. Intranets and other forms of technology make cost-effective on-the-job training programs available 24 hours a day. Computer systems can monitor workers' input and give them instructions if they become confused about what to do next.

apprentice programs
Training programs during which a learner works alongside an experienced employee to master the skills and procedures of a craft.

- In **apprentice programs** a learner works alongside an experienced employee to master the skills and procedures of a craft. Some apprentice programs include classroom training. Trade unions in skilled crafts, such as bricklaying and plumbing, require a new worker to serve as an apprentice for several years to ensure excellence as well as to limit entry to the union. Workers who successfully complete an apprenticeship earn the classification *journeyman*. As baby boomers retire from skilled trades such as pipefitting, welding, and carpentry, shortages of trained workers will result. Apprentice programs may be shortened to prepare people for skilled jobs in changing industries such as auto repair and aircraft maintenance that require increased knowledge of computer technology. About 450,000 apprentices are registered with the U.S. Department of Labor.[20]

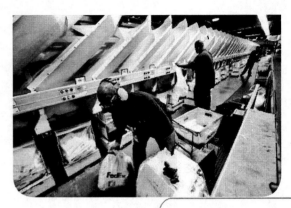

At FedEx, time is money. That's why the company spends six times more on employee training than the average firm. Does the added expense pay off? You bet. FedEx enjoys a remarkably low 4 percent employee turnover rate. Should other companies follow FedEx's financial commitment to training? Why?

- **Off-the-job training** occurs away from the workplace and consists of internal or external programs to develop any of a variety of skills or to foster personal development. Training is becoming more sophisticated as jobs become more sophisticated. Furthermore, training is expanding to include education (through the Ph.D.) and personal development. Subjects may include time management, stress management, health and wellness, physical education, nutrition, and even art and languages.

- **Online training** demonstrates how technology is improving the efficiency of many off-the-job training programs. Most colleges and universities now offer a wide variety of online classes, sometimes called *distance learning,* including introductory business courses. Both nonprofit and profit-seeking businesses make extensive use of online training. The Red Cross offers an online tutorial called "Be Red Cross Ready" to help citizens prepare for disasters such as floods, tornadoes, or hurricanes.[21] Technology giants like EMC and large manufacturers like Timken use the online training tool GlobeSmart to teach employees how to operate in different cultures.[22] Online training's key advantage is the ability to provide a large number of employees with consistent content tailored to specific training needs at convenient times.

- **Vestibule training** (or near-the-job training) is done in classrooms with equipment similar to that used on the job so that employees learn proper methods and safety procedures before assuming a specific job assignment. Computer and robotics training is often completed in a vestibule classroom.

- **Job simulation** is the use of equipment that duplicates job conditions and tasks so that trainees can learn skills before attempting them on the job. It differs from vestibule training in that it duplicates the *exact* combination of conditions that occur on the job. This is the kind of training given to astronauts, airline pilots, army tank operators, ship captains, and others who must learn difficult procedures off the job.

Management Development

Managers often need special training. To be good communicators, they need to learn listening skills and empathy. They also need time management,

off-the-job training
Internal or external training programs away from the workplace that develop any of a variety of skills or foster personal development.

online training
Training programs in which employees complete classes via the Internet.

vestibule training
Training done in schools where employees are taught on equipment similar to that used on the job.

job simulation
The use of equipment that duplicates job conditions and tasks so trainees can learn skills before attempting them on the job.

NASA's KC-135 aircraft helps astronauts like these train for space missions. After the plane makes a fast and steep ascent, it suddenly free-falls for 20 to 30 seconds enabling the passengers to experience "apparent weightlessness." (For obvious reasons the plane is also known as the Vomit Comet.) Do you think simulation training is effective for jobs like this? Why or why not?

management development
The process of training and educating employees to become good managers, and then monitoring the progress of their managerial skills over time.

planning, and human relations skills. **Management development**, then, is the process of training and educating employees to become good managers, and then monitoring the progress of their managerial skills over time. Management development programs are widespread, especially at colleges, universities, and private management development firms. Managers may participate in role-playing exercises, solve various management cases, and attend films and lectures.[23]

Management development is increasingly being used as a tool to accomplish business objectives. General Electric's and Motorola's management teams were built with significant investment in their development. Most management training programs include several of the following:

- *On-the-job coaching.* A senior manager assists a lower-level manager by teaching needed skills and providing direction, advice, and helpful feedback. E-coaching is being developed to coach managers electronically, though it will take time and experimentation before firms figure out how to make coaches come to life online.[24]

- *Understudy positions.* Job titles such as *undersecretary* and *assistant* are part of a relatively successful way of developing managers. Selected employees work as assistants to higher-level managers and participate in planning and other managerial functions until they are ready to assume such positions themselves.

- *Job rotation.* So that they can learn about different functions of the organization, managers are often given assignments in a variety of departments. Such job rotation gives them the broad picture of the organization they need to succeed.[25]

- *Off-the-job courses and training.* Managers periodically go to classes or seminars for a week or more to hone technical and human relations skills. Major universities like the University of Michigan, MIT, and the University of Chicago offer specialized short courses to assist managers in performing their jobs more efficiently. McDonald's Corporation has its own Hamburger University. Managers and potential franchisees attend six days of classes and complete a course of study equivalent to 36 hours of college business-school credit.[26]

Networking

Networking is the process of establishing and maintaining contacts with key managers in your own and other organizations, and using those contacts to weave strong relationships that serve as informal development systems. Of equal or greater importance may be a **mentor**, a corporate manager who supervises, coaches, and guides selected lower-level employees by introducing them to the right people and generally acting as their organizational sponsor. In most organizations informal mentoring occurs as experienced employees assist less experienced workers. However, many organizations formally assign mentors to employees considered to have strong potential.[27]

It's also important to remember that networking and mentoring go beyond the business environment. For example, college is a perfect place to begin networking. Associations you nurture with professors, with local businesspeople through internships, and especially with your classmates can provide a valuable network to turn to for the rest of your career.

Informal networking gatherings like this help professionals make new connections with people in their fields. Why do you think younger workers prefer such informal gatherings?

Diversity in Management Development

As more women moved into management, they learned the importance of networking and of having mentors. Unfortunately, women often have more difficulty than men in networking or finding mentors, since most senior managers are male. Women, however, won a major legal victory when the U.S. Supreme Court ruled it illegal to bar women from certain clubs, long open to men only, where business activity flows and contacts are made. This decision allowed more women to enter established networking systems or, in some instances, create their own.

Similarly, African American and Hispanic managers learned the value of networking. Both groups are forming pools of capital and new opportunities helping many individuals overcome traditional barriers to success. *Black Enterprise* magazine sponsors several networking forums each year for African American professionals. The Hispanic Alliance for Career Enhancement (HACE) is committed to building career opportunities and career advancement for Hispanics. Monte Jade is an association that helps Taiwanese and Chinese assimilate in U.S. business. Sulekha is an Indian networking group that unites Indians in the United States and around the world.

Companies that take the initiative to develop female and minority managers understand three crucial principles: (1) grooming women and minorities for management positions isn't about legality, morality, or even morale but rather about bringing more talent in the door, the key to long-term profitability; (2) the best women and minorities will become harder to attract and retain, so companies that commit to development early have an edge; and (3) having more women and minorities at all levels lets businesses serve their increasingly female and minority customers better. If you don't have a diversity of people working in the back room, how are you going to satisfy the diversity of people coming in the front door?

networking
The process of establishing and maintaining contacts with key managers in and outside the organization and using those contacts to weave strong relationships that serve as informal development systems.

mentor
An experienced employee who supervises, coaches, and guides lower-level employees by introducing them to the right people and generally being their organizational sponsor.

LEARNING goal 7

Trace the six steps in appraising employee performance.

APPRAISING EMPLOYEE PERFORMANCE TO GET OPTIMUM RESULTS

Managers must be able to determine whether their workers are doing an effective and efficient job, with a minimum of errors and disruptions. They do so by using a **performance appraisal**, an evaluation that measures employee performance against established standards in order to make decisions about promotions, compensation, training, or termination. Performance appraisals have six steps:

1. *Establishing performance standards.* This step is crucial. Standards must be understandable, subject to measurement, and reasonable. Both manager and subordinate must accept them.

2. *Communicating those standards.* It's dangerous to assume that employees know what is expected of them. They must be told clearly and precisely what the standards and expectations are, and how to meet them.

3. *Evaluating performance.* If the first two steps are done correctly, performance evaluation is relatively easy. It is a matter of evaluating the employee's behavior to see whether it matches standards.

4. *Discussing results with employees.* Employees often make mistakes and fail to meet expectations at first. It takes time to learn a job and do it well. Discussing an employee's successes and areas that need improvement can provide managers an opportunity to be understanding and helpful and guide the employee to better performance. The performance appraisal can also allow employees to suggest how a task could be done better.

5. *Taking corrective action.* As part of performance appraisal, a manager can take corrective action or provide feedback to help the employee perform better. The key word is *perform*. The primary purpose of an appraisal is to improve employee performance if possible.

6. *Using the results to make decisions.* Decisions about promotions, compensation, additional training, or firing are all based on performance evaluations. An effective performance appraisal system is also a way of satisfying legal requirements about such decisions.

Managing effectively means getting results through top performance. That's what performance appraisals are for at all levels of the organization, including at the top where managers benefit from reviews by their subordinates and peers.

In the *360-degree review,* management gathers opinions from all around the employee, including those under, above, and on the same level, to get an accurate, comprehensive idea of the worker's abilities. Figure 11.5 illustrates how managers can make performance appraisals more meaningful.

performance appraisal
An evaluation that measures employee performance against established standards in order to make decisions about promotions, compensation, training, or termination.

progress assessment

- Name and describe four training techniques.
- What is the primary purpose of a performance appraisal?
- What are the six steps in a performance appraisal?

figure 11.5

**CONDUCTING EFFECTIVE
APPRAISALS AND REVIEWS**

I. **DON'T** attack the employee personally. Critically evaluate his or her work.

2. **DO** allow sufficient time, without distractions, for appraisal. (Take the phone off the hook or close the office door.)

3. **DON'T** make the employee feel uncomfortable or uneasy. *Never* conduct an appraisal where other employees are present (such as on the shop floor).

4. **DO** include the employee in the process as much as possible. (Let the employee prepare a self-improvement program.)

5. **DON'T** wait until the appraisal to address problems with the employee's work that have been developing for some time.

6. **DO** end the appraisal with positive suggestions for employee improvement.

figure 11.5

**CONDUCTING EFFECTIVE
APPRAISALS AND REVIEWS**

LEARNING goal **8**

Summarize the objectives of employee compensation programs, and describe various pay systems and fringe benefits.

COMPENSATING EMPLOYEES: ATTRACTING AND KEEPING THE BEST

Companies don't just compete for customers; they also compete for employees. Compensation is one of the main tools companies use to attract qualified employees, and one of their largest operating costs. The long-term success of a firm—perhaps even its survival—may depend on how well it can control employee costs and optimize employee efficiency. Service organizations like hospitals and airlines struggle with high employee costs since these firms are *labor-intensive* (the primary cost of operations is the cost of labor). Manufacturing firms in the auto and steel industries have asked employees to take reductions in wages (called givebacks) to make the firms more competitive. (We discuss this in Chapter 12.) Those are just a few reasons compensation and benefit packages require special attention. In fact, some experts believe determining how best to compensate employees is today's greatest human resources challenge.[28]

A carefully managed and competitive compensation and benefit program can accomplish several objectives:

- Attracting the kinds of people the organization needs, and in sufficient numbers.

- Providing employees with the incentive to work efficiently and productively.

- Keeping valued employees from going to competitors or starting competing firms.

- Maintaining a competitive position in the marketplace by keeping costs low through high productivity from a satisfied workforce.

- Providing employees with some sense of financial security through fringe benefits such as insurance and retirement benefits.

Pay Systems

The way an organization chooses to pay its employees can have a dramatic effect on efficiency and productivity. Managers thus look for a system that compensates employees fairly.

Many companies still use the pay system known as the Hay system, devised by Edward Hay. This plan is based on job tiers, each of which has a strict pay range. The system is set up on a point basis with three key factors considered: know-how, problem solving, and accountability.

Firms like San Francisco–based Skyline Construction let workers pick their own pay system. They can earn a fixed salary or collect a lower salary with potential for a bonus. John Whitney, author of *The Trust Factor*, believes that companies should set pay at the market level or better and then award all employees the same percentage merit raise. Doing so, he says, sends the message that everyone in the company is important. Figure 11.6 outlines some of the most common pay systems. Which do you think is the fairest?

Compensating Teams

Thus far, we've talked about compensating individuals. What about teams? Since you want your teams to be more than simply a group of individuals, would you compensate them like individuals? If you can't answer that question immediately, you're not alone. Most managers believe in using teams, but fewer are sure about how to pay them. Team-based pay programs are not as effective or as fully developed as managers would hope. Measuring and rewarding individual performance on teams, while at the same time rewarding team performance, is tricky—but it can be done. Professional football players, for example, are rewarded as a team when they go to the playoffs and to the Super Bowl, but they are paid individually as well. Companies are now experimenting with and developing similar incentive systems.

Jim Fox, founder and senior partner of compensation and human resource specialist firm Fox Lawson & Associates, insists that setting up the team right in the first place is the key element to designing an appropriate team compensation plan. He believes the pay model to enhance performance will be a natural outcome of the team's development process. Jay Schuster, coauthor of a study of team pay, found that when pay is based strictly on individual performance, it erodes team cohesiveness and makes the team less likely meet its goals as a collaborative effort. Workplace studies indicate over 50 percent of team compensation plans are based on team goals. Skill-based pay and gain-sharing systems are the two most common compensation methods for teams.

Skill-based pay rewards the growth of both the individual and the team. Base pay is raised when team members learn and apply new skills. Baldrige Award winner Eastman Chemical Company rewards its teams for proficiency in technical, social, and business knowledge skills. A cross-functional compensation policy team defines the skills. The drawbacks of skill-based pay are twofold: the system is complex, and it is difficult to relate the acquisition of skills directly to profit gains.

Most *gain-sharing systems* base bonuses on improvements over previous performance. Nucor Steel, one of the largest U.S. steel producers, calculates bonuses on quality—tons of steel that go out the door with no defects. There are no limits on bonuses a team can earn; they usually average around $20,000 per employee each year.[29]

Competitive compensation and benefit programs can have a tremendous impact on employee efficiency and productivity. Sometimes businesses reward exceptional performance by awarding bonuses. Does your instructor ever award bonuses for exceptional performance in class?

Some of the different pay systems are as follows:

- **Salary:** Fixed compensation computed on weekly, biweekly, or monthly pay periods (e.g., $1,600 per month or $400 per week). Salaried employees do not receive additional pay for any extra hours worked.
- **Hourly wage or daywork:** Wage based on number of hours or days worked, used for most blue-collar and clerical workers. Often employees must punch a time clock when they arrive at work and when they leave. Hourly wages vary greatly. The federal minimum wage is $7.25, and top wages go as high as $40 per hour or more for skilled craftspeople. This does not include benefits such as retirement systems, which may add 30 percent or more to the total package.
- **Piecework system:** Wage based on the number of items produced rather than by the hour or day. This type of system creates powerful incentives to work efficiently and productively.
- **Commission plans:** Pay based on some percentage of sales. Often used to compensate salespeople, commission plans resemble piecework systems.
- **Bonus plans:** Extra pay for accomplishing or surpassing certain objectives. There are two types of bonuses: monetary and cashless. Money is always a welcome bonus. Cashless rewards include written thank-you notes, appreciation notes sent to the employee's family, movie tickets, flowers, time off, gift certificates, shopping sprees, and other types of recognition.
- **Profit-sharing plans:** Annual bonuses paid to employees based on the company's profits. The amount paid to each employee is based on a predetermined percentage. Profit sharing is one of the most common forms of performance-based pay.
- **Gain-sharing plans:** Annual bonuses paid to employees based on achieving specific goals such as quality measures, customer satisfaction measures, and production targets.
- **Stock options:** Right to purchase stock in the company at a specific price over a specific period. Often this gives employees the right to buy stock cheaply despite huge increases in the price of the stock. For example, if over the course of his employment a worker received options to buy 10,000 shares of the company stock at $10 each and the price of the stock eventually grows to $100, he can use those options to buy the 10,000 shares (now worth $1 million) for $100,000.

figure 11.6

PAY SYSTEMS
Competitive compensation and benefit programs can have a tremendous impact on employee efficiency and productivity. Sometimes businesses reward exceptional performance by awarding bonuses. Does your instructor ever award bonuses for exceptional performance in class?

It is important to reward individual team players also. Outstanding team players—who go beyond what is required and make an outstanding individual contribution—should be separately recognized, with cash or noncash rewards. A good way to compensate for uneven team participation is to let the team decide which members get what type of individual award. After all, if you really support the team process, you need to give teams freedom to reward themselves.

Fringe Benefits

Fringe benefits include sick-leave pay, vacation pay, pension plans, and health plans that provide additional compensation to employees beyond base wages. Benefits in recent years grew faster than wages and can't really be considered fringe anymore. In 1929, such benefits accounted for less than 2 percent of payroll; today they account for about 30 percent. Health care costs have soared, forcing employees to pay a larger share of their own health insurance bill. Since 2000, the cost to the employee for employee-only coverage has increased 86 percent; the cost of family coverage premiums has increased 80

fringe benefits
Benefits such as sick-leave pay, vacation pay, pension plans, and health plans that represent additional compensation beyond base wages.

The workers at DreamWorks Studios who helped create the popular Shrek movies enjoy perks like free breakfast and lunch, afternoon yoga classes, free movie screenings, on-campus art classes, and monthly parties. How might fringe benefits like these affect employee performance?

percent.[30] Employees often request more fringe benefits instead of salary, in order to avoid higher taxes. This has resulted in increased debate and government investigation.

Fringe benefits can include recreation facilities, company cars, country club memberships, discounted massages, special home-mortgage rates, paid and unpaid sabbaticals, day care services, and executive dining rooms. Employees often want dental care, mental health care, elder care, legal counseling, eye care, and even short workweeks.[31]

Understanding that it takes many incentives to attract and retain the best employees, dozens of firms among *Fortune* magazine's "100 Best Companies to Work For" list offer so-called soft benefits. *Soft benefits* help workers maintain the balance between work and family life that is often as important to hardworking employees as the nature of the job itself.[32] These perks include onsite haircuts and shoe repair, concierge services, and free breakfasts.[33] Freeing employees from errands and chores gives them more time for family—and work. Biotechnology firm Genentech even offers doggie day care and an onsite farmer's market.[34]

At one time, most employees sought benefits that were similar. Today, however, some may seek child-care benefits while others prefer attractive pension plans. To address such growing demands, over half of all large firms offer **cafeteria-style fringe benefits**, in which employees can choose the benefits they want up to a certain dollar amount. Such plans let human resource managers equitably and cost-effectively meet employees' individual needs by allowing them choice.

As the cost of administering benefits programs has accelerated, many companies have chosen to outsource this function. Managing benefits can be especially complicated when employees are located in other countries. The Reaching Beyond Our Borders box discusses the human resource challenges faced by global businesses. To put it simply, benefits are often as important to recruiting top talent as salary and may even become more important in the future.

cafeteria-style fringe benefits
Fringe benefits plan that allows employees to choose the benefits they want up to a certain dollar amount.

LEARNING goal 9

Demonstrate how managers use scheduling plans to adapt to workers' needs.

SCHEDULING EMPLOYEES TO MEET ORGANIZATIONAL AND EMPLOYEE NEEDS

Workplace trends and the increasing costs of transportation have led employees to look for scheduling flexibility. Flextime, in-home employment, and job sharing are becoming important benefits employees seek.

REACHING BEYOND
our borders

www.shrm.org

Working Worldwide

Human resource management of a global workforce begins with an understanding of the customs, laws, and local business needs of every country in which the organization operates. Country-specific cultural and legal standards can affect a variety of human resource functions:

- *Compensation.* Salaries must be converted to and from foreign currencies. Often employees with international assignments receive special allowances for relocation, children's education, housing, travel, and other business-related expenses.

- *Health and pension standards.* There are different social contexts for benefits in other countries. In the Netherlands the government provides retirement income and health care.

- *Paid time off.* Four weeks of paid vacation is the standard of many European employers. But many other countries lack the short-term and long-term absence policies offered in the United States, including sick leave, personal leave, and family and medical leave. Global companies need a standard definition of *time off.*

- *Taxation.* Different countries have varying taxation rules, and the payroll department is an important player in managing immigration information.

- *Communication.* When employees leave to work in another country, they often feel disconnected from their home country. Wise companies use their intranet and the Internet to help these faraway employees keep in direct contact.

Human resource policies at home are influenced more and more by conditions and practices in other countries and cultures. Human resource managers need to sensitize themselves and their organizations to overseas cultural and business practices.

Sources: Anne Vo and Pauline Stanton, "The Transfer of HRM Policies and Practices to a Transitional Business System," *The Journal of Human Resource Management,* April 1, 2011; and Liisa Mäkelä and Vesa Suutari, "Coping with Work-Family Conflicts in the Global Career Context," *International Business Review,* April 14, 2011.

Flextime Plans

A **flextime plan** gives employees some freedom to choose which hours to work, as long as they work the required number of hours or complete their assigned tasks. The most popular plans allow employees to arrive between 7:00 and 9:00 a.m. and leave between 4:00 and 6:00 p.m. Flextime plans generally incorporate core time. **Core time** is the period when all employees are expected to be at their job stations. An organization may designate core time as 9:00 to 11:00 a.m. and 2:00 to 4:00 p.m. During these hours all employees are required to be at work (see Figure 11.7 on p. 314). Flextime allows employees to adjust to work/life demands. Two-income families find them especially helpful. Companies that use flextime say that it boosts employee productivity and morale.[35]

flextime plan
Work schedule that gives employees some freedom to choose when to work, as long as they work the required number of hours or complete their assigned tasks.

core time
In a flextime plan, the period when all employees are expected to be at their job stations.

figure 11.7

A FLEXTIME CHART
At this company, employees can start work anytime between 6:30 and 9:30 a.m. They take a half hour for lunch anytime between 11:00 a.m. and 1:30 p.m. and can leave between 3:00 and 6:30 p.m. Everyone works an eight-hour day. The blue arrows show a typical employee's flextime day.

compressed workweek
Work schedule that allows an employee to work a full number of hours per week but in fewer days.

Flextime is not for all organizations, however. It doesn't suit shift work like fast-food or assembly processes like manufacturing, where everyone on a given shift must be at work at the same time. Another disadvantage is that managers often have to work longer days to assist and supervise in organizations that may operate from 6:00 a.m. to 6:00 p.m. Flextime also makes communication more difficult since certain employees may not be there when others need to talk to them. Furthermore, if not carefully supervised, some employees could abuse the system, causing resentment among others.[36]

Another option that about one in four companies uses is a **compressed workweek**. An employee works the full number of hours, but in fewer than the standard number of days. For example, an employee may work four 10-hour days and then enjoy a long weekend, instead of working five 8-hour days with a traditional weekend. There are obvious advantages of compressed workweeks, but some employees get tired working such long hours, and productivity can decline. Others find the system a great benefit, however, and are enthusiastic about it. Nurses often work compressed weeks.

Home-Based Work

Nearly 10 million U.S. workers now telecommute, working at home at least several days per month. Approximately 12 percent of businesses use some home-based work.[37] Home-based workers can choose their own hours, interrupt work for child care or other tasks, and take time out for personal reasons. Working at home isn't for everyone. It requires discipline to stay focused on the job and not be easily distracted.

Home-based work can be a cost saver for employers. For example, Bank of America introduced a program it calls My Work that saves an estimated $5,500 per enrolled employee every year (this adds up to a $100 million a year savings). Employees in the program work remotely about 60 percent of the time. When they do come into the office, they work in communal areas or plug laptops into mobile workstations on a first-come, first-served basis. Bank of America was able to terminate leases and sublease space it no longer needed.[38] Many other large companies offer "hot-desking," or sharing a desk with other employees who work at different times.

Many companies are hiring U.S. home-based call agents rather than using either more expensive in-house operators or less-qualified offshore call centers. Office Depot shifted to home-based call agents and saved 30 or 40 percent on the cost of each call by not providing workspace (or benefits) for its home-based call-center workers. Figure 11.8 outlines the benefits and challenges of home-based work to organizations, individuals, and society.

	BENEFITS	CHALLENGES
To Organization	• Increases productivity due to fewer sick days, fewer absences, higher job satisfaction, and higher work performance ratings • Broadens available talent pool • Reduces costs of providing on-site office space	• Makes it more difficult to appraise job performance • Can negatively affect the social network of the workplace and can make it difficult to promote team cohesiveness • Complicates distribution of tasks (should office files, contact lists, and such be allowed to leave the office?)
To Individual	• Makes more time available for work and family by reducing or eliminating commute time • Reduces expenses of buying and maintaining office clothes • Avoids office politics • Helps balance work and family • Expands employment opportunities for disabled individuals	• Can cause feeling of isolation from social network • Can raise concerns regarding promotions and other rewards due to being out of sight, out of mind • May diminish individual's influence within company due to limited opportunity to learn the corporate culture
To Society	• Decreases traffic congestion • Discourages community crime that might otherwise occur in bedroom communities • Increases time available to build community ties	• Increases need to resolve zoning regulations forbidding business deliveries in residential neighborhoods • May reduce ability to interact with other people in a personal, intimate manner

Job-Sharing Plans

Job sharing lets two or more part-time employees share one full-time job. Students and parents with small children, for instance, may work only during school hours, and older workers can work part-time before fully retiring or after retiring. Benefits of job sharing include:

- Employment opportunities for those who cannot or prefer not to work full-time.
- An enthusiastic and productive workforce.
- Reduced absenteeism and tardiness.
- Ability to schedule part-time workers into peak demand periods (e.g., banks on payday).
- Retention of experienced employees who might otherwise have retired.

Disadvantages include the need to hire, train, motivate, and supervise at least twice as many people and perhaps prorate some fringe benefits. But firms are finding that the advantages generally outweigh the disadvantages.

figure II.8

BENEFITS AND CHALLENGES OF HOME-BASED WORK
Home-based work (also known as telecommuting) offers many benefits and challenges to organizations, individuals, and society as a whole.

job sharing
An arrangement whereby two part-time employees share one full-time job.

LEARNING goal 10

Describe how employees can move through a company: promotion, reassignment, termination, and retirement.

Working from home gives workers the flexibility to choose their own hours and to take time out for personal tasks. It requires self-discipline in order to stay focused on the job and not allow yourself to be distracted. Do you think you have the discipline to be a home-based worker?

MOVING EMPLOYEES UP, OVER, AND OUT

Employees don't always stay in the position they were hired to fill. They may excel and move up the corporate ladder or fail and move out the door. Employees can also be reassigned or retire. Of course, some choose to move themselves by going to another company.

Promoting and Reassigning Employees

Many companies find that promotion from within the company improves employee morale. It's also cost-effective in that the promoted employees are already familiar with the corporate culture and procedures and don't need to spend valuable time on basic orientation.

In the new, flatter corporate structures (see Chapter 8), there are fewer levels for employees to reach than in the past. Thus they often move *over* to a new position rather than *up*. Such lateral transfers allow employees to develop and display new skills and learn more about the company overall. Reassignment is one way of motivating experienced employees to remain in a company with few advancement opportunities.[39]

Terminating Employees

We've seen that the relentless pressure of global competition, shifts in technology, increasing customer demands for greater value, and uncertain economic conditions have human resource managers struggling to manage layoffs and firings. Even if the economy is booming, many companies are hesitant to hire or rehire workers full-time. Why is that the case? One reason is that the cost of terminating employees is prohibitively high in terms of lost training costs and possible damages and legal fees for wrongful discharge suits. That's why many companies are either using temporary employees or outsourcing certain functions.

At one time the prevailing employment doctrine in the United States was "employment at will." This meant managers had as much freedom to fire workers as workers had to leave voluntarily. Most states now limit the at-will doctrine to protect employees from wrongful firing. An employer can no longer fire someone for exposing the company's illegal actions or refusing to violate a law. Employees who are members of a minority or other protected group also may have protections under equal employment law. In some cases, workers fired for using illegal drugs have sued on the ground that they have an illness (addiction) and are therefore protected by laws barring discrimination under the Americans with Disabilities Act (ADA). Well-intended legislation has in some ways restricted management's ability to terminate employees as it increased workers' rights to their jobs. See Figure 11.9 for advice about how to minimize the chance of wrongful discharge lawsuits.

> *As the economic crisis grew, managers had to terminate a growing number of employees. Do you think they will rehire full-time employees when the economy recovers? Why or why not? What alternatives do employers have?*

Retiring Employees

Companies looking to downsize sometimes offer early retirement benefits to entice older (and more expensive) workers to retire. Such benefits can include one-time cash payments, known in some companies as *golden handshakes.* The advantage early retirement benefits have over layoffs or firing is the increased morale of surviving employees. Retiring senior workers earlier also increases promotion opportunities for younger employees.

Losing Valued Employees

In spite of a company's efforts to retain them, some talented employees will choose to pursue opportunities elsewhere. Knowing their reasons for leaving can be invaluable in preventing the loss of other good people in the future. One way to learn the reasons is to have an outside expert conduct an *exit interview.* Outsiders can provide confidentiality and anonymity that earns more honest feedback than employees are comfortable giving in face-to-face interviews with their bosses. Web-based systems can capture, track, and statistically analyze employee exit interview data to generate reports that identify trouble areas. Such programs can also coordinate exit interview data with employee satisfaction surveys to predict which departments should expect turnover to occur.

Consultants offer this advice to minimize the chance of a lawsuit for wrongful discharge:

- Prepare before hiring by requiring recruits to sign a statement that retains management's freedom to terminate at will.
- Don't make unintentional promises by using such terms as *permanent employment.*
- Document reasons before firing and make sure you have an unquestionable business reason for the firing.
- Fire the worst first and be consistent in discipline.
- Buy out bad risk by offering severance pay in exchange for a signed release from any claims.
- Be sure to give employees the true reasons they are being fired. If you do not, you cannot reveal it to a recruiter asking for a reference without risking a defamation lawsuit.
- Disclose the reasons for an employee's dismissal to that person's potential new employers. For example, if you fired an employee for dangerous behavior and you withhold that information from your references, you can be sued if the employee commits a violent act at his or her next job.

figure II.9

HOW TO AVOID WRONGFUL-DISCHARGE LAWSUITS

Sources: "In Economics Old and New, Treatment of Workers Is Paramount," *The Washington Post,* February II, 200I, p. LI; and U.S. Law, www.uslaw.com.

Attracting and retaining the best employees is the key to success in the competitive global business environment. Dealing with controversial issues employees have on the job is challenging and never-ending. Chapter 12 discusses such issues.

progress assessment

- Can you name and describe five alternative compensation techniques?
- What advantages do compensation plans such as profit sharing offer an organization?
- What are the benefits and challenges of flextime? Telecommuting? Job sharing?

summary

Learning Goal 1. Explain the importance of human resource management, and describe current issues in managing human resources.

- **What are current challenges and opportunities in the human resource area?**

Many current challenges and opportunities arise from changing demographics: more women, minorities, immigrants, and older workers in the workforce. Others include a shortage of trained workers and an abundance of unskilled workers, skilled workers in declining industries requiring retraining, changing employee work attitudes, and complex laws and regulations.

Learning Goal 2. Illustrate the effects of legislation on human resource management.

- **What are some of the key laws?**

See the Legal Briefcase box on page 295 and review the text section on laws.

Learning Goal 3. Summarize the five steps in human resource planning.

- **What are the steps in human resource planning?**

The five steps are (1) preparing a human resource inventory of the organization's employees; (2) preparing a job analysis; (3) assessing future demand; (4) assessing future supply; and (5) establishing a plan for recruiting, hiring, educating, appraising, compensating, and scheduling employees.

Learning Goal 4. Describe methods that companies use to recruit new employees, and explain some of the issues that make recruitment challenging.

- **What methods do human resource managers use to recruit new employees?**

Recruiting sources are classified as either internal or external. Internal sources include those hired from within (transfers, promotions, reassignments) and employees who recommend others to hire. External recruitment sources include advertisements, public and private employment agencies, college placement bureaus, management consultants, professional organizations, referrals, walk-in applications, and the Internet.

- **Why has recruitment become more difficult?**

Legal restrictions complicate hiring and firing practices. Finding suitable employees can be more difficult if companies are considered unattractive workplaces.

Learning Goal 5. Outline the six steps in selecting employees.
- **What are the six steps in the selection process?**

The steps are (1) obtaining complete application forms, (2) conducting initial and follow-up interviews, (3) giving employment tests, (4) conducting background investigations, (5) obtaining results from physical exams, and (6) establishing a trial period of employment.

Learning Goal 6. Illustrate employee training and development methods.
- **What are some training activities?**

Training activities include employee orientation, on- and off-the-job training, apprentice programs, online training, vestibule training, and job simulation.
- **What methods help develop managerial skills?**

Management development methods include on-the-job coaching, understudy positions, job rotation, and off-the-job courses and training.
- **How does networking fit in this process?**

Networking is the process of establishing contacts with key managers within and outside the organization to get additional development assistance.

Learning Goal 7. Trace the six steps in appraising employee performance.
- **How do managers evaluate performance?**

The steps are (1) establish performance standards; (2) communicate those standards; (3) compare performance to standards; (4) discuss results; (5) take corrective action when needed; and (6) use the results for decisions about promotions, compensation, additional training, or firing.

Learning Goal 8. Summarize the objectives of employee compensation programs, and describe various pay systems and fringe benefits.
- **What are common types of compensation systems?**

They include salary systems, hourly wages, piecework, commission plans, bonus plans, profit-sharing plans, and stock options.
- **What types of compensation are appropriate for teams?**

The most common are gain-sharing and skill-based compensation programs. Managers also reward outstanding individual performance within teams.
- **What are fringe benefits?**

Fringe benefits include sick leave, vacation pay, company cars, pension plans, and health plans that provide additional compensation to employees beyond base wages. Cafeteria-style fringe benefits plans let employees choose the benefits they want, up to a certain dollar amount.

Learning Goal 9. Demonstrate how managers use scheduling plans to adapt to workers' needs.
- **What scheduling plans can adjust work to employees' need for flexibility?**

Such plans include job sharing, flextime, compressed workweeks, and working at home.

320

Learning Goal 10. Describe how employees can move through a company: promotion, reassignment, termination, and retirement.

• **How can employees move within a company?**

Employees can be moved up (promotion), over (reassignment), or out (termination or retirement) of a company. They can also choose to leave a company to pursue opportunities elsewhere.

key terms

affirmative action 294	**job analysis** 297	**on-the-job training** 304
apprentice programs 304	**job description** 297	**orientation** 303
cafeteria-style fringe benefits 312	**job sharing** 315	**performance appraisal** 308
compressed workweek 314	**job simulation** 305	**recruitment** 298
contingent workers 302	**job specifications** 297	**reverse discrimination** 294
core time 313	**management development** 306	**selection** 300
flextime plan 313	**mentor** 307	**training and development** 303
fringe benefits 311	**networking** 307	**vestibule training** 305
human resource management (HRM) 290	**off-the-job training** 305	
	online training 305	

critical thinking

1. Does human resource management interest you as a career? What are your experiences working with human resource professionals?

2. What effects have dual-career families had on the human resource function?

3. What problems can arise when family members work together in the same firm?

4. If you were a human resource manager, how would you address the brain drain that occurs as knowledgeable workers retire?

5. Imagine you must fire an employee. What effect might the dismissal have on remaining employees? Explain how you would tell the employee and your other subordinates.

developing workplace skills

1. Look in the classified ads in your local newspaper or on the Internet and find at least two positions you might like to have when you graduate. List the qualifications specified in each of the ads and identify methods the companies might use to determine how well applicants meet them.

2. Read several current business periodicals to find information about the latest court rulings on benefits, affirmative action, and other human resource issues. Summarize your findings. Is there a trend in these decisions? If so, what is it, and what will it mean for tomorrow's college graduates?

3. Recall any on-the-job and off-the-job training sessions you've experienced. Write a brief critique of each. How would you improve them? Share your ideas with the class.

4. Consider the following occupations: doctor, computer salesperson, computer software developer, teacher, and assembly worker. Identify the method of compensation you think is appropriate for each. Explain your answer.

5. Choose one of these positions: a human resource manager notifying employees of mandatory drug testing or an employee representative protesting such testing. Write a memorandum supporting your position.

taking it to the net

Purpose

To illustrate the types of questions managers typically ask during interviews and practice answering such questions in a safe environment.

Exercise

Go to HYPERLINK "http://Monster.com" Monster.com's Interview Cheat Sheet page at http://career-advice.monster.com/job-interview/interview-preparation/interview-cheat-sheet/article.aspx. This page provides links to articles that will give you hints for what to do before, during, and after job interviews. Practice answering some of the interview questions provided in one or two of these links. This will give you the opportunity to practice your answers so that when you do go on an actual interview you are less likely to fumble for an answer.

casing the web

To access the case "Dual-Career Planning," visit **www.mhhe.com/ubl0e**

video case

To access the video case featuring SAS, visit **www.mhhe.com/ubl0e**

MARKETING:
HELPING
Buyers Buy

13

LEARNING goals

After you have read and studied this chapter, you should be able to

1 Define *marketing*, and apply the marketing concept to both for-profit and nonprofit organizations.

2 Describe the four Ps of marketing.

3 Summarize the marketing research process.

4 Show how marketers use environmental scanning to learn about the changing marketing environment.

5 Explain how marketers apply the tools of market segmentation, relationship marketing, and the study of consumer behavior.

6 Compare the business-to-business market and the consumer market.

profile

Getting to Know

X *Joseph Jimenez*

CEO of Novartis

Joseph (Joe) Jimenez was a collegiate all-American swimmer and captain of the swim team at Stanford University. He credits competitive swimming with helping him build an inner strength that sustains him to this day. Today Jimenez is CEO of Novartis, one of the world's largest pharmaceutical companies.

After earning an M.B.A. from the University of California, Berkeley, Jimenez began his career in marketing as a brand manager at Clorox. Success in marketing at Clorox led him to ConAgra Foods where he became a division head and finally to H.J. Heinz Company where he became President and CEO of Heinz Europe and Heinz North America. In 2010, he became the first American CEO of Swiss-based Novartis.

On assuming the CEO job at Novartis, Jimenez put his marketing experience to good use. Instead of lamenting the problems faced in the pharmaceutical industry, such as the uncertain Food & Drug Administration (FDA) approval process in the United States, he decided Novartis "was not going to complain—but was going to change." One decision Jimenez made was to "geo tailor" the sales force at Novartis to fit particular markets. He restructured the sales force to address specific trends in individual markets where payer organizations (i.e. insurance companies) have a great influence on what pharmaceutical products are purchased. In other areas where physicians make decisions, a more traditional sales model was retained. His intention was to focus on the individual needs of specific customers and develop better relationships with them as they make purchasing decisions. In other words, he wanted to help buyers buy.

Like all good marketers, Jimenez sees Novartis as more than just a pharmaceutical company. He understands that to exemplify marketing at its best, social responsibility needs to be part of the Novartis mission. For example, Novartis teamed with Americas's VetDogs to train and provide guide dogs for veterans who are blind or visually impaired, and service dogs for those with disabilities other than blindness—at no cost to the veteran. The program trains over 1,000 dogs a year.

Novartis and Jimenez are also proud of the company's access-to-medicine program that has reached more than 80 million patients worldwide. The company offers discounts and support programs to patients who lack medical insurance or cannot afford treatment. Such strategies emphasize Jimenez's belief that marketing is a multidimensional discipline and is not just centered on issues of selling and advertising.

This chapter and the following three chapters are about marketing. You will learn about traditional marketing practices, but you will also learn about new marketing practices, including the use of social media. Joseph Jimenez is a role model for other progressive managers who see marketing from a broader perspective.

Sources: David Bach and David Bruce Allen, "What Every CEO Needs to Know about Nonmarket Strategy," *MIT Sloan Management Review*, Spring 2010; www.forbes.com, accessed April 2011; www.youtube, accessed in April 2011; www.novartis.com; and Dominic Barton, "Capitalism for the Long Term," *Harvard Business Review*, May 2011.

NOVARTIS

NAME THAT
company

Where's the beef? Many people don't care about the answer to that question anymore. As the trend toward vegetarianism grows, this well-known company in Canada offers a vegan version of its chicken sandwich in 500 of its 750 stores. What is the name of this company? (Find the answer in the chapter.)

LEARNING goal **1**

Define *marketing,* and apply the marketing concept to both for-profit and nonprofit organizations.

WHAT IS MARKETING?

The term marketing means different things to different people. Many think of marketing as simply "selling" or "advertising."[1] Yes, selling and advertising are part of marketing, but it's much more. The American Marketing Association has defined **marketing** as the activity, set of institutions, and processes for creating, communicating, delivering, and exchanging offerings that have value for customers, clients, partners, and society at large. We can also think of marketing, more simply, as the activities buyers and sellers perform to facilitate mutually satisfying exchanges.

In the past marketing focused almost entirely on helping the seller sell. That's why many people still think of it as mostly selling, advertising, and distribution *from the seller to the buyer.* Today, much of marketing is instead about *helping the buyer buy.* One author calls it "The Power of Pull."[2] Let's examine a couple of examples.

Today, when people want to buy a new or used car, they often turn to the Internet first. They go to a website like Vehix (www.vehix.com) to search for the vehicle they want and even take a virtual ride.[3] At other websites they compare prices and features. By the time they go to the dealer, they may know exactly which car they want and the best price available.

The websites have *helped the buyer buy.* Not only are customers spared searching one dealership after another to find the best price, but manufacturers and dealers are eager to participate so that they don't lose customers. The future of marketing is doing everything you can to help the buyer buy.[4]

Let's look at another case. In the past, one of the few ways students and parents could find the college with the right "fit" was to travel from campus to campus, a grueling and expensive process. Today, colleges use podcasts, virtual tours, live chats, and other interactive technologies to make on-campus visits less necessary. Such virtual tours help students and their parents buy.

Of course, helping the buyer buy also helps the seller sell. Think about that for a minute.

Here's an example from *The Wall Street Journal:* In the vacation market, many people find the holiday they want themselves. They use the Internet to

marketing
The activity, set of institutions, and processes for creating, communicating, delivering, and exchanging offerings that have value for customers, clients, partners, and society at large.

find the right spot, and then make choices, sometimes questioning potential sellers online. In industries like this, the role of marketing is to make sure that a company's products or services are easily found online, and that the company responds effectively to potential customers.[5]

These are only a few examples of the marketing trend toward helping buyers buy. Consumers today spend hours searching the Internet for good deals. Wise marketers provide a wealth of information online and even cultivate customer relationships using blogs and social networking sites such as Facebook and Twitter.[6]

Online communities provide an opportunity to observe people (customers and others) interacting with one another, expressing their own opinions, forming relationships, and commenting on various goods and services.[7] It is important for marketers to track what relevant bloggers are writing by doing blog searches using key terms that define their market. Vendors who have text-mining tools can help companies measure conversations about their products and their personnel. Much of the future of marketing lies in mining such online conversations and responding appropriately.[8]

Retailers and other marketers who rely solely on *traditional* advertising and selling are losing out to the new ways of marketing. The Spotlight on Small Business box on p. 354 discusses how some theaters are being creative with their marketing efforts.[9]

The Evolution of Marketing

What marketers do at any particular time depends on what they need to do to fill customers' needs and wants, which continually change. Let's take a brief look at how those changes have influenced the evolution of marketing. Marketing in the United States has passed through four eras: (1) production, (2) selling, (3) marketing concept, and (4) customer relationship (see Figure 13.1).

The Production Era From the time the first European settlers began their struggle to survive in America until the early 1900s, the general philosophy of business was "Produce as much as you can, because there is a limitless market for it." Given the limited production capability and vast demand for products in those days, a production philosophy was both logical and profitable. Business owners were mostly farmers, carpenters, and trade workers. They needed to produce more and more, so their goals centered on

figure 13.1

MARKETING ERAS
The evolution of marketing in the United States involved four eras: (1) production, (2) selling, (3) marketing concept, and (4) customer relationship.

SPOTLIGHT ON SMALL
business

Let's Go to the Movies

Imagine you own a small movie theater. How can you differentiate your theater from the others in your town? Some theaters have had success with 3D movies. Others offer bigger and more screens. For many theaters today, the answer is to provide food with the movie. In fact, about 400 of the 5,750 theaters are doing just that. In-theater dining is said to be one of the biggest bets for increasing the theater-going audience. Thus, you should expect to see more such theaters in the future.

It is a risk to offer an eat-in experience. For example, it is more difficult than you might imagine to keep such theaters clean. After all, there isn't that much time between showings. You can imagine the difficulty some theaters have had trying to create a menu that allows people to eat in the dark. You can also imagine the work it takes to add a kitchen and luxury facilities to an old theater. Nonetheless, theater owners have decided that to fill a need they would have to go to such lengths. It may turn out that such theaters only appeal to a niche market and may not prove profitable.

To further enhance the experience, some theaters are offering alcohol, luxury seats, footrests, blankets, pillows, and the like. Have you experienced these theaters yet? What did you think? Was the additional cost worth it? Do you have other suggestions for how to improve the movie-going experience?

Sources: Lauren A. E. Schuker, "Double Feature: Dinner and a Movie," *The Wall Street Journal*, January 5, 2011; and Judy Hedding, "iPic Theatres—A Scottsdale Luxury Theatre Experience," About.com, accessed April 2011.

In the selling era, the focus of marketing was on selling, with little service afterward and less customization. What economic and social factors made this approach appropriate for the times?

production. You can see this same process occurring in the oil industry today, where producers can often sell as much oil as they can produce. For a long time, GE thought that they would sell all the products they produced.[10] Now they know better, of course. The greatest marketing need in this industry is for more production and less expensive distribution and storage.

The Selling Era   By the 1920s, businesses had developed mass-production techniques (such as automobile assembly lines), and production capacity often exceeded the immediate market demand. Therefore, the business philosophy turned from producing to *selling.*[11] Most companies emphasized selling and advertising in an effort to persuade consumers to buy existing products; few offered extensive service after the sale.

The Marketing Concept Era   After World War II ended in 1945, returning soldiers starting new careers and beginning families sparked a tremendous demand for goods and services. The postwar years launched the sudden increase in the birthrate that we now call the baby boom, and also a boom in consumer spending. Competition for the consumer's dollar was fierce. Businesses recognized that they needed to be responsive to consumers if they wanted to get their business, and a philosophy emerged in the 1950s called the marketing concept.

The **marketing concept** had three parts:

1. *A customer orientation.* Find out what consumers want and provide it for them. (Note the emphasis on meeting consumer needs rather than on promotion or sales.)
2. *A service orientation.* Make sure everyone in the organization has the same objective: customer satisfaction. This should be a total and integrated organizational effort. That is, everyone from the president of the firm to the delivery people should be customer-oriented. Does that seem to be the norm today?
3. *A profit orientation.* Focus on those goods and services that will earn the most profit and enable the organization to survive and expand to serve more consumer wants and needs.

It took a while for businesses to implement the marketing concept. The process went slowly during the 1960s and 70s. During the 1980s, businesses began to apply the marketing concept more aggressively than they had done over the preceding 30 years. That led to a focus on customer relationship management (CRM) that has become very important today. We explore that concept next.

The Customer Relationship Era In the 1990s and early 2000s managers extended the marketing concept by adopting the practice of customer relationship management. **Customer relationship management (CRM)** is the process of learning as much as possible about present customers and doing everything you can over time to satisfy them—or even to exceed their expectations—with goods and services. The idea is to enhance customer satisfaction and stimulate long-term customer loyalty.[12] For example, most airlines offer frequent-flier programs that reward loyal customers with free flights. The newest in customer relationship building, as mentioned earlier, involves social networks, online communities, tweets, and blogs.[13]

Clearly, the degree of consumer dissatisfaction that exists, especially with services such as airlines and phone companies, shows that marketers have a long way to go to create customer satisfaction and loyalty. According to a recent study, only 6.8 percent of marketers said they have excellent knowledge of their customers when it comes to demographic, behavioral, and psychographic (how they think) data.

The newest in CRM efforts is customer-managed relationships (CMR). The idea is to give the customer the power to build relationships with suppliers and consumers. Websites like Expedia, Travelocity, and Priceline allow customers to find the best price or set their own.[14] Since consumers are interested in green marketing today, relationship building also means responding to that desire. The Thinking Green box on p. 356, for example, explores "going green" in the apparel industry.

Nonprofit Organizations and Marketing

Even though the marketing concept emphasizes a profit orientation, marketing is a critical part of almost all organizations, including nonprofits. Charities use marketing to raise funds for combating world hunger, for instance, or to obtain other resources.[15] The Red Cross uses promotion to encourage people to donate blood when local or national supplies run low. Greenpeace uses marketing to promote ecologically safe technologies. Environmental groups use marketing to try to cut

marketing concept
A three-part business philosophy: (1) a customer orientation, (2) a service orientation, and (3) a profit orientation.

customer relationship management (CRM)
The process of learning as much as possible about customers and doing everything you can to satisfy them—or even exceed their expectations—with goods and services.

The Ad Council sponsors many public service ads like this one. The idea is to make the public more aware of various needs that only nonprofit organizations are meeting. The ads then encourage the public to get engaged in the issue somehow, if only by donating money. Have you reponded to any Ad Council advertisements?

THINKING green

How Green Is Green?

How far will companies go with relationship building through green marketing? Well, the clothing industry is developing a software tool to help them measure the environmental impact of their apparel and footwear, from raw material to garbage dump. You may be surprised by how "dirty" the apparel industry can be. For example, tanning leather often involves toxic chemicals. Making polyester uses large amounts of crude oil and other materials that release volatile compounds.

A series of questions is used to determine just how "green" some products are. The questions cover every step in the life of a product from raw-material production to manufacturing, shipping, and even disposal. Levi's gets points for having a recycling program that lets consumers drop off their old jeans at Goodwill.

Would you look at a label to determine whether or not you would buy tennis shoes or a garment based on its eco-friendliness? The apparel industry is counting on you to do so. And it is preparing for that choice by changing fabrics, distribution procedures, and more, all with the goal of establishing and maintaining good relationships with their customers.

Sources: Christina Binkley, "How Green Is My Sneaker?" *The Wall Street Journal*, July 22, 2010; and "Levi's New Jeans Design Cuts Water Use by 96 Percent," www.greenbiz.com, accessed June 2011.

---

carbon emissions. Churches use marketing to attract new members and raise funds. Politicians use marketing to get votes.

States use marketing to attract new businesses and tourists. Many states, for example, have competed to get automobile companies from other countries to locate plants in their area.[16] Schools use marketing to attract new students. Other organizations, such as arts groups, unions, and social groups, also use marketing.[17] The Ad Council, for example, uses public service ads to create awareness and change attitudes on such issues as drunk driving and fire prevention.

Organizations use marketing, in fact, to promote everything from environmentalism and crime prevention ("Take A Bite Out Of Crime") to social issues ("Choose Life").

LEARNING goal 2

Describe the four Ps of marketing.

THE MARKETING MIX

We can divide much of what marketing people do into four factors, called the four Ps to make them easy to remember. They are:

1. Product
2. Price
3. Place
4. Promotion

figure 13.2

MARKETING MANAGERS AND THE MARKETING MIX
Marketing managers must choose how to implement the four Ps of the marketing mix: product, price, place, and promotion. The goals are to please customers and make a profit.

Marketing manager

Marketing mix

Product   Price   Place   Promotion

Managing the controllable parts of the marketing process means (1) designing a want-satisfying *product*, (2) setting a *price* for the product, (3) putting the product in a *place* where people will buy it, and (4) *promoting* the product, including how "green" it is. These four factors are called the **marketing mix** because businesses blend them together in a well-designed marketing program (see Figure 13.2).

marketing mix
The ingredients that go into a marketing program: product, price, place, and promotion.

Applying the Marketing Process

The four Ps are a convenient way to remember the basics of marketing, but they don't necessarily include everything that goes into the marketing process for all products. One of the best ways to understand the entire marketing process is to take a product or a group of products and follow the process that led to their development and sale (see Figure 13.3 on p. 358).

Imagine, for example, that you and your friends want to start a money-making business near your college. You've noticed a lot of vegetarians among your acquaintances. You do a quick survey in a few dorms, sororities, and fraternities and find many vegetarians—and other students who like to eat vegetarian meals once in a while.[18] Your preliminary research indicates some demand for a vegetarian restaurant nearby. You check the fast-food stores in the area and find that none offer more than one or two vegetarian meals. In fact, most don't have any, except salads and some soups.

Further research identifies a number of different kinds of vegetarians. Lacto-ovo vegetarians eat dairy products and eggs. Lacto-vegetarians eat dairy products but no eggs. Fruitarians eat mostly raw fruits, grains, and nuts. Vegans eat neither eggs nor dairy products. Flexitarians eat the occasional cheesecake, hamburger, or whatever.

Your research identifies vegan farmers who don't use any synthetic chemical fertilizers, pesticides, herbicides, or genetically modified ingredients. You also find that KFC Canada offers a vegan version of its chicken sandwich in 500 of its 750 outlets. Is the Colonel on to something? He may be, since there are successful vegetarian restaurants even in Argentina, where the per-capita consumption of beef is the highest in the world. You conclude that a vegetarian restaurant would have to appeal to all kinds of vegetarians to be a success.

THE MARKETING PROCESS WITH THE FOUR PS

Find opportunities

Conduct research

Identify a target market

Product

Design a product to meet the need based on research

Do product testing

Price

Determine a brand name, design a package, and set a price

Place

Select a distribution system

Promotion

Design a promotional program

Build a relationship with customers

product
Any physical good, service, or idea that satisfies a want or need plus anything that would enhance the product in the eyes of consumers, such as the brand.

test marketing
The process of testing products among potential users.

brand name
A word, letter, or group of words or letters that differentiates one seller's goods and services from those of competitors.

You've just performed the first few steps in the marketing process. You noticed an opportunity (a need for vegetarian food near campus). You conducted some preliminary research to see whether your idea had any merit. And then you identified groups of people who might be interested in your product. They will be your *target market* (the people you will try to persuade to come to your restaurant).

Designing a Product to Meet Consumer Needs

Once you've researched consumer needs and found a target market (which we'll discuss in more detail later) for your product, the four Ps of marketing come into play. You start by developing a product or products. A **product** is any physical good, service, or idea that satisfies a want or need, plus anything that would enhance the product in the eyes of consumers, such as the brand name. In this case, your proposed product is a restaurant that would serve different kinds of vegetarian meals.

It's a good idea at this point to do *concept testing*. That is, you develop an accurate description of your restaurant and ask people, in person or online, whether the idea of the restaurant and the kind of meals you intend to offer appeals to them. If it does, you might go to a supplier, like Amy's Kitchen, that makes vegetarian meals, to get samples you can take to consumers to test their reactions. The process of testing products among potential users is called **test marketing**.

If consumers like the products and agree they would buy them, you have the information you need to find investors and look for a convenient location to open a restaurant. You'll have to think of a catchy name. (For practice, stop for a minute and try to think of one.) We'll use Very Vegetarian in this text, although we're sure you can think of a better name. Meanwhile, let's continue with the discussion of product development.

You may want to offer some well-known brand names to attract people right away. A **brand name** is a word, letter, or group of words or letters that differentiates one seller's goods and services from those of competitors. Brand names of vegetarian products include Tofurky, Mori-Nu, and Yves Veggie Cuisine. We'll discuss the product development process in detail in Chapter 14, and follow the Very Vegetarian case to show you how all marketing and other business decisions tie together. For now, we're simply sketching the whole marketing process to give you an overall picture. So far, we've covered the first P of the marketing mix: product. Next comes price.

Setting an Appropriate Price

After you've decided what products and services you want to offer consumers, you have to set appropriate prices.[19] Those depend on a number of factors. In the restaurant business, the price could be close to what other restaurants charge to stay competitive. Or you might charge less to attract business, especially at the beginning. Or you may offer high-quality products for which customers are willing to pay a little more (as Starbucks does). You also have to consider the costs of producing, distributing, and promoting the product, which all influence your price. We'll discuss pricing issues in more detail in Chapter 14.

Getting the Product to the Right Place

There are several ways you can serve the market for vegetarian meals. You can have people come in, sit down, and eat at the restaurant, but that's not the only alternative—think of pizza. You could deliver the food to customers' dorms, apartments, and student unions. You may want to sell your products in supermarkets or health-food stores, or through organizations that specialize in distributing food products. Such *intermediaries* are the middle links in a series of organizations that distribute goods from producers to consumers. (The more traditional word for them is *middlemen*.) Getting the product to consumers when and where they want it is critical to market success.[20] Don't forget to consider the Internet as a way to reach consumers. We'll discuss the importance of marketing intermediaries and distribution in detail in Chapter 15.

promotion
All the techniques sellers use to inform people about and motivate them to buy their products or services.

Developing an Effective Promotional Strategy

The last of the four Ps of marketing is promotion. **Promotion** consists of all the techniques sellers use to inform people about and motivate them to buy their products or services. Promotion includes advertising; personal selling; public relations; publicity; word of mouth (viral marketing); and various sales promotion efforts, such as coupons, rebates, samples, and cents-off deals.[21] We'll discuss promotion in detail in Chapter 16.

Promotion often includes relationship building with customers. Among other activities, that means responding to suggestions consumers make to improve the products or their marketing, including price and packaging. For Very Vegetarian, postpurchase, or after-sale, service may include refusing payment for meals that weren't satisfactory and stocking additional vegetarian products customers say they would like. Listening to customers and responding to their needs is the key to the ongoing process that is marketing. The Social Media in Business box on p. 360 discusses how businesses can use social media and smartphones to build relationships with customers.

A vegetarian restaurant might fill a popular need in the neighborhood of many college campuses today. Is there one near your school? What can you tell about its manager's application of the four Ps of marketing – product, price, place, and promotion?

SOCIAL MEDIA IN
business

Calling All Businesses!

In this digital age, setting up shop online is vital for most retail businesses. But having only an online presence that customers can access at home isn't enough anymore. Now consumers have an array of smartphones and digital tablets that can get them online from anywhere. For social networks and retailers alike, the mobile market has already enjoyed tremendous growth. Amazon, for instance, earned more than $1 billion from purchases made on phones in 2009. The online auction house eBay predicts that its mobile sales will double in 2011 to $4 billion.

Translating a company's current online presence into something suited for a smartphone isn't difficult for large retailers with vast resources. For small businesses, however, migrating to the mobile medium can be tricky. The array of devices available and lack of uniform design standards present a challenge to web designers, thus increasing the cost of going mobile. But as Amazon's mobile sales suggests, making the leap from laptop to touchscreen may become essential for the survival of small retailers.

Boulder-based company mShopper is helping small retailers break into the mobile market with the introduction of the Mobile Commerce Platform, or mStore. The service takes the guesswork out of constructing a mobile site by providing design and search engine tools along with an analytics dashboard to track traffic and sales. It also streamlines records and retains customer service processes. mShopper charges a licensing fee on a sliding scale ranging from $99 to $999, depending on web traffic. Since mShopper doesn't get paid if their clients' stores don't get hits, the company also offers a marketing system that sends out promotional texts and discounts to customers on an mStore's mailing list.

Some retailers are hoping to use social media to enter the mobile market. Although many companies use social media to create awareness, there is a trend now of setting up direct outlets on social platforms. JCPenney and Delta Airlines have been in talks for months about obtaining a direct presence on Facebook. In three to five years, economists estimate that as much as 15 percent of total consumer spending may go through social networking sites. That means that many companies could be poised for a fortune if all those friends turn into customers.

Sources: Jason Ankeny, "Setting Sale on Smartphones," *Entrepreneur*, December 2010; and Sarah Shannon, "Fashion Retailer ASOS Sets Up Shop on Facebook," *Bloomberg Businessweek*, February 17, 2011.

progress assessment

- What does it mean to "help the buyer buy"?
- What are the three parts of the marketing concept?
- What are the four Ps of the marketing mix?

LEARNING goal 3

Summarize the marketing research process.

PROVIDING MARKETERS WITH INFORMATION

marketing research
The analysis of markets to determine opportunities and challenges, and to find the information needed to make good decisions.

Every decision in the marketing process depends on information. When they conduct **marketing research**, marketers analyze markets to determine opportunities and challenges, and to find the information they need to make good decisions.

Marketing research helps identify what products customers have purchased in the past, and what changes have occurred to alter what they want now and what they're likely to want in the future. Marketers also conduct research on business trends, the ecological impact of their decisions, global trends, and more. Businesses need information to compete effectively, and marketing research is the activity that gathers it. Besides listening to customers, marketing researchers also pay attention to what employees, shareholders, dealers, consumer advocates, media representatives, and other stakeholders have to say. As noted earlier, some of that research is now being gathered online through blogs and social networks.

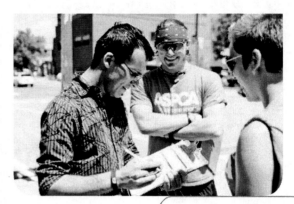

Personal interviews are one way of collecting primary research data about customers' needs, wants, and buying habits. Perhaps someone has stopped you in a shopping mall recently to ask you some questions about a product or product category you use. What might contribute to the difficulty of collecting information through such interviews, and how can marketers improve the process?

The Marketing Research Process

A simplified marketing research process consists of at least four key steps:

1. Defining the question (the problem or opportunity) and determining the present situation.
2. Collecting research data.
3. Analyzing the research data.
4. Choosing the best solution and implementing it.

The following sections look at each of these steps.

Defining the Question and Determining the Present Situation   Marketing researchers need the freedom to discover what the present situation is, what the problems or opportunities are, what the alternatives are, what information they need, and how to go about gathering and analyzing data.

Collecting Data   Usable information is vital to the marketing research process. Research can become quite expensive, however, so marketers must often make a trade-off between the need for information and the cost of obtaining it. Normally the least expensive method is to gather information already compiled by others and published in journals and books or made available online.

Such existing data are called **secondary data**, since you aren't the first one to gather them. Figure 13.4 on p. 362 lists the principal sources of secondary marketing research information. Despite its name, *secondary* data is what marketers should gather *first* to avoid incurring unnecessary expense. To find secondary data about vegetarians, go to the website for *Vegetarian Times* (www.vegetariantimes.com) or search other websites on vegetarianism.

Often, secondary data don't provide all the information managers need for important business decisions. To gather additional in-depth information, marketers must do their own research. The results of such *new studies* are called **primary data**. One way to gather primary data is to conduct a survey.

Telephone surveys, online surveys, mail surveys, and personal interviews are the most common forms of primary data collection. Focus groups (defined below) are another popular method of surveying individuals. What do you think would be the best way to survey students about your potential new restaurant? Would you do a different kind of survey after it had been open a few months? How could you help vegetarians find your restaurant? That is, how

secondary data
Information that has already been compiled by others and published in journals and books or made available online.

primary data
Data that you gather yourself (not from secondary sources such as books and magazines).

PRIMARY SOURCES	SECONDARY SOURCES		
Interviews	**Government Publications**		
Surveys	*Statistical Abstract of the United States*		*Census of Transportation*
Observation	*Survey of Current Business*		*Annual Survey of Manufacturers*
Focus groups	*Census of Retail Trade*		
Online surveys			
Questionnaires	**Commercial Publications**		
Customer comments	ACNielsen Company studies on retailing and media		
Letters from customers	Marketing Research Corporation of America studies on consumer purchases		
	Selling Areas—Marketing Inc. reports on food sales		

Magazines

Entrepreneur	*Journal of Retailing*	*Journal of Advertising Research*
Bloomberg Businessweek	*Journal of Consumer Research*	
Fortune		Trade magazines appropriate to your industry such as *Progressive Grocer*
Inc.	*Journal of Advertising*	
Advertising Age	*Journal of Marketing Research*	
Forbes	*Marketing News*	Reports from various chambers of commerce
Harvard Business Review	*Hispanic Business*	
Journal of Marketing	*Black Enterprise*	

Newspapers
The Wall Street Journal, Barron's, your local newspapers

Internal Sources

Company records	Income statements
Balance sheets	Prior research reports

General Sources

Internet searches	Commercial databases
Google-type searches	

figure 13.4

SELECTED SOURCES OF PRIMARY AND SECONDARY INFORMATION You should spend a day or two at the library becoming familiar with these sources. You can read about primary research in any marketing research text from the library.

focus group
A small group of people who meet under the direction of a discussion leader to communicate their opinions about an organization, its products, or other given issues.

could you help your buyers buy? One question researchers pay close attention to is: "Would you recommend this product to a friend?"

A **focus group** is a group of people who meet under the direction of a discussion leader to communicate their opinions about an organization, its products, or other given issues. This textbook is updated periodically using many focus groups made up of faculty and students. They tell us, the authors, what subjects and examples they like and dislike, and the authors follow their suggestions for changes.

Marketers can now gather both secondary and primary data online. The authors of this text, for example, do much research online, but they also gather data from books, articles, interviews, and other sources.

Analyzing the Research Data   Marketers must turn the data they collect in the research process into useful information. Careful, honest interpretation of the data can help a company find useful alternatives to specific marketing challenges. For example, by doing primary research, Fresh Italy, a small Italian

The authors of this text enjoy the benefits of using focus groups. College faculty and students come to these meetings and tell us how to improve this book and its support material. We listen carefully and make as many changes as we can in response. Suggestions have included adding more descriptive captions to the photos in the book and making the text as user-friendly as possible. How are we doing so far?

pizzeria, found that its pizza's taste was rated superior to that of the larger pizza chains. However, the company's sales lagged behind the competition. Secondary research on the industry revealed that free delivery (which Fresh Italy did not offer) was more important to customers than taste. Fresh Italy now delivers—and has increased its market share.

Choosing the Best Solution and Implementing It   After collecting and analyzing data, market researchers determine alternative strategies and make recommendations about which may be best and why. This final step in a research effort also includes following up on actions taken to see whether the results were what was expected. If not, the company can take corrective action and conduct new studies in its ongoing attempt to provide consumer satisfaction at the lowest cost. You can see, then, that marketing research is a *continuous process* of responding to changes in the marketplace and in consumer preferences.

LEARNING goal **4**

Show how marketers use environmental scanning to learn about the changing marketing environment.

THE MARKETING ENVIRONMENT

Marketing managers must be aware of the surrounding environment when making marketing mix decisions. **Environmental scanning** is the process of identifying factors that can affect marketing success. As you can see in Figure 13.5 on p. 364, they include global, technological, sociocultural,

environmental scanning
The process of identifying the factors that can affect marketing success.

figure I3.5

THE MARKETING
ENVIRONMENT

competitive, and economic influences. We discussed these factors in some detail in Chapter 1, but now let's review them from a strictly marketing perspective.

Global Factors

Using the Internet, businesses can reach many of the world's consumers relatively easily and carry on a dialogue with them about the goods and services they want. By 2018, half of all small businesses will be engaged in global trade.

The globalization process puts more pressure on those whose responsibility it is to deliver products. Many marketers outsource delivery to companies like FedEx, UPS, and DHL, which have a solid reputation for shipping goods quickly.[22]

Technological Factors

The most important technological changes also relate to the Internet. Using consumer databases, blogs, social networking, and the like, companies can develop products and services that closely match consumers' needs. As you read in Chapter 9, firms can now produce customized goods and services for about the same price as mass-produced goods. Thus flexible manufacturing and mass customization are also major influences on marketers. You can imagine, for example, using databases to help you devise custom-made fruit mixes and various salads for your customers at Very Vegetarian.

Sociocultural Factors

Marketers must monitor social trends to maintain their close relationship with customers, since population growth and changing demographics can have an effect on sales. One of the fastest-growing segments of the U.S. population in the 21st century is people over 65. The increase in the number of older adults creates growing demand for nursing homes, health care, prescription drugs, recreation, continuing education, and more.

Other shifts in the U.S. population are creating new challenges for marketers as they adjust their products to meet the tastes and preferences of Hispanic, Asian, and other growing ethnic groups.[23] To appeal to diverse groups, marketers must listen better and be more responsive to unique ethnic needs. What might you do to appeal to specific ethnic groups with Very Vegetarian?

Competitive Factors

Of course, marketers must pay attention to the dynamic competitive environment. Many brick-and-mortar companies must be aware of new competition from the Internet, including firms that sell automobiles, insurance, music, and clothes. In the book business, Barnes & Noble is still adjusting to the new reality of Amazon.com's huge selection of books at good prices. Borders Books went out of business.[24] What will the challenge from Kindle and other eReaders provide? Now that consumers can literally search the world for the best buys through the Internet, marketers must adjust their pricing, delivery, and services accordingly. Can you see any opportunities for Very Vegetarian to make use of the Internet and social media?

Economic Factors

Marketers must pay close attention to the economic environment. As we began the new millennium, the United States was experiencing unparalleled growth, and customers were eager to buy even the most expensive automobiles, watches, and vacations. But as the economy slowed, marketers had to adapt by offering products that were less expensive and more tailored to consumers with modest incomes.[25]

The economic collapse beginning in 2008 really slowed sales and became global in scope. You can see why environmental scanning is critical to a company's success during rapidly changing economic times. What economic changes are occurring around your school that might affect a new restaurant? How have the economic crisis, the wars in Iraq, Afghanistan, and Libya, or natural disasters affected your area?

TWO DIFFERENT MARKETS: CONSUMER AND BUSINESS-TO-BUSINESS (B2B)

Marketers must know as much as possible about the market they wish to serve. As we defined it in Chapter 6, a *market* consists of people with unsatisfied wants and needs who have both the resources and the willingness to buy. There are two major markets in business: the *consumer market* and the *business-to-business market*. The **consumer market** consists of all the individuals or households that want goods and services for personal consumption or use and have the resources to buy them.

The **business-to-business (B2B) market** consists of all the individuals and organizations that want goods and services to use in producing other goods and services or to sell, rent, or supply goods to others. Oil-drilling bits, cash registers, display cases, office desks, public accounting audits, and business software are B2B goods and services. Traditionally, they have been known

consumer market
All the individuals or households that want goods and services for personal consumption or use.

business-to-business (B2B) market
All the individuals and organizations that want goods and services to use in producing other goods and services or to sell, rent, or supply goods to others.

The B2B market consists of individuals and organizations that sell goods and services to other businesses. For example, manufacturer E.G.O. makes components for appliances and supplies them to virtually every stove, washing machine, and dishwasher manufacturer. How many ways can you think of in which B2B products differ from those you buy, like toothpaste and laundry detergent?

as *industrial* goods and services because they are used in industry.

The important thing to remember is that the buyer's reason for buying—that is, the end use of the product—determines whether a product is a consumer product or a B2B product. A cup of yogurt that a student buys for breakfast is a consumer product. However, when Very Vegetarian purchases the same cup of yogurt to sell to its breakfast customers, it has purchased a B2B product. The following sections outline consumer and B2B markets.

progress assessment

- What are the four steps in the marketing research process?
- What is environmental scanning?
- What factors are included in environmental scanning?

LEARNING goal 5

Explain how marketers apply the tools of market segmentation, relationship marketing, and the study of consumer behavior.

THE CONSUMER MARKET

The total potential consumer market consists of the 7 billion or so people in global markets. Because consumer groups differ greatly by age, education level, income, and taste, a business usually can't fill the needs of every group. It must decide which groups to serve, and then develop products and services specially tailored to their needs.

Take the Campbell Soup Company, for example. You know Campbell for its traditional soups such as chicken noodle and tomato. You may also have noticed that Campbell has expanded its U.S. product line to appeal to a number of different tastes. Aware of population growth in the South and in Latino communities in cities across the nation, it introduced a Creole soup for the southern market and a red bean soup for the Latino market. In Texas and California, where people like their food with a bit of kick, Campbell makes its nacho cheese soup spicier than in other parts of the country. It's just one company that has had some success studying the consumer market, breaking it down into categories, and developing products for separate groups.

The process of dividing the total market into groups with similar characteristics is called **market segmentation**. Selecting which groups or segments an organization can serve profitably is **target marketing**. For example, a shoe store may choose to sell only women's shoes, only children's shoes, or only athletic shoes. The issue is finding the right *target market*—the most profitable segment—to serve.

market segmentation
The process of dividing the total market into groups whose members have similar characteristics.

target marketing
Marketing directed toward those groups (market segments) an organization decides it can serve profitably.

figure 13.6

MARKET SEGMENTATION

This table shows some of the methods marketers use to divide the market. The aim of segmentation is to break the market into smaller units.

MAIN DIMENSION	SAMPLE VARIABLES	TYPICAL SEGMENTS
Geographic segmentation	Region	Northeast, Midwest, South, West
	City or county size	Under 5,000; 5,000-10,999; 20,000-49,000; 50,000 and up
	Density	Urban, suburban, rural
Demographic segmentation	Gender	Male, female
	Age	Under 5; 5-10; 11-18; 19-34; 35-49; 50-64; 65 and over
	Education	Some high school or less, high school graduate, some college, college graduate, postgraduate
	Race	Caucasian, African American, Indian, Asian, Hispanic
	Nationality	American, Asian, Eastern European, Japanese
	Life stage	Infant, preschool, child, teenager, collegiate, adult, senior
	Income	Under $15,000; $15,000-$24,999; $25,000-$44,999; $45,000-$74,999; $75,000 and over
	Household size	1; 2; 3-4; 5 or more
	Occupation	Professional, technical, clerical, sales supervisors, farmers, students, home-based business owners, retired, unemployed
Psychographic segmentation	Personality	Gregarious, compulsive, extroverted, aggressive, ambitious
	Values	Actualizers, fulfillers, achievers, experiencers, believers, strivers, makers, strugglers
	Lifestyle	Upscale, moderate
Benefit segmentation	Comfort	(Benefit segmentation divides an already established market into smaller, more homogeneous segments. Those people who desire economy in a car would be an example. The benefit desired varies by product.)
	Convenience	
	Durability	
	Economy	
	Health	
	Luxury	
	Safety	
	Status	
Volume segmentation	Usage	Heavy users, light users, nonusers
	Loyalty status	None, medium, strong

Segmenting the Consumer Market

A firm can segment the consumer market several ways (see Figure 13.6). Rather than selling your product throughout the United States, you might focus on just one or two regions where you can be most successful, say southern states such as Florida, Texas, and South Carolina. Dividing a market by cities, counties, states, or regions is **geographic segmentation**.

Alternatively, you could aim your product's promotions toward people ages 25 to 45 who have some college education and above-average incomes.

geographic segmentation
Dividing a market by cities, counties, states, or regions.

demographic segmentation
Dividing the market by age, income, and education level.

psychographic segmentation
Dividing the market using groups' values, attitudes, and interests.

benefit segmentation
Dividing the market by determining which benefits of the product to talk about.

volume (or usage) segmentation
Dividing the market by usage (volume of use).

niche marketing
The process of finding small but profitable market segments and designing or finding products for them.

The Internet has dramatically increased the ways in which companies can reach out to customers and conduct relationship marketing. For example, it can assist marketers in customizing products like photo books and calendars shown here. What appeals to you about these firms?

Automobiles such as Lexus are often targeted to this audience. Age, income, and education level are criteria for **demographic segmentation**. So are religion, race, and occupation. Demographics are the most widely used segmentation variable, but not necessarily the best.

You may want your ads to portray a target group's lifestyle. To do that, you would study the group's values, attitudes, and interests in a strategy called **psychographic segmentation**. If you decide to target Generation Y, you would do an in-depth study of members' values and interests, like which TV shows they watch and which personalities they like best. With that information you would develop advertisements for those TV shows using those stars.

In marketing for Very Vegetarian, what benefits of vegetarianism might you talk about? Should you emphasize freshness, heart-healthiness, taste, or something else? Determining which product benefits your target market prefers and using those benefits to promote a product is **benefit segmentation**.

You can also determine who are the big eaters of vegetarian food. Does your restaurant seem to attract more men or more women? More students or more faculty members? Are your repeat customers from the local community or are they commuters? Separating the market by volume of product use is called **volume (or usage) segmentation**. Once you know who your customer base is, you can design your promotions to better appeal to that specific group or groups.

The best segmentation strategy is to use all the variables to come up with a consumer profile that represents a sizable, reachable, and profitable target market. That may mean not segmenting the market at all and instead going after the total market (everyone). Or it may mean going after ever-smaller segments. We'll discuss that strategy next.

Reaching Smaller Market Segments

Niche marketing is identifying small but profitable market segments and designing or finding products for them. Because it so easily offers an unlimited choice of goods, the Internet is transforming a consumer culture once based on big hits and best-sellers into one that supports more specialized niche products.[26] Just how small such a segment can be is illustrated by FridgeDoor.com. This company sells refrigerator magnets on the Internet. It keeps some 1,500 different magnets in stock and sells as many as 400 a week.

One-to-one marketing means developing a unique mix of goods and services for *each individual customer.* Travel agencies often develop such packages, including airline reservations, hotel reservations, rental cars, restaurants, and admission to museums and other attractions for individual customers. This is relatively easy to do in B2B markets where each customer may buy in huge volume. But one-to-one marketing is now becoming possible in consumer markets as well. Dell produces a unique computer system for each customer. Can you envision designing special Very Vegetarian menu items for individual customers?

Moving toward Relationship Marketing

In the world of mass production following the Industrial Revolution, marketers responded by practicing mass marketing. **Mass marketing** means developing products and promotions to please large groups of people. That is, there is little market segmentation. The mass marketer tries to sell the same products to as many people as possible. That means using mass media, such as TV, radio, and newspapers to reach them. Although mass marketing led many firms to success, marketing managers often got so caught up with their products and competition that they became less responsive to the market. Airlines, for example, are so intent on meeting competition that they often annoy their customers.

Relationship marketing tends to lead away from mass production and toward custom-made goods and services. The goal is to keep individual customers over time by offering them new products that exactly meet their requirements. The latest in technology enables sellers to work with individual buyers to determine their wants and needs and to develop goods and services specifically designed for them, like hand-tailored shirts and unique vacations.

Understanding consumers is so important to marketing that a whole area of marketing emerged called consumer behavior. We explore that area next.

The Consumer Decision-Making Process

Figure 13.7 on p. 370 shows the consumer decision-making process and some outside factors that influence it. The five steps in the process are often studied in courses on consumer behavior.

The first step is *problem recognition,* which may occur when your washing machine breaks down and you realize you need a new one. This leads to an *information search*—you look for ads and brochures about washing machines. You may consult a secondary data source like *Consumer Reports* or other information, perhaps online. And you'll likely seek advice from other people who have purchased washing machines.

After compiling all this information, you *evaluate alternatives* and make a *purchase decision.* But your buying process doesn't end here. After the purchase, you may ask the people you spoke to previously how their machines perform and then do other comparisons to your new washer.

Marketing researchers investigate these consumer thought processes and behavior at each stage in a purchase to determine the best way to help the buyer buy. This area of study is called *consumer behavior.*

Consumer behavior researchers also study the influences that affect consumer behavior. Figure 13.7 shows several: marketing mix variables (the four Ps); psychological influences, such as perception and attitudes; situational influences, such as the type of purchase and the physical surroundings; and sociocultural influences, such as reference groups and culture. Other important factors include these:

- *Learning* creates changes in an individual's behavior resulting from previous experiences and information. If you've tried a particular brand of shampoo and don't like it, you've learned not to buy it again.

- *Reference group* is the group an individual uses as a reference point in forming beliefs, attitudes, values, or behavior. A college student who carries a briefcase instead of a backpack may see businesspeople as his or her reference group.

- *Culture* is the set of values, attitudes, and ways of doing things transmitted from one generation to another in a given society. The U.S. culture emphasizes and transmits the values of education, freedom, and diversity.

Consumer behavior researchers investigate people's buying decisions and the factors that influence their choices. Social, psychological, and marketing-mix factors are important when we decide what to buy. So are the store environment and our previous buying experiences. What influences the choices you make in your local supermarket?

one-to-one marketing
Developing a unique mix of goods and services for each individual customer.

mass marketing
Developing products and promotions to please large groups of people.

relationship marketing
Marketing strategy with the goal of keeping individual customers over time by offering them products that exactly meet their requirements.

figure 13.7

THE CONSUMER DECISION-MAKING PROCESS AND OUTSIDE INFLUENCES
There are many influences on consumers as they decide which goods and services to buy. Marketers have some influence, but it's not usually as strong as sociocultural influences. Helping consumers in their information search and their evaluation of alternatives is a major function of marketing.

Marketing mix influences
- Product
- Price
- Place
- Promotion

Sociocultural influences
- Reference groups
- Family
- Social class
- Culture
- Subculture

Psychological influences
- Perception
- Attitudes
- Learning
- Motivation

Situational influences
- Type of purchase
- Social surroundings
- Physical surroundings
- Previous experience

Decision-making process
1. Problem recognition
2. Information search
3. Alternative evaluation
4. Purchase decision/or no purchase
5. Postpurchase evaluation (cognitive dissonance)

- *Subculture* is the set of values, attitudes, and ways of doing things that results from belonging to a certain ethnic group, racial group, or other group with which one closely identifies (e.g., teenagers).

- *Cognitive dissonance* is a type of psychological conflict that can occur after a purchase. Consumers who make a major purchase may have doubts about whether they got the best product at the best price. Marketers must reassure such consumers after the sale that they made a good decision. An auto dealer, for example, may send positive press articles about the particular car a consumer purchased, offer product guarantees, and provide certain free services.

Many universities have expanded the marketing curriculum to include courses in business-to-business marketing. As you'll learn below, that market is huge.

LEARNING goal 6

Compare the business-to-business market and the consumer market.

THE BUSINESS-TO-BUSINESS MARKET

Business-to-business (B2B) marketers include manufacturers; intermediaries such as retailers; institutions like hospitals, schools, and charities; and the government. The B2B market is larger than the consumer market because items are often sold and resold several times in the B2B process before they reach the final consumer. B2B marketing strategies also differ from consumer marketing because business buyers have their own decision-making process. Several factors make B2B marketing different, including these:

1. Customers in the B2B market are relatively few; there are just a few construction firms or mining operations compared to the 70 million or so households in the U.S. consumer market.

2. Business customers are relatively large; that is, big organizations account for most of the employment and production of various goods and services. Nonetheless, there are many small- to medium-sized firms in the United States that together make an attractive market.

3. B2B markets tend to be geographically concentrated. For example, oilfields are found in the Southwest and Alaska. Thus B2B marketers can concentrate their efforts on a particular area and minimize distribution problems by locating warehouses near industrial centers.

4. Business buyers are generally more rational and less emotional than ultimate consumers; they use product specifications to guide buying choices and often more carefully weigh the total product offer, including quality, price, and service.

5. B2B sales tend to be direct, but not always. Tire manufacturers sell directly to auto manufacturers but use intermediaries, such as wholesalers and retailers, to sell to ultimate consumers.

6. Whereas consumer promotions are based more on *advertising,* B2B sales are based on *personal selling.* There are fewer customers and they usually demand more personal service.

Figure 13.8 shows some of the differences between buying behavior in the B2B and consumer markets. B2B buyers also use the Internet to make purchases. You'll learn more about the business-to-business market in advanced marketing courses.

figure 13.8

COMPARING BUSINESS-TO-BUSINESS AND CONSUMER BUYING BEHAVIOR

	BUSINESS-TO-BUSINESS MARKET	CONSUMER MARKET
Market Structure	Relatively few potential customers Larger purchases Geographically concentrated	Many potential customers Smaller purchases Geographically dispersed
Products	Require technical, complex products Frequently require customization Frequently require technical advice, delivery, and after-sale service	Require less technical products Sometimes require customization Sometimes require technical advice, delivery, and after-sale service
Buying Procedures	Buyers are trained Negotiate details of most purchases Follow objective standards Formal process involving specific employees Closer relationships between marketers and buyers Often buy from multiple sources	No special training Accept standard terms for most purchases Use personal judgment Informal process involving household members Impersonal relationships between marketers and consumers Rarely buy from multiple sources

YOUR PROSPECTS IN MARKETING

There is a wider variety of careers in marketing than in most business disciplines. If you major in marketing, an array of career options will be available to you. You could become a manager in a retail store like Saks or Target. You could do marketing research or work in product management. You could go into selling, advertising, sales promotion, or public relations. You could work in transportation, storage, or international distribution. You could design interactive websites to implement CRM. These are just a few of the possibilities. Think, for example, of the many ways to use Facebook, Google, and other new technologies in marketing. As you read through the following marketing chapters, consider whether a marketing career would interest you.

progress assessment

- Can you define the terms *consumer market* and *business-to-business market?*
- Can you name and describe five ways to segment the consumer market?
- What is niche marketing, and how does it differ from one-to-one marketing?
- What are four key factors that make B2B markets different from consumer markets?

summary

Learning Goal 1. Define *marketing,* and apply the marketing concept to both for-profit and nonprofit organizations.

- **What is marketing?**

Marketing is the activity, set of institutions, and processes for creating, communicating, delivering, and exchanging offerings that have value for customers, clients, partners, and society at large.

- **How has marketing changed over time?**

During the *production era,* marketing was largely a distribution function. Emphasis was on producing as many goods as possible and getting them to markets. By the early 1920s, during the *selling era,* the emphasis turned to selling and advertising to persuade customers to buy the existing goods produced by mass production. After World War II, the tremendous demand for goods and services led to the *marketing concept era,* when businesses recognized the need to be responsive to customers' needs. During the 1990s, marketing entered the *customer relationship era,* focusing on enhancing customer satisfaction and stimulating long-term customer loyalty. The newest in customer relationship building involves social networks, online communities, and blogs.

- **What are the three parts of the marketing concept?**

The three parts of the marketing concept are (1) a customer orientation, (2) a service orientation, and (3) a profit orientation (that is, marketing goods and services that will earn a profit and enable the firm to survive and expand).

- **What kinds of organizations are involved in marketing?**

All kinds of organizations use marketing, including for-profit and nonprofit organizations like states, charities, churches, politicians, and schools.

Learning Goal 2. Describe the four Ps of marketing.
- **How do marketers implement the four Ps?**
The idea behind the four Ps is to design a *product* people want, *price* it competitively, *place* it where consumers can find it easily, and *promote* it so consumers know it exists.

Learning Goal 3. Summarize the marketing research process.
- **What are the steps in conducting marketing research?**
(1) Define the problem or opportunity and determine the present situation, (2) collect data, (3) analyze the data, and (4) choose the best solution.

Learning Goal 4. Show how marketers use environmental scanning to learn about the changing marketing environment.
- **What is environmental scanning?**
Environmental scanning is the process of identifying factors that can affect marketing success. Marketers pay attention to all the environmental factors that create opportunities and threats.
- **What are some of the more important environmental trends in marketing?**
The most important global and technological change is probably the growth of the Internet. Another is the growth of consumer databases, with which companies can develop products and services that closely match consumers' needs. Marketers must monitor social trends like population growth and shifts to maintain their close relationship with customers. They must also monitor the dynamic competitive and economic environments.

Learning Goal 5. Explain how marketers apply the tools of market segmentation, relationship marketing, and the study of consumer behavior.
- **What are some of the ways marketers segment the consumer market?**
Geographic segmentation means dividing the market into different regions. Segmentation by age, income, and education level is *demographic segmentation*. We study a group's values, attitudes, and interests using *psychographic segmentation*. Determining which benefits customers prefer and using them to promote a product is *benefit segmentation*. Separating the market by usage is called *volume segmentation*. The best segmentation strategy is to use all the variables to come up with a consumer profile for a target market that's sizable, reachable, and profitable.
- **What is the difference between mass marketing and relationship marketing?**
Mass marketing means developing products and promotions to please large groups of people. Relationship marketing tends to lead away from mass production and toward custom-made goods and services. Its goal is to keep individual customers over time by offering them products or services that meet their needs.
- **What are some of the factors that influence the consumer decision-making process?**
See Figure 13.7 on p. 370 for some of the major influences on consumer decision-making. Other factors are learning, reference group, culture, subculture, and cognitive dissonance.

Learning Goal 6. Compare the business-to-business market and the consumer market.
- **What makes the business-to-business market different from the consumer market?**
Customers in the B2B market are relatively few and large. B2B markets tend to be geographically concentrated, and industrial buyers generally are more rational than ultimate consumers in their selection of goods and services. B2B sales tend to be direct, and there is much more emphasis on personal selling than in consumer markets.

key terms

benefit
  segmentation 368
brand name 358
business-to-business
  (B2B) market 365
consumer market 365
customer relationship
  management (CRM) 355
demographic
  segmentation 368
environmental
  scanning 363

focus group 362
geographic
  segmentation 367
marketing 352
marketing concept 355
marketing mix 357
marketing research 360
market
  segmentation 366
mass marketing 369
niche marketing 368
one-to-one marketing 369

primary data 361
product 358
promotion 359
psychographic
  segmentation 368
relationship
  marketing 369
secondary data 361
target marketing 366
test marketing 358
volume (or usage)
  segmentation 368

critical thinking

1. When businesses buy goods and services from other businesses, they usually buy in large volume. Salespeople in the business-to-business area usually are paid on a commission basis; that is, they earn a certain percentage of each sale they make. Why might B2B sales be a more financially rewarding career area than consumer sales?

2. Industrial companies sell goods such as steel, lumber, computers, engines, parts, and supplies. Name three such companies in your region.

3. What environmental changes are occurring in your community? What has been the impact of the recent economic crisis? What environmental changes in marketing are most likely to change your career prospects in the future? How can you learn more about those changes? What might you do to prepare for them?

4. Which of your needs are not being met by businesses and/or nonprofit organizations in your area? Are there enough people with similar needs to attract an organization that would meet those needs? How would you find out?

developing workplace skills

1. Think of an effective marketing mix for a new electric car or a brushless car wash for your neighborhood. Be prepared to discuss your ideas in class.

2. Working in teams of five (or on your own), think of a product or service your friends want but cannot get on or near campus. You might ask your friends at other schools what's available there. What kind of product would fill that need? Discuss your results in class and how you might go about marketing that new product or service.

3. Business has fallen off greatly at your upscale restaurant because of the economic crisis. List four things you can do to win back the loyalty of your past customers.

4. Working in teams of four or five (or on your own), list as many brand names of pizza as you can, including from pizza shops, restaurants, supermarkets, and so on. Merge your list with the lists from other groups or classmates. Then try to identify the target market for each brand. Do they all seem to be after the same market, or are there different brands for different markets? What are the separate appeals?

5. Take a little time to review the concepts in this chapter as they apply to Very Vegetarian, the restaurant we used as an example throughout. Have an open discussion in class about (a) a different name for the restaurant, (b) a location for the restaurant, (c) a promotional program, and (d) a way to establish a long-term relationship with customers.

taking it to the net

Purpose

To demonstrate how the Internet can be used to enhance marketing relationships.

Exercise

Nike wants to help its customers add soul to their soles and express their individuality by customizing their own shoes. See for yourself at www.nike.com. Enter "customize" in the search box and build a shoe that fits your style.

1. What if you're in the middle of your shoe design and have questions about what to do next? Where can you go for help?

2. How does Nike's website help the company strengthen its relationships with its stakeholders? Give examples to support your answer.

3. How do the elements of the website reflect Nike's target market?

4. Does Nike invite comments from visitors to its website? If so, how does this affect its attempt to build positive relationships with its customers?

casing the web

To access the case "Measuring Marketing Effectiveness," visit **www.mhhe.com/ubl0e**

video case

To access the video case featuring Energizer, visit **www.mhhe.com/ubl0e**

DEVELOPING AND
Pricing
Goods and
Services

14

LEARNING goals

After you have read and studied this chapter, you should be able to

1 Describe a total product offer.

2 Identify the various kinds of consumer and industrial goods.

3 Summarize the functions of packaging.

4 Contrast *brand, brand name,* and *trademark,* and show the value of brand equity.

5 Explain the steps in the new-product development process.

6 Describe the product life cycle.

7 Identify various pricing objectives and strategies.

profile

Getting to Know
X _Mary Barra_
GM Senior Vice President

When General Motors (GM) faced bankruptcy in 2009, the government invested $50 billion in the company. That means that U.S. citizens now have an ownership interest in the carmaker. With our money on the line, we certainly have an interest in what the company plans to do to regain profitability. Many of the most important decisions will involve developing new products that consumers will want to buy. The new GM senior vice president of global product development is Mary Barra. Barra was already GM's highest-ranking woman, having served as vice president for global human resources. She has also been vice president for global manufacturing engineering and manager of an assembly plant in Detroit.

Barra earned her undergraduate degree in electrical engineering at Kettering University and her MBA at Stanford. The GM chairman and CEO said that Barra will bring a fresh perspective to the critically important job of managing global vehicle programs for GM. She will focus on the customer in the areas of global design, vehicle and power train engineering, program management, and quality with the goal of delivering the world's best vehicles. With more than 36,000 members, her team will also manage global strategic product alliances. GM is working to gain market share in highly competitive segments like small fuel-efficient cars, and it plans to expand its lineup of plug-in hybrids beyond the Chevy Volt.

Barra doesn't emphasize her status as the first female to head product development for an American automaker. But, "If it encourages more young girls in junior high to stick with math and science, that's great," she said. "We need more women in engineering in general." Perhaps there are women in college today who will be inspired by Barra's success.

Barra faces a substantial task: figuring out how to cut the time it takes to design, engineer, and build new vehicles while turning out cars and trucks that respond to consumer needs from all nations. GM's new-vehicle development process was slowed leading up to the company's bankruptcy reorganization and is now entering a period in which few new models will be introduced. About 12 percent of GM's U.S. vehicle sales in 2011 was from "new" or heavily redesigned vehicles. That number is expected to rise to 30 percent in 2012. The automaker's sales rose 7 percent in 2010 (from a year earlier) despite removing eight brands from its lineup.

Developing and pricing goods and services will be a major goal of firms around the world as they begin to dig themselves out of the financial problems they are now facing. This chapter will introduce you to the many facets of new product development in both goods and services. You will also learn about packaging, branding, and the other elements of a total product offer. It will be interesting to follow the auto industry as it introduces new electric cars, the new, smaller, fuel-efficient cars, and the like. With people like Mary Barra leading the charge, we would expect the U.S. auto industry to be right up with the global leaders in the coming years.

Sources: Sharon Terlep, "GM Product Chief's Job: New Cars Fast," *The Wall Street Journal*, January 21, 2011; LinkedIn profile accessed March 2011; and "GM Appoints Mary Barra to Lead Global Product Development," *GM News*, accessed March 2011.

NAME THAT

company

It's no secret that the airline industry is extremely competitive and many airlines have cut basic services like free baggage and food. In order to set itself apart from its competitors, this company takes a different path by offering door-to-door limousine service and in-flight massages. What is the name of this company? (Find the answer in the chapter.)

LEARNING goal **1**

Describe a total product offer.

PRODUCT DEVELOPMENT AND THE TOTAL PRODUCT OFFER

value
Good quality at a fair price. When consumers calculate the value of a product, they look at the benefits and then subtract the cost to see if the benefits exceed the costs.

Global managers will be challenging U.S. managers with new products at low prices.[1] The best way to compete is to design and promote better products, meaning products that customers perceive to have the best **value**—good quality at a fair price.[2] You may have noticed that many restaurants were pushing "value meals" when the economy slowed from 2008 to 2011. Have you tried, for example, the new, smaller Blizzard from Dairy Queen?[3]

One of the American Marketing Association's definitions of marketing says it's "a set of processes for creating, communicating, and delivering *value* to customers." When consumers calculate the value of a product, they look at the benefits and then subtract the cost (price) to see whether the benefits exceed the costs, including the cost of driving to the store (or shipping fees if they buy the product online). Note that L.L. Bean eliminated shipping charges. That lowers the cost for consumers and makes their products more desirable (valuable).[4]

Whether consumers perceive a product as the best value depends on many factors, including the benefits they seek and the service they receive. To satisfy consumers, marketers must learn to listen better and constantly adapt to changing market demands. For example, traditional phone companies must now compete with Voice over Internet Protocol (VoIP)—a system that allows people to make very inexpensive phone calls through the Internet. And U.S. automobile companies must adapt to foreign producers by offering more competitive cars, or face extinction.[5]

Marketers have learned that adapting products to new competition and new markets is an ongoing need. We're sure you've noticed menu changes at your local fast-food restaurant over time. An organization can't do a one-time survey of consumer wants and needs, design a group of products to meet those needs, put them in the stores, and then just relax. It must constantly monitor changing consumer wants and needs, and adapt products, policies, and services accordingly. Did you know that McDonald's sells as much chicken as beef these days?[6] Some is being sold as a Chicken Biscuit for breakfast. Those double cheeseburgers fast-food restaurants were serving for $1.00 turned out to be a money loser, even though they were popular with consumers. You can't give consumers *too* good a deal or you can go out of business.

McDonald's and other restaurants are constantly trying new ideas. It added smoothies and oatmeal with fruit.[7] In Kokomo, Indiana, McDonald's tried waiter service and a more varied menu. In New York, it offered McDonuts to compete with Krispy Kreme. In Atlanta and other cities, McDonald's had computer stations linked to the Internet. In Hawaii, it tried a Spam breakfast platter, and in Columbus, Ohio, a mega-McDonald's had a karaoke booth. McDonald's has a McCafé in Chicago's Loop that sells premium coffee, pastries, and wrapped sandwiches. It has more than 300 such cafés in other countries and most McDonald's in the United States are putting in something similar. Watch out Starbucks. Some McDonald's even have digital-media kiosks that allow customers to burn custom CDs from a catalog of 70,000 songs, print digital photos, and download ringtones for mobile phones.

How would you like a beer or glass of wine with your Big Mac? You can get both at this McDonald's in Paris. Notice how the restaurant's architecture fits the style of the city. The same is true of the food in McDonald's other restaurants outside the United States. In Europe, the menus and interior designs are frequently adapted to fit the tastes and cultural preferences of each country.

What was Starbucks' answer to the new challenges from McDonald's, Dunkin' Donuts, Target, and others? It began offering more food products. Oatmeal has become a huge success at Starbucks as well. The new menu also includes fruit smoothies and more—like regular coffee at lower prices.

All fast-food organizations must constantly monitor all sources of information for new-product ideas. McDonald's isn't alone in that. Look at those baguettes and cream cheese croissants at 7-Eleven—they're right next to the cappuccino machine. KFC put in a line of chicken sandwiches. Burger King tried an X-treme Double Cheeseburger. Wendy's is trying a major coffee program in Mississippi, including iced coffee, and introducing a whole new lineup of other products.

Offerings may differ in various locations according to the wants of the local community. In Iowa pork tenderloin is big, but in Oklahoma City it's tortilla scramblers. Globally, companies must adapt to local tastes. At Bob's Big Boy in Thailand, you can get Tropical Shrimp; at Carl's Junior in Mexico, you can order the Machaca Burrito; and at Shakey's Pizza in the Philippines, you can get Cali Shandy, a Filipino beer. Product development, then, is a key activity in any modern business, anywhere in the world.

You can imagine what could happen when your product loses some of its appeal. Zippo lighters, for example, may lose some market as people turn away from smoking. Zippo, therefore, tried offering products such as key holders, tape measures and belt buckles. They are no longer being sold, but Zippo has recently introduced a new men's fragrance and a clothing line that includes hoodies, ball caps and jeans.[8]

Distributed Product Development

The increase in outsourcing and alliance building has resulted in innovation efforts that often require using multiple organizations separated by cultural, geographic and legal boundaries. **Distributed product development** is the

distributed product development
Handing off various parts of your innovation process—often to companies in other countries.

figure 14.1

**POTENTIAL COMPONENTS OF
A TOTAL PRODUCT OFFER**

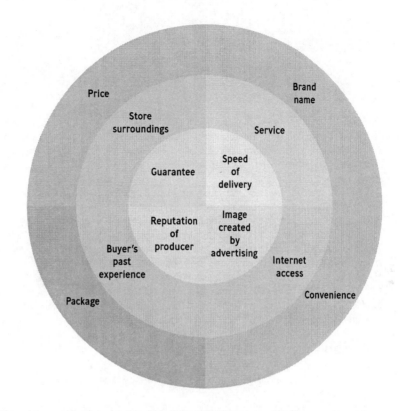

total product offer
Everything that consumers evaluate when deciding whether to buy something; also called a value package.

Apple's iPhone offers a range of features and functions, including the ability to make video calls, take photos, check e-mail, browse websites, get directions, tell time, keep a shopping list, record appointments in your calendar, download songs, sync with your other devices, and even make and receive phone calls. The product will likely continue to evolve and improve. What would you like Apple to add to the iPhone's total product offer?

term used to describe handing off various parts of your innovation process—often to companies in other countries. It is difficult enough to coordinate processes within a firm; it becomes substantially more difficult when trying to coordinate multifirm processes.[9] Great care must be taken to establish goals and procedures and standards before any such commitment is made.[10] One company that has collaborated with many other firms to make innovative products is 3M Company. It has developed some 55,000 products from Scotch tape to Thinsulate, and many of those products are embedded in other products such as the iPhone.[11]

Developing a Total Product Offer

From a strategic marketing viewpoint, a product is more than just the physical good or service. A **total product offer** consists of everything consumers evaluate when deciding whether to buy something. Thus, the basic product or service may be a washing machine, an insurance policy, or a beer, but the total product offer includes some or all the *value* enhancers in Figure 14.1. You may hear some people call the basic product the "core product" and the total product offer the "augmented product." Can you see how sustainability can be part of the augmented product? The nearby Thinking Green box discusses quality and sustainability.

When people buy a product, they may evaluate and compare total product offers on many dimensions. Some are tangible (the product itself and its package); others are intangible (the producer's reputation

THINKING green

www.tridentseafoods.com

Quality and Sustainability

One product that concerns consumers for both its health benefits and environmental aspects is fish. Trident Seafoods is one company that brings customers the freshest and healthiest fish possible and still assures sustainability by staying well within catch limits.

Trident Seafoods started with one boat. It focused on Alaska, fishing for salmon, pollock, crab, halibut and cod. Ignoring the cries that "It can't be done," Chuck Bundrant, the owner, decided to build a boat that both caught and processed crab. Despite that focus, the boat still catches salmon and bottom fish for diversity's sake. Bundrant and his partners now supply wild-caught salmon to warehouse giant Costco and have 40 vessels and 16 shore-based plants.

One focus of the firm is on quality. Quality control includes everything from temperature control to X-raying the fish for bones. Everything is carefully weighed to make sure that weights are honest and accurate.

Quality control goes hand in hand with sustainability. The company works with the North Pacific Fishery Management Council and the Marine Stewardship Council, which promote world sustainability practices. One part of its sustainability practices is to use all of the fish. That results in fish oil, fishmeal, and byproducts used in fertilizer and fishmeal. Bundrant says that none of what he does will amount to anything if there are no fish to catch.

Sources: Stephanie E. Ponder, "Success at Sea," *The Costco Connection,* February 2011; and Trident Seafoods Corporation, tridentseafoods.com, accessed April 2011.

and the image created by advertising). A successful marketer must begin to think like a consumer and evaluate the total product offer as a collection of impressions created by all the factors listed in Figure 14.1. It is wise to talk with consumers to see which features and benefits are most important to them and which value enhancers they want or don't want in the final offering. Frito-Lay, for example, had to drop biodegradable bags because they were "too noisy."

What questions might you ask consumers when developing the total product offer for Very Vegetarian? (Recall the business idea we introduced in Chapter 13.) Remember, store surroundings are important in the restaurant business, as are the parking lot and the condition of bathrooms. When designing services, some have even suggested the importance of things like trust and feelings in general.[12]

Sometimes an organization can use low prices to create an attractive total product offer. For example, outlet stores offer brand-name goods for less. Shoppers like getting high-quality goods and low prices, but they must be careful. Outlets also carry lower-quality products with similar but not exactly the same features as goods carried in regular stores. Different consumers may want different total product offers, so a company must develop a variety of offerings.

Product Lines and the Product Mix

Companies usually don't sell just one product. A **product line** is a group of products that are physically similar or intended for a similar market. They usually face similar competition. In one product line, there may be several competing brands. Notice, for example, Diet Coke, Diet Coke with Splenda, Coke Zero, Diet Coke with Lemon, Diet Coke with Lime, Diet Vanilla Coke, and Diet Cherry Coke. Makes it kind of hard to choose, doesn't it? Even Coke

product line
A group of products that are physically similar or are intended for a similar market.

commercials have product managers who can't tell the difference between Coke and Coke Zero. Have you seen the new aluminum Coke bottle? It's recyclable, resealable, less costly to make than a plastic or glass bottle, and feels cooler to the touch. Both Coke and Pepsi have added water and sports drinks to their product lines to meet new consumer tastes.

Procter & Gamble (P&G) has many brands in its laundry detergent product line, including Tide, Era, Downy, and Bold. P&G's product lines together make up its **product mix**, the combination of all product lines offered by a manufacturer. Have you noticed that there are some 352 distinct types of toothpastes available in stores?[13] Do you think that is too many or not?

Service providers have product lines and product mixes as well. A bank or credit union may offer a variety of services from savings accounts, automated teller machines, and computer banking to money market funds, safety deposit boxes, car loans, mortgages, traveler's checks, online banking, and insurance. AT&T combines services (communications) with goods (phones) in its product mix, with special emphasis on wireless.

> **product mix**
> The combination of product lines offered by a manufacturer.

LEARNING goal 2

> Identify the various kinds of consumer and industrial goods.

PRODUCT DIFFERENTIATION

Product differentiation is the creation of real or perceived product differences. Actual product differences are sometimes quite small, so marketers must use a creative mix of pricing, advertising, and packaging (value enhancers) to create a unique, attractive image. Various bottled water companies, for example, have successfully attempted product differentiation. The companies made their bottled waters so attractive through pricing and promotion that now restaurant customers often order water by brand name.

There's no reason why you couldn't create a similar attractive image for Very Vegetarian, your vegetarian restaurant. Small businesses can often win market share with creative product differentiation. Yearbook photographer Charlie Clark competes by offering multiple clothing changes, backgrounds, and poses along with special allowances, discounts, and guarantees. His small business has the advantage of being more flexible in adapting to customer needs and wants, and he's able to offer attractive product options. Clark has been so successful that companies use him as a speaker at photography conventions. How could you respond creatively to the consumer wants of vegetarians?

> **product differentiation**
> The creation of real or perceived product differences.
>
> **convenience goods and services**
> Products that the consumer wants to purchase frequently and with a minimum of effort.
>
> **shopping goods and services**
> Those products that the consumer buys only after comparing value, quality, price, and style from a variety of sellers.
>
> **specialty goods and services**
> Consumer products with unique characteristics and brand identity. Because these products are perceived as having no reasonable substitute, the consumer puts forth a special effort to purchase them.

Marketing Different Classes of Consumer Goods and Services

One popular classification of consumer goods and services has four general categories—convenience, shopping, specialty, and unsought.

1. **Convenience goods and services** are products the consumer wants to purchase frequently and with a minimum of effort, like candy, gum,

milk, snacks, gas, and banking services. One store that sells mostly convenience goods is 7-Eleven. Location, brand awareness, and image are important for marketers of convenience goods and services. The Internet has taken convenience to a whole new level, especially for banks and other service companies. Companies that don't offer such services are likely to lose market share to those that do unless they offer outstanding service to customers who visit in person.

2. **Shopping goods and services** are products the consumer buys only after comparing value, quality, price, and style from a variety of sellers. Shopping goods and services are sold largely through *shopping centers* where consumers can make comparisons of products like clothes, shoes, appliances, and auto repair services. Target is one store that sells mostly shopping goods. Because many consumers carefully compare such products, marketers can emphasize price differences, quality differences, or some combination of the two. Think of how the Internet has helped you find the right shopping goods..

3. **Specialty goods and services** are consumer products with unique characteristics and brand identity. Because consumers perceive that specialty goods have no reasonable substitute, they put forth a special effort to purchase them. Examples include fine watches, expensive wine, fur coats, jewelry, imported chocolates, and services provided by medical specialists or business consultants.

    Specialty goods are often marketed through specialty magazines. Specialty skis may be sold through sports magazines and specialty foods through gourmet magazines. Again, the Internet helps buyers find specialty goods. In fact, some specialty goods can be sold exclusively on the Internet.

4. **Unsought goods and services** are products consumers are unaware of, haven't necessarily thought of buying, or suddenly find they need to solve an unexpected problem. They include emergency car-towing services, burial services, and insurance.

Tap the "Gift a Drink" button on Pepsi's new Social Vending Machine, enter your info, choose a drink, record an optional video message, enter your friends' info, and instantly they'll receive a text message with a code to redeem their drink at another sociable machine. Do you think this new machine will be popular with your friends?

unsought goods and services
Products that consumers are unaware of, haven't necessarily thought of buying, or find that they need to solve an unexpected problem.

The marketing task varies according to the category of product; convenience goods are marketed differently from specialty goods. The best way to promote convenience goods is to make them readily available and create the proper image. Some combination of price, quality, and service is the best appeal for shopping goods. Specialty goods rely on reaching special market segments through advertising. Unsought goods such as life insurance often rely on personal selling. Car towing relies heavily on Yellow Pages advertising.

Whether a good or service falls into a particular class depends on the individual consumer. Coffee can be a shopping good for one consumer, while flavored gourmet roast is a specialty good for another. Some people shop around to compare different dry cleaners, so dry cleaning is a shopping service for them. Others go to the closest store, making it a convenience service. Marketers must carefully monitor their customer base to determine how consumers perceive their products.[14]

PART 5   ✳   Marketing: Developing and Implementing Customer-Oriented Marketing Plans

Marketing Industrial Goods and Services

Many goods could be classified as consumer goods or industrial goods, based on their uses. A computer kept at home for personal use is clearly a consumer good. But in a commercial setting, such as an accounting firm or manufacturing plant, the same computer is an industrial good.

industrial goods
Products used in the production of other products. Sometimes called business goods or B2B goods.

Industrial goods (sometimes called business goods or B2B goods) are products used in the production of other products. They are sold in the business-to-business (B2B) market. Some products can be both consumer and industrial goods. We've just mentioned how personal computers fit in both categories. As a consumer good, a computer might be sold through electronics stores like Best Buy or computer magazines. Most of the promotion would be advertising. As an industrial good, personal computers are more likely to be sold through salespeople or on the Internet. Advertising is less of a factor when selling industrial goods. Thus, you can see that classifying goods by user category helps marketers determine the proper marketing-mix strategy.

Figure 14.2 shows some categories of both consumer goods and industrial goods and services. *Installations* consist of major capital equipment such as new factories and heavy machinery. *Capital items* are expensive products that last a long time. A new factory building is both a capital item and an installation. *Accessory equipment* consists of capital items that are not quite as long-lasting or expensive as installations—like computers, copy machines, and various tools. Various categories of industrial goods are shown in the figure.

Many goods could be classified as consumer goods or industrial goods, based on their uses. For example, a computer that a person uses at home for personal use would clearly be a consumer good. But that same computer used in a commercial setting, such as a hospital, would be classified as an industrial good. What difference does it make how a good is classified?

progress assessment

- What value enhancers may be included in a total product offer?
- What's the difference between a product line and a product mix?
- Name the four classes of consumer goods and services, and give examples of each.
- Describe three different types of industrial goods.

figure 14.2

VARIOUS CATEGORIES OF CONSUMER AND INDUSTRIAL GOODS AND SERVICES

LEARNING goal **3**

Summarize the functions of packaging.

PACKAGING CHANGES THE PRODUCT

We've said that consumers evaluate many aspects of the total product offer, including the brand. It's surprising how important packaging can be in such evaluations. Many companies have used packaging to change and improve their basic product. We have squeezable ketchup bottles that stand upside down; square paint cans with screw tops and integrated handles; plastic bottles for motor oil that eliminate the need for funnels; toothpaste pumps; packaged dinners and other foods, like popcorn, that can be cooked in a microwave oven; single-use packets of spices; and so forth. Another interesting innovation is aromatic packaging. Arizona Beverage Company now has aromatic caps on its flavored iced teas.

In each case, the package changed the product in consumers' minds and opened large new markets. Do you sometimes have difficulty opening plastic packaging? Which packaging innovations do you like best? Can you see some market potential in developing better packaging? Packaging has even become a profession. Check out the Michigan State University School of Packaging, for example. Packages must perform the following functions:

1. Attract the buyer's attention.
2. Protect the goods inside, stand up under handling and storage, be tamperproof, and deter theft.
3. Be easy to open and use.
4. Describe and give information about the contents.
5. Explain the benefits of the good inside.
6. Provide information on warranties, warnings, and other consumer matters.
7. Give some indication of price, value, and uses.

Packaging can also make a product more attractive to retailers. The Universal Product Codes (UPCs) on many packages help stores control inventory. They combine a bar code and a preset number that gives the retailer information about the product's price, size, color, and other attributes. In short, packaging changes the product by changing its visibility, usefulness, or attractiveness.

One relatively new packaging technology for tracking products is the radio frequency identification (RFID) chip, especially the ones made with nanoparticle powder. When attached to a product, the chip sends out signals telling a company where the product is at all times. RFID chips carry more information than bar codes, don't have to be read one at a time (whole pallets can be read in an instant), and can be read at a distance. Walmart has been a leader in using RFID technology.

The Growing Importance of Packaging

Packaging has always been an important aspect of the product offer, but today it's carrying more of the promotional burden than in the past. Many products once sold by salespersons are now sold in self-service outlets, and the package has acquired more sales responsibility. The Fair Packaging and Labeling Act was passed to give consumers much more quantity and value information on product packaging.

bundling
Grouping two or more products together and pricing them as a unit.

Even industrial products can benefit from innovative packaging. The new Heinz Dip & Squeeze ketchup package allows restaurant owners to offer their customers a choice of peeling off the lid for dipping or tearing off the top for squeezing. The new package contains 3 times the ketchup of traditional sachets and uses less packaging. Shaped like the iconic bottles, the packets reinforce the Heinz Ketchup brand.

Packaging may make use of a strategy called **bundling**, which combines goods and/or services for a single price. Virgin Airlines has bundled door-to-door limousine service and in-flight massages in its total product offer. Financial institutions are offering everything from financial advice to help in purchasing insurance, stocks, bonds, mutual funds, and more. When combining goods or services into one package, marketers must not include so much that the price gets too high. It's best to work with customers to develop value enhancers that meet their individual needs.[15]

LEARNING goal 4

Contrast *brand, brand name,* and *trademark,* and show the value of brand equity.

brand
A name, symbol, or design (or combination thereof) that identifies the goods or services of one seller or group of sellers and distinguishes them from the goods and services of competitors.

BRANDING AND BRAND EQUITY

A **brand** is a name, symbol, or design (or combination thereof) that identifies the goods or services of one seller or group of sellers and distinguishes them from the goods and services of competitors. The word *brand* includes practically all means of identifying a product. As we noted in Chapter 13, a *brand name* consists of a word, letter, or group of words or letters that differentiates one seller's goods and services from those of competitors. Brand names you may be familiar with include Red Bull, Sony, Del Monte, Campbell, Levi's, Google, Borden, Michelob, and of course many more. Brand names give products a distinction that tends to make them attractive to consumers. The Reaching Beyond Our Borders box on p. 388 discusses product names in more depth.

A **trademark** is a brand that has exclusive legal protection for both its brand name and its design. Trademarks like McDonald's golden arches are widely recognized and help represent the company's reputation and image. McDonald's might sue to prevent a company from selling, say, McDonnel hamburgers. Did you know there are Starsbuck coffee shops in China? (Look closely at that name.)

trademark
A brand that has exclusive legal protection for both its brand name and its design.

People are often impressed by certain brand names, even though they say there's no difference between brands in a given product category. For example, even when people say that all aspirin is alike, if you put two aspirin bottles in front of them—one with the Anacin label and one with an unknown name—most choose the one with the well known brand name. Gasoline buyers often choose a brand name (e.g., Exxon) over price.

For the buyer, a brand name ensures quality, reduces search time, and adds prestige to purchases. For the seller, brand names facilitate new-product introductions, help promotional efforts, add to repeat purchases, and differentiate products so that prices can be set higher. What brand names do you prefer?

Whether its contained in a name like Cheerios, a symbol like Nike's swoosh, a design like Coca-Cola's logo, or a combination of those, a brand distinguishes one marketer's goods and services from everyone else's. How do familiar brands influence consumers' choices of products every day?

Brand Categories

Several categories of brands are familiar to you. **Manufacturers' brands** represent manufacturers that distribute products nationally—Xerox, Kodak, Sony, and Dell, for example.

Dealer (private-label) brands are products that don't carry the manufacturer's name but carry a distributor or retailer's name instead. Kenmore and Diehard are dealer brands sold by Sears. These brands are also known as *house brands* or *distributor brands.*

Many manufacturers fear having their brand names become generic names. A *generic name* is the name for a whole product category. Did you know that aspirin and linoleum were once brand names? So were nylon, escalator,

manufacturers' brands
The brand names of manufacturers that distribute products nationally.

dealer (private-label) brands
Products that don't carry the manufacturer's name but carry a distributor or retailer's name instead.

REACHING BEYOND
our borders

The Name Game

So, you've developed a product and you're ready to take it on the market. So what should you call it? America's favorite cookie, Oreo, is said to be a great name because the two O's nicely mirror the shape of the cookie itself. Could the name be part of the charm? Twitter has become the most-used word in the English language according to Global Language Monitor data. Think of the names that come to your mind when you think of American products: Coke, Pepsi, Häagen-Dazs (yes, an American product) and so on.

At one time, finding a name for a product was relatively simple. Now, with a couple hundred countries on the cyber-platform, choosing the right name is a global issue. For example, a Web development company in New Zealand chose the name hairyLemon. It has been estimated that at least a third of hairyLemon's business came from its name. Not all do-it-yourself names have been successful. For example, when Russian gas company Gazprom formed a joint venture with Nigeria's NNPC, the company was called NiGaz. Not a great name, we'd say.

Every once in a while, a successful name is created by accident. For example, the popular search engine was supposed to be called Googol (a scientific name for 1 followed by one hundred zeros). However, the founders made a typo when registering the domain name. The error resulted in a warm, catchy, human-sounding name.

In the marketing chapter, we chose the name Very Vegetarian for our new vegetarian restaurant. Have you come up with a better name? Would it help to brainstorm names with others? Would it be worthwhile to bring in an expert?

What if you wanted to build vegetarian restaurants at schools around the world? Would that make a difference? Can you see why names are critical to the long-run success of many firms?

Sources: Susan Purcell and Jay Jurisich, "Enter the Lexicon," *Bloomberg Businessweek*, October 25–October 31, 2010; and Igor International Naming and Branding Agency, www.igorinternational.com, accessed April 2011.

---

kerosene, and zipper. All those names became so popular, so identified with the product, that they lost their brand status and became generic. (Such issues are decided in the courts.) Their producers then had to come up with new names. The original Aspirin, for example, became Bayer aspirin. Companies working hard to protect their brand names today include Xerox and Rollerblade (in-line skates).

generic goods
Nonbranded products that usually sell at a sizable discount compared to national or private-label brands.

Generic goods are nonbranded products that usually sell at a sizable discount compared to national or private-label brands. They feature basic packaging and are backed with little or no advertising. Some are of poor quality, but many come close to the same quality as the national brand-name goods they copy. There are generic tissues, generic cigarettes, generic drugs, and so on. Consumers today are buying large amounts of generic products because their overall quality has improved so much in recent years. What has been your experience trying generic products?

knockoff brands
Illegal copies of national brand-name goods.

Knockoff brands are illegal copies of national brand-name goods. If you see an expensive brand-name item such as a Polo shirt or a Rolex watch for sale at a ridiculously low price, you can be pretty sure it's a knockoff. Often the brand name is just a little off, too, like Palo (Polo) or Bolex (Rolex). Look carefully. Zippo has taken to calling counterfeit copies "Rippos."[16]

Generating Brand Equity and Loyalty

A major goal of marketers in the future will be to reestablish the notion of brand equity. **Brand equity** is the value of the brand name and associated symbols. Usually, a company cannot know the value of its brand until it sells it to another company. Brand names with high reported brand equity ratings include Reynolds Wrap aluminum foil and Ziploc food bags. What's the most valuable brand name today? It's Apple. Microsoft is not far behind.[17]

The core of brand equity is **brand loyalty**, the degree to which customers are satisfied, like the brand, and are committed to further purchases. A loyal group of customers represents substantial value to a firm, and that value can be calculated. One way manufacturers are trying to create more brand loyalty is by lowering the carbon footprint of their products.

In the past, companies tried to boost their short-term performance by offering coupons and price discounts to move goods quickly. This eroded consumers' commitment to brand names, especially of grocery products. Many consumers complain when companies drop brand names like Carnation Breakfast Bars or Flex shampoo.[18] Such complaints show the power of brand names.[19] Now companies realize the value of brand equity and are trying harder to measure the earning power of strong brand names.

Brand awareness refers to how quickly or easily a given brand name comes to mind when someone mentions a product category. Advertising helps build strong brand awareness. Established brands, such as Coca-Cola and Pepsi, are usually among the highest in brand awareness. Sponsorship of events, like football's Orange Bowl and NASCAR's Cup Series, helps improve brand awareness. Simply being there over and over also increases brand awareness. That's one way Google became such a popular brand..

Perceived quality is an important part of brand equity. A product that's perceived as having better quality than its competitors can be priced accordingly. The key to creating a perception of quality is to identify what consumers look for in a high-quality product, and then to use that information in every message the company sends out. Factors influencing the perception of quality include price, appearance, and reputation.

Consumers often develop *brand preference*—that is, they prefer one brand over another—because of such cues. When consumers reach the point of *brand insistence*, the product becomes a specialty good. For example, a consumer may insist on Goodyear tires for his or her car.

It's now so easy to copy a product's benefits that off-brand products can draw consumers away from brand-name goods. Brand-name manufacturers like Intel Corporation have to develop new products and new markets faster and promote their names better than ever before to hold off challenges from competitors.

Creating Brand Associations

The name, symbol, and slogan a company uses can assist greatly in brand recognition for that company's products. **Brand association** is the linking of a brand to other favorable images, like famous product users, a popular celebrity, or a particular geographic area. Note, for example, how ads for Mercedes-Benz associate its company's cars with successful people who live luxurious lives. The person responsible for building brands is known as a brand manager or product manager. We'll discuss that position next.

---

brand equity
The value of the brand name and associated symbols.

brand loyalty
The degree to which customers are satisfied, like the brand, and are committed to further purchases.

brand awareness
How quickly or easily a given brand name comes to mind when a product category is mentioned.

brand association
The linking of a brand to other favorable images.

Brand Management

brand manager
A manager who has direct responsibility for one brand or one product line; called a *product manager* in some firms.

A **brand manager** (known as a *product manager* in some firms) has direct responsibility for one brand or product line, and manages all the elements of its marketing mix: product, price, place, and promotion. Thus, you might think of the brand manager as the president of a one-product firm.

One reason many large consumer-product companies created this position was to have greater control over new-product development and product promotion. Some companies have brand-management *teams* to bolster the overall effort. In B2B companies, brand managers are often known as product managers.

progress assessment

- What six functions does packaging now perform?
- What's the difference between a brand name and a trademark?
- Can you explain the difference between a manufacturer's brand, a dealer brand, and a generic brand?
- What are the key components of brand equity?

LEARNING goal 5

Explain the steps in the new-product development process.

THE NEW-PRODUCT DEVELOPMENT PROCESS

The odds a new product will fail are high.[20] Over 80 percent of products introduced in any year fail to reach their business objectives. Not delivering what is promised is a leading cause of new-product failure. Other causes include getting ready for marketing too late, poor positioning, too few differences from competitors, and poor packaging. Small firms especially may experience a low success rate unless they do proper product planning and new product development. As Figure 14.3 shows, new-product development for producers consists of six stages.

New products continue to pour into the market every year, and their profit potential looks tremendous. Think, for example, of the potential of home video conferencing, interactive TV, Wii games and products, smart phones, iPads, and other innovations.[21] Where do these ideas come from? How are they tested? What's the life span for an innovation? Let's look at these issues.

Generating New-Product Ideas

It now takes about seven ideas to generate one commercial product. Most ideas for new industrial products come from employee suggestions rather than research and development. Research and development, nonetheless, is a major source of new products. Employees are a major source for new consumer-goods ideas. Firms should also listen to their suppliers for new-product ideas because suppliers are often exposed to new ideas. Present customers are also a good source for new product ideas.[22]

Product Screening

Product screening reduces the number of new-product ideas a firm is working on at any one time so it can focus on the most promising. *Screening* applies criteria to determine whether the product fits well with present products, has good profit potential, and is marketable. The company may assign each of these factors a weight and compute a total score for each new product so that it can compare their potentials.

Product Analysis

After product screening comes **product analysis**, or making cost estimates and sales forecasts to get a feeling for the profitability of new-product ideas. Products that don't meet the established criteria are withdrawn from consideration.

Product Development and Testing

If a product passes the screening and analysis phase, the firm begins to develop it further, testing many different product concepts or alternatives. A firm that makes packaged meat products may develop the concept of a chicken dog—a hot dog made of chicken that tastes like an all-beef hot dog. It will develop a prototype, or sample, so that consumers can try the taste. The Spotlight on Small Business box on p. 392 discusses some new ideas for products.

Idea generation (based on consumer wants and needs)

Product screening

Product analysis

Development (including building prototypes)

Testing

Commercialization (bringing the product to the market)

figure 14.3

THE NEW-PRODUCT DEVELOPMENT PROCESS
Product development is a six-stage process. Which stage do you believe to be the most important?

product screening
A process designed to reduce the number of new-product ideas being worked on at any one time.

product analysis
Making cost estimates and sales forecasts to get a feeling for profitability of new-product ideas.

Tom Szaky of TerraCycle makes new products such as plant food, planters, pencil cases, and tote bags from discarded products made by other companies. (To see his bags made from drink pouches and Oreo cookie wrappers, go to www.terracycle.net.) What products do you own that are made of recycled material?

SPOTLIGHT ON SMALL
business

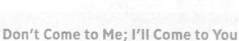

Don't Come to Me; I'll Come to You

In many cities, street vendors hawking hot dogs and other traditional fare is part of Americana. They are American icons. But that icon is changing. Not only is their menu changing from greasy hot dogs and salty pretzels to crème brulee and organic drinks, but also how customers find them is becoming more high tech. Some vendors now use Twitter and other social media to reveal their current locations and build customer relationships.

There are some cities, like Chicago, where legislation restricts food trucks for health and sanitary reasons. But in cities like New York and Portland and Austin, you can find these mobile units selling hot dogs and, often, more gourmet offerings. French rotisserie Roli Roti in San Francisco, Vietnamese bahn mi at Nom Nom in L.A., and Gruyere grilled cheese in Austin are offering gourmet food items not usually found in standard street vendor carts. Here are just a few of the mobile units you can find online:

- Clover Food Truck in Boston/Cambridge offers a rotating menu of local organic materials.

- Sugar Philly Truck in Philadelphia offers crème brulee hot off the truck.

- Dim and Den Sum in Cleveland has some of the best food truck art in America.

- Koi Fusion PDX in Portland is one of the few mobile eateries in that town.

You may enjoy looking online for a mobile unit near you. Such exploring may give you an idea about how you may start your own small business on a truck. The possibilities seem endless. You should be able to put into practice all of the product concepts you learned in this chapter. Say, how about a vegetarian truck?

Sources: Leslie Robarge, "Gourmet Food Truck Smackdown," *Bloomberg Businessweek*, March 14–March 20, 2011; Matt Vilano, "The Secret Sauce Part II," *Entrepreneur*, April 2011; and Cloverfoodlab.com, DimandDenSum.com, accessed in April 2011.

---

concept testing
Taking a product idea to consumers to test their reactions.

Concept testing takes a product idea to consumers to test their reactions. Do they see the benefits of this new product? How frequently would they buy it? At what price? What features do they like and dislike? What changes in it would they make? The firm tests samples using different packaging, branding, and ingredients until a product emerges that's desirable from both production and marketing perspectives. Some new hotels are being built to match the trendy W chain. They are said to have "hipness." Such innovations must be tried on consumers to see if they indeed recognize and appreciate the new "hip" design.[23] As you plan for Very Vegetarian, can you see the importance of concept testing for new vegetarian dishes?

How do firms test services? American Airlines conducted a six-month trial of a new self-tagging system that allowed customers to print and put the tags on their own checked bags. What features and benefits was American Airlines probably testing for?

Commercialization

Even if a product tests well, it may take quite a while to achieve success in the market. Take the zipper, for example, the result of one of the longest development efforts on record for a consumer product. After Whitcomb Judson received the first patents for his clothing fastener in the early 1890s, it took more than 15 years to perfect the product—and even then consumers weren't interested. Judson's company suffered numerous financial setbacks, name changes, and relocations before settling in Meadville, Pennsylvania. Finally, the U.S. Navy started using zippers during World War I. Today, Talon Inc. is the leading U.S. maker of zippers, producing some 500 million of them a year.

The example of the zipper shows why the marketing effort must include **commercialization**, which includes (1) promoting the product to distributors and retailers to get wide distribution, and (2) developing strong advertising and sales campaigns to generate and maintain interest in the product among distributors and consumers. New products are now getting rapid exposure to global markets through commercialization on the Internet and social media. Websites enable consumers to view new products, ask questions, and make purchases easily and quickly.[24]

commercialization
Promoting a product to distributors and retailers to get wide distribution, and developing strong advertising and sales campaigns to generate and maintain interest in the product among distributors and consumers.

LEARNING goal **6**

Describe the product life cycle.

product life cycle
A theoretical model of what happens to sales and profits for a product class over time; the four stages of the cycle are introduction, growth, maturity, and decline.

THE PRODUCT LIFE CYCLE

Once a product has been developed and tested, it goes to market. There it may pass through a **product life cycle** of four stages: introduction, growth, maturity, and decline (see Figure 14.4). This cycle is a *theoretical* model of what happens

figure 14.4

SALES AND PROFITS DURING THE PRODUCT LIFE CYCLE
Note that profit levels start to fall *before* sales reach their peak. This is due to increasing price competition. When profits and sales start to decline, it's time to come out with a new product or to remodel the old one to maintain interest and profits.

to sales and profits for a *product class* over time. However, not all individual products follow the life cycle, and particular brands may act differently. For example, while frozen foods as a generic class may go through the entire cycle, one brand may never get beyond the introduction stage. Some product classes, such as microwave ovens, stay in the introductory stage for years. Some products, like catsup, become classics and never experience decline. Others, such as fad clothing, may go through the entire cycle in a few months. Still others may be withdrawn from the market altogether. Nonetheless, the product life cycle may provide some basis for anticipating future market developments and for planning marketing strategies.

Example of the Product Life Cycle

The product life cycle can give marketers valuable clues to successfully promoting a product over time. Some products, like crayons and sidewalk chalk, have very long product life cycles, change very little, and never seem to go into decline. Crayola Crayons has been successful for 100 years! How long do you think the new virtual video games will last?[25]

You can see how the theory works by looking at the product life cycle of instant coffee. When it was introduced, most people didn't like it as well as "regular" coffee, and it took several years for instant coffee to gain general acceptance (introduction stage). At one point, though, instant coffee grew rapidly in popularity, and many brands were introduced (growth stage). After a while, people became attached to one brand and sales leveled off (maturity stage). Sales then went into a slight decline when freeze-dried coffees were introduced (decline stage). Now freeze-dried coffee is, in turn, at the decline stage as consumers are buying bags of coffee from Starbucks and brewing them at home. It's extremely important for marketers to recognize what stage a product is in so that they can make intelligent and efficient marketing decisions about it.

figure 14.5

SAMPLE STRATEGIES FOLLOWED DURING THE PRODUCT LIFE CYCLE

	MARKETING MIX ELEMENTS			
LIFE CYCLE STAGE	**PRODUCT**	**PRICE**	**PLACE**	**PROMOTION**
Introduction	Offer market-tested product; keep mix small	Go after innovators with high introductory price (skimming strategy) or use penetration pricing	Use wholesalers, selective distribution	Dealer promotion and heavy investment in primary demand advertising and sales promotion to get stores to carry the product and consumers to try it
Growth	Improve product; keep product mix limited	Adjust price to meet competition	Increase distribution	Heavy competitive advertising
Maturity	Differentiate product to satisfy different market segments	Further reduce price	Take over wholesaling function and intensify distribution	Emphasize brand name as well as product benefits and differences
Decline	Cut product mix; develop new-product ideas	Consider price increase	Consolidate distribution; drop some outlets	Reduce advertising to only loyal customers

LIFE CYCLE STAGE	SALES	PROFITS	COMPETITORS
Introduction	Low sales	Losses may occur	Few
Growth	Rapidly rising sales	Very high profits	Growing number
Maturity	Peak sales	Declining profits	Stable number, then declining
Decline	Falling sales	Profits may fall to become losses	Declining number

figure I4.6

HOW SALES, PROFITS, AND COMPETITION VARY OVER THE PRODUCT LIFE CYCLE

Using the Product Life Cycle

Different stages in the product life cycle call for different marketing strategies. Figure 14.5 outlines the marketing mix decisions you might make. As you go through the figure, you'll see that each stage calls for multiple marketing mix changes. Remember, these concepts are largely theoretical and you should use them only as guidelines. We'll discuss the price strategies mentioned in the figure later in this chapter.

Figure 14.6 shows in theory what happens to sales volume, profits, and competition during the product life cycle. Compare it to Figure 14.4. Both figures show that a product at the mature stage may reach the top in sales growth while profit is decreasing. At that stage, a marketing manager may decide to create a new image for the product to start a new growth cycle. You may have noticed how Arm & Hammer baking soda gets a new image every few years to generate new sales. One year it's positioned as a deodorant for refrigerators and the next as a substitute for harsh chemicals in swimming pools. Knowing what stage in the cycle a product has reached helps marketing managers decide when such strategic changes are needed.

Theoretically, all products go through these stages at various times in their life cycle. What happens to sales as a product matures?

progress assessment

- What are the six steps in the new-product development process?
- What is the difference between product screening and product analysis?
- What are the two steps in commercialization?
- What is the theory of the product life cycle?

LEARNING goal 7

Identify various pricing objectives and strategies.

COMPETITIVE PRICING

Pricing is so important to marketing and the development of total product offers that it has been singled out as one of the four Ps in the marketing mix, along with product, place, and promotion. It's one of the most difficult of the four Ps for a manager to control, however, because price is such a critical ingredient in consumer evaluations of the product. In this section, we'll explore price both as an ingredient of the total product offer and as a strategic marketing tool.

Pricing Objectives

A firm may have several objectives in mind when setting a pricing strategy. When pricing a new vegetarian offering, we may want to promote the product's image. If we price it *high* and use the right promotion, maybe we can make it the Evian of vegetarian meals. We also might price it high to achieve a certain profit objective or return on investment. We could also price our product *lower* than its competitors, because we want low-income people to afford this healthy meal. That is, we could have some social or ethical goal in mind. Low pricing may also discourage competition because it reduces the profit potential, but it may help us capture a larger share of the market.

Thus a firm may have several pricing objectives over time, and it must formulate these objectives clearly before developing an overall pricing strategy. Popular objectives include the following:

1. *Achieving a target return on investment or profit.* Ultimately, the goal of marketing is to make a profit by providing goods and services to others. Naturally, one long-run pricing objective of almost all firms is to optimize profit. One way companies have tried to increase profit is by reducing the amount provided to customers. Thus cereal companies have cut the amount of cereal in a box, toilet paper companies are making their products smaller, and so on.[26] Have you noticed this happening for products you buy?

2. *Building traffic.* Supermarkets often advertise certain products at or below cost to attract people to the store. These products are called *loss leaders.* The long-run objective is to make profits by following the short-run objective of building a customer base. The Internet portal Yahoo once provided a free auction service to compete with eBay. Why give such a service away? To increase advertising revenue on the Yahoo site and attract more people to Yahoo's other services.

3. *Achieving greater market share.* One way to capture a larger part of the market is to offer lower prices, low finance rates (like 0 percent financing), low lease rates, or rebates.

4. *Creating an image.* Certain watches, perfumes, and other socially visible products are priced high to give them an image of exclusivity and status.

5. *Furthering social objectives.* A firm may want to price a product low so people with little money can afford it. The government often subsidizes the price of farm products to keep basic necessities like milk and bread easily affordable.

A firm may have short-run objectives that differ greatly from its long-run objectives. Managers should understand both types at the beginning and put both into their strategic marketing plan. They should also set pricing objectives in the context of other marketing decisions about product design, packaging, branding, distribution, and promotion. All these marketing decisions are interrelated.

Intuition tells us the price charged for a product must bear some relationship to the cost of producing it. Prices usually *are*

Some products are priced high to create a high-status image of exclusivity and desirability. Salvatore Ferragamo shoes fall into this category. What is the total product offer for a product like this?

set somewhere above cost. But as we'll see, price and cost aren't always related. In fact, there are three major approaches to pricing strategy: cost-based, demand-based (target costing), and competition-based.

Cost-Based Pricing

Producers often use cost as a primary basis for setting price. They develop elaborate cost accounting systems to measure production costs (including materials, labor, and overhead), add in a margin of profit, and come up with a price. Picture the process in terms of producing a car. You add up all the various components—engine parts, body, tires, radio, door locks and windows, paint, and labor—add a profit margin, and come up with a price. The question is whether the price will be satisfactory to the market as well. How has the market responded to the prices of U.S. cars lately? In the long run, the market—not the producer—determines what the price will be (see Chapter 2). Pricing should take into account costs, but it should also include the expected costs of product updates, the marketing objectives for each product, and competitor prices.

Demand-Based Pricing

Unlike cost-based pricing, **target costing** is demand-based. That means we design a product so it not only satisfies customers but also meets the profit margins we've set. Target costing makes the final price an *input* to the product development process, not an outcome of it. You first estimate the selling price people would be willing to pay for a product and then subtract your desired profit margin. The result is your target cost of production, or what you can spend to profitably produce the item. Imagine how you would use this process to make custom-made jewelry.

target costing
Designing a product so that it satisfies customers and meets the profit margins desired by the firm.

Competition-Based Pricing

Competition-based pricing is a strategy based on what all the other competitors are doing. The price can be at, above, or below competitors' prices. Pricing depends on customer loyalty, perceived differences, and the competitive climate. **Price leadership** is the strategy by which one or more dominant firms set pricing practices all competitors in an industry follow. You may have noticed that practice among oil companies.

competition-based pricing
A pricing strategy based on what all the other competitors are doing. The price can be set at, above, or below competitors' prices.

price leadership
The strategy by which one or more dominant firms set the pricing practices that all competitors in an industry follow.

Break-Even Analysis

Before you begin selling a new vegetarian sandwich, it may be wise to determine how many sandwiches you'd have to sell before making a profit. You'd then determine whether you could reach such a sales goal. **Break-even analysis** is the process used to determine profitability at various levels of sales. The break-even point is the point where revenues from sales equal all costs. The formula for calculating the break-even point is as follows:

$$\text{Break-even point (BEP)} = \frac{\text{Total fixed costs (FC)}}{\text{Price of one unit (P)} - \text{Variable costs (VC) of one unit}}$$

Total fixed costs are all the expenses that remain the same no matter how many products are made or sold. Among the expenses that make up fixed costs are the amount paid to own or rent a factory or warehouse and the amount paid for business insurance. **Variable costs** change according to the level of production. Included are the expenses for the materials used in making products and

break-even analysis
The process used to determine profitability at various levels of sales.

total fixed costs
All the expenses that remain the same no matter how many products are made or sold.

variable costs
Costs that change according to the level of production.

the direct costs of labor used in making those goods. For producing a specific product, let's say you have a fixed cost of $200,000 (for mortgage interest, real estate taxes, equipment, and so on). Your variable cost (e.g., labor and materials) per item is $2. If you sold the products for $4 each, the break-even point would be 100,000 items. In other words, you wouldn't make any money selling this product unless you sold more than 100,000 of them:

$$\text{BEP} = \frac{\text{FC}}{\text{P–VC}} = \frac{\$200,000}{\$4.00 - \$2.00} = \frac{\$200,000}{\$2.00} = 100,000 \text{ boxes}$$

Other Pricing Strategies

Let's say a firm has just developed a new line of products, such as Blu-ray players. The firm has to decide how to price these sets at the introductory stage of the product life cycle. A **skimming price strategy** prices a new product high to recover research and development costs and make as much profit as possible while there's little competition. Of course, those large profits will eventually attract new competitors.

A second strategy is to price the new players low. Low prices will attract more buyers and discourage other companies from making sets because profits are slim. This **penetration strategy** enables the firm to penetrate or capture a large share of the market quickly.

Retailers use several pricing strategies. **Everyday low pricing (EDLP)** is the choice of Home Depot and Walmart. They set prices lower than competitors and don't usually have special sales. The idea is to bring consumers to the store whenever they want a bargain rather than having them wait until there is a sale.

Department stores and some other retailers most often use a **high–low pricing strategy**. Regular prices are higher than at stores using EDLP, but during special sales they're lower. The problem with such pricing is that it encourages consumers to wait for sales, thus cutting into profits. As online shopping continues to grow, you may see fewer stores with a high–low strategy because consumers will be able to find better prices on the Internet.

Retailers can use price as a major determinant of the goods they carry. Some promote goods that sell only for 99 cents, or only for $10. Some of those 99-cent stores have raised their prices to over a dollar because of rising costs.

You learned earlier in this chapter that bundling means grouping two or more products together and pricing them as a unit. For example, a store might

skimming price strategy
Strategy in which a new product is priced high to make optimum profit while there's little competition.

penetration strategy
Strategy in which a product is priced low to attract many customers and discourage competition.

everyday low pricing (EDLP)
Setting prices lower than competitors and then not having any special sales.

high–low pricing strategy
Setting prices that are higher than EDLP stores, but having many special sales where the prices are lower than competitors'.

price washers and dryers as a unit. Jiffy Lube offers an oil change and lube, checks your car's fluid levels and air pressure, and bundles all these services into one price. Research suggests that a discount will increase sales more effectively if it's offered on an attractive, pleasurable item.[27]

Psychological pricing means pricing goods and services at price points that make the product appear less expensive than it is. A house might be priced at $299,000 because that sounds like a lot less than $300,000. Gas stations almost always use psychological pricing.

psychological pricing
Pricing goods and services at price points that make the product appear less expensive than it is.

How Market Forces Affect Pricing

Recognizing that different consumers may be willing to pay different prices, marketers sometimes price on the basis of consumer demand rather than cost or some other calculation. That's called *demand-oriented pricing,* and you can observe it at movie theaters with low rates for children and drugstores with discounts for senior citizens. The Washington Opera Company in Washington, DC, raised prices on prime seating and lowered them on less-attractive seats. This strategy raised the company's revenues 9 percent.

Marketers are facing a new pricing problem: Customers can now compare prices of many goods and services on the Internet, at websites like DealTime.com and MySimon.com. Priceline.com introduced consumers to a "demand collection system," in which buyers post the prices they are willing to pay and invite sellers to accept or decline the price. Consumers can get great prices on airlines, hotels, and other products by naming their price. They can also buy used goods online. Clearly, price competition is going to heat up as consumers have more access to price information from all around the world.[28] As a result, nonprice competition is likely to increase.

NONPRICE COMPETITION

Marketers often compete on product attributes other than price. You may have noted that price differences are small for products like gasoline, candy bars, and even major products such as compact cars and private colleges.

You won't typically see price as a major promotional appeal on television. Instead, marketers tend to stress product images and consumer benefits such as comfort, style, convenience, and durability.

Many small organizations promote the services that accompany basic products rather than price in order to compete with bigger firms. Good service will enhance a relatively homogeneous product. Danny O'Neill, for example, is a small wholesaler who sells gourmet coffee to upscale restaurants. He has to watch competitors' prices *and* the services they offer so that he can charge the premium prices he wants. To charge high prices, he has to offer and then provide superior service. Larger companies often do the same thing. Some airlines stress friendliness, large "sleeping" seats, promptness, abundant flights, and other such services. Many hotels stress "no surprises," business services, health clubs, and other extras.

progress assessment

- Can you list two short-term and two long-term pricing objectives? Can the two be compatible?
- What are the limitations of a cost-based pricing strategy?
- What is psychological pricing?

summary

Learning Goal 1. Describe a total product offer.
- **What's included in a total product offer?**

A total product offer consists of everything consumers evaluate when deciding whether to buy something. It includes price, brand name, and satisfaction in use.

- **What's the difference between a product line and a product mix?**

A product line is a group of physically similar products with similar competitors. A product line of gum may include bubble gum and sugarless gum. A product mix is a company's combination of product lines. A manufacturer may offer lines of gum, candy bars, and breath mints in its product mix.

- **How do marketers create product differentiation for their goods and services?**

Marketers use a combination of pricing, advertising, and packaging to make their products seem unique and attractive.

Learning Goal 2. Identify the various kinds of consumer and industrial goods.
- **What are consumer goods?**

Consumer goods are sold to ultimate consumers like you and me for personal use.

- **What are the four classifications of consumer goods and services, and how are they marketed?**

There are convenience goods and services (requiring minimum shopping effort); shopping goods and services (for which people search and compare price and quality); specialty goods and services (which consumers go out of their way to get, and for which they often demand specific brands); and unsought goods and services (products consumers are unaware of, haven't thought of buying, or need to solve an unexpected problem). Convenience goods and services are best promoted by location, shopping goods and services by some price/quality appeal, and specialty goods and services by specialty magazines and interactive websites.

- **What are industrial goods, and how are they marketed differently from consumer goods?**

Industrial goods are products sold in the business-to-business (B2B) market and used in the production of other products. They're sold largely through salespeople and rely less on advertising.

Learning Goal 3. Summarize the functions of packaging.
- **What are the seven functions of packaging?**

Packaging must (1) attract the buyer's attention; (2) protect the goods inside, stand up under handling and storage, be tamperproof, and deter theft; (3) be easy to open and use; (4) describe the contents; (5) explain the benefits of the good inside; (6) provide information about warranties, warnings, and other consumer matters; and (7) indicate price, value, and uses. Bundling means grouping two or more products into a unit, through packaging, and charging one price for them.

Learning Goal 4. Contrast *brand, brand name,* and *trademark,* and show the value of brand equity.
- **Can you define brand, brand name, and trademark?**

A *brand* is a name, symbol, or design (or combination thereof) that identifies the goods or services of one seller or group of sellers and distinguishes them from the goods and services of competitors. The word *brand* includes all means of identifying a product. A *brand name* consists of a word, letter, or group of words or letters that differentiates one seller's goods and services from those of competitors. A *trademark* is a brand that has exclusive legal protection for both its brand name and design.

- **What is brand equity, and how do managers create brand associations?**

Brand equity is the value of a brand name and associated symbols. Brand association is the linking of a brand to other favorable images such as product users, a popular celebrity, or a geographic area.

- **What do brand managers do?**

Brand managers coordinate product, price, place, and promotion decisions for a particular product.

Learning Goal 5. Explain the steps in the new-product development process.

- **What are the six steps of the product development process?**

The steps of product development are (1) generation of new-product ideas, (2) product screening, (3) product analysis, (4) development, (5) testing, and (6) commercialization.

Learning Goal 6. Describe the product life cycle.

- **What is the product life cycle?**

The product life cycle is a theoretical model of what happens to sales and profits for a product class over time.

- **What are the four stages in the product life cycle?**

The four product life cycle stages are introduction, growth, maturity, and decline.

Learning Goal 7. Identify various pricing objectives and strategies.

- **What are pricing objectives?**

Pricing objectives include achieving a target profit, building traffic, increasing market share, creating an image, and meeting social goals.

- **What strategies can marketers use to determine a product's price?**

A skimming strategy prices the product high to make big profits while there's little competition. A penetration strategy uses low price to attract more customers and discourage competitors. Demand-oriented pricing starts with consumer demand rather than cost. Competition-oriented pricing is based on all competitors' prices. Price leadership occurs when all competitors follow the pricing practice of one or more dominant companies.

- **What is break-even analysis?**

Break-even analysis is the process used to determine profitability at various levels of sales. The break-even point is the point where revenues from sales equal all costs.

- **Why do companies use nonprice strategies?**

Pricing is one of the easiest marketing strategies to copy. It's often not a good long-run competitive tool.

key terms

brand 387	**bundling** 386	**dealer (private-label) brands** 387
brand association 389	**commercialization** 393	
brand awareness 389	**competition-based pricing** 397	**distributed product development** 379
brand equity 389		
brand loyalty 389	**concept testing** 392	**everyday low pricing (EDLP)** 398
brand manager 390	**convenience goods and services** 382	
break-even analysis 397		**generic goods** 388

critical thinking

1. What value enhancers affected your choice of the school you attend? Did you consider size, location, price, reputation, WiFi services, library and research services, sports, and courses offered? What factors were most important? Why? What schools were your alternatives? Why didn't you choose them?

2. What could you do to enhance the product offer of Very Vegetarian, other than changing the menu from time to time?

3. How could you use psychological pricing when making up the menu at Very Vegetarian?

4. Are you impressed by the use of celebrities in product advertisements? What celebrity could you use to promote Very Vegetarian?

developing workplace skills

1. Look around your classroom and notice the different types of shoes students are wearing. What product qualities were they looking for when they chose their shoes? How important were price, style, brand name, and color? Describe the product offerings you would feature in a new shoe store designed to appeal to college students.

2. A total product offer consists of everything consumers evaluate when choosing among products, including price, package, service, and reputation. Working in teams, compose a list of factors consumers might consider when evaluating the total product offer of a vacation resort, a cell phone, and a rental apartment.

3. How important is price to you when buying the following: clothes, milk, computers, haircuts, rental cars? What nonprice factors, if any, are more important than price? How much time do you spend evaluating factors other than price when making such purchases?

4. Go through several local stores of different types and note how often they use psychological pricing. Discuss the practice with the class to see whether students recognize the influence psychological pricing has upon them.

taking it to the net

Purpose

To assess how consumers can use the Internet to shop for various goods.

Exercise

Shopbots are Internet sites for finding the best prices on goods you need. No shopbot searches the entire Internet, so it's a good idea to use more than one to get the best deals. Furthermore, not all shopbots quote shipping and handling costs. Here are some to try: MySimon.com, PriceGrabber.com, PriceSCAN.com, and YahooShopping.com.

1. Which of the shopbots offers the most goods and the most information? How helpful are the consumer reviews? The product descriptions?

2. Which shopbot is easiest to use? The hardest? Why?

3. Write down some of the prices you find on the Internet and then go to a local store, such as Walmart or Target, and compare prices. Does either source (online or brick-and-mortar) consistently offer the best price?

4. Compare shopping on the Internet to shopping in stores. What are the advantages and disadvantages of each? Which has the best total product offer?

casing the web

To access the case, "Everyday Low Pricing," visit a **www.mhhe.com/ubl0e**

video case

To access the video case featuring Dream Dinners, visit **www.mhhe.com/ubl0e**

DISTRIBUTING
PRODUCTS

15

LEARNING
goals

After you have read and studied this chapter, you should be able to

1 Explain the concept of marketing channels and their value.

2 Demonstrate how intermediaries perform the six marketing utilities.

3 Identify the types of wholesale intermediaries in the distribution system.

4 Compare the distribution strategies retailers use.

5 Explain the various kinds of nonstore retailing.

6 Explain the various ways to build cooperation in channel systems.

7 Describe logistics and outline how intermediaries manage the transportation and storage of goods.

www.zappos.com

Although many online shopping sites have been extremely successful, e-tailers often fall short of their brick-and-mortar rivals in terms of customer service. After all, dealing with an issue face-to-face with a salesperson is usually easier than negotiating an issue over a series of e-mails. At the online shoe store Zappos, however, a unique company culture demonstrates that online shoppers need not sacrifice quality service for convenience.

When Tony Hsieh sold his first company to Microsoft for $265 million, he joined Zappos as CEO. One of the first things he wanted to do was change the company's corporate work environment. To set Zappos apart from the pack of online retailers, he wanted his service representatives to wow customers with their energy and expertise. Accomplishing that task meant keeping employees upbeat and motivated through the love of their work. He gave his call-center staffers remarkable freedom, allowing them to talk to customers for hours at a time or send flowers and thank-you notes on the company dime. In Hsieh's mind, a customer may only call Zappos once in their lifetime, but the experience is guaranteed to stick with them.

Hsieh's commitment to a fun work environment and quality service helped grow Zappos from a $32 million company to a $1.2 billion powerhouse. Nevertheless, Zappos didn't become the success it is today based on Hsieh's freewheeling managerial style alone. Hsieh also decided that the company needed total control of its supply chain. Up until 2003 Zappos earned 25 percent of its annual revenue through a drop shipping system (passing the customer orders to producers who would ship the products directly to the customers). While this saved the company the hassle of handling, stocking, or delivering the products, it also prevented the company from knowing exactly what it had in stock at any given time, thus impeding its customer service

profile

Getting to Know
X   Tony Hsieh
CEO of Zappos

capabilities. In order to provide the top-notch service it promised, Zappos needed to control the whole process from beginning to end.

After assuming total control over its inventory, Zappos' service department knows exactly what is in stock and what is out. If a customer wants a pair of shoes Zappos doesn't have, an employee may even direct the customer to a competitor that does. Maintaining its own inventory and order fulfillment gives Zappos' company culture the independence it needs to succeed by getting the products its customers want where they want them.

The four Ps of marketing are product, place, promotion, and price. This chapter is all about place. The place function goes by many other names as well, including shipping, warehousing, distribution, logistics, and supply-chain management. We'll explore all these concepts in this chapter. At the end, you will have a much better understanding of the many steps required to get products from the producer to the consumer.

Sources: Christopher Palmeri, "Now For Sale, The Zappos Culture," *Bloomberg Businessweek,* January 11, 2010; Brian Solis, "Zappos' Tony Hsieh Delivers Happiness Through Service and Innovation," *Fast Company,* April 12, 2011; Adam Bryant, "On a Scale of 1 to 10, How Weird Are You?" *The New York Times,* January 9, 2010; and Paul B. Carroll, "Getting a Foothold Online," *The Wall Street Journal,* June 7, 2010.

NAME THAT
company

Although this automobile manufacturer builds its cars in South Korea, the 30,000 components come from all over the world. For example, the airbags come from a Swedish company that makes them in Utah. Its supply chain is truly interfirm and international. What is the name of this company? (Find the answer in the chapter.)

marketing intermediaries Organizations that assist in moving goods and services from producers to businesses (B2B) and from businesses to consumers (B2C).

channel of distribution A whole set of marketing intermediaries, such as agents, brokers, wholesalers, and retailers, that join together to transport and store goods in their path (or channel) from producers to consumers.

Distribution warehouses store goods until they are needed. Have you ever thought about the benefits of having food, furniture, clothing, and other needed goods close at hand?

LEARNING goal 1

Explain the concept of marketing channels and their value.

THE EMERGENCE OF MARKETING INTERMEDIARIES

It's easy to overlook distribution and storage in marketing, where the focus is often on advertising, selling, marketing research, and other functions. But it doesn't take much to realize how important distribution is. Imagine the challenge Timberland faces of getting raw materials together, making 12 million pairs of shoes, and then distributing those shoes to stores throughout the world. That's what thousands of manufacturing firms—making everything from automobiles to toys—have to deal with every day. Imagine further that there has been a major volcano eruption or tsunami that has caused a disruption in the supply of goods. Such issues are commonplace for distribution managers.[1]

Fortunately there are hundreds of thousands of companies and individuals whose job it is to help move goods from the raw-material state to producers and then on to consumers. Then, as is often the case, the products are sent from consumers to recyclers and back to manufacturers or assemblers. Did you know that only 20 percent of plastic water bottles are recycled? See the Thinking Green box for more on sustainability and the distribution process.[2]

Managing the flow of goods has become one of the most important managerial functions for many organizations. Let's look at how this function is carried out.

Marketing intermediaries (once called *middlemen*) are organizations that assist in moving goods and services from producers to businesses (B2B) and from businesses to consumers (B2C). They're called intermediaries because they're in the middle of a series of organizations that join together to help distribute goods from producers to consumers. A **channel of distribution** consists of a whole set of marketing intermediaries, such as agents, brokers, wholesalers, and retailers, that

THINKING green

Distribution and Sustainability

Throughout this text we've talked about companies that have adopted a "greener" attitude toward producing and selling goods and services. But such companies will not be successful in implementing a "green" strategy without the cooperation and participation of other companies in their supply chain. Thus environmentally aware companies are pushing their supply chain partners to work with them to come up with a distribution plan that would minimize pollution and optimize profits. Such a plan is good to not only halt negative publicity, but to make the whole system more profitable.

Recently, transportation accounted for over 28 percent of U.S. energy consumption and over 33 percent of carbon dioxide emissions. Motor transportation is four times less fuel efficient per ton-mile than rail, and emissions from airfreight are 600 times higher than rail or ocean shipping. Clearly, the decision of what distribution mode to use is more complex than first imagined—if you keep the environment in mind. Companies throughout the world are taking such measurements and are responding accordingly. The era of sustainability has entered into distribution as well as the other aspects of marketing.

Sources: Michael S. Hopkins, "How Sustainability Creates New Opportunity," *MIT Sloan Management Review,* Summer 2010; Susan L. Golicic, Courtney N. Boerstler and Lisa M. Ellram, " 'Greening' in the Supply Chain," *MIT Sloan Management Review,* Winter 2010; and Todd W. Price, "Making Resource Management Work: Sustainability and the Supply Chain," *Harvard Business Review,* March 2011.

join together to transport and store goods in their path (or channel) from producers to consumers. **Agents/brokers** are marketing intermediaries who bring buyers and sellers together and assist in negotiating an exchange but don't take title to the goods—that is, at no point do they own the goods. Think of real estate agents as an example.

A **wholesaler** is a marketing intermediary that sells to other organizations, such as retailers, manufacturers, and hospitals. Wholesalers are part of the B2B system. Because of high distribution costs, Walmart has been trying to eliminate independent wholesalers from its system and do the job itself. That is, Walmart provides its own warehouses and has its own trucks. It has over 120 distribution centers and 53,000 trailers to distribute goods to its stores.[3] Finally, a **retailer** is an organization that sells to ultimate consumers (people like you and me).

Channels of distribution help ensure communication flows *and* the flow of money and title to goods. They also help ensure that the right quantity and assortment of goods will be available when and where needed. Figure 15.1 on p. 408 shows selected channels of distribution for both consumer and industrial goods.

You can see the distribution system in the United States at work when you drive down any highway and see the thousands of trucks and trains moving goods from here to there. Less visible, however, are the many distribution warehouses that store goods until they are needed. Have you ever thought about the benefits of having food, furniture, and other needed goods close at hand? Have you seen distribution warehouses along the road as you drive from town to town?

Why Marketing Needs Intermediaries

Figure 15.1 shows that some manufacturers sell directly to consumers. So why have marketing intermediaries at all? The answer is that intermediaries perform certain marketing tasks—such as transporting, storing, selling, advertising, and

agents/brokers
Marketing intermediaries who bring buyers and sellers together and assist in negotiating an exchange but don't take title to the goods.

wholesaler
A marketing intermediary that sells to other organizations.

retailer
An organization that sells to ultimate consumers.

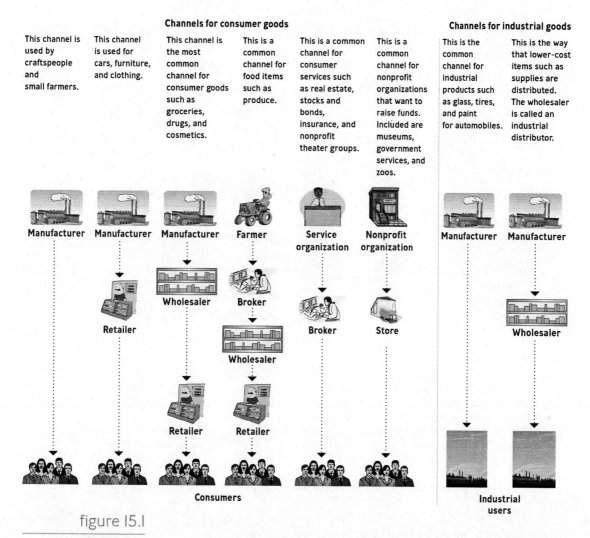

Channels for consumer goods

This channel is used by craftspeople and small farmers.

This channel is used for cars, furniture, and clothing.

This channel is the most common channel for consumer goods such as groceries, drugs, and cosmetics.

This is a common channel for food items such as produce.

This is a common channel for consumer services such as real estate, stocks and bonds, insurance, and nonprofit theater groups.

This is a common channel for nonprofit organizations that want to raise funds. Included are museums, government services, and zoos.

Channels for industrial goods

This is the common channel for industrial products such as glass, tires, and paint for automobiles.

This is the way that lower-cost items such as supplies are distributed. The wholesaler is called an industrial distributor.

Manufacturer · Manufacturer · Manufacturer · Farmer · Service organization · Nonprofit organization · Manufacturer · Manufacturer

Retailer · Wholesaler · Broker · Broker · Store · Wholesaler

Wholesaler

Retailer · Retailer

Consumers

Industrial users

figure 15.1

SELECTED CHANNELS OF DISTRIBUTION FOR CONSUMER AND INDUSTRIAL GOODS AND SERVICES

relationship building—faster and more cheaply than most manufacturers could.[4] Here's a simple analogy: You could personally deliver packages to people anywhere in the world, but usually you don't. Why not? Because it's generally cheaper and faster to have them delivered by the U.S. Postal Service or a private firm such as UPS.[5]

Similarly, you could sell your home by yourself or buy stock directly from individual companies, but you probably wouldn't. Why? Again, because agents and brokers are marketing intermediaries who make the exchange process easier and more efficient and profitable.[6] In the next section, we'll explore how intermediaries improve the efficiency of various exchanges.

How Intermediaries Create Exchange Efficiency

Here is an easy way to see the benefits of using marketing intermediaries. Suppose five manufacturers of various food products each tried to sell directly to five retailers. The number of exchange relationships needed to create this market is 5 times 5, or 25.

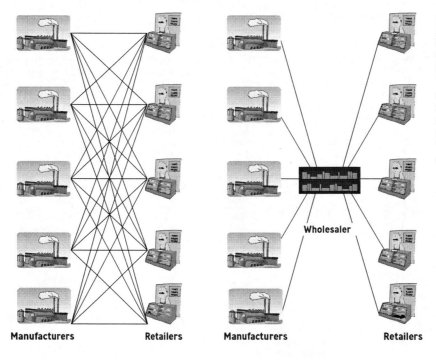

figure 15.2

HOW INTERMEDIARIES CREATE EXCHANGE EFFICIENCY
This figure shows that adding a wholesaler to the channel of distribution cuts the number of contacts from 25 to 10. This improves the efficiency of distribution.

But picture what happens when a wholesaler enters the system. The five manufacturers each contact the wholesaler, establishing five exchange relationships. The wholesaler then establishes contact with the five retailers, creating five more exchange relationships. The wholesaler's existence reduces the number of exchanges from 25 to only 10. Figure 15.2 shows this process.

Some economists have said that intermediaries add *costs* and should be eliminated. Marketers say intermediaries add *value,* and that the *value greatly exceeds the cost.* Let's explore this debate and see what value intermediaries provide.[7]

The Value versus the Cost of Intermediaries

The public has often viewed marketing intermediaries with a degree of suspicion. Some surveys show about half the cost of what we buy is marketing costs that go largely to pay for the work of intermediaries. If we could only get rid of intermediaries, people reason, we could greatly reduce the cost of everything we buy. Sounds good, but is the solution really that simple?

Take a box of cereal that sells for $4. How could we, as consumers, get the cereal for less? Well, we could all drive to Michigan, where some cereal is produced, and save shipping costs. But imagine millions of people getting in their cars and driving to Michigan just to buy cereal. No, it doesn't make sense. It's much cheaper to have intermediaries bring the cereal to major cities. That might make transportation and warehousing by wholesalers necessary. These steps add cost, don't they? Yes, but they add value as well—the value of not having to drive to Michigan.

The cereal is now in a warehouse somewhere on the outskirts of the city. We could all drive down to the wholesaler and pick it up. But that still isn't the most economical way to buy cereal. If we figure in the cost of gas and time, the cereal will again be too expensive. Instead, we prefer to have someone

410   PART 5   ✳   **Marketing: Developing and Implementing Customer-Oriented Marketing Plans**

figure I5.3

DISTRIBUTION'S EFFECT ON YOUR FOOD DOLLAR
Note that the farmer gets only 25 cents of your food dollar. The bulk of your money goes to intermediaries to pay distribution costs. Their biggest cost is labor (truck drivers, clerks), followed by warehouses and storage.

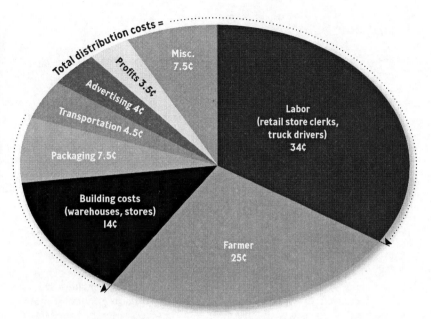

move the cereal from the warehouse to a truck, drive it to the corner super-market, unload it, unpack it, price it, shelve it, and wait for us to come in to buy it. To make it even more convenient, the supermarket may stay open for 24 hours a day, seven days a week. Think of the costs. But think also of the value! For $4, we can get a box of cereal *when* we want it, and with little effort.

If we were to get rid of the retailer, we could buy a box of cereal for slightly less, but we'd have to drive farther and spend time in the warehouse looking through rows of cereals. If we got rid of the wholesaler, we could save a little more money, not counting our drive to Michigan. But a few cents here and there add up—to the point where distribution (marketing) may add up to 75 cents for every 25 cents in manufacturing costs. Figure 15.3 shows where your money goes in the distribution process. The largest percentage goes to people who drive trucks and work in wholesale and retail organizations. Note that only 3.5 cents goes to profit.

Here are three basic points about intermediaries:

1. Marketing intermediaries can be eliminated, but their activities can't; that is, you can eliminate some wholesalers and retailers, but then consumers or someone else would have to perform the intermediaries' tasks, including transporting and storing goods, finding suppliers, and establishing communication with suppliers.

2. Intermediary organizations have survived because they perform marketing functions faster and more cheaply than others can. To maintain their competitive position in the channel, they now must adopt the latest technology. That includes search engine optimization, social networking (on sites like Facebook), and analyzing website statistics to understand their customers better.

3. Intermediaries add costs to products, but these costs are usually more than offset by the values they create.

LEARNING goal 2

Demonstrate how intermediaries perform the six marketing utilities.

THE UTILITIES CREATED BY INTERMEDIARIES

Utility, in economics, is the want-satisfying ability, or value, that organizations add to goods or services by making them more useful or accessible to consumers than they were before. The six kinds of utility are form, time, place, possession, information, and service. Although producers provide some utilities, marketing intermediaries provide most. Let's look at how.

Form Utility

Traditionally, producers rather than intermediaries have provided form utility (see Chapter 9) by changing raw materials into useful products. Thus, a farmer who separates the wheat from the chaff and the processor who turns the wheat into flour are creating form utility. Retailers and other marketers sometimes provide form utility as well. For example, retail butchers cut pork chops from a larger piece of meat and trim off the fat. The servers at Starbucks make coffee just the way you want it. Dell assembles computers according to customers' wishes.

Time Utility

Intermediaries, such as retailers, add **time utility** to products by making them available when consumers need them. Devar Tennent lives in Boston. One winter evening while watching TV with his brother, Tennent suddenly got the urge for a hot dog and a Coke. The problem was there were no hot dogs or Cokes in the house.

Devar ran down to the corner delicatessen and bought some hot dogs, buns, Cokes, and potato chips. He also bought some frozen strawberries and ice cream. Devar was able to get these groceries at midnight because the local deli was open 24 hours a day. That's time utility. You can buy goods at any time on the Internet, but you can't beat having them available right around the corner *when you want them*. On the other hand, note the value an Internet company provides by staying accessible 24 hours a day.

Place Utility

Intermediaries add **place utility** to products by placing them *where* people want them. While traveling through the badlands of South Dakota, Juanita Ruiz got hungry and thirsty. There are no stores for miles in this part of the country, but Juanita saw signs along the road saying a 7-Eleven was ahead. Following the signs, she stopped at the store for refreshments. She also bought some sunglasses and souvenir items there. The goods and services provided by 7-Eleven are in a convenient place for vacationers. Throughout the United States, 7-Eleven stores remain popular because they are usually in easy-to-reach locations. They provide place utility. As more and more sales become global, place utility will grow in importance.

utility
In economics, the want-satisfying ability, or value, that organizations add to goods or services.

time utility
Adding value to products by making them available when they're needed.

place utility
Adding value to products by having them where people want them.

Think of how many stores provide time utility by making goods and services available to you 24 hours a day, seven days a week. Have you ever needed to renew a prescription late at night or needed a late night snack? Can you see how time utility offers added value?

Possession Utility

possession utility
Doing whatever is necessary to transfer ownership from one party to another, including providing credit, delivery, installation, guarantees, and follow-up service.

Intermediaries add **possession utility** by doing whatever is necessary to transfer ownership from one party to another, including providing credit. Activities associated with possession utility include delivery, installation, guarantees, and follow-up service. Larry Rosenberg wanted to buy a nice home in the suburbs. He found just what he wanted, but he didn't have the money he needed. So he went with the real estate broker to a local savings and loan and borrowed money to buy the home. Both the real estate broker and the savings and loan are marketing intermediaries that provide possession utility. For those who don't want to own goods, possession utility makes it possible for them to use goods through renting or leasing.

Information Utility

information utility
Adding value to products by opening two-way flows of information between marketing participants.

Intermediaries add **information utility** by opening two-way flows of information between marketing participants. Jerome Washington couldn't decide what kind of TV set to buy. He looked at various ads in the newspaper, talked to salespeople at several stores, read material at the library and on the Internet, and tweeted his friends. Newspapers, salespeople, libraries, websites, and government publications are all information sources made available by intermediaries. They provide information utility.

Service Utility

service utility
Adding value by providing fast, friendly service during and after the sale and by teaching customers how to best use products over time.

Intermediaries add **service utility** by providing fast, friendly service during and after the sale and by teaching customers how to best use products over time. Sze Leung bought a personal computer for his home office. Both the computer manufacturer and the retailer Leung used continue to offer help whenever he needs it. He also gets software updates for a small fee to keep his computer up-to-date. What attracted Leung to the retailer in the first place was the helpful, friendly service he received from the salesperson in the store. Service utility is rapidly becoming the most important utility for many retailers, because without it they would lose business to direct marketing (e.g., marketing by catalog or on the Internet). Can you see how the Internet can provide some forms of service utility?

Service after the sale is one of the contributing factors to Apple's success. Customers can call to make an appointment with an Apple Genius who will help them learn how to use their computers, iPhones, or iPads. How does this service add value to Apple's products?

progress assessment

- What is a channel of distribution, and what intermediaries participate in it?
- Why do we need intermediaries? Illustrate how intermediaries create exchange efficiency.
- How would you defend intermediaries to someone who said getting rid of them would save consumers millions of dollars?
- Can you give examples of the utilities intermediaries create and how they provide them?

LEARNING goal **3**

Identify the types of wholesale intermediaries in the distribution system.

WHOLESALE INTERMEDIARIES

Let's distinguish wholesaling from retailing and clearly define the functions of each. Some producers deal only with wholesalers and won't sell directly to retailers or to end users (consumers). Some producers deal with both wholesalers and retailers, but give wholesalers a bigger discount. In turn, some wholesalers sell to both retailers and consumers. The office superstore Staples is a good example. It sells office supplies to small businesses and to consumers as well. Warehouse clubs such as Sam's Club and Costco are other companies with both wholesale and retail functions.

The difference is this: A *retail sale* is the sale of goods and services to consumers *for their own use*. A *wholesale sale* is the sale of goods and services to businesses and institutions, like schools or hospitals, *for use in the business,* or to wholesalers or retailers *for resale.*

Wholesalers make business-to-business sales. Most people are not as familiar with the various kinds of wholesalers as they are with retailers. Let's explore some of these helpful wholesale intermediaries. Most of them provide a lot of marketing jobs and offer you a good opportunity.

Merchant Wholesalers

Merchant wholesalers are independently owned firms that take title to the goods they handle. About 80 percent of wholesalers fall in this category. There are two types of merchant wholesalers: full-service and limited-function. *Full-service wholesalers* perform all the distribution functions (see Figure 15.4 on p. 414). *Limited-function wholesalers* perform only selected functions, but try to do them especially well. Three common types of limited-function wholesalers are rack jobbers, cash-and-carry wholesalers, and drop shippers.

Rack jobbers furnish racks or shelves full of merchandise, like music, toys, hosiery, and health and beauty aids, to retailers. They display the products and sell them on consignment, meaning they keep title to the goods until they're sold and then share the profits with the retailer. Have you seen shelves at the supermarket full of CDs and related items? Rack jobbers likely put them there.

Cash-and-carry wholesalers serve mostly smaller retailers with a limited assortment of products. Traditionally, retailers went to such wholesalers, paid cash, and carried the goods back to their stores—thus the term *cash-and-carry.* Today, stores such as Staples allow retailers and others to use credit cards for wholesale purchases. Thus the term *cash-and-carry* is becoming obsolete for wholesalers.

Drop shippers solicit orders from retailers and other wholesalers and have the merchandise shipped directly from a producer to a buyer. They own the merchandise but don't handle, stock, or deliver it. That's done by the producer. Drop shippers tend to handle bulky products such as coal, lumber, and chemicals.

---

merchant wholesalers
Independently owned firms that take title to the goods they handle.

rack jobbers
Wholesalers that furnish racks or shelves full of merchandise to retailers, display products, and sell on consignment.

cash-and-carry wholesalers
Wholesalers that serve mostly smaller retailers with a limited assortment of products.

drop shippers
Wholesalers that solicit orders from retailers and other wholesalers and have the merchandise shipped directly from a producer to a buyer.

figure 15.4

A FULL-SERVICE WHOLESALER

A FULL-SERVICE WHOLESALER WILL:	THE WHOLESALER MAY PERFORM THE FOLLOWING SERVICES FOR CUSTOMERS:
1. Provide a sales force to sell the goods to retailers and other buyers.	1. Buy goods the end market will desire and make them available to customers.
2. Communicate manufacturers' advertising deals and plans.	2. Maintain inventory, thus reducing customers' costs.
3. Maintain inventory, thus reducing the level of the inventory suppliers have to carry.	3. Transport goods to customers quickly.
4. Arrange or undertake transportation.	4. Provide market information and business consulting services.
5. Provide capital by paying cash or quick payments for goods.	5. Provide financing through granting credit, which is especially critical to small retailers.
6. Provide suppliers with market information they can't afford or can't obtain themselves.	6. Order goods in the types and quantities customers desire.
7. Undertake credit risk by granting credit to customers and absorbing any bad debts, thus relieving the supplier of this burden.	
8. Assume the risk for the product by taking title.	

Source: Thomas C. Kinnear, *Principles of Marketing*, 4th ed., © 1995, p. 394. Reprinted by permission of Pearson Education, Inc., Upper Saddle River, NJ.

Agents and Brokers

Agents and brokers bring buyers and sellers together and assist in negotiating an exchange. However, unlike merchant wholesalers, agents and brokers never own the products they distribute. Usually they do not carry inventory, provide

Agents and brokers are a familiar type of intermediary. Typically they don't take possession of the goods they sell. A real estate broker, for instance, facilitates the transaction between seller and buyer but never holds title to the house. What functions does a realtor provide in a home sale?

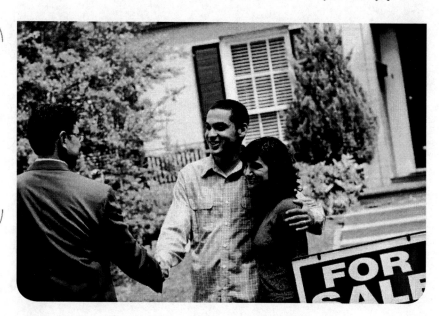

credit, or assume risks. While merchant wholesalers earn a profit from the sale of goods, agents and brokers earn commissions or fees based on a percentage of the sales revenues. Agents maintain long-term relationships with the people they represent, whereas brokers are usually hired on a temporary basis.

Agents who represent producers are either *manufacturer's agents* or *sales agents*. As long as they do not carry competing products, manufacturer's agents may represent several manufacturers in a specific territory. They often work in the automotive supply, footwear, and fabricated steel industries. Sales agents represent a single producer in a typically larger territory.

Brokers have no continuous relationship with the buyer or seller. Once they negotiate a contract between the parties, their relationship ends. Producers of seasonal products like fruits and vegetables often use brokers, as does the real estate industry.

LEARNING goal 4

Compare the distribution strategies retailers use.

RETAIL INTERMEDIARIES

A retailer, remember, is a marketing intermediary, like a supermarket, that sells to ultimate consumers. The United States boasts approximately 2.3 million retail stores, not including retail websites. Retail organizations employ more than 11 million people and are one of the major employers of marketing graduates. The recent recession has affected retailers, forcing many to cut back on employees, but large retailers like Macy's and Sears have been making a comeback.[8] Figure 15.5 lists, describes, and gives examples of various kinds of retailers. Have you shopped in each kind of store? What seem to be the

figure 15.5

TYPES OF RETAIL STORES

TYPE	DESCRIPTION	EXAMPLE
Department store	Sells a wide variety of products (clothes, furniture, housewares) in separate departments	Sears, JCPenney, Nordstrom
Discount store	Sells many different products at prices generally below those of department stores	Walmart, Target
Supermarket	Sells mostly food with other nonfood products such as detergent and paper products	Safeway, Kroger, Albertson's
Warehouse club	Sells food and general merchandise in facilities that are usually larger than supermarkets and offer discount prices; membership may be required	Costco, Sam's Club
Convenience store	Sells food and other often-needed items at convenient locations; may stay open all night	7-Eleven
Category killer	Sells a huge variety of one type of product to dominate that category of goods	Toys "R" Us, Bass Proshops, Office Depot
Outlet store	Sells general merchandise directly from the manufacturer at a discount; items may be discontinued or have flaws ("seconds")	Nordstrom Rack, Liz Claiborne, Nike, TJ Maxx
Specialty store	Sells a wide selection of goods in one category	Jewelry stores, shoe stores, bicycle shops

SPOTLIGHT ON SMALL
business

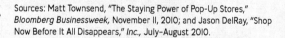

Pop Goes the Retail Store

With online shopping sites like Amazon continuing to gather market share, brick-and-mortar retailers have had to step up their game in order to compete. In the early 2000s, companies experimented with so-called "pop-up stores" to create a new shopping experience for consumers. These temporary outlets remained open for a short amount of time in small spaces and offered promotional offers and/or items not found in traditional stores. Though some excused the strategy as too gimmicky at the time, many are now willing to give the pop-up experience another shot.

While the decline of the American mall dealt a major blow to retailers, the empty storefronts provide lots of space for pop-up stores. In fact, this past holiday season Toys 'R' Us opened more than 600 pop-up stores with many of them in malls that used to house the bankrupt KB Toys. Of the 25 pop-ups that Borders opened last year, the majority were placed in malls where the retailer used to have a presence itself.

Still, pop-up stores aren't guaranteed to bring a company out of the doldrums, as evidenced by Borders' recent closing.

The most ambitious pop-ups don't even sell items. Instead, they try to create a unique experience between the consumers and the company's products, often opting to give products away rather than sell them. For instance, Procter & Gamble recently opened a pop-up in New York solely for promotion. Visitors could get a free Cover Girl makeover or take home complimentary samples of Febreeze candles and Head & Shoulders shampoo. The idea was to engage in a different conversation with customers and let them interact with the products. The aim of these types of pop-ups is to create lasting relationships with customers rather than just distribute products quickly. And if the strategy works, people will talk, text and tweet about the experience they had, giving the company invaluable exposure.

Sources: Matt Townsend, "The Staying Power of Pop-Up Stores," *Bloomberg Businessweek,* November 11, 2010; and Jason DelRay, "Shop Now Before It All Disappears," *Inc.,* July–August 2010.

advantages of each? Would you enjoy working in a retail store of some kind? Some retailers seem to compete mostly on price, but others, such as specialty stores, use variety as a competitive tool. The nearby Spotlight on Small Business box describes a new innovation in retail stores popping up across the country. Marketers use several strategies for retail distribution. We explain them next.

Retail Distribution Strategy

Because different products call for different retail distribution strategies, a major decision marketers must make is selecting the right retailers to sell their products. There are three categories of retail distribution: intensive, selective, and exclusive.

Intensive distribution puts products into as many retail outlets as possible, including vending machines. Products that need intensive distribution include convenience goods such as candy, cigarettes, gum, and popular magazines.

intensive distribution
Distribution that puts products into as many retail outlets as possible.

Selective distribution uses only a preferred group of the available retailers in an area. Such selection helps ensure producers of quality sales and service. Manufacturers of appliances, furniture, and clothing (shopping goods) use selective distribution.

Exclusive distribution is the use of only one retail outlet in a given geographic area. The retailer has exclusive rights to sell the product and is therefore likely to carry a large inventory, give exceptional service, and pay more attention to this brand than to others. Luxury auto manufacturers often use exclusive distribution, as do producers of specialty goods such as skydiving equipment and fly-fishing products.

selective distribution
Distribution that sends products to only a preferred group of retailers in an area.

exclusive distribution
Distribution that sends products to only one retail outlet in a given geographic area.

progress assessment

- Describe the activities of rack jobbers and drop shippers.
- What kinds of products would call for each of the different distribution strategies: intensive, selective, exclusive?

LEARNING goal 5

Explain the various kinds of nonstore retailing.

NONSTORE RETAILING

Nothing else in retailing has received more attention recently than electronic retailing. Internet retailing is just one form of nonstore retailing. Other categories are telemarketing; vending machines, kiosks, and carts; direct selling; multilevel marketing; and direct marketing. Small businesses can use nonstore retailing to open up new channels of distribution for their products.

Electronic Retailing

Electronic retailing consists of selling goods and services to ultimate consumers over the Internet. Thanks to website improvements and discounting, online retail sales have risen dramatically over the last few years.[9] But getting customers is only half the battle. The other half is delivering the goods, providing helpful service, and keeping your customers. When electronic retailers lack sufficient inventory or fail to deliver goods on time (especially at holidays and other busy periods), customers often give up and go back to brick-and-mortar stores.

Most Internet retailers now offer e-mail order confirmation. But sometimes they are less good at handling complaints, accepting returns, and providing personal help. Some are improving customer service by adding help buttons that lead customers to real-time online assistance from a human employee.

Old brick-and-mortar stores that add online outlets are sometimes called brick-and-click stores. They allow customers to choose which shopping technique suits them best. Most companies that want to compete in the future will probably need both a real store and an online presence to provide consumers with all the options they want. Walmart has added same-day in-store pickup of online purchases to its services.[10]

electronic retailing
Selling goods and services to ultimate customers (e.g., you and me) over the Internet.

Many brick-and-mortar stores have added Internet services for the added convenience of their customers. Some people shop online and then go to the store to buy the merchandise. Others both shop and buy on the Internet. What are the advantages and disadvantages of shopping and buying online?

telemarketing
The sale of goods and services by telephone.

Traditional retailers like Sears have learned that selling on the Internet calls for a new kind of distribution. Sears's warehouses were accustomed to delivering truckloads of goods to the company's retail outlets. But they were not prepared to deliver to individual consumers, except for large orders like furniture and appliances. It turns out, therefore, that both traditional and Internet retailers have to develop new distribution systems to meet the demands of today's Internet-savvy shoppers. It's often easy to sell goods and services on eBay, but there is always the need to distribute those goods. Most people outsource that function to FedEx or UPS, which have the needed expertise.

Telemarketing

Telemarketing is the sale of goods and services by telephone. Some 80,000 companies use it to supplement or replace in-store selling and complement online selling. Many send a catalog to consumers, who order by calling a toll-free number. Many electronic retailers provide a help feature online that serves the same function.

Vending Machines, Kiosks, and Carts

Vending machines dispense convenience goods when consumers deposit sufficient money. They carry the benefit of location—they're found in airports, office buildings, schools, service stations, and other areas where people want convenience items. In Japan, they sell everything from bandages and face cloths to salads and spiced seafood. Vending by machine will be an interesting area to watch as more innovations are introduced in the United States. U.S. vending machines are already selling iPods, Bose headphones, sneakers, digital cameras, and DVD movies. You can even find earthworms, medical marijuana, and Chardonnay in vending machines.[11] An ATM machine in Abu Dhabi dispenses gold.[12]

Carts and kiosks have lower overhead costs than stores do, so they can offer lower prices on items such as T-shirts, purses, watches, and cell phones. You often see vending carts outside stores or along walkways in malls. Many mall owners love them because they're colorful and create a marketplace atmosphere. Kiosk workers often dispense coupons and helpful product information. You may have noticed airlines are using kiosks to speed the process of getting on the plane. Most provide a boarding pass and allow you to change your seat. Many kiosks serve as gateways to the Internet, so in one place consumers can shop at a store and still have access to all the products available on the Internet. What's your reaction to such kiosks?

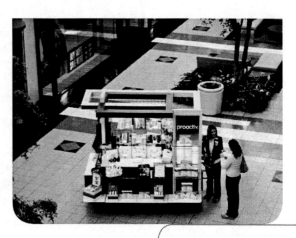

Direct Selling

Direct selling reaches consumers in their homes or workplaces. Because so many men and women work outside the home and aren't in during the day, companies that use direct selling are sponsoring parties at workplaces or evenings and weekends. Major users of this sales category include cosmetics producers and vacuum cleaner manufacturers. Trying to copy their success, other businesses are venturing into direct selling with lingerie, artwork, and candles sold at house parties they sponsor. Some companies, however, such as those in encyclopedia sales, have dropped most of their direct selling efforts in favor of Internet selling.

Vending machines and kiosks are convenient and easy for customers to use. They also have lower overhead than stores do. What do stores provide that kiosks and vending machines don't?

Multilevel Marketing

Over 1,000 U.S. companies have had success using multilevel marketing (MLM) and salespeople who work as independent contractors. One of the most successful MLM firms today is called Team. It sells MonaVie, a fruit juice in a wine bottle for $39. Salespeople earn commissions on their own sales, create commissions for the "upliners" who recruited them, and receive commissions from any "downliners" they recruit to sell. When you have hundreds of downliners—people recruited by the people you recruit—your commissions can be sizable. Some people make tens of thousands of dollars a month this way. That doesn't mean you should get involved with such schemes. More often than not, people at the bottom buy the products themselves and sell a bare minimum to others.

The main attraction of multilevel marketing for employees, other than the potential for making money, is the low cost of entry. For a small investment, the average person can start up a business and begin recruiting others. Many people question MLM because some companies using it have acted unethically. Potential employees must be very careful to examine the practices of such firms. Nonetheless, MLM's sales of $30 billion a year demonstrate the potential for success in this form of marketing.

direct selling
Selling to consumers in their homes or where they work.

Direct Marketing

Direct marketing includes any activity that directly links manufacturers or intermediaries with the ultimate consumer. One of the fastest-growing types of retailing, it includes direct mail, catalog sales, and telemarketing as well as online marketing. Popular consumer catalog companies that use direct marketing include Coldwater Creek, L.L. Bean, and Lands' End (now owned by Sears). Direct marketing has created tremendous competition in some high-tech areas as well.

Direct marketing has become popular because shopping from home or work is more convenient for consumers than going to stores. Instead of driving to a mall, people can shop in catalogs and advertising supplements in the newspaper and then buy by phone, mail, or computer. Interactive online selling

direct marketing
Any activity that directly links manufacturers or intermediaries with the ultimate consumer.

is expected to provide increasing competition for retail stores. Recently, L.L. Bean put pressure on rivals by eliminating shipping charges. That made L.L. Bean even more attractive to people who like to shop by catalog or online.[13]

Direct marketing took on a new dimension with *interactive video*. Producers now provide all kinds of information on websites. Consumers can ask questions, seek the best price, and order goods and services—all online. Companies that use interactive video have become major competitors for those who market through paper catalogs.

To offer consumers the maximum benefit, marketing intermediaries must work together to ensure a smooth flow of goods and services. There hasn't always been total harmony in the channel of distribution. As a result, channel members have created systems to make the flows more efficient. We'll discuss those next.

corporate distribution system
A distribution system in which all of the organizations in the channel of distribution are owned by one firm.

contractual distribution system
A distribution system in which members are bound to cooperate through contractual agreements.

LEARNING goal 6

Explain the various ways to build cooperation in channel systems.

BUILDING COOPERATION IN CHANNEL SYSTEMS

One way traditional retailers can compete with online retailers is to be so efficient that online retailers can't beat them on cost—given the need for customers to pay for delivery. That means manufacturers, wholesalers, and retailers must work closely to form a unified system. How can manufacturers get wholesalers and retailers to cooperate in such a system? One way is to link the firms in a formal relationship. Four systems have emerged to tie firms together: corporate systems, contractual systems, administered systems, and supply chains.

Corporate Distribution Systems

In a **corporate distribution system** one firm owns all the organizations in the channel of distribution. If the manufacturer owns the retail firm, clearly it can maintain a great deal of control over its operations. Sherwin Williams, for example, owns its own retail stores and coordinates everything: display, pricing, promotion, inventory control, and so on.

Franchisors like Chocolate Chocolate Chocolate Company use a contractual distribution system that requires franchisees to follow the franchisors' rules and procedures. How does such a system ensure consistent quality and level of service?

Contractual Distribution Systems

If a manufacturer can't buy retail stores, it can try to get retailers to sign a contract to cooperate with it. In a **contractual distribution system** members are bound to cooperate through contractual agreements. There are three forms of contractual systems:

1. *Franchise systems* such as McDonald's, KFC, Baskin-Robbins, and AAMCO. The franchisee agrees to all the rules, regulations, and procedures established by the franchisor. This results in the consistent quality and level of service you find in most franchised organizations.

2. *Wholesaler-sponsored chains* such as Ace Hardware and IGA food stores. Each store signs an agreement to use the same name, participate in chain promotions, and cooperate as a unified system of stores, even though each is independently owned and managed.

3. *Retail cooperatives* such as Associated Grocers. This arrangement is much like a wholesaler-sponsored chain except it is initiated by the retailers. The same degree of cooperation exists, and the stores remain independent. Normally in such a system, retailers agree to focus their purchases on one wholesaler, but cooperative retailers could also purchase a wholesale organization to ensure better service.

Administered Distribution Systems

If you were a producer, what would you do if you couldn't get retailers to sign an agreement to cooperate? You might manage all the marketing functions yourself, including display, inventory control, pricing, and promotion. A system in which producers manage all the marketing functions at the retail level is called an **administered distribution system**. Kraft does that for its cheeses. Scott does it for its seed and other lawn care products. Retailers cooperate with producers in such systems because they get a great deal of free help. All the retailer has to do is ring up the sale.

Supply Chains

A **supply chain** (or **value chain**) consists of all the linked activities various organizations must perform to move goods and services from the source of raw materials to ultimate consumers. A supply chain is longer than a channel of distribution because it includes links from suppliers to manufacturers, whereas the channel of distribution begins with manufacturers.[14] Channels of distribution are part of the overall supply chain (see Figure 15.6).

Included in the supply chain are farmers, miners, suppliers of all kinds (parts, equipment, supplies), manufacturers, wholesalers, and retailers. **Supply-chain management** is the process of managing the movement of raw materials, parts, work in progress, finished goods, and related information through all the organizations in the supply chain; managing the return of such goods if necessary; and recycling materials when appropriate.[15]

One complex supply chain is that for the automaker Kia's Sorento model. The Sorento is assembled in South Korea and made of over 30,000 components from all over the world. The shock and front-loading system is from AF Sachs AG, the front-wheel drive is from BorgWarner, and the tires are from Michelin. Airbags are sometimes flown in from Swedish company Autoliv Inc., which makes them in Utah. As you can see, supply-chain management is

administered distribution system
A distribution system in which producers manage all of the marketing functions at the retail level.

supply chain (value chain)
The sequence of linked activities that must be performed by various organizations to move goods from the sources of raw materials to ultimate consumers.

supply-chain management
The process of managing the movement of raw materials, parts, work in progress, finished goods, and related information through all the organizations involved in the supply chain; managing the return of such goods, if necessary; and recycling materials when appropriate.

figure 15.6

THE SUPPLY CHAIN

REACHING BEYOND
our borders

The Global Supply Chain for Services

It is easy to imagine the supply chain for parts and materials that go into goods. For example, you can easily imagine components traveling from Thailand, the Philippines, Malaysia, and Taiwan to a factory in China where they are assembled before being sold as iPods or iPad 2s in an Apple store in New York. In the future, it may be more important to study and understand the supply chain for services. Imagine call centers as part of the service supply chain. They are relatively easy to establish and most of us have experienced talking to someone on the phone from Asia when we've had technology problems. Now imagine outsourcing other services such as the programming of software, reviewing legal documents, processing expense reports and the like.

Much movie animation is now taking place in the Philippines, and companies in China are providing research and development services. One article stated, "We're heading for a day when a Malaysian architect will sketch out a new office tower for London, a Philippine architect will prepare detailed renderings, and a Chinese engineer will assess the structural soundness of the design. Or a specialist firm in Bangalore will administer health benefits for a Kansas company." The competition among foreign suppliers is intense, including the need to find workers with strong language skills. Those countries that excel in providing supply chains for goods (e.g., China) may not be the same as those providing expertise in services (e.g., India). Of course, one of the countries that could become a leader in supplying supply-chain services is the United States. One important step is to make supply chains secure. The 2011 disasters in Japan showed people that the supply chain is only as good as the weakest link.

Sources: Joseph Sternberg, "Now Comes the Global Revolution in Services," *The Wall Street Journal,* February 10, 2011; Janet Napolitano, "How to Secure the Global Supply Chain," *The Wall Street Journal,* January 6, 2011; and Bruce Einhorn, Tim Culpan and Alan Ohnsman, "Now, A Weak Link in the Supply Chain," *Bloomberg Businessweek,* March 21–March 27, 2011.

interfirm and international.[16] Increasingly, it also involves services. To learn about supply chains and services, see the nearby Reaching Beyond Our Borders box.

Companies like SAP, i2, and Oracle have developed software to coordinate the movement of goods and information so that producers can translate consumer wants into products with the least amount of materials, inventory, and time. Firms can move parts and information so smoothly, they look like one firm.

Computers make such links possible. Naturally, the systems are quite complex and expensive, but they can pay for themselves in the long run because of inventory savings, customer service improvement, and responsiveness to market changes. Because such systems are so effective and efficient, they are sometimes called *value chains* instead of supply chains.[17]

Not all supply chains are as efficient as they can be. Some companies have struggled with high distribution costs, including the cost of gas, inefficient truck routes, and excess inventory.[18] The complexity of supply-chain management often leads firms to outsource the whole process to experts that know how to integrate it. Richardson Electronics of La Fox, Illinois, does business in 125 countries with 37 different currencies. It relies on Oracle's PeopleSoft Supply Chain Management and Financial Management solutions. Oracle's PeopleSoft also provides financial help, making it easier and less expensive to ship goods anywhere in the world and be sure of payment. Outsourcing is on the rise as more firms realize how complex distribution is.

Outsourcing this function can have serious consequences as companies learned when they found lead paint in toys and contaminants in the drug Heparin.[19] Cardinal Health, the nation's second largest drug distributor, became much more successful when the CEO reorganized the supply chain.[20] All companies must be careful to evaluate each of the components of the supply chain to make sure the whole system is sustainable.[21] Emphasis today is focused on "green" technology because so much of what affects the environment is caused by distribution.[22]

LEARNING goal 7

Describe logistics and outline how intermediaries manage the transportation and storage of goods.

LOGISTICS: GETTING GOODS TO CONSUMERS EFFICIENTLY

Shipping costs have risen dramatically in recent years. When shipping from country to country, it is often impossible to use trucks or trains because the goods have to travel over water. Shipping by air is often prohibitively expensive, which sometimes narrows the choice to moving goods by ship. But how do you get the goods to the ship—and from the ship to the buyer? How do you keep costs low enough to make exchanges beneficial for you and your customers? And how do you handle foreign trade duties and taxes? Distributing goods globally is complicated. As transportation and distribution have grown more complex, marketers have responded by developing more sophisticated systems.

To better manage customs problems, for instance, many turn to web-based trade compliance systems. Firms like TradePoint and Xporta determine what paperwork is needed, cross-checking their databases for information about foreign trade duties and taxes, U.S. labor law restrictions, and federal regulations from the Food and Drug Administration or the Bureau of Alcohol, Tobacco, and Firearms. In other words, they manage logistics.[23]

Logistics is the planning, implementing, and controlling of the physical flow of materials, final goods, and related information from points of origin to

logistics
The marketing activity that involves planning, implementing, and controlling the physical flow of materials, final goods, and related information from points of origin to points of consumption to meet customer requirements at a profit.

How do you move heavy raw materials like timber from one country to another? This photo shows some of the firms engaged in the logistics process. A trucking firm brings the logs to a dock where huge cranes lift them into the hold of a ship. The ship must be unloaded and the logs put on another truck to travel to a processing plant. Why is managing the logistics process a key to survival in some industries?

inbound logistics
The area of logistics that involves bringing raw materials, packaging, other goods and services, and information from suppliers to producers.

materials handling
The movement of goods within a warehouse, from warehouses to the factory floor, and from the factory floor to various workstations.

outbound logistics
The area of logistics that involves managing the flow of finished products and information to business buyers and ultimate consumers (people like you and me).

reverse logistics
The area of logistics that involves bringing goods back to the manufacturer because of defects or for recycling materials.

points of consumption to meet customer requirements at a profit. **Inbound logistics** brings raw materials, packaging, other goods and services, and information from suppliers to producers.

Materials handling is the movement of goods within a warehouse, from warehouses to the factory floor, and from the factory floor to various workstations. *Factory processes* change raw materials and parts and other inputs into outputs, such as finished goods like shoes, cars, and clothes.

Outbound logistics manages the flow of finished products and information to business buyers and ultimately to consumers like you and me. **Reverse logistics** brings goods back to the manufacturer because of defects or for recycling materials.[24]

Logistics is as much about the movement of *information* as it is about the movement of goods. Customer wants and needs must flow through the system all the way to suppliers and must do so in real time. Information must also flow down through the system with no delay. That, of course, demands sophisticated hardware and software. One company in India, Fabindia (a seller of hand-woven garments and home furnishings), ensures close relationships with its suppliers by having its suppliers become shareholders.

Third-party logistics is the use of outside firms to help move goods from here to there. It is part of the trend to outsource functions your firm cannot do more efficiently than outside firms.[25] The 3PLs (third-party logistics providers) that have superior capability in business intelligence and are proactively sharing that knowledge are the ones who will grow in the future.[26] Greatwide Logistics Services, for example, does business with six of the top 10 grocery retailers and wholesalers in the United States.[27]

Texas Instruments (TI) is one of the world's largest makers of silicon chips. About 75 percent of its semiconductor products move through its distribution network. The company uses a regional distribution center in Singapore to serve customers in Asia; one in Dallas to serve North America; one in Utrecht, the Netherlands, to serve Europe; and one in Tsubuka, Japan, to serve markets in that country. TI uses a 3PL service to handle the day-to-day operations of those warehouses. Moving goods from one place to another is a major part of logistics.

How do you get products to people around the world after the sale? What are your options? You could send goods by truck, by train, ship, or pipeline. You could use a shipping specialist, such as UPS, FedEx, or the U.S. Postal Service, but often that is expensive, especially for large items. Nonetheless, some of the most sophisticated marketers outsource the distribution process to such specialists.[28] All transportation modes can be evaluated on basic service criteria: cost, speed, dependability, flexibility, frequency, and reach. Figure 15.7 compares the various transportation modes on these criteria.

figure I5.7

COMPARING TRANSPORTATION MODES
Combining trucks with railroads lowers cost and increases the number of locations reached. The same is true when combining trucks with ships. Combining trucks with airlines speeds goods over long distances and gets them to almost any location.

MODE	COST	SPEED	ON-TIME DEPENDABILITY	FLEXIBILITY HANDLING PRODUCTS	FREQUENCY OF SHIPMENTS	REACH
Railroad	Medium	Slow	Medium	High	Low	High
Trucks	High	Fast	High	Medium	High	Highest
Pipeline	Low	Medium	Highest	Lowest	Highest	Lowest
Ships (water)	Lowest	Slowest	Lowest	Highest	Lowest	Low
Airplane	Highest	Fastest	Low	Low	Medium	Medium

Railroads carry over a third of all goods shipped within the United States and are expected to remain a dominant transportation mode. What are some of the advantages of shipping by rail, for both large and small producers?

Trains Are Great for Large Shipments

The largest percentage of goods in the United States (by volume) is shipped by rail. As a whole, the rail industry carries about 43 percent of all freight (as measured in ton miles), but uses only 7 percent of the total energy used to move freight.[29] Railroad shipment is best for bulky items such as coal, wheat, automobiles, and heavy equipment. In *piggyback* shipping, a truck trailer is detached from the cab, loaded onto a railroad flatcar, and taken to a destination where it will be offloaded, attached to a truck, and driven to the customer's plant. Railroads should continue to hold their own in competition with other modes of transportation. They offer a relatively energy-efficient way to move goods and could experience significant gains if fuel prices climb.

A company may not ship enough goods to think of using a railroad. Such smaller manufacturers or marketers can get good rates and service by using a **freight forwarder**, which puts many small shipments together to create a single large one that can be transported cost-effectively by truck or train. Some freight forwarders also offer warehousing, customs assistance, and other services along with pickup and delivery. You can see the benefits of such a company to a smaller seller. A freight forwarder is just one of many distribution specialists that have emerged to help marketers move goods from one place to another.

freight forwarder
An organization that puts many small shipments together to create a single large shipment that can be transported cost-effectively to the final destination.

Trucks Are Good for Small Shipments to Remote Locations

The second largest surface transportation mode is motor vehicles (trucks and vans). As Figure 15.7 shows, trucks reach more locations than trains and can deliver almost any commodity door-to-door.

You could buy your own truck to make deliveries, but for widespread delivery you can't beat trucking specialists. Like freight forwarders, they have emerged to supply one important marketing function—transporting goods. Railroads have joined with trucking firms to further the process of piggybacking with 20-foot-high railroad cars, called double stacks, that carry two truck trailers, one on top of the other.

When fuel prices rise, trucking companies look for ways to cut costs. The newest measure of transportation from farm to consumer is the *carbon cost*. Some argue that the fewer miles food travels, the better for the environment, but that may not always be true.

Water Transportation Is Inexpensive but Slow

When sending goods overseas, often the least expensive way is by ship. Obviously, ships are slower than ground or air transportation, so water transportation isn't appropriate for goods that need to be delivered quickly. There was a huge dropoff in shipping when oil prices skyrocketed, improved somewhat when oil prices came down, and dropped off again when oil prices rose again. Water transport is local as well as international. If you live near the Mississippi River, you've likely seen towboats hauling as many as 30 barges at a time, with a cargo of up to 35,000 tons. On smaller rivers, towboats can haul about eight barges, carrying up to 20,000 tons—that's the equivalent of four 100-car railroad trains. Add to that Great Lakes shipping, shipping from coast to coast and along the coasts, and international shipments, and water transportation takes on a new dimension as a key transportation mode. When truck trailers are placed on ships to travel long distances at lower rates, it's called *fishyback* (see the explanation of piggyback above). When they are placed in airplanes, by the way, that's *birdyback*.

Pipelines Are Fast and Efficient

One transportation mode we don't often observe is pipeline. Pipelines primarily transport water, petroleum, and petroleum products—but a lot more products than you may imagine are shipped by pipelines. For example, coal can be sent by pipeline by first crushing it and mixing it with water.

Air Transportation Is Fast but Expensive

Today, only a small proportion of shipping goes by air. Nonetheless, air transportation is a critical factor in many industries, carrying everything from small packages to luxury cars and elephants. Its primary benefit is speed. No firms know this better than FedEx and UPS. As just two of several competitors vying for the fast-delivery market, FedEx and UPS have used air transport to expand into global markets.

The air freight industry is starting to focus on global distribution. Emery has been an industry pioneer in establishing specialized sales and operations teams aimed at serving the distribution needs of specific industries. KLM Royal Dutch Airlines has cargo/passenger planes that handle high-profit items such as diplomatic pouches and medical supplies. Specializing in such cargo has enabled KLM to compete with FedEx, TNT, and DHL.

Intermodal Shipping

intermodal shipping
The use of multiple modes of transportation to complete a single long-distance movement of freight.

Intermodal shipping uses multiple modes of transportation—highway, air, water, rail—to complete a single long-distance movement of freight. Services that specialize in intermodal shipping are known as intermodal marketing companies. Today, railroads are merging with each other and with other transportation companies to offer intermodal distribution.

Picture an automobile made in Japan for sale in the United States. It's shipped by truck to a loading dock, and from there moved by ship to a port in the United States. It may be placed on another truck and then taken to a railroad station for loading on a train that will take it across the country, to again be loaded on a truck for delivery to a local dealer. No doubt you've seen automobiles being hauled across the country by train and by truck. Now imagine that one integrated shipping firm handled all that movement. That's what intermodal shipping is all about.

The Storage Function

The preceding sections detailed the various ways of shipping goods once the company has sold them. But that's only the first step in understanding the system that moves goods from one point to another. Another important part of a complex logistics system is storage.

Buyers want goods delivered quickly. That means marketers must have goods available in various parts of the country ready to be shipped locally when ordered. A good percentage of the total cost of logistics is for storage. This includes the cost of the storage warehouse (distribution facility) and its operation, plus movement of goods within the warehouse.

There are two major kinds of warehouses: storage and distribution. A *storage warehouse* holds products for a relatively long time. Seasonal goods such as lawn mowers are kept in such a warehouse. *Distribution warehouses* are facilities used to gather and redistribute products. You can picture a distribution warehouse for FedEx or UPS handling thousands of packages in a very short time. The packages are picked up at places throughout the country and then processed for reshipment at these centers. General Electric's combination storage and distribution facility in San Gabriel Valley, California, gives you a feel for how large such buildings can be. It is nearly half a mile long and 465 feet wide—that's enough to hold almost 27 football fields.

Tracking Goods

How do producers keep track of where their goods are at any given time? As we noted in Chapter 14, companies use Universal Product Codes—the familiar black-and-white bar codes and a preset number—to keep track of inventory. Bar codes got a big lift when camera phone apps made it possible to compare prices and read reviews about products from different suppliers.[30]

Radio frequency identification (RFID), which we also mentioned earlier, is newer technology that tags merchandise so that it can be tracked from its arrival on the supplier's docks to its exit through the retailer's door. Walmart, Target, and other organizations all plan to require suppliers to use RFID. Currently, RFID tags cost about 10 cents each, but the goal is to get the cost down to about 1 cent.

Few companies are more interested in tracking items than UPS, which now uses a mix of Bluetooth's short-range radio capability and wireless receivers to track merchandise. It claims the system is even better than RFID. The U.S. State Department is producing an electronic passport card as a substitute for booklet passports to be used by U.S. citizens who travel often to Canada, Mexico, and the Caribbean. It uses an RFID chip to provide data about the user. The card is very controversial, however, because some people believe it can be easily altered.

RFID tags are being used in all kinds of situations, from the movement of goods to the tracking of livestock. RFID tags in products like these jeans helps retailers and producers track products from the suppliers' docks through the retailers' doors. How can RFID tags help you avoid losing your luggage, car keys, and other things?

WHAT ALL THIS MEANS TO YOU

The life or death of a firm often depends on its ability to take orders, process orders, keep customers informed about the progress of their orders, get the goods out to customers quickly, handle returns, and manage any recycling issues. Some of the most exciting firms in the marketplace are those that assist in some aspect of supply-chain management.

What all this means to you is that many new jobs are becoming available in the exciting area of supply-chain management. These include jobs in distribution: trains, airplanes, trucks, ships, and pipelines. It also means jobs handling information flows between and among companies, including website development. Other jobs include processing orders, keeping track of inventory, following the path of products as they move from seller to buyer and back, recycling goods, and much more.

progress assessment

- What four systems have evolved to tie together members of the channel of distribution?
- How does logistics differ from distribution?
- What are inbound logistics, outbound logistics, and reverse logistics?

summary

Learning Goal 1. Explain the concept of marketing channels and their value.

- **What is a channel of distribution?**

A channel of distribution consists of a whole set of marketing intermediaries, such as agents, brokers, wholesalers, and retailers, that join together to transport and store goods in their path (or channel) from producers to consumers.

- **How do marketing intermediaries add value?**

Intermediaries perform certain marketing tasks—such as transporting, storing, selling, advertising, and relationship building—faster and more cheaply than most manufacturers could. Channels of distribution ensure communication flows and the flow of money and title to goods. They also help ensure that the right quantity and assortment of goods will be available when and where needed.

- **What are the principles behind the use of such intermediaries?**

Marketing intermediaries can be eliminated, but their activities can't. Without wholesalers and retailers, consumers would have to perform the tasks of transporting and storing goods, finding suppliers, and establishing communication with them. Intermediaries add costs to products, but these costs are usually more than offset by the values they create.

Learning Goal 2. Demonstrate how intermediaries perform the six marketing utilities.

- **How do intermediaries perform the six marketing utilities?**

A retail grocer may cut or trim meat, providing some form utility. But marketers are more often responsible for the five other utilities. They provide time utility by having goods available *when* people want them, and place utility by having goods *where* people want them. Possession utility makes it possible for people to own things and includes credit, delivery, installation, guarantees, and anything else that completes the sale. Marketers also inform consumers of the availability of goods and services with advertising, publicity, and other means. That provides information utility. Finally, marketers provide fast, friendly, and efficient service during and after the sale (service utility).

Learning Goal 3. Identify the types of wholesale intermediaries in the distribution system.

- **What is a wholesaler?**

A wholesaler is a marketing intermediary that sells to organizations and individuals, but not to final consumers.

- **What are some wholesale organizations that assist in the movement of goods from manufacturers to consumers?**

Merchant wholesalers are independently owned firms that take title to the goods they handle. *Rack jobbers* furnish racks or shelves full of merchandise to retailers, display products, and sell on consignment. *Cash-and-carry wholesalers* serve mostly small retailers with a limited assortment of products. *Drop shippers* solicit orders from retailers and other wholesalers and have the merchandise shipped directly from a producer to a buyer.

Learning Goal 4. Compare the distribution strategies retailers use.

- **What is a retailer?**

A retailer is an organization that sells to ultimate consumers. Marketers develop several strategies based on retailing.

- **What are three distribution strategies marketers use?**

Marketers use three basic distribution strategies: intensive (putting products in as many places as possible), selective (choosing only a few stores in a chosen market), and exclusive (using only one store in each market area).

Learning Goal 5. Explain the various kinds of nonstore retailing.

- **What are some of the forms of nonstore retailing?**

Nonstore retailing includes online marketing; telemarketing (marketing by phone); vending machines, kiosks, and carts (marketing by putting products in convenient locations, such as in the halls of shopping centers); direct selling (marketing by approaching consumers in their homes or places of work); multilevel marketing (marketing by setting up a system of salespeople who recruit other salespeople and help them to sell directly to customers); and direct marketing (direct mail and catalog sales). Telemarketing and online marketing are also forms of direct marketing.

Learning Goal 6. Explain the various ways to build cooperation in channel systems.

- **What are the four types of distribution systems?**

The four distribution systems that tie firms together are (1) *corporate systems,* in which all organizations in the channel are owned by one firm; (2) *contractual systems,* in which members are bound to cooperate through contractual agreements; (3) *administered systems,* in which all marketing functions at the retail level are managed by manufacturers; and (4) *supply chains,* in which the various firms in the supply chain are linked electronically to provide the most efficient movement of information and goods possible.

Learning Goal 7. Describe logistics and outline how intermediaries manage the transportation and storage of goods.

- **What is logistics?**

Logistics includes planning, implementing, and controlling the physical flow of materials, final goods, and related information from points of origin to points of consumption to meet customer requirements at a profit.

- **What is the difference between logistics and distribution?**

Distribution generally means transportation. Logistics is more complex. *Inbound logistics* brings raw materials, packaging, other goods and services, and information from suppliers to producers. *Materials handling* is the moving of goods from warehouses to the factory floor and to various workstations. *Outbound logistics* manages the flow of finished products and information to business buyers and ultimate consumers (people like you and me). *Reverse logistics* brings goods back to the manufacturer because of defects or for recycling materials.

- **What are the various transportation modes?**

Transportation modes include rail (for heavy shipments within the country or between bordering countries); trucks (for getting goods directly to consumers); ships (for slow, inexpensive movement of goods, often internationally); pipelines (for moving water and oil and other such goods); and airplanes (for shipping goods quickly).

- **What is intermodal shipping?**

Intermodal shipping uses multiple modes of transportation—highway, air, water, rail—to complete a single long-distance movement of freight.

- **What are the different kinds of warehouses?**

A storage warehouse stores products for a relatively long time. Distribution warehouses are used to gather and redistribute products.

key terms

administered distribution system 421	exclusive distribution 417	possession utility 412
agents/brokers 407	freight forwarder 425	rack jobbers 413
cash-and-carry wholesalers 413	inbound logistics 424	retailer 407
channel of distribution 406	information utility 412	reverse logistics 424
contractual distribution system 420	intensive distribution 416	selective distribution 417
corporate distribution system 420	intermodal shipping 426	service utility 412
direct marketing 419	logistics 423	supply chain (value chain) 421
direct selling 419	marketing intermediaries 406	supply-chain management 421
drop shippers 413	materials handling 424	telemarketing 418
electronic retailing 417	merchant wholesalers 413	time utility 411
	outbound logistics 424	utility 411
	place utility 411	wholesaler 407

critical thinking

1. Imagine that we have eliminated marketing intermediaries, and you need groceries and shoes. How would you find out where the shoes and groceries are? How far would you have to travel to get them? How much money do you think you'd save for your time and effort?

2. Which intermediary do you think is most important today and why? What changes are happening to companies in that area?

3. One scarce item in the future will be water. If you could think of an inexpensive way to get water from places of abundance to places where it is needed for drinking, farming, and other uses, you could become a wealthy marketing intermediary. Pipelines are an alternative, but could you also freeze the water and ship it by train or truck? Could you use ships to tow icebergs to warmer climates? What other means of transporting water might there be?

developing workplace skills

1. The six utilities of marketing are form, time, place, possession, information, and service. Give examples of organizations in your area that perform each of these functions.

2. Form small groups and diagram how Dole might get pineapples from a field in Thailand to a canning plant in California to a store near your college. Include the intermediaries and the forms of transportation each one might use.

3. Compare the merits of buying and selling goods in stores and over the Internet. What advantages do stores have? Has anyone in the class tried to sell anything on the Internet? How did he or she ship the product?

4. In class, discuss the differences between wholesaling and retailing and why retailing has more appeal for students considering jobs. Since fewer students seek jobs in wholesaling than in retailing, do you think wholesaling jobs may be easier to get?

5. One part of retailing is using auction sites like eBay to sell new and used merchandise. Form small groups and discuss group members' experiences using eBay. What tips have they learned? How do eBay users minimize the problems associated with shipping?

taking it to the net

Purpose

To examine how small businesses can learn to use the Internet to distribute their products directly to customers.

Exercise

Many small-business owners have no idea how to begin selling goods over the Internet. Several free websites have been developed to help them get started with tasks from setting up their site to doing online marketing, handling credit purchases, and more. Go to Homestead.com or BlueVoda.com and listen to the presentations they make. Search the Web to find other sources of help in designing your own website. Then answer the following questions:

1. How long do the websites say that it takes to get started?

2. Does the process seem easier or harder than you imagined?

3. Do you have questions that the websites did not answer?

4. What help are you given, if any, in planning how to ship your goods?

casing the web

To access the case "Multilevel Marketing," visit **www.mhhe.com/ub10e**

video case

To access the video case featuring Netflix, visit **www.mhhe.com/ub10e**

USING
Effective
Promotions

16

LEARNING

LEARNING
goals

After you have read and studied this chapter, you should be able to

1 Identify the new and traditional tools that make up the promotion mix.

2 Contrast the advantages and disadvantages of various advertising media, including the Internet and social media.

3 Illustrate the steps of the B2B and B2C selling processes.

4 Describe the role of the public relations department, and show how publicity fits in that role.

5 Assess the effectiveness of various forms of sales promotion, including sampling.

6 Show how word of mouth, e-mail marketing, viral marketing, blogging, podcasting, and mobile marketing work.

After falling out of fashion in the free-spending 1990s and early 2000s, deal hunting returned with a vengeance when the recession hit. In this digital age, cost-conscious shoppers have far more options than just print coupons to aid them in their quest for value. Deal sites like Groupon combine aspects of social networking with clearance-level discounts, driving foot traffic to local businesses and giving consumers more bang for their buck.

Founded in 2008 by Andrew Mason, Groupon posts a single local deal every day. Typical promotions include coupons for $40 worth of food at an area restaurant for only $20. In order for the coupon to become valid, Groupon requires that a certain number of people first buy into the deal. Businesses hope that in the long run the deal will convert bargain hunters into lifelong customers, all while bringing in a healthy number of immediate sales. Groupon splits the revenue from the purchased coupons with merchants, claiming as much as 40 to 50 percent of each deal.

Such high commissions turned Groupon into a dot-com goldmine. In fact, it grew faster than any Web company in history, ballooning from $740 million in revenue in 2010 to approximately $4 billion in 2011. The company was valued at $1.4 billion at the start of 2010 and quickly grew to $3 billion by November. Google offered to buy the company for $6 billion in December 2010, but Mason astonished the market by rejecting the offer. Now with talks of an initial public offering (first public sale of stock) on the rise, Groupon could be worth as much as $25 billion when it finally reaches the open market.

The one constant throughout Groupon's turbulently successful initial years has been its founder and CEO Andrew Mason. As an idealistic public policy grad student at University of Chicago, Mason first tried his hand at crowdsourcing (an open call to interested people to contribute ideas or perform tasks) with a website called The Point. The idea of the site was to gather large groups of consumers to lobby companies and government officials for various policy changes, such as making Election Day a national holiday. Although The Point attracted few users, Mason recognized that he could harness the same technology to bring clusters of bargain hunting customers to local businesses' doorsteps. Within 13 months of The Point's conversion to Groupon, Mason attracted $1.3 billion of venture capital investment.

Much of Mason's success can be attributed to Groupon's simplicity. Unfortunately, that simplicity is also responsible for Groupon's increasing number of competitors. Several high profile startups such as Tippr and the Amazon-backed LivingSocial basically mirror the Groupon model. While these sites haven't experienced the same explosive popularity, they nevertheless command a big enough share of the market to worry Mason.

In response to competitors, Mason and his staff introduced a new venture dubbed Groupon Now. As opposed to the regular site's single daily deal, Groupon Now offers a variety of discounts filtered through a smartphone app. When users activate the app they are greeted with two buttons: "I'm bored" and "I'm hungry." If they select the latter, a map will pop up with a selection of restaurants in the area offering deals. The catch is that the coupons are only valid at certain times during the day. This way, restaurants can fill up tables during off times when they aren't busy. Mason is optimistic about Groupon Now, predicting that it will bring in $1 billion in revenue by the end of its first year. On the other hand, some skeptical insiders wonder if merchants will want to handle even more discount-related hassles. Still, as with all forms of promotion, only time will tell whether or not Mason's service will succeed.

In this chapter, we explore all the traditional and new elements of promotion. We'll explain how marketers use different media for promotion and the advantages and disadvantages of each. We'll compare B2C and B2B promotions and look at the role of public relations. Throughout the chapter we'll pay particular attention to promotional uses of electronic media like blogging, social networking, and podcasts.

profile

Getting to Know

X *Andrew Mason*

CEO of Groupon

Sources: Brad Stone and Douglas MacMillan, "Are Four Words Worth $25 Billion for Groupon?" *Bloomberg Businessweek,* March 17, 2011; Christopher Steiner, "The Next Web Phenom," *Forbes,* September 9, 2010; Jayne O'Donnell and Rachel Huggins, "Crave Coupons, Bargains? Group-Buying Sites Offer Deals," *USA Today,* May 14, 2010; Brad Stone and Douglas MacMillan, "When Groupon Dodged Google," *Bloomberg Businessweek,* December 8, 2010.

NAME THAT
company

This beverage company has 8.5 million Facebook fans. It posts two daily messages and then monitors how many times each message is reviewed, how many times it is shared, and what the fan response to the messages are. It also uses Facebook to test potential ads before airing them on traditional media like TV. What is the name of this company? (Find the answer in the chapter.)

LEARNING goal 1

Identify the new and traditional tools that make up the promotion mix.

PROMOTION AND THE PROMOTION MIX

Promotion is one of the four Ps of marketing. As noted in Chapter 13, promotion consists of all the techniques sellers use to motivate people to buy their products or services. Both profit-making and nonprofit organizations use promotional techniques to communicate with people in their target market about goods and services, and to persuade them to participate in a marketing exchange.[1] Marketers use many different tools to promote their products.[2] Traditionally, those tools were advertising, personal selling, public relations, and sales promotion. Today they also include e-mail promotions, mobile promotions (those that use cell phones), social networking, blogging, podcasting, tweets, and more.[3] The Spotlight on Small Business box explores what happens when a small business seems too busy to do traditional marketing.

The combination of promotional tools an organization uses is called its **promotion mix;** see Figure 16.1. We show the product in the middle of the

promotion mix
The combination of promotional tools an organization uses.

figure 16.1

THE TRADITIONAL PROMOTION MIX

figure to illustrate that the product itself can also be a promotional tool, such as when marketers give away free samples.

Integrated marketing communication (IMC) combines the promotional tools into one comprehensive, unified promotional strategy. With IMC, marketers can create a positive brand image, meet the needs of the consumer, and meet the strategic marketing and promotional goals of the firm. Emphasis today is on integrating traditional media, like TV, with social media[4] or integrating print media with online sites.[5]

integrated marketing communication (IMC)
A technique that combines all the promotional tools into one comprehensive, unified promotional strategy.

figure 16.2

STEPS IN A PROMOTIONAL CAMPAIGN

1. Identify a target market. (Refer back to Chapter 13 for a discussion of segmentation and target marketing.)
2. Define the objectives for each element of the promotion mix. Goals should be clear and measurable.
3. Determine a promotional budget. The budgeting process will clarify how much can be spent on advertising, personal selling, and other promotional efforts.
4. Develop a unifying message. The goal of an integrated promotional program is to have one clear message communicated by advertising, public relations, sales, and every other promotional effort.
5. Implement the plan. Advertisements, blogs, and other promotional efforts must be scheduled to complement efforts being made by public relations and sales promotion. Salespeople should have access to all materials to optimize the total effort.
6. Evaluate effectiveness. Measuring results depends greatly on clear objectives. Each element of the promotional mix should be evaluated separately, and an overall measure should be taken as well. It is important to learn what is working and what is not.

Figure 16.2 on p. 437 shows the six steps in a typical promotional campaign. Let's begin exploring promotional tools by looking at advertising—the most visible tool.

LEARNING goal 2

Contrast the advantages and disadvantages of various advertising media, including the Internet and social media.

ADVERTISING: INFORMING, PERSUADING, AND REMINDING

advertising
Paid, nonpersonal communication through various media by organizations and individuals who are in some way identified in the advertising message.

Advertising is paid, nonpersonal communication through various media by organizations and individuals who are in some way *identified in the message.* Identification of the sender separates advertising from *propaganda,* which is nonpersonal communication that *does not have an identified sponsor.* Propaganda is often distributed by the government in various countries. Figure 16.3 lists various categories of advertising. Take a minute to look it over; you'll see there's a lot more to advertising than just television commercials.

It's also easy to appreciate the impact of advertising spending on the U.S. economy; see Figure 16.4. Total ad volume exceeds $241 billion yearly. Note that direct mail is the number one medium, with expenditures over $52

Figure 16.3

MAJOR CATEGORIES OF ADVERTISING
Different kinds of advertising are used by various organizations to reach different market targets.

- *Retail advertising*—advertising to consumers by various retail stores such as supermarkets and shoe stores.
- *Trade advertising*—advertising to wholesalers and retailers by manufacturers to encourage them to carry their products.
- *Business-to-business advertising*—advertising from manufacturers to other manufacturers. A firm selling motors to auto companies would use business-to-business advertising.
- *Institutional advertising*—advertising designed to create an attractive image for an organization rather than for a product. "We Care about You" at Giant Food is an example. "Virginia Is for Lovers" and "I ❤ New York" were two institutional campaigns by government agencies.
- *Product advertising*—advertising for a good or service to create interest among consumer, commercial, and industrial buyers.
- *Advocacy advertising*—advertising that supports a particular view of an issue (e.g., an ad in support of gun control or against nuclear power plants). Such advertising is also known as cause advertising.
- *Comparison advertising*—advertising that compares competitive products. For example, an ad that compares two different cold care products' speed and benefits is a comparative ad.
- *Interactive advertising*—customer-oriented communication that enables customers to choose the information they receive, such as interactive video catalogs that let customers select which items to view.
- *Online advertising*—advertising messages that appear on computers as people visit different websites.
- *Mobile advertising*—advertising that reaches people on their cell phones.

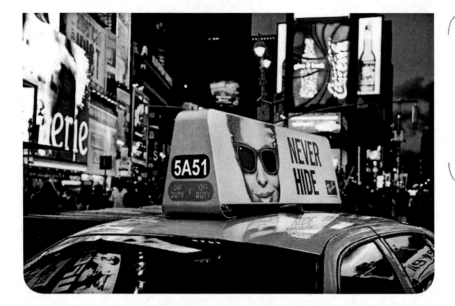

Advertising seems to be everywhere as we go about our daily lives. How many advertisements can you spot in this photo? Can the noise created by so many ads interfere with the messages the advertisers are trying to communicate?

billion. Would you have guessed that direct mail is number one? Broadcast TV is number two, with expenditures of over $36 billion. Cable networks bring in another $27 billion. Note that the Internet is at $25 billion. That's double what it was in 2005. The leading advertising agencies still take the bulk of promotional dollars and still have a major impact on consumers.[6]

How do we, as consumers, benefit from these advertising expenditures? First, ads are informative. Direct mail is full of information about products, prices, features, store policies, and more; so is newspaper advertising. Newspaper advertising is down because more and more people are getting their news on mobile devices.[7]

Second, not only does advertising inform us, but the money advertisers spend for commercial time pays the production costs of TV and radio programs. Advertising also covers the major costs of producing newspapers and magazines. Subscriptions and newsstand revenues cover only mailing and promotional costs. Figure 16.5 compares the advantages and disadvantages

RANK	MEDIUM	PROJECTED ADVERTISING SPENDING
1	Direct mail	52.3
2	Broadcast TV (network, spot, synd.)	36.8
3	Newspaper	23.4
4	Cable TV networks	27.0
5	Radio	15.9
6	Yellow Pages	11.9
7	Consumer magazine	9.1
8	Internet	25.3
9	All other	39.7
Total		241.4 billion

Source: www.businessinsider.com, 2011.

figure 16.4

ESTIMATED U.S ADVERTISING SPENDING BY MEDIUM, 2010 (IN BILLIONS OF DOLLARS)

MEDIUM	ADVANTAGES	DISADVANTAGES
Newspapers	Good coverage of local markets; ads can be placed quickly; high consumer acceptance; ads can be clipped and saved.	Ads compete with other features in paper; poor color; ads get thrown away with paper (short life span).
Television	Uses sight, sound, and motion; reaches all audiences; high attention with no competition from other material.	High cost; short exposure time; takes time to prepare ads. Digital video recorders skip over ads.
Radio	Low cost; can target specific audiences; very flexible; good for local marketing.	People may not listen to ad; depends on one sense (hearing); short exposure time; audience can't keep ad.
Magazines	Can target specific audiences; good use of color; long life of ad; ads can be clipped and saved.	Inflexible; ads often must be placed weeks before publication; cost is relatively high.
Outdoor	High visibility and repeat exposures; low cost; local market focus.	Limited message; low selectivity of audience.
Direct mail	Best for targeting specific markets; very flexible; ad can be saved.	High cost; consumers may reject ad as junk mail; must conform to post office regulations.
Yellow Pages–type advertising	Great coverage of local markets; widely used by consumers; available at point of purchase.	Competition with other ads; cost may be too high for very small businesses.
Internet	Inexpensive global coverage; available at any time; interactive.	Customers may leave the site before buying.
Mobile advertising	Great reach among younger shoppers.	Easy to ignore, avoid.
Social media	Wonderful communication tools.	Time drain.

figure 16.5

ADVANTAGES AND DISADVANTAGES OF VARIOUS ADVERTISING MEDIA
The most effective media are often very expensive. The inexpensive media may not reach your market. The goal is to use the medium that can reach your desired market most effectively and efficiently.

for marketers of various advertising media. Notice that newspapers, radio, and the Yellow Pages are especially attractive to local advertisers.

Marketers must choose which media will best reach the audience they desire. Radio advertising, for example, is less expensive than TV advertising and often reaches people when they have few other distractions, such as while they're driving. Radio is thus especially effective at selling *services* people don't usually read about in print media—banking, mortgages, continuing education, and brokerage services, to name a few. On the other hand, radio has become so commercial-ridden that many people are paying to switch to commercial-free satellite radio. Marketers also search for other places to put advertising, such as on video screens mounted in elevators. Have you noticed ads on park benches and grocery carts? You've certainly seen them on websites you visit.

Mobile marketing via cell phones started out mostly as text messages, but now Starbucks can send signals to your phone as you approach the store, reminding you to stop in for a latte. Kraft Foods developed the iPhone Assistant, an iPhone application that serves up recipes for users—recipes made with Kraft products. Other retailers use e-mail advertisements to build brand awareness and drive people to their stores or websites.[8] Social media in general is growing so fast that marketers can hardly keep up.[9] Take the restaurant industry for example. Starbucks is number one in social media with 12 million Twitter followers. It registers 19.3 million "likes" on Facebook. McDonald's has over 80,000 followers with Twitter and 7 million friends on Facebook.[10]

Another way to get more impact from advertising is to appeal to the interest in green marketing among consumers and businesses.[11] A brief glance through magazines and the business press reveals all kinds of new appeals to sustainability and carbon-cutting measures. In the next sections, we'll look in more depth at some other popular advertising media.

Television Advertising

Television offers many advantages to national advertisers, but it's expensive. Thirty seconds of advertising during the Super Bowl telecast cost about $3 million.[12] How many bottles of beer or automobiles must a company sell to pay for such commercials? A lot, but few media besides television allow advertisers to reach so many people with such impact, although not all ads are equally effective.[13]

Despite what you may read about the growth of alternative promotional tools, TV advertising is still a dominant medium.[14] Digital video recorders (DVRs) enable consumers to skip the ads on TV. This may make TV less attractive to advertisers unless commercials get so much better that people *want* to watch them. New program delivery systems, such as video on demand, make it even more difficult for TV advertisers to catch consumers' eyes. Thus marketers are demanding better and more accurate measures of TV advertising's effectiveness, and many are switching to social media as a result.[15]

Product Placement

TV advertising isn't limited to traditional commercials; sometimes the products appear in the programs themselves. With **product placement**, advertisers pay to put their products into TV shows and movies where the audience will see them. One classic example of product placement is the trail of Reese's Pieces in the movie E.T.[16] Did you ever notice the Coca-Cola cups on the judges' table on *American Idol?* Many placements are more subtle, like the wheeled luggage from Zuca Inc. that appeared on the TV show *CSI.*

The latest wrinkle in product placement puts virtual products into video games. If you're a gamer, you've seen in-game ads, like ads around the court in

product placement
Putting products into TV shows and movies where they will be seen.

Product placement is often subtle. You can see it in the products used in movies like the ones shown on the table in this one. The goal is to influence you to want that product yourself. What product placements have you noticed in your favorite TV shows and movies?

basketball games. New technology allows vending machines in racing games to be branded and rebranded over time, depending on whether Coke, Pepsi, Exxon, or Shell has purchased ad time.[17]

Infomercials

infomercial
A full-length TV program devoted exclusively to promoting goods or services.

An **infomercial** is a full-length TV program devoted exclusively to promoting a particular good or service. Infomercials have been successful because they show the product and how it works in great detail. They are the equivalent of sending your very best salespeople to a person's home and having them use all of their techniques to make the sale: drama, demonstration, testimonials, graphics, and more. Because of their success, infomercials are expected to rise to over $170 billion in 2014.[18]

Products that have earned over $1 billion in sales through infomercials include Proactiv (acne cream), Soloflex, Total Gym, Bowflex (exercise machines), the George Foreman Grill, and Ron Popeil's Rotisserie and Grill. Some products, such as personal development seminars, real estate programs, and workout tapes, are hard to sell without showing people a sample of their contents and using testimonials. Have you purchased any products that you saw in an infomercial?

Online Advertising

When marketers advertise on an online search engine such as Google or Bing, they can reach the people they most want to reach—consumers researching vacations, exploring the car market, or checking stocks. One goal of online advertising is to get potential customers to a website where they can learn more about the company and its products—and the company can learn more about them.[19] If users click through an ad to get to the website, the company has an opportunity to gather their names, addresses, opinions, and preferences.[20] Online advertising thus brings customers and companies together. Another advantage is that it enables advertisers to see just how many people have clicked on a commercial and how much of it each potential customer has read or watched. It has been one of the fastest-growing parts of advertising. Spending on online advertising and social media is expected to increase greatly in the next three years.[21]

E-mail marketing has become a big component of online advertising. However, advertisers have to be careful not to overuse it because customers don't like to see too many promotional e-mails in their in-boxes. Thus some companies use e-mail as an alert to send users to other social media such as Facebook and Twitter. The nearby Social Media in Business box discusses the link between social media and other promotional tools in more depth.[22]

interactive promotion
Promotion process that allows marketers to go beyond a monologue, where sellers try to persuade buyers to buy things, to a dialogue in which buyers and sellers work together to create mutually beneficial exchange relationships.

Interactive promotion allows marketers to go beyond a *monologue,* in which sellers try to persuade buyers to buy things, to a *dialogue,* in which buyers and sellers work together to create mutually beneficial exchange relationships.[23] Garden.com is an online retailer of garden products and services.[23] Dionn Schaffner, the company's vice president of marketing, once said that gardening is an information-intensive activity. Customers obviously want to learn about gardening, but they also seek inspiration by communicating with fellow gardeners and experts. Garden.com's answer to such customers has been to include a forum on its website where people can chat with each other and ask gardening questions.

Technology has greatly improved customer communications.[24] Many companies provide online videos, chat rooms, and other services in a *virtual*

SOCIAL MEDIA IN
business

Social Media Complements Other Promotions

If there is one thing that advertisers agree upon, it is the growing importance of social media in product promotion. Here are a few examples of what executives have to say about the need to integrate social media in the promotion mix:

Linda LoRe, the President of Frederick's of Hollywood Group, Inc., says, "Social media needs to work hand-in-hand with other channels, whether it's direct mail or an in-store promotion, to create a wholistic marketing campaign that drives consumers to the branding you want to get in front of them."

David J. Brown, Executive Vice President of the National Trust for Historic Preservation, says that investing in social media helps the Trust reach certain goals, such as building awareness for preservation—because it reaches new and nontraditional audiences. He goes on to say that social media followers get direct mail from his organization because people don't use just one form of communication any more. He thinks that social media and direct mail are quite complementary.

Kassie Rempel, the owner of SimplySoles, sends out handwritten thank-you notes. She feels that the common ground between handwritten notes and social media is accessibility. Both can help marketers relate to customers on a personal level.

Sources: "Does Return on Social Media Justify the Spending?" *Deliver Magazine,* July 2010, www.simplysoles.com, accessed April 2011; and www.preservationnation.org, accessed April 2011.

store where customers are able to talk to each other, ask questions of salespeople, examine goods and services, and buy products. The Internet is fundamentally changing the way marketers are working with customers. Notice we said *working with* rather than *promoting to.* Marketers now want to *build relationships* with customers over time. That means carefully listening to what consumers want, tracking their purchases, providing them with excellent service, and giving them access to a full range of information.[25]

Here's how online interactive promotion helped one traditional marketer stay competitive. Vita-Mix Corporation makes expensive food blenders. In the beginning, when there was little competition, the company relied mostly on 140 independent contractors to sell the blenders at state fairs, food events, and

Online advertising is the fastest-growing type of advertising and can offer more than just a list of products and their features. For example, Tissot will introduce a new 3-D reality application on its website that allows customers to try on a 3-D virtual watch and interact with its features. Do you think some types of products or services are promoted more effectively online than others?

stores. Eventually Vita-Mix began using infomercials, and sales passed $100 million. Then commercial blender maker K-Tec in Orem, Utah, began going after Vita-Mix's consumer market. K-Tec promoted its new product on a website that showed the CEO blending things like golf balls, a rotisserie chicken, and, believe it or not, an Apple iPhone. The video eventually got on YouTube, and sales of this new competitor took off. Vita-Mix successfully responded by creating its own site called Vita-Village, showing how to create healthy meals and snacks, and a social network that enables blender fans to share recipes.[26] Online marketers should strive to make sure that their efforts fit into an overall multimedia strategy.

Using Social Media to Monitor Ad Effectiveness

Dr Pepper has an 8.5 million fan base on Facebook. Now the company can track and test users who say they "like" the soft drink. The company posts two messages daily on a Facebook fan page and then monitors the results. The company can thus measure how many times a message is reviewed, how many times it is shared, and what the fan response is. The company believes that if it is to engage in social media, it has to listen and understand the nature of the conversation, the volume, and the topics being discussed. In short, social media, such as Facebook and Twitter, have made it possible for organizations to test ads before airing them on traditional media like TV and to listen to the reasons why people like and dislike some messages.

It is best, if a company wants to establish a base with customers, to include top managers in the dialogue. For example, Richard Branson of Virgin Group Ltd and Tony Hsieh of Zappos tweet their customers.[27] Sherry Chris of Better Homes & Gardens Real Estate LLC spends two hours each day reading and contributing to Twitter, Facebook, LinkedIn, and Foursquare. Such involvement with customers has become a major part of many company's listening strategy. It may take time, but there is not a better way to learn about what customers are thinking and saying about your firm.

Many firms are allowing employees to use their personal phones for business purposes. That includes, of course, using Facebook, Twitter, and other social media. The nearby Making Ethical Decisions box explores some issues that may come up as a result.

Global Advertising

Global advertising requires the marketer to develop a single product and promotional strategy it can implement worldwide, like MasterCard's "Priceless" campaign. Certainly global advertising that's the same everywhere can save companies money in research and design. In some cases, however, promotions tailored to specific countries or regions may be more successful since each country or region has its own culture, language, and buying habits.

Some problems do arise when marketers use one campaign in all countries. When a Japanese company tried to use English words to name a popular drink, it came up with Pocari Sweat, not a

This Maybelline ad is designed for African-American women. There are many ads directed toward the Latina and Asian markets as well. What other groups are attractive candidates for targeted ads?

MAKING ethical decisions

Electronic Ethics

Many companies let employees use their personal gadgets such as their smartphones to do their jobs. What happens, though, when a phone loaded with sensitive business documents gets lost? Most companies insist that workers use the password feature found in every smartphone. The password prevents other users from accessing any of the phone's basic functions. This is important because employees often store e-mails and attachments with company data on their phones.

Imagine that you have received personal information about fellow workers, including some of your bosses, on your phone. You know that the information could lead to discipline or firing of many of those workers and managers. You also know that other workers have received the same information. You are wondering what would be the ethical thing to do with such information. Should you pass it along to your immediate supervisor or not? What are the ethical issues involved? What would you do? What do you expect to be the consequences of your actions?

good image for most English-speaking people.[28] In England, the Ford Probe didn't go over too well because the word *probe* made people think of doctors' waiting rooms and medical examinations.[29] People in the United States may have difficulty with Krapp toilet paper from Sweden. But perhaps worse was the translation of Coors' slogan "Turn it loose," which became "Suffer from diarrhea." Clairol introduced its curling iron, the Mist Stick, to the German market, not realizing *mist* in German can mean "manure." A T-shirt promoting the Pope's visit to Miami read *la papa,* which in Spanish means "the potato." (It should have said *el Papa.*) As you can see, getting the words right in international advertising is tricky and critical. So is understanding the culture, which calls for researching each country, designing appropriate ads, and testing them.

In the United States, some groups are large enough and different enough to call for specially designed promotions. Masterfoods USA, for example, tried to promote dulce de leche (caramel) M&M's to the Hispanic market in cities like Los Angeles, Miami, and San Antonio. The promotion was not successful, however. Knowing the market had potential, Masterfoods changed course and bought a candy company called the Lucas Group, which has had success selling such candies as Felix Sour Fruit and Lucas Hot and Spicy in Mexico. Masterfoods had much more success selling those candies in the United States.[30]

Many marketers today are moving from globalism (one ad for everyone in the world) to regionalism (specific ads for each country or for specific groups within a country). In the future, marketers will prepare more custom-designed promotions to reach even smaller audiences—audiences as small as one person.[31] The Reaching Beyond Our Borders box on p. 446 presents an example of how advertising is done in remote areas such as rural villages in India.

LEARNING goal 3

Illustrate the steps of the B2B and B2C selling processes.

REACHING BEYOND
our borders

www.interpublic.com

Promotion in Rural India

While advertisers in the United States use the latest technology to promote their products, global advertising agencies in India can't rely on even the most traditional media such as TV, radio or newspapers to reach the country's 700 million rural consumers. So they use traveling performers like Sandeep Sharma. The former wedding singer cracks jokes, gives demonstrations, and stages game shows in order to bring the world's biggest brands to small audiences in the remotest areas of India.

Insulated from the worst of the global recession, India's rural consumers are spending more than ever. International brands are sending out armies of salesmen like Sharma to reach these customers. Overall advertising spending climbed about 10 percent in India last year; while rural advertising grew at more than four times that rate. Sharma gives free Castrol oil changes for tractors, passes out bowls of Nestlé noodles in village schools, and sells Unilever soaps, creams, and promotes tooth powder. He starts by asking the village elders for permission to set up his mobile stage. He then rouses the villagers by driving around with music blaring and passes out candy to the children telling them to bring their neighbors. The crowds are all male. Selling takes a lot of interaction—but very little with women. When Sharma does talk to women about the wonders of Unilever soaps and skin creams, he does so from behind flip charts so there is no direct eye contact that could offend the men. Usually a husband or brother stands nearby and asks all the questions, even for women's products.

Sharma has been working the circuit for five years for Linterland Rural Communication, the rural outreach company connected to Lowe Worldwide, an agency owned by Interpublic Group PLC. He earns about $350 a month, a higher-than-average rural wage. Sharma is on the road more than 5,000 miles a month, visiting as many as three villages a day. He sleeps in cheap hotel rooms with the four others on his team, or in his truck. He can't go home for months at a time. No, this isn't as good as his dream of singing in the best hotels, but Sharma makes a lot more money than he made singing at weddings.

Sources: Eric Bellman, "The Infomercial Comes to Life in India's Remotest Villages," *The Wall Street Journal*, June 10, 2009; and Interpublic Group, www.interpublic.com, accessed May 2011.

PERSONAL SELLING: PROVIDING PERSONAL ATTENTION

personal selling
The face-to-face presentation and promotion of goods and services

Personal selling is the face-to-face presentation and promotion of goods and services, including the salesperson's search for new prospects and follow-up service after the sale. Effective selling isn't simply a matter of persuading others to buy. In fact, it's more accurately described today as helping others satisfy their wants and needs (again, helping the buyer buy).

Given that perspective, you can see why salespeople use the Internet, laptop computers, iPads, and other technology to help customers search for information, design custom-made products, look over prices, and generally do everything it takes to complete the order. The benefit of personal selling is having a person help you complete a transaction. The salesperson should listen to your needs, help you reach a solution, and do everything possible to make accomplishing it smoother and easier.

It's costly for firms to provide customers with personal attention, so those companies that retain salespeople must train them to be especially effective, efficient, and helpful. To attract new salespeople, companies are paying them quite well. The average cost of a single sales call to a potential business-to-business (B2B) buyer is about $400. Surely no firm would pay that much to send anyone but a skillful and highly trained professional salesperson and consultant.

Steps in the Selling Process

The best way to understand personal selling is to go through the selling process. Imagine you are a software salesperson whose job is to show business users the advantages of various programs your firm markets. One product critically important to establishing long-term relationships with customers is customer relationship management (CRM) software, particularly social CRM that integrates social media to create a community-based relationship with customers.[32] Let's go through the seven steps of the selling process to see what you can do to sell social CRM software.

Although this is a business-to-business (B2B) example, the process in consumer selling is similar but less complex. In both cases the salesperson must have deep *product* knowledge—that is, he or she must know the product—and competitors' products—thoroughly.

You're familiar with all kinds of situations in which people do personal selling. They work in local stores such as the one shown here. They also sell all kinds of goods and services like automobiles, insurance, and real estate. What could they do to be more helpful to you, the customer?

1. Prospect and Qualify   The first step in the selling process is **prospecting**, researching potential buyers and choosing those most likely to buy. The selection process is called **qualifying**. To qualify people means to make sure they have a need for the product, the authority to buy, and the willingness to listen to a sales message. Some people call prospecting and qualifying the process of *lead generation.*

A person who meets the qualifying criteria is called a **prospect**. You often meet prospects at trade shows, where they come to booths sponsored by manufacturers and ask questions. Others may visit your website seeking information. But often the best prospects are people recommended to you by others who use or know about your product. Salespeople often e-mail prospects with proposals to see whether there is any interest before making a formal visit.

2. Preapproach   The selling process may take a long time, and gathering information before you approach the customer is critical. Before making a sales call, you must do some further research. In the preapproach phase, you learn as much as possible about customers and their wants and needs.[33] Before you try to sell the social CRM software, you'll want to know which people in the company are most likely to buy or use it. What kind of customers do they deal with? What kind of relationship strategies are they using now? How is their system set up, and what kind of improvements are they looking for? All that information should be in a database so that, if one representative leaves the firm, the company can carry information about customers to the new salesperson.

3. Approach   "You don't have a second chance to make a good first impression." That's why the approach is so important. When you call on a customer for the first time, you want to give an impression of friendly professionalism, create rapport, build credibility, and start a business relationship.[34] Often a company's decision to use a new software package is based on the buyer's perception of reliable service from the salesperson. In selling social CRM products, you can make it known from the start that you'll be available to help your customer train its employees and to upgrade the package when necessary.

prospecting
Researching potential buyers and choosing those most likely to buy.

qualifying
In the selling process, making sure that people have a need for the product, the authority to buy, and the willingness to listen to a sales message.

prospect
A person with the means to buy a product, the authority to buy, and the willingness to listen to a sales message.

trial close
A step in the selling process that consists of a question or statement that moves the selling process toward the actual close.

Making the sale isn't the end of the salesperson's relationship with the customer. The salesperson should follow up on the sale to make sure the customer is happy and perhaps suggest something to complement what the customer purchased. Have salespeople been able to sell you more because they used effective follow-up procedures? How did they do it?

4. Make a Presentation In your actual presentation of the software, you'll match the benefits of your value package to the client's needs. Companies such as Ventaso Inc. and the Sant Group now provide sales proposal software that includes everything from PowerPoint presentations to competitive analysis. Since you've done your homework and know the prospect's wants and needs, you can tailor your sales presentation accordingly.[35] The presentation is a great time to use testimonials showing potential buyers that they're joining leaders in other firms who are using the product.

5. Answer Objections You should anticipate any objections the prospect may raise and determine the proper responses. Think of questions as opportunities for creating better relationships, not as challenges to what you're saying. Customers may have legitimate doubts, and you are there to resolve them. Successfully and honestly working with others helps you build relationships based on trust. Often you can introduce the customer to others in your firm who can answer their questions and provide them with anything they need. Using a laptop computer, you may set up a virtual meeting in which the customer can chat with your colleagues and begin building a relationship.

6. Close the Sale After you've answered questions and objections, you may present a **trial close**, a question or statement that moves the selling process toward the actual purchase. You might ask, "When would be the best time to train your staff to use the new software?" The final step is to ask for the order and show the client where to sign. Once you've established a relationship, the goal of your sales call may be to get a testimonial from the customer.

7. Follow Up The selling process isn't over until the order is approved and the customer is happy. Salespeople need to be providers of solutions for their customers and to think about what happens after the sale. The follow-up step includes handling customer complaints, making sure the customer's questions are answered, and quickly supplying what the customer wants. Often, customer service is as important to the sale as the product itself. That's why most manufacturers have websites where customers can find information and get questions answered. You can see why we describe selling as a process of *establishing relationships*, not just exchanging goods or services. The sales relationship may continue for years as you respond to new requests for information and provide new services.

The selling process varies somewhat among different goods and services, but the general idea stays the same. Your goals as a salesperson are to help the buyer buy and make sure the buyer is satisfied after the sale. Sales force automation (SFA) includes hundreds of software programs that help salespeople design products, close deals, tap into company intranets, and more. Some salespeople use it to conduct virtual reality tours of the manufacturing plant for the customer. An IBM salesperson may rely on everything from a BlackBerry and sales management software to wikis (collaborative websites that users can edit), blogs, podcasts, IBM's intranet, and more.

The Business-to-Consumer Sales Process

Most sales to consumers take place in retail stores, where the role of the salesperson differs somewhat from that in B2B selling. In both cases, knowing the product comes first.[36] However, in business-to-consumer (B2C) sales, the salesperson does not have to do much prospecting or qualifying. The seller assumes most people who come to the store are qualified to buy the merchandise (except in sales of expensive products such as automobiles and furniture, during which salespeople may have to ask a few questions to qualify prospective customers before spending too much time with them).

Similarly, retail salespeople don't usually have to go through a preapproach step, although they should understand as much as possible about the type of people who shop at a given store. The salesperson does need to focus on the customer and refrain from talking to fellow salespeople, however—or, worse, to friends on the phone. Have you ever experienced such rude behavior from salespeople? What did you think?

The first formal step in the B2C sales process is the approach. Too many salespeople begin with a line like "May I help you?" but the answer too often is "No." A better approach is "How can I help you?" or, simply, "Welcome to our store." The idea is to show the customer you are there to help and are friendly and knowledgeable.

Discover what the customer wants first, and then make a presentation. Show customers how your products meet their needs and answer questions that help them choose the right products for them.

As in B2B selling, it is important to make a trial close, like "Would you like me to put that on hold?" or "Will you be paying for that with your store credit card?" Selling is an art, and a salesperson must learn how to walk the fine line between being helpful and being pushy. Often individual buyers need some time alone to think about the purchase. The salesperson must respect that need but still be clearly available when needed.

After-sale follow-up is an important but often neglected step in B2C sales. If the product is to be delivered, the salesperson should follow up to be sure it is delivered on time. The same is true if the product has to be installed. There is often a chance to sell more merchandise when a salesperson follows up on a sale. Figure 16.6 shows the whole B2C selling process. Compare it to the seven-step process we outlined earlier for B2B selling.

figure 16.6

STEPS IN THE BUSINESS-TO-CONSUMER (B2C) SELLING PROCESS

progress assessment

- What are the four traditional elements of the promotion mix?
- What are the three most important advertising media in order of dollars spent?
- What are the seven steps in the B2B selling process?

LEARNING goal 4

Describe the role of the public relations department, and show how publicity fits in that role.

PUBLIC RELATIONS: BUILDING RELATIONSHIPS

public relations (PR)
The management function that evaluates public attitudes, changes policies and procedures in response to the public's requests, and executes a program of action and information to earn public understanding and acceptance.

Public relations (PR) is the management function that evaluates public attitudes, changes policies and procedures in response to the public's requests, and executes a program of action and information to earn public understanding and acceptance. In other words, a good public relations program has three steps:

1. *Listen to the public.* Public relations starts with good marketing research to evaluate public attitudes.
2. *Change policies and procedures.* Businesses earn understanding not by bombarding the public with propaganda but by creating programs and practices in the public interest. The best way to learn what the public wants is to listen to people often—in different forums, including on the Internet. That includes being able to handle a crisis by communicating online.
3. *Inform people you're responsive to their needs.* It's not enough to simply have programs in the public interest. You have to *tell* the public about those programs. Public relations has more power to influence consumers than other corporate communications because the message comes via the media, a source usually perceived as trustworthy.

Recent events have emphasized the need for good public relations. Such events include Toyota Motor's safety problems, Apple's iPhone antenna problems, BPs oil spill, Japan's nuclear power problems, and the issues surrounding some key actors and sports personalities.[37]

The PR department maintains close ties with company stakeholders (customers, media, community leaders, government officials, and other corporate stakeholders). Marketers are looking for alternatives to advertising. Public relations is a good alternative. As newspapers cut back on their reporting staff, people are looking for other sources of news information, including publicity releases. Linking up with bloggers has become an important way to keep company names in the news.

Publicity: The Talking Arm of PR

Publicity is the talking arm of public relations and one of the major functions of almost all organizations. Here's how it works: Suppose you want to introduce your store, Very Vegetarian, to consumers, but you have little money to promote it. You need to get some initial sales to generate funds. One effective way to reach the public is through publicity.

Publicity is any information about an individual, product, or organization that's distributed to the public through the media and is not paid for or controlled by the seller. It takes skill to write interesting or newsworthy press releases that the media will want to publish. You may need to write different stories for different media. One may introduce the new owners. Another may describe the unusual product offerings. If the stories are published, news about your store will reach many potential consumers (and investors, distributors, and dealers), and you may be on your way to becoming a successful marketer. John D. Rockefeller once remarked, "Next to doing the right thing, the most important thing is to *let people know* that you are doing the right thing." What might Very Vegetarian do to help the community and thus create more publicity?

Besides being free, publicity has several further advantages over other promotional tools like advertising. It may reach people who wouldn't read an ad. It may appear on the front page of a newspaper or in some other prominent position, or be given air time on a television news show. Perhaps the greatest advantage of publicity is its believability. When a newspaper or magazine publishes a story as news, the reader treats that story as news—and news is more believable than advertising.

Publicity has several disadvantages as well. For example, marketers have no control over whether, how, and when the media will use the story. The media aren't obligated to use a publicity release, most of which are thrown away. Furthermore, the media may alter the story so that it's not positive. There's good publicity (iPod sales are taking off) and bad publicity (GM is going bankrupt). Also, once a story has run, it's not likely to be repeated. Advertising, in contrast, can be repeated as often as needed. One way to see that the media handle your publicity well is to establish a friendly relationship with media representatives and be open with them. Then, when you want their support, they're more likely to cooperate.

Some companies will race to extremes to generate publicity. This streaker avoided Super Bowl XXXVIII security to show off a tattooed message for Internet casino GoldenPalace.com. Which do you think attracts more attention for a firm, an appealing news story or a paid ad?

LEARNING goal 5

Assess the effectiveness of various forms of sales promotion, including sampling.

SALES PROMOTION: GIVING BUYERS INCENTIVES

Sales promotion is the promotional tool that stimulates consumer purchasing and dealer interest by means of short-term activities. These activities include such things as displays, trade shows and exhibitions, event sponsorships, and contests. Figure 16.7 lists some B2B sales promotion techniques.

Trade shows	Catalogs
Portfolios for salespeople	Conventions
Deals (price reductions)	

publicity
Any information about an individual, product, or organization that's distributed to the public through the media and that's not paid for or controlled by the seller.

sales promotion
The promotional tool that stimulates consumer purchasing and dealer interest by means of short-term activities

figure 16.7

BUSINESS-TO-BUSINESS SALES PROMOTION TECHNIQUES

figure I6.8

**CONSUMER SALES
PROMOTION TECHNIQUES**

Coupons	Bonuses (buy one, get one free)
Cents-off promotions	Catalogs
Sampling	Demonstrations
Premiums	Special events
Sweepstakes	Lotteries
Contests	In-store displays

For consumer sales promotion activities, think of those free samples you get in the mail, cents-off coupons you clip from newspapers, contests that various retail stores sponsor, and prizes in cereal boxes (see Figure 16.8). You can stimulate sales at Very Vegetarian by putting half-off coupons in the school paper and home mailers. Do you see any problems that might emerge by using Groupon to bring in customers?

Sales promotion programs are designed to supplement personal selling, advertising, public relations, and other promotional efforts by creating enthusiasm for the overall promotional program. There was a big increase in such promotions as the 21st century began, especially online. The recent financial crisis has people looking more closely for coupons and other promotional deals.

Sales promotion can take place both within and outside the company. The most important internal sales promotion efforts are directed at salespeople and other customer-contact people, such as customer service representatives and clerks. Internal sales promotion efforts include (1) sales training; (2) the development of sales aids such as flip charts, portable audiovisual displays, and videos; and (3) participation in trade shows where salespeople can get leads. Other employees who deal with the public may also receive special training to improve their awareness of the company's offerings and make them an integral part of the total promotional effort.

After generating enthusiasm internally, marketers want to make distributors and dealers eager to help promote the product. Trade shows allow marketing intermediaries to see products from many different sellers and make comparisons among them. Today, virtual trade shows on the Internet, called

The International Manufacturing Trade Show in Chicago featured 4,000 booths, giving buyers for other businesses thousands of new products to explore and purchase. Can you see why trade shows in many industries are an efficient and necessary way to stay abreast of the latest developments, competitors, and consumer reactions and needs?

Webinars, enable buyers to see many products without leaving the office. Such promotions are usually interactive, so buyers can ask questions, and the information is available 24 hours a day, seven days a week.

After the company's employees and intermediaries have been motivated with sales promotion efforts, the next step is to promote to final consumers using samples, coupons, cents-off deals, displays, store demonstrations, premiums, contests, rebates, and so on. Sales promotion is an ongoing effort to maintain enthusiasm, so sellers use different strategies over time to keep the ideas fresh. You could put food displays in your Very Vegetarian store to show customers how attractive the products look. You could also sponsor in-store cooking demonstrations to attract new vegetarians. You can imagine the success of a promotion using Groupon or LivingSocial.

One popular sales promotion tool is **sampling**—letting consumers have a small sample of the product for no charge. Because many consumers won't buy a new product unless they've had a chance to see it or try it, grocery stores often have people standing in the aisles handing out small portions of food and beverage products. Sampling is a quick, effective way of demonstrating a product's superiority when consumers are making a purchase decision. Standing outside Very Vegetarian and giving out samples would surely attract attention.

Pepsi introduced its SoBe (herbal fortified drinks) product line with a combination of sampling, event marketing, and a new website. *Event marketing* means sponsoring events such as rock concerts or being at various events to promote your products. In the case of SoBe, Pepsi first sent samples to beach cities during spring break where students got samples of the drinks. Similar sampling and event marketing efforts had been successful with Snapple (fruit drinks and iced teas).

Everyone likes a free sample. Sampling is a promotional strategy that lets people try a new product, often in a situation when they can buy it right away if they like it. What are some advantages of sampling food products that advertising can't duplicate?

progress assessment

- What are the three steps in setting up a public relations program?
- What are the sales promotion techniques used to reach consumers?
- What sales promotion techniques are used to reach businesses?

sampling
A promotional tool in which a company lets consumers have a small sample of a product for no charge.

LEARNING goal 6

Show how word of mouth, e-mail marketing, viral marketing, blogging, podcasting, and mobile marketing work.

WORD OF MOUTH AND OTHER PROMOTIONAL TOOLS

Although word of mouth was not traditionally listed as one of the major promotional efforts (it was not considered to be manageable), it is now one of the most effective, especially on the Internet. In **word-of-mouth promotion**, people tell other people about products they've purchased.

When James and Ann Scaggs started a company that repairs iPods, customers were hesitant to part with their units without assurance they would be fixed properly. The Scaggs went to RatePoint, a Web 2.0 system for collecting

word-of-mouth promotion
A promotional tool that involves people telling other people about products they've purchased.

and displaying word of mouth in the form of customer feedback. Sales immediately went up.

Anything that encourages people to talk favorably about an organization can be effective word of mouth. Notice, for example, how stores use clowns, banners, music, fairs, and other attention-getting devices to create word of mouth. Clever commercials can also generate word of mouth. The more that people talk about your products and your brand name, the more easily customers remember them when they shop. You might enjoy brainstorming strategies for creating word of mouth about Very Vegetarian.

Viral Marketing

A number of companies have begun creating word of mouth by rewarding customers for promoting their products to others. One such strategy encourages people to go into Internet chat rooms and hype bands, movies, video games, and sports teams. People who agree to promote products in this way may get what the industry calls *swag*—free tickets, backstage passes, T-shirts, and other such merchandise. What do you think of the ethics of rewarding people to promote goods and services? What do you think of people sending messages to friends on Facebook and Twitter talking about products?

Viral marketing describes everything from paying customers to say positive things on the Internet (e.g., using Twitter) to setting up multilevel selling schemes whereby consumers get commissions for directing friends to specific websites.

One especially effective strategy for spreading positive word of mouth is to send testimonials to current customers. Most companies use these only in promoting to new customers, but testimonials are also effective in confirming customers' belief that they chose the right company. Therefore, some companies make it a habit to ask customers for referrals.

Word of mouth is so powerful that negative word of mouth can hurt a firm badly. Criticism of a product or company can spread through online forums, social media, and websites. Addressing consumer complaints quickly and effectively is one of the best ways to reduce the effects of negative word of mouth.

Blogging

A **blog**—short for web log—is an online diary that looks like a web page but is easier to create and update by posting text, photos, or links to other sites. There are millions of blogs on the Internet, and thousands of new ones are added each day. How do blogs affect marketing? When a book called *Freakonomics* was about to be released, the publisher sent advance copies to 100 bloggers. These bloggers sent reviews to other bloggers (word of mouth), and soon *Freakonomics* was number three on Amazon.com's list of most-ordered books. You can imagine what blogging can do to promote movies, TV shows, and more.

Podcasting

Podcasting is a means of distributing audio and video programs via the Internet. It lets users subscribe to a number of files, also known as feeds, and then hear or view the material when they choose. Podcasting allows you to become your own newscaster, since—besides giving broadcast radio and TV a new distribution medium—it enables independent producers to create self-published, syndicated "radio shows." Many companies have also found success in creating video for YouTube.

viral marketing
The term now used to describe everything from paying customers to say positive things on the Internet to setting up multilevel selling schemes whereby consumers get commissions for directing friends to specific websites.

blog
An online diary (Web log) that looks like a Web page but is easier to create and update by posting text, photos, or links to other sites.

podcasting
A means of distributing audio and video programs via the Internet that lets users subscribe to a number of files, also known as feeds, and then hear or view the material at the time they choose.

E-Mail Promotions

Armstrong, the flooring manufacturer, has an e-mail marketing program designed to increase brand awareness among commercial suppliers. At one time it sent out monthly e-mails to announce new products and product updates and to keep people loyal to the brand. Over time, however, those e-mails lost their power. Armstrong then turned to an e-mail service provider that completely revamped the program. The provider divided the market into four separate segments and tracked the success of the e-mails much more closely.

E-mail promotions are gaining in popularity. Most marketers make sure their e-newsletters are also viewable on mobile devices like BlackBerrys or iPhones. One key to success, therefore, is to keep the message brief, because mobile users don't want to go through much text.

Mobile Media

With mobile media, marketers make use of the cell phone, using text messaging to promote sweepstakes, send customers news or sports alerts, and give them company information. We've seen that companies can now determine where you are and send you messages about restaurants and other services in your vicinity. Despite some technological glitches to work through, mobile marketing is catching on.[38]

Are you getting the idea that traditional promotional methods are slowly but surely being replaced by new technology? If so, you're getting the right idea. By keeping up with the latest trends, you may be able to grab a good job in promotion while traditionalists are still wondering what happened. [39]

Mobile media allow marketers to reach customers through text messaging. Have you received such promotional messages? For which products are they most effective?

MANAGING THE PROMOTION MIX: PUTTING IT ALL TOGETHER

Each target group calls for a separate promotion mix. Advertising is most efficient for reaching large groups of consumers whose members share similar traits. Personal selling is best for selling to large organizations. To motivate people to buy now rather than later, marketers use sales promotions like sampling, coupons, discounts, special displays, and premiums. Publicity supports other efforts and can create a good impression among all consumers. Word of mouth is often the most powerful promotional tool. Generate it by listening, being responsive, and creating an impression worth passing on to others that you spread through blogging, podcasting, and tweeting.

Promotional Strategies

How do producers move products to consumers? In a **push strategy**, the producer uses advertising, personal selling, sales promotion, and all other promotional tools to convince wholesalers and retailers to stock and sell merchandise, *pushing* it through the distribution system to the stores. If the push strategy works, consumers will walk into a store, see the product, and buy it.

A **pull strategy** directs heavy advertising and sales promotion efforts toward *consumers*. If the pull strategy works, consumers will go to the store and ask for the products. The store owner will order them from the wholesaler, who in turn will order them from the producer. Products are thus *pulled* through the distribution system.

push strategy
Promotional strategy in which the producer uses advertising, personal selling, sales promotion, and all other promotional tools to convince wholesalers and retailers to stock and sell merchandise.

pull strategy
Promotional strategy in which heavy advertising and sales promotion efforts are directed toward consumers so that they'll request the products from retailers.

Ads in bus shelters are nothing new, but Absolut furnished this shelter with seating that reflects the style and luxury it attributes to its products. Do you think giving consumers experiences (like luxury seating) is an effective way to remind them of a product?

pick economy
Customers who pick out their products from online outlets or who do online comparison shopping.

Dr Pepper has used TV advertising in a pull strategy to increase distribution. Tripledge, a maker of windshield wipers, also tried to capture the interest of retail stores through a pull strategy. Of course, a company could use both strategies in a major promotional effort. The latest pull and push strategies are being conducted on the Internet, with companies sending messages to both consumers and businesses.

It has been important to make promotion part of a total systems approach to marketing. That is, promotion was part of supply-chain management. In such cases, retailers would work with producers and distributors to make the supply chain as efficient as possible. Then a promotional plan would be developed for the whole system. The idea would be to develop a total product offer that would appeal to everyone: manufacturers, distributors, retailers, and consumers.

Today push and pull strategies have lost some of their effectiveness. Still, customers are interested in searching online outlets like Drugstore.com or Zappos and doing online comparison shopping as they pick the products that appeal to them. Some leading marketers sell directly to consumers with products that really stand out because of their design, packaging, price, or color, like the Dyson vacuum. The idea is to help the consumer distinguish your product from the competitors. The term **pick economy** refers to those consumers who pick out their products from online outlets or who do online comparison shopping.

progress assessment

- What is viral marketing?
- What are blogging and podcasting?
- Describe a push strategy, a pull strategy, and the pick economy.

summary

Learning Goal 1. Identify the new and traditional tools that make up the promotion mix.

- **What is promotion?**

Promotion is an effort by marketers to inform and remind people in the target market about products and to persuade them to participate in an exchange.

- **What are the four traditional promotional tools that make up the promotion mix?**

The four traditional promotional tools are advertising, personal selling, public relations, and sales promotion. The product itself can also be a promotional tool—that's why it is shown in the middle of Figure 16.1.

- **What are some of the newer tools used in promotion?**
Today's promotional tools include e-mail promotions, mobile promotions (those that use cell phones), social networks, blogging, podcasts, and YouTube.

Learning Goal 2. Contrast the advantages and disadvantages of various advertising media, including the Internet and social media.
- **What is advertising?**
Advertising is limited to paid, nonpersonal (not face-to-face) communication through various media by organizations and individuals who are in some way identified in the advertising message.
- **What are the advantages of using the various media?**
Review the advantages and disadvantages of the various advertising media in Figure 16.5.
- **Why the growing use of infomercials?**
Infomercials are growing in importance because they show products in use and present testimonials to help sell goods and services.

Learning Goal 3. Illustrate the steps of the B2B and B2C selling processes.
- **What is personal selling?**
Personal selling is the face-to-face presentation and promotion of products and services. It includes the search for new prospects and follow-up service after the sale.
- **What are the seven steps of the B2B selling process?**
The steps of the selling process are (1) prospect and qualify, (2) preapproach, (3) approach, (4) make presentation, (5) answer objections, (6) close sale, and (7) follow up.
- **What are the steps in the B2C selling process?**
The steps are the approach, which includes asking questions; the presentation, which includes answering questions; the close; and the follow-up.

Learning Goal 4. Describe the role of the public relations department, and show how publicity fits in that role.
- **What is public relations?**
Public relations (PR) is the function that evaluates public attitudes, changes policies and procedures in response to the public's requests, and executes a program of action and information to earn public understanding and acceptance.
- **What are the three major steps in a good public relations program?**
(1) Listen to the public; (2) develop policies and procedures in the public interest; and (3) tell people you're being responsive to their needs.
- **What is publicity?**
Publicity is the talking part of sales promotion; it is information distributed by the media that's not paid for, or controlled by, the seller. Publicity's greatest advantage is its believability.

Learning Goal 5. Assess the effectiveness of various forms of sales promotion, including sampling.
- **How are sales promotion activities used both within and outside the organization?**
Internal sales promotion efforts are directed at salespeople and other customer-contact people to keep them enthusiastic about the company. Internal sales promotion activities include sales training, sales aids, audiovisual displays, and trade shows. External sales promotions to consumers rely on samples, coupons, cents-off deals, displays, store demonstrators, premiums, and other incentives.

Learning Goal 6. Show how word of mouth, e-mail marketing, viral marketing, blogging, podcasting, and mobile marketing work.

- **Is word of mouth a major promotional tool?**

Word of mouth was not one of the traditional forms of promotion because it was not considered to be manageable, but it has always been an effective way of promoting goods and services.

- **How is word of mouth used in promotion today?**

Some companies reward people to blog or go into Internet chat rooms and talk enthusiastically about bands, movies, video games, and sports teams. People who agree to hype products in this way get *swag*—free tickets, backstage passes, T-shirts, and other merchandise. *Viral marketing* is everything from paying people to say positive things on the Internet to setting up multilevel selling schemes whereby consumers get commissions for directing friends to specific websites. Podcasting is like blogging with an audiovisual focus.

- **What are the major promotional strategies?**

In a *push strategy*, the producer uses advertising, personal selling, sales promotion, and all other promotional tools to convince wholesalers and retailers to stock and sell merchandise. In a *pull strategy*, heavy advertising and sales promotion efforts are directed toward consumers so they'll request the products from retailers. The term *pick economy* refers to those consumers who pick out their products from online outlets such as Drugstore.com or Zappos or who do online comparison shopping.

key terms

advertising 438	**pick economy** 456	**pull strategy** 455
blog 454	**podcasting** 454	**push strategy** 455
infomercial 442	**product placement** 441	**qualifying** 447
integrated marketing communication (IMC) 437	**promotion mix** 436	**sales promotion** 451
	prospect 447	**sampling** 453
interactive promotion 442	**prospecting** 447	**trial close** 448
	publicity 451	**viral marketing** 454
personal selling 446	**public relations (PR)** 450	**word-of-mouth promotion** 453

critical thinking

1. What kinds of problems can emerge if a firm doesn't communicate with environmentalists, the news media, and the local community? Do you know of any firms that aren't responsive to your community? What are the consequences?

2. How often do you buy online? If you don't actually buy, do you use the Internet to compare goods and prices? Do you or your friends take advantage of low prices on used goods at eBay or other online sites like Craig's List? Do you look at ads on the Internet? Do they seem to be effective? Do you think you will use the Internet for more purchases over time?

3. As interactive communications between companies and customers grow, do you think traditional advertising will grow or decline? What will be the

effect of growth or decline on the price we pay for TV programs, newspapers, and magazines?

4. How have blogging, podcasting, and social media affected other media you use, like news sites, newspapers, or television? Do you think blogging is an influential word-of-mouth promotional tool? Do you read newspapers now or do you get your news some other way?

developing workplace skills

1. Using at least two different media—a newspaper, magazine, television, radio, the Internet—choose two ads you consider effective and two you find ineffective. Be prepared to rationalize your choices.

2. Scan your local newspaper for examples of publicity (stories about new products) and sales promotion (coupons, contests, sweepstakes). Share your examples and discuss the effectiveness of such promotional efforts with the class.

3. Many students shy away from careers in selling, often because they think they are not outgoing enough or that salespeople are dishonest or pushy. Prepare a one-page document about your experience with salespeople and what you think of selling as a career.

4. In small groups, discuss whether you are purchasing more goods using catalogs and/or the Internet and why. Do you look up information on the Internet before buying goods and services? How helpful are such searches? Present your findings to the class.

5. In small groups or individually, list six goods and services most students own or use and discuss promotional techniques that prompt you to buy them: advertising, personal selling, social media, publicity, sales promotion, or word of mouth. Which seems most effective for your group? Why?

taking it to the net

Purpose

To learn about business blogs.

Exercise

Go to www.google.com/blogger to learn how easy it is to start your own blog. Then go to the following business-oriented blogs: VentureBlog.com (www.ventureblog.com) and PatentPending.blogs.com (http://patentpending.blogs.com).

1. What kind of subjects are covered in each blog?

2. What are the advantages and disadvantages of reading such blogs?

3. Would you like to see a blog for this course? For your school?

casing the web

To access the case "Developing a Promotional Strategy for Biltmore Estate," visit **www.mhhe.com/ubl0e**

video case

To access the video case featuring Groupon, visit **www.mhhe.com/ubl0e**

UNDERSTANDING
Accounting
& Financial
Information

17

LEARNING goals

After you have read and studied this chapter, you should be able to

1 Demonstrate the role that accounting and financial information play for a business and for its stakeholders.

2 Identify the different disciplines within the accounting profession.

3 List the steps in the accounting cycle, distinguish between accounting and bookkeeping, and explain how computers are used in accounting.

4 Explain how the major financial statements differ.

5 Demonstrate the application of ratio analysis in reporting financial information.

When Siggi Hilmarsson left his native Iceland at age 25 to pursue a business degree at Columbia University, he was certain of one thing: working for a large corporation was not the way he wanted to go. However, after graduation he accepted a job with accounting giant Deloitte. Hilmarsson knew he was an entrepreneur at heart and had trouble adjusting to life in corporate America. He also had problems adjusting to sugar-laden American food, and particularly missed an Icelandic treat called skyr—a thick, strained, protein-rich yogurt. Armed with a 1913 recipe his mother found in the Reykjavik library in Iceland, he set about to prepare his own skyr in his kitchen sink.

According to Hilmarsson, his first few batches of skyr were sometimes okay and sometimes awful. One of his problems was that proper skyr requires preparation in specific and exact temperatures, something his small kitchen could not provide. So Hilmarsson took a vacation from his job and traveled to upstate New York to a dairy plant that he could rent that was attached to an agricultural college. It was there that he made his first professional batch of yogurt that he thought tasted wonderful. He resigned from Deloitte to make his own yogurt full time.

With his recipe perfected, he was ready for his friends to try his yogurt. His colleagues gave the taste a unanimous thumbs-up. Then Hilmarsson got his first break. A friend who tried the yogurt brought a sample to a staff tasting at Murray's Cheese in New York City. Impressed with his product Murray's Cheese became his first client.

Knowing he needed financing, Hilmarsson contacted a professor from Columbia University who had tried his yogurt. The professor agreed to invest a small amount in the company if Hilmarsson was investing his own money as well. His next step was to search for a small dairy plant where he could start production. He found an underused dairy plant in Norwich, New York, that had been producing cheese, yogurt, and goat's milk for several years.

After donating skyr to a fundraising event, a Whole Foods employee tasted the yogurt and loved it. Before he knew it Hilmarsson was at Whole Foods' headquarters signing a contract to supply his yogurt to half the Whole Food stores in America. Unfortunately, the company couldn't make the yogurt and cool it fast enough to meet the jump from 15 to 100 stores. The plant shut down for three months to expand, creating a cash flow problem. Hilmarsson worried the company would not be able to recover from the setback. However, his education and work experience at Deloitte helped him face the financial challenge head on. Using careful financial and logistics control, he restarted production in three months.

Going forward, Hilmarsson faces continued cost issues. The core of his product is skim milk from grass-fed cows that's completely strained of whey that requires three times the milk of regular yogurt. This causes the price of his yogurt to approach $3 for a 6-ounce cup in an industry where price competition can be intense. Distribution of a product that must be continuously refrigerated also raises cost problems that can affect cash flow. Hilmarsson knows that all companies have to face such financial challenges. He is, fortunately, familiar with measures of business health—like financial analysis, cost control, financial statements, and return on equity and assets.

Controlling costs, managing cash flows, understanding profit margins and taxes, and financial reporting are keys to growth and survival for large yogurt producers like Dannon and Yoplait, as well as small producers like Siggi's Yogurt. This chapter will introduce you to the accounting fundamentals and financial information critical to business success. It also briefly explores financial ratios that businesses use to measure performance in a large or small business.

profile

Getting to Know

X *Siggi Hilmarsson*

Founder of Siggi's Yogurt

Sources: Jill Priluck, "The Yogurt Chronicles," *Slate*, August 13, 2010; Alexandra Wolfe, "Learning to Milk a Profit," *Bloomberg Businessweek*, August 12, 2010; and Courtney Rubin, "The Sugar Made Him Do It," *Inc.*, February 15, 2011.

Until the development of accounting software simplified the accounting process, accountants had to enter all financial information by hand. Today accounting software makes it possible for businesses to have financial information available whenever they need it. Name two companies that provide accounting software for small businesses. (Find the answer in the chapter.)

LEARNING goal 1

Demonstrate the role that accounting and financial information play for a business and for its stakeholders.

THE ROLE OF ACCOUNTING INFORMATION

Stories like Siggi's Yogurt are repeated every day throughout the business community. Small and large businesses often survive or fail according to how well they handle financial procedures. Financial management is the heartbeat of competitive businesses, and accounting information helps keep the heartbeat stable.

Accounting reports and financial statements reveal as much about a business's health as pulse and blood pressure readings tell us about a person's health. Thus, you have to know something about accounting if you want to succeed in business. It's almost impossible to understand business operations without being able to read, understand, and analyze accounting reports and financial statements.

By the end of the chapter, you should have a good idea what accounting is, how it works, and the value it offers businesses. You should also know some accounting terms and understand the purpose of accounting statements. Your new understanding will pay off as you become more active in business or will help you in simply understanding what's going on in the world of business and finance.

What Is Accounting?

accounting
The recording, classifying, summarizing, and interpreting of financial events and transactions to provide management and other interested parties the information they need to make good decisions.

Accounting is the recording, classifying, summarizing, and interpreting of financial events and transactions in an organization to provide management and other interested parties the financial information they need to make good decisions about its operation. Financial transactions include buying and selling goods and services, acquiring insurance, paying employees, and using supplies. Usually we group all purchases together, and all sales transactions together. The method we use to record and summarize accounting data into reports is an *accounting system* (see Figure 17.1).

A major purpose of accounting is to help managers make well-informed decisions. Another is to report financial information about the firm to interested stakeholders, such as employees, owners, creditors, suppliers, unions, community activists, investors, and the government (for tax purposes) (see Figure 17.2). Accounting is divided into several major disciplines. Let's look at those next.

figure 17.1

THE ACCOUNTING SYSTEM
The inputs to an accounting system include sales documents and other documents. The data are recorded, classified, and summarized. They're then put into summary financial statements such as the income statement and balance sheet and statement of cash flows.

LEARNING goal 2

Identify the different disciplines within the accounting profession.

ACCOUNTING DISCIPLINES

You may think accounting is only for profit-seeking firms. Nothing could be further from the truth. Accounting, often called the language of business, allows us to report financial information about nonprofit organizations such as churches, schools, hospitals, fraternities, and government agencies.[1] The accounting profession is divided into five key working areas: managerial accounting, financial accounting, auditing, tax accounting, and governmental and not-for-profit accounting.[2] All five are important, and all create career opportunities.[3] Let's explore each.

Managerial Accounting

Managerial accounting provides information and analysis to managers *inside* the organization to assist them in decision making. Managerial accounting is concerned with measuring and reporting costs of production, marketing, and other functions; preparing budgets (planning); checking whether or not units are staying within their budgets (controlling); and designing strategies to minimize taxes.

If you are a business major, you'll probably take a course in managerial accounting. You may even pursue a career as a certified management

managerial accounting
Accounting used to provide information and analyses to managers inside the organization to assist them in decision making.

USERS	TYPE OF REPORT
Government taxing authorities (e.g., the Internal Revenue Service)	Tax returns
Government regulatory agencies	Required reports
People interested in the organization's income and financial position (e.g., owners, creditors, financial analysts, suppliers)	Financial statements found in annual reports (e.g., income statement, balance sheet, statement of cash flows)
Managers of the firm	Financial statements and various internally distributed financial reports

figure 17.2

USERS OF ACCOUNTING INFORMATION AND THE REQUIRED REPORTS
Many types of organizations use accounting information to make business decisions. The reports needed vary according to the information each user requires. An accountant must prepare the appropriate forms.

Assembling an airplane engine requires many tools, parts, raw materials, and other components, as well as labor costs. Keeping these costs at a minimum and setting realistic production schedules is critical to a business's survival. What other internal departments must management accountants team with to ensure company competitiveness?

certified management accountant (CMA)
A professional accountant who has met certain educational and experience requirements, passed a qualifying exam, and been certified by the Institute of Certified Management Accountants.

financial accounting
Accounting information and analyses prepared for people outside the organization.

annual report
A yearly statement of the financial condition, progress, and expectations of an organization.

private accountant
An accountant who works for a single firm, government agency, or nonprofit oranization.

public accountant
An accountant who provides accounting services to individuals or businesses on a fee basis.

accountant.[4] A **certified management accountant (CMA)** is a professional accountant who has met certain educational and experience requirements, passed a qualifying exam, and been certified by the Institute of Certified Management Accountants.[5] With the growing emphasis on global competition, outsourcing, and organizational cost-cutting, managerial accounting is one of the most important areas you may study in your college career.

Financial Accounting

Financial accounting differs from managerial accounting in that the financial information and analyses it generates are for people primarily *outside* the organization. The information goes not only to company owners, managers, and employees, but also to creditors and lenders, employee unions, customers, suppliers, government agencies, and the general public. External users are interested in questions like: Is the organization profitable? Is it able to pay its bills? How much debt does it owe? These questions and others are often answered in the company's **annual report**, a yearly statement of the financial condition, progress, and expectations of an organization. As pressure from stakeholders for detailed financial information has grown, companies have poured more information than ever into their annual reports.

It's critical for firms to keep accurate financial information. Therefore, many organizations employ a **private accountant** who works for a single firm, government agency, or nonprofit organization. However, not all firms or nonprofit organizations want or need a full-time accountant. Fortunately, thousands of accounting firms in the United States provide the accounting services an organization needs through public accountants.[6]

For a fee, a **public accountant** provides accounting services to individuals or businesses. Such services can include designing an accounting system, helping select the correct software to run the system, and analyzing an organization's financial performance. An accountant who passes a series of examinations established by the American Institute of Certified Public Accountants (AICPA) and meets the state's requirement for education and experience is recognized as a **certified public accountant (CPA)** . CPAs find careers as private or public accountants and are often sought to fill other financial positions within organizations.[7] Today, there are over 650,000 CPAs in the United States, 370,000 of whom are members of the AICPA.[8]

Accountants know it's vital for users of a firm's accounting information to be assured the information is accurate. The independent Financial Accounting Standards Board (FASB) defines the *generally accepted accounting principles (GAAP)* that accountants must follow. If accounting reports are prepared in accordance with GAAP, users can expect the information to meet standards upon which accounting professionals have agreed.

The accounting profession suffered a dark period in the early 2000s when accounting scandals at WorldCom, Enron, and Tyco raised public suspicions about the profession and corporate integrity in general. Arthur Andersen, one of the nation's leading accounting firms, was forced out of business after being convicted of obstruction of justice for shredding records in the Enron case (the conviction was later overturned by the U.S. Supreme Court).

Scrutiny of the accounting industry intensified, and resulted in the U.S. Congress's passage of the Sarbanes-Oxley Act (called Sarbox). This legislation created new government reporting standards for publicly traded companies. It also created the Public Company Accounting Oversight Board (PCAOB), which is charged with overseeing the AICPA.[9] Prior to the passage of Sarbox, the accounting profession was self-regulated.[10] Figure 17.3 lists some of the major provisions of Sarbanes-Oxley.

The financial crisis beginning in 2008 led Congress to pass the Dodd-Frank Wall Street Reform and Consumer Protection Act. The Dodd-Frank Act increased financial regulation affecting accounting by increasing the power of the PCAOB to oversee auditors of brokers and dealers in securities markets.[11] We'll discuss the Dodd-Frank Act in more depth in Chapter 19.

The accounting profession understands that to be effective, accountants must be considered as professional as doctors or lawyers. Besides completing more than 150 hours of intense training and a rigorous exam, CPAs on

certified public accountant (CPA)
An accountant who passes a series of examinations established by the American Institute of Certified Public Accountants (AICPA).

- Prohibits accounting firms from providing certain non-auditing work (such as consulting services) to companies they audit.
- Strengthens the protection for whistle-blowers who report wrongful actions of company officers.
- Requires company CEOs and CFOs to certify the accuracy of financial reports and imparts strict penalties for any violation of securities reporting (e.g., earnings misstatements).
- Prohibits corporate loans to directors and executives of the company.
- Establishes the five-member Public Company Accounting Oversight Board (PCAOB) under the Securities and Exchange Commission (SEC) to oversee the accounting industry.
- Stipulates that altering or destroying key audit documents will result in felony charges and significant criminal penalties.

figure 17.3

KEY PROVISIONS OF THE SARBANES-OXLEY ACT

LEGAL
briefcase

www.forensisgroup.com

Fighting Accounting Fraud Line-by-Line

According to the Association of Certified Fraud Examiners, it is likely many companies are losing money in the worst way possible—through fraud. Sam E. Antar, a CPA, agrees with that assessment and he should know. While he was Chief Financial Officer (CFO) of Crazy Eddie, a consumer electronics retailer, Antar was convicted of inflating sales figures, money laundering, and inventory fraud in a corporate scam that cost investors and creditors hundreds of millions of dollars. Today, he lectures companies concerning fraud and how to prevent it from occurring and is a strong proponent of training auditors in forensic accounting.

According to Mr. Antar, auditors are trained to look for bookkeeping errors while forensic accountants are trained as crime-scene investigators. Steve Pedneault of Forensic Accounting Services suggests that more fraud and embezzlement exist in businesses today than there was 10 years ago when Enron, WorldCom, and Tyco were in the news. When a company suspects financial wrongdoings, companies like Mr. Pedneault's are called in to search out fraud by analyzing computer hard drives, financial papers, bank records, e-mail, and billing receipts. *Accounting Today* magazine estimates almost 80 percent of the nation's top CPA firms use forensic accounting in fraud and litigation.

If you think accountants are just glorified pencil pushers think again. Forensic accountants see their job as investigative. In most cases internal informants who have concerns about supervisors encouraging them to falsify financial records or hide some costs are their first line of investigation. With financial problems like the subprime mortgage crisis of the late 2000s and the Bernie Madoff Ponzi scheme that cost investors billions of dollars, forensic accountants won't have any trouble keeping busy in the future.

Sources: Marie Leone, "Something Wicked This Way Comes," *CFO*, June 1, 2010; Laton McCartney, "Where There's Smoke, There's Fraud," *CFO*, March 1, 2011; and "AICPA Adds More Options for Specialty Credentials," *Accounting Today*, April 27, 2011.

average take 40 hours of continuing education training a year, are subject to recertification, undergo ethics training requirements, and must pass an ethics exam.

Auditing

auditing
The job of reviewing and evaluating the information used to prepare a company's financial statements.

independent audit
An evaluation and unbiased opinion about the accuracy of a company's financial statements.

Reviewing and evaluating the information used to prepare a company's financial statements is referred to as **auditing**. Private accountants within an organization often perform internal audits to guarantee that it is carrying out proper accounting procedures and financial reporting.[12] Public accountants also conduct independent audits of accounting information and related records. An **independent audit** is an evaluation and unbiased opinion about the accuracy of a company's financial statements. Annual reports often include an auditor's unbiased written opinion.

After the accounting scandals of the early 2000s, questions surfaced about the ethics of allowing an accounting firm to do both auditing and consulting work for the same company. In response, the Sarbanes-Oxley Act put in place new rules about auditing and consulting to ensure the integrity of the auditing process. Auditing procedures again came under fire in 2011.[13] Many called for stricter controls over auditing procedures after analyzing the failure of Lehman Brothers in 2008 and the financial crisis that followed.[14] The nearby Legal Briefcase discusses the problem of accounting fraud and how companies can help prevent it.

In doing their job, auditors not only examine the financial health of an organization but also its operational efficiencies and effectiveness.[15] Accountants who have a bachelor's degree and two years of experience in internal auditing, and who pass an exam administered by the Institute of Internal Auditors, can earn professional accreditation as a **certified internal auditor (CIA)**.[16]

Tax Accounting

Taxes enable governments to fund roads, parks, schools, police protection, the military, and other functions. Federal, state, and local governments require individuals and organizations to file tax returns at specific times and in a precise format. A **tax accountant** is trained in tax law and is responsible for preparing tax returns or developing tax strategies. Since governments often change tax policies according to specific needs or objectives, the job of the tax accountant is always challenging.[17] And as the burden of taxes grows in the economy, the role of the tax accountant becomes increasingly valuable to the organization, individual, or entrepreneur.[18]

Government and Not-for-Profit Accounting

Government and not-for-profit accounting supports organizations whose purpose is not generating a profit, but serving ratepayers, taxpayers, and others according to a duly approved budget. Federal, state, and local governments require an accounting system that helps taxpayers, special interest groups, legislative bodies, and creditors ensure that the government is fulfilling its obligations and making proper use of taxpayers' money. Government accounting standards are set by an organization called the Governmental Accounting Standards Board (GASB).[19] The Federal Bureau of Investigation, the Internal Revenue Service, the Missouri Department of Natural Resources, and the Cook County Department of Revenue are just a few of the many government agencies that offer career possibilities to accountants seeking to work in government accounting.

Not-for-profit organizations also require accounting professionals. Charities like the Salvation Army, Red Cross, museums, and hospitals all hire accountants to show contributors how their money is spent. In fact, their need for trained accountants is growing since donors to nonprofits want to see exactly how and where the funds they contribute are being spent. During the deep recession beginning in 2008, many businesses and individuals cut back on donations making it more important than ever to account for every dollar contributed.[20]

As you can see, managerial and financial accounting, auditing, tax accounting, and governmental and not-for-profit accounting each require specific training and skill. After the Progress Assessment, we will clarify the difference between accounting and bookkeeping.

The National Park Service, with its workforce of over 26,000 employees, maintains and protects places special to the people of the United States, like the faces on Mount Rushmore. Such government organizations employ accountants, auditors, and financial managers.

certified internal auditor (CIA)
An accountant who has a bachelor's degree and two years of experience in internal auditing, and who has passed an exam administered by the Institute of Internal Auditors.

tax accountant
An accountant trained in tax law and responsible for preparing tax returns or developing tax strategies.

government and not-for-profit accounting
Accounting system for organizations whose purpose is not generating a profit but serving ratepayers, taxpayers, and others according to a duly approved budget.

progress assessment

- What is the key difference between managerial and financial accounting?
- How is the job of a private accountant different from that of a public accountant?
- What is the job of an auditor? What's an independent audit?

LEARNING goal 3

List the steps in the accounting cycle, distinguish between accounting and bookkeeping, and explain how computers are used in accounting.

THE ACCOUNTING CYCLE

accounting cycle
A six-step procedure that results in the preparation and analysis of the major financial statements.

bookkeeping
The recording of business transactions.

journal
The record book or computer program where accounting data are first entered.

double-entry bookkeeping
The practice of writing every business transaction in two places.

ledger
A specialized accounting book or computer program in which information from accounting journals is accumulated into specific categories and posted so that managers can find all the information about one account in the same place.

The **accounting cycle** is a six-step procedure that results in the preparation and analysis of the major financial statements (see Figure 17.4). It relies on the work of both a bookkeeper and an accountant. **Bookkeeping**, the recording of business transactions, is a basic part of financial reporting. Accounting, however, goes far beyond the mere recording of financial information. Accountants classify and summarize financial data provided by bookkeepers, and then interpret the data and report the information to management. They also suggest strategies for improving the firm's financial condition and prepare financial analyses and income tax returns.

A bookkeeper's first task is to divide all the firm's transactions into meaningful categories such as sales documents, purchasing receipts, and shipping documents, being very careful to keep the information organized and manageable. Bookkeepers then record financial data from the original transaction documents (sales slips and so forth) into a record book or computer program called a **journal**. The word *journal* comes from the French word *jour*, which means "day." Therefore, a journal is where the day's transactions are kept.

It's quite possible to make a mistake when recording financial transactions, like entering $10.98 as $10.89. That's why bookkeepers record all transactions in two places so they can check one list of transactions against the other to make sure both add up to the same amount. If the amounts are not equal, the bookkeeper knows there is a mistake. The practice of writing every transaction in two places is called **double-entry bookkeeping**. It requires two entries in the journal and in the ledgers (discussed next) for each transaction.

Suppose a business wanted to determine how much it paid for office supplies in the first quarter of the year. Without a specific bookkeeping tool, that would be difficult—even with accurate accounting journals. Therefore, bookkeepers use a specialized accounting book or computer program called a **ledger**. In the ledger, they transfer (or post) information from accounting journals into specific categories so managers can find all the information about a single account, like office supplies or cash, in one place.

. figure 17.4

STEPS IN THE ACCOUNTING CYCLE

1	2	3	4	5	6
Analyze source documents (sales slips, travel records, etc.)	Record transactions in journals	Transfer (post) journal entries to ledger	Take a trial balance	Prepare financial statements	Analyze financial statements

Balance sheet   Income statement   Statement of cash flows

The next step in the accounting cycle is to prepare a **trial balance**, a summary of all the financial data in the account ledgers that ensures the figures are correct and balanced. If the information in the account ledgers is not accurate, the accountant must correct it before preparing the firm's financial statements. Using the correct information, the accountant then prepares the firm's financial statements—including a balance sheet, an income statement, and a statement of cash flows—according to generally accepted accounting principles.

> **trial balance**
> A summary of all the financial data in the account ledgers that ensures the figures are correct and balanced.

Accounting Technology

Not long ago, accountants and bookkeepers needed to enter all of a firm's financial information by hand. Today, technology has simplified the accounting process considerably.[21] Computerized accounting programs post information from journals instantaneously, even from remote locations, so that financial information is readily available whenever the organization needs it. Such assistance frees accountants' time for more important tasks such as financial analysis. Computerized accounting programs are particularly helpful to small-business owners who often lack the strong accounting support within their companies that larger firms enjoy. Accounting software—such as Intuit's QuickBooks and Sage's Peachtree—addresses the specific needs of small businesses, often significantly different from the needs of a major corporation.[22] Small business owners, however, need to understand exactly which computer systems and programs are best suited for their particular company needs.[23] That's one reason why entrepreneurs planning to start a business should either hire or consult with an accountant to identify the particular needs of their firm. They can then develop a specific computer accounting system that works with the accounting software they've chosen.

With sophisticated accounting software available, you might wonder why you need to study and understand accounting. Without question a computer is a wonderful tool for businesspeople and certainly helps ease the monotony of bookkeeping and accounting work. Unfortunately the work of an accountant requires training and very specific competencies that computers are not programmed to handle. It's the partnership of technology and an accountant's knowledge that helps a firm make the right financial decisions. After the Progress Assessment, we'll explore the balance sheet, income statement, and statement of cash flows. It's from the information contained in these financial statements that the accountant analyzes and evaluates the financial condition of the firm.

progress assessment

- How is the job of the bookkeeper different from that of an accountant?
- What's the purpose of accounting journals and of a ledger?
- Why does a bookkeeper prepare a trial balance?
- How has computer software helped businesses in maintaining and compiling accounting information?

LEARNING goal 4

Explain how the major financial statements differ.

UNDERSTANDING KEY FINANCIAL STATEMENTS

financial statement
A summary of all the transactions that have occurred over a particular period.

An accounting year is either a calendar or fiscal year. A calendar year begins January 1st and ends December 31st. A fiscal year can begin at any date designated by the business. A **financial statement** is a summary of all the financial transactions that have occurred over a particular period. Financial statements indicate a firm's financial health and stability and are key factors in management decision making.[24] That's why stockholders (the owners of the firm), bondholders and banks (people and institutions that lend money to the firm), labor unions, employees, and the Internal Revenue Service are all interested in a firm's financial statements. The key financial statements of a business are:

1. The *balance sheet*, which reports the firm's financial condition *on a specific date*.

2. The *income statement*, which summarizes revenues, cost of goods, and expenses (including taxes), for a specific period and highlights the total profit or loss the firm experienced *during that period*.

3. The *statement of cash flows*, which provides a summary of money coming into and going out of the firm. It tracks a company's cash receipts and cash payments.

The differences among the financial statements can best be summarized this way: The balance sheet details what the company owns and owes on a certain day; the income statement shows the revenue a firm earned selling its products compared to its selling costs (profit or loss) over a specific period of time; and the statement of cash flows highlights the difference between cash coming in and cash going out of a business. To fully understand this important financial information, you need to know the purpose of an organization's financial statements.[25] To help with this task, we'll explain each statement in more detail next.

Service businesses like dog groomers rely on the same set of financial statements as manufacturers like Ford and retail sales firms like Macy's. What are some of the assets and liabilities a typical service business, like this, one would carry on its balance sheet?

The Fundamental Accounting Equation

Imagine you don't owe anybody money. That is, you have no liabilities (debts). In this case, your assets (cash and so forth) are equal to what you *own* (your equity). However, if you borrow some money from a friend, you have incurred a liability. Your assets are now equal to what you *owe* plus what you own. Translated into business terms, Assets = Liabilities + Owners' equity.

In accounting, this equation must always be balanced. For example, suppose you have $50,000 in cash and decide to use that money to open a small coffee shop. Your business has assets of $50,000 and no debts. The accounting equation would look like this:

$$\text{Assets} = \text{Liabilities} + \text{Owner's equity}$$
$$\$50,000 = \$0 \quad\quad + \$50,000$$

You have $50,000 cash and $50,000 owners' equity (the amount of your investment in the business—sometimes referred to as net worth). However, before opening the business, you borrow $30,000 from a local bank; now the equation changes. You have $30,000 of additional cash, but you also have a debt (liability) of $30,000. (Remember, in double-entry bookkeeping we record each business transaction in two places.)

Your financial position within the business has changed. The equation is still balanced but we change it to reflect the borrowing transaction:

$$\text{Assets} = \text{Liabilities} + \text{Owner's equity}$$
$$\$80,000 = \$30,000 \quad + \$50,000$$

fundamental accounting equation
Assets = Liabilities + Owners' equity; this is the basis for the balance sheet.

This **fundamental accounting equation** is the basis for the balance sheet.

The Balance Sheet

A **balance sheet** is the financial statement that reports a firm's financial condition at a specific time. As highlighted in the sample balance sheet in Figure 17.5 (for our hypothetical vegetarian restaurant Very Vegetarian introduced in Chapter 13), assets are listed in a separate column from liabilities and owners' (or stockholders') equity. The assets are equal to, or *balanced* with, the liabilities and owners' (or stockholders') equity. The balance sheet is that simple.

balance sheet
Financial statement that reports a firm's financial condition at a specific time and is composed of three major accounts: assets, liabilities, and owners' equity.

VERY VEGETARIAN
Balance Sheet
December 31, 2012

Assets
① Current assets

Cash	$ 15,000	
Accounts receivable	200,000	
Notes receivable	50,000	
Inventory	335,000	
Total current assets		$600,000

② Fixed assets

Land		$ 40,000	
Building and improvements	$200,000		
Less: Accumulated depreciation	−90,000		
		110,000	
Equipment and vehicles	$ 120,000		
Less: Accumulated depreciation	−80,000		
		40,000	
Furniture and fixtures	$ 26,000		
Less: Accumulated depreciation	−10,000		
		16,000	
Total fixed assets			206,000

③ Intangible assets

Goodwill	$ 20,000	
Total intangible assets		20,000
Total assets		$ 826,000

Liabilities and Owners' Equity
④ Current liabilities

Accounts payable	$ 40,000	
Notes payable (due June 2011)	8,000	
Accrued taxes	150,000	
Accrued salaries	90,000	
Total current liabilities		$ 288,000

⑤ Long-term liabilities

Notes payable (due Mar. 2015)	$ 35,000	
Bonds payable (due Dec. 2020)	290,000	
Total long-term liabilities		325,000
Total liabilities		$ 613,000

⑥ Owners' equity

Common stock (1,000,000 shares)	$ 100,000	
Retained earnings	113,000	
Total owners' equity		213,000
Total liabilities & owners' equity		$ 826,000

figure 17.5

SAMPLE VERY VEGETARIAN BALANCE SHEET

① Current assets: Items that can be converted to cash within one year.

② Fixed assets: Items such as land, buildings, and equipment that are relatively permanent.

③ Intangible assets: Items of value such as patents and copyrights that don't have a physical form.

④ Current liabilities: Payments that are due in one year or less.

⑤ Long-term liabilities: Payments not due for one year or longer.

⑥ Owner's equity: The value of what stockholders own in a firm (also called stockholder's equity).

Let's say you want to know what your financial condition is at a given time. Maybe you want to buy a house or car and therefore need to calculate your available resources. One of the best measuring sticks is your balance sheet. First, add up everything you own—cash, property, and money owed you. These are your assets. Subtract from that the money you owe others—credit card debt, IOUs, car loan, and student loan. These are your liabilities. The resulting figure is your net worth, or equity. This is fundamentally what companies do in preparing a balance sheet: they follow the procedures set in the fundamental accounting equation. In that preparation, it's important to follow generally accepted accounting principles (GAAP).

Since it's critical that you understand the financial information on the balance sheet, let's take a closer look at what is in a business's asset account and what is in its liabilities and owners' equity accounts.

Classifying Assets

assets
Economic resources (things of value) owned by a firm.

Assets are economic resources (things of value) owned by a firm. Assets include productive, tangible items such as equipment, buildings, land, furniture, and motor vehicles that help generate income, as well as intangible items with value like patents, trademarks, copyrights, and goodwill. Goodwill represents the value attached to factors such as a firm's reputation, location, and superior products. Goodwill is included on a balance sheet when one firm acquires another and pays more for it than the value of its tangible assets. Intangible assets like brand names can be among the firm's most valuable resources. Think of the value of brand names such as Starbucks, Coca-Cola, McDonald's, and Apple. Not all companies, however, list intangible assets on their balance sheets.

liquidity
The ease with which an asset can be converted into cash.

Accountants list assets on the firm's balance sheet in order of their **liquidity**, or the ease with which they can convert them to cash. Speedier conversion means higher liquidity. For example, an *account receivable* is an amount of money owed to the firm that it expects to receive within one year. It is considered a liquid asset because it can be quickly converted to cash. Land, however, is not considered a liquid asset because it takes time, effort, and paperwork to sell. It is considered as a fixed or long-term asset. Assets are thus divided into three categories, according to how quickly they can be turned into cash:

current assets
Items that can or will be converted into cash within one year.

1. **Current assets** are items that can or will be converted into cash within one year. They include cash, accounts receivable, and inventory.

fixed assets
Assets that are relatively permanent, such as land, buildings, and equipment.

2. **Fixed assets** are long-term assets that are relatively permanent such as land, buildings, and equipment. (On the balance sheet we also refer to these as property, plant, and equipment.)

intangible assets
Long-term assets (e.g., patents, trademarks, copyrights) that have no real physical form but do have value.

3. **Intangible assets** are long-term assets that have no physical form but do have value. Patents, trademarks, copyrights, and goodwill are intangible assets.

Liabilities and Owners' Equity Accounts

liabilities
What the business owes to others (debts).

Liabilities are what the business owes to others—its debts. *Current liabilities* are debts due in one year or less. *Long-term liabilities* are debts not due for one year or more. The following are common liability accounts recorded on a balance sheet (look at Figure 17.5 again):

accounts payable
Current liabilities are bills the company owes to others for merchandise or services purchased on credit but not yet paid for.

1. **Accounts payable** are current liabilities or bills the company owes others for merchandise or services it purchased on credit but has not yet paid for.

2. **Notes payable** can be short-term or long-term liabilities (like loans from banks) that a business promises to repay by a certain date.
3. **Bonds payable** are long-term liabilities; money lent to the firm that it must pay back. (We discuss bonds in depth in Chapters 18 and 19.)

As you saw in the fundamental accounting equation, the value of things you own (assets) minus the amount of money you owe others (liabilities) is called *equity*. The value of what stockholders own in a firm (minus liabilities) is called *stockholders' equity* or *shareholders' equity*. Because stockholders are the owners of a firm, we also call stockholders' equity **owners' equity**, or the amount of the business that belongs to the owners, minus any liabilities the business owes. The formula for owners' equity, then, is assets minus liabilities.

The owners' equity account will differ according to the type of organization. For sole proprietors and partners, owners' equity means the value of everything owned by the business minus any liabilities of the owner(s), such as bank loans. Owners' equity in these firms is called the *capital account*.

For corporations, the owners' equity account records the owners' claims to funds they have invested in the firm (such as stock), as well as retained earnings. **Retained earnings** are accumulated earnings from the firm's profitable operations that are reinvested in the business and not paid out to stockholders in distributions of company profits. (Distributions of profits, called dividends, are discussed in Chapter 19.) Take a few moments to look again at Figure 17.5 and see what facts you can determine about the vegetarian restaurant, Very Vegetarian, from its balance sheet. After the Progress Assessment, have some fun and estimate your own personal net worth, following the directions in Figure 17.6.

notes payable
Short-term or long-term liabilities that a business promises to repay by a certain date.

bonds payable
Long-term liabilities that represent money lent to the firm that must be paid back.

owners' equity
The amount of the business that belongs to the owners minus any liabilities owed by the business.

retained earnings
The accumulated earnings from a firm's profitable operations that were reinvested in the business and not paid out to stockholders in dividends.

progress assessment

- What do we call the formula for the balance sheet? What three accounts does it include?
- What does it mean to list assets according to liquidity?
- What's the difference between long-term and short-term liabilities on the balance sheet?
- What is owners' equity and how do we determine it?

ASSETS		LIABILITIES	
Cash	$ _____	Installment loans & interest	$ _____
Savings account	_____	Other loans & interest	_____
Checking account	_____	Credit card accounts	_____
Home	_____	Mortgage	_____
Stocks & bonds	_____	Taxes	_____
Automobile	_____	Cell phone service	_____
IRA or Keogh	_____		
Personal property	_____		
Other assets	_____		
Total assets	$ _____	Total liabilities	$ _____
Determine your net worth:			
Total assets	$ _____		
Total liabilities	− _____		
Net worth	$ _____		

figure 17.6.

YOU INCORPORATED
How do you think You Inc. stacks up financially? Let's take a little time to find out. You may be pleasantly surprised, or you may realize that you need to think hard about planning your financial future. Remember, your net worth is nothing more than the difference between what you own (assets) and what you owe (liabilities). Be honest, and do your best to give a fair evaluation of your private property's value.

The Income Statement

income statement
The financial statement that shows a firm's profit after costs, expenses, and taxes; it summarizes all of the resources that have come into the firm (revenue), all the resources that have left the firm (expenses), and the resulting net income or net loss.

The financial statement that shows a firm's bottom line—that is, its profit after costs, expenses, and taxes—is the **income statement**. The income statement summarizes all the resources, called *revenue*, that have come into the firm from operating activities, money resources the firm used up, expenses it incurred in doing business, and resources it has left after paying all costs and expenses, including taxes. The resources (revenue) left over or depleted are referred to as **net income or net loss** (see Figure 17.7).

The income statement reports the firm's financial operations over a particular period of time, usually a year, a quarter of a year, or a month. It's the financial statement that reveals whether the business is actually earning a profit or losing money. The income statement includes valuable financial information for stockholders, lenders, potential investors, employees, and of course the government. Because it's so valuable, let's take a quick look at how to compile the income statement. Then we will discuss what each element in it means.

net income or net loss
Revenue left over after all costs and expenses, including taxes, are paid.

Revenue
− Cost of goods sold
= Gross Profit (gross margin)
− Operating expenses
= Net income before taxes
− Taxes
= Net income or loss

cost of goods sold (or cost of goods manufactured)
A measure of the cost of merchandise sold or cost of raw materials and supplies used for producing items for resale.

Revenue

Revenue is the monetary value of what a firm received for goods sold, services rendered, and other payments (such as rents received, money paid to the firm for use of its patents, interest earned, etc.). Be sure not to confuse the terms *revenue* and *sales;* they are not the same thing. True, most revenue the firm earns does come from sales, but companies can also have other sources of revenue. Also, a quick glance at the income statement shows you that *gross sales* refers to the total of all sales the firm completed. *Net sales* are gross sales minus returns, discounts, and allowances.

Drew Albert owns popular CJ's All-American Grill in Walnut Creek, California. The restaurant earns revenue by selling American fare like this "danger dog." What is the difference between revenue and gross profit? Between gross profit and net income before taxes?

Cost of Goods Sold

The **cost of goods sold (or cost of goods manufactured)** measures the cost of merchandise the firm sells or the cost of raw materials and supplies it used in producing items for resale. It makes sense to compare how much a business earned by selling merchandise and how much it spent to make or buy the merchandise. The cost of goods sold includes the purchase price plus any freight charges paid to transport goods, plus any costs associated with storing the goods.

In financial reporting, it doesn't matter when a firm places a particular item in its inventory, but it does matter how an accountant records the cost of the item when the firm sells it. To find out why, read the Spotlight on Small Business box on p. 478 about two different inventory valuation methods.

When we subtract the cost of goods sold from net sales, we get gross profit or gross margin. **Gross profit (or gross margin)** is how much a firm earned

VERY VEGETARIAN
Income Statement
For the Year Ended December 31, 2012

① Revenues

Gross sales		$720,000	
Less: Sales returns and allowances	$ 12,000		
Sales discounts	8,000	−20,000	
Net sales			$700,000

② Cost of goods sold

Beginning inventory, Jan. 1		$200,000	
Merchandise purchases	$400,000		
Freight	40,000		
Net purchases		440,000	
Cost of goods available for sale	$640,000		
Less ending inventory, Dec. 31		−230,000	
Cost of goods sold			−410,000

③ Gross profit $290,000

④ Operating expenses

Selling expenses

Salaries for salespeople	$ 90,000		
Advertising	18,000		
Supplies	2,000		
Total selling expenses		$ 110,000	

General expenses

Office salaries	$ 67,000		
Depreciation	1,500		
Insurance	1,500		
Rent	28,000		
Light, heat, and power	12,000		
Miscellaneous	2,000		
		112,000	

Total operating expenses		222,000
Net income before taxes		$ 68,000
Less: Income tax expense		19,000
⑤ Net income after taxes		$ 49,000

figure 17.7

SAMPLE VERY VEGETARIAN INCOME STATEMENT

① Revenue: Value of what's received from goods sold, services rendered, and other financial sources.

② Cost of goods sold: Cost of merchandise sold or cost of raw materials or parts used for producing items for resale.

③ Gross profit: How much the firm earned by buying or selling merchandise.

④ Operating expenses: Cost incurred in operating a business.

⑤ Net income after taxes: Profit or loss over a specific period after subtracting all costs and expenses, including taxes.

by buying (or making) and selling merchandise. In a service firm, there may be no cost of goods sold; therefore, gross profit could *equal* net sales. Gross profit does not tell you everything you need to know about the firm's financial performance. To get that, you must also subtract the business's expenses.

Operating Expenses

In selling goods or services, a business incurs certain **operating expenses** such as rent, salaries, supplies, utilities, and insurance. Other operating expenses that appear on an income statement, like depreciation, are a bit more complex. For example, have you ever heard that a new car depreciates in market value as soon as you drive it off the dealer's lot? The same principle holds true for assets such as equipment and machinery. **Depreciation** is the systematic write-off of the cost of a tangible asset over its estimated useful life. Under accounting rules set by GAAP and the Internal Revenue Service (which are beyond the scope of this chapter), companies are permitted to recapture the cost of these assets over time by using depreciation as an operating expense.

gross profit (or gross margin)
How much a firm earned by buying (or making) and selling merchandise.

operating expenses
Costs involved in operating a business, such as rent, utilities, and salaries.

depreciation
The systematic write-off of the cost of a tangible asset over its estimated useful life.

SPOTLIGHT ON SMALL business

www.aicpa.org

What's Coming and Going at the College Bookstore?

Generally accepted accounting principles (GAAP) sometimes permit an accountant to use different methods of accounting for a firm's inventory. Let's look at two possible treatments—FIFO and LIFO.

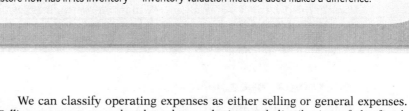

Say a college bookstore buys 100 copies of a particular textbook in July at $100 a copy. When classes begin, the bookstore sells 50 copies of the text to students at $120 each. Since the book will be used again next term, the store places the 50 copies it did not sell in its inventory until then.

In late December, when the bookstore orders 50 additional copies of the text to sell for the coming term, the publisher's price has increased to $110 a copy due to inflation and other production and distribution costs. The bookstore now has in its inventory 100 copies of the same textbook from different purchase cycles. If it sells 50 copies to students at $120 each at the beginning of the new term, what's the bookstore's cost of the book for accounting purposes? Actually, it depends.

The books are identical, but the accounting treatment could be different. If the bookstore uses a method called first in, first out (FIFO), the cost of goods sold is $100 for each textbook, because the textbook the store bought first—the *first in*—cost $100. The bookstore could use another method, however. Under last in, first out (LIFO), its *last* purchase of the textbooks, at $110 each, determines the cost of each of the 50 textbooks sold.

If the book sells for $120, what is the difference in gross profit (margin) between using FIFO and using LIFO? As you can see, the inventory valuation method used makes a difference.

We can classify operating expenses as either selling or general expenses. *Selling expenses* are related to the marketing and distribution of the firm's goods or services, such as advertising, salespeople's salaries, and supplies. *General expenses* are administrative expenses of the firm such as office salaries, depreciation, insurance, and rent. Accountants are trained to help you record all applicable expenses and find other relevant expenses you can deduct from your taxable income as a part of doing business.

Net Profit or Loss

After deducting all expenses, we can determine the firm's net income before taxes, also referred to as net earnings or net profit (see Figure 17.7 again). After allocating for taxes, we get to the *bottom line,* which is the net income (or perhaps net loss) the firm incurred from revenue minus sales returns, costs, expenses, and taxes over a period of time. We can now answer the question "Did the business earn or lose money in the specific reporting period?"

As you can see, the basic principles of the balance sheet and income statement are already familiar to you. You know how to keep track of costs and expenses when you prepare your own budget. If your rent and utilities exceed your earnings, you know you're in trouble. If you need more money, you may need to sell some of the things you own to meet your expenses. The same is true in business. Companies need to keep track of how much money they earn

Most businesses incur operating expenses including rent, salaries, utilities, supplies, and insurance. What are some of the likely operating expenses for this firm?

and spend, and how much cash they have on hand. The only difference is that they tend to have more complex problems and a good deal more information to record than you do.

Users of financial statements are interested in how a firm handles the flow of cash coming into a business and the cash flowing out of the business. Cash flow problems can plague both businesses and individuals. Keep this in mind as we look at the statement of cash flows next.

The Statement of Cash Flows

The **statement of cash flows** reports cash receipts and cash disbursements related to the three major activities of a firm:

- *Operations* are cash transactions associated with running the business.
- *Investments* are cash used in or provided by the firm's investment activities.
- *Financing* is cash raised by taking on new debt, or equity capital or cash used to pay business expenses, past debts, or company dividends.

Accountants analyze all changes in the firm's cash that have occurred from operating, investing, and financing in order to determine the firm's net cash position. The statement of cash flows also gives the firm some insight into how to handle cash better so that no cash-flow problems occur—such as having no cash on hand for immediate expenses.[26]

Figure 17.8 on p. 480 shows a sample statement of cash flows, again using the example of Very Vegetarian. As you can see, the statement of cash flows answers such questions as: How much cash came into the business from current operations, such as buying and selling goods and services? Did the firm use cash to buy stocks, bonds, or other investments? Did it sell some investments that brought in cash? How much money did the firm take in from issuing stock?

statement of cash flows
Financial statement that reports cash receipts and disbursements related to a firm's three major activities: operations, investments, and financing.

figure 17.8

SAMPLE VERY VEGETARIAN STATEMENT OF CASH FLOWS

① Cash receipts from sales, commissions, fees, interest, and dividends. Cash payments for salaries, inventories, operating expenses, interest, and taxes.
② Includes cash flows that are generated through a company's purchase or sale of long-term operational assets, investments in other companies, and its lending activities.
③ Cash inflows and outflows associated with the company's own equity transactions or its borrowing activities.

VERY VEGETARIAN
Statement of Cash Flows
For the Year Ended December 31, 2012

① Cash flows from operating activities		
Cash received from customers	$700,000	
Cash paid to suppliers and employees	(567,000)	
Interest paid	(64,000)	
Income tax paid	(19,000)	
Interest and dividends received	2,000	
Net cash provided by operating activities		$52,000
② Cash flows from investing activities		
Proceeds from sale of plant assets	$ 4,000	
Payments for purchase of equipment	(23,000)	
Net cash provided by investing activities		(19,000)
③ Cash flows from financing activities		
Proceeds from issuance of short-term debt	$ 2,000	
Payment of long-term debt	(8,000)	
Payment of dividends	(15,000)	
Net cash inflow from financing activities		(21,000)
Net change in cash and equivalents		$ 12,000
Cash balance (beginning of year)		3,000
Cash balance (end of year)		$ 15,000

Cash flow is the difference between money coming into and going out of a business. Careful cash flow management is a must for a business of any size, but it's particularly important for small businesses and for seasonal businesses like ski resorts. Have you read of any firms that were forced into bankruptcy because of cash flow problems?

We analyze these and other financial transactions to see their effect on the firm's cash position. Managing cash flow can mean success or failure of any business, which is why we analyze it in more depth in the next section.

The Need for Cash Flow Analysis

Cash flow, if not properly managed, can cause a business much concern. Understanding cash flow analysis is important and not difficult to understand.[27] Let's say you borrow $100 from a friend to buy a used bike and agree to pay her back at the end of the week. You then sell the bike for $150 to someone else, who also agrees to pay you by the end of the week. Unfortunately, by the weekend your buyer does not have the money as promised, and says he will have to pay you next month. Meanwhile, your friend wants the $100 you agreed to pay her by the end of the week!

What seemed a great opportunity to make an easy $50 profit is now a cause for concern. You owe $100 and have no cash. What do you do? If you were a business, you might default on the loan and possibly go bankrupt, even though you had the potential for profit.

It's possible for a business to increase its sales and profits yet still suffer cash flow problems.[28] **Cash flow** is simply the difference between cash coming in and cash going out of a business. Poor cash flow constitutes a major operating problem for many companies and is particularly difficult for small

Barking Up the Wrong Financial Statement

The recession of the late 2000s hit small manufacturers very hard. Many did not survive the downturn. You are the lone accountant employed by Keegan's Feast, a small producer of premium dog food that sells directly online. Many of the company's customers became cost-conscious during the downturn and purchased lower-cost brands. Fortunately with the economy recovering, many of the firm's old customers are returning and things are looking up. The problem is the company's cash flow suffered during the recession, and the firm needs immediate funding to continue to pay its bills. You know the CEO has prepared a proposal to a local bank asking for short-term financing. Unfortunately, you are aware that Keegan's financial statements for the past year will not show good results. Your expectation is the bank will not approve the loan on the basis of the financial information even though the firm seems to be coming back.

Before you close the books for the end of the year, the CEO suggests you might "improve" the company's financial statements by treating the sales made at the beginning of January of the current year as if they were made in December of the past year. He is confident the company auditors will not discover the discrepancy.

You know this is against the rules of the Financial Accounting Standards Board (FASB), and you refuse to alter the information. The CEO warns that without the bank loan, the business is likely to close, meaning you and everyone else will be out of a job. You know he's probably right, and also know it's unlikely the firm's employees will find new jobs. What are your alternatives? What are the likely consequences of each? What will you do?

and seasonal businesses.[29] Accountants sometimes face tough ethical challenges in reporting the flow of funds into a business. Read the Making Ethical Decisions box to see how such an ethical dilemma can arise.

How do cash flow problems start? Often in order to meet the growing demands of customers, a business buys goods on credit (using no cash). If it then sells a large number of goods on credit (getting no cash), the company needs more credit from a lender (usually a bank) to pay its immediate bills. If a firm has reached its credit limit and can borrow no more, it has a severe cash flow problem. It has cash coming in at a later date, but no cash to pay current expenses. That problem could, unfortunately, force the firm into bankruptcy, even though sales may be strong—all because no cash was available when it was most needed. Cash flow analysis shows that a business's relationship with its lenders is critical to preventing cash flow problems. Accountants can provide valuable insight and advice to businesses in managing cash flow, suggesting whether they need cash and how much.[30] After the Progress Assessment, we will see how accountants analyze financial statements using ratios.

cash flow
The difference between cash coming in and cash going out of a business.

progress assessment

- What are the key steps in preparing an income statement?
- What's the difference between revenue and income on the income statement?
- Why is the statement of cash flows important in evaluating a firm's operations?

LEARNING goal 5

Demonstrate the application of ratio analysis in reporting financial information.

ANALYZING FINANCIAL PERFORMANCE USING RATIOS

The firm's financial statements—its balance sheet, income statement, and statement of cash flows—form the basis for financial analyses performed by accountants inside and outside the firm. **Ratio analysis** is the assessment of a firm's financial condition, using calculations and financial ratios developed from the firm's financial statements. Financial ratios are especially useful in comparing the company's performance to its financial objectives and to the performance of other firms in its industry. You probably are already familiar with the use of ratios. For example, in basketball, we express the number of shots made from the foul line with a ratio: shots made to shots attempted. A player who shoots 85 percent from the foul line is considered an outstanding foul shooter; you don't want to foul this player in a close game.

Whether ratios measure an athlete's performance or the financial health of a business, they provide valuable information. Financial ratios provide key insights into how a firm compares to other firms in its industry on liquidity, amount of debt, profitability, and overall business activity. Understanding and interpreting business ratios is important to sound financial analysis. Let's look briefly at four key types of ratios businesses use to measure financial performance.

ratio analysis
The assessment of a firm's financial condition using calculations and interpretations of financial ratios developed from the firm's financial statements.

Liquidity Ratios

We've discussed that *liquidity* refers to how fast an asset can be converted to cash. Liquidity ratios measure a company's ability to turn assets into cash to pay its short-term debts (liabilities that must be repaid within one year). These short-term debts are of particular importance to the firm's lenders who expect to be paid on time. Two key liquidity ratios are the current ratio and the acid-test ratio.[31]

The *current ratio* is the ratio of a firm's current assets to its current liabilities. This information appears on the firm's balance sheet. Look back at Figure 17.5, which details Very Vegetarian's balance sheet. The company lists current assets of $600,000 and current liabilities of $288,000, yielding a current ratio of 2.08, which means Very Vegetarian has $2.08 of current assets for every $1 of current liabilities. See the following calculation:

$$\text{Current ratio} = \frac{\text{Current assets}}{\text{Current liabilities}} = \frac{\$600,000}{\$288,000} = \$2.08$$

The question the current ratio attempts to answer is: Is Very Vegetarian financially secure for the short term (less than one year)? It depends! Usually a company with a current ratio of 2 or better is considered a safe risk for lenders granting short-term credit, since it appears to be performing in line with market expectations. However, lenders will also compare Very Vegetarian's current ratio to that of competing firms in its industry and to its current ratio from the previous year to note any significant changes.

Another key liquidity ratio, called the *acid-test* or *quick ratio,* measures the cash, marketable securities (such as stocks and bonds), and receivables of a firm, compared to its current liabilities. Again, this information is on a firm's balance sheet.

$$\text{Acid-test ratio} = \frac{\text{Cash + Accounts receivable + Marketable securities}}{\text{Current liabilities}}$$

$$= \frac{\$265,000}{\$288,000} = 0.92$$

This ratio is particularly important to firms with difficulty converting inventory into quick cash. It helps answer such questions as: What if sales drop off and we can't sell our inventory? Can we still pay our short-term debt? Though ratios vary among industries, an acid-test ratio between 0.50 and 1.0 is usually considered satisfactory, but bordering on cash-flow problems. Therefore, Very Vegetarian's acid-test ratio of 0.92 could raise concerns that perhaps the firm may not meet its short-term debt and may have to go to a high-cost lender for financial assistance.

Leverage (Debt) Ratios

Leverage (debt) ratios measure the degree to which a firm relies on borrowed funds in its operations. A firm that takes on too much debt could experience problems repaying lenders or meeting promises made to stockholders. The *debt to owners' equity ratio* measures the degree to which the company is financed by borrowed funds that it must repay. Again, let's use Figure 17.5 to measure Very Vegetarian's level of debt:

$$\text{Debt to owners' equity ratio} = \frac{\text{Total liabilities}}{\text{Owners' equity}}$$

$$= \frac{\$613,000}{\$213,000} = 288\%$$

Building luxury hotels, like the Vdara at City Center in Las Vegas, generally requires taking on a high degree of debt before the hotel ever earns its first dollar. Once opened, the company incurs heavy expenses daily just to keep the business functioning efficiently. Would monitoring the four key accounting ratios be a major part of the accountant's job at the Vdara?

Anything above 100 percent shows a firm has more debt than equity. With a ratio of 288 percent, Very Vegetarian has a rather high degree of debt compared to its equity, which implies that lenders and investors may perceive the firm to be quite risky. However, again *it's important to compare a firm's debt ratios to those of other firms in its industry,* because debt financing is more acceptable in some industries than in others. Comparisons with the same firm's past debt ratios can also identify possible trends within the firm or industry.

Profitability (Performance) Ratios

Profitability (performance) ratios measure how effectively a firm's managers are using its various resources to achieve profits. Three of the more important ratios are earnings per share (EPS), return on sales, and return on equity.

PART 6 ✳ **Managing Financial Resources**

EPS is a revealing ratio because earnings help stimulate the firm's growth and provide for stockholders' dividends. The Financial Accounting Standards Board requires companies to report their quarterly EPS in two ways: basic and diluted. The *basic earnings per share (basic EPS) ratio* helps determine the amount of profit a company earned for each share of outstanding common stock.[32] The *diluted earnings per share (diluted EPS) ratio* measures the amount of profit earned for each share of outstanding common stock, but also considers stock options, warrants, preferred stock, and convertible debt securities the firm can convert into common stock. For simplicity's sake, we will compute only the basic EPS for Very Vegetarian:

$$\text{Basic earnings per share} = \frac{\text{Net income after taxes}}{\text{Number of common stock shares outstanding}}$$

$$= \frac{\$49,000}{1,000,000} = \$.049 \text{ per share}$$

Another reliable indicator of performance is *return on sales,* which tells us whether the firm is doing as well as its competitors in generating income from sales. We calculate it by comparing net income to total sales. Very Vegetarian's return on sales is 7 percent, a figure we must measure against similar numbers for competing firms to judge Very Vegetarian's performance:

$$\text{Return on sales} = \frac{\text{Net income}}{\text{Net sales}} = \frac{\$49,000}{\$700,000} = 7\%$$

The higher the risk of failure or loss in an industry, the higher the return investors expect on their investment; they expect to be well compensated for shouldering such odds. *Return on equity* indirectly measures risk by telling us how much a firm earned for each dollar invested by its owners. We calculate it by comparing a company's net income to its total owners' equity. Very

Inventory turnover is critical to just about any business, particularly restaurants that serve perishable items and that must turn over tables to keep the flow of food moving and profits up. Can you think of other businesses that need to watch their inventory turnover closely?

Balance Sheet Accounts			Income Statement Accounts			
ASSETS	**LIABILITIES**	**OWNERS' EQUITY**	**REVENUES**	**COST OF GOODS SOLD**	**EXPENSES**	
Cash	Accounts payable	Capital stock	Sales revenue	Cost of buying goods	Wages	Interest
Accounts receivable	Notes payable	Retained earnings	Rental revenue	Cost of storing goods	Rent	Donations
Inventory	Bonds payable	Common stock	Commissions revenue		Repairs	Licenses
Investments	Taxes payable	Treasury stock	Royalty revenue		Travel	Fees
Equipment					Insurance	Supplies
Land					Utilities	Advertising
Buildings					Entertainment	Taxes
Motor vehicles					Storage	
Goodwill						

figure I7.9

ACCOUNTS IN THE BALANCE SHEET AND INCOME STATEMENT

Vegetarian's return on equity looks reasonably sound since some believe anything over 15 percent is considered a reasonable return:

$$\text{Return on equity} = \frac{\text{Net income after tax}}{\text{Total owners' equity}} = \frac{\$49,000}{\$213,000} = 23\%$$

Remember that profits help companies like Very Vegetarian grow. That's why profitability ratios are such closely watched measurements of company growth and management performance.

Activity Ratios

Converting the firm's inventory to profits is a key function of management. Activity ratios tell us how effectively management is turning over inventory.

The *inventory turnover ratio* measures the speed with which inventory moves through the firm and gets converted into sales. Idle inventory sitting in a warehouse earns nothing and costs money. The more efficiently a firm sells or turns over its inventory, the higher its revenue. We can measure the inventory turnover ratio for Very Vegetarian as follows:

$$\text{Inventory turnover} = \frac{\text{Costs of goods sold}}{\text{Average inventory}} = \frac{\$410,000}{\$215,000} = 1.19 \text{ times}$$

A lower-than-average inventory turnover ratio often indicates obsolete merchandise on hand or poor buying practices. Managers need to be aware of proper inventory control and anticipated inventory turnover to ensure proper performance. For example, have you ever worked as a food server in a restaurant like Very Vegetarian? How many times did your employer expect you to *turn over* a table (keep changing customers at the table) in an evening? The more times a table turns, the higher the return to the owner. Of course, like other ratios, rates of inventory turnover vary from industry to industry.

REACHING BEYOND
our borders

Accountants of the World United

Throughout this text you've read about the tremendous impact the global market has on business. U.S. companies like Coca-Cola earn the majority of their revenues from global markets, which helps their profitability but creates considerable accounting headaches. Since no global accounting system exists, multinationals like Coca-Cola must adapt their accounting procedures to different countries' rules. However, if the Financial Accounting Standards Board (FASB) in the United States and the London-based International Accounting Standards Board (IASB) get their way, that situation could change.

The governing bodies of the accounting profession have made significant progress toward integrating the U.S. accounting code with the International Financial Reporting Standards (IFRS) used around the world. The U.S. Securities and Exchange Commission (SEC) seems to support such a change and has suggested the IFRS replace the long standing generally accepted accounting principles (GAAP) in the near future. However, moving to one accounting standard is not likely to

happen before 2015 in order to allow companies and auditors in the United States ample time to prepare for the change. Many accountants also question if the international standards under IFRS would provide the same quality of financial reporting as the GAAP.

James Quigley, chief executive officer of Deloitte Touche Tohmatsu, one of the Big Four accounting firms in the United States, favors the move to IFRS. He believes that since we have global capital markets, we need global standards for accounting. Colleges and accounting firms across the country are waiting to see if they need to get ready for implementation of IFRS. Like it or not, it appears that IFRS is coming sooner or later to an accounting department near you.

Sources: Doug DeLoach, "IFRS: International Methods on Convergent Path," *Atlanta Business Chronicle*, January 14, 2011; "Global Accounting Standards Move Forward," *South Florida Business Journal*, April 21, 2011; and Adam Jones, "IASB Optimistic on U.S. Rules Timing, *The Financial Times*, April 22, 2011.

Accountants and other finance professionals use several other specific ratios, in addition to the ones we've discussed. To review where the accounting information in ratio analysis comes from, see Figure 17.9 on p. 485 for a quick reference. Remember, financial analysis begins where the accounting financial statements end.

Like other business disciplines, accounting is subject to change. Currently, the accounting profession is feeling the impact of the global market. The Reaching Beyond Our Borders box discusses a movement taking hold to globalize accounting procedures. It's something that accountants will be following closely. Before leaving this chapter, it's worth saying once more that, as the language of business, accounting is a worthwhile language to learn.

progress assessment

- What is the primary purpose of performing ratio analysis using the firm's financial statements?
- What are the four main categories of financial ratios?

summary

Learning Goal 1. Demonstrate the role that accounting and financial information play for a business and for its stakeholders.

- **What is accounting?**

Accounting is the recording, classifying, summarizing, and interpreting of financial events and transactions that affect an organization. The methods we use to record and summarize accounting data into reports are called an accounting system.

Learning Goal 2. Identify the different disciplines within the accounting profession.

- **How does managerial accounting differ from financial accounting?**

Managerial accounting provides information and analyses to managers within the firm to assist them in decision making. Financial accounting provides information and analyses to external users of data such as creditors and lenders.

- **What is the job of an auditor?**

Auditors review and evaluate the standards used to prepare a company's financial statements. An independent audit is conducted by a public accountant and is an evaluation and unbiased opinion about the accuracy of a company's financial statements.

- **What is the difference between a private accountant and a public accountant?**

A public accountant provides services for a fee to a variety of companies, whereas a private accountant works for a single company. Private and public accountants do essentially the same things with the exception of independent audits. Private accountants do perform internal audits, but only public accountants supply independent audits.

Learning Goal 3. List the steps in the accounting cycle, distinguish between accounting and bookkeeping, and explain how computers are used in accounting.

- **What are the six steps of the accounting cycle?**

The six steps of the accounting cycle are (1) analyzing documents; (2) recording information into journals; (3) posting that information into ledgers; (4) developing a trial balance; (5) preparing financial statements— the balance sheet, income statement, and statement of cash flows; and (6) analyzing financial statements.

- **What is the difference between bookkeeping and accounting?**

Bookkeeping is part of accounting and includes the systematic recording of data. Accounting includes classifying, summarizing, interpreting, and reporting data to management.

- **What are journals and ledgers?**

Journals are the first place bookkeepers record transactions. Bookkeepers then summarize journal entries by posting them to ledgers. Ledgers are specialized accounting books that arrange the transactions by homogeneous groups (accounts).

- **How do computers help accountants?**

Computers can record and analyze data and provide financial reports. Software can continuously analyze and test accounting systems to be sure they are functioning correctly. Computers can help decision making by providing appropriate information, but they cannot themselves make good financial decisions. Accounting applications and creativity are still human functions.

Learning Goal 4. Explain how the major financial statements differ.

* **What is a balance sheet?**
A balance sheet reports the financial position of a firm on a particular day. The fundamental accounting equation used to prepare the balance sheet is Assets = Liabilities + Owners' equity.
* **What are the major accounts of the balance sheet?**
Assets are economic resources owned by the firm, such as buildings and machinery. Liabilities are amounts the firm owes to creditors, bondholders, and others. Owners' equity is the value of everything the firm owns— its assets—minus any liabilities; thus, Owners' equity = Assets − Liabilities.
* **What is an income statement?**
An income statement reports revenues, costs, and expenses for a specific period of time (say, the year ended December 31, 2012). The formulas we use in preparing the income statement are:
* **Revenue − Cost of goods sold = Gross margin**
* **Gross margin − Operating expenses = Net income before taxes**
* **Net income before taxes − Taxes = Net income (or net loss)**
Net income or loss is also called the bottom line.
* **What is a statement of cash flows?**
Cash flow is the difference between cash receipts (money coming in) and cash disbursements (money going out). The statement of cash flows reports cash receipts and disbursements related to the firm's major activities: operations, investments, and financing.

Learning Goal 5. Demonstrate the application of ratio analysis in reporting financial information.

* **What are the four key categories of ratios?**
The four key categories of ratios are liquidity ratios, leverage (debt) ratios, profitability (performance) ratios, and activity ratios.
* **What is the major value of ratio analysis to the firm?**
Ratio analysis provides the firm with information about its financial position in key areas *for comparison to other firms in its industry and its own past performance.*

key terms

accounting 464
accounting cycle 470
accounts
  payable 474
annual report 466
assets 474
auditing 468
balance sheet 473
bonds payable 475
bookkeeping 470
cash flow 481
certified internal
  auditor (CIA) 469

certified management
  accountant (CMA) 466
certified public
  accountant (CPA) 467
cost of goods sold
  (or cost of goods
  manufactured) 476
current assets 474
depreciation 477
double-entry
  bookkeeping 470
financial accounting 466
financial statement 472

fixed assets 474
fundamental accounting
  equation 472
government and not-
  for-profit
  accounting 469
gross profit (or gross
  margin) 477
income statement 476
independent audit 468
intangible assets 474
journal 470
ledger 470

critical thinking

1. As a potential investor in a firm or perhaps the buyer of a particular business, would it be advisable to evaluate the company's financial statements? Why or why not? What key information would you seek from a firm's financial statements?

2. Why must accounting reports be prepared according to specific procedures (GAAP)? Should we allow businesses some flexibility or creativity in preparing financial statements? Why or why not?

3. What value do financial ratios offer investors in reviewing the financial performance of a firm?

4. Why is it important to remember financial ratios can differ from industry to industry?

developing workplace skills

1. Contact a CPA at a firm in your area, or talk with a CPA in your college's business department. Ask what challenges, changes, and opportunities he or she foresees in the accounting profession in the next five years. List the CPA's forecasts on a sheet of paper and then compare them with the information in this chapter.

2. Go to the websites of the American Institute of Certified Public Accountants (www.aicpa.org) and the Institute of Management Accountants (www.imanet.org). Browse the sites and find the requirements for becoming a certified public accountant (CPA) and a certified management accountant (CMA). Compare the requirements of the programs and decide which program is more appealing to you.

3. Suppose you are a new board member for an emerging not-for-profit organization hoping to attract new donors. Contributors want to know how efficiently not-for-profit organizations use their donations. Unfortunately, your fellow board members see little value in financial reporting and analysis and believe the good works of the organization speak for themselves. Prepare a fact sheet convincing the board of the need for effective financial reporting with arguments about why it helps the organization's fundraising goals.

4. Obtain a recent annual report for a company of your choice. (Hints: *The Wall Street Journal* has a free annual reports service, and virtually all major companies post their annual reports on their websites.) Look over the firm's financial statements and see whether they match the information in

this chapter. Read the auditor's opinion (usually at the end of the report) and evaluate what you think are the most important conclusions of the auditors.

5. Obtain a recent annual report for a company of your choice (see the hints just above in exercise 4) and try your hand at computing financial ratios. Compute the current ratio, debt to owners' equity ratio, and basic earnings per share ratio. Then request an annual report from one of the firm's major competitors and compute the same ratios for that company. What did you find?

taking it to the net

Purpose

To calculate and analyze the current and quick (acid-test) ratios of different businesses.

Exercise

Potz and Pans, a small gift shop, has current assets of $45,000 (including inventory valued at $30,000) and $9,000 in current liabilities. WannaBees, a specialty clothing store, has current assets of $150,000 (including inventory valued at $125,000) and $85,000 in current liabilities. Both businesses have applied for loans. Click the calculators box on the tool bar at www.bankrate.com and then go to small business to answer the following questions:

1. Calculate the current ratio for each company. Which company is more likely to get the loan? Why?

2. The acid-test ratio subtracts the value of the firm's inventory from its total current assets. Because inventory is often difficult to sell, this ratio is considered an even more reliable measure of a business's ability to repay loans than the current ratio. Calculate the acid-test ratio for each business and decide whether you would give either the loan? Why or why not?

casing the web

To access the case "Between a Rock and a Hard Rock," visit **www.mhhe.com/ubl0e**

video case

To access the video case featuring Goodwill, visit **www.mhhe.com/ubl0e**

Financial
MANAGEMENT

18

LEARNING goals

After you have read and studied this chapter, you should be able to

1 Explain the role and responsibilities of financial managers.

2 Outline the financial planning process, and explain the three key budgets in the financial plan.

3 Explain why firms need operating funds.

4 Identify and describe different sources of short-term financing.

5 Identify and describe different sources of long-term financing.

In the business world, just because you're on top today doesn't mean you'll be there tomorrow. Uncertainty abounds even at the nation's largest companies as the commercial landscape constantly changes. The savviest businesspeople are always on the lookout for new avenues of opportunity. After all, it's either that or get swept up in the tide.

Carol Tomé, Chief Financial Officer (CFO) at Home Depot, knows a thing or two about adapting to unforeseen circumstances. She first learned about the ins and outs of finance in her hometown of Jackson, Wyoming, where her father owned the Jackson State Bank. Tomé grew up assuming that one day she would become the first female CEO of the family business. Fate dropped a bombshell, however, while she was studying for an MBA at the University of Denver. Tomé's father informed her that after 27 years of marriage he would be divorcing her mother and selling the bank.

Though the news devastated Tomé, she didn't let it destroy her ambition. "When I calmed down, I said to myself, 'Carol, you are going to be a banker. So be a banker.'" She did exactly that, landing a job at the United Bank of Denver after graduation. She then moved on to a series of corporate finance jobs before ending up at Home Depot in 1995. By the time she worked her way up to CFO in 2001, the company was caught up in a store building frenzy. With Tomé in control of the expansion committee, Home Depot added more than 100 locations a year through 2005. "We were very much like that Kevin Costner movie: 'Build a store, and they will come,'" says Tomé.

But the company's obsession with expansion led it to neglect other key areas, primarily technology. Up until 2010 most Home Depot stores kept track of stock with 15-year-old computers, some powered by motorboat batteries set on bulky carts. The company was also slow to offer customers the option of ordering online and picking up the merchandise at a store, as its chief competitor Lowe's did. Even the product information the company offered on its website was minimal. With studies showing that 7 out of 10 consumers first check out products online before buying, Home Depot executives realized that their

reliance on aged technology was hurting sales and growth. It was clearly time for a change at the home improvement giant.

By focusing on improving its technological foothold rather than opening new stores, Home Depot's entire business plan shifted to improving sales at existing outlets. As CFO, Tomé was at the center of this transition. In 2010 she oversaw the distribution of $350 million in tech spending, $60 million of that money going to purchasing 40,000 handheld devices to replace the company's outdated in-store computers. The rest went toward beefing up online sales. Digital purchases accounted for a mere 1.5 percent of the $68 billion Home Depot made in 2010. By the end of that year Tomé unveiled a new purchasing app for iPhones and iPads, a technological triumph that not even Lowe's could match at the time. Still, to succeed in the future Tomé will need to strike a middle ground between Home Depot's new customers who shop online and the old contractors who prefer to shop in a store. Tomé will continue working to close that gap and ensure Home Depot's future dominance but, as she knows well already, nothing is certain.

Risk and uncertainty clearly define the role of financial management. In this chapter, you'll explore the role of finance in business. We'll discuss the challenges as well as the tools top managers like Carol Tomé use to attain financial stability and growth.

Sources: Chris Burritt, "Home Depot's Fix-It Lady," *Bloomberg Businessweek*, January 13, 2011; "Senior Leadership Team: Carol Tomé," Home Depot, corporate.homedepot.com, accessed May 2011; and Maxwell Murphy, "Home Depot Beats Sales, EPS Views, Raises Guidance," *The Wall Street Journal*, February 22, 2011.

profile

Getting to Know
X *Carol Tomé*
CFO of Home Depot

NAME THAT
company

At one time this company was the largest automobile maker in the world. Due to severe financial problems in 2009, the company came very close to extinction. A $7 billion government-backed loan and an additional $43 billion government investment in the company helped it survive. It is now attempting a comeback as a much smaller company. What is the name of this company? (Find the answer in the chapter.)

LEARNING goal **1**

Explain the role and responsibilities of financial managers.

THE ROLE OF FINANCE AND FINANCIAL MANAGERS

finance
The function in a business that acquires funds for the firm and manages those funds within the firm.

The goal of this chapter is to answer two major questions: "What is finance?" and "What do financial managers do?" **Finance** is the function in a business that acquires funds for the firm and manages them within the firm. Finance activities include preparing budgets; doing cash flow analysis; and planning for the expenditure of funds on such assets as plant, equipment, and machinery. **Financial management** is the job of managing a firm's resources to meet its goals and objectives. Without a carefully calculated financial plan, a firm has little chance for survival, regardless of its product or marketing effectiveness. Let's briefly review the roles of accountants and financial managers.

financial management
The job of managing a firm's resources so it can meet its goals and objectives.

We can compare an accountant to a skilled laboratory technician who takes blood samples and other measures of a person's health and writes the findings on a health report (in business, this process is the preparation of financial statements). A financial manager is like the doctor who interprets the report and makes recommendations that will improve the patient's health. In short, **financial managers** examine financial data prepared by accountants and recommend strategies for improving the financial performance of the firm.

financial managers
Managers who examine financial data prepared by accountants and recommend strategies for improving the financial performance of the firm.

Clearly financial managers can make sound financial decisions only if they understand accounting information. That's why we examined accounting in Chapter 17. Similarly, a good accountant needs to understand finance. Accounting and finance go together like peanut butter and jelly. In large and medium-sized organizations, both the accounting and finance functions are generally under the control of a chief financial officer (CFO).[1] However, financial management could also be in the hands of a person who serves as company treasurer or vice president of finance. A comptroller is the chief *accounting* officer.

Figure 18.1 highlights a financial manager's tasks. As you can see, two key responsibilities are to obtain funds and to effectively control the use of those funds. Controlling funds includes managing the firm's cash, credit accounts (accounts receivable), and inventory. Finance is a critical activity in both profit-seeking and nonprofit organizations.

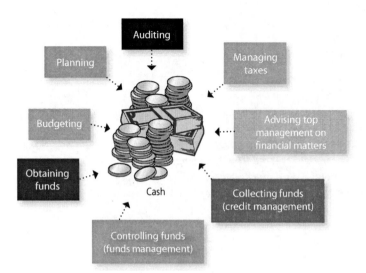

figure 18.1

WHAT FINANCIAL MANAGERS DO

Finance is important, no matter what the firm's size. As you may remember from Chapter 6, financing a small business is essential if the firm expects to survive its important first five years. But the need for careful financial management remains a challenge that any business, large or small, must face throughout its existence.[2] This is a lesson the U.S. businesses learned the hard way in the late 2000s when a financial crisis threatened the economy.[3]

General Motors, once the world's dominant automaker, faced extinction in 2009 because of severe financial problems. The company survived due to a direct government loan of $7 billion and an additional $43 billion in bailout funds provided by the U.S. Treasury.[4] (The $43 billion gave the government a 60 percent ownership stake in the company.) That same year, the government also approved an $85 billion loan to save insurance giant American International Group (AIG) and passed the $700 billion Troubled Assets Relief Program (TARP) to help restore confidence in the financial system.[5]

The Value of Understanding Finance

Three of the most common reasons a firm fails financially are:

1. Undercapitalization (insufficient funds to start the business).
2. Poor control over cash flow.
3. Inadequate expense control.

You can see all three in the following classic story:

Two friends, Elizabeth Bertani and Pat Sherwood, started a company called Parsley Patch on what can best be described as a shoestring budget. It began when Bertani prepared

Michael Miller overhauled the underperforming Goodwill Industries operation in Portland, Oregon, by treating the nonprofit like a for-profit business. He trimmed operating expenses 30 percent by comparing sales by store, closing weak outlets and opening new ones in better locations, and cutting distribution costs. Sales soared from $4 million to over $50 million.

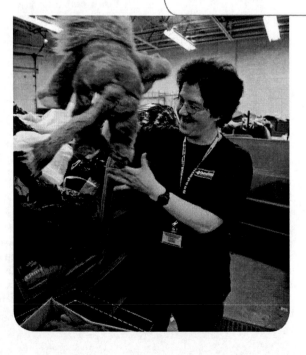

salt-free seasonings for her husband, who was on a no-salt diet. Her friend Sherwood thought the seasonings were good enough to sell. Bertani agreed, and Parsley Patch Inc. was born. The business began with an investment of $5,000 that was rapidly depleted on a logo and label design. Bertani and Sherwood quickly learned about the need for capital in getting a business going. Eventually, they invested more than $100,000 of their own money to keep the business from being undercapitalized.

Everything started well, and hundreds of gourmet shops adopted the product line. But when sales failed to meet expectations, the women decided the health-food market offered more potential because salt-free seasonings were a natural for people with restricted diets. The choice was a good one. Sales soared, approaching $30,000 a month. Still, the company earned no profits.

Bertani and Sherwood weren't trained in monitoring cash flow or in controlling expenses. In fact, they were told not to worry about costs, and they hadn't. They eventually hired a certified public accountant (CPA) and an experienced financial manager, who taught them how to compute the costs of their products, and how to control expenses as well as cash moving in and out of the company (cash flow). Soon Parsley Patch was earning a comfortable margin on operations that ran close to $1 million a year. Luckily, the owners were able to turn things around before it was too late. Eventually, they sold the firm to spice and seasonings giant McCormick.[6]

If Bertani and Sherwood had understood finance before starting their business, they might have been able to avoid the problems they encountered. The key word here is *understood*. You do not have to pursue finance as a career to understand it. Financial understanding is important to anyone who wants to start a small business, invest in stocks and bonds, or plan a retirement fund. In short, finance and accounting are two areas everyone in business should study. Since we discussed accounting in Chapter 17, let's look more closely at what financial management is all about.

What Is Financial Management?

Financial managers are responsible for paying the company's bills at the appropriate time, and for collecting overdue payments to make sure the company does not lose too much money to bad debts (people or firms that don't pay their bills). Therefore, finance functions, such as buying merchandise on credit (accounts payable) and collecting payment from customers (accounts receivable), are key components of the financial manager's job.[7] While these functions are vital to all types of businesses, they are particularly critical to small and medium-sized businesses, which typically have smaller cash or credit cushions than large corporations.

Most businesses have predictable day-to-day needs, like the need to buy supplies, pay for fuel and utilities and pay employees. Financial management is the function that helps ensure firms have the funds they need when they need them. What would happen to the company providing the work in this photo if it couldn't buy fuel for its trucks?

It's essential that financial managers stay abreast of changes or opportunities in finance, such as changes in tax law, since taxes represent an outflow of cash from the business.[8] Financial managers must also analyze the tax implications of managerial decisions to minimize the taxes the business must pay. Usually a member of the firm's finance department, the internal auditor, also checks the journals, ledgers, and financial statements the accounting department prepares, to make sure all transactions are in accordance with generally accepted accounting principles (GAAP). Without such audits, accounting statements would be less reliable. Therefore, it is important that internal auditors be objective and critical of any improprieties or deficiencies noted in their evaluation.[9] Thorough internal audits assist the firm in financial planning, which we'll look at next.[10]

LEARNING goal **2**

> Outline the financial planning process, and explain the three key budgets in the financial plan.

FINANCIAL PLANNING

Financial planning means analyzing short-term and long-term money flows to and from the firm.[11] Its overall objective is to optimize the firm's profitability and make the best use of its money. It has three steps: (1) forecasting the firm's short-term and long-term financial needs, (2) developing budgets to meet those needs, and (3) establishing financial controls to see whether the company is achieving its goals (see Figure 18.2). Let's look at each step and the role it plays in improving the organization's financial health.

Forecasting Financial Needs

Forecasting is an important part of any firm's financial plan.[12] A **short-term forecast** predicts revenues, costs, and expenses for a period of one year or less. Part of the short-term forecast may be a **cash flow forecast**, which predicts the cash inflows and outflows in future periods, usually months or quarters. The

short-term forecast
Forecast that predicts revenues, costs, and expenses for a period of one year or less.

cash flow forecast
Forecast that predicts the cash inflows and outflows in future periods, usually months or quarters.

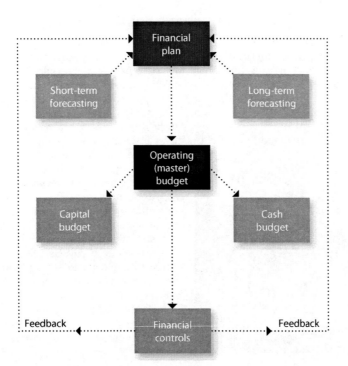

figure 18.2

FINANCIAL PLANNING
Note the close link between financial planning and budgeting.

inflows and outflows of cash recorded in the cash flow forecast are based on expected sales revenues and various costs and expenses incurred, as well as when they are due for payment. The company's sales forecast estimates projected sales for a particular period. A business often uses its past financial statements as a basis for projecting expected sales and various costs and expenses.

A **long-term forecast** predicts revenues, costs, and expenses for a period longer than 1 year, sometimes as long as 5 or 10 years. This forecast plays a crucial part in the company's long-term strategic plan, which asks questions such as: What business are we in? Should we be in it five years from now? How much money should we invest in technology and new plant and equipment over the next decade? Will we have cash available to meet long-term obligations? Innovations in Web-based software help financial managers address these long-term forecasting questions.

The long-term financial forecast gives top management, as well as operations managers, some sense of the income or profit potential of different strategic plans.[13] It also helps in preparing company budgets.

Working with the Budget Process

A **budget** sets forth management's expectations for revenues and, on the basis of those expectations, allocates the use of specific resources throughout the firm. As a financial plan, it depends heavily on the accuracy of the firm's balance sheet, income statement, statement of cash flows, and short-term and long-term financial forecasts, which all need to be as accurate as possible. To prepare budgets, financial managers must therefore take their forecasting responsibilities seriously.[14] A budget becomes the primary guide for the firm's financial operations and expected financial needs.

There are usually several types of budgets in a firm's financial plan:

- A capital budget.
- A cash budget.
- An operating or master budget.

Let's look at each.

A **capital budget** highlights a firm's spending plans for major asset purchases that often require large sums of money, like property, buildings, and equipment.

A **cash budget** estimates cash inflows and outflows during a particular period, like a month or a quarter. It helps managers anticipate borrowing needs, debt repayment, operating expenses, and short-term investments, and is often the last budget prepared. A sample cash budget for our example company, Very Vegetarian, is provided in Figure 18.3.

The **operating (or master) budget** ties together the firm's other budgets and summarizes its proposed financial activities. More formally, it estimates costs and expenses needed to run a business, given projected revenues. The firm's spending on supplies, travel, rent, technology, advertising, and salaries is determined in the operating budget, generally the most detailed a firm prepares.

Financial planning obviously plays an important role in the firm's operations and often determines what long-term investments it makes, when it will need specific funds, and how it will generate them. Once a company forecasts its short-term and long-term financial needs and compiles budgets to show how it will allocate funds, the final step in financial planning is to establish financial controls. Before we talk about those, however, Figure 18.4 on p. 500 challenges you to check your personal financial-planning skill by developing a monthly budget for "You Incorporated."

long-term forecast
Forecast that predicts revenues, costs, and expenses for a period longer than 1 year, and sometimes as far as 5 or 10 years into the future.

budget
A financial plan that sets forth management's expectations and, on the basis of those expectations, allocates the use of specific resources throughout the firm.

capital budget
A budget that highlights a firm's spending plans for major asset purchases that often require large sums of money.

cash budget
A budget that estimates cash inflows and outflows during a particular period like a month or a quarter.

operating (or master) budget
The budget that ties together the firm's other budgets and summarizes its proposed financial activities.

VERY VEGETARIAN
Monthly Cash Budget

figure 18.3

A SAMPLE CASH BUDGET FOR
VERY VEGETARIAN

	January	February	March
Sales forecast	$50,000	$45,000	$40,000
Collections			
Cash sales (20%)		$ 9,000	$ 8,000
Credit sales (80% of past month)		$40,000	$ 36,000
Monthly cash collection		$49,000	$44,000
Payments schedule			
Supplies and material		$ 11,000	$ 10,000
Salaries		12,000	12,000
Direct labor		9,000	9,000
Taxes		3,000	3,000
Other expenses		7,000	6,000
Monthly cash payments		$42,000	$39,000
Cash budget			
Cash flow		$ 7,000	$ 5,000
Beginning cash		−1,000	6,000
Total cash		$ 6,000	$ 11,000
Less minimum cash balance		−6,000	−6,000
Excess cash to market securities		$ 0	$ 5,000
Loans needed for minimum balance		0	0

Establishing Financial Controls

Financial control is a process in which a firm periodically compares its actual revenues, costs, and expenses with its budget. Most companies hold at least monthly financial reviews as a way to ensure financial control. Such control procedures help managers identify variances to the financial plan and allow them to take corrective action if necessary. Financial controls also help reveal which specific accounts, departments, and people are varying from the financial plan. Finance managers can judge whether these variances are legitimate and thereby merit adjustments to the plan. Shifts in the economy or unexpected global events can also alter financial plans. For example, unrest in the Middle East and the spike in oil prices in 2011 caused many companies to consider adjusting their financial plans.[15] The Legal Briefcase box on p. 501 highlights how one state is implementing financial control to deal with severe financial problems. After the Progress Assessment, we'll see why firms need readily available funds.

financial control
A process in which a firm periodically compares its actual revenues, costs, and expenses with its budget.

progress assessment

- Name three finance functions important to the firm's overall operations and performance.
- What three primary financial problems cause firms to fail?
- How do short-term and long-term financial forecasts differ?
- What is the purpose of preparing budgets in an organization? Can you identify three different types of budgets?

	EXPECTED	ACTUAL	DIFFERENCE
Monthly income			
Wages (net pay after taxes)	_____	_____	_____
Savings account withdrawal	_____	_____	_____
Family support	_____	_____	_____
Loans	_____	_____	_____
Other sources	_____	_____	_____
Total monthly income	_____	_____	_____
Monthly expenses			
Fixed expenses			
Rent or mortgage	_____	_____	_____
Car payment	_____	_____	_____
Health insurance	_____	_____	_____
Life insurance	_____	_____	_____
Tuition or fees	_____	_____	_____
Other fixed expenses	_____	_____	_____
Subtotal of fixed expenses	_____	_____	_____
Variable expenses			
Food	_____	_____	_____
Clothing	_____	_____	_____
Entertainment	_____	_____	_____
Transportation	_____	_____	_____
Phone	_____	_____	_____
Utilities	_____	_____	_____
Publications	_____	_____	_____
Internet connection	_____	_____	_____
Cable television	_____	_____	_____
Other expenses	_____	_____	_____
Subtotal of variable expenses	_____	_____	_____
Total expenses	_____	_____	_____
Total income − Total expenses = Cash on hand/(Cash deficit)	_____	_____	_____

figure 18.4

YOU INCORPORATED MONTHLY BUDGET

In Chapter 17, you compiled a sample balance sheet for You Inc. (see p. 475). Now, let's develop a monthly budget for You Inc. Be honest and think of everything that needs to be included for an accurate monthly budget for You!

LEARNING goal 3

Explain why firms need operating funds.

THE NEED FOR OPERATING FUNDS

In business, the need for operating funds never seems to end. That's why sound financial management is essential to all businesses. And like our personal financial needs, the capital needs of a business change over time. Remember the example of Parsley Patch to see why a small business's financial requirements can shift considerably. The same is true for large corporations such as Apple, Johnson & Johnson, and Nike when they venture into new-product

LEGAL briefcase

Financial Order or Financial Martial Law?

The recession that began in 2008 not only brought tough economic times to millions of Americans; it also exposed severe economic problems in many of the governments of the states and cities where they live. Perhaps nowhere has the economic fallout been more severe than in Michigan where half of the state's communities are in financial distress. These severe financial problems led the state to pass the Local Government and School District Fiscal Accountability Act that allows cities, towns, and school districts to be taken over by state-appointed emergency financial managers (EFMs) selected by the Governor. The emergency managers have broad and far-reaching powers that allow them to void union contracts and in some instances remove elected officials. Supporters of the program insist that a number of struggling communities have been saved from bankruptcy by the actions of the EFMs. Others claim the Governor has become a dictator and has imposed nothing short of martial law.

According to the Governor's office the intention of the law is to protect the health, welfare, and safety of local government. In many instances it blames the financial shortcomings facing many communities on elected officials who were unwilling or unable to address the financial problems they faced. Michael Imber, of accounting firm Grant Thornton, supports the law and believes that many of the same techniques and processes used to bring private sector businesses back on firm financial footing can be used to get communities back on track as well. Directors of big public pension funds in Detroit are not so sure and have filed a lawsuit testing the law's constitutionality.

It's likely that EFMs will expand beyond Michigan. Indiana is considering similar legislation to create its own version of EFMs. In New York and several other states, receivers and oversight boards have been given similar power to EFMs to bring financial stability back to local communities. Whether EFMs are the financial solutions distressed communities need remains to be seen. One thing is for certain: responsible financial management is something that cannot be ignored.

Sources: "Bankrupt Cities Using Emergency Financial Managers to Recover," ABCNews.com, accessed May 2011; Jeff Green and Jonathan Keehner, "Muni Bankruptcy Threat Makes Michigan Train Financial SWAT Team," *Bloomberg Businessweek,* April 18, 2011; John F. Mogk, "Emergency Manager Law No Mistake," *The Detroit News,* April 15, 2011; and Susan Berfield, "Michigan's Extreme Measures," *Bloomberg Businessweek,* May 8, 2011.

---

areas or new markets. Virtually all organizations have operational needs for which they need funds. Key areas include:

- Managing day-by-day needs of the business.
- Controlling credit operations.
- Acquiring needed inventory.
- Making capital expenditures.

Let's look carefully at the financial needs of these key areas, which affect both the smallest and the largest of businesses.

Managing Day-by-Day Needs of the Business

If workers expect to be paid on Friday, they don't want to wait until Monday for their paychecks. If tax payments are due on the 15th of the month, the government expects the money on time. If the interest payment on a business loan is due on the 30th of this month, the lender doesn't mean the 1st of next month. As you can see, funds have to be available to meet the daily operational costs of the business.

Financial managers must ensure that funds are available to meet daily cash needs without compromising the firm's opportunities to invest money for its future.[16] Money has a *time value*. In other words, if someone offered to give you $200 either today or one year from today, you would benefit by taking the $200 today. Why? It's very simple. You could invest the $200 you receive today and over a year's time it would grow. The same is true in business; the interest a firm gains on its investments is important in maximizing the profit it will gain. That's why financial managers often try to minimize cash expenditures to free up funds for investment in interest-bearing accounts. They suggest the company pay its bills as late as possible (unless a cash discount is available for early payment). They also advise companies to try to collect what's owed them as fast as possible, to maximize the investment potential of the firm's funds.[17] Efficient cash management is particularly important to small firms since their access to capital is much more limited than larger businesses. Software from companies like Peachtree can assist small firms in handling day-to-day cash management.

Controlling Credit Operations

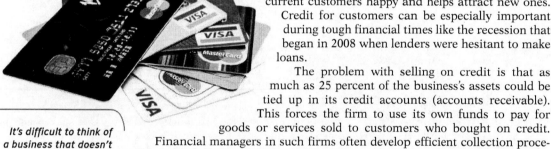

Financial managers know that in today's highly competitive business environment making credit available helps keep current customers happy and helps attract new ones. Credit for customers can be especially important during tough financial times like the recession that began in 2008 when lenders were hesitant to make loans.

The problem with selling on credit is that as much as 25 percent of the business's assets could be tied up in its credit accounts (accounts receivable). This forces the firm to use its own funds to pay for goods or services sold to customers who bought on credit.

Financial managers in such firms often develop efficient collection procedures, like offering cash or quantity discounts to buyers who pay their accounts by a certain time. They also scrutinize old and new credit customers to see whether they have a history of meeting credit obligations on time.

One convenient way to decrease the time and expense of collecting accounts receivable is to accept bank credit cards such as MasterCard or Visa. The banks that issue these cards have already established the customer's creditworthiness, which reduces the business's risk. Businesses must pay a fee to accept credit cards, but they are usually offset by the benefits.[18]

It's difficult to think of a business that doesn't make credit available to its customers. However, collecting accounts receivable can be time-consuming and expensive. Accepting credit cards such as Visa, MasterCard, and American Express can simplify transactions for sellers and guarantee payment. What types of products do you regularly purchase with a credit card?

Acquiring Needed Inventory

As we saw in Chapter 13, effective marketing requires focusing on the customer and providing high-quality service and readily available goods. A carefully constructed inventory policy helps manage the firm's available funds and maximize profitability. Doozle's, an ice cream parlor in St. Louis, Missouri, deliberately ties up fewer funds in its inventory of ice cream in winter. It's obvious why: demand for ice cream is lower in winter.

Just-in-time inventory control (see Chapter 9) and other such methods can reduce the funds a firm must tie up in inventory. Carefully evaluating its inventory turnover ratio (see Chapter 17) can also help a firm control the outflow of cash for inventory. A business of any size must understand that poorly managed inventory can seriously affect cash flow and drain its finances dry.[19] The nearby Making Ethical Decisions box raises an

MAKING
ethical decisions

Good Finance or Bad Medicine?

Imagine that you have just earned your business degree and have been hired as a hospital administrator at a small hospital that, like many others, is experiencing financial problems. Having studied finance, you know that efficient cash management is important to all firms in all industries to meet the day-by-day operations of the firm. One way to ensure such efficiency is to use a carefully planned and managed inventory control system that can reduce the amount of cash an organization has tied up in inventory. Being familiar with just-in-time inventory, you know it is a proven system that helps reduce the costs of managing inventory.

At a meeting of the hospital's executive committee you recommend that the hospital save money by using a just-in-time inventory system to manage its drug supply. You suggest discontinuing the hospital's large stockpile of drugs, especially expensive cancer treatment drugs that tie up a great deal of the hospital's cash and shift to ordering them just when they are needed. Several members seem to like the idea, but the doctors in charge of practicing medicine and oncology are outraged, claiming you are sacrificing patients' well-being for cash. After debate, the committee says the decision is up to you. What will you do? What could result from your decision?

interesting question about sound financial management and inventory control in a critical industry.

Making Capital Expenditures

Capital expenditures are major investments in either tangible long-term assets such as land, buildings, and equipment, or intangible assets such as patents, trademarks, and copyrights. In many organizations the purchase of major assets—such as land for future expansion, manufacturing plants to increase production capabilities, research to develop new-product ideas, and equipment to maintain or exceed current levels of output—is essential. Expanding into new markets can be expensive with no guarantee of success. Therefore, it's critical that companies weigh all possible options before committing a large portion of available resources.

Consider a firm that needs to expand its production capabilities due to increased customer demand. It could buy land and build a new plant, purchase an existing plant, or rent space. Can you think of financial and accounting considerations at play in this decision?

The need for operating funds raises several questions for financial managers: How does the firm obtain funds to finance operations and other business needs? Will it require specific funds in the long or the short term? How much will it cost (i.e. interest) to obtain these funds? Will they come from internal or external sources? We address these questions next.

capital expenditures
Major investments in either tangible long-term assets such as land, buildings, and equipment or intangible assets such as patents, trademarks, and copyrights.

Alternative Sources of Funds

We described finance earlier as the function in a business responsible for acquiring and managing funds. Sound financial management determines the amount of money needed and the most appropriate sources from which to obtain it. A firm can raise needed capital by borrowing money (debt), selling

figure 18.5

WHY FIRMS NEED FUNDS

SHORT-TERM FUNDS	LONG-TERM FUNDS
Monthly expenses	New-product development
Unanticipated emergencies	Replacement of capital equipment
Cash flow problems	Mergers or acquisitions
Expansion of current inventory	Expansion into new markets (domestic or global)
Temporary promotional programs	New facilities

debt financing
Funds raised through various forms of borrowing that must be repaid.

equity financing
Money raised from within the firm, from operations or through the sale of ownership in the firm (stock or venture capital).

short-term financing
Funds needed for a year or less.

long-term financing
Funds needed for more than a year (usually 2 to 10 years).

ownership (equity), or earning profits (retained earnings).[20] **Debt financing** refers to funds raised through various forms of borrowing that must be repaid. **Equity financing** is money raised from within the firm, from operations or through the sale of ownership in the firm (stock). Firms can borrow funds either short-term or long-term. **Short-term financing** refers to funds needed for a year or less. **Long-term financing** covers funds needed for more than a year (usually 2 to 10 years). Figure 18.5 highlights why firms may need short-term and long-term funds.

We'll explore the different sources of short- and long-term financing next. Let's first pause to check your understanding by doing the Progress Assessment.

progress assessment

- Money has time value. What does this mean?
- Why is accounts receivable a financial concern to the firm?
- What's the primary reason an organization spends a good deal of its available funds on inventory and capital expenditures?
- What's the difference between debt and equity financing?

LEARNING goal **4**

Identify and describe different sources of short-term financing.

OBTAINING SHORT-TERM FINANCING

The bulk of a finance manager's job does not relate to obtaining *long-term* funds. In small businesses, for example, long-term financing is often out of the question. Instead, day-to-day operations call for the careful management of *short-term* financial needs. Firms may need to borrow short-term funds for purchasing additional inventory or for meeting bills that come due unexpectedly. Like an individual, a business, especially a small business, sometimes needs to secure short-term funds when its cash reserves are low. Let's see how it does so.

Trade Credit

trade credit
The practice of buying goods and services now and paying for them later.

Trade credit is the practice of buying goods or services now and paying for them later. It is the most widely used source of short-term funding, the least expensive, and the most convenient.[21] Small businesses rely heavily on trade credit from firms such as United Parcel Service, as do large firms such as Kmart or Macy's. When a firm buys merchandise, it receives an invoice (a bill) much like the one you receive when you buy something with a credit card. As you'll see, however, the terms businesses receive are often different from those on your monthly statement.

Business invoices often contain terms such as *2/10, net 30*. This means the buyer can take a 2 percent discount for paying the invoice within 10 days. Otherwise the total bill (net) is due in 30 days. Finance managers pay close attention to such discounts because they create opportunities to reduce the firm's costs. Think about it for a moment: If the terms are 2/10, net 30, the customer will pay 2 percent more by waiting an extra 20 days to pay the invoice. If the firm *can* pay its bill within 10 days, it is needlessly increasing its costs by not doing so.

Some suppliers hesitate to give trade credit to an organization with a poor credit rating, no credit history, or a history of slow payment. They may insist the customer sign a **promissory note**, a written contract with a promise to pay a supplier a specific sum of money at a definite time. Promissory notes are negotiable. The supplier can sell them to a bank at a discount (the amount of the promissory note less a fee for the bank's services in collecting the amount due) and the business is then responsible to pay the bank.

promissory note
A written contract with a promise to pay a supplier a specific sum of money at a definite time.

Family and Friends

As we discussed in Chapter 17, firms often have several bills coming due at the same time with no sources of funds to pay them. Many small firms obtain short-term funds by borrowing money from family and friends. Such loans can create problems, however, if all parties do not understand cash flow. That's why it's sometimes better, when possible, to go to a commercial bank that fully understands the business's risk and can help analyze its future financial needs rather than borrow from friends or relatives.

Entrepreneurs appear to be listening to this advice. According to the National Federation of Independent Business, entrepreneurs today are relying less on family and friends as a source of borrowed funds than they have in the past.[22] If an entrepreneur decides to ask family or friends for financial assistance, it's important that both parties (1) agree to specific loan terms, (2) put the agreement in writing, and (3) arrange for repayment in the same way they would for a bank loan. Such actions help keep family relationships and friendships intact.[23]

One thing you can never have too much of is cash. Financial managers must make certain there is enough cash available to meet daily financial needs and still have funds to invest in its future. What does it mean when we say cash has time value?

Commercial Banks

Banks, being sensitive to risk, generally prefer to lend short-term money to larger, established businesses. Imagine the different types of businesspeople who go to banks for a loan, and you'll get a better idea of the requests bankers evaluate. Picture, for example, a farmer going to the bank in spring to borrow funds for seed, fertilizer, equipment, and other needs that will be repaid after the fall harvest. Or consider a local toy store buying merchandise for Christmas sales. The store borrows the money for such purchases in the summer and plans to pay it back after Christmas. Restaurants often borrow funds at the beginning of the month and pay at the end of the month.

How much a business borrows and for how long depends on the kind of business it is, and how quickly it can resell the merchandise

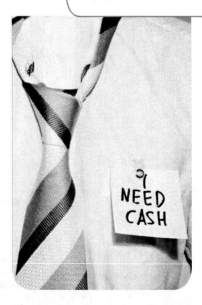

Did you ever wonder how retail stores get the money to buy all the treasures we splurge on during the holidays? Department stores and other large retailers make extensive use of commercial banks and other lenders to borrow the funds they need to buy merchandise and stock their shelves. How do the stores benefit from using this type of financing?

it purchases with a bank loan or use it to generate funds. In a large business, specialists in a company's finance and accounting departments do a cash flow forecast.[24] Small-business owners generally lack such specialists and must monitor cash flow themselves.

The financial crisis beginning in 2008 severely curtailed bank lending to small businesses. It was difficult for even a promising and well-organized small business to obtain a bank loan. Fortunately, the situation seems to be changing.[25] What's important for a small firm to remember is if it gets a bank loan, the owner or person in charge of finance should keep in close touch with the bank and send regular financial statements to keep the bank up-to-date on its operations. The bank may spot cash flow problems early or be more willing to lend money in a crisis if the business has established a strong relationship built on trust and sound management. The Spotlight on Small Business highlights the problems and opportunities small businesses face in attempting to secure financing.

Different Forms of Short-Term Loans

secured loan
A loan backed by collateral, something valuable such as property.

Commercial banks offer different types of short-term loans. A **secured loan** is backed by *collateral*, something valuable such as property. If the borrower fails to pay the loan, the lender may take possession of the collateral. An automobile loan is a secured loan. If the borrower doesn't repay it, the lender will repossess the car. Inventory of raw materials like coal and steel often serves as collateral for business loans. Collateral removes some of the bank's risk in lending the money.

Accounts receivable are company assets often used as collateral for a loan; this process is called *pledging* and works as follows: A percentage of the value of a firm's accounts receivable pledged (usually about 75 percent) is advanced to the borrowing firm.[26] As customers pay off their accounts, the funds received are forwarded to the lender in repayment of the funds that were advanced.

SPOTLIGHT ON SMALL
business

www.lendingclub.com

Exploring the Financing Universe

Many small businesses had limited access to financing during the recession that began in 2008. Unfortunately, small businesses across the nation are still in a death struggle to stay afloat as many don't qualify for bank loans and financing through alternative sources is very expensive. Estimates are that less than one-third of small business owners qualify for traditional bank or SBA loans. Over 55 percent of small-business owners seek financing through a patchwork of sources such as factoring, unsecured lines of credit, and credit cards that can cost 20 percent or higher. The remaining 15 percent of small businesses are often ineligible for any financing at all.

Securing capital is the lifeblood to launching and expanding a small business. While often attempts at securing financing can be frustrating and fruitless, with some research and dedicated effort small businesses may find unexpected sources of financing. *Peer-to-peer lending* sites like Lending Club match small businesses with lenders and receive a fee for their services. Lending Club borrowers apply on line through a free application process in which they supply information about the company and explain exactly why the funds they are requesting are needed. Unfortunately, only about 10 percent of

the requests receive funding, but those that do receive their financing quickly. *Crowdfunding* pools a large number of small loans (or some may say donations) from backers who do not expect to get interest or even their investment back. Instead they receive some type of "reward" if the business succeeds.

Small businesses can also turn to *fee-based services* like Lendio to seek a financing match for their business. Lendio claims to have developed a technology that matches business owners with the right type of business loan and lender. The company also offers services such as a business plan makeover and website design for a fee. Lendio does not guarantee funding for its clients. Small businesses are advised to carefully research fee-based companies before paying for services. With 50 percent of GDP and 60 to 80 percent of new jobs created by small business, the need for small business financing remains critical to the economy.

Sources: Laura Petrecca, "Crowdfunding and Peer-to-Peer Lending Help Small Businesses," *USA Today,* May 9, 2011; Emily Maltby, "Costly Financing Only Choice for Most Small Firms," *The Wall Street Journal,* May 6, 2011; and Helen Coster, "Pay to Play," *Forbes,* March 14, 2011.

An **unsecured loan** is more difficult to obtain because it doesn't require any collateral. Normally, lenders give unsecured loans only to highly regarded customers—long-standing businesses or those considered financially stable.

If a business develops a strong relationship with a bank, the bank may open a **line of credit** for the firm, a given amount of unsecured short-term funds a bank will lend to a business, provided the funds are readily available. A line of credit is *not* guaranteed to a business. However, it speeds up the borrowing process since a firm does not have to apply for a new loan every time it needs funds. As businesses mature and become more financially secure, banks will often increase their line of credit. Some even offer a **revolving credit agreement**, a line of credit that's guaranteed but usually comes with a fee. Both lines of credit and revolving credit agreements are particularly good sources of funds for unexpected cash needs.[27]

If a business is unable to secure a short-term loan from a bank, the financial manager may seek short-term funds from **commercial finance companies**. These non-deposit-type organizations make short-term loans to borrowers who offer tangible assets like property, plant, and equipment as collateral. Commercial finance companies will often make loans to businesses that cannot get short-term funds elsewhere. Since commercial finance companies assume higher degrees of risk than commercial banks, they usually charge higher interest rates. General Electric Capital is one of the world's

unsecured loan
A loan that doesn't require any collateral.

line of credit
A given amount of unsecured short-term funds a bank will lend to a business, provided the funds are readily available.

revolving credit agreement
A line of credit that's guaranteed but usually comes with a fee.

commercial finance companies
Organizations that make short-term loans to borrowers who offer tangible assets as collateral.

A secured loan is backed by collateral, a tangible item of value. A car loan, for instance, is a secured loan in which the car itself is the collateral. What is the collateral in a mortgage loan?

largest commercial finance companies, with $576 billion in assets and operations in over 50 countries around the world.[28]

Factoring Accounts Receivable

factoring
The process of selling accounts receivable for cash.

One relatively expensive source of short-term funds for a firm is **factoring**, the process of selling accounts receivable for cash. Factoring dates as far back as 4,000 years, during the days of ancient Babylon. Here's how it works: Let's say a firm sells many of its products on credit to consumers and other businesses, creating a number of accounts receivable. Some buyers may be slow in paying their bills, so a large amount of money is due the firm. A *factor* is a market intermediary (usually a financial institution or a commercial bank) that agrees to buy the firm's accounts receivable, at a discount, for cash.[29] The discount depends on the age of the accounts receivable, the nature of the business, and the condition of the economy. When it collects the accounts receivable that were originally owed to the firm, the factor keeps them.

While factors charge more than banks' loan rates, remember many small businesses cannot qualify for a loan. So even though factoring is an expensive way of raising short-term funds, it is popular among small businesses.[30] A company can often reduce its factoring cost if it agrees to reimburse the factor for slow-paying accounts, or to assume the risk for customers who don't pay at all. Remember factoring is not a loan; it is the sale of a firm's asset (accounts receivable). Factoring is common in the clothing and furniture businesses, and in growing numbers of global trade ventures.[31]

Commercial Paper

commercial paper
Unsecured promissory notes of $100,000 and up that mature (come due) in 270 days or less.

Often a corporation needs funds for just a few months and prefers not to have to negotiate with a commercial bank. One strategy available to larger firms is to sell commercial paper. **Commercial paper** consists of *unsecured* promissory notes, in amounts of $100,000 and up, that mature or come due in 270 days or less. Commercial paper states a fixed amount of money the business agrees to repay to the lender (investor) on a specific date at a specified rate of interest.

Because commercial paper is unsecured, only financially stable firms (mainly large corporations with excellent credit reputations) are able to sell it. Commercial paper can be a quick path to short-term funds at lower interest than charged by commercial banks. Even very stable firms, however, had trouble selling commercial paper during the financial crisis. The Federal Reserve stepped in and assisted many companies with their short-term financing by purchasing their short-term commercial paper. Since most commercial paper matures in 30 to 90 days, it can be an investment opportunity for buyers who can afford to put up cash for short periods to earn some interest on their money.

Credit Cards

According to the National Small Business Association (NSBA), nearly half of all small firms now use credit cards to finance their businesses. Even though more businesses are turning to credit cards for financing, two-thirds believe the terms of their cards are getting worse and it's very likely they are correct. When the Credit Card Responsibility Accountability and Disclosure Act of 2009 was passed, it reduced consumer interest rates and approved many protections for consumers against card-company abuses. Unfortunately rates for small business credit cards increased almost 30 percent since small businesses did not fall under the protection of the law.[32] Still with many traditional financing options closed to them, entrepreneurs are being forced to finance their firms with credit cards.

Credit cards provide a readily available line of credit that can save time and the likely embarrassment of being rejected for a bank loan. Of course, in contrast to the convenience they offer, credit cards are extremely risky and costly. Interest rates can be exorbitant, and there can be considerable penalties if users fail to make their payments on time. Savvy businesspersons study the perks that are offered with many cards and determine which might be the most beneficial to their companies. Joe Speiser, of pet-food distributor Petflow.com, found a cash-back card that helped put additional dollars back into his business.[33] Still, when dealing with credit cards remember it's an expensive way to borrow money and credit cards are probably best used as a last resort.

After checking your progress below, we'll look into long-term financing options.

progress assessment

- What does an invoice containing the terms *2/10, net 30* mean?
- What's the difference between trade credit and a line of credit?
- What's the key difference between a secured and an unsecured loan?
- What is factoring? What are some of the considerations factors consider in establishing their discount rate?

LEARNING goal 5

Identify and describe different sources of long-term financing.

OBTAINING LONG-TERM FINANCING

In a financial plan, forecasting determines the amount of funding the firm will need over various periods and the most appropriate sources for obtaining those funds. In setting long-term financing objectives, financial managers generally ask three questions:

1.   What are our organization's long-term goals and objectives?
2.   What funds do we need to achieve the firm's long-term goals and objectives?
3.   What sources of long-term funding (capital) are available, and which will best fit our needs?

Firms need long-term capital to purchase expensive assets such as plant and equipment, to develop new products, or perhaps finance their expansion. In major corporations, the board of directors and top management usually make decisions about long-term financing, along with finance and accounting executives. Pfizer, one of the world's largest research-based biomedical and pharmaceutical company, spends over $9 billion a year researching and developing new products. The development of a single new drug could take 10 years and cost the firm close to $1.3 billion before it brings in any profit.[34] It's easy to see why high-level managers make the long-term financing decisions at Pfizer. Owners of small- and medium-sized businesses are almost always actively engaged in analyzing their long-term financing decisions.

As we noted earlier, long-term funding comes from two major sources, debt financing and equity financing. Let's look at these sources next.

Debt Financing

Debt financing is borrowing money the company has a legal obligation to repay. Firms can borrow by either getting a loan from a lending institution or issuing bonds.

term-loan agreement
A promissory note that requires the borrower to repay the loan in specified installments.

Debt Financing by Borrowing from Lending Institutions
Long-term loans are usually due within 3 to 7 years but may extend to 15 or 20 years. A **term-loan agreement** is a promissory note that requires the borrower to repay the loan with interest in specified monthly or annual installments. A major advantage is that the interest is tax deductible.

Long-term loans are both larger and more expensive to the firm than short-term loans. Since the repayment period can be quite long, lenders assume more risk and usually require collateral, which may be real estate, machinery, equipment, company stock, or other items of value. Lenders may also require certain restrictions to force the firm to act responsibly. The interest rate is based on the adequacy of collateral, the firm's credit rating, and the general level of market interest rates. The greater the risk a lender takes in making a loan, the higher the rate of interest. This principle is known as the **risk/return trade-off**.

risk/return trade-off
The principle that the greater the risk a lender takes in making a loan, the higher the interest rate required.

indenture terms
The terms of agreement in a bond issue.

Debt Financing by Issuing Bonds
If an organization is unable to obtain its long-term financing needs by getting a loan from a lending institution it may try to issue bonds. To put it simply, a bond is like an IOU with a promise to repay the amount borrowed, with interest, on a certain date. The terms of the agreement in a bond issue are the **indenture terms**. The types of organizations that can issue bonds include federal, state, and local governments; federal government agencies; foreign governments; and corporations.

Major League Baseball is a big business, and building a new stadium requires big dollars. When the St. Louis Cardinals needed financing to replace their old stadium with a new state-of-the-art facility, St. Louis County issued bonds that helped finance the construction of the Cardinals' new home. What organizations in your community have issued bonds, and for what purpose?

You may already be familiar with bonds. You may own investments like U.S. government savings bonds, or perhaps you volunteered your time to help a local school district pass a bond issue. If your community is building a new stadium or cultural center, it may sell bonds to finance the project. Businesses and governments compete when issuing bonds. Potential investors (individuals and institutions) measure the risk of purchasing a bond against the return the bond promises to pay—the interest—and the issuer's ability to repay when promised.

Like other forms of long-term debt, bonds can be secured or unsecured. A **secured bond** is issued with some form of collateral, such as real estate, equipment, or other pledged assets. If the bond's indenture terms are violated (e.g., not paying interest payments), the bondholder can issue a claim on the collateral. An **unsecured bond**, called a debenture bond, is backed only by the reputation of the issuer. Investors in such bonds simply trust that the organization issuing the bond will make good on its financial commitments.

Bonds are a key means of long-term financing for many organizations. They can also be valuable investments for private individuals or institutions. Given this importance, we will discuss bonds in depth in Chapter 19.

secured bond
A bond issued with some form of collateral.

unsecured bond
A bond backed only by the reputation of the issuer; also called a debenture bond.

Equity Financing

If a firm cannot obtain a long-term loan from a lending institution or is unable to sell bonds to investors, it may seek equity financing. Equity financing makes funds available when the owners of the firm sell shares of ownership to outside investors in the form of stock, when they reinvest company earnings in the business, or obtain funds from venture capitalists.

Equity Financing by Selling Stock   The key thing to remember about stock is that stockholders become owners in the organization. Generally, the corporation's board of directors decides the number of shares of stock that will be offered to investors for purchase. The first time a company offers to sell its stock to the general public is called an *initial public offering (IPO)*.[35] Selling stock to the public to obtain funds is by no means easy or automatic. U.S.

PART 6 ✳ **Managing Financial Resources**

John Krech created an inventory management product that he believed would sell well if he could find the money to bring it to market. When credit grew tight in the recent financial crisis, Krech sold his home and tapped his retirement funds to obtain start-up money for his new venture. Why is this financing strategy considered risky?

venture capital
Money that is invested in new or emerging companies that are perceived as having great profit potential.

companies can issue stock for public purchase only if they meet requirements set by the U.S. Securities and Exchange Commission (SEC) and various state agencies. They can offer different types of stock such as common and preferred. We'll discuss IPOs and common and preferred stock in depth in Chapter 19.

Equity Financing from Retained Earnings You probably remember from Chapter 17 that the profits the company keeps and reinvests in the firm are called *retained earnings*. Retained earnings often are a major source of long-term funds, especially for small businesses. They often have fewer financing alternatives, such as selling stock or bonds, than large businesses do. However, large corporations also depend on retained earnings for needed long-term funding. In fact, retained earnings are usually the most favored source of meeting long-term capital needs. A company that uses them saves interest payments, dividends (payments for investing in stock), and any possible underwriting fees for issuing bonds or stock. Retained earnings also create no new ownership in the firm, as stock does.

Suppose you wanted to buy an expensive personal asset such as a new car. Ideally you would go to your personal savings account and take out the necessary cash. No hassle! No interest! Unfortunately, few people have such large amounts of cash available. Most businesses are no different. Even though they would like to finance long-term needs from operations (retained earnings), few have the resources available to accomplish this.

Equity Financing from Venture Capital The hardest time for a business to raise money is when it is starting up or just beginning to expand. A start-up business typically has few assets and no market track record, so the chances of borrowing significant amounts of money from a bank are slim. **Venture capital** is money invested in new or emerging companies that some investors— venture capitalists—believe have great profit potential. Venture capital helped firms like Intel, Apple, and Cisco Systems get started and let Facebook and Google expand and grow. Venture capitalists invest in a business in return for part ownership of the business. They expect higher-than-average returns and competent management performance for their investment.

The venture capital industry originally began as an alternative investment vehicle for wealthy families. The Rockefeller family, for example (whose vast fortune came from John D. Rockefeller's Standard Oil Company, started in the 19th century), financed Sanford McDonnell when he was operating his company from an airplane hangar. That small venture eventually grew into McDonnell Douglas, a large aerospace and defense contractor that merged with Boeing Corporation in 1997. The venture capital industry grew significantly in the 1990s, especially in high-tech centers like California's Silicon Valley, where venture capitalists concentrated on Internet-related companies. In the early 2000s, problems in the technology industry and a slowdown in the overall economy reduced venture capital expenditures. The recent financial crisis caused venture capital spending to drop to new lows. However, as the economy began to grow in 2011, venture capital again returned to the market.[36]

Comparing Debt and Equity Financing

Figure 18.6 compares debt and equity financing options. Raising funds through borrowing to increase the firm's rate of return is referred to as **leverage**. Though debt increases risk because it creates a financial obligation that must be repaid, it also enhances the firm's ability to increase profits. Recall that two key jobs of the financial manager or CFO are forecasting the firm's need for borrowed funds and planning how to manage these funds once they are obtained.

Firms are very concerned with the cost of capital. **Cost of capital** is the rate of return a company must earn in order to meet the demands of its lenders and expectations of its equity holders (stockholders or venture capitalists). If the firm's earnings are larger than the interest payments on borrowed funds, business owners can realize a higher rate of return than if they used equity financing. Figure 18.7 on p. 514 describes an example, again involving our vegetarian restaurant, Very Vegetarian (introduced in Chapter 13). If Very Vegetarian needed $200,000 in new financing, it could consider debt by selling bonds or equity through offering stock. Comparing the two options in this situation, you can see that Very Vegetarian would benefit by selling bonds since the company's earnings are greater than the interest paid on borrowed funds (bonds). However, if the firm's earnings were less than the interest paid on borrowed funds (bonds), Very Vegetarian could lose money. It's also important to remember that bonds, like all debt, have to be repaid at a specific time.

Individual firms must determine exactly how to balance debt and equity financing by comparing the costs and benefits of each. Leverage ratios (discussed in Chapter 17) can also give companies an industry standard for this balance, to which they can compare themselves. Still debt varies considerably among major companies and industries. For example, automaker Ford Motor Company has almost $100 billion of debt on its balance sheet. This seems mild compared to General Electric that has over $400 billion of debt on theirs.[37] Leisure industry giants Sands and Trump Hotels and Casinos carry billions of dollars of debt to finance their hotels, condos, and golf courses. In contrast, tech leaders Apple and Microsoft have no long-term debt and both have had almost $50 billion in cash available at times. According to Standard & Poor's and Moody's Investor Services (firms that provide corporate and financial research), the debt of a large industrial corporation typically ranges between 33 and 40 percent of its total assets. The amount of small-business debt obviously varies considerably from firm to firm.

leverage
Raising needed funds through borrowing to increase a firm's rate of return

cost of capital
The rate of return a company must earn in order to meet the demands of its lenders and expectations of its equity holders.

figure 18.6
DIFFERENCES BETWEEN DEBT AND EQUITY FINANCING

	Type of Financing	
CONDITIONS	**DEBT**	**EQUITY**
Management influence	There's usually none unless special conditions have been agreed on.	Common stockholders have voting rights.
Repayment	Debt has a maturity date. Principal must be repaid.	Stock has no maturity date. The company is never required to repay equity.
Yearly obligations	Payment of interest is a contractual obligation.	The firm isn't legally liable to pay dividends.
Tax benefits	Interest is tax deductible.	Dividends are paid from after-tax income and aren't deductible.

figure 18.7

USING LEVERAGE (DEBT) VERSUS EQUITY FINANCING
Very Vegetarian wants to raise $200,000 in new capital. Compare the firm's debt and equity options.

ADDITIONAL DEBT		ADDITIONAL EQUITY	
Stockholders' equity	$500,000	Stockholders' equity	$500,000
Additional equity	—	Additional equity	$200,000
Total equity	$500,000	Total equity	$700,000
Bond @ 8% interest	200,000	Bond interest	—
Total shareholder equity	$700,000	Total shareholder equity	$700,000

YEAR-END EARNINGS			
Gross profit	$100,000	Gross profit	$100,000
Less bond interest	−16,000	Less interest	—
Operating profit	$84,000	Operating profit	$100,000
Return on equity	16.6%	Return on equity	14.2%
($84,000 ÷ $500,000 = 16.6%)		($100,000 ÷ $700,000 = 14.2%)	

Lessons from the Financial Crisis

The financial crisis that started in 2008 caused financial markets to suffer their worst fall since the Great Depression of the 1920s and 1930s. The collapse of financial markets could be laid at the feet of financial managers for failing to do their job effectively. Poor investment decisions and risky financial dealings (especially in real estate) caused long-standing financial firms such as Lehman Brothers to close their doors.[38] The multibillion-dollar Ponzi scheme of once respected financial manager Bernie Madoff further caused the public's trust in financial managers to disappear.[39] Unfortunately, it also caused many investors' funds to disappear as well.

The financial meltdown of the late 2000s led the U.S. Congress to pass sweeping financial regulatory reform. The Dodd-Frank Wall Street Reform and Consumer Protection Act affects almost every aspect of the U.S. financial services industry.[40] As the government increases its involvement and intervention in financial markets, the requirements of financial institutions and financial managers have become more stringent. This means that the job of the financial manager promises to become even more challenging. The events in late 2000s questioned the integrity and good judgment of financial managers much like events in the early 2000s questioned the integrity and judgment of the accounting industry (see Chapter 17). Without a doubt, financial managers have a long road back to earning the trust of the public.

Chapter 19 takes a close look at securities markets as a source of securing long-term financing for businesses and as a base for investment options for private investors. You will learn how securities exchanges work, how firms issue stocks and bonds, how to choose the right investment strategy, how to buy and sell stock, where to find up-to-date information about stocks and bonds, and more. Finance takes on a new dimension when you see how you can participate in financial markets yourself.

progress assessment

- What are the two major forms of debt financing available to a firm?
- How does debt financing differ from equity financing?
- What are the three major forms of equity financing available to a firm?
- What is leverage, and why do firms choose to use it?

summary

Learning Goal 1. Explain the role and responsibilities of financial managers.
- **What are the most common ways firms fail financially?**

The most common financial problems are (1) undercapitalization, (2) poor control over cash flow, and (3) inadequate expense control.
- **What do financial managers do?**

Financial managers plan, budget, control funds, obtain funds, collect funds, conduct audits, manage taxes, and advise top management on financial matters.

Learning Goal 2. Outline the financial planning process, and explain the three key budgets in the financial plan.
- **What are the three budgets in a financial plan?**

The capital budget is the spending plan for expensive assets such as property, plant, and equipment. The cash budget is the projected cash balance at the end of a given period. The operating (master) budget summarizes the information in the other two budgets. It projects dollar allocations to various costs and expenses given various revenues.

Learning Goal 3. Explain why firms need operating funds.
- **What are firms' major financial needs?**

Businesses need financing for four major tasks: (1) managing day-by-day operations, (2) controlling credit operations, (3) acquiring needed inventory, and (4) making capital expenditures.
- **What's the difference between debt financing and equity financing?**

Debt financing raises funds by borrowing. Equity financing raises funds from within the firm through investment of retained earnings, sale of stock to investors, or sale of part ownership to venture capitalists.
- **What's the difference between short-term and long-term financing?**

Short-term financing raises funds to be repaid in less than a year, whereas long-term financing raises funds to be repaid over a longer period.

Learning Goal 4. Identify and describe different sources of short-term financing.
- **Why should businesses use trade credit?**

Trade credit is the least expensive and most convenient form of short-term financing. Businesses can buy goods today and pay for them sometime in the future.
- **What is meant by a line of credit and a revolving credit agreement?**

A line of credit is an agreement by a bank to lend a specified amount of money to the business at any time, if the money is available. A revolving credit agreement is a line of credit that guarantees a loan will be available— for a fee.
- **What's the difference between a secured loan and an unsecured loan?**

An unsecured loan has no collateral backing it. Secured loans have collateral backed by assets such as accounts receivable, inventory, or other property of value.
- **Is factoring a form of secured loan?**

No, factoring means selling accounts receivable at a discounted rate to a factor (an intermediary that pays cash for those accounts and keeps the funds it collects on them).
- **What's commercial paper?**

Commercial paper is a corporation's unsecured promissory note maturing in 270 days or less.

Learning Goal 5. Identify and describe different sources of long-term financing.

- **What are the major sources of long-term financing?**

Debt financing is the sale of bonds to investors and long-term loans from banks and other financial institutions. Equity financing is obtained through the sale of company stock, from the firm's retained earnings, or from venture capital firms.

- **What are the two major forms of debt financing?**

Debt financing comes from two sources: selling bonds and borrowing from individuals, banks, and other financial institutions. Bonds can be secured by some form of collateral or unsecured. The same is true of loans.

- **What's leverage, and how do firms use it?**

Leverage is borrowing funds to invest in expansion, major asset purchases, or research and development. Firms measure the risk of borrowing against the potential for higher profits.

key terms

budget 498	**finance** 494	**revolving credit agreement** 507
capital budget 498	**financial control** 499	**risk/return trade-off** 510
capital expenditures 503	**financial management** 494	**secured bond** 511
cash budget 498	**financial managers** 494	**secured loan** 506
cash flow forecast 497	**indenture terms** 510	**short-term financing** 504
commercial finance companies 507	**leverage** 513	**short-term forecast** 497
commercial paper 508	**line of credit** 507	**term-loan agreement** 510
cost of capital 513	**long-term financing** 504	**trade credit** 504
debt financing 504	**long-term forecast** 498	**unsecured bond** 511
equity financing 504	**operating (or master) budget** 498	**unsecured loan** 507
factoring 508	**promissory note** 505	**venture capital** 512

critical thinking

1. What are the primary sources of short-term funds for new business owners? What are their sources of long-term funds?

2. Why does a finance manager need to understand accounting information if the firm has a trained accountant on its staff?

3. Why do firms generally prefer to borrow funds to obtain long-term financing rather than issue shares of stock?

developing workplace skills

1. Go to your college's website and see whether its operating budget is online. If not, go to the campus library and see whether the reference librarian has a copy of your college's operating budget for the current year. Try to identify major capital expenditures your college has planned for the future.

2. One of the most difficult concepts to get across to small-business owners is the need to take all the trade credit they can get. For example, the credit terms 2/10, net 30 can save businesses money if they pay their bills in the first 10 days. Work with a group of classmates to build a convincing argument for using trade credit.

3. Go online and check the capitalization required to open a franchise of your choice, like Subway or McDonald's. Does the franchisor offer financial assistance to prospective franchisees? Evaluate the cost of the franchise versus its business potential using the risk/return trade-off discussed in the chapter.

4. Contact a lending officer at a local bank in your community, or visit the bank's website, to check the bank's policies on providing a business a line of credit and a revolving line of credit. Evaluate the chances that this bank will give a small business either form of short-term loan.

5. Factoring accounts receivable is a form of financing used since the days of Babylonian King Hammurabi 4,000 years ago. Today it's still a source of short-term funds used by small businesses. Visit www.21stfinancialsolutions.com to get more in-depth information about factoring and be prepared to discuss the pros and cons of factoring.

taking it to the net

Purpose

To identify which types of companies qualify for financing through the Small Business Administration.

Exercise

Many small-business owners have a difficult time finding financing to start or expand their business. The Small Business Administration is one potential source of financing for many types of small businesses, but there are also some businesses that do not qualify for SBA loans. Go to www.sba.gov/content/businesses-eligible-ineligible-sba-assistance and see whether the following businesses are eligible to apply for SBA financing:

1. Growing Like a Weed is a lawn care business that needs funding to buy additional equipment in order to expand. Does it meet SBA criteria? Why or why not?

2. Glamour Galore is a cosmetic company that pays sales commissions based on a system that depends upon salespeople recruiting additional salespeople. It needs funding to build a marketing campaign. Does it meet SBA criteria? Why or why not?

3. Bells'n'Whistles is a pinball refurbishing company. Its founding partners need funding to buy inventory. Do they meet SBA criteria? Why or why not?

4. Lettuce Entertain You is a company needing funding to remodel an old warehouse to house its latest restaurant. Does it meet SBA criteria? Why or why not?

casing the web

To access the case "Surviving Financially in the Nonprofit World," visit
www.mhhe.com/ubl0e

video case

To access the video case featuring Tom & Eddie's, visit **www.mhhe.com/ubl0e**

USING Securities Markets for Financing & Investing Opportunities

19

LEARNING goals

After you have read and studied this chapter, you should be able to

1 Describe the role of securities markets and of investment bankers.

2 Identify the stock exchanges where securities are traded.

3 Compare the advantages and disadvantages of equity financing by issuing stock, and detail the differences between common and preferred stock.

4 Compare the advantages and disadvantages of obtaining debt financing by issuing bonds, and identify the classes and features of bonds.

5 Explain how to invest in securities markets and set

investment objectives such as long-term growth, income, cash, and protection from inflation.

6 Analyze the opportunities stocks offer as investments.

7 Analyze the opportunities bonds offer as investments.

8 Explain the investment opportunities in mutual funds and exchange-traded funds (ETFs).

9 Describe how indicators like the Dow Jones Industrial Average affect the market.

profile

In some ways, investing has become almost too easy today. Anybody with an e-mail address and a bank account can open an account with an online brokerage like E-Trade or Schwab and instantly start trading stocks from around the world. At the same time, though, the tangle of toxic investments that fueled the economic meltdown beginning in 2008 taught many investors just how complicated the financial world can be.

Many people hoping to find ways to better understand investing have turned to media such as CNBC to help guide them through the sea of easily available information. CNBC's multiple Emmy Award–winning Maria Bartiromo's accessible analysis of the day-to-day intricacies of Wall Street has made her the face of investing for millions of Americans. A recent study of Bartiromo's CNBC peers, both men and women, found that many are inclined to stir up media stunts that cause investors to sell their stocks. Bartiromo, on the other hand, uses her well-earned "street cred" wisely and incites far fewer sells than her colleagues. And in a 24-hour news cycle that sometimes resembles a circus more than actual journalism, Bartiromo's integrity is all the more valuable.

Born and raised in Brooklyn, Bartiromo spent her youth working in the coat checkroom of her family's Italian restaurant. Eventually she made it to the kitchen, where she closely observed her father's dogged work ethic as head chef. "Every day, I witnessed my father dedicate himself and his life to his family," said Bartiromo. "He'd regularly work long hours, day after day and he never complained." After graduating from New York University, Bartiromo brought that same dedication to her work as an overnight producer at CNN. Though her responsibilities were limited strictly to behind the camera, she quietly began gathering taped segments of herself as anchor in her off hours. None of these pieces ever made it to air, but they were promising enough to land her a job at CNBC.

After working for two years at the network, Bartiromo distinguished herself by becoming the first journalist to broadcast directly from the hectic floor of the New York Stock Exchange. By the late 1990s she was a CNBC fixture, earning the nickname the "Money Honey." But Bartiromo is far more than a pretty face in an anchor's chair. Her dislike for sensationalism and her candid interviews with everyone from former General Electric CEO Jack Welch to Bono made her a top draw at the station. By the 2000s she was lead anchor at two of the network's biggest shows, *Closing Bell* and *The Wall Street Journal Report with Maria Bartiromo.* She has written several books and numerous columns and articles in publications such as *Businessweek, Milano Finanza, Individual Investor, Ticker, Financial Times, Newsweek,* and the *New York Post.* In 2009, the *Financial Times* named her one of the "50 Who Shaped the Decade." In 2011 she was the first journalist to be inducted into the Cable Hall of Fame.

When the stock market tanked in 2008, Bartiromo provided front-line insight on the extent of the crisis. Her lengthy relationship with the NYSE gave her a unique perspective on events.

Also, her years of experience helped translate the complicated technical language and concepts of the financial sector into more digestible terms. As she watched Wall Street burn around her, Bartiromo felt saddened for her investment friends who were losing their jobs in droves. Still, she did not fail to recognize those unethical individuals who managed to profit from the crisis. "At the heart of everything on Wall Street has to be integrity," said Bartiromo. "I am outraged to see some of these executives walk away with giant pay packages . . . however, I also believe that an across-the-board, blanket statement that all business is 'bad' is just not true." To be a successful investor, you need a little education. In this chapter you'll learn about the many ways that money can be invested in securities markets.

Getting to Know

X *Maria Bartiromo*

CNBC Financial Analyst

Sources: Michael Martin, "How Maria Bartiromo May Become the Best Teacher You've Ever Had," *The Huffington Post,* April 15, 2010; Kristina Peterson, "CNBC CEO Chats Seldom Break News: Study," *The Wall Street Journal,* February 17, 2011; and "Maria Bartiromo" CNBC TV Profiles, http://www.cnbc.com/id/15838253, accessed May 2011.

NAME THAT company

When the price of their stock rises to a certain level, many companies will split the stock (i.e., exchanging two shares worth $50 for each original share worth $100) in order to make the stock appear more affordable. However, this company, run by America's most successful investor, has never split its stock even when the price of the company's stock reached $150,000 a share (that's right $150,000 for one share). What is the name of this company? (Find the answer in the chapter.)

initial public offering (IPO)
The first public offering of a corporation's stock.

David and Tom Gardner, the Motley Fools, are passionate about spreading the message that securities markets can provide opportunities for all. The brothers have built their careers on providing high-quality financial information to investors regardless of education or income. Visit their web site at www.fool.com for more information.

LEARNING goal 1

Describe the role of securities markets and of investment bankers.

THE FUNCTION OF SECURITIES MARKETS

Securities markets—financial marketplaces for stocks, bonds, and other investments—serve two major functions. First, they assist businesses in finding long-term funding to finance capital needs, such as expanding operations, developing new products, or buying major goods and services. Second, they provide private investors a place to buy and sell securities (investments) such as stocks and bonds that can help them build their financial future. In this chapter, we look at securities markets first from the perspective of funding for businesses and second as markets for private investors to buy and trade investments.

Securities markets are divided into primary and secondary markets. *Primary markets* handle the sale of *new* securities. This is an important point to understand. Corporations make money on the sale of their securities (stock) only once—when they sell it on the primary market. The first public offering of a corporation's stock is called an **initial public offering (IPO)**. After that, the *secondary market* handles the trading of these securities between investors, with the proceeds of the sale going to the investor selling the stock, not to the corporation whose stock is sold. For example, imagine your vegetarian restaurant, Very Vegetarian, has grown into a chain and your products are available in many retail stores throughout the country. You want to raise additional funds to expand further. If you offer 1 million shares of stock in your company at $10 a share, you can raise $10 million at this initial offering. However, after the initial sale, if Shareholder Jones decides to sell 100 shares of her Very Vegetarian stock to Investor Smith, Very Vegetarian collects nothing from that transaction. Smith buys the stock from Jones, not from Very Vegetarian. It is possible, however, for companies like Very Vegetarian to offer additional shares of stock for sale to raise additional capital.

As mentioned in Chapter 18, we can't overemphasize the importance of long-term funding to businesses. Given a choice, businesses normally prefer to meet their long-term financial needs by using retained earnings or borrowing funds either from a lending institution (bank, pension fund, insurance company) or corporate bond issue. However, if long-term funds are not available from retained earnings or lenders, a company may be able to raise capital by issuing corporate stock. (Recall from Chapter 18 that selling stock in the corporation is a form of *equity financing* and issuing corporate bonds is a form of *debt financing*.) Social networking giants Groupon and Facebook are expected to have initial public offerings in 2011 that will raise billions for the companies.[1] Visa, the world's largest processor of debit and credit cards, raised $18 billion from its IPO in 2008; Facebook is expected to dwarf that amount.[2] These sources of equity and bond financing are not available to all companies, especially small businesses.

Let's imagine you need further long-term financing to *expand* operations at Very Vegetarian. Your chief financial officer (CFO) says the company lacks sufficient retained earnings and she doesn't think it can secure the needed funds from a lending institution. She suggests that you offer shares of stock or issue corporate bonds to private investors to secure the funding. She warns, however, that issuing shares of stock or corporate bonds is not simple or automatic. To get approval for stock or bond issues you must make extensive financial disclosures and undergo detailed scrutiny by the U.S. Securities and Exchange Commission (SEC). Because of these requirements, your CFO recommends that the company turn to an investment banker for assistance. Let's see why.

The Role of Investment Bankers

Investment bankers are specialists who assist in the issue and sale of new securities. These large financial firms can help companies like Very Vegetarian prepare the extensive financial analyses necessary to gain SEC approval for bond or stock issues. Investment bankers can also *underwrite* new issues of stocks or bonds. That is, the investment banking firm buys the entire stock or bond issue at an agreed-on discount, which can be quite sizable, and then sells the issue to private or institutional investors at full price.[3]

Institutional investors are large organizations—such as pension funds, mutual funds, and insurance companies—that invest their own funds or the funds of others. Because of their vast buying power, institutional investors are a powerful force in securities markets.

Before we look at stocks and bonds as long-term financing and investment opportunities in more depth, it's important to understand stock exchanges—the places where stocks and bonds are traded.

> **investment bankers**
> Specialists who assist in the issue and sale of new securities.

> **institutional investors**
> Large organizations—such as pension funds, mutual funds, and insurance companies—that invest their own funds or the funds of others.

LEARNING goal **2**

Identify the stock exchanges where securities are traded.

STOCK EXCHANGES

As the name implies, a **stock exchange** is an organization whose members can buy and sell (exchange) securities on behalf of companies and individual investors. The New York Stock Exchange (NYSE) was founded in 1792 and was primarily a floor-based exchange, which means trades physically took place on the floor of the stock exchange. Things changed in 2005 when the NYSE

> **stock exchange**
> An organization whose members can buy and sell (exchange) securities for companies and individual investors.

The NYSE Euronext was the largest floor-based exchange. Stock trades were made on the crowded floor of the exchange. Today stocks are bought and sold primarily on electronic networks. The illustration (on the right) of the exchange floor that will be completed in 2012 seems deserted compared to the old days.

over-the-counter (OTC) market
Exchange that provides a means to trade stocks not listed on the national exchanges.

NASDAQ
A nationwide electronic system that links dealers across the nation so that they can buy and sell securities electronically.

merged with Archipelago, a securities trading company that specialized in electronic trades. Two years later, it merged with Europe's Euronext exchange, and became the NYSE Euronext. In 2011, the NYSE Euronext agreed to be acquired by Deutsche Borse AG of Germany in a deal valued at approximately $10 billion.[4]

Today, the floor of the NYSE Euronext is now largely symbolic.[5] Most trading takes place on computers that can transact thousands of stock trades within seconds.[6] In fact, trading stocks has become a very small part of the exchange's revenue. The bulk of the company's revenue comes from selling complex financial contracts and market information to companies like Yahoo and Google that offer stock quotes as a service on their websites.[7] They also earn revenue from fees paid by over 8,000 companies to be listed on the NYSE Euronext.[8]

Not all securities are traded on registered stock exchanges. The **over-the-counter (OTC) market** provides companies and investors with a means to trade stocks not listed on the large securities exchanges. The OTC market is a network of several thousand brokers who maintain contact with one another and buy and sell securities through a nationwide electronic system. Trading is conducted between two parties directly, instead of through an exchange like the NYSE Euronext.

The **NASDAQ** (originally known as the National Association of Securities Dealers Automated Quotations) was the world's first electronic stock market. It evolved from the OTC market but is no longer part of it. The NASDAQ is an electronic-based network that links dealers so they can buy and sell securities electronically rather than in person. In 2007, the NASDAQ purchased the Swedish OMX Group and is now the NASDAQ OMX Group.[9] It is the largest U.S. electronic stock trading market and has more trading volume than any electronic exchange in the world. The NASDAQ originally dealt mostly with smaller firms, but today well-known companies such as Microsoft, Intel, Google, Starbucks, Cisco, and Dell trade their stock on the NASDAQ. The NASDAQ also handles federal, state, and city government bonds and lists approximately 3,000 companies.

Adding a company to an exchange is a highly competitive undertaking, and the battle between the stock exchanges for a stock listing is often fierce.[10] If a company fails to meet the requirements of an exchange, the stock can be de-listed from the exchange.[11] You can find the requirements for registering (listing) stocks on the NYSE Euronext and NASDAQ in their websites www.nyse.com and www.nasdaq.com. The nearby Spotlight on Small Business box presents an interesting idea of adding a new exchange for smaller businesses to the securities landscape.

SPOTLIGHT ON SMALL business

A Place for Small Companies to Call Home

Since the beginning of the financial crisis in 2008, small businesses have found it difficult, if not impossible, to secure financing from banks. Even the old "air-ball loans" that banks would grant to businesses they had a personal relationship with disappeared. David Weild, former vice-chairman of NASDAQ, thinks he has a solution to this problem. He would like to see the creation of a new stock exchange where small companies can raise needed capital.

Weild's suggested exchange would move slower than the large exchanges that rely on electronic trading, and it would cost more to buy and sell a stock. It would also involve a larger role for stockbrokers who would go back to the old days of calling clients about new companies they have discovered that offer investment potential. To lure stockbrokers into the exchange, he would consider setting minimum and maximum brokerage commissions to make their efforts worthwhile. He also feels the exchange would be a source for attracting venture capitalists.

While Weild's proposed exchange is a new idea in the United States, it's important to note that China recently established the ChiNext stock exchange that is designed for start-up companies. The ChiNext was created as part of the Shenzhen exchange with the purpose of making it easier for "strategically important emerging companies" to gain access to capital. Liu Zehui, executive director of Legend Capital, feels the ChiNext exchange is doing exactly what it's intended to do. "The ChiNext market has released the pent-up passion for innovation and entrepreneurship in China," he says. "It tells everyone that you don't have to have a powerful dad to get rich."

Sources: Kevin Hamlin, Eva Woo, Dexter Roberts, and Frances Liu, "In China, a Stock Market Where Start-Ups Thrive," *Bloomberg Businessweek,* November 28, 2010; Reinhardt Krause, "China, Emerging-Market Stocks Rising, but Experts Still Cautious," *Investor's Business Daily,* April 7, 2011; and Emily Lambert, "Trading Places," *Forbes,* April 11, 2011.

Securities Regulations and the Securities and Exchange Commission

The **Securities and Exchange Commission (SEC)** is the federal agency responsible for regulating the various stock exchanges. The Securities Act of 1933 helps protect investors by requiring full disclosure of financial information by firms selling bonds or stock. The U.S. Congress passed this legislation to deal with the free-for-all atmosphere that existed in the securities markets during the 1920s and the early 1930s that helped cause the Great Depression. The Securities and Exchange Act of 1934 created the SEC.

Companies trading on the national exchanges must register with the SEC and provide it with annual updates. The 1934 act also established specific guidelines that companies must follow when issuing financial securities such as stocks or bonds. For example, before issuing either stocks or bonds for sale to the public, a company must file a detailed registration statement with the SEC that includes extensive economic and financial information. The condensed version of that registration document—called a **prospectus**—must be sent to prospective investors.

The 1934 act also established guidelines to prevent insiders within the company from taking advantage of privileged information they may have. *Insider trading* is using knowledge or information that individuals gain through

Securities and Exchange Commission (SEC)
The federal agency that has responsibility for regulating the various stock exchanges.

prospectus
A condensed version of economic and financial information that a company must file with the SEC before issuing stock; the prospectus must be sent to prospective investors.

figure 19.1

IS IT INSIDER TRADING OR NOT?

Insider trading involves buying or selling a stock on the basis of company information not available to the investing public. It's sometimes difficult to identify insider trading. The following hypothetical examples will give you an idea of what's legal and what's illegal. See how many of the questions you can answer. The answers are at the end of this box.

1. You work in research and development at a large company and have been involved in a major effort that should lead to a blockbuster new product coming to the market. News about the product is not public, and very few other workers even know about it. Can you purchase stock in the company?

2. Pertaining to the above situation, you are in a local coffee bar and mention to a friend about what's going on at the company. Another customer seated at an adjoining table overhears your discussion. Can this person legally buy stock in the company before the public announcement?

3. You work as an executive secretary at a major investment banking firm. You are asked to copy documents that detail a major merger about to happen that will keenly benefit the company being taken over. Can you buy stock in the company before the announcement is made public?

4. Your stockbroker recommends that you buy shares in a little-known company. The broker seems to have some inside information, but you don't ask any questions about his source. Can you buy stock in this company?

5. You work as a cleaning person at a major securities firm. At your job you come across information from the trash cans and computer printers of employees of the firm that provide detailed information about several upcoming deals the firm will be handling. Can you buy stock in the companies involved?

Answers: 1. No; 2. Yes; 3. No; 4. Yes; 5. No.

their position that allows them to benefit unfairly from fluctuations in security prices. The key words here are *benefit unfairly*. Insiders within a firm are permitted to buy and sell stock in the company they work for, so long as they do not take unfair advantage of information unknown to the public.

Originally, the SEC defined the term *insider* rather narrowly as covering a company's directors and employees and their relatives. Today the term has been broadened to include just about anyone with securities information not available to the general public. Let's say the CFO of Very Vegetarian tells her next-door neighbor she is finalizing paperwork to sell the company to a large corporation, and the neighbor buys the stock based on this information. A court may well consider the purchase an insider trade. Penalties for insider trading can include fines or imprisonment. For example, billionaire hedge fund manager Raj Rajaratnam was convicted of insider trading in a high profile case in 2011 and could face up to 200 years in prison.[12] Look at Figure 19.1 and test your skill in identifying insider trading.

Foreign Stock Exchanges

Thanks to expanded communications and the relaxation of many legal barriers, investors can buy securities from companies almost anywhere in the world. If you uncover a foreign company you feel has great potential for growth, you can purchase shares of its stock with little difficulty from U.S. brokers who have access to foreign stock exchanges. Foreign investors can also invest in U.S. securities, and large foreign stock exchanges, like those in London and Tokyo, trade large amounts of U.S. securities daily. The number of U.S. companies listed on foreign stock exchanges is growing. In addition to the London and Tokyo exchanges, other major stock exchanges are located in Shanghai, Sydney, Hong Kong, São Paolo, and Toronto. There are stock exchanges in Africa as well.[13]

Raising long-term funds using equity financing by issuing stock is an option many companies pursue. After the Progress Assessment, let's look in more depth at how firms raise capital by issuing stock.

progress assessment

- What is the primary purpose of a securities exchange?
- What does NASDAQ stand for? How does this exchange work?

LEARNING goal 3

Compare the advantages and disadvantages of equity financing by issuing stock, and detail the differences between common and preferred stock.

HOW BUSINESSES RAISE CAPITAL BY SELLING STOCK

Stocks are shares of ownership in a company. A **stock certificate** represents stock ownership. It specifies the name of the company, the number of shares owned, and the type of stock it represents. Today, companies are not required to issue paper stock certificates to owners since stock is generally held electronically.

Stock certificates sometimes indicate a stock's *par value,* which is a dollar amount assigned to each share of stock by the corporation's charter. Today, since par values do not reflect the market value of the stock (what the stock is actually worth), most companies issue *no-par* stock. **Dividends** are part of a firm's profits that the firm may (but is not required to) distribute to stockholders as either cash payments or additional shares of stock. Dividends are declared by a corporation's board of directors and are generally paid quarterly.

Advantages and Disadvantages of Issuing Stock

Some advantages to a firm of issuing stock include:

- As owners of the business, stockholders never have to be repaid their investment.
- There's no legal obligation to pay dividends to stockholders; therefore, the firm can reinvest income (retained earnings) to finance future needs.
- Selling stock can improve the condition of a firm's balance sheet since issuing stock creates no debt. (A corporation may also buy back its stock to improve its balance sheet and make the company appear stronger financially.)

Disadvantages of issuing stock include:

- As owners, stockholders (usually only common stockholders) have the right to vote for the company's board of directors. (Typically, one vote

stocks
Shares of ownership in a company.

stock certificate
Evidence of stock ownership that specifies the name of the company, the number of shares it represents, and the type of stock being issued.

dividends
Part of a firm's profits that the firm may distribute to stockholders as either cash payments or additional shares of stock.

When LinkedIn issued its initial public offering (IPO), the company gained more than $4 billion from the sale. Can you see why issuing stock can be an appealing option for financing a company's growth?

common stock
The most basic form of ownership in a firm; it confers voting rights and the right to share in the firm's profits through dividends, if approved by the firm's board of directors.

preferred stock
Stock that gives its owners preference in the payment of dividends and an earlier claim on assets than common stockholders if the company is forced out of business and its assets sold.

is granted for each share of stock.) Issuing new shares of stock can thus alter the control of the firm.

- Dividends are paid from profit after taxes and are not tax-deductible.
- The need to keep stockholders happy can affect managers' decisions.

Companies can issue two classes of stock: common and preferred. Let's see how these two forms of equity financing differ.

Issuing Shares of Common Stock

Common stock is the most basic form of ownership in a firm. In fact, if a company issues only one type of stock, by law it must be common stock. Holders of common stock have the right to (1) elect members of the company's board of directors and vote on important issues affecting the company and (2) share in the firm's profits through dividends, if approved by the firm's board of directors. Having voting rights in a corporation allows common stockholders to influence corporate policy because the board members they elect choose the firm's top management and make major policy decisions. Common stockholders also have a *preemptive right* to purchase new shares of common stock before anyone else. This allows common stockholders to maintain their proportional share of ownership in the company.

Issuing Shares of Preferred Stock

Owners of **preferred stock** are given preference in the payment of company dividends and must be paid their dividends in full before any common stock dividends can be distributed (hence the term *preferred*). They also have a prior claim on company assets if the firm is forced out of business and its assets sold.[14] Normally, however, preferred stockholders do not get voting rights in the firm.

Preferred stock may be issued with a par value that becomes the base for a fixed dividend the firm is willing to pay. For example, if a preferred stock's par value is $50 a share and its dividend rate is 4 percent, the dividend is $2 a share. An owner of 100 preferred shares receives a fixed yearly dividend of $200 if dividends are declared by the board of directors.

Preferred stock can have other special features that common stock doesn't have. For example it can be *callable*, which means preferred stockholders could be required to sell their shares back to the corporation. Preferred stock can also be converted to shares of common stock (but not the other way around), and it can be *cumulative*. That is, if one or more dividends are not paid when promised, they accumulate and the corporation must pay them in full at a later date before it can distribute any common stock dividends.

Companies often prefer to raise capital by debt financing. One debt funding option frequently used by larger firms is issuing corporate bonds. Let's look at what's involved with issuing corporate bonds and how they differ from issuing stock.

progress assessment

- Name at least two advantages and two disadvantages of a company's issuing stock as a form of equity financing.
- What are the major differences between common stock and preferred stock?

LEARNING goal 4

Compare the advantages and disadvantages of obtaining debt financing by issuing bonds, and identify the classes and features of bonds.

HOW BUSINESSES RAISE CAPITAL BY ISSUING BONDS

A **bond** is a corporate certificate indicating that an investor has lent money to a firm (or a government). An organization that issues bonds has a legal obligation to make regular interest payments to investors and to repay the entire bond principal amount at a prescribed time.[15] Let's further explore the language of bonds so you understand exactly how they work.

bond
A corporate certificate indicating that a person has lent money to a firm (or a government).

Learning the Language of Bonds

Corporate bonds are usually issued in units of $1,000 (government bonds can be in much larger amounts). The *principal* is the face value (dollar value) of a bond, which the issuing company is legally bound to repay in full to the bondholder on the **maturity date**. **Interest** is the payment the bond issuer makes to the bondholders to compensate them for the use of their money. If Very Vegetarian issues a $1,000 bond with an interest rate of 5 percent and a maturity date of 2022, it is agreeing to pay the bondholder a total of $50 interest each year until a specified date in 2022, when it must repay the full $1,000. Maturity dates can vary. Firms such as Disney, IBM and Coca-Cola have issued bonds with 100-year maturity dates.[16]

Bond interest is sometimes called the *coupon rate,* a term that dates back to when bonds were issued as *bearer* bonds. The holder, or bearer, was considered the bond's owner. Back then, the company issuing the bond kept no record of changes in ownership. Bond interest was paid to whoever clipped coupons attached to the bond and sent them to the issuing company for payment. Today, bonds are registered to specific owners and changes in ownership are recorded electronically.

The interest rate paid by U.S. government bonds influences the bond interest rate businesses must pay. U.S. government bonds are considered safe investments, so they can pay lower interest. Figure 19.2 on p. 530 describes several types of government bonds that compete with U.S. corporate bonds in securities markets. Bond interest rates also vary according to the state of the economy, the reputation of the issuing company, and the interest rate for bonds of similar companies. Though bond interest is quoted for an entire year, it is usually paid in two installments, and the rate generally cannot be changed.

maturity date
The exact date the issuer of a bond must pay the principal to the bondholder.

interest
The payment the issuer of the bond makes to the bondholders for use of the borrowed money.

BOND	DESCRIPTION
U.S. government bond	Issued by the federal government; considered the safest type of bond investment
Treasury bill (T-bill)	Matures in less than a year; issued with a minimum denomination of $1,000
Treasury note	Matures in 10 years or less; sold in denominations of $1,000 and $5,000
Treasury bond	Matures in 25 years or more; sold in denominations of $1,000 and $5,000
Municipal bond	Issued by states, cities, counties, and other state and local government agencies; usually exempt from federal taxes
Yankee bond	Issued by a foreign government; payable in U.S. dollars

Bond rating organizations access the creditworthiness of a corporation's bond issues. Independent rating firms such as Standard & Poor's, Moody's Investors Service, and Fitch Ratings rate bonds according to their degree of risk. Bonds can range from the highest quality to junk bonds (which we discuss later in this chapter).[17] Figure 19.3 gives an example of the range of bond ratings.

Advantages and Disadvantages of Issuing Bonds

Bonds offer long-term financing advantages to an organization:

- Bondholders are creditors of the firm, not owners. They seldom vote on corporate matters; thus, management maintains control over the firm's operations.
- Bond interest is a business expense and tax-deductible to the firm (see Chapter 17).
- Bonds are a temporary source of funding. They're eventually repaid and the debt obligation is eliminated.
- Bonds can be repaid before the maturity date if they contain a *call provision*. They can also be converted to common stock. (We discuss both features below.)

Bonds also have drawbacks:

- Bonds increase debt (long-term liabilities) and may adversely affect the market's perception of the firm.
- Paying interest on bonds is a legal obligation. If interest is not paid, bondholders can take legal action to force payment.
- The face value of the bond must be repaid on the maturity date. Without careful planning, this obligation can cause cash flow problems when the repayment comes due.

debenture bonds
Bonds that are unsecured
(i.e., not backed by any
collateral such as
equipment).

Different Classes of Bonds

Corporations can issue two different classes of corporate bonds. *Unsecured bonds,* usually called **debenture bonds**, are not backed by any specific collateral (such as land or equipment). Only firms with excellent reputations and

BOND RATING AGENCIES			
MOODY'S	**STANDARD & POOR'S**	**FITCH RATINGS**	**DESCRIPTIONS**
Aaa	AAA	AAA	Highest quality (lowest default risk)
Aa	AA	AA	High quality
A	A	A	Upper medium grade
Baa	BBB	BBB	Medium grade
Ba	BB	BB	Lower medium grade
B	B	B	Speculative
Caa	CCC, CC	CCC	Poor (high default risk)
Ca	C	DDD	Highly speculative
C	D	D	Lowest grade

figure 19.3

BOND RATINGS: MOODY'S INVESTORS SERVICE, STANDARD & POOR'S INVESTOR SERVICE, AND FITCH RATINGS

credit ratings can issue debenture bonds, due to the lack of security they provide investors. *Secured bonds,* sometimes called mortgage bonds, are backed by collateral such as land or buildings that is pledged to bondholders if interest or principal isn't paid when promised. A corporate bond issuer can choose to include different bond features. Let's look at some special features.

Special Bond Features

By now you should understand that bonds are issued with an interest rate, are unsecured or secured by some type of collateral, and must be repaid at their maturity date. This repayment requirement often leads companies to establish a reserve account called a **sinking fund**. Its primary purpose is to ensure that enough money will be available to repay bondholders on the bond's maturity date. Firms issuing sinking-fund bonds periodically *retire* (set aside) some part of the principal prior to maturity so that enough funds will accumulate by the maturity date to pay off the bond. Sinking funds are generally attractive to both issuing firms and investors for several reasons:

sinking fund
A reserve account in which the issuer of a bond periodically retires some part of the bond principal prior to maturity so that enough capital will be accumulated by the maturity date to pay off the bond.

- They provide for an orderly retirement (repayment) of a bond issue.
- They reduce the risk the bond will not be repaid.
- They support the market price of the bond because they reduce the risk the bond will not be repaid.

A *callable bond* permits the bond issuer to pay off the principal before its maturity date. This gives companies some discretion in their long-term forecasting. Suppose Very Vegetarian issued $10 million in 20-year bonds at 10 percent interest. Its yearly interest expense is $1 million ($10 million times 10 percent). If market conditions change and bonds of the same quality now pay only 7 percent, Very Vegetarian will be paying 3 percent, or $300,000 ($10 million times 3 percent), in excess interest yearly. The company could benefit by calling in (paying off) the old bonds and issuing new bonds at the lower rate. If a company calls a bond before maturity, it often pays investors a price above the bond's face value.

Investors can convert *convertible bonds* into shares of common stock in the issuing company.[18] This can be an incentive for an investor because common stock value tends to grow faster than a bond. Therefore, if the value of the firm's common stock grows sizably over time, bondholders can compare the value of continued bond interest earned with the potential profit of a specified number of shares of common stock.[19]

PART 6 ✳ Managing Financial Resources

Now that you understand the advantages and disadvantages of stocks and bonds as a financing tool from a company's perspective, let's explore the opportunities stocks and bonds provide for *investors*. First, though, let's check your progress.

progress assessment

- Why are bonds considered a form of debt financing?
- What does it mean if a firm issues a 9 percent debenture bond due in 2025?
- Explain the difference between an unsecured and a secured bond.
- Why are convertible bonds attractive to investors?

LEARNING goal 5

Explain how to invest in securities markets and various investment objectives such as long-term growth, income, cash, and protection from inflation.

stockbroker
A registered representative who works as a market intermediary to buy and sell securities for clients.

Online brokers like Scottrade and E*Trade specialize in providing information for investors. What are some of the features of this website (www. scottrade.com) that are designed to provide investment information?

HOW INVESTORS BUY SECURITIES

Investing in stocks and bonds is not difficult. First, you decide what stock or bond you want to buy. After that, you find a brokerage firm authorized to trade securities to execute your order. A **stockbroker** is a registered representative who works for a brokerage firm as a market intermediary to buy and sell securities for clients. Stockbrokers place an order and negotiate a price. After the transaction is completed, the trade is reported to your broker, who notifies you. Today, large brokerage firms maintain automated order systems that allow brokers to enter your order the instant you make it. The order can be confirmed in seconds.

A stockbroker can also be a source of information about what stocks or bonds would best meet your financial objectives, but it's still important to learn about stocks and bonds on your own.[20] Investment analysts' advice may not always meet your specific expectations and needs.

Investing through Online Brokers

Today, investors can choose from multiple online trading services to buy and sell stocks and bonds. Ameritrade, E*Trade, Scottrade, and Fidelity are among the leaders.[21] Investors who trade online are willing to do their own research and make investment decisions without the direct assistance of a broker. This allows online brokers the ability to charge much lower trading fees than traditional stockbrokers. The leading online services do provide important market information, such as company financial data, price histories of a stock, and analysts' reports. Often the level of information services you receive depends on the size of your account and your level of trading.

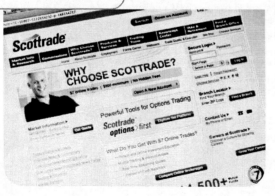

MAKING ethical decisions

Money Going Up in Smoke

You recently received news that your Uncle Alex passed away after a long battle with lung cancer. To your surprise, he left you $25,000 in his will, saying you were his favorite nephew. You remember your uncle as a hard-working man who loved baseball and liked nothing better than to watch you pitch for your college team. Unfortunately, your uncle started smoking as a young man and eventually became a heavy chain smoker. His doctors said that smoking was the primary cause of his lung cancer.

After receiving the inheritance, you wonder where to invest the money. Your old teammate Jack, who is now a financial advisor, recommends that you buy stock in a well-known multinational firm that offers a good dividend and has solid growth potential. He tells you the firm's primary product is tobacco, but assures you it produces many other products as well. You know Jack has your best interests at heart. You also believe Uncle Alex would like to see the money he left you grow. However, you wonder if a company that markets tobacco is an appropriate place to invest your inheritance. What are the ethical alternatives in this situation? What are the consequences of the alternatives? What will you do?

Whether you decide to use an online broker or to invest through a traditional stockbroker, remember that investing means committing your money with the hope of making a profit. The dot-com bubble in the early 2000s and the financial crisis beginning in 2008 proved again that investing is a risky business. Therefore, the first step in any investment program is to analyze your level of risk tolerance. Other factors to consider include your desired income, cash requirements, and need to hedge against inflation, along with the investment's growth prospects. The Making Ethical Decisions box describes an interesting stock investment decision.

You are never too young or too old to invest, but you should first ask questions and consider investment alternatives. Let's take a look at several strategies.

Choosing the Right Investment Strategy

Investment objectives change over the course of a person's life. A young person can better afford to invest in high-risk investment options such as stocks than a person nearing retirement. Younger investors generally look for significant growth in the value of their investments over time. If stocks go into a tailspin and decrease in value, as they did in 2008, a younger person has time to wait for stock values to rise again. Older people, perhaps on a fixed income, lack the luxury of waiting and may be more inclined to invest in bonds that offer a steady return as a protection against inflation.

Consider five key criteria when selecting investment options:

1. *Investment risk.* The chance that an investment will be worth less at some future time than it's worth now.
2. *Yield.* The expected return on an investment, such as interest or dividends, usually over a period of one year.
3. *Duration.* The length of time your money is committed to an investment.

REACHING BEYOND
our borders

www.charlesschwab.com

The Sun Never Sets on Stock Opportunities

Reading about the ups-and-downs of U.S. stocks may frighten you out of even thinking about investing in global stocks. Add in the news about unstable governments under attack in Middle East countries, European debt problems, and natural disasters in Japan and Indonesia and the thought of investing in global stocks may seem even less attractive. Recalling the risk/return trade-off, your inclination may be to forget about global stocks and stick with safe U.S. securities like IBM, Apple, and Procter and Gamble. Financial analysts disagree and argue that investing in some global stocks can be a good idea.

Consider some statistics that support their suggestion. The growth rate in the United States from 2002 to 2010 was 37 percent. This pales compared with the growth rate in the BRIC (Brazil, Russia, India, and China) nations (see Chapter 3). China experienced growth of 628 percent, Brazil 1,171 percent, India 1,229 percent, and Russia 1,512 percent. The risk/return trade-off still applies, but given the potential returns, we would be remiss to not at least explore the opportunities that exist in global markets. The following suggestions may help build your financial future:

- Invest in global companies you are familiar with and that have a solid record of performance. Names like Honda (Japan), Shell Oil (Netherlands), Nestlé (Switzerland), Samsung (South Korea), and Siemens (Germany) come to mind.

- Invest in global stocks listed on U.S. stock exchanges since they must comply with U.S. accounting standards and rules of the Securities and Exchange Commission.

- Contact U.S. brokers about American depository receipts (ADRs) that you can purchase that represent a set number of shares in a foreign company that are held on deposit at a foreign branch of a U.S. bank.

- Countless mutual and exchange-traded funds offer a bevy of global opportunities that focus on countries such as China and Brazil or entire regions such as Africa, Asia, Europe, or Latin America.

- Use extreme caution or completely avoid investing in stocks from countries that have a history of currency problems or political instability.

Keep your long-term financial goals in mind when considering any investments, and stay abreast of the news daily, especially when risking your capital in global markets.

Sources: "Global Stock Markets," *Charles Schwab On Investing,* Spring 2011; Anna Prior, "Investing in Smaller Emerging Markets," *Smart Money,* April 4, 2011; Jason Raznick, "Dividends, Emerging Markets . . . Oh My," *Forbes,* May 9, 2011; and Andrew Tanzer, "The World's Best Stocks," *Kiplinger's Personal Finance,* February 2011.

4. *Liquidity.* How quickly you can get back your invested funds in cash if you want or need them.
5. *Tax consequences.* How the investment will affect your tax situation.

What's important in any investment strategy is the risk/return trade-off. Setting investment objectives such as *growth* (choosing stocks you believe will increase in price) or *income* (choosing bonds that pay consistent interest) should set the tone for your investment strategy.

Reducing Risk by Diversifying Investments

diversification
Buying several different investment alternatives to spread the risk of investing.

Diversification involves buying several different types of investments to spread the risk of investing. An investor may put 25 percent of his or her money into U.S. stocks that have relatively high risk but strong growth potential, another 25 percent in conservative government bonds, 25 percent in dividend-paying stocks that provide income, 10 percent in an international mutual fund (discussed later), and the rest in the bank for emergencies and other possible investment opportunities. By diversifying with such a *portfolio strategy* or *allocation model*, investors decrease the chance of losing everything they have invested.[22]

Both stockbrokers and certified financial planners (CFPs) are trained to give advice about the investment portfolio that would best fit each client's financial objectives. However, the more investors themselves read and study the market, the higher their potential for gain.[23] A short course in investments can also be useful. Stocks and bonds are investment opportunities individuals can use to enhance their financial future. The Reaching Beyond our Borders box discusses growing opportunities investors can find in global stocks. Before we look at stocks and bonds in depth, let's check your understanding with the Progress Assessment.

Securities markets are like financial supermarkets—there are lots of investment options to choose from. That's why it's important to determine what investment strategy is right for you. Watching investment programs like CNBC's Mad Money with Jim Cramer could be a good starting point. How do you think your investment objectives will change over your lifetime?

progress assessment

- What is the key advantage of investing through online brokers? What is the key disadvantage?
- What is the primary purpose of diversifying investments?

LEARNING goal 6

Analyze the opportunities stocks offer as investments.

INVESTING IN STOCKS

Buying stock makes investors part owners of a company. This means that as stockholders they can participate in its success. Unfortunately, they can also lose money if a company does not do well or the overall stock market declines. The stock market fall beginning in 2008 was proof of that.

Stock investors are often called bulls or bears according to their perceptions of the market. *Bulls* believe that stock prices are going to rise; they buy stock in anticipation of the increase. A bull market is when overall stock prices are rising. *Bears* expect stock prices to decline and sell their stocks in anticipation of falling prices. That's why when stock prices are declining steadily, the market is called a bear market.

The market price and growth potential of most stock depends heavily on how well the corporation is meeting its business objectives. A company that achieves its objectives offers great potential for **capital gains**, the positive difference between the price at which you bought a stock and what you sell it for.[24] For example, an investment of $2,250 in 100 shares of McDonald's when the company first offered its stock to the public in 1965 would have grown to 74,360 shares (after the company's 12 stock splits) worth approximately $5.7 million as of year-end market close on December 31, 2010.[25] Now that's a lot of Big Macs!

Investors often select stocks depending on their investment strategy. Stocks issued by higher-quality companies such as Coca-Cola, Johnson & Johnson,

capital gains
The positive difference between the purchase price of a stock and its sale price.

stock splits
An action by a company that gives stockholders two or more shares of stock for each one they own.

and Procter & Gamble are referred to as *blue-chip stocks* (a term derived from poker where the highest value chip was the blue chip). These stocks generally pay regular dividends and experience consistent price appreciation.

Stocks of corporations in emerging fields such as technology, biotechnology, or Internet-related firms, whose earnings are expected to grow at a faster rate than other stocks, are referred to as *growth stocks*. While riskier, growth stocks offer the potential for higher returns. Stocks of public utilities are considered *income stocks* because they usually offer investors a high dividend yield that generally keeps pace with inflation. There are even *penny stocks*, representing ownership in companies that compete in high-risk industries like oil exploration. Penny stocks sell for less than $2 (some analysts say less than $5) and are considered risky investments.

When purchasing stock, investors have choices when placing buy orders. A *market order* tells a broker to buy or to sell a stock immediately at the best price available. A *limit order* tells the broker to buy or sell a stock at a specific price, if that price becomes available. Let's say a stock is selling for $40 a share. You believe the price will eventually go higher but could drop to $36 first. You can place a limit order at $36, so your broker will buy the stock at $36 if it drops to that price. If the stock never falls to $36, the broker will not purchase it for you.

Stock Splits

Brokers prefer stock purchases in *round lots* of 100 shares at a time. Investors, however, often cannot afford to buy 100 shares, which may sell for as much as

If you stroll through Times Square in New York City, you never have to wonder how stocks on the NASDAQ exchange are performing. The NASDAQ price wall continuously updates prices and the number of shares being traded. Originally, the NASDAQ dealt primarily with small companies; today, it competes with the NYSE Euronet for new stock listings.

$100 each, and therefore often buy in *odd lots*, or fewer than 100 shares at a time. High per-share prices can induce companies to declare **stock splits**, in which they issue two or more shares for every one that's outstanding. If Very Vegetarian stock were selling for $100 a share, the firm could declare a two-for-one stock split. Investors who owned one share of Very Vegetarian would now own two, each worth only $50 (half as much as before the split).

Stock splits cause no change in the firm's ownership structure and no immediate change in the investment's value. Investors generally approve of stock splits, however, because demand for a stock may be greater at $50 than at $100, and the price may then go up in the near future. A company cannot be forced to split its stock, and today stock splits are becoming less common.[26] Legendary American investor Warren Buffett's firm, Berkshire Hathaway, has never split its Class A stock even when its per-share price surpassed $150,000.[27]

Buying Stock on Margin

Buying stock on margin means borrowing some of the stocks' purchase cost from the brokerage firm. The margin is the portion of the stocks' purchase price that investors must pay with their own money. The board of governors of the Federal Reserve System sets *margin rates* in the U.S. market. Briefly, if the margin rate is 50 percent, an investor who qualifies for a margin account may borrow up to 50 percent of the stock's purchase price from the broker.

Although buying on margin sounds like an easy way to buy more stocks, the downside is that investors must repay the credit extended by the broker, plus interest. If the investor's account goes down in value, the broker may issue *a margin call,* requiring the investor to come up with funds to cover the losses the account has suffered.[28] If the investor is unable to fulfill the margin call, the broker can legally sell off shares of the investor's stock to reduce the broker's chance of loss. Margin calls can force an investor to repay a significant portion of his or her account's loss within days or even hours. Buying on margin is thus a risky way to invest in stocks.

buying stock on margin
Purchasing stocks by borrowing some of the purchase cost from the brokerage firm.

Understanding Stock Quotations

Publications like *The Wall Street Journal, Barron's,* and *Investor's Business Daily* carry a wealth of information concerning stocks and other investments. Your local newspaper may carry similar information as well. Financial websites like MSN Money, Yahoo! Finance, and CNBC carry up-to-the-minute information about companies that is much more detailed and only a click away. Take a look at Figure 19.4 to see an example of a stock quote from MSN Money for Microsoft. Microsoft trades on the NASDAQ exchange under the symbol MSFT. Preferred stock is identified by the letters *pf* following the company symbol. Remember, corporations can have several different preferred stock issues.

The information provided in the quote is easy to understand. It includes the highest and lowest price the stock traded for that day, the stock's high and low over the past 52 weeks, the dividend paid (if any), the stock's dividend yield (annual dividend as a percentage of the stock's price per share), important ratios like the price/earnings (P/E) ratio (the price of the stock divided by the firm's per-share earnings), and the return on equity. Investors can also see the number of shares outstanding and the total market capitalization of the firm. More technical features, such as the stock's beta (which measures the degree of the stock's risk), may also appear. Figure 19.4 illustrates the stock's intraday trading (trading throughout the current day), but you can also click to see charts for different time periods. Similar information about bonds, mutual funds, and other investments is also available online.

You might want to follow the market behavior of specific stocks that catch your interest, even if you lack the money to invest in them. Many successful investors started in college by building hypothetical portfolios of stocks and tracking their performance. The more you know about investing before you

figure 19.4

UNDERSTANDING STOCK QUOTATIONS

actually risk your money, the better. (The Developing Workplace Skills and Taking It to the Net exercises at the end of this chapter have exercises you can use for practice.)

LEARNING goal 7

Analyze the opportunities bonds offer as investments.

INVESTING IN BONDS

Investors looking for guaranteed income and limited risk often turn to U.S. government bonds for a secure investment. These bonds have the financial backing and full faith and credit of the federal government. Municipal bonds are offered by local governments and often have advantages such as tax-free interest.[29] Some may even be insured. Corporate bonds are a bit more risky and challenging.

First-time corporate bond investors often ask two questions. The first is, "If I purchase a corporate bond, do I have to hold it until the maturity date?" No, you do not. Bonds are bought and sold daily on major securities exchanges (the secondary market we discussed earlier). However, if you decide to sell your bond to another investor before its maturity date, you may not get its face value (usually $1,000). If your bond does not have features that make it attractive to other investors, like a high interest rate or early maturity, you may have to sell at a *discount,* that is, a price less than the bond's face value. But if other investors do highly value it, you may be able to sell your bond at a *premium,* a price above its face value. Bond prices generally fluctuate inversely with current market interest rates. This means *as interest rates go up, bond prices fall, and vice versa.* Like all investments, however, bonds have a degree of risk.

The second question is, "How can I evaluate the investment risk of a particular bond issue?" Standard & Poor's, Moody's Investors Service, and Fitch Ratings rate the risk of many corporate and government bonds (look back at Figure 19.3). In evaluating the ratings, recall the risk/return trade-off: The higher the risk of a bond, the higher the interest rate the issuer must offer. Investors will invest in a bond considered risky only if the potential return (interest) is high enough. In fact, some will invest in bonds considered junk.

Investing in High-Risk (Junk) Bonds

junk bonds
High-risk, high-interest bonds.

Although bonds are considered relatively safe investments, some investors look for higher returns through riskier bonds called **junk bonds**. Standard & Poor's, Moody's Investors Service, and Fitch Ratings define junk bonds as those with high risk *and* high default rates. Junk bonds pay investors interest as long as the value of the company's assets remains high and its cash flow stays strong.[30] Although the interest rates are attractive and often tempting, if the company can't pay off the bond, the investor is left with an investment that isn't worth more than the paper it's written on—in other words, junk.

Understanding Bond Quotations

Bond prices are quoted as a percentage of $1,000, and their interest rate is often followed by an *s* for easier pronunciation. For example, 9 percent bonds due in 2022 are called 9s of 22. Figure 19.5 is an example of a bond

GOLDMAN SACHS GROUP INC

OVERVIEW	
Price:	104.32
Coupon (%):	7.350
Maturity Date:	1-Oct-2012
Yield to Maturity (%):	-3.289
Current Yield (%):	7.045
Fitch Ratings:	A
Coupon Payment Frequency:	Semi-Annual
First Coupon Date:	1-Apr-2000
Type:	Corporate
Callable:	No

figure 19.5

UNDERSTANDING BOND QUOTATIONS

quote for Goldman Sachs from Yahoo! Finance. The quote highlights the bond's interest rate (coupon rate), maturity date, rating, current price, and whether it's callable. The more you know about bonds, the better prepared you will be to discuss with investment advisers and brokers your financial objectives and be sure their advice is consistent with your best interests and objectives.

LEARNING goal 8

Explain the investment opportunities in mutual funds and exchange-traded funds (ETFs).

INVESTING IN MUTUAL FUNDS AND EXCHANGE-TRADED FUNDS

A **mutual fund** buys stocks, bonds, and other investments and then sells shares in those securities to the public. A mutual fund is like an investment company that pools investors' money and then buys stocks or bonds (for example) in many companies in accordance with the fund's specific purpose.[31] Mutual fund managers are specialists who pick what they consider to be the best stocks and bonds available and help investors diversify their investments.

Mutual funds range from very conservative funds that invest only in government securities to others that specialize in emerging biotechnology firms, Internet companies, foreign companies, precious metals, and other investments with greater risk. Some funds will have a mix of investments like stocks and bonds. The number of mutual funds available today is staggering. For example, there were 3,286 stock mutual funds investing in U.S. stocks in 2011.[32] Investors have invested over $11 trillion in mutual funds. Figure 19.6 on p. 540 gives you a list of some mutual fund investment options.

Young or new investors are often advised to buy shares in *index funds* that invest in a certain kind of stocks or bonds or in the market as a whole. An index fund may focus on large companies, small companies, emerging countries, or real estate (real estate investment trusts, or REITs). One way to diversify your investments is by investing in a variety of index funds. A stockbroker, certified financial planner (CFP), or banker can help you find the option that best fits your investment objectives. The *Morningstar Investor* newsletter is an

mutual fund
An organization that buys stocks and bonds and then sells shares in those securities to the public.

figure 19.6

MUTUAL FUND OBJECTIVES
Mutual funds have a wide array of investment categories. They range from low-risk, conservative funds to others that invest in high-risk industries. Listed here are abbreviations of funds and what these abbreviations stand for.

AB	Investment-grade corporate bonds	MP	Stock and bond fund
AU	Gold oriented	MT	Mortgage securities
BL	Balanced	MV	Mid-cap value
EI	Equity income	NM	Insured municipal bonds
EM	Emerging markets	NR	Natural resources
EU	European region	PR	Pacific region
GL	Global	SB	Short-term corporate bonds
GM	General municipal bond	SC	Small-cap core
GT	General taxable bonds	SE	Sector funds
HB	Health/biotech	SG	Small-cap growth
HC	High-yield bonds	SM	Short-term municipal bonds
HM	High-yield municipal bonds	SP	S&P 500
IB	Intermediate-term corporate bonds	SQ	Specialty
IG	Intermediate-term government bonds	SS	Single-state municipal bonds
IL	International	SU	Short-term government bonds
IM	Intermediate-term municipal bonds	SV	Small-cap value
LC	Large-cap core	TK	Science & technology
LG	Large-cap growth	UN	Unassigned
LT	Latin America	UT	Utility
LU	Long-term U.S. bonds	WB	World bonds
LV	Large-cap value	XC	Multi-cap core
MC	Mid-cap core	XG	Multi-cap growth
MG	Mid-cap growth	XV	Multi-cap value

Sources: *The Wall Street Journal* and *Investor's Business Daily*.

excellent resource for evaluating mutual funds, as are business publications such as *Bloomberg Businessweek, The Wall Street Journal, Money, Forbes, Investor's Business Daily* and many others.

With mutual funds it's simple to change your investment objectives if your financial objectives change. For example, moving your money from a bond fund to a stock fund is no more difficult than making a phone call or clicking a mouse. Another advantage of mutual funds is that you can generally buy directly from the fund and avoid broker fees or commissions. However, check for fees and charges of the mutual fund because they can differ significantly. A *load fund,* for example, charges investors a commission to buy or sell its shares; a *no-load fund* charges no commission.[33]

It's important to check the long-term performance of the fund's managers; the more consistent the performance of the fund's management, the better.[34] Mutual funds called *open-end funds* will accept the investments of any interested investors. *Closed-end funds,* however, limit the number of shares; once the fund reaches its target number, no new investors can buy into the fund.

Exchange-traded funds (ETFs) resemble both stocks and mutual funds. They are collections of stocks, bonds, and other investments that are traded on securities exchanges but are traded more like individual stocks than like mutual funds. Mutual funds, for example, permit investors to buy and sell shares only at the close of the trading day. ETFs can be purchased or sold at any time during the trading day just like individual stocks.

The key points to remember about mutual funds and ETFs is that they offer small investors a way to spread the risk of stock and bond ownership and have their investments managed by a financial specialist for a fee. Financial advisers put mutual funds and ETFs high on the list of recommended investments, particularly for small or first-time investors.[35]

exchange-traded funds (ETFs)
Collections of stocks, bonds, and other investments that are traded on exchanges but are traded more like individual stocks than like mutual funds.

Understanding Mutual Fund Quotations

You can investigate the specifics of various mutual funds by contacting a broker or contacting the fund directly by phone or through its website. Business publications and online sources also provide information about mutual funds.

Look at the example of the T. Rowe Price Blue Chip Growth fund from Yahoo! Finance in Figure 19.7. The fund's name is listed in large letters. The net asset value (NAV) is the price per share of the mutual fund. The NAV is calculated by dividing the market value of the mutual fund's portfolio by the number of shares it has outstanding. The chart also shows the fund's year-to-date (YTD) return, the change in the NAV from the previous day's trading, and the fund's net assets.

Figure 19.8 evaluates bonds, stocks, mutual funds, and ETFs according to risk, income, and possible investment growth (capital gain).

figure 19.7

UNDERSTANDING MUTUAL FUND QUOTATIONS

figure 19.8

COMPARING INVESTMENTS

Investment	Degree of risk	Expected income	Possible growth (capital gain)
Bonds	Low	Secure	Little
Preferred stock	Medium	Steady	Little
Common stock	High	Variable	Good
Mutual funds	Medium	Variable	Good
ETFs	Medium	Variable	Good

progress assessment

- What is a stock split? Why do companies sometimes split their stock?
- What does buying stock on margin mean?
- What are mutual funds and ETFs?
- What is the key benefit to investors in investing in a mutual fund or ETF?

LEARNING goal 9

Describe how stock market indicators like the Dow Jones Industrial Average affect the market.

UNDERSTANDING STOCK MARKET INDICATORS

Investors today have an enormous wealth of investment information available to them. Newspapers like *The Wall Street Journal, Barron's, Investor's Business Daily,* and *USA Today* provide vast amounts of information about companies and global markets. Television networks like MSNBC and CNBC offer daily investment analysis and different viewpoints to assist investors. Websites like MSN Money and Yahoo! Finance offer financial information to investors free of charge that not long ago was only available to brokers for a hefty fee. But keep in mind that investing is an inexact science. Every time someone sells a stock, believing it will fall, someone else is buying it, believing its price will go higher.

Dow Jones Industrial Average (the Dow)
The average cost of 30 selected industrial stocks, used to give an indication of the direction (up or down) of the stock market over time.

You often hear news reports end with a comment like, "The Dow was up 190 points today in active trading." Ever wonder what that's all about? The **Dow Jones Industrial Average (the Dow)** is the average cost of 30 selected industrial stocks. The financial industry uses it to give an indication of the direction (up or down) of the stock market over time. Charles Dow began the practice of measuring stock averages in 1884, using the prices of 12 key stocks. In 1982, the Dow was broadened to include 30 stocks. The 12 original and the 30 current stocks in the Dow are illustrated in Figure 19.9. Do you recognize any of the 12 original companies?

Today, Dow Jones & Company substitutes new stocks in the Dow when it's deemed appropriate. In 1991, Disney was added to reflect the increased economic importance of the service sector. In 1999, the Dow added Home Depot and SBC Communications along with its first NASDAQ stocks, Intel and

figure 19.9

THE ORIGINAL DOW AND CURRENT DOW

THE ORIGINAL DOW 12	THE 30 CURRENT DOW COMPANIES	
American Cotton Oil	Alcoa	Intel
American Sugar Refining Co.	American Express	Johnson & Johnson
American Tobacco	AT&T	JPMorgan Chase
Chicago Gas	Bank of America	Kraft
Distilling & Cattle Feeding Co.	Boeing	McDonald's
General Electric Co.	Caterpillar	Merck
Laclede Gas Light Co.	Chevron	Microsoft
National Lead	Cisco	Pfizer
North American Co.	Coca-Cola	Procter & Gamble
Tennessee Coal, Iron & Railroad Co.	DuPont	3M
U.S. Leather	ExxonMobil	United Technologies
U.S. Rubber Co.	General Electric	Travelers
	Hewlett-Packard	Verizon
	Home Depot	Wal-Mart Stores
	IBM	Walt Disney

Microsoft. In 2004, American International Group (AIG), Pfizer, and Verizon replaced AT&T, International Paper, and Eastman Kodak. (In 2005, AT&T rejoined the Dow when it merged with SBC.) In 2008, Chevron, Bank of America, and Kraft Foods replaced Altria Group, Honeywell, and AIG. In 2009, Travelers and Cisco replaced Citigroup and General Motors.

Critics argue that the 30-company Dow sample is too small to get a good statistical representation of the direction of the market over time. Many investors and analysts prefer to follow stock indexes like the Standard & Poor's 500 (S&P 500), which tracks the performance of 400 industrial, 40 financial, 40 public utility, and 20 transportation stocks. Investors also closely follow the NASDAQ average, which is quoted each trading day to show trends in this important exchange.

Staying abreast of the market will help you decide what investments seem most appropriate to your needs and objectives. Remember two key investment realities: Your personal financial objectives and needs change over time, and markets can be volatile. Let's look at market volatility and the challenges that present investors with new risks and opportunities.

Riding the Market's Roller Coaster

Throughout the 1900s, the stock market had its ups and downs, spiced with several major tremors. The first major crash occurred on Tuesday, October 29, 1929 (called Black Tuesday), when the stock market lost almost 13 percent of its value in a single day. This day, and the deep depression that followed, reinforced the reality of market volatility, especially to those who bought stocks heavily on margin. On October 19, 1987, the stock market suffered the largest one-day drop in its history, losing over 22 percent of its value. On October 27, 1997, investors again felt the market's fury. Fears of an impending economic crisis in Asia caused panic and widespread losses. Luckily, the market regained its strength after a short downturn.

After regaining strength in the late 1990s, the market again suffered misfortune in the early 2000s. All told, investors lost $7 trillion in market value

Investing in the stock market has never been for the weak-hearted. The market seems to have continuous steep climbs and sharp falls. Do you have the risk tolerance to survive the wild market swings?

from 2000 through 2002. A recovery that started in the mid-2000s was cut short in 2008, when the financial crisis fueled a massive exodus from the stock market, resulting in record losses.

What caused the market turmoil of 1987, 1997, 2000–2002, and 2008? In 1987, analysts agreed it was **program trading**, in which investors give their computers instructions to sell automatically to avoid potential losses if the price of their stock dips to a certain point. On October 19, 1987, computers' sell orders caused many stocks to fall to unbelievable depths. The crash prompted the U.S. exchanges to create mechanisms called *curbs* and *circuit breakers* to restrict program trading whenever the market moves up or down by a large number of points in a trading day. A key computer is turned off and program trading is halted. If you watch programming on CNBC or MSNBC, you'll see the phrase *curbs in* appear on the screen.

Circuit breakers are more drastic than curbs and are triggered when the Dow falls 10, 20, or 30 percent in a day. That happened on October 27, 1997, when the market suffered an approximate 7 percent decline and the market closed for the day at 3:30 p.m. instead of 4:00. Many believe the 1997 market drop (caused by the financial crisis in Asia) could have been much worse without the trading restrictions. Depending on the rate of decline and the time of day, circuit breakers will halt trading for half an hour to two hours so traders have time to assess the situation.

In the late 1990s the stock market reached unparalleled heights only to collapse into a deep decline in 2000–2002. The bursting of the dot-com bubble was the primary reason. A bubble is caused when too many investors drive the price of something (in this case dot-com stocks) unrealistically high.

The dot-com crash was, unfortunately, accompanied by disclosures of financial fraud at companies such as WorldCom, Enron, Global Crossing, and Tyco. Investors had trusted that the real value of these companies was fairly reflected in their financial statements. This trust was shattered when they found investment analysts often provided clients with wildly optimistic evaluations and recommendations about companies they knew were not worth their current prices.

After the financial downturn caused by the dot-com bubble, the stock market surged in the mid-2000s with the Dow setting a record high in October 2007. The market's growth was dramatic, especially in the real estate sector. From 2000 to 2006 prices of existing homes rose 50 percent; however, between 2006 and 2011, housing values fell $6.3 trillion.[36] The real estate bubble was like the dot-com bubble before it: Investors believed that home prices would increase forever. Financial institutions reduced their lending requirements for buyers, homebuilders overbuilt, and buyers overspent, all sharing blame for the crisis. The government also contributed to the problem by requiring more mortgages be given to low- and moderate-income buyers, many with weak credit scores or no verification of income or assets. These *subprime* loans were pooled together and repackaged as mortgage-backed securities that were sold to investors (discussed in Chapter 20). What followed was huge numbers of foreclosures, the failure of government-sponsored mortgage giants Fannie Mae and Freddie Mac, and more than 350 bank failures.[37]

The collapse of the real estate market caused the economy a combined loss of $8 trillion in

program trading
Giving instructions to computers to automatically sell if the price of a stock dips to a certain point to avoid potential losses.

The economic crisis that began in 2008 caused much anguish among Wall Street workers and people in general. How effective has the government's response been thus far?

Cleaning Up the Street

In response to a historic economic meltdown, Congress passed the Dodd-Frank Financial Reform and Consumer Protection Act into law on July 21, 2010. While the bill is far from the miracle cure that many politicians and consumers demanded, Dodd-Frank nevertheless represents the most sweeping change in financial regulation since the Great Depression. Its provisions will affect every layer of the economy from home buyers and merchants to giant investment banks.

The articles included in Dodd-Frank will have a dramatic effect on the future of American commerce. First of all, the new legislation gives the government power to seize and shutter large financial institutions on the verge of collapse in an effort to prevent further bailouts. It also subjects derivatives, complicated financial deals (including those that packaged subprime mortgages that helped fuel the crisis), to strict governmental oversight. Hedge funds will have to register with the SEC as investment advisers and provide information about trades and portfolio holdings. Perhaps most important to the general public, however, is the law's formation of an independent consumer protection agency housed within the Federal Reserve. The new agency protects borrowers against a host of financial abuses associated with payday loans, mortgages, and credit cards.

Still, the bill is far from perfect. Some advocates worry about the Consumer Financial Protection Bureau's location within the Federal Reserve. Also, a number of entities, such as car dealers, are exempt from regulation by the agency. In the law's most controversial move, it leaves all of the nation's largest financial institutions almost completely intact, even those that remain on taxpayer support. For all its faults, though, the Dodd-Frank Act at least resolves some of the most pressing issues facing our economy today while setting the stage for a stronger financial future.

Sources: Brady Dennis, "Congress Passes Financial Reform Bill," *The Washington Post,* July 16, 2010; Paul Davidson, Paul Wiseman and John Waggoner, "Will New Financial Regulations Prevent Future Meltdowns?" *USA Today,* June 28, 2010; and Phil Mattingly, "Dodd-Frank Consumer Protection Bureau Changes Approved by U.S. House Panel," *Bloomberg Businessweek,* May 13, 2011.

housing and commercial property (more than the GDP of China).[38] Financial institutions, like Lehman Brothers, went out of business and Wall Street icon Merrill Lynch was purchased by Bank of America. With financial markets in the worst condition since the Great Depression and the economy in a deep recession, the federal government took action. Congress passed a $700 billion financial package called the Troubled Assets Relief Program (TARP) that allowed the Treasury Department to purchase or insure "troubled assets" to bolster banks and bail out the automotive industry and insurer American International Group (AIG). Unfortunately in 2009, the economy continued to decline and unemployment grew to double digits causing President Obama to encourage passage of an $800 billion economic stimulus package—a blend of tax cuts and increased government spending—that was intended to reduce unemployment and provide a "significant boost" to the crippled economy.

As the economy slowly moves to recovery today from the financial crisis beginning in 2008, a few positive economic signs have surfaced. The amount of TARP funds spent did not approximate the $700 billion Congress allocated. Plus troubled banks have repaid most of the money they received through TARP, and AIG and General Motors expect to repay the government in full. However, unemployment and slow economic growth continue to be major causes for concern. It's very likely the financial crisis will affect the economy for a long time.[39]

Investing Challenges in the 21st-Century Market

As you can see from the previous section, in the stock market, what goes up also goes down. Financial markets will likely experience changes in the future that will only heighten investor risk. The financial crisis also reinforced that the world's economies are closely linked. The United States was not the only nation affected by the financial crisis; financial markets in Europe, Asia, and South America felt the pain as well. Persistent challenges and even political and social change promise to make securities markets exciting but not stable places to be in the 21st century. The nearby Legal Briefcase box on p. 545 discusses new government regulations designed to address some of these challenges.

Diversify your investments, and be mindful of the risks of investing. Taking a long-term perspective is also a wise idea. There's no such thing as easy money or a sure thing. If you carefully research companies and industries, keep up with the news, and make use of investment resources—such as newspapers, magazines, newsletters, the Internet, and TV programs—the payoff can be rewarding over time.

progress assessment

- What does the Dow Jones Industrial Average measure? Why is it important?
- Why do the 30 companies comprising the Dow change periodically?
- Explain program trading and the problems it can create.

summary

Learning Goal 1. Describe the role of securities markets and of investment bankers.

- **What opportunities do securities markets provide businesses and individual investors?**

By issuing securities businesses are able to raise much-needed funding to help finance their major expenses. Individual investors can share in the success and growth of emerging or established firms by investing in them.

- **What role do investment bankers play in securities markets?**

Investment bankers are specialists who assist in the issue and sale of new securities.

Learning Goal 2. Identify the stock exchanges where securities are traded.

- **What are stock exchanges?**

Stock exchanges are securities markets whose members are engaged in buying and selling securities such as stocks and bonds.

- **What are the different exchanges?**

The NYSE Euronext lists the stock of over 8,000 companies. The NASDAQ is a telecommunications network that links dealers across the nation so that they can buy and sell securities electronically rather than in person. It is the largest U.S. electronic stock trading market. There are stock exchanges all over the world.

- **What is the over-the-counter (OTC) market?**

The OTC market is a system for exchanging stocks not listed on the national exchanges.

- **How are securities exchanges regulated?**

The Securities and Exchange Commission (SEC) regulates securities exchanges and requires companies that intend to sell bonds or stock to provide a prospectus to potential investors.

- **What is insider trading?**

Insider trading is the use of information or knowledge individuals gain that allows them to benefit unfairly from fluctuations in security prices.

Learning Goal 3. Compare the advantages and disadvantages of equity financing by issuing stock, and detail the differences between common and preferred stock.

- **What are the advantages and disadvantages to a firm of selling stock?**

The advantages of selling stock include the following: (1) the stock price never has to be repaid to stockholders, since they become owners in the company; (2) there is no legal obligation to pay stock dividends; and (3) the company incurs no debt, so it may appear financially stronger. Disadvantages of selling stock include the following: (1) stockholders become owners of the firm and can affect its management by voting for the board of directors; (2) it is more costly to pay dividends since they are paid in after-tax profits; and (3) managers may be tempted to make stockholders happy in the short term rather than plan for long-term needs.

- **What are the differences between common and preferred stock?**

Holders of common stock have voting rights in the company. In exchange for having no voting rights, preferred stockholders receive a fixed dividend that must be paid in full before common stockholders receive a dividend. Preferred stockholders are also paid back their investment before common stockholders if the company is forced out of business.

Learning Goal 4. Compare the advantages and disadvantages of obtaining debt financing by issuing bonds, and identify the classes and features of bonds.

- **What are the advantages and disadvantages of issuing bonds?**

The advantages of issuing bonds include the following: (1) management retains control since bondholders cannot vote; (2) interest paid on bonds is tax-deductible; (3) bonds are only a temporary source of financing, and after they are paid off the debt is eliminated; (4) bonds can be paid back early if they are issued with a call provision; and (5) sometimes bonds can be converted to common stock. The disadvantages of bonds include the following: (1) because bonds are an increase in debt, they may adversely affect the market's perception of the company; (2) the firm must pay interest on its bonds; and (3) the firm must repay the bond's face value on the maturity date.

- **What are the different types of bonds?**

Unsecured (debenture) bonds are not supported by collateral, whereas secured bonds are backed by tangible assets such as mortgages, buildings, and equipment.

Learning Goal 5. Explain how to invest in securities markets and set investment objectives such as long-term growth, income, cash, and protection from inflation.

- **How do investors normally make purchases in securities markets?**

Investors purchase investments through market intermediaries called stockbrokers, who provide many different services. Online investing has become increasingly popular.

- **What are the criteria for selecting investments?**

Investors should determine their overall financial objectives and evaluate investments according to (1) risk, (2) yield, (3) duration, (4) liquidity, and (5) tax consequences.

- **What is diversification?**

Diversification means buying several different types of investments (government bonds, corporate bonds, preferred stock, common stock, global stock) with different degrees of risk. The purpose is to reduce the overall risk an investor would assume by investing in just one type of security.

Learning Goal 6. Analyze the opportunities stocks offer as investments.
- **What is a market order?**

A market order tells a broker to buy or to sell a security immediately at the best price available.
- **A limit order?**

A limit order tells the broker to buy or sell if the stock reaches a specific price.
- **What does it mean when a stock splits?**

When a stock splits, stockholders receive two (or more) shares of stock for each share they own. Each is worth half (or less) of the original share, so while the number of the shares increases, the total value of stockholders' holdings stays the same. The lower per-share price that results may increase demand for the stock.
- **What does buying on margin mean?**

An investor buying on margin borrows part (the percentage allowed to be borrowed is set by the Federal Reserve) of the cost of a stock from the broker to get shares of stock without immediately paying the full price.
- **What type of information do stock quotations give you?**

Stock quotations provide the highest and lowest price in the last 52 weeks; the dividend yield; the price/earnings ratio; the total shares traded that day; and the closing price and net change in price from the previous day.

Learning Goal 7. Analyze the opportunities bonds offer as investments.
- **What is the difference between a bond selling at a discount and a bond selling at a premium?**

In the secondary market a bond selling at a premium is priced above its face value. A bond selling at a discount sells below its face value.
- **What is a junk bond?**

Junk bonds are high-risk (rated BB or below), high-interest debenture bonds that speculative investors often find attractive.
- **What information does a bond quotation give you?**

A bond quotation gives the bond's interest rate (coupon rate), maturity date, rating, current price, and whether it's callable.

Learning Goal 8. Explain the investment opportunities in mutual funds and exchange-traded funds (ETFs).
- **How can mutual funds help individuals diversify their investments?**

A mutual fund is an organization that buys stocks and bonds and then sells shares in those securities to the public, enabling individuals to invest in many more companies than they could otherwise afford.
- **What are ETFs?**

Like mutual funds ETFs are collections of stocks that are traded on securities exchanges, but they are traded more like individual stocks.

Learning Goal 9. Describe how stock market indicators like the Dow Jones Industrial Average affect the market.
- **What is the Dow Jones Industrial Average?**

The Dow Jones Industrial Average is the average price of 30 specific stocks that analysts use to track the direction (up or down) of the stock market.

key terms

bond 529

buying stock on
margin 537

capital gains 535

common stock 528

debenture bonds 530

diversification 534

dividends 527

Dow Jones Industrial
Average (the Dow) 542

exchange-traded funds
(ETFs) 540

initial public offering
(IPO) 522

institutional
investors 523

interest 529

investment bankers 523

junk bonds 538

maturity date 529

mutual fund 539

NASDAQ 524

over-the-counter (OTC)
market 524

preferred stock 528

program trading 544

prospectus 525

Securities and
Exchange
Commission (SEC) 525

sinking fund 531

stockbroker 532

stock certificate 527

stock exchange 523

stocks 527

stock splits 536

critical thinking

1. Imagine you inherited $50,000 and you want to invest it to meet two financial goals: (*a*) to save for your wedding, which you plan to have in two years, and (*b*) to save for your retirement a few decades from now. How would you invest the money? Explain your answer.

2. If you are considering investing in the bond market, how could information provided by Standard & Poor's, Moody's Investors Service, and Fitch Ratings help you?

3. Why do companies like callable bonds? Why are investors generally not very fond of them?

4. If you were thinking about investing in the securities market, would you prefer individual stocks, mutual funds, or ETFs? Explain your choice by comparing the advantages and disadvantages of each.

5. Consider the companies added and subtracted from the Dow Jones Industrial Average over the past five years. (Go to www.djaverages.com to learn more about these companies.) What types of companies were added and deleted? Why do you think the changes were made? Do you think new changes will be made in the next five years? Why?

developing workplace skills

1. Go to the websites of Charles Schwab (www.schwab.com), E*Trade (www.etrade.com), and Ameritrade (www.ameritrade.com). Investigate each of these brokerage companies to compare their fees and what they offer in terms of research and advice. Which firm seems most appropriate to your investment objectives? Be prepared to defend your choice to the class.

2. Visit MSN Money or Yahoo! Finance and select six stocks for your portfolio—three from the NYSE and three from the NASDAQ. Track the stocks daily for three weeks using the graphs provided on the websites to see how

market trends and information affected your stock's performance. Report your observations.

3. U.S. government bonds compete with corporations for investors' dollars. Check out the different types of bonds the federal government offers and list the types most appealing to you. Be sure to check out TIPs.

4. See whether anyone in class is interested in forming an investment group. If so, each member should choose one stock and one mutual fund or ETF. Record each student's selections and the corresponding prices. In two weeks measure the percentage of change in the investments and discuss the results.

5. Go to the websites of Charles Schwab (www.schwab.com), E*Trade (www.etrade.com), or Ameritrade (www.ameritrade.com) and find two IPOs offered in the past year or so. Track the performance of each from its introduction to its present market price. Report your observations.

taking it to the net

Purpose
To evaluate and understand the advantages and disadvantages of ETFs.

Exercise
Exchange-traded funds (ETFs) are a low-cost, flexible way to diversify a portfolio. To learn more, go to Yahoo! Finance (www.finance.yahoo.com) and click on investing, then on the ETFs tab.

1. What are the pros and cons of investing in ETFs?

2. What are the five most actively traded ETFs?

3. Which ETFs grew the most in the last three years?

4. In which industry sectors or countries do these high-growth ETFs specialize?

casing the web

To access the case "Making Dreams Come True," visit **www.mhhe.com/ubl0e**

video case

To access the video case featuring Morningstar, visit **www.mhhe.com/ubl0e**

Money,
Financial INSTITUTIONS, AND
the Federal Reserve

20

LEARNING
goals

After you have read and studied this chapter, you should be able to

1 Explain what money is and what makes money useful.

2 Describe how the Federal Reserve controls the money supply.

3 Trace the history of banking and the Federal Reserve System.

4 Classify the various institutions in the U.S. banking system.

5 Briefly trace the causes of the banking crisis starting in 2008 and explain how the government protects your funds during such crises.

6 Describe how technology helps make banking more efficient.

7 Evaluate the role and importance of international banking, the World Bank, and the International Monetary Fund.

en Bernanke (pronounced ber-*nan̄*-kee) is the head of the Federal Reserve. As you will learn in this chapter, the Federal Reserve is in charge of the U.S. monetary policy (managing the money supply and interest rates). Lately, the Fed has flooded the world with dollars, which many believe caused stock and other asset prices to rise, eliminated the risk of deflation, and prevented a double-dip recession. Many other people, however, believe that the Fed's actions created more inflation and put the United States deeper into a debt crisis that may never be resolved. In short, Ben Bernanke is the center of much attention when it comes to monetary issues. No doubt it was this attention that led *Time* magazine to name Bernanke as "Person of the Year" in 2010.

Bernanke was born in Augusta, Georgia. He taught himself calculus in high school, scored 1590 of a possible 1600 on his college entrance exams, and graduated from Harvard summa cum laude with a bachelor's degree in economics. After earning a PhD from MIT, he was an economics professor and department chair at Princeton. He then served as chair of the President's Council of Economic Advisors in 2005 and was a member of the Board of Governors at the Federal Reserve from 2002 to 2005.

Former president George W. Bush appointed Bernanke to the Fed, making him one of the most powerful people in the United States. The Senate approved a second term for Bernanke as Fed chief under President Obama. It was Bernanke, along with former Treasury secretary Henry Paulson, who convinced Congress to commit about $700 billion to try to end the banking collapse. Bernanke lowered interest rates for banks to near zero and kept them there for a couple of years, and was among the group of advisers who made billions of dollars available to banks in an effort to ease the credit crisis.

Bernanke's challenges today include keeping inflation in check, increasing the value of the dollar, and getting the economy moving upward again. Part of that plan includes credit easing and buying more than a trillion dollars in debt and mortgage-backed securities. As you can see, almost everything about the economy is affected by the choices Bernanke makes.

You will learn more about the Federal Reserve and the banking system in general in this chapter. Using that information, you can better understand Bernanke's decisions. Keep up with what he is doing by reading the business press and listening to business reports. His successes and failures will be making headlines for a long time.

profile

Getting to Know

X *Ben S. Bernanke*

Chairman of the Federal Reserve

Sources: "Bernanke's Inflation Paradox," *The Wall Street Journal,* April 26, 2011; J. Alex Tarquinio, "When QE2 Weighs Anchor," *Smart Money,* May 2011; George Melloan, "The Fed Can Create Money, Not Confidence," *The Wall Street Journal,* August 24, 2010; Sean Fieler and Jeffrey Bell, "Our Unaccountable Fed," *The Wall Street Journal,* April 6, 2011; David J. Lynch and Craig Torres, "Lifting the Veil at the Fed—Sort of," *Bloomberg Businessweek,* April 4–April 10, 2011; Steve Stanek, "It's Inflation When More Dollars Are Needed to Print More Dollars," *Washington Examiner,* March 24, 2011; Neil Irwin, "Bernanke Defends U.S. Policies," *The Washington Post,* February 19, 2011; Patrice Hill, "Senate OKs 2nd Term for Bernanke as Fed Chief," *The Washington Times,* January 29, 2011; and "How the Fed Works," *Time,* January 4, 2010.

This bank-like store in Austin, Texas, was designed to serve low-income clients who don't have traditional bank accounts. Customers pay a one-time $10 fee that allows them to cash checks and put the money onto debit cards. What is the name of this company? (The answer can be found in the chapter.)

LEARNING goal 1

Explain what money is and what makes money useful.

WHY MONEY IS IMPORTANT

The Federal Reserve, or the Fed, is the organization in charge of money in the United States. You will be hearing a lot about it and its head, Ben Bernanke, in the coming years. That is why we chose him to be the subject of the Profile for this chapter. The banking crisis and the moves being made globally by the Fed and other banks to halt a global financial crisis are too complex to discuss in detail here. Our goal in this chapter is simply to introduce you to the world of banking and the role of the Federal Reserve.

Two of the most critical issues in the United States today, economic growth and the creation of jobs, depend on the ready availability of money. Money is so important to the economy that many institutions have evolved to manage it and make it available when you need it. Today you can get cash from an automated teller machine (ATM) almost anywhere in the world, and most organizations will also accept a check, credit card, debit card, or smart card for purchases.[1] Behind the scenes is a complex system of banking that makes the free flow of money possible. Each day, about $4 trillion is exchanged in the world's currency markets. Therefore, what happens to any major country's economy has an effect on the U.S. economy and vice versa. That's why the financial crisis in the United States affected economies throughout the world.

New engraved bills make counterfeiting much more difficult than in the past. The bills look a little different from older ones and are different colors. If you owned a store, what would you do to make sure employees don't accept counterfeit bills?

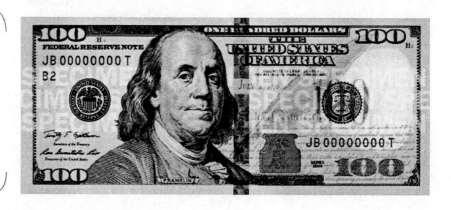

There's no way to understand the U.S. economy without understanding global money exchanges and the institutions involved in the creation and management of money. Let's start at the beginning by discussing exactly what the word *money* means and how the supply of money affects the prices you pay for goods and services.

What Is Money?

Money is anything people generally accept as payment for goods and services. In the past, objects as diverse as salt, feathers, fur pelts, stones, rare shells, tea, and horses have served as money. In fact, until the 1880s, cowrie shells were one of the world's most popular currencies.

    Barter is the direct trading of goods or services for other goods or services. Though barter may sound like something from the past, many people have discovered the benefits of bartering online.[2] Others barter goods and services the old-fashioned way—face-to-face. In Siberia people have bought movie tickets with two eggs, and in Ukraine people have paid their energy bills with sausages and milk. Today you can go to a *barter exchange* where you can put goods or services into the system and get trade credits for other goods and services that you need. The barter exchange makes it easier to barter because you don't have to find people with whom to barter. The exchange does that for you.

    The problem with traditional barter is that eggs and milk are difficult to carry around. Most people need some object that's portable, divisible, durable, and stable so that they can trade goods and services without carrying the actual goods around with them. One solution is coins and paper bills. The five standards for a useful form of money are:

- *Portability.* Coins and paper money are a lot easier to take to market than pigs or other heavy products.
- *Divisibility.* Different-sized coins and bills can represent different values. Prior to 1963, a U.S. quarter had half as much silver content as a half-dollar coin, and a dollar had four times the silver of a quarter. Because silver is now too expensive, today's coins are made of other metals, but the accepted values remain.
- *Stability.* When everybody agrees on the value of coins, the value of money is relatively stable. In fact, U.S. money has become so stable that much of the world has used the U.S. dollar as the measure of value. If the value of the dollar fluctuates too rapidly, the world may turn to some other form of money, such as the euro, for the measure of value.
- *Durability.* Coins last for thousands of years, even when they've sunk to the bottom of the ocean, as you've seen when divers find old coins in sunken ships.
- *Uniqueness.* It's hard to counterfeit, or copy, elaborately designed and minted coins. With the latest color copiers, people are able to duplicate the look of paper money relatively easily. Thus, the government has had to go to extra lengths to make sure *real* dollars are readily identifiable. That's why you have newer paper money with the picture slightly off center and with invisible lines that quickly show up when reviewed by banks and stores. The new $100 bill has features such as a three dimensional ribbon as well as ink that contains microscopic

Although people have long used barter to exchange goods without money, one problem is that objects like chickens and eggs are harder to carry around than a ten-dollar bill. What other drawbacks does bartering have?

money
Anything that people generally accept as payment for goods and services.

barter
The direct trading of goods or services for other goods or services.

flakes that shift color with movement.[3] The new bill had its problems, however, and the Bureau of Engraving and Printing had to sort through millions of bills to eliminate faulty ones.[4]

Coins and paper money simplified exchanges. Most countries have their own currencies, and they're all about equally portable, divisible, and durable. However, they're not always equally stable.[5]

Electronic cash (e-cash) is one of the newest forms of money. You can make online payments using Quicken or Microsoft Money or e-mail e-cash using PayPal. Recipients can choose automatic deposit to their bank, e-dollars for spending online, or a traditional check in the mail. Bitcoin is a digital version of money that is tougher to forge, cuts across international boundaries, and can be stored on your hard drive instead of in a bank. However, the Bitcoin is not yet generally accepted and some of the transactions may be illegal.[6] Nonetheless, efforts will be made in the future to create a cashless society using some other form of currency than the bills and coins we now use.[7]

LEARNING goal 2

Describe how the Federal Reserve controls the money supply.

What Is the Money Supply?

As Fed chairman, Ben Bernanke is in control of the U.S. money supply. Two questions emerge from that sentence. What is the money supply? Why does it need to be controlled?

money supply
The amount of money the Federal Reserve Bank makes available for people to buy goods and services.

The **money supply** is the amount of money the Federal Reserve makes available for people to buy goods and services. And, yes, the Federal Reserve, in tandem with the U.S. Treasury, can print more money if it is needed. For example, some of the trillions of dollars that are being spent over the next few years to get the economy moving again were printed with authorization from the Federal Reserve. The terms QE 1 and QE 2 literally mean quantitative easing one and two, but the real meaning is that the Fed is creating more money because it believes that money is needed to get the economy moving again.[8]

There are several ways of referring to the U.S. money supply. They're called M-1, M-2, and M-3. The *M* stands for money, and the 1, 2, and 3 stand for different definitions of the money supply.

M-1
Money that can be accessed quickly and easily (coins and paper money, checks, traveler's checks, etc.)

M-1 includes coins and paper bills, money that's available by writing checks (demand deposits and share drafts), and money held in traveler's checks—that is, money that can be accessed quickly and easily. **M-2** includes everything in M-1 plus money in savings accounts, and money in money market accounts, mutual funds, certificates of deposit, and the like—that is, money that may take a little more time to obtain than coins and paper bills. M-2 is the most commonly used definition of money.[9] **M-3** is M-2 plus big deposits like institutional money market funds..

M-2
Money included in M-1 plus money that may take a little more time to obtain (savings accounts, money market accounts, mutual funds, certificates of deposit, etc.).

M-3
M-2 plus big deposits like institutional money market funds.

Managing Inflation and the Money Supply

Imagine what would happen if governments (or in the case of the United States, the Federal Reserve, a nongovernmental organization) were to generate twice as much money as exists now.[10] There would be twice as much money available, but still the same amount of goods and services. What would happen to prices? (Hint: Remember the laws of supply and demand from Chapter 2.) Prices would go up, because more people would try to buy goods and services with their money and bid up the price to get what they wanted. This rise in price is called *inflation,* which some people call "too much money chasing too few goods."

Now think about the opposite: What would happen if the Fed took money out of the economy? Prices would go down because there would be an over-supply of goods and services compared to the money available to buy them; this decrease in prices is called *deflation.*

Now we come to our second question about the money supply: Why does it need to be controlled? The reason is that doing so allows us to manage, somewhat, the prices of goods and services. The size of the money supply also affects employment and economic growth or decline. That's why the Fed and Ben Bernanke are so important.[11]

The Global Exchange of Money

A *falling dollar value* means that the amount of goods and services you can buy with a dollar decreases. A *rising dollar value* means that the amount of goods and services you can buy with a dollar goes up. Thus, the price in euros you pay for a German car will be lower if the U.S. dollar rises relative to the euro.[12] However, if the euro rises relative to the dollar, the cost of cars from Germany will go up and U.S. consumers may buy fewer German cars.

What makes the dollar weak (falling value) or strong (rising value) is the position of the U.S. economy relative to other economies. When the economy is strong, the demand for dollars is high and the value of the dollar rises. When the economy is perceived as weakening, however, the demand for dollars declines and the value of the dollar falls. The value of the dollar thus depends on a relatively strong economy. (See Chapter 3 for further discussion of effects of changes in currency values or exchange rates.) In the following section, we'll discuss in more detail the money supply and how it's managed. Then we'll explore the U.S. banking system and how it lends money to businesses and individuals, like you and me.

CONTROL OF THE MONEY SUPPLY

Theoretically, with the proper monetary policy in place to control the money supply, one can keep the economy growing without causing inflation. (See Chapter 2 to review monetary policy.) Again, the organization in charge of monetary policy is the Federal Reserve.

Basics about the Federal Reserve

The Federal Reserve System consists of five major parts: (1) the board of governors; (2) the Federal Open Market Committee (FOMC); (3) 12 Federal Reserve banks; (4) three advisory councils; and (5) the member banks of the system. Figure 20.1 shows where the 12 Federal Reserve banks are located.[13]

The board of governors administers and supervises the 12 Federal Reserve banks. The seven members of the board are appointed by the president and confirmed by the senate. The board's primary function is to set monetary policy. The

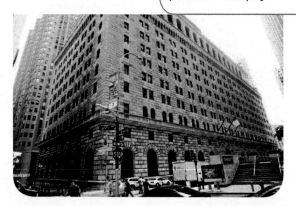

The Federal Reserve system includes 12 member banks (see Figure 20.1). This is the Federal Reserve Bank in New York City. What special role in the Fed does the president of this particular bank play?

figure 20.1

**THE 12 FEDERAL RESERVE
DISTRICT BANKS**

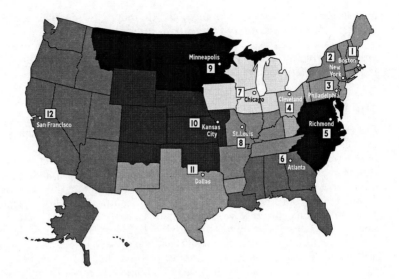

Federal Open Market Committee (FOMC) has 12 voting members and is the policymaking body. The committee is made up of the seven-member board of governors plus the president of the New York reserve bank and four members who rotate in from the other reserve banks. The advisory councils represent the various banking districts, consumers, and member institutions, including banks, savings and loan institutions, and credit unions. They offer suggestions to the board and to the FOMC.

The Fed buys and sells foreign currencies, regulates various types of credit, supervises banks, and collects data on the money supply and other economic activity. As part of monetary policy, the Fed determines the reserve requirement, that is, the level of reserve funds all financial institutions must keep at one of the 12 Federal Reserve banks.[14] It buys and sells government securities

figure 20.2

**HOW THE FEDERAL RESERVE
CONTROLS THE
MONEY SUPPLY**

CONTROL METHOD	IMMEDIATE RESULT	LONG-TERM EFFECT
Reserve Requirements		
A. Increase.	Banks put more money into the Fed, *reducing* money supply; thus, there is less money available to lend to customers.	Economy slows.
B. Decrease.	Banks put less money into the Fed, *increasing* the money supply; thus, there is more money available to lend to customers.	Economy speeds up.
Open-Market Operations		
A. Fed sells bonds.	Money flows from the economy to the Fed.	Economy slows.
B. Fed buys bonds.	Money flows into the economy from the Fed.	Economy speeds up.
Managing the Discount Rate		
A. Rate increases.	Banks borrow less from the Fed; thus, there is less money to lend.	Economy slows.
B. Rate decreases.	Banks borrow more from the Fed; thus, there is more money to lend.	Economy speeds up.

in *open-market operations*. Finally, it lends money to member banks at an interest rate called the *discount rate*.

As noted, the three basic tools the Fed uses to manage the money supply are reserve requirements, open-market operations, and the discount rate (see Figure 20.2). Let's explore how it administers each.

The Reserve Requirement

The **reserve requirement** is a percentage of commercial banks' checking and savings accounts they must keep in the bank (as cash in the vault) or in a non-interest-bearing deposit at the local Federal Reserve district bank.[15] The reserve requirement is one of the Fed's most powerful tools. When it increases the reserve requirement, money becomes scarcer, which in the long run tends to reduce inflation. For instance, if Omaha Security Bank holds deposits of $100 million and the reserve requirement is, say, 10 percent, then the bank must keep $10 million on reserve. If the Fed were to increase the reserve requirement to 11 percent, then the bank would have to put an additional $1 million on reserve, reducing the amount it could lend out. Since this increase in the reserve requirement would affect all banks, the money supply would be reduced and prices would likely fall.

A decrease of the reserve requirement, in contrast, *increases* the funds available to banks for loans, so they make more loans and money becomes more readily available. An increase in the money supply can *stimulate the economy* to achieve higher growth rates, but it can also create inflationary pressures. That is, the prices of goods and services may go up. Can you see why the Fed may want to decrease the reserve requirement when the economy is in a recession?

reserve requirement
A percentage of commercial banks' checking and savings accounts that must be physically kept in the bank.

Open-Market Operations

Open-market operations consist of the buying and selling of government bonds. To decrease the money supply, the federal government sells U.S. government bonds to the public. The money it gets as payment is no longer in circulation, decreasing the money supply. If the Fed wants to increase the money supply, it buys government bonds back from individuals, corporations, or organizations that are willing to sell. The money the Fed pays for these securities enters circulation, increasing the money supply. That's why the Fed's Bernanke bought bonds during the recent recession. The idea was to get the economy growing again.[16]

open-market operations
The buying and selling of U.S. government bonds by the Fed with the goal of regulating the money supply.

The Discount Rate

The Fed has often been called the bankers' bank, because member banks can borrow money from the Fed and pass it on to their customers in the form of loans. The **discount rate** is the interest rate the Fed charges for loans to member banks. An increase in the discount rate discourages banks from borrowing and reduces the number of available loans, decreasing the money supply. In contrast, lowering the discount rate encourages member banks to borrow money and increases the funds they have available for loans, which increases the money supply. For many months, the Fed lowered the discount rate to almost zero, hoping to increase bank lending. Nonetheless, many banks still seemed reluctant to make loans.[17]

The discount rate is one of two interest rates the Fed controls. The other is the rate banks charge each other, called the *federal funds rate*.

discount rate
The interest rate that the Fed charges for loans to member banks.

The Federal Reserve's Check-Clearing Role

If you write a check to a local retailer that uses the same bank you do, it is a simple matter to reduce your account by the amount of the check and increase the amount in the retailer's account. But what happens if you write a check to a retailer in another state? That's where the Fed's check-clearing function comes into play.

That retailer will take the check to its bank. That bank will deposit the check for credit in the closest Federal Reserve bank. That bank will send the check to your local Federal Reserve bank for collection. The check will then be sent to your bank and the amount of the check will be withdrawn. Your bank will authorize the Federal Reserve bank in your area to deduct the amount of the check. That bank will pay the Federal Reserve bank that began the process in the first place. It will then credit the deposit account in the bank where the retailer has its account. That bank will then credit the account of the retailer. (See Figure 20.3 for a diagram of such an interstate transaction.) This long

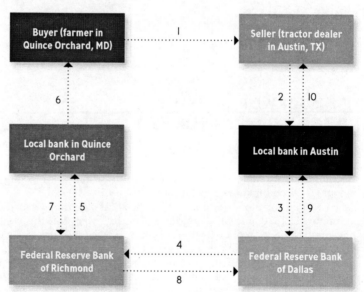

Suppose Mr. Brown, a farmer from Quince Orchard, Maryland, purchases a tractor from a dealer in Austin, Texas.

1. Mr. Brown sends his check to the tractor dealer.
2. The dealer deposits the check in his account at a local bank in Austin.
3. The Austin bank deposits the check for credit in its account at the Federal Reserve Bank of Dallas.
4. The Federal Reserve Bank of Dallas sends the check to the Federal Reserve Bank of Richmond for collection.
5. The Federal Reserve Bank of Richmond forwards the check to the local bank in Quince Orchard, where Mr. Brown has his account.
6. The local bank in Quince Orchard deducts the check amount from Mr. Brown's account.
7. The Quince Orchard bank authorizes the Federal Reserve Bank of Richmond to deduct the check amount from its deposit account with the Federal Reserve Bank.
8. The Federal Reserve Bank of Richmond pays the Federal Reserve Bank of Dallas.
9. The Federal Reserve Bank of Dallas credits the Austin bank's deposit account.
10. The Austin bank credits the tractor dealer's account.

figure 20.3

CHECK-CLEARING PROCESS THROUGH THE FEDERAL RESERVE BANK SYSTEM

and involved process is a costly one; therefore, banks take many measures to lessen the use of checks. Such efforts include the use of credit cards, debit cards, and other electronic transfers of money.[18]

As you can see, the whole economy is affected by the Federal Reserve System's actions. Next we'll briefly discuss the history of banking to give you some background about why the Fed came into existence. Then we'll explore what's happening in banking today.

progress assessment

- What is money?
- What are the five characteristics of useful money?
- What is the money supply, and why is it important?
- How does the Federal Reserve control the money supply?
- What are the major functions of the Federal Reserve? What other functions does it perform?

LEARNING goal 3

Trace the history of banking and the Federal Reserve System.

THE HISTORY OF BANKING AND THE NEED FOR THE FED

At first, there were no banks in the United States. Strict laws in Europe limited the number of coins people could bring to the colonies in the New World. Thus, colonists were forced to barter for goods; for example, they might trade cotton and tobacco for shoes and lumber.

The demand for money was so great that Massachusetts issued its own paper money in 1690, and other colonies soon followed suit. But continental money, the first paper money printed in the United States, became worthless after a few years because people didn't trust its value.

Land banks were established to lend money to farmers. But Great Britain, still in charge of the colonies at that point, ended land banks by 1741. The colonies rebelled against these and other restrictions on their freedom, and a new bank was formed in Pennsylvania during the American Revolution to finance the war against England.

In 1791, after the United States gained independence, Alexander Hamilton persuaded Congress to form a *central bank* (a bank at which other banks could keep their funds and borrow funds if needed). This first version of a federal bank closed in 1811, only to be replaced in 1816 because state-chartered banks couldn't support the War of 1812. The battle between the Second (Central) Bank of the United States and state banks got hot in the 1830s. Several banks in Tennessee were hurt by pressure from the Central Bank. The fight ended when the Central Bank was closed in 1836. You can see that there was great resistance to a central bank, like the Federal Reserve, through much of U.S. history.

By the time of the Civil War, the U.S. banking system was a mess. Different banks issued different kinds of currencies. People hoarded gold and silver coins because they were worth more as precious metal than as money. That may be happening again today. In any case, the chaos continued long after the war ended, reaching something of a climax in 1907, when many banks failed. People got nervous about the safety of banks and in a run on the banks attempted to withdraw their funds. Soon the cash was depleted and some banks had to refuse money to depositors. This caused people to distrust the banking system in general.

Despite the long history of opposition to a central bank, the cash shortage problems of 1907 led to the formation of an organization that could lend money to banks—the Federal Reserve System. It was to be a "lender of last resort" in such emergencies. Under the Federal Reserve Act of 1913, all federally chartered banks had to join the Federal Reserve. State banks could also join. The Federal Reserve became the bankers' bank. If banks had excess funds, they could deposit them in the Fed; if they needed extra money, they could borrow from the Fed. The Federal Reserve System has been intimately related to banking ever since, but never more than now.

Banking and the Great Depression

The Federal Reserve System was designed to prevent a repeat of the 1907 panic. Nevertheless, the stock market crash of 1929 led to bank failures in the early 1930s. When the stock market began tumbling, people hurried to banks to withdraw cash. In spite of the Federal Reserve System, the banks ran out of money and states were forced to close them. President Franklin D. Roosevelt extended the period of bank closings in 1933, to gain time to come up with a solution to the problem. In 1933 and 1935, Congress passed legislation to strengthen the banking system. The most important move was to establish federal deposit insurance to further protect the public from bank failures. As you can see, bank crises are nothing new; they often occur during a recession. From 1945 to 2007, the United States experienced 10 recessions. The average duration was 10 months.

The Federal Reserve System was designed in 1913 to prevent the kind of run on banks that occurred in 1907. Yet the stock market crash of 1929 caused depositors to make another run on their banks and take big withdrawals. Federal deposit insurance was established in 1933 to protect depositors' money. Do you think these protections are enough?

LEARNING goal 4

Classify the various institutions in the U.S. banking system.

THE U.S. BANKING SYSTEM

The U.S. banking system consists of commercial banks, savings and loan associations, and credit unions. In addition, there are various financial organizations, or nonbanks, that accept no deposits but offer many of the services of regular banks. Let's discuss the activities and services of each, starting with commercial banks.

Commercial Banks

A **commercial bank** is a profit-seeking organization that receives deposits from individuals and corporations in the form of checking and savings accounts and uses these funds to make loans. It has two types of customers—depositors and borrowers—and is equally responsible to both. A commercial bank makes a profit by efficiently using depositors' funds as inputs (on which it pays interest) to invest in interest-bearing loans to other customers.[19] If the revenue generated by loans exceeds the interest paid to depositors plus operating expenses, the bank makes a profit.

commercial bank
A profit-seeking organization that receives deposits from individuals and corporations in the form of checking and savings accounts and then uses some of these funds to make loans.

Services Provided by Commercial Banks

Individuals and corporations that deposit money in a checking account can write personal checks to pay for almost any purchase or transaction. The technical name for a checking account is a **demand deposit** because the money is available on demand from the depositor. Typically, banks impose a service charge for check-writing privileges or demand a minimum deposit. They might also charge a small handling fee for each check written. For corporate depositors, the amount of the service charge depends on the average daily balance in the checking account, the number of checks written, and the firm's credit rating and credit history.

In the past, checking accounts paid no interest to depositors, but interest-bearing checking accounts have experienced phenomenal growth in recent years. Commercial banks also offer a variety of savings account options. A savings account is technically a **time deposit** because the bank can require a prior notice before you make a withdrawal. Compare online and neighborhood banks to find where your money can earn the most interest.

A **certificate of deposit (CD)** is a time-deposit (savings) account that earns interest, to be delivered on the certificate's maturity date. The depositor agrees not to withdraw any of the funds until then. CDs are now available for periods of months to years; usually the longer the period, the higher the interest rate. The interest rates also depend on economic conditions. At the present time, interest rates are very low because the economy is not robust.

Commercial banks also offer credit cards to creditworthy customers, life insurance, inexpensive brokerage services, financial counseling, automatic payment of bills, safe-deposit boxes, individual retirement accounts (IRAs), traveler's checks, trust departments, automated teller machines, and overdraft checking account privileges. The latter means preferred customers can automatically get loans when they've written checks exceeding their account balance. The Social Media in Business box on p. 564 discusses how banks are using social media to reach new market segments.

demand deposit
The technical name for a checking account; the money in a demand deposit can be withdrawn anytime on demand from the depositor.

time deposit
The technical name for a savings account; the bank can require prior notice before the owner withdraws money from a time deposit.

certificate of deposit (CD)
A time-deposit (savings) account that earns interest to be delivered at the end of the certificate's maturity date.

SOCIAL MEDIA IN
business

Banking on Social Media

Just like any other business, banks must know who their customers are and how to best meet their needs. When it comes to reaching Gen Y customers (those born between 1980 and 2000) banks know that to converse and interact with this valued customer group, they have to do it online. That's one reason why banks are committing more resources to using social media.

Take Bank of America (BofA) for example. BofA introduced its mobile banking platform four years ago as cell phones got "smarter" with GPS capabilities and faster Internet access. Today 29 million BofA's customers use online banking, including 6.5 million who use their cell phones for banking. An additional 1.1 million of the bank's customers use text messages on their phones to access account information. This cultural shift led the bank to understand it needs to talk in real time with its customers online. In 2012, the bank plans to introduce two-way text alerts that allow customers to transfer funds between accounts if they receive a text message warning them that one

of their account balances is low. BofA admits that it's Gen Y's expectation that banks be accessible by social media that is driving the company's social media focus.

Banks were slow to adapt to social media due to regulatory and privacy concerns, but that's all changing. Reaching the coveted Gen Y demographic requires tweeting or texting rather than hoping they visit a local bank branch. Banks are following the lead of consumer products companies like Starbucks, Adidas, and Victoria's Secret that have used social media to get more customers. As Karen Gutierrez, social media manager for US Bank commented, "It's where our customers are, and we can better meet their needs if we are there."

Sources: Maryann Omidi, "Banks Spooked by Social Media," *Financial News*, May 4, 2011; Meghna Kothari, "Playing a Role in Social Websites," *CPI Financial*, May 11, 2011; and Lisa Brown, "Banks Woo Youth with Social Media," *St. Louis Post Dispatch*, April 17, 2011.

ATMs can dispense maps and directions, phone cards, and postage stamps. They can sell tickets to movies, concerts, and sporting events and show movie trailers, news tickers, and video ads. Some can take orders for flowers and DVDs and download music and games.

Services to Borrowers

Commercial banks offer a variety of services to individuals and corporations in need of a loan. Generally, loans are given on the basis of the recipient's creditworthiness, although the real estate collapse beginning in 2008 was partially due to banks' ignoring that rule. Banks want to manage their funds effectively and are supposed to screen loan applicants carefully to ensure that the loan plus interest will be paid back on time. Clearly banks failed to do that in the period leading up to the banking crisis. We will discuss why that happened later in the chapter. The nearby Making Ethical Decisions box explores a more minor issue that could occur in your banking efforts.

Savings and Loan Associations (S&Ls)

savings and loan association (S&L)
A financial institution that accepts both savings and checking deposits and provides home mortgage loans.

A **savings and loan association (S&L)** is a financial institution that accepts both savings and checking deposits and provides home mortgage loans. S&Ls are often known as thrift institutions because their original purpose (starting in 1831) was to promote consumer thrift and home ownership. To help them encourage home ownership, thrifts were permitted for many years to offer slightly higher interest rates on savings deposits than banks. Those rates

MAKING ethical decisions

What to Tell the Teller

You are at the teller window of your bank making a withdrawal. The teller counts out your money and says: "OK, here's your $300." You count the money and see the teller has given you $320 by mistake. When you point this out, the teller replies indignantly, "I don't think so. I counted the money in front of you."

You are upset by her quick denial of a mistake and her attitude. You have to decide whether or not to give her back the overpayment of $20. What are your alternatives? What would you do? Is that the ethical thing to do?

attracted a large pool of funds, which S&Ls used to offer long-term fixed-rate mortgages. They no longer offer better rates than banks, however.

Between 1979 and 1983, about 20 percent of the nation's S&Ls failed. Perhaps the biggest reason is that capital gains taxes were raised, making it less attractive to invest in real estate (because the added tax reduced profits). Investors therefore walked away from their real estate loans, leaving S&Ls with lots of properties worth less than the outstanding loans on them. When they sold those properties, the S&Ls lost money. The recent drop in real estate prices has caused similar problems for banks and S&Ls.

In the 1980s, the government stepped in to strengthen S&Ls, permitting them to offer higher interest rates, allocate up to 10 percent of their funds to commercial loans, and offer mortgages with adjustable interest rates based on market conditions. You can learn more about this by looking up the Glass-Steagall Act.[20] In addition, S&Ls were permitted to offer a variety of new banking services, such as financial counseling to small businesses and credit cards. As a result, they became much more similar to commercial banks.

credit unions
Nonprofit, member-owned financial cooperatives that offer the full variety of banking services to their members.

Credit Unions

Credit unions are nonprofit, member-owned financial cooperatives that offer the full variety of banking services to their members—interest-bearing checking accounts at relatively high rates, short-term loans at relatively low rates, financial counseling, life insurance policies, and a limited number of home mortgage loans. They are organized by government agencies, corporations, unions, and professional associations.

As nonprofit institutions, credit unions enjoy an exemption from federal income taxes. You might want to visit a local credit union to see whether you are eligible to belong, and then compare the rates to those at local banks. Ed Mierzwinski, a consumer program director for the U.S. Public Interest Research Group says, "The average consumer does much better at a credit union than a bank. Credit unions have lower requirements for waiving fees, offer better deals on car loans, and are generally more flexible in responding to customer's problems."[21]

Credit unions are member-owned financial cooperatives that offer their members a wide range of banking services and, because they are non-profits, are exempt from federal income tax. Which credit unions are available in your area?

565

Credit unions often have fewer branches than banks and less access to ATMs. It's best to determine what services you need and then compare those services to the same services offered by banks.

Other Financial Institutions (Nonbanks)

nonbanks
Financial organizations that accept no deposits but offer many of the services provided by regular banks (pension funds, insurance companies, commercial finance companies, consumer finance companies, and brokerage houses).

Nonbanks are financial organizations that accept no deposits but offer many of the services provided by regular banks. Nonbanks include life insurance companies, pension funds, brokerage firms, commercial finance companies, and corporate financial services (like GE Capital). Nonbanks cut back their lending considerably during the banking crisis beginning in 2008. Such a drop-off in lending contributed to slowing the economy greatly.

As competition between banks and nonbanks has increased, the dividing line between them has become less apparent. This is equally true in Europe, where U.S. companies compete with European banks. The diversity of financial services and investment alternatives nonbanks offer has led banks to expand their own services. In fact, many banks have merged with brokerage firms to offer full-service financial assistance.

Life insurance companies provide financial protection for policyholders, who periodically pay premiums. In addition, insurers invest the funds they receive from policyholders in corporate and government bonds. In recent years, more insurance companies have begun to provide long-term financing for real estate development projects. Do you think that was a wise decision?

pension funds
Amounts of money put aside by corporations, nonprofit organizations, or unions to cover part of the financial needs of members when they retire.

Pension funds are monies put aside by corporations, nonprofit organizations, or unions to help fund their members' financial needs when they retire. Contributions to pension funds are made by employees, employers, or both. To generate additional income, pension funds typically invest in low-return but safe corporate stocks or other conservative investments such as government securities and corporate bonds.

Many financial services organizations that provide retirement and health benefits, such as TIAA-CREF, are becoming a major force in U.S. financial markets. They also lend money directly to corporations.

Brokerage firms have traditionally offered investment services in stock exchanges in the United States and abroad. They have also made serious inroads into regular banks' domain by offering high-yield combination savings and checking accounts. In addition, they offer money market accounts with check-writing privileges and allow investors to borrow, using their securities as collateral.

Commercial and consumer finance companies offer short-term loans to those who cannot meet the credit requirements of regular banks, such as new businesses, or who have exceeded their credit limit and need more funds. College students with no credit history often turn to consumer finance companies for education loans. Be careful when borrowing from such institutions because their interest rates can be quite high. The nearby Spotlight on Small Business box offers an example of a newer type of nonbank that offers services to people who do not have traditional checking accounts.

progress assessment

- Why did the United States need a Federal Reserve Bank?
- What's the difference between a bank, a savings and loan association, and a credit union?
- What is a consumer finance company?

SPOTLIGHT ON SMALL
business

The Rise of the Nonbank

About a fourth of American households don't have a bank account. That creates a huge market for alternative banking such as that provided by Mango Store. It is a banklike facility in Austin, Texas. Clients pay a one-time $10 fee that lets them cash as many checks as they want by putting the money onto debit cards. More sophisticated services cost extra. Nonetheless, Mango's fees are much less than a typical local bank.

Mango hopes its customers will increase their earning power and remain customers over time. First, however, the company must get customers through the door and onto its system. Because the majority of Mango's cash is stored in the outside ATM, the interior can emphasize open spaces and security cameras. Customers can use self-serve kiosks to check card balances and transfer funds. Bilingual counselors help customers understand the system. To help customers

better understand the services available and the costs, the store has banners clearly displaying fees.

Sources: Dan Macsai, "The Mango Store Lets You Bank without Commitment," *Fast Company*, July I, 2010; "Mango Financial, Inc., Debuts First U.S. Store in Austin," PR Newswire.com, accessed May 2011; and mangomoney.com, accessed May 2011.

LEARNING goal 5

Briefly trace the causes of the banking crisis starting in 2008 and explain how the government protects your funds during such crises.

THE RECENT BANKING CRISIS AND HOW THE GOVERNMENT PROTECTS YOUR MONEY

What led to the recent banking crisis? There is no simple answer. Some people believe the Federal Reserve is partly responsible because it kept the cost of borrowing so low that people were tempted to borrow more than they could afford to pay back. Congress, very interested in creating more "affordable housing," prodded banks to lend to people with minimal assets. The Community Reinvestment Act further encouraged loans to families with questionable ability to repay.

Other organizations pressured banks, normally quite risk-averse, to make risky loans. Banks learned they could avoid much of the risk by dividing their portfolios of mortgages up and selling the mortgage-backed securities (MBSs) to other banks and other organizations all over the world. These securities seemed quite safe because they were backed by the homes that were mortgaged. Fannie Mae and Freddie Mac are both quasi-government agencies that seemed to guarantee the value of MBSs. Banks sold more and more of such seemingly safe

The bursting of the housing bubble forced a sharp decline in home values. When homeowners discovered they owed more on their mortgages than their homes were worth, many stopped paying off their loans and the banks foreclosed on their homes. This forced home prices to fall lower still and put even more people in jeopardy of losing their homes. What can the government do to help homeowners?

Federal Deposit Insurance Corporation (FDIC)
An independent agency of the U.S. government that insures bank deposits.

securities, hoping to make lots of money. Bankers were also accused of pushing loans onto naive consumers.

Meanwhile, the Federal Reserve and the Securities and Exchange Commission failed to issue sufficient warnings. That is, they failed in their regulatory duties. When the value of homes began to decline, people began defaulting on their loans (not paying them) and turned the properties back over to the banks. Since the banks owned the mortgages on those homes, their profits declined dramatically, leading to the recent banking crisis—and the need for the government to help the banks out. Not doing so was considered too risky because the whole economy might fail. The long-term effects of that process are not yet known.

So whom do we blame for the banking crisis? The answer is that we could blame the Fed for suppressing interest rates, the Congress for promoting questionable loans, the banks for making such loans and creating mortgage-backed securities that were not nearly as safe as promoted, government regulatory agencies for not doing their job, and people who took advantage of low interest rates to borrow money they couldn't reasonably hope to repay. No matter who was to blame, the crisis still needed to be solved.

Toward the end of George W. Bush's presidency, the Treasury Department proposed a $700 billion "bailout" package, known as the Troubled Assets Relief Program (TARP). The program was enacted in October 2008. President Barack Obama, who took office in January 2009, proposed over $800 billion in additional government spending plus a stimulus package. We are just now seeing the results of that spending.

Protecting Your Funds

The recent banking crisis is nothing new. The government had seen similar problems during the Great Depression of the 1930s. To prevent investors from ever again being completely wiped out during an economic downturn, it created three major organizations to protect your money: the Federal Deposit Insurance Corporation (FDIC); the Savings Association Insurance Fund (SAIF); and the National Credit Union Administration (NCUA). All three insure deposits in individual accounts up to a certain amount. Because these organizations are so important to the safety of your money, let's explore them individually in more depth.

The Federal Deposit Insurance Corporation (FDIC)

The **Federal Deposit Insurance Corporation (FDIC)** is an independent agency of the U.S. government that insures bank deposits. If a bank were to fail, the FDIC would arrange to have that bank's accounts transferred to another bank or reimburse depositors up to $250,000. The FDIC covers about 13,000 institutions, mostly commercial banks.

The Savings Association Insurance Fund (SAIF)

The **Savings Association Insurance Fund (SAIF)** insures holders of accounts in savings and loan associations. A brief history will show why it was created. Some 1,700 bank and thrift institutions had failed during the early 1930s, and people were losing confidence in them. The FDIC and the Federal Savings and Loan Insurance Corporation (FSLIC) were designed (in 1933 and 1934, respectively) to create more confidence in banking institutions by protecting people's savings from loss. In the 1980s, to get more control over the banking system in general, the government placed the FSLIC under the FDIC and gave it a new name: the Savings Association Insurance Fund (SAIF).

The National Credit Union Administration (NCUA)

The National Credit Union Administration (NCUA) provides up to $250,000 coverage per individual depositor per institution. This coverage includes all accounts—checking accounts, savings accounts, money market accounts, and certificates of deposit. Depositors qualify for additional protection by holding accounts jointly or in trust. Individual retirement accounts (IRAs) are also separately insured up to $250,000. Credit unions, like banks, suffered from the banking crisis beginning in 2008 and got money from the federal government to make more loans.

LEARNING goal 6

Describe how technology helps make banking more efficient.

USING TECHNOLOGY TO MAKE BANKING MORE EFFICIENT

Imagine the cost to a bank of approving a written check, physically processing it through the banking system, and mailing it back to you. It's expensive. Bankers have long looked for ways to make the system more efficient.

One solution was to issue credit cards to reduce the flow of checks, but they too have their costs: there's still paper to process. Accepting Visa and MasterCard costs retailers about $2 per $100 purchase; Amex costs them about $2.50. In the future we'll see much more electronic rather than physical exchange of money, because it is the most efficient way to transfer funds.

If you must use a credit card, be sure to search for one that offers the best deal for you. Some offer cash back, others offer free travel, and so forth. Don't just sign up for whatever card is offering free T-shirts on campus. Do your research.

In an **electronic funds transfer (EFT) system**, messages about a transaction are sent from one computer to another. Thus, organizations can transfer funds more quickly and economically than

Savings Association Insurance Fund (SAIF)
The part of the FDIC that insures holders of accounts in savings and loan associations.

electronic funds transfer (EFT) system
A computerized system that electronically performs financial transactions such as making purchases, paying bills, and receiving paychecks.

Smartphone apps, such as FaceCash, allow users to pay for purchases with their phones. What problems could there be with such capabilities?

Need to pass the security check in your office building, put gas in your car, and get cash at the ATM? No problem. Smart cards with embedded RFID chips can take care of these tasks and then some. Has cash become a thing of the past?

debit card
An electronic funds transfer tool that serves the same function as checks: it withdraws funds from a checking account.

smart card
An electronic funds transfer tool that is a combination credit card, debit card, phone card, driver's license card, and more.

with paper checks. EFT tools include electronic check conversion, debit cards, smart cards, direct deposits, and direct payments. The latest technology, developed by information commerce company First Data, is the GO-Tag, a pea-shaped chip with a radio transmitter inside that can stick to a cell phone or ID badge to make payments fast and easy. It takes only a second to complete a transaction with a GO-Tag, much faster than even a credit card.

A **debit card** serves the same function as a check—it withdraws funds from a checking account. It looks like a credit card but withdraws (debits) money that is already in your account. When the sale is recorded, the debit card sends an electronic signal to the bank, automatically transferring funds from your account to the store's. A record of transactions immediately appears online. Debit transactions surpassed credit years ago and continue to grow twice as fast.[22]

Payroll debit cards are an efficient way for some firms to pay their workers and an alternative to cash for those who don't qualify for a credit or debit card—the so-called unbanked. Employees can access funds in their accounts immediately after they are posted, withdraw them from an ATM, pay bills online, or transfer funds to another cardholder. The system is much cheaper for companies than issuing checks and more convenient for employees. On the other hand, debit cards don't offer the same protection as credit cards. If someone steals your credit card, you are liable only for a certain amount. You are liable for everything when someone steals your debit card.

A **smart card** is an electronic funds transfer tool that combines a credit card, debit card, phone card, driver's license card, and more. Smart cards replace the typical magnetic strip on a credit or debit card with a microprocessor. The card can then store a variety of information, including the holder's bank balance. Merchants can use this information to check the card's validity and spending limits, and transactions can debit up to the amount on the card.

Some smart cards have embedded radio-frequency identification (RFID) chips that make it possible to enter buildings and secure areas and to buy gas and other items with a swipe of the card. A biometric function lets you use your fingerprint to boot up your computer. Students are using smart cards to open locked doors to dorms and identify themselves to retailers near campus and online. The cards also serve as ATM cards.

For many, the ultimate convenience in banking is automatic transactions such as direct deposit and direct payments. A *direct deposit* is a credit made directly to a checking or savings account in place of a paycheck. The employer contacts the bank and orders it to transfer funds from the employer's account to the worker's account. Individuals can use direct deposits to transfer funds to other accounts, such as from a checking account to a savings or retirement account.

A *direct payment* is a preauthorized electronic payment. Customers sign a separate form for each company whose bill they would like to automatically pay from their checking or savings account on a specified date. The customer's bank completes each transaction and records it on the customer's monthly statement.

Online Banking

All top U.S. retail banks now allow customers to access their accounts online, and most have bill-paying capacity. Thus, you can complete all your financial transactions from home, using your telephone or your computer to transfer funds from one account to another, pay your bills, and check the balance in each of your accounts. You can apply for a car loan or mortgage and get a response while you wait. Buying and selling stocks and bonds is equally easy.

Internet banks such as E*Trade Bank offer online banking only, not physical branches. They can offer customers higher interest rates and lower fees because they do not have the overhead costs traditional banks have. While many consumers are pleased with the savings and convenience, not all are happy with the service. Why? Some are nervous about security. People fear putting their financial information into cyberspace, where others may see it despite all the assurances of privacy. Further, some people want to be able to talk to a knowledgeable person one-on-one when they have banking problems.

The future thus seems to be with traditional banks that offer both online services and brick-and-mortar facilities. Even small, local banks offer online services now.

LEARNING goal **7**

> Evaluate the role and importance of international banking, the World Bank, and the International Monetary Fund.

INTERNATIONAL BANKING AND BANKING SERVICES

Banks help companies conduct business in other countries by providing three services: letters of credit, banker's acceptances, and money exchange. If a U.S. company wants to buy a product from Germany, the company could pay a bank to issue a letter of credit. A **letter of credit** is a promise by the bank to pay the seller a given amount if certain conditions are met. For example, the German company may not be paid until the goods have arrived at the U.S. company's warehouse. A **banker's acceptance** promises that the bank will pay some specified amount at a particular time. No conditions are imposed. Finally, a company can go to a bank and exchange U.S. dollars for euros to use in Germany; that's called *currency* or *money exchange*.

Banks are making it easier than ever for travelers and businesspeople to buy goods and services overseas. Automated teller machines now provide yen, euros, and other foreign currencies through your personal Visa, MasterCard, Cirrus, or American Express card.

letter of credit
A promise by the bank to pay the seller a given amount if certain conditions are met.

banker's acceptance
A promise that the bank will pay some specified amount at a particular time.

Leaders in International Banking

It would be shortsighted to discuss the U.S. economy apart from the world economy. If the Federal Reserve decides to lower interest rates, within minutes foreign investors can withdraw their money from the United States and put it in countries with higher rates. Of course, the Fed's increasing of interest rates can draw money to the United States equally quickly.

Today's money markets thus form a global market system of which the United States is just a part. International bankers make investments in any country where they can get a maximum return for their money at a reasonable risk. That's how about $4 trillion is traded daily! The net result of international banking and finance has been to link the economies of the world into one interrelated system with no regulatory control. U.S. firms must compete for funds with firms all over the world. An efficient firm in London or Tokyo is more likely to get international financing than a less efficient firm in Detroit or Chicago. Global markets mean that banks do not necessarily keep their money in their own countries. They make investments where they get the maximum return.

What this means for you is that banking is no longer a domestic issue; it's a global one. To understand the U.S. financial system, you must learn about the global financial system. To understand the state of the U.S. economy, you need to learn about the economic condition of countries throughout the world. In the new world economy financed by international banks, the United States is just one player. To be a winner, it must stay financially secure and its businesses must stay competitive in world markets. Is that happening today?

World Bank
The bank primarily responsible for financing economic development; also known as the International Bank for Reconstruction and Development.

International Monetary Fund (IMF)
Organization that assists the smooth flow of money among nations.

The World Bank and the International Monetary Fund (IMF)

The bank primarily responsible for financing economic development is the International Bank for Reconstruction and Development, or the **World Bank**.[23] After World War II, it lent money to countries in Western Europe so they could rebuild. Today, it lends most of its money to developing nations to improve their productivity and help raise standards of living and quality of life. That includes working to eliminate diseases that kill millions of people each year.

The World Bank has faced considerable criticism and protests around the world. Environmentalists charge that it finances projects damaging to the ecosystem. Human rights activists and unionists say the bank supports countries that restrict religious freedoms and tolerate sweatshops. AIDS activists complain that it does not do enough to get low-cost AIDS drugs to developing nations.

Despite its efforts to improve, the World Bank still has many critics. Some want it to forgive the debts of developing countries and others want it to stop making such loans until the countries institute free markets and the right to own property. Some changes in World Bank policy may lie ahead.[24]

In contrast to the World Bank, the **International Monetary Fund (IMF)** was established to foster cooperative monetary policies that stabilize the exchange of one national currency for another.[25] About 185 countries are voluntary members of the IMF and allow their money to be freely exchanged for foreign money, keep the IMF informed about

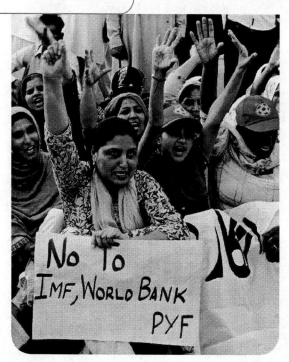

The World Bank and the International Monetary Fund (IMF) are intergovernmental organizations that help support the global banking community. Both draw protests for their actions. Why?

REACHING BEYOND
our borders

New Issues Facing the World Bank and the IMF

In the past, the World Bank and the IMF have had to face major crises throughout the world. Today, the issues seem to be as great as ever. For example, the United States has very high unemployment and a debt crisis that exceeds anything in the past. A similar debt crisis is occurring in many European countries. Japan is trying to recover from its earthquake and tsunami and other disasters (e.g., the nuclear problems). There are major disruptions occurring in the Middle East, and the United States is uncertain as to what to do. Emerging nations such as China and Brazil are having problems with high inflation, and food prices are rising all over the planet. Poorer nations are having a particularly hard time because of the high food prices.

The Chair of the IMF's governing body says, "There are significant vulnerabilities still in the global financial and economic systems. That reflects the legacy of an international monetary system that is still not in what we consider satisfactory shape."

The IMF and the World Bank are both trying to come up with answers to the global issues that have become very serious. The United States is a major contributor to those organizations, but there is not enough money to pay down the U.S. debt, much less solve the problems of the rest of the world.

Sources: Neil Irwin, "World Bank, IMF Leaders: Recovery Still a Shaky One," *The Washington Post,* April 17, 2011; and Howard Schneider, "IMF Panel Seeks a New Consensus," *The Washington Post,* March 8, 2011.

changes in monetary policy, and modify those policies on the advice of the IMF to accommodate the needs of the entire membership.

The IMF is designed to oversee member countries' monetary and exchange rate policies. Its goal is to maintain a global monetary system that works best for all nations and enhances world trade. While it is not primarily a lending institution like the World Bank, its members do contribute funds according to their ability, and those funds are available to countries in financial difficulty.[26] The IMF saw a slowing in the global economy in 2010 and was prepared to give certain countries a boost if necessary.[27] The IMF is usually in favor of free capital inflows, but recently it has allowed countries to put up barriers to protect their economies from inflation or bubbles in their stock markets. Countries included in this effort included Brazil, South Korea, and Turkey.[28] The nearby Reaching Beyond Our Borders box discusses what is happening today at the World Bank and the IMF.

progress assessment

- What are some of the causes for the banking crisis that began in 2008?
- What is the role of the FDIC?
- How does a debit card differ from a credit card?
- What is the World Bank and what does it do?
- What is the IMF and what does it do?

summary

Learning Goal 1. Explain what money is and what makes money useful.

- **What is money?**

Money is anything people generally accept as payment for goods and services.

- **What are the five standards for a useful form of money?**

The five standards for a useful form of money are portability, divisibility, stability, durability, and uniqueness.

Learning Goal 2. Describe how the Federal Reserve controls the money supply.

- **How does the Federal Reserve control the money supply?**

The Federal Reserve makes financial institutions keep funds in the Federal Reserve System (reserve requirement), buys and sells government securities (open-market operations), and lends money to banks (the discount rate). To increase the money supply, the Fed can cut the reserve requirement, buy government bonds, and lower the discount rate.

Learning Goal 3. Trace the history of banking and the Federal Reserve System.

- **How did banking evolve in the United States?**

Massachusetts issued its own paper money in 1690; other colonies followed suit. British land banks lent money to farmers but ended such loans by 1741. After the American Revolution, there was much debate about the role of banking, and heated battles between the Central Bank of the United States and state banks. Eventually, a federally chartered and state-chartered system was established, but chaos continued until many banks failed in 1907. The system was revived by the Federal Reserve only to fail again during the Great Depression. There have been 10 recessions since then, including the recession starting in 2008. The Federal Reserve is doing all it can to solve the banking crisis again.

Learning Goal 4. Classify the various institutions in the U.S. banking system.

- **What institutions make up the banking system?**

Savings and loans, commercial banks, and credit unions are all part of the banking system.

- **How do they differ from one another?**

Before deregulation in 1980, commercial banks were unique in that they handled both deposits and checking accounts. At that time, savings and loans couldn't offer checking services; their main function was to encourage thrift and home ownership by offering high interest rates on savings accounts and providing home mortgages. Deregulation closed the gaps between banks and S&Ls and they now offer similar services.

- **What kinds of services do they offer?**

Banks and thrifts offer such services as savings accounts, checking accounts, certificates of deposit, loans, individual retirement accounts (IRAs), safe-deposit boxes, online banking, life insurance, brokerage services, and traveler's checks.

- **What is a credit union?**

A credit union is a member-owned cooperative that offers everything a bank does—it takes deposits, allows you to write checks, and makes loans. It also may sell life insurance and offer mortgages. Credit union interest rates are sometimes higher than those from banks, and loan rates are often lower.

- **What are some of the other financial institutions that make loans and perform banklike operations?**

Nonbanks include life insurance companies that lend out their funds, pension funds that invest in stocks and bonds and make loans, brokerage firms that offer investment services, and commercial finance companies.

Learning Goal 5. Briefly trace the causes of the banking crisis starting in 2008 and explain how the government protects your funds during such crises.

- **What caused the banking crisis that began in 2008?**

The goal was to have affordable housing, so the government urged banks to make loans to some who could not afford to repay. The banks wanted to minimize the risk of such loans, so they created mortgage-backed securities and sold them to other banks and organizations throughout the world. The government did not regulate these transactions well, and many banks failed because housing values fell and people defaulted on their loans. Many have been blamed for the loss: the Fed, Congress, bank managers, Fannie Mae, and Freddie Mac among them.

- **What agencies insure the money you put into a bank, S&L, or credit union?**

Money deposited in banks is insured by the Federal Deposit Insurance Corporation (FDIC). Money in S&Ls is insured by another agency connected to the FDIC, the Savings Association Insurance Fund (SAIF). Money in credit unions is insured by the National Credit Union Administration (NCUA). Accounts are now insured to $250,000.

Learning Goal 6. Describe how technology helps make banking more efficient.

- **What are debit cards and smart cards?**

A debit card looks like a credit card but withdraws money that is already in your account. When the sale is recorded, the debit card sends an electronic signal to the bank, automatically transferring funds from your account to the store's. A smart card is an electronic funds transfer tool that combines a credit card, debit card, phone card, driver's license card, and more. Smart cards replace the typical magnetic strip on a credit or debit card with a microprocessor.

- **What is the benefit of automatic transactions and online banking?**

A *direct deposit* is a credit made directly to a checking or savings account in place of a paycheck. A *direct payment* is a preauthorized electronic payment. Customers sign a separate form for each company whose bill they would like to automatically pay from their checking or savings account on a specified date. The customer's bank completes each transaction and records it on the customer's monthly statement. All top U.S. retail banks now allow customers to access their accounts online, and most have bill-paying capacity.

Learning Goal 7. Evaluate the role and importance of international banking, the World Bank, and the International Monetary Fund.

- **What do we mean by global markets?**

Global markets mean that banks do not necessarily keep their money in their own countries. They make investments where they get the maximum return. What this means for you is that banking is no longer a domestic issue; it's a global one.

- **What roles do the World Bank and the IMF play?**

The World Bank (also called the International Bank for Reconstruction and Development) is primarily responsible for financing economic development. The International Monetary Fund (IMF), in contrast, was established to assist the smooth flow of money among nations. It requires members (who join voluntarily) to allow their own money to be exchanged for foreign money freely, to keep the IMF informed about changes in monetary policy, and to modify those policies on the advice of the IMF to accommodate the needs of the entire membership. Lately the IMF has been lending money to countries affected by the U.S. banking crisis, and the U.S. has promised more money to the IMF.

key terms

banker's acceptance 571	**Federal Deposit Insurance Corporation (FDIC)** 568	**open-market operations** 559
barter 555		**pension funds** 566
certificate of deposit (CD) 563	**International Monetary Fund (IMF)** 572	**reserve requirement** 559
commercial bank 563	**letter of credit** 571	**savings and loan association (S&L)** 564
credit unions 565	**M-1** 556	**Savings Association Insurance Fund (SAIF)** 569
debit card 570	**M-2** 556	
demand deposit 563	**M-3** 556	**smart card** 570
discount rate 559	**money** 555	**time deposit** 563
electronic funds transfer (EFT) system 569	**money supply** 556	**World Bank** 572
	nonbanks 566	

critical thinking

1. If you were Ben Bernanke, chairman of the Federal Reserve, what economic figures might you use to determine how well you were doing? What role did Bernanke play in the recent banking crisis?

2. How much cash do you usually carry with you? What other means do you use to pay for items at the store or on the Internet? What trends do you see in such payments? How might those trends make your purchase experience more satisfactory?

3. If the value of the dollar declines relative to the euro, what will happen to the price of French wine sold in U.S. stores? Will people in France be more or less likely to buy a U.S.-made car? Why or why not?

4. Do you keep your savings in a bank, an S&L, a credit union, or some combination? Have you compared the benefits you could receive from each? Where would you expect to find the best loan values?

developing workplace skills

1. In a small group, discuss the following: What services do you use from banks and S&Ls? Does anyone use online banking? What seem to be its pluses and minuses? Use this opportunity to compare the rates and services of various local banks and S&Ls.

2. Poll the class to see who uses a bank and who uses a credit union. Have class members compare the services at each (interest rates on savings accounts, services available, loan rates). If anyone uses an online service, see how those rates compare. If no one uses a credit union or online bank, discuss the reasons.

3. One role of the Federal Reserve is to help process your checks. In small groups discuss when and where you use checks, credit cards, debit cards, and cash. Do you often write checks for small amounts? Would you stop if

you calculated how much it costs to process such checks? Have you switched to debit cards as a result? Discuss your findings with the class.

4. Form several smaller groups and discuss the recent banking crisis. How has it affected the people in the class? What has happened to banks and the economy in general since the start of the banking crisis? What have been the political implications of recent economic changes?

5. Write a one-page paper on the role of the World Bank and the International Monetary Fund in providing loans to countries. Is it important for U.S. citizens to lend money to people in other countries through such organizations? Why or why not? Be prepared to debate the value of these organizations in class.

taking it to the net

Purpose

To learn more about the banking crisis that began in 2008 and what has happened since.

Exercise

1. Do an Internet search to find the latest articles on the global financial crisis. What has happened to banking in the United States and around the world since 2009? What role has the Fed played in trying to end the crisis in the United States?

2. How many search items have appeared covering this issue? What does the number of articles tell you about the importance of this issue?

3. Develop your own story about the causes of the banking crisis. Talk to others in the class and compare stories. What organizations share the blame for the crisis?

casing the web

To access the case "Learning about the Federal Reserve System," visit **www.mhhe.com/ubl0e**

video case

To access the video case featuring the Financial Crisis-Banking Disaster, visit **www.mhhe.com/ubl0e**

glossary

401(k) plan (p. D-14) A savings plan that allows you to deposit pretax dollars and whose earnings compound tax free until withdrawal, when the money is taxed at ordinary income tax rates.

absolute advantage (p. 62) The advantage that exists when a country has a monopoly on producing a specific product or is able to produce it more efficiently than all other countries.

accounting (p. 464) The recording, classifying, summarizing, and interpreting of financial events and transactions to provide management and other interested parties the information they need to make good decisions.

accounting cycle (p. 470) A six-step procedure that results in the preparation and analysis of the major financial statements.

accounts payable (p. 474) Current liabilities involving money owed to others for merchandise or services purchased on credit but not yet paid for.

acquisition (p. 131) One company's purchase of the property and obligations of another company.

administered distribution system (p. 421) A distribution system in which producers manage all of the marketing functions at the retail level.

administrative agencies (p. A-3) Federal or state institutions and other government organizations created by Congress or state legislatures with delegated power to pass rules and regulations within their mandated area of authority.

advertising (p. 438) Paid, nonpersonal communication through various media by organizations and individuals who are in some way identified in the advertising message.

affiliate marketing (p. 156) An Internet-based marketing strategy in which a business rewards individuals or other businesses (affiliates) for each visitor or customer the affiliate sends to its website.

affirmative action (p. 294) Employment activities designed to "right past wrongs" by increasing opportunities for minorities and women.

agency shop agreement (p. 331) Clause in a labor–management agreement that says employers may hire nonunion workers; employees are not required to join the union but must pay a union fee.

agents/brokers (p. 407) Marketing intermediaries who bring buyers and sellers together and assist in negotiating an exchange but don't take title to the goods.

American Federation of Labor (AFL) (p. 326) An organization of craft unions that championed fundamental labor issues; founded in 1886.

annual report (p. 466) A yearly statement of the financial condition, progress, and expectations of an organization.

annuity (p. D-11) A contract to make regular payments to a person for life or for a fixed period.

apprentice programs (p. 304) Training programs involving a period during which a learner works alongside an experienced employee to master the skills and procedures of a craft.

arbitration (p. 334) The agreement to bring in an impartial third party (a single arbitrator or a panel of arbitrators) to render a binding decision in a labor dispute.

assembly process (p. 240) That part of the production process that puts together components.

assets (p. 474) Economic resources (things of value) owned by a firm.

auditing (p. 468) The job of reviewing and evaluating the information used to prepare a company's financial statements.

autocratic leadership (p. 192) Leadership style that involves making managerial decisions without consulting others.

balance of payments (p. 65) The difference between money coming into a country (from exports) and money leaving the country (for imports) plus money flows from other factors such

Note: Terms and definitions printed in italics are considered business slang, or jargon.

as tourism, foreign aid, military expenditures, and foreign investment.

balance of trade (p. 64) The total value of a nation's exports compared to its imports over a particular period.

balance sheet (p. 473) Financial statement that reports a firm's financial condition at a specific time and is composed of three major accounts: assets, liabilities, and owners' equity.

ballyhooed *Talked about in an exaggerated way.*

banker's acceptance (p. 571) A promise that the bank will pay some specified amount at a particular time.

bankruptcy (p. A-15) The legal process by which a person, business, or government entity unable to meet financial obligations is relieved of those obligations by a court that divides any assets among creditors, allowing creditors to get at least part of their money and freeing the debtor to begin anew.

bargaining zone (p. 333) The range of options between the initial and final offer that each party will consider before negotiations dissolve or reach an impasse.

barter (p. 555) The direct trading of goods or services for other goods or services.

bear market *Situation where the stock market is declining in value and investors feel it will continue to decline.*

been there, done that *Prior experience.*

benchmarking (p. 221) Comparing an organization's practices, processes, and products against the world's best.

benefit segmentation (p. 368) Dividing the market by determining which benefits of the product to talk about.

blog (p. 454) An online diary (Web log) that looks like a Web page but is easier to create and update by posting text, photos, or links to other sites.

bond (p. 529) A corporate certificate indicating that a person has lent money to a firm.

bonds payable (p. 475) Long-term liabilities that represent money lent to the firm that must be paid back.

bookkeeping (p. 470) The recording of business transactions.

bottom line *The last line in a profit and loss statement; it refers to net profit or loss.*

brain drain (p. 42) The loss of the best and brightest people to other countries.

brainstorming (p. 187) Coming up with as many solutions to a problem as possible in a short period of time with no censoring of ideas.

brand (p. 387) A name, symbol, or design (or combination thereof) that identifies the goods or services of one seller or group of sellers and distinguishes them from the goods and services of competitors.

brand association (p. 389) The linking of a brand to other favorable images.

brand awareness (p. 389) How quickly or easily a given brand name comes to mind when a product category is mentioned.

brand equity (p. 389) The value of the brand name and associated symbols.

brand loyalty (p. 389) The degree to which customers are satisfied, like the brand, and are committed to further purchases.

brand manager (p. 390) A manager who has direct responsibility for one brand or one product line; called a product manager in some firms.

brand name (p. 358) A word, letter, or group of words or letters that differentiates one seller's goods and services from those of competitors.

breach of contract (p. A-10) When one party fails to follow the terms of a contract.

break-even analysis (p. 397) The process used to determine profitability at various levels of sales.

brightest days *The best of times for a person or organization.*

broadband technology (p. B-10) Technology that offers users a continuous connection to the Internet and allows them to send and receive mammoth files that include voice, video, and data much faster than ever before.

budget (p. 498) A financial plan that sets forth management's expectations, and, on the basis of those expectations, allocates the use of specific resources throughout the firm.

bull market *Situation where the stock market is increasing in value and investors feel it will continue to grow.*

bundling (p. 386) Grouping two or more products together and pricing them as a unit.

G-2   **GLOSSARY**

bureaucracy (p. 209) An organization with many layers of managers who set rules and regulations and oversee all decisions.

business (p. 4) Any activity that seeks to provide goods and services to others while operating at a profit.

business cycles (p. 49) The periodic rises and falls that occur in economies over time.

business environment (p. II) The surrounding factors that either help or hinder the development of businesses.

business intelligence (BI) (p. B-3) Any of a variety of software applications that analyze an organization's raw data and take out useful insights from it.

business law (p. A-2) Rules, statutes, codes, and regulations that are established to provide a legal framework within which business may be conducted and that are enforceable by court action.

business plan (p. 163) A detailed written statement that describes the nature of the business, the target market, the advantages the business will have in relation to competition, and the resources and qualifications of the owner(s).

business-to-business (B2B) market (p. 365) All the individuals and organizations that want goods and services to use in producing other goods and services or to sell, rent, or supply goods to others.

buying stock on margin (p. 537) Purchasing stocks by borrowing some of the purchase cost from the brokerage firm.

cafeteria-style fringe benefits (p. 312) Fringe benefits plan that allows employees to choose the benefits they want up to a certain dollar amount.

cannibalize a business *One franchise pulls business away from another franchise, for example.*

capital budget (p. 498) A budget that highlights a firm's spending plans for major asset purchases that often require large sums of money.

capital expenditures (p. 503) Major investments in either tangible long-term assets such as land, buildings, and equipment or intangible assets such as patents, trademarks, and copyrights.

capital gains (p. 535) The positive difference between the purchase price of a stock and its sale price.

capitalism (p. 35) An economic system in which all or most of the factors of production and distribution are privately owned and operated for profit.

cash-and-carry wholesalers (p. 413) Wholesalers that serve mostly smaller retailers with a limited assortment of products.

cash budget (p. 498) A budget that estimates cash inflows and outflows during a particular period like a month or a quarter.

cash flow (p. 480) The difference between cash coming in and cash going out of a business.

cash flow forecast (p. 487) Forecast that predicts the cash inflows and outflows in future periods, usually months or quarters.

center stage *A very important position.*

centralized authority (p. 210) An organization structure in which decision-making authority is maintained at the top level of management at the company's headquarters.

certificate of deposit (CD) (p. 563) A time-deposit (savings) account that earns interest to be delivered at the end of the certificate's maturity date.

certification (p. 329) Formal process whereby a union is recognized by the National Labor Relations Board (NLRB) as the bargaining agent for a group of employees.

certified internal auditor (CIA) (p. 469) An accountant who has a bachelor's degree and two years of experience in internal auditing, and who has passed an exam administered by the Institute of Internal Auditors.

certified management accountant (CMA) (p. 466) A professional accountant who has met certain educational and experience requirements, passed a qualifying exam in the field, and been certified by the Institute of Certified Management Accountants.

certified public accountant (CPA) (p. 467) An accountant who passes a series of examinations established by the American Institute of Certified Public Accountants (AICPA).

chain of command (p. 209) The line of authority that moves from the top of a hierarchy to the lowest level.

channel of distribution (p. 406) A whole set of marketing intermediaries, such as agents, brokers, wholesalers, and retailers, that join together to transport and store goods in their path (or channel) from producers to consumers.

claim (p. C-7) A statement of loss that the insured sends to the insurance company to request payment.

climate change (p. 19) The movement of the temperature of the planet up or down over time.

climbed the ladder *Promoted to higher-level jobs.*

closed shop agreement (p. 331) Clause in a labor–management agreement that specified workers had to be members of a union before being hired (was outlawed by the Taft-Hartley Act in 1947).

cloud computing (p. B-14) A form of virtualization in which a company's data and applications are stored at offsite data centers that are accessed over the Internet (the cloud).

collective bargaining (p. 328) The process whereby union and management representatives form a labor–management agreement, or contract, for workers.

command economies (p. 43) Economic systems in which the government largely decides what goods and services will be produced, who will get them, and how the economy will grow.

commercial bank (p. 563) A profit-seeking organization that receives deposits from individuals and corporations in the form of checking and savings accounts and then uses some of these funds to make loans.

commercial finance companies (p. 507) Organizations that make short-term loans to borrowers who offer tangible assets as collateral.

commercialization (p. 393) Promoting a product to distributors and retailers to get wide distribution, and developing strong advertising and sales campaigns to generate and maintain interest in the product among distributors and consumers.

commercial paper (p. 508) Unsecured promissory notes of $100,000 and up that mature (come due) in 270 days or less.

common law (p. A-3) The body of law that comes from decisions handed down by judges; also referred to as unwritten law.

common market (p. 77) A regional group of countries that have a common external tariff, no internal tariffs, and a coordination of laws to facilitate exchange; also called a *trading bloc.* An example is the European Union.

common stock (p. 528) The most basic form of ownership in a firm; it confers voting rights and the right to share in the firm's profits through dividends, if offered by the firm's board of directors.

communism (p. 42) An economic and political system in which the government makes almost all economic decisions and owns almost all the major factors of production.

comparative advantage theory (p. 62) Theory that states that a country should sell to other countries those products that it produces most effectively and efficiently, and buy from other countries those products that it cannot produce as effectively or efficiently.

competition-based pricing (p. 397) A pricing strategy based on what all the other competitors are doing. The price can be set at, above, or below competitors' prices.

compliance-based ethics codes (p. 96) Ethical standards that emphasize preventing unlawful behavior by increasing control and by penalizing wrongdoers.

compressed workweek (p. 314) Work schedule that allows an employee to work a full number of hours per week but in fewer days.

computer-aided design (CAD) (p. 241) The use of computers in the design of products.

computer-aided manufacturing (CAM) (p. 241) The use of computers in the manufacturing of products.

computer-integrated manufacturing (CIM) (p. 241) The uniting of computer-aided design with computer-aided manufacturing.

concept testing (p. 392) Taking a product idea to consumers to test their reactions.

conceptual skills (p. 190) Skills that involve the ability to picture the organization as a whole and the relationship among its various parts.

conglomerate merger (p. 131) The joining of firms in completely unrelated industries.

Congress of Industrial Organizations (CIO) (p. 326) Union organization of unskilled workers; broke away from the American Federation of Labor (AFL) in 1935 and rejoined it in 1955.

consideration (p. A-9) Something of value; consideration is one of the requirements of a legal contract.

consumerism (p. A-13) A social movement that seeks to increase and strengthen the rights and powers of buyers in relation to sellers.

consumer market (p. 365) All the individuals or households that want goods and services for personal consumption or use.

consumer price index (CPI) (p. 48) Monthly statistics that measure the pace of inflation or deflation.

contingency planning (p. 186) The process of preparing alternative courses of action that may be used if the primary plans don't achieve the organization's objectives.

contingent workers (p. 302) Workers who do not have the expectation of regular, full-time employment.

continuous process (p. 240) A production process in which long production runs turn out finished goods over time.

contract (p. A-9) A legally enforceable agreement between two or more parties.

contract law (p. A-9) Set of laws that specify what constitutes a legally enforceable agreement.

contract manufacturing (p. 68) A foreign country's production of private-label goods to which a domestic company then attaches its brand name or trademark; part of the broad category of *outsourcing*.

contractual distribution system (p. 420) A distribution system in which members are bound to cooperate through contractual agreements.

contrarian approach (p. D-8) Buying stock when everyone else is selling or vice versa.

controlling (p. 183) A management function that involves establishing clear standards to determine whether or not an organization is progressing toward its goals and objectives, rewarding people for doing a good job, and taking corrective action if they are not.

convenience goods and services (p. 382) Products that the consumer wants to purchase frequently and with a minimum of effort.

conventional (C) corporation (p. 123) A state-chartered legal entity with authority to act and have liability separate from its owners.

cookies (p. B-21) Pieces of information, such as registration data or user preferences, sent by a website over the Internet to a Web browser that the browser software is expected to save and send back to the server whenever the user returns to that website.

cooking the books *Making accounting information look better than it actually is to outside observers and users of financial information of a company.*

cooling-off period (p. 335) When workers in a critical industry return to their jobs while the union and management continue negotiations.

cooperative (p. 140) A business owned and controlled by the people who use it—producers, consumers, or workers with similar needs who pool their resources for mutual gain.

copyright (p. A-7) A document that protects a creator's rights to materials such as books, articles, photos, and cartoons.

core competencies (p. 222) Those functions that the organization can do as well as or better than any other organization in the world.

core time (p. 313) In a flextime plan, the period when all employees are expected to be at their job stations.

corporate distribution system (p. 420) A distribution system in which all of the organizations in the channel of distribution are owned by one firm.

corporate philanthropy (p. 99) The dimension of social responsibility that includes charitable donations.

corporate policy (p. 99) The dimension of social responsibility that refers to the position a firm takes on social and political issues.

corporate responsibility (p. 99) The dimension of social responsibility that includes everything from hiring minority workers to making safe products.

corporate social initiatives (p. 99) Enhanced forms of corporate philanthropy directly related to the company's competencies.

corporate social responsibility (CSR) (p. 98) A business's concern for the welfare of society.

corporation (p. 116) A legal entity with authority to act and have liability separate from its owners.

cost of capital (p. 513) The rate of return a company must earn in order to meet the demands of its lenders and expectations of its equity holders.

cost of goods sold (or cost of goods manufactured) (p. 476) A measure of the cost of merchandise sold or cost of raw materials and supplies used for producing items for resale.

couch potatoes *People who sit and watch TV for hours at a time.*

countertrading (p. 74) A complex form of bartering in which several countries may be involved, each trading goods for goods or services for services.

counting on it *Expecting it.*

craft union (p. 326) An organization of skilled specialists in a particular craft or trade.

credit unions (p. 565) Nonprofit, member-owned financial cooperatives that offer the full variety of banking services to their members.

critical path (p. 252) In a PERT network, the sequence of tasks that takes the longest time to complete.

cross-functional self-managed teams (p. 218) Groups of employees from different departments who work together on a long-term basis.

current assets (p. 474) Items that can or will be converted into cash within one year.

customer relationship management (CRM) (p. 355) The process of learning as much as possible about customers and doing everything you can over time to satisfy them—or even exceed their expectations—with goods and services.

damages (p. A-10) The monetary settlement awarded to a person who is injured by a breach of contract.

database (p. 16) An electronic storage file for information.

data processing (DP) (p. B-2) Name for business technology in the 1970s; included technology that supported an existing business and was primarily used to improve the flow of financial information.

dealer (private-label) brands (p. 387) Products that don't carry the manufacturer's name but carry a distributor or retailer's name instead.

debenture bonds (p. 530) Bonds that are unsecured (i.e., not backed by any collateral such as equipment).

debit card (p. 570) An electronic funds transfer tool that serves the same function as checks: it withdraws funds from a checking account.

debt financing (p. 504) Funds raised through various forms of borrowing that must be repaid.

decentralized authority (p. 210) An organization structure in which decision-making authority is delegated to lower-level managers more familiar with local conditions than headquarters management could be.

decertification (p. 329) The process by which workers take away a union's right to represent them.

decision making (p. 187) Choosing among two or more alternatives.

deflation (p. 48) A situation in which prices are declining.

demand (p. 37) The quantity of products that people are willing to buy at different prices at a specific time.

demand deposit (p. 563) The technical name for a checking account; the money in a demand deposit can be withdrawn anytime on demand from the depositor.

demographic segmentation (p. 368) Dividing the market by age, income, and education level.

demography (p. 17) The statistical study of the human population with regard to its size, density, and other characteristics such as age, race, gender, and income.

departmentalization (p. 212) The dividing of organizational functions into separate units.

depreciation (p. 477) The systematic write-off of the cost of a tangible asset over its estimated useful life.

depression (p. 49) A severe recession, usually accompanied by deflation.

deregulation (p. A-17) Government withdrawal of certain laws and regulations that seem to hinder competition.

devaluation (p. 74) Lowering the value of a nation's currency relative to other currencies.

digital natives (p. 222) Young people who have grown up using the Internet and social networking.

direct marketing (p. 419) Any activity that directly links manufacturers or intermediaries with the ultimate consumer.

direct selling (p. 419) Selling to consumers in their homes or where they work.

disability insurance (p. D-11) Insurance that pays part of the cost of a long-term sickness or an accident.

discount rate (p. 559) The interest rate that the Fed charges for loans to member banks.

disinflation (p. 48) A situation in which price increases are slowing (the inflation rate is declining).

distributed product development (p. 379) Handing off various parts of your innovation process—often to companies in other countries

diversification (p. 534) Buying several different investment alternatives to spread the risk of investing.

dividends (p. 527) Part of a firm's profits that the firm may distribute to stockholders as either cash payments or additional shares of stock.

double-entry bookkeeping (p. 470) The practice of writing every business transaction in two places.

Dow Jones Industrial Average (the Dow) (p. 542) The average cost of 30 selected industrial stocks, used to give an indication of the direction (up or down) of the stock market over time.

drop shippers (p. 413) Wholesalers that solicit orders from retailers and other wholesalers and have the merchandise shipped directly from a producer to a buyer.

dumping (p. 66) Selling products in a foreign country at lower prices than those charged in the producing country.

e-commerce (p. 14) The buying and selling of goods over the Internet.

economic pie *The money available in the economy.*

economics (p. 30) The study of how society chooses to employ resources to produce goods and services and distribute them for consumption among various competing groups and individuals.

economies of scale (p. 206) The situation in which companies can reduce their production costs if they can purchase raw materials in bulk; the average cost of goods goes down as production levels increase.

electronic funds transfer (EFT) system (p. 569) A computerized system that electronically performs financial transactions such as making purchases, paying bills, and receiving paychecks.

electronic retailing (p. 417) Selling goods and services to ultimate customers (e.g., you and me) over the Internet.

e-mail snooped *When someone other than the addressee reads e-mail messages.*

embargo (p. 76) A complete ban on the import or export of a certain product, or the stopping of all trade with a particular country.

empowerment (p. 17) Giving frontline workers the responsibility, authority, freedom, training, and equipment they need to respond quickly to customer requests.

enabling (p. 194) Giving workers the education and tools they need to make decisions.

enterprise resource planning (ERP) (p. 247) A newer version of materials requirement planning (MRP) that combines the computerized functions of all the divisions and subsidiaries of the firm—such as finance, human resources, and order fulfillment—into a single integrated software program that uses a single database.

enterprise zones (p. 157) Specific geographic areas to which governments try to attract private business investment by offering lower taxes and other government support.

entrepreneur (p. 4) A person who risks time and money to start and manage a business.

entrepreneurial team (p. 152) A group of experienced people from different areas of business who join together to form a managerial team with the skills needed to develop, make, and market a new product.

entrepreneurship (p. 149) Accepting the risk of starting and running a business.

environmental scanning (p. 363) The process of identifying the factors that can affect marketing success.

equity financing (p. 504) Money raised from within the firm, from operations or through the sale of ownership in the firm (stock or venture capital).

equity theory (p. 272) The idea that employees try to maintain equity between inputs and outputs compared to others in similar positions.

ethics (p. 91) Standards of moral behavior, that is, behavior accepted by society as right versus wrong.

everyday low pricing (EDLP) (p. 398) Setting prices lower than competitors and then not having any special sales.

exchange rate (p. 74) The value of one nation's currency relative to the currencies of other countries.

exchange-traded funds (ETFs) (p. 540) Collections of stocks that are traded on exchanges but are traded more like individual stocks than like mutual funds.

exclusive distribution (p. 417) Distribution that sends products to only one retail outlet in a given geographic area.

executor (p. D-16) A person who assembles and values your estate, files income and other taxes, and distributes assets.

expectancy theory (p. 271) Victor Vroom's theory that the amount of effort employees exert on a specific task depends on their expectations of the outcome.

exporting (p. 61) Selling products to another country.

express warranties (p. A-9) Specific representations by the seller that buyers rely on regarding the goods they purchase.

external customers (p. 196) Dealers, who buy products to sell to others, and ultimate customers (or end users), who buy products for their own personal use.

extranet (p. B-9) A semiprivate network that uses Internet technology and allows more than one company to access the same information or allows people on different servers to collaborate.

extrinsic reward (p. 261) Something given to you by someone else as recognition for good work; extrinsic rewards include pay increases, praise, and promotions.

facility layout (p. 246) The physical arrangement of resources (including people) in the production process.

facility location (p. 244) The process of selecting a geographic location for a company's operations.

factoring (p. 508) The process of selling accounts receivable for cash.

factors of production (p. 9) The resources used to create wealth: land, labor, capital, entrepreneurship, and knowledge.

Federal Deposit Insurance Corporation (FDIC) (p. 568) An independent agency of the U.S. government that insures bank deposits.

finance (p. 494) The function in a business that acquires funds for the firm and manages those funds within the firm.

financial accounting (p. 466) Accounting information and analyses prepared for people outside the organization.

financial control (p. 499) A process in which a firm periodically compares its actual revenues, costs, and expenses with its budget.

financial management (p. 494) The job of managing a firm's resources so it can meet its goals and objectives.

financial managers (p. 494) Managers who examine financial data prepared by accountants and recommend strategies for improving the financial performance of the firm.

financial statement (p. 472) A summary of all the transactions that have occurred over a particular period.

fiscal policy (p. 50) The federal government's efforts to keep the economy stable by increasing or decreasing taxes or government spending.

fixed assets (p. 474) Assets that are relatively permanent, such as land, buildings, and equipment.

flat organization structure (p. 210) An organization structure that has few layers of management and a broad span of control.

flexible manufacturing (p. 242) Designing machines to do multiple tasks so that they can produce a variety of products.

flextime plan (p. 313) Work schedule that gives employees some freedom to choose when to work, as long as they work the required number of hours.

focus group (p. 362) A small group of people who meet under the direction of a discussion leader to communicate their opinions about an organization, its products, or other given issues.

foreign direct investment (FDI) (p. 70) The buying of permanent property and businesses in foreign nations.

foreign subsidiary (p. 70) A company owned in a foreign country by another company, called the *parent company*.

formal organization (p. 225) The structure that details lines of responsibility, authority, and position; that is, the structure shown on organization charts.

form utility (p. 239) The value producers add to materials in the creation of finished goods and services.

franchise (p. 133) The right to use a specific business's name and sell its products or services in a given territory.

franchise agreement (p. 133) An arrangement whereby someone with a good idea for a business sells the rights to use the business name and sell a product or service to others in a given territory.

franchisee (p. 133) A person who buys a franchise.

franchisor (p. 133) A company that develops a product concept and sells others the rights to make and sell the products.

free-for-all atmosphere *A situation where all order seems to be lost in conducting business.*

free-market economies (p. 43) Economic systems in which the market largely determines what goods and services get produced, who gets them, and how the economy grows.

free-rein leadership (p. 194) Leadership style that involves managers setting objectives and employees being relatively free to do whatever it takes to accomplish those objectives.

free trade (p. 62) The movement of goods and services among nations without political or economic barriers.

freight forwarder (p. 425) An organization that puts many small shipments together to create a single large shipment that can be transported cost-effectively to the final destination.

fringe benefits (p. 311) Benefits such as sick-leave pay, vacation pay, pension plans, and health plans that represent additional compensation to employees beyond base wages.

from scratch *From the beginning.*

fundamental accounting equation (p. 472) Assets = Liabilities + Owners' equity; this is the basis for the balance sheet.

Gantt chart (p. 252) Bar graph showing production managers what projects are being worked on and what stage they are in at any given time.

General Agreement on Tariffs and Trade (GATT) (p. 77) A 1948 agreement that established an international forum for negotiating mutual reductions in trade restrictions.

general partner (p. 119) An owner (partner) who has unlimited liability and is active in managing the firm.

general partnership (p. 119) A partnership in which all owners share in operating the business and in assuming liability for the business's debts.

generic goods (p. 388) Nonbranded products that usually sell at a sizable discount compared to national or private-label brands.

geographic segmentation (p. 367) Dividing the market by cities, counties, states, or regions.

get in on the dough *Take the opportunity to make some money.*

givebacks (p. 336) Concessions made by union members to management; gains from labor negotiations are given back to management to help employers remain competitive and thereby save jobs.

go for the gold *To work to be the very best (figuratively winning a gold medal).*

go out with me *Go with me to dinner or to a movie or some other entertainment.*

goals (p. 183) The broad, long-term accomplishments an organization wishes to attain.

goal-setting theory (p. 270) The idea that setting ambitious but attainable goals can motivate workers and improve performance if the goals are accepted, accompanied by feedback, and facilitated by organizational conditions.

gone off the deep end *Doing something risky, almost crazy—like jumping into the deep end of a swimming pool when you can't swim.*

goods (p. 4) Tangible products such as computers, food, clothing, cars, and appliances.

goofing off *Doing things at work not associated with the job, such as talking with others at the drinking fountain.*

government and not-for-profit accounting (p. 469) Accounting system for organizations whose purpose is not generating a profit but serving ratepayers, taxpayers, and others according to a duly approved budget.

greening (p. 19) The trend toward saving energy and producing products that cause less harm to the environment.

grievance (p. 333)   A charge by employees that management is not abiding by the terms of the negotiated labor–management agreement.

gross domestic product (GDP) (p. 46)   The total value of final goods and services produced in a country in a given year.

gross profit (or gross margin) (p. 477)   How much a firm earned by buying (or making) and selling merchandise.

hand over the keys   *Give access to others.*

hard copy   *Copy printed on paper.*

Hawthorne effect (p. 262)   The tendency for people to behave differently when they know they are being studied.

health maintenance organizations (HMOs) (p. C-9)   Health care organizations that require members to choose from a restricted list of doctors.

health savings accounts (HSAs) (p. C-10)   Tax-deferred savings accounts linked to low-cost, high-deductible health insurance policies.

heart   *The most important part of something; the central force or idea.*

hierarchy (p. 208)   A system in which one person is at the top of the organization and there is a ranked or sequential ordering from the top down of managers who are responsible to that person.

high–low pricing strategy (p. 398)   Setting prices that are higher than EDLP stores, but having many special sales where the prices are lower than competitors'.

horizontal merger (p. 131)   The joining of two firms in the same industry.

hot second   *Immediately.*

human relations skills (p. 190)   Skills that involve communication and motivation; they enable managers to work through and with people.

human resource management (HRM) (p. 290)   The process of determining human resource needs and then recruiting, selecting, developing, motivating, evaluating, compensating, and scheduling employees to achieve organizational goals.

hygiene factors (p. 265)   In Herzberg's theory of motivating factors, job factors that can cause dissatisfaction if missing but that do not necessarily motivate employees if increased.

identity theft (p. 16)   The obtaining of individuals' personal information, such as Social Security and credit card numbers, for illegal purposes.

If it isn't broken, don't fix it   *Don't risk making things worse by changing things that don't need to be changed.*

implied warranties (p. A-9)   Guarantees legally imposed on the seller.

importing (p. 61)   Buying products from another country.

import quota (p. 76)   A limit on the number of products in certain categories that a nation can import.

inbound logistics (p. 424)   The area of logistics that involves bringing raw materials, packaging, other goods and services, and information from suppliers to producers.

income statement (p. 476)   The financial statement that shows a firm's profit after costs, expenses, and taxes; it summarizes all of the resources that have come into the firm (revenue), all the resources that have left the firm, expenses, and the resulting net income or net loss.

incubators (p. 158)   Centers that offer new businesses low-cost offices with basic business services.

indenture terms (p. 510)   The terms of agreement in a bond issue.

independent audit (p. 468)   An evaluation and unbiased opinion about the accuracy of a company's financial statements.

individual retirement account (IRA) (p. D-13)   A tax-deferred investment plan that enables you (and your spouse, if you are married) to save part of your income for retirement; a traditional IRA allows people who qualify to deduct from their reported income the money they put into an account.

industrial goods (p. 384)   Products used in the production of other products. Sometimes called business goods or B2B goods.

industrial unions (p. 326)   Labor organizations of unskilled and semiskilled workers in mass-production industries such as automobiles and mining.

inflation (p. 47)   A general rise in the prices of goods and services over time.

infomercial (p. 442)   A full-length TV program devoted exclusively to promoting goods or services.

informal organization (p. 225) The system that develops spontaneously as employees meet and form cliques, relationships, and lines of authority outside the formal organization; that is, the human side of the organization that does not appear on any organization chart.

information systems (IS) (p. B-2) Technology that helps companies do business; includes such tools as automated teller machines (ATMs) and voice mail.

information technology (IT) (p. B-2) Technology that helps companies change business by allowing them to use new methods.

information utility (p. 412) Adding value to products by opening two-way flows of information between marketing participants.

initial public offering (IPO) (p. 522) The first public offering of a corporation's stock.

injunction (p. 336) A court order directing someone to do something or to refrain from doing something.

insider trading (p. 101) An unethical activity in which insiders use private company information to further their own fortunes or those of their family and friends.

institutional investors (p. 523) Large organizations—such as pension funds, mutual funds, and insurance companies—that invest their own funds or the funds of others.

insurable interest (p. C-5) The possibility of the policyholder to suffer a loss.

insurable risk (p. C-5) A risk that the typical insurance company will cover.

insurance policy (p. C-6) A written contract between the insured and an insurance company that promises to pay for all or part of a loss.

intangible assets (p. 474) Long-term assets (e.g., patents, trademarks, copyrights) that have no real physical form but do have value.

integrated marketing communication (IMC) (p. 437) A technique that combines all the promotional tools into one comprehensive and unified promotional strategy.

integrity-based ethics codes (p. 96) Ethical standards that define the organization's guiding values, create an environment that supports ethically sound behavior, and stress a shared accountability among employees.

intensive distribution (p. 416) Distribution that puts products into as many retail outlets as possible.

interactive promotion (p. 442) Promotion process that allows marketers to go beyond a monologue, where sellers try to persuade buyers to buy things, to a dialogue in which buyers and sellers work together to create mutually beneficial exchange relationships.

interest (p. 529) The payment the issuer of the bond makes to the bondholders for use of the borrowed money.

intermittent process (p. 241) A production process in which the production run is short and the machines are changed frequently to make different products.

intermodal shipping (p. 426) The use of multiple modes of transportation to complete a single long-distance movement of freight.

internal customers (p. 196) Individuals and units within the firm that receive services from other individuals or units.

International Monetary Fund (IMF) (p. 572) Organization that assists the smooth flow of money among nations.

Internet2 (p. B-10) The private Internet system that links government supercomputer centers and a select group of universities; it runs more than 22,000 times faster than today's public infrastructure and supports heavy-duty applications.

intranet (p. B-9) A companywide network, closed to public access, that uses Internet-type technology.

intrapreneurs (p. 157) Creative people who work as entrepreneurs within corporations.

intrinsic reward (p. 261) The personal satisfaction you feel when you perform well and complete goals.

inverted organization (p. 223) An organization that has contact people at the top and the chief executive officer at the bottom of the organization chart.

investment bankers (p. 523) Specialists who assist in the issue and sale of new securities.

invisible hand (p. 33) A phrase coined by Adam Smith to describe the process that turns self-directed gain into social and economic benefits for all.

involuntary bankruptcy (p. A-15) Bankruptcy procedures filed by a debtor's creditors.

IOUs *Debt; abbreviation for "I owe you."*

ISO 14000 (p. 251) A collection of the best practices for managing an organization's impact on the environment.

ISO 9000 (p. 251) The common name given to quality management and assurance standards.

job analysis (p. 297) A study of what is done by employees who hold various job titles.

job description (p. 297) A summary of the objectives of a job, the type of work to be done, the responsibilities and duties, the working conditions, and the relationship of the job to other functions.

job enlargement (p. 274) A job enrichment strategy that involves combining a series of tasks into one challenging and interesting assignment.

job enrichment (p. 273) A motivational strategy that emphasizes motivating the worker through the job itself.

job rotation (p. 274) A job enrichment strategy that involves moving employees from one job to another.

job sharing (p. 315) An arrangement whereby two part-time employees share one full-time job.

job simulation (p. 305) The use of equipment that duplicates job conditions and tasks so that trainees can learn skills before attempting them on the job.

job specifications (p. 297) A written summary of the minimum qualifications required of workers to do a particular job.

joint venture (p. 70) A partnership in which two or more companies (often from different countries) join to undertake a major project.

journal (p. 470) The record book or computer program where accounting data are first entered.

judiciary (p. A-2) The branch of government chosen to oversee the legal system through the court system.

jumped headfirst *Began quickly and eagerly without hesitation.*

junk bonds (p. 538) High-risk, high-interest bonds.

just-in-time (JIT) inventory control (p. 249) A production process in which a minimum of inventory is kept on the premises and parts, supplies, and other needs are delivered just in time to go on the assembly line.

Keynesian economic theory (p. 50) The theory that a government policy of increasing spending and cutting taxes could stimulate the economy in a recession.

key player *Important participant.*

kick back and relax *To take a rest.*

Knights of Labor (p. 326) The first national labor union; formed in 1869.

knockoff brands (p. 388) Illegal copies of national brand-name goods.

know-how *A level of specific expertise.*

knowledge management (p. 195) Finding the right information, keeping the information in a readily accessible place, and making the information known to everyone in the firm.

latchkey kids *School-age children who come home to empty houses since all of the adults are at work.*

law of large numbers (p. C-7) Principle that if a large number of people are exposed to the same risk, a predictable number of losses will occur during a given period of time.

leading (p. 183) Creating a vision for the organization and guiding, training, coaching, and motivating others to work effectively to achieve the organization's goals and objectives.

lean manufacturing (p. 242) The production of goods using less of everything compared to mass production.

ledger (p. 470) A specialized accounting book or computer program in which information from accounting journals is accumulated into specific categories and posted so that managers can find all the information about one account in the same place.

letter of credit (p. 571) A promise by the bank to pay the seller a given amount if certain conditions are met.

level playing field *Treating everyone equally.*

leverage (p. 513) Raising needed funds through borrowing to increase a firm's rate of return.

leveraged buyout (LBO) (p. 131) An attempt by employees, management, or a group of investors to purchase an organization primarily through borrowing.

liabilities (p. 474) What the business owes to others (debts).

licensing (p. 66) A global strategy in which a firm (the licensor) allows a foreign company (the licensee) to produce its product in exchange for a fee (a royalty).

limited liability (p. II9) The responsibility of a business's owners for losses only up to the amount they invest; limited partners and shareholders have limited liability.

limited liability company (LLC) (p. I28) A company similar to an S corporation but without the special eligibility requirements.

limited liability partnership (LLP) (p. II9) A partnership that limits partners' risk of losing their personal assets to only their own acts and omissions and to the acts and omissions of people under their supervision.

limited partner (p. II9) An owner who invests money in the business but does not have any management responsibility or liability for losses beyond the investment.

limited partnership (p. II9) A partnership with one or more general partners and one or more limited partners.

line of credit (p. 507) A given amount of unsecured short-term funds a bank will lend to a business, provided the funds are readily available.

line organization (p. 215) An organization that has direct two-way lines of responsibility, authority, and communication running from the top to the bottom of the organization, with all people reporting to only one supervisor.

line personnel (p. 215) Employees who are part of the chain of command that is responsible for achieving organizational goals.

liquidity (p. 474) The ease with which an asset can be converted into cash.

lockout (p. 335) An attempt by management to put pressure on unions by temporarily closing the business.

logistics (p. 423) The marketing activity that involves planning, implementing, and controlling the physical flow of materials, final goods, and related information from points of origin to points of consumption to meet customer requirements at a profit.

long-term financing (p. 504) Funds needed for more than a year (usually 2 to 10 years).

long-term forecast (p. 498) Forecast that predicts revenues, costs, and expenses for a period longer than 1 year, and sometimes as far as 5 or 10 years into the future.

loss (p. 4) When a business's expenses are more than its revenues.

M-I (p. 556) Money that can be accessed quickly and easily (coins and paper money, checks, traveler's checks, etc.).

M-2 (p. 556) Money included in M-1 plus money that may take a little more time to obtain (savings accounts, money market accounts, mutual funds, certificates of deposit, etc.).

M-3 (p. 556) M-2 plus big deposits like institutional money market funds.

Ma Bell *Telecommunication giant, AT&T.*

macroeconomics (p. 30) The part of economics study that looks at the operation of a nation's economy as a whole.

management (p. I8I) The process used to accomplish organizational goals through planning, organizing, leading, and controlling people and other organizational resources.

management by objectives (MBO) (p. 270) Peter Drucker's system of goal setting and implementation; it involves a cycle of discussion, review, and evaluation of objectives among top and middle-level managers, supervisors, and employees.

management development (p. 306) The process of training and educating employees to become good managers and then monitoring the progress of their managerial skills over time.

managerial accounting (p. 465) Accounting used to provide information and analyses to managers within the organization to assist them in decision making.

manufacturers' brands (p. 387) The brand names of manufacturers that distribute products nationally.

market (p. I69) People with unsatisfied wants and needs who have both the resources and the willingness to buy.

marketing (p. 352) The activity, set of institutions, and processes for creating, communicating, delivering, and exchanging offerings that have value for customers, clients, partners, and society at large.

marketing concept (p. 355) A three-part business philosophy: (1) a customer orientation, (2) a service orientation, and (3) a profit orientation.

marketing intermediaries (p. 406) Organizations that assist in moving goods and services from producers to businesses (B2B) and from businesses to consumers (B2C).

marketing mix (p. 357) The ingredients that go into a marketing program: product, price, place, and promotion.

marketing research (p. 360) The analysis of markets to determine opportunities and challenges, and to find the information needed to make good decisions.

market price (p. 39) The price determined by supply and demand.

market segmentation (p. 366) The process of dividing the total market into groups whose members have similar characteristics.

marriage of software, hardware, etc. *Combination of various technologies.*

Maslow's hierarchy of needs (p. 263) Theory of motivation based on unmet human needs from basic physiological needs to safety, social, and esteem needs to self-actualization needs.

mass customization (p. 242) Tailoring products to meet the needs of individual customers.

mass marketing (p. 369) Developing products and promotions to please large groups of people.

master limited partnership (MLP) (p. 119) A partnership that looks much like a corporation (in that it acts like a corporation and is traded on a stock exchange) but is taxed like a partnership and thus avoids the corporate income tax.

materials handling (p. 424) The movement of goods within a warehouse, from warehouses to the factory floor, and from the factory floor to various workstations.

materials requirement planning (MRP) (p. 247) A computer-based operations management system that uses sales forecasts to make sure that needed parts and materials are available at the right time and place.

matrix organization (p. 216) An organization in which specialists from different parts of the organization are brought together to work on specific projects but still remain part of a line-and-staff structure.

maturity date (p. 529) The exact date the issuer of a bond must pay the principal to the bondholder.

measuring stick *Tool used to evaluate or compare something.*

mediation (p. 334) The use of a third party, called a mediator, who encourages both sides in a dispute to continue negotiating and often makes suggestions for resolving the dispute.

mentor (p. 307) An experienced employee who supervises, coaches, and guides lower-level employees by introducing them to the right people and generally being their organizational sponsor.

merchant wholesalers (p. 413) Independently owned firms that take title to the goods they handle.

merger (p. 131) The result of two firms forming one company.

Mickey D's *Nickname for McDonald's.*

microeconomics (p. 30) The part of economics study that looks at the behavior of people and organizations in particular markets.

micropreneurs (p. 152) Entrepreneurs willing to accept the risk of starting and managing the type of business that remains small, lets them do the kind of work they want to do, and offers them a balanced lifestyle.

middle management (p. 189) The level of management that includes general managers, division managers, and branch and plant managers who are responsible for tactical planning and controlling.

mine the knowledge *Make maximum use of the knowledge employees have.*

mission statement (p. 183) An outline of the fundamental purposes of an organization.

mixed economies (p. 44) Economic systems in which some allocation of resources is made by the market and some by the government.

monetary policy (p. 50) The management of the money supply and interest rates by the Federal Reserve Bank.

money (p. 555) Anything that people generally accept as payment for goods and services.

money supply (p. 556) The amount of money the Federal Reserve Bank makes available for people to buy goods and services.

monopolistic competition (p. 39) The degree of competition in which a large number of sellers produce very similar products that buyers nevertheless perceive as different.

monopoly (p. 40) A degree of competition in which only one seller controls the total supply of a product or service, and sets the price.

more than meets the eye *More than one can see with his or her own eyes; much is happening that is not visible.*

motivators (p. 265) In Herzberg's theory of motivating factors, job factors that cause employees to be productive and that give them satisfaction.

mouse-click away *Ease of doing something by using the computer or Internet.*

muddy the water *Making things even more difficult than they currently are.*

multinational corporation (p. 70) An organization that manufactures and markets products in many different countries and has multinational stock ownership and multinational management.

mutual fund (p. 539) An organization that buys stocks and bonds and then sells shares in those securities to the public.

mutual insurance company (p. C-7) A type of insurance company owned by its policyholders.

NASDAQ (p. 524) A nationwide electronic system that communicates over-the-counter trades to brokers.

national debt (p. 50) The sum of government deficits over time.

negligence (p. A-4) In tort law, behavior that causes unintentional harm or injury.

negotiable instruments (p. A-9) Forms of commercial paper (such as checks) that are transferable among businesses and individuals and represent a promise to pay a specified amount.

negotiated labor–management agreement (labor contract) (p. 330) Agreement that sets the tone and clarifies the terms under which management and labor agree to function over a period of time.

net income or net loss (p. 476) Revenue left over after all costs and expenses, including taxes, are paid.

network computing system (or client/server computing) (p. B-14) Computer systems that allow personal computers (clients) to obtain needed information from huge databases in a central computer (the server).

networking (pp. 219, 307) The process of establishing and maintaining contacts with key managers in one's own organization and other organizations and using those contacts to weave strong relationships that serve as informal development systems.

niche marketing (p. 368) The process of finding small but profitable market segments and designing or finding products for them.

nonbanks (p. 556) Financial organizations that accept no deposits but offer many of the services provided by regular banks (pension funds, insurance companies, commercial finance companies, consumer finance companies, and brokerage houses).

nonprofit organization (p. 7) An organization whose goals do not include making a personal profit for its owners or organizers.

North American Free Trade Agreement (NAFTA) (p. 79) Agreement that created a free-trade area among the United States, Canada, and Mexico.

notes payable (p. 475) Short-term or long-term liabilities that a business promises to repay by a certain date.

objectives (p. 184) Specific, short-term statements detailing how to achieve the organization's goals.

off-the-job training (p. 305) Training that occurs away from the workplace and consists of internal or external programs to develop any of a variety of skills or to foster personal development.

oligopoly (p. 39) A degree of competition in which just a few sellers dominate the market.

one-to-one marketing (p. 369) Developing a unique mix of goods and services for each individual customer.

online training (p. 305) Training programs in which employees complete classes via the Internet.

on-the-job training (p. 304) Training at the workplace that lets the employee learn by doing or by watching others for a while and then imitating them.

open-market operations (p. 559) The buying and selling of U.S. government bonds by the Fed with the goal of regulating the money supply.

open shop agreement (p. 332) Agreement in right-to-work states that gives workers the option to join or not join a union, if one exists in their workplace.

operating (or master) budget (p. 498) The budget that ties together the firm's other budgets and summarizes its proposed financial activities.

operating expenses (p. 477) Costs involved in operating a business, such as rent, utilities, and salaries.

operational planning (p. 186) The process of setting work standards and schedules necessary to implement the company's tactical objectives.

operations management (p. 238) A specialized area in management that converts or transforms resources (including human resources) into goods and services.

organizational (or corporate) culture (p. 224) Widely shared values within an organization that provide unity and cooperation to achieve common goals.

organization chart (p. 188) A visual device that shows relationships among people and divides the organization's work; it shows who is accountable for the completion of specific work and who reports to whom.

organizing (p. 182) A management function that includes designing the structure of the organization and creating conditions and systems in which everyone and everything work together to achieve the organization's goals and objectives.

orientation (p. 303) The activity that introduces new employees to the organization; to fellow employees; to their immediate supervisors; and to the policies, practices, and objectives of the firm.

other side of the tracks *The area where people with less money live.*

out of the office loop *Out of the line of communication that occurs in the workplace.*

outbound logistics (p. 424) The area of logistics that involves managing the flow of finished products and information to business buyers and ultimate consumers (people like you and me).

outsourcing (p. 7) Contracting with other companies (often in other countries) to do some or all of the functions of a firm, like its production or accounting tasks.

over-the-counter (OTC) market (p. 524) Exchange that provides a means to trade stocks not listed on the national exchanges.

owners' equity (p. 475) The amount of the business that belongs to the owners minus any liabilities owed by the business.

participative (democratic) leadership (p. 193) Leadership style that consists of managers and employees working together to make decisions.

partnership (p. 116) A legal form of business with two or more owners.

patent (p. A-6) A document that gives inventors exclusive rights to their inventions for 20 years.

pave the way *Process of making a task easier.*

peanut butter and jelly *Popular combination for sandwich; the two are seen as perfect complementary products.*

penetration strategy (p. 398) Strategy in which a product is priced low to attract many customers and discourage competition.

pension funds (p. 566) Amounts of money put aside by corporations, nonprofit organizations, or unions to cover part of the financial needs of members when they retire.

perks *Short for* perquisites; *compensation in addition to salary, such as day care or a company car.*

perfect competition (p. 39) The degree of competition in which there are many sellers in a market and none is large enough to dictate the price of a product.

performance appraisal (p. 308) An evaluation that measures employee performance against established standards in order to make decisions about promotions, compensation, training, or termination.

personal selling (p. 446) The face-to-face presentation and promotion of goods and services.

pick economy (p. 456) Customers who pick out their products from online outlets or who do online comparison shopping.

piece of the action   *A share in the opportunity.*

pink slip   *A notice that you've lost your job.*

pitch in   *To help as needed.*

place utility (p. 411)   Adding value to products by having them where people want them.

planning (p. 182)   A management function that includes anticipating trends and determining the best strategies and tactics to achieve organizational goals and objectives.

PMI (p. 187)   Listing all the pluses for a solution in one column, all the minuses in another, and the implications in a third column.

podcasting (p. 454)   A means of distributing audio and video programs via the Internet that lets users subscribe to a number of files, also known as feeds, and then hear or view the material at the time they choose.

possession utility (p. 412)   Doing whatever is necessary to transfer ownership from one party to another, including providing credit, delivery, installation, guarantees, and follow-up service.

poster child   *Best example.*

precedent (p. A-3)   Decisions judges have made in earlier cases that guide the handling of new cases.

preferred provider organizations (PPOs) (p. C-10)   Health care organizations similar to HMOs except that they allow members to choose their own physicians (for a fee).

preferred stock (p. 528)   Stock that gives its owners preference in the payment of dividends and an earlier claim on assets than common stockholders if the company is forced out of business and its assets sold.

premium (p. C-6)   The fee charged by an insurance company for an insurance policy.

price leadership (p. 397)   The strategy by which one or more dominant firms set the pricing practices that all competitors in an industry follow.

primary boycott (p. 335)   When a union encourages both its members and the general public not to buy the products of a firm involved in a labor dispute.

primary data (p. 361)   Data that you gather yourself (not from secondary sources such as books and magazines).

principle of motion economy (p. 262)   Theory developed by Frank and Lillian Gilbreth that every job can be broken down into a series of elementary motions.

private accountant (p. 466)   An accountant who works for a single firm, government agency, or nonprofit organization.

problem solving (p. 187)   The process of solving the everyday problems that occur. Problem solving is less formal than decision making and usually calls for quicker action.

process manufacturing (p. 240)   That part of the production process that physically or chemically changes materials.

producer price index (PPI) (p. 48)   An index that measures prices at the wholesale level.

product (p. 358)   Any physical good, service, or idea that satisfies a want or need plus anything that would enhance the product in the eyes of consumers, such as the brand name.

product analysis (p. 391)   Making cost estimates and sales forecasts to get a feeling for profitability of new-product ideas.

product differentiation (p. 382)   The creation of real or perceived product differences.

product liability (p. A-4)   Part of tort law that holds businesses liable for harm that results from the production, design, sale, or use of products they market.

product life cycle (p. 393)   A theoretical model of what happens to sales and profits for a product class over time; the four stages of the cycle are introduction, growth, maturity, and decline.

product line (p. 381)   A group of products that are physically similar or are intended for a similar market.

product mix (p. 382)   The combination of product lines offered by a manufacturer.

product placement (p. 441)   Putting products into TV shows and movies where they will be seen.

product screening (p. 391)   A process designed to reduce the number of new-product ideas being worked on at any one time.

production (p. 237)   The creation of finished goods and services using the factors of production: land, labor, capital, entrepreneurship, and knowledge.

production management (p. 237) The term used to describe all the activities managers do to help their firms create goods.

productivity (p. 15) The amount of output you generate given the amount of input (e.g., hours worked).

profit (p. 4) The amount of money a business earns above and beyond what it spends for salaries and other expenses.

program evaluation and review technique (PERT) (p. 252) A method for analyzing the tasks involved in completing a given project, estimating the time needed to complete each task, and identifying the minimum time needed to complete the total project.

program trading (p. 544) Giving instructions to computers to automatically sell if the price of a stock dips to a certain point to avoid potential losses.

promissory note (p. 505) A written contract with a promise to pay a supplier a specific sum of money at a definite time.

promotion (p. 359) All the techniques sellers use to inform people about and motivate them to buy their products or services.

promotion mix (p. 436) The combination of promotional tools an organization uses.

pros and cons *Arguments for and against something.*

prospect (p. 447) A person with the means to buy a product, the authority to buy, and the willingness to listen to a sales message.

prospecting (p. 447) Researching potential buyers and choosing those most likely to buy.

prospectus (p. 525) A condensed version of economic and financial information that a company must file with the SEC before issuing stock; the prospectus must be sent to prospective investors.

psychographic segmentation (p. 367) Dividing the market using the group's values, attitudes, and interests.

psychological pricing (p. 399) Pricing goods and services at price points that make the product appear less expensive than it is.

public accountant (p. 466) An accountant who provides accounting services to individuals or businesses on a fee basis.

public domain software (or freeware) (p. B-16) Software that is free for the taking.

publicity (p. 451) Any information about an individual, product, or organization that's distributed to the public through the media and that's not paid for or controlled by the seller.

public relations (PR) (p. 450) The management function that evaluates public attitudes, changes policies and procedures in response to the public's requests, and executes a program of action and information to earn public understanding and acceptance.

pull strategy (p. 455) Promotional strategy in which heavy advertising and sales promotion efforts are directed toward consumers so that they'll request the products from retailers.

pump up the profits *Making profits in a company appear larger than they actually are under recognized accounting rules.*

purchasing (p. 249) The function in a firm that searches for quality material resources, finds the best suppliers, and negotiates the best price for goods and services.

pure risk (p. C-3) The threat of loss with no chance for profit.

push strategy (p. 455) Promotional strategy in which the producer uses advertising, personal selling, sales promotion, and all other promotional tools to convince wholesalers and retailers to stock and sell merchandise.

qualifying (p. 447) In the selling process, making sure that people have a need for the product, the authority to buy, and the willingness to listen to a sales message.

quality (p. 249) Consistently producing what the customer wants while reducing errors before and after delivery to the customer.

quality of life (p. 6) The general well-being of a society in terms of its political freedom, natural environment, education, health care, safety, amount of leisure, and rewards that add to the satisfaction and joy that other goods and services provide.

quid pro quo *Latin phrase meaning "something given in return for something else."*

quite a stir *Something that causes a feeling of concern.*

rack jobbers (p. 413) Wholesalers that furnish racks or shelves full of merchandise to retailers, display products, and sell on consignment.

ratio analysis (p. 482) The assessment of a firm's financial condition using calculations and interpretations of financial ratios developed from the firm's financial statements.

real time (p. 220) The present moment or the actual time in which something takes place.

recession (p. 49) Two or more consecutive quarters of decline in the GDP.

recruitment (p. 298) The set of activities used to obtain a sufficient number of the right people at the right time.

reinforcement theory (p. 272) Theory that positive and negative reinforcers motivate a person to behave in certain ways.

relationship marketing (p. 369) Marketing strategy with the goal of keeping individual customers over time by offering them products that exactly meet their requirements.

reserve requirement (p. 559) A percentage of commercial banks' checking and savings accounts that must be physically kept in the bank.

resource development (p. 31) The study of how to increase resources and to create the conditions that will make better use of those resources.

restructuring (p. 223) Redesigning an organization so that it can more effectively and efficiently serve its customers.

retailer (p. 407) An organization that sells to ultimate consumers.

retained earnings (p. 475) The accumulated earnings from a firm's profitable operations that were reinvested in the business and not paid out to stockholders in dividends.

revenue (p. 4) The total amount of money a business takes in during a given period by selling goods and services.

reverse discrimination (p. 294) Discrimination against whites or males in hiring or promoting.

reverse logistics (p. 424) The area of logistics that involves bringing goods back to the manufacturer because of defects or for recycling materials.

revolving credit agreement (p. 507) A line of credit that is guaranteed but usually comes with a fee.

right-to-work laws (p. 332) Legislation that gives workers the right, under an open shop, to join or not join a union if it is present.

risk (p. 5) The chance an entrepreneur takes of losing time and money on a business that may not prove profitable.

risk (p. C-3) The chance of loss, the degree of probability of loss, and the amount of possible loss.

risk/return trade-off (p. 510) The principle that the greater the risk a lender takes in making a loan, the higher the interest rate required.

Roth IRA (p. D-14) An IRA where you don't get upfront deductions on your taxes as you would with a traditional IRA, but the earnings grow tax-free and are also tax-free when they are withdrawn.

rule of indemnity (p. C-7) Rule saying that an insured person or organization cannot collect more than the actual loss from an insurable risk.

rules-of-the-road orientation *Introduction to the proper procedures within an organization.*

sales promotion (p. 451) The promotional tool that stimulates consumer purchasing and dealer interest by means of short-term activities.

sampling (p. 453) A promotional tool in which a company lets consumers have a small sample of a product for no charge.

savings and loan association (S&L) (p. 564) A financial institution that accepts both savings and checking deposits and provides home mortgage loans.

Savings Association Insurance Fund (SAIF) (p. 569) The part of the FDIC that insures holders of accounts in savings and loan associations.

scientific management (p. 261) Studying workers to find the most efficient ways of doing things and then teaching people those techniques.

S corporation (p. 127) A unique government creation that looks like a corporation but is taxed like sole proprietorships and partnerships.

sea of information *Lots of information, often too much to process.*

secondary boycott (p. 335) An attempt by labor to convince others to stop doing business with a firm that is the subject of a primary boycott; prohibited by the Taft-Hartley Act.

secondary data (p. 36I) Information that has already been compiled by others and published in journals and books or made available online.

secured bond (p. 5II) A bond issued with some form of collateral.

secured loan (p. 506) A loan backed by collateral (something valuable, such as property).

Securities and Exchange Commission (SEC) (p. 525) Federal agency that has responsibility for regulating the various exchanges.

selection (p. 300) The process of gathering information and deciding who should be hired, under legal guidelines, for the best interests of the individual and the organization.

selective distribution (p. 4I7) Distribution that sends products to only a preferred group of retailers in an area.

self-insurance (p. C-4) The practice of setting aside money to cover routine claims and buying only "catastrophe" policies to cover big losses.

Service Corps of Retired Executives (SCORE) (p. I7I) An SBA office with volunteers from industry, trade associations, and education who counsel small businesses at no cost (except for expenses).

services (p. 4) Intangible products (i.e., products that can't be held in your hand) such as education, health care, insurance, recreation, and travel and tourism.

service utility (p. 4I2) Adding value by providing fast, friendly service during and after the sale and by teaching customers how to best use products over time.

sexual harassment (p. 34I) Unwelcome sexual advances, requests for sexual favors, and other conduct (verbal or physical) of a sexual nature that creates a hostile work environment.

shaky ground *Idea that possible problems lie ahead.*

shareware (p. B-I6) Software that is copyrighted but distributed to potential customers free of charge.

Sherlock Holmes *A famous fictional detective who was particularly adept at uncovering information to solve very difficult mysteries.*

shoestring budget *A budget that implies the company is short on funds and only includes a minimal amount of financial expenditures (i.e., it's as thin as a shoestring).*

shopping goods and services (p. 382) Those products that the consumer buys only after comparing value, quality, price, and style from a variety of sellers.

shop stewards (p. 333) Union officials who work permanently in an organization and represent employee interests on a daily basis.

short-term financing (p. 504) Funds needed for a year or less.

short-term forecast (p. 497) Forecast that predicts revenues, costs, and expenses for a period of one year or less.

sift through mountains of information *Sort through large volumes of information.*

sin taxes *Taxes used to discourage the use of goods like liquor or cigarettes.*

sinking fund (p. 53I) A reserve account in which the issuer of a bond periodically retires some part of the bond principal prior to maturity so that enough capital will be accumulated by the maturity date to pay off the bond.

Six Sigma quality (p. 250) A quality measure that allows only 3.4 defects per million opportunities.

skimming price strategy (p. 398) Strategy in which a new product is priced high to make optimum profit while there's little competition.

small business (p. I59) A business that is independently owned and operated, is not dominant in its field of operation, and meets certain standards of size (set by the Small Business Administration) in terms of employees or annual receipts.

Small Business Administration (SBA) (p. I68) A U.S. government agency that advises and assists small businesses by providing management training and financial advice and loans.

Small Business Investment Company (SBIC) Program (p. I68) A program through which private investment companies licensed by the Small Business Administration lend money to small businesses.

smart card (p. 570) An electronic funds transfer tool that is a combination credit card, debit card, phone card, driver's license card, and more.

smoking gun *An issue or other disclosure that could prove a person or organization has done something wrong.*

G-20   GLOSSARY

social audit (p. 104) A systematic evaluation of an organization's progress toward implementing socially responsible and responsive programs.

Social Security (p. D-13) The term used to describe the Old-Age, Survivors, and Disability Insurance Program established by the Social Security Act of 1935.

socialism (p. 41) An economic system based on the premise that some, if not most, basic businesses should be owned by the government so that profits can be more evenly distributed among the people.

sole proprietorship (p. 116) A business that is owned, and usually managed, by one person.

sovereign wealth funds (SWFs) (p. 70) Investment funds controlled by governments holding large stakes in foreign companies.

span of control (p. 210) The optimum number of subordinates a manager supervises or should supervise.

specialty goods and services (p. 382) Consumer products with unique characteristics and brand identity. Because these products are perceived as having no reasonable substitute, the consumer puts forth a special effort to purchase them.

speculative risk (p. C-3) A chance of either profit or loss.

squeezing franchisees' profits *Tightening or reducing profits.*

staffing (p. 190) A management function that includes hiring, motivating, and retaining the best people available to accomplish the company's objectives.

staff personnel (p. 216) Employees who advise and assist line personnel in meeting their goals.

stagflation (p. 48) A situation when the economy is slowing but prices are going up anyhow.

stakeholders (p. 6) All the people who stand to gain or lose by the policies and activities of a business and whose concerns the business needs to address.

standard of living (p. 5) The amount of goods and services people can buy with the money they have.

state-of-the-art *The most modern type available.*

statement of cash flows (p. 479) Financial statement that reports cash receipts and disbursements related to a firm's three major activities: operations, investments, and financing.

statistical process control (SPC) (p. 250) The process of taking statistical samples of product components at each stage of the production process and plotting those results on a graph. Any variances from quality standards are recognized and can be corrected if beyond the set standards.

statistical quality control (SQC) (p. 250) The process some managers use to continually monitor all phases of the production process to assure that quality is being built into the product from the beginning.

statutory law (p. A-2) State and federal constitutions, legislative enactments, treaties of the federal government, and ordinances—in short, written law.

staying afloat *Staying in business during tough times.*

stockbroker (p. 532) A registered representative who works as a market intermediary to buy and sell securities for clients.

stock certificate (p. 527) Evidence of stock ownership that specifies the name of the company, the number of shares it represents, and the type of stock being issued.

stock exchange (p. 523) An organization whose members can buy and sell (exchange) securities for companies and investors.

stock insurance company (p. C-7) A type of insurance company owned by stockholders.

stocks (p. 527) Shares of ownership in a company.

stock splits (p. 536) An action by a company that gives stockholders two or more shares of stock for each one they own.

strategic alliance (p. 70) A long-term partnership between two or more companies established to help each company build competitive market advantages.

strategic planning (p. 185) The process of determining the major goals of the organization and the policies and strategies for obtaining and using resources to achieve those goals.

strict product liability (p. A-5) Legal responsibility for harm or injury caused by a product regardless of fault.

strike (p. 335) A union strategy in which workers refuse to go to work; the purpose is to further workers' objectives after an impasse in collective bargaining.

strikebreakers (p. 336)   Workers hired to do the jobs of striking workers until the labor dispute is resolved.

supervisory management (p. 189)   Managers who are directly responsible for supervising workers and evaluating their daily performance.

supply (p. 37)   The quantity of products that manufacturers or owners are willing to sell at different prices at a specific time.

supply chain (or value chain) (p. 421)   The sequence of linked activities that must be performed by various organizations to move goods from the sources of raw materials to ultimate consumers.

supply-chain management (p. 421)   The process of managing the movement of raw materials, parts, work in progress, finished goods, and related information through all the organizations involved in the supply chain; managing the return of such goods, if necessary; and recycling materials when appropriate.

SWOT analysis (p. 184)   A planning tool used to analyze an organization's strengths, weaknesses, opportunities, and threats.

tactical planning (p. 186)   The process of developing detailed, short-term statements about what is to be done, who is to do it, and how it is to be done.

tall organization structure (p. 210)   An organizational structure in which the pyramidal organization chart would be quite tall because of the various levels of management.

target costing (p. 397)   Designing a product so that it satisfies customers and meets the profit margins desired by the firm.

target marketing (p. 367)   Marketing directed toward those groups (market segments) an organization decides it can serve profitably.

tariff (p. 76)   A tax imposed on imports.

tax accountant (p. 469)   An accountant trained in tax law and responsible for preparing tax returns or developing tax strategies.

tax-deferred contributions (p. D-13)   Retirement account deposits for which you pay no current taxes, but the earnings gained are taxed as regular income when they are withdrawn at retirement.

taxes (p. A-14)   How the government (federal, state, and local) raises money.

technical skills (p. 190)   Skills that involve the ability to perform tasks in a specific discipline or department.

technology (p. 14)   Everything from phones and copiers to computers, medical imaging devices, personal digital assistants, and the various software programs that make business processes more effective, efficient, and productive.

telecom   *Short for telecommunications.*

telecommuting (p. 246)   Working from home via computer and modem.

telemarketing (p. 418)   The sale of goods and services by telephone.

telephone tag   *To leave a telephone message when you attempt to return a message left for you.*

term insurance (p. D-10)   Pure insurance protection for a given number of years.

term-loan agreement (p. 510)   A promissory note that requires the borrower to repay the loan in specified installments.

test marketing (p. 358)   The process of testing products among potential users.

thorny issue   *An issue that can cause pain or difficulty (as a thorn on a rose bush may).*

through the grapevine   *Informal information communication; stories told by one person to the next.*

time deposit (p. 563)   The technical name for a savings account; the bank can require prior notice before the owner withdraws money from a time deposit.

time in the trenches   *Working with the other employees and experiencing what they contend with as opposed to managing from an office and relying solely on reports about what is happening in the workplace.*

time-motion studies (p. 261)   Studies, begun by Frederick Taylor, of which tasks must be performed to complete a job and the time needed to do each task.

time utility (p. 411)   Adding value to products by making them available when they're needed.

to take a break   *To slow down and do something besides work.*

top management (p. 188) Highest level of management, consisting of the president and other key company executives who develop strategic plans.

tort (p. A-4) A wrongful act that causes injury to another person's body, property, or reputation.

total fixed costs (p. 397) All the expenses that remain the same no matter how many products are made or sold.

total product offer (p. 380) Everything that consumers evaluate when deciding whether to buy something; also called a *value package*.

trade credit (p. 504) The practice of buying goods and services now and paying for them later.

trade deficit (p. 64) An unfavorable balance of trade; occurs when the value of a country's imports exceeds that of its exports.

trademark (p. 387) A brand that has exclusive legal protection for both its brand name and its design.

trade protectionism (p. 76) The use of government regulations to limit the import of goods and services.

trade surplus (p. 64) A favorable balance of trade; occurs when the value of a country's exports exceeds that of its imports.

training and development (p. 303) All attempts to improve productivity by increasing an employee's ability to perform. Training focuses on short-term skills, whereas development focuses on long-term abilities.

transparency (p. 192) The presentation of a company's facts and figures in a way that is clear and apparent to all stakeholders.

trial balance (p. 471) A summary of all the financial data in the account ledgers that ensures the figures are correct and balanced.

trial close (p. 448) A step in the selling process that consists of a question or statement that moves the selling process toward the actual close.

trigger-happy *Term that refers to people reacting too fast to the circumstances facing them in a difficult situation.*

turn a blind eye *Ignore something of importance.*

turn the work off *Stop working.*

umbrella policy (p. D-12) A broadly based insurance policy that saves you money because you buy all your insurance from one company.

unemployment rate (p. 47) The number of civilians at least 16 years old who are unemployed and tried to find a job within the prior four weeks.

Uniform Commercial Code (UCC) (p. A-8) A comprehensive commercial law, adopted by every state in the United States, that covers sales laws and other commercial laws.

uninsurable risk (p. C-5) A risk that no insurance company will cover.

union (p. 324) An employee organization that has the main goal of representing members in employee–management bargaining over job-related issues.

union security clause (p. 331) Provision in a negotiated labor–management agreement that stipulates that employees who benefit from a union must either officially join or at least pay dues to the union.

union shop agreement (p. 331) Clause in a labor–management agreement that says workers do not have to be members of a union to be hired, but must agree to join the union within a prescribed period.

unlimited liability (p. 118) The responsibility of business owners for all of the debts of the business.

unsecured bond (p. 511) A bond backed only by the reputation of the issuer; also called a debenture bond.

unsecured loan (p. 507) A loan that doesn't require any collateral.

unsought goods and services (p. 383) Products that consumers are unaware of, haven't necessarily thought of buying, or find that they need to solve an unexpected problem.

utility (p. 411) In economics, the want-satisfying ability, or value, that organizations add to goods or services when the products are made more useful or accessible to consumers than they were before.

value (p. 378) Good quality at a fair price. When consumers calculate the value of a product, they look at the benefits and then subtract the cost to see if the benefits exceed the costs.

variable costs (p. 397) Costs that change according to the level of production.

variable life insurance (p. D-11) Whole life insurance that invests the cash value of the policy in stocks or other high-yielding securities.

venture capital (p. 512) Money that is invested in new or emerging companies that are perceived as having great profit potential.

venture capitalists (p. 167) Individuals or companies that invest in new businesses in exchange for partial ownership of those businesses.

vertical merger (p. 131) The joining of two companies involved in different stages of related businesses.

vestibule training (p. 305) Training done in schools where employees are taught on equipment similar to that used on the job.

viral marketing (p. 454) The term now used to describe everything from paying customers to say positive things on the Internet to setting up multilevel selling schemes whereby consumers get commissions for directing friends to specific websites.

virtual corporation (p. 220) A temporary networked organization made up of replaceable firms that join and leave as needed.

virtualization (p. B-14) A process that allows networked computers to run multiple operating systems and programs through one central computer at the same time.

virtual private network (VPN) (p. B-9) A private data network that creates secure connections, or "tunnels," over regular Internet lines.

virus (p. B-18) A piece of programming code inserted into other programming to cause some unexpected and, for the victim, usually undesirable event.

vision (p. 183) An encompassing explanation of why the organization exists and where it's trying to head.

volume (or usage) segmentation (p. 368) Dividing the market by usage (volume of use).

voluntary bankruptcy (p. A-15) Legal procedures initiated by a debtor.

walk out the door Leave the company; quit your job.

watching over your shoulder Looking at everything you do.

Web 2.0 (p. B-12) The set of tools that allow people to build social and business connections, share information, and collaborate on projects online (including blogs, wikis, social networking sites and other online communities, and virtual worlds).

Web 3.0 (p. B-12) A combination of technologies that adds intelligence and changes how people interact with the Web, and vice versa (consists of the semantic Web, mobile Web, and immersive Internet).

whistleblowers (p. 97) Insiders who report illegal or unethical behavior.

whole life insurance (p. D-10) Life insurance that stays in effect until age 100.

wholesaler (p. 407) A marketing intermediary that sells to other organizations.

will (p. D-16) A document that names the guardian for your children, states how you want your assets distributed, and names the executor for your estate.

word-of-mouth promotion (p. 453) A promotional tool that involves people telling other people about products they've purchased.

World Bank (p. 572) The bank primarily responsible for financing economic development; also known as the International Bank for Reconstruction and Development.

World Trade Organization (WTO) (p. 77) The international organization that replaced the General Agreement on Tariffs and Trade, and was assigned the duty to mediate trade disputes among nations.

yellow-dog contract (p. 328) A type of contract that required employees to agree as a condition of employment not to join a union; prohibited by the Norris-LaGuardia Act in 1932.